Library of
Davidson College

IMPRISONED IN A TESSERACT

Portrait of Blish appearing on the back of the dustjacket of *Earthman, Come Home* (New York: G. P. Putnam's Sons, 1955) (Dep. Blish 406/1)

IMPRISONED IN A TESSERACT

The Life and Work of James Blish

David Ketterer

THE KENT STATE UNIVERSITY PRESS
Kent, Ohio, and London, England

© 1987 by The Kent State University Press, Kent, Ohio 44242
All rights reserved
Library of Congress Catalog Card Number 86-16074
ISBN 0-87338-334-6
Manufactured in the United States of America

The paper in this book meets the guidelines for permanence and durability of the Committee on Production Guidelines for Book Longevity of the Council on Library Resources.

Library of Congress Cataloging-in-Publication Data

Ketterer, David.
  Imprisoned in a tesseract.

  Includes bibliographies and index.
  1. Blish, James. 2. Science fiction, American—History and criticism. 3. Authors, American—20th century—Biography. I. Title.
PS3503.L64Z74   1987   813'.54   86-16074
ISBN 0-87338-334-6

British Library Cataloguing in Publication data are available

For Xenia

▍What had been Jack Ginsberg's room in the palazzo now looked a great deal more like the cabinet of Dr. Caligari. Every stone, every window frame, every angle, every wall was out of true, so that there was no place to stand where he did not feel as though he had been imprisoned in a tesseract—except that even the planes of the prison were crazed with jagged cracks without any geometry whatsoever. The window panes were out, and the ceiling dripped; the floor was invisible under fallen plaster, broken glass and anonymous dirt; and in the *gabinetto* the toilet was pumping continuously as though trying to flush away the world. The satin-sheeted bed was sandy to the touch, and when he took his clothes out of the wardrobe, his beautiful clothes so carefully selected from *Playboy,* dust fumed out of them like spores from a puffball.

                                        First Station, *The Day After Judgment*

OTHER BOOKS BY DAVID KETTERER

New Worlds for Old: The Apocalyptic Imagination, Science Fiction, and American Literature
The Rationale of Deception in Poe
Frankenstein's Creation: The Book, the Monster, and Human Reality
The Science Fiction of Mark Twain (editor)

CONTENTS

Illustrations	x
Acknowledgments	xi
Abbreviations	xiii
Chronology	xiv
1. A Life for Science Fiction	1
I. SCIENCE-FICTION FUTURES	31
2. A Pulp Apprenticeship	33
3. Pantropy, Polyploidy, and Tectogenesis	55
4. Covering *A Case of Conscience*	79
II. HISTORICAL MODELS	105
5. "New Paradigms" and Problematic Endings	107
6. Wagnerian Spenglerian Space Opera: *Cities in Flight*	160
7. "Explosive Doctrine": *Doctor Mirabilis*	192
III. THE NUB OF FANTASY	217
8. A Transfinite Mathematics	219
9. The Branching Tree: Juveniles, Poetry, Criticism, Miscellany	249
10. "Imprisoned in a Tesseract": *Black . . . Judgment*	290
Notes	320
Primary Bibliography	366
Secondary Bibliography	385
Index	390

ILLUSTRATIONS

Portrait of Blish on the dustjacket of *Earthman, Come Home*	*frontispiece*
Cover of the first SF magazine Blish saw	5
Pencil drawing of Blish by Judith Lawrence Blish	20
Blish aged 52	26
An analog for Blish's vision	68
Diagram by Norman L. Knight for *A Torrent of Faces*	74
Notes for "How Beautiful with Banners"	147
Cover that inspired the Okie stories	162
Analog cover for *A Life for the Stars*	166
"James Blish at Roger Bacon"	193
Cover that inspired "Common Time"	224
Judith Lawrence Blish's cover for *The Magazine of Fantasy & Science Fiction*	238
Diagrammatic synopsis for "Circles"/*The Breath of Brahma*	247
The Haertel Network	258
The Triangle of Solomon and the Magical Circle	299
The Goëtic Circle of Pacts	300
If cover for *Black Easter*	302

ACKNOWLEDGMENTS

▎I have attempted in this book to provide the first full-scale and complete treatment of a contemporary writer of science fiction. Such would not have been possible without the availability of that author's papers and the cooperation of the people who knew James Blish personally, in particular, Judith Blish and Virginia Kidd. They both read through, and commented helpfully on, manuscript versions of my opening biographical chapter. I am also grateful to Brian W. Aldiss, Alfred Bester, Algis Budrys, Damon Knight, Robert A. W. Lowndes, Frederik Pohl, and Josephine Saxton, all of whom played significant roles in Blish's life.

During the time I spent at the New Bodleian Library, Oxford, repository of the Blish Papers, I was ably assisted by Timothy Rogers, assistant librarian in the Department of Western Manuscripts. "Dep. Blish" and the appropriate numbers follow all citations from this source. One other substantial accumulation of Blish correspondence is located in the archives of Faber & Faber, the most important of Blish's English publishers. At the Faber offices matters were greatly facilitated by the archivist, Mrs. Constance B. Cruickshank. There also Charles Monteith, director of Faber & Faber between 1954 and 1974 and the man responsible for his firm's originally publishing Blish, took time to discuss with me his association with the writer. The file identifications "CM 51," "CM 84," or "PdS 120" follow all citations from the Faber Archives. "CM" stands for Charles Monteith, "PdS" for Peter du Sautoy, vice-chairman (1960–71), then chairman (1971–76) of Faber & Faber.

Various kinds of help and information were provided by Joyce Day, secretary of the Science Fiction Foundation and by the Foundation Library at the North East London Polytechnic, by the Interlibrary Loan Department of Concordia University, my employer, and by the following individuals: Jerome Bixby, Cy Chauvin, John Clute, Malcolm Edwards, John Feather, William Godshalk, George Hay, Sam Moskowitz, Robert M. Philmus, super sleuth Bernard Queenan, Brian Stableford, and Darko Suvin.

The English fan Paul Shackley supplied both valuable information and photocopies of the often lengthy letters he received from Blish, quotations from which are identified by the abbreviation "PS" followed by a date. Blish's copies of some of these letters together with Shackley's letters to him may be found in the New Bodleian Library, Dep. Blish 431/11.

I am especially grateful to Karin L. Laflin (the former Karin Laflin Adams), who provided me with photocopies of Blish's letters to her (her side of the correspondence is also in the New Bodleian Library—Dep. Blish 411/1; his is not), and allowing me to quote from them. My quotations from Blish's letters to Karin are identified by the abbreviation "KLA" followed by a date.

My debt to fellow Blishian Gregory Feeley deserves special mention. In the course of our interchange of information, Feeley (who is at work on a biography of Blish) provided me with copies of a mass of useful material.

But without the support of the Social Sciences and Humanities Research Council of Canada all might have come to nought. SSHRCC awarded me a 1982–83 Research Grant and Salary Replacement Stipend and a 1984–85 follow-up Research Grant. My thanks also to the Dean of Arts office, Concordia University, which made available a sum of money that covered the cost of word processing (just one of the manifestations of our SF world).

My teaching assistants, Yolande Kuzmicki and Jeannette Winter, worked on the bibliography. Patricia Berger, Veronica Hollinger, Rosalind Lester, and Richard Thompson typed some parts of my manuscript; Roslyn Yearwood and Jeannette Winter word-processed others. The resulting final manuscript was then expertly copyedited by Laura Nagy of the Kent State University Press.

A version of section ii of chapter 2 was published in *Extrapolation* (Spring 1985). Earlier versions of chapters 3 and 4, section iv of chapter 5, section vi of chapter 8, and section ii of chapter 9 were published in *Science-Fiction Studies* (July 1983, July 1982, July 1984, March 1984, November 1984); an earlier version of chapter 6 was published in *Foundation* (July 1984), and a version of all but section 1 of chapter 10 was published in a special SF and fantasy issue of *The Missouri Review* (March 1984).

ABBREVIATIONS

CM	Charles Monteith Blish files, Faber & Faber Archives, London
Dep. Blish	Blish Papers, Department of Western Manuscripts, the New Bodleian Library, Oxford University
KLA	Letters from Blish to Karin Laflin Adams, in Laflin's possession
PdS	Peter du Sautoy Blish file, Faber & Faber Archives, London
PS	Letters from Blish to Paul Shackley, in Shackley's possession

CHRONOLOGY

1921	James Benjamin, only child of Asa Rhodes Blish and Dorothea Schneewind Blish, born on May 23 in East Orange, New Jersey.
1931	Sees April issue of *Astounding Stories* in June.
1934–38	Attends East Orange High School.
1937	Attends first SF convention, the Second Science Fiction Convention in New York, on February 21.
1938	Begins attending meetings of the Futurian Society of New York in November.
1939–42	Majors in zoology at Rutgers University and graduates with a B.Sc. in Education.
1940	Publishes first SF story, "Emergency Refueling," in *Super Science Stories* (March).
1941	Begins freelance writing.
1942–44	Drafted into the U.S. Army where he becomes a medical technician, "rises" to the rank of private, first class, and is demoted to buck private. After his discharge he takes part in a nationwide draft card burning demonstration.
1944–46	Attends graduate school at Columbia University. Switches from study of zoology to literature, sells his Ezra Pound thesis, but does not complete his M.A.
1945	In April Blish and fellow Futurian, Robert A. W. Lowndes, move into an apartment ("Blowndsh") on West 11th Street, Manhattan. Futurians break up.
1945–52	Edits various trade journals for the drug and food industries.
1946	Moves into double apartment ("Fort Wit") with Virginia Kidd Emden in the spring. Works as reader for the Scott Meredith Literary Agency.
1947	Marries Virginia Kidd on May 23.
1948	First failed bid at survival as a freelance writer.
1950	"Okie" appears in *Astounding* (April).
1953	Second failed bid at survival as a freelance writer. Blishes move to "Arrowhead," a brookside house in Milford, Pennsylvania, in April. Publishes "A Case of Conscience" in *If* (September).
1954	Elisabeth Blish born on June 28.

CHRONOLOGY

1955	Joins the Civil Air Patrol and learns to fly. In August, hurricane Diane causes the flooding of the Blishes' home and they move to a Brooklyn apartment.
1955–59	Works for drug company, Chas. Pfizer & Co., as a public relations counsel and science editor.
1956	Helps Damon Knight and Judith Merril organize the first Milford Science Fiction Writers' Conference in June (following New York Worldcon). Charles Benjamin Blish born on July 18.
1957	Publishes *The Seedling Stars*.
1958	In August the Blishes return to "Arrowhead" in Milford. Publishes *A Case of Conscience,* for which he receives the Hugo award.
1960–62	Works for Hill & Knowlton, Inc., a public relations firm.
1960	Guest of honor at the 18th World Science Fiction Convention in Pittsburgh in September.
1962–68	Works as an account executive for the Washington, D.C. office of The Tobacco Institute (part of the Hill & Knowlton operation).
1964	Divorce granted from Virginia Kidd on 20 February. Lives in New York. Operation for tongue cancer in July, but the spread of the cancer necessitates a radical neck dissection on September 1. Marries Judith Ann Lawrence on November 7. Publishes *Doctor Mirabilis* in England, and a critical collection, *The Issue at Hand,* in the U.S.
1965	First trip abroad—the Blishes attend the 23d World Science Fiction Convention in London.
1966	In the spring the Blishes move to an apartment in Alexandria, Virginia. Science Fiction Writers of America founded. Blish serves as vice-president of the SFWA for two terms, beginning in 1966.
1967	Guest of honor, Lunacon. The Blishes spend three weeks in England.
1968	Publishes *Black Easter.* Principal speaker at Phillycon.
1968–75	Third and this time successful bid at survival as a freelance writer, thanks, in part, to a series of contracts with Bantam Books to write *Star Trek* collections.
1969	The Blishes move to England in April. After renting a house in Marlow, they buy "Treetops" in Harpsden, a hamlet 20 miles from Oxford. Blish serves on jury at the Trieste Film Festival in June.

1970	Guest of honor at the British Science Fiction Association Eastercon in London. Publishes one volume edition of *Cities in Flight,* and *More Issues at Hand*.
1971	Publishes *The Day After Judgment*.
1972	Special Blish issue of *The Magazine of Fantasy & Science Fiction* (April). In the autumn, at the first English Milford Conference, organized by the Blishes and held at Milford-on-Sea, Hampshire, Blish becomes acquainted with Josephine Saxton.
1974	Operation for lung cancer in October at Battle Hospital, Reading.
1975	Dies at "Treetops" on July 30. Buried on August 4 in St. Cross Church cemetery, Oxford.

ONE
A LIFE FOR SCIENCE FICTION

■ Death is beginning to claim the second generation of genre SF writers, the generation that includes many of the best-known names. James Blish came a little late to that generation and left tragically early. Yet, within an abbreviated but intense career, he created a large body of work which exhibits a certain completeness in its overall shape and contains a number of titles that may not only be counted among SF's most successful achievements but also prized as genuine works of literature.

Although not as familiar a name to the average reader as that of Isaac Asimov, Ray Bradbury, Arthur C. Clarke, or Robert Heinlein, James Blish certainly would figure in any list of the twenty or so most significant writers of SF. His 1958 Hugo-award-winning novel, *A Case of Conscience,* which successfully fused complex religious issues with the theme of alien contact, remains one of the few genuine classics of the genre—far superior to most of the titles loosely touted as such. While much of Blish's output is as ephemeral and tawdry as most SF, his best work both invites and rewards close scrutiny. It is, of course, too early to know which works published in the years since 1926, when (with the appearance of Hugo Gernsback's *Amazing Stories*) science fiction became a publishing category, will best withstand the test of time. But I would hazard the guess that the work of the four writers who are today best known will wear less well than *A Case of Conscience* and some other works by James Blish.

(i) Childhood and Adolescence (1921–38)

James Benjamin Blish was born on 23 May 1921 in East Orange, New Jersey, the only child of Asa Rhodes and Dorothea Schneewind Blish. According to the *Supplement to Genealogy of the Blish Family in*

America (1957), compiled by Matthew Rhodes Blish, James Blish (Matthew Rhodes's grandson) constitutes the tenth Blish (or "Blush" or "Bliss," as the old records sometimes have it) generation, counting from Abraham Blish, while his roots apparently go back to Edward and Samuel Fuller of the *Mayflower,* to the Reverend John Lathrop, and to Dr. Matthew Fuller, a physician of Barnstable.[1] Asa Blish, who came from a New England family, was the advertising manager for Bernarr McFadden's *True Story* and, after McFadden's death, eastern advertising manager for *Esquire*. Three years after he and James's mother divorced in 1927, he married Katherine Hosking.

Damon Knight notes that James was "'some fractional part' Jewish on his mother's side; his maternal grandfather, Benjamin von Schneewind, was a candy manufacturer who packaged two large boxes of chocolates, very popular in the Midwest at one time, named the Dorothea and Babette Selection after his two daughters."[2] After the divorce Dorothea and her six-year-old son moved to Chicago, into an apartment in her father's house—"The Mansards," 1344 East 48th Street. It was there, at the age of nine, that James set up his first laboratory in what had been the butler's pantry. At that time his major ambition was to be a scientist and he already owned a small Wollensak toy microscope and a Chemcraft chemistry set which he had received as a Christmas present. A toy printing set enabled him to make cards reading

BLISH LABORATORIES
MICROSCOPIC WORK

which he distributed to relatives. At the same time he made use of another present, a second-hand Smith Corona portable, to type up short disaster stories in the form of single-copy booklets. Subsequently, James, Dorothea, and her parents moved into a brownstone around the corner at 4750 Kenwood.[3]

Money was a problem. Dorothea, a talented pianist with perfect pitch and organist at the local Christian Science Church, was living on alimony and her earnings as a piano teacher. James, however, hated piano lessons and it was not, it seems, particularly thanks to her influence that he later came to love music and learned successively to play the piano, glockenspiel, trumpet, baritone horn, and French horn.[4] James's grandfather had lost his candy company as a result of the 1929 crash and thereafter lived on his dwindling capital. On one occasion James caused "considerable outright financial anguish" when he "broke a glass lampshade." He would later recreate a similar scene when he has the narrator of *The Frozen Year* (1957) recall, at the beginning of chapter 8, breaking his eyeglasses. With the passage of time, his grandparents "dwindled into smaller and smaller households" until at their deaths, several years apart, "they were both living with us rather than we with them."[5]

Blish remembered his father, an intelligent, "tall, handsome, blond erratic man with a fine singing voice," as a financially successful Simon Dedalus, but also as a selfish man and "a figure of terror" who would visit and take him out every other Saturday. On one of those Saturdays, his father took him to the 1933 Chicago World's Fair ("A Century of Progress") where they boarded a Giant Ford Trimotor for an aerial tour of the city and Blish's first wondrous experience of flying. Blish, however, was already thoroughly familiar with the World's Fair (especially the Hall of Science), since he visited the place, notebook in hand, every Friday (the reduced-price Children's Day) of its two-year existence. Blish also recalled another Saturday when his father "imprisoned me in his deserted office in the Wrigley Building until I learned how to tie my own shoes." Contact virtually ceased after his father's remarriage until Blish "was on the verge of college" at which time "I learned to love him, rather too late. . . ."[6]

He never, it seems, learned to love his mother, by his own account "a stupid and phenomenally selfish woman." Late in his life he recalls that his distaste for her

> deepened inexorably into something not very short of hatred. Now that she has declined into the usual stumblings, broken hips, and inability to manage her own bank balance which is characteristic of the senile who have never led any sort of intellectual life, I cannot even begin to pity her more than abstractly. I would give quite a lot to be shut of her. . . .[7]

The intemperate brutality of this account, even if only truly applicable to the last cancer-wracked years of Blish's life, comes as something of a shock and might lead the psychiatrically inclined to question Blish's own lovableness and the likely psycho-sexual consequences of his childhood situation. At the time of the breakup of his first marriage, Blish was persuaded to visit various psychiatrists but throughout his life he professed total skepticism regarding the possibility that his early emotional experiences could have in any significant way formed the outwardly somewhat icy man that he became. Blish deemed "to have been crucial" the intellectual rather than the sexual and emotional experiences of his childhood. At any rate his mother gets little credit for protecting her priggish, mildly dyslexic, bookish child, the block sissy, from other boys, and even Blish's "love for the whole art of music" he credits to one Erwin Lane's "passion for Italian opera." On the other hand, Blish's mother is credited with foisting on him a gimcrack religious affiliation that he quickly abandoned. Around the age of fifteen "a budding chemist" friend named Andy "converted me from my mother's wobbly Christian Science—which must be the silliest and least exciting religion the West has ever contrived—to an atheism [or agnosticism, as other earlier statements have it] around which I have been wobbling uneasily ever since."[8]

Blish's first experience of the pulp magazines seems to have begun around the age of six or seven. At that time it was "those which specialized in stories about World War I aerial fighting," like *Battle Aces, Flying Aces* and *War Birds,* that captured his attention. Determined some day to be a pilot, he could identify "all of the major military aircraft of 1914–1918." He built models of some of the German craft (which were generally deemed to be of superior design to the Allied ones) and followed the air-war magazines until their demise.[9]

In June 1931 a block friend, knowing of nine-year-old James's interest in astronomy (observational astronomy would become one of his hobbies), gave him "a book that tells all about life on other planets": the April 1931 issue of *Astounding Stories*.[10] This was Blish's introduction to the SF pulp magazines. The issue was a good one; it featured a cover by "Wesso" (Hans Waldemar Wessoloski) (see p. 5) and such stories as "Monsters of Mars" by Edmond Hamilton, the first segment of "The Exile of Time" by Ray Cummings, and "The Lake of Light" (a South Pole fantasy) by Jack Williamson. Blish was instantly addicted and soon frustrated to discover that, since the July issue of *Astounding* was then the only one on the stands, he had missed the two intermediate installments of Ray Cummings's time-travel serial. *Astounding* (which the twelve-year-old Blish broke into with a published letter) was, of course, the magazine that John W. Campbell was to edit (so influentially up to around 1950) from 1937 until his death in 1971. Blish was influenced by Campbell's prospectus for a realistic species of SF in which whatever hypotheses might be advanced were treated as serious literary thought-experiments (the average SF story having declined into transposed romantic melodrama since Gernsback's day). Like Campbell, Blish believed that SF dealt with the realm of the possible (known scientific facts must not be violated) and that it could and should be well written.

In the "Discussions" letter column of *Astounding Stories* Donald Wollheim proposed a single-character magazine entitled *The Plan-*

The cover by "Wesso" (Hans Waldeman Wessolowski) of the first SF magazine that Blish saw, *Astounding Stories,* April 1931

eteer—"planeteers" figure in Campbell's "Penton and Blake" series in *Thrilling Wonder Stories* (1936–38). In November 1935 the fourteen-year-old Blish (who can now be considered a member of Sam Moskowitz's third stratum of SF fandom) put out the hectographed first issue of a fan magazine of the same title to which he contributed a story entitled "Neptunian Refuge." By 1936 Blish was back in East Orange, New Jersey, where he and his mother had moved to a shabby first-floor apartment at 91 Halstead Street. Blish was not happy about the move although it did bring him into proximity with the New York World's Fair, "The World of Tomorrow," which was in its final building stage in 1938, and into closer contact with a group of young people who called themselves the International Cosmos Science Club (ICSC) and later the Science Fiction Advancement Association (SFAA).

Blish became one of the most regular contributors to *Tesseract*, the SFAA's official organ and one of the more important fanzines of the time. Its first issue had appeared in March 1936. Blish's two-part article, "Notes on Writing Science Fiction," in the May and June 1936 issues, appears as by "Niles [sic] H. Frome." Nils Frome, a Canadian fan in Fraser Mills, British Columbia, with whom Blish corresponded, was a gifted artist but a less gifted author of generally Lovecraftian stories, one of which, "Spacecast," he mailed to Blish to be completed and typed. The story did not sell nor did the first of Blish's collaborations with Frome, "Empty City," which Blish submitted to *Astounding*. Eventually Blish lost touch with Frome, who apparently never sold a story, or a drawing for that matter, but the unfortunate Frome was not forgotten. Blish wonders what became of him in his late autobiographical piece, "A Science-Fiction Coming of Age," and used "Nilsson Frome" as a pseudonym on a potentially embarrassing questionnaire that he filled out on 2 January 1974, just over a year and a half before his death. In addition to "Frome," at one time or another Blish used the following pseudonyms: William Atheling, Jr., V. K. Emden, Donald Laverty (with Damon Knight), Marcus Lyons, John MacDougal (with Robert W. Lowndes), Arthur Merlyn, and Luke Torley.

Blish produced six issues of *The Planeteer* in which appeared not only Blish's own tales of interplanetary adventure but two weak stories purchased from professionals (Edmond Hamilton and Lawrence Manning) at the then outrageously generous rate of a penny a word. Blish's associate editor was a friend named William H. Miller, Jr., who illustrated issues four through six and with whom Blish, at fifteen, had his only fistfight over a girl. Blish arranged to take over *Tesseract* and combine it with *The Planeteer* but this fell through when C. Hamilton

Bloomer of the SFAA, who had invested a loan of $10.00 in *The Planeteer* for the purchase of a hand printing press, had Blish expelled from the SFAA when he was unable to refund the money. The aborted issue of *Tesseract Combined with The Planeteer* (September 1936) contains an unfinished Blish story, the title of which, "Death's Crystal Towers," indicates an early preoccupation with death. In the meantime Blish had also joined the Queens chapter of the Science Fiction League, a promotional club launched in 1934 by Gernsback's *Wonder Stories,* which published Blish's response to part of a League test—an essay on his favorite SF character, Hawk Carse—and James V. Taurasi, director of that chapter, took over the editorship of *The Planeteer.* Blish was also a member of the short-lived Fantasy Legion which David A. Kyle originated in late 1936 with Miller as president and Kyle as vice-president. At the same time Blish produced two humor fanzines, *Grotesque* and *Phantascience League Digest* (a caricature of Donald Wollheim's *The Phantagraph*). On 21 February 1937 he went to his first SF convention, the Second Science Fiction Convention, in New York.[11]

Between 1934 and 1938 Blish attended East Orange High School but without much enthusiasm. Given a choice of three curricula—classical, scientific, and technical—he opted for the scientific. This included courses in physics, chemistry, and the one in which he excelled, biology. He eventually received the Bausch and Lomb Science Award for his graduating class. He was also required to take a shop course which, after some misadventures with woodworking, turned out to be printing, and a modern language—he chose German. He stayed with both subjects for the four years. He was poor in Latin and, because of "unnecessarily formidable teaching methods," a mediocre math student. In English, however, he maintained "an [almost] unbroken A+ record." From the English courses he "developed an enduring passion for most of Shakespeare, a qualified one for Poe, Dickens and Thackeray," and a love of poetry in spite of Carl Sandburg, "publicity-saint of American education."[12]

At the age of fifteen, Blish took an aptitude test at the Stevens Institute of Technology in Hoboken, New Jersey. David Mack of the Institute summarized the results as follows:

(1) The solution of an enormous problem would offer you the greatest opportunity to use your outstanding characteristics. (2) Although the laboratory knows of no specific job which will offer you a chance to use all your aptitudes, administrative work along statistical lines would most nearly do so. (3) Most important of all, you should make yourself do an almost impossi-

bly difficult school job in order to form the work habits which will carry you through college. (4) You should certainly acquire a college or university background. (Dep. Blish 406/5)

Mack finally proposed that Blish become an engineering executive. In any event an extremely objective personality like Blish's would definitely not be suited to the solitary occupation of writing.

(ii) The Futurians (1938-46)

Damon Knight has told the story of the Futurian [Science Literary] Society of New York, the group that (as his subtitle has it) "Produced Today's Top SF Writers and Editors." The group first met on 18 September 1938 and, in addition to Knight, it eventually included, among others, Isaac Asimov, Virginia Kidd, Cyril Kornbluth, Robert A. W. Lowndes, Judith Zissman (later Judith Merril), Frederik Pohl, Donald A. Wollheim, and Blish. Blish joined when he was seventeen and still living with his mother in New Jersey. Beginning with the third Futurian meeting (in November [?] 1938) Blish attended meetings regularly until the fall of 1939 when he became a freshman at Rutgers University.[13] There he "minored in languages and literature, the curriculum for which included a splendid philosophy course . . . that generated what became a lifelong interest." But he majored in biology "with emphasis on limnology (the biology of shorelines) and fresh-water ecology . . . when the very word was virtually unknown" (KLA, 18 February 1973), and graduated with a Bachelor of Science in Education in 1942.

While at Rutgers Blish became a member of the Fortean Society and undertook some temporary editorial and teaching work and some freelance writing. Pohl, as editor of *Super Science Stories,* published Blish's "Emergency Refueling" in the March 1940 issue—Blish's first commercial sale—and in the May 1942 issue published the most important story from the earliest phase of Blish's career, "Sunken Universe," which later became part of "Surface Tension" (1952) and *The Seedling Stars* (1957). As editor of *Astonishing Stories,* Pohl was also responsible for Blish's tenth story publication, "Solar Plexus" (September 1941). For these stories Blish was paid the substandard rate of one-half cent a word. Wollheim, who had inaugurated the short-lived *Stirring Science Fiction,* gave Blish his fourth and sixth publications, "Citadel of Thought" and "Callistan Cabal," in the first and second issues

(February and April 1941).[14] Other stories of this early period were published in *Cosmic Stories* (also edited by Wollheim) and R. W. Lowndes's *Future Fiction*.

World War II interrupted the careers of some of the Futurians and, a few months after graduation, Blish was drafted into the U.S. Army. After "starting out as the world's worst infantryman," Blish became a laboratory medical technician, thanks to his training in biology and a year's hard campaigning.[15] For reasons that Knight explains, Blish, who remained in the States during his entire army career (1942–44), never did rise above the rank of private, first class:

> [He] did not take well to military discipline; he was always in trouble over unshined shoes, or pajamas showing under his trousers at reveille. At Fort Dix, he did not let the army interfere with his writing: he set up a card table in the canteen, lined up several containers of beer around the edges, with his typewriter in the middle, and wrote for three or four hours every night, while the other draftees were playing pool or listening to the jukebox. The end of his military career came when he refused an order to clean the grease trap under the kitchen sink. Since it was wartime, he could have been court-martialed, but his father pulled strings in Washington and got him discharged.[16]

When Blish returned from the army the Futurians gave a dinner party for him at the Dragon Inn in Greenwich Village. It was there that he first met Damon Knight. Alone among the Futurians, Blish was to become a conscientious objector when, after his army service, he symbolically "burned" his by-then lost draft card in a nationwide demonstration organized by Dwight Macdonald of the Break with Conscription Committee. Blish and others present at the War Resisters League meeting where this event took place were photographed by the FBI.[17]

The GI Bill enabled Blish to attend graduate school at Columbia (1944–46), where one more year of zoology (he was thinking of becoming a limnobiologist) "convinced me that I did not have the makings of a scientist and I switched to literature."[18] He never did complete his M.A. but he did sell his thesis as a long article ("Rituals on Ezra Pound") to *The Sewanee Review* for $375, a large sum of money for such an essay even today.[19] And he did begin writing in earnest for most of the pulp magazine spectrum—westerns, detectives, jungle stories, sports, and popular science—and the SF pulps, newly revived after being discontinued during the war because of the paper shortage. Blish also wrote poetry and criticism, which began appearing in various literary quarterlies in 1948. Most of the pulps in which Blish's early stories appeared—*Crack Detective Stories, Famous Detective Stories, Western Action, Super Sports,* and, after the war, *Dynamic Science Fiction, Science Fiction Quarterly,* and the revived *Future Fiction*—were edited by Robert A. W. Lowndes who, from 1942 until 1960, was editor of all the Columbia Publications pulp magazines except for their two love pulps.

According to Lowndes, he and the five-years-younger Blish became aware of each other through the letter columns in *Wonder Stories* and *Astounding Stories* in 1935 but first became acquainted in late 1942 or early 1943 over a Chinese dinner and developed a friendship that lasted the thirty or so years until Blish's death. It was Lowndes who, in December 1944, introduced Blish to his wife-to-be and fellow Gemini, Virginia Kidd, who became a Futurian shortly thereafter. Virginia (she had dropped her given name of Mildred at age fourteen) had been briefly engaged by correspondence with Lowndes when he was sixteen but later married Jack Emden, a handsome baritone who had sung with her in the Unitarian Church choir in Baltimore. In April 1945 Blish, Lowndes, and Lowndes's cat Blackout moved into an apartment on the top floor of a five-story walk-up building on West 11th Street, Manhattan, which they called "Blowndsh." Blish, a cat lover, later angered Blackout by bringing home a tricolor kitten, "Curfew," not to be confused with "Poor Original Curfew," the white cat referred to hopefully as "Formed Stool Conway" in Knight's account. Blish also loved beer. Lowndes notes that "his metabolism was such that he could kill a quart or two a night and never gain an ounce." During this period (1945–46) Blish wrote his first SF novel, *The Duplicated Man,* in collaboration with Lowndes, a novel not published until 1953. Lowndes recalls that he was Watson to Blish's Holmes.[20]

Earlier in 1945, Lowndes, Wollheim, and fellow Futurian John B. Michel had persuaded Blish to join the new Gothic, Modern and finally (without Wollheim and Michel) Vanguard Amateur Press Association (VAPA), which was to have higher standards and in Lowndes's phrase a "more liberal left orientation" than the Fantasy Amateur Press Association. At this time, Knight recalls that Blish "described himself as a 'book fascist,' meaning that he agreed with the theory of fascism, not with its practice." In the VAPA mailings Knight and Blish hammered out the standards which would inform their subsequent critical writings. The second VAPA mailing (May 1945) carried sheets of Blish's musical score for a brief anguished poem by Cyril Kornbluth called "Cry in the Night." A poll covering VAPA's first year voted Blish the best article writer. Subsequently he was voted best writer. *Tumbrils,*

Blish's personal magazine, appeared in most of the VAPA mailings from the first (March 1945) to the near-to-last (February 1950). Between August 1945 and September 1946 Blish edited seven issues of *Renascence,* "a dogmatic review which welcomes critical contributions in all the arts," and printed pieces by Ezra Pound and Kenneth Patchen. Lowndes was Blish's co-editor for all but the last two issues. Lowndes writes that "*Renascence* started out as an entry in the mailings of the Vanguard Amateur Press Association" but "after a few issues [the first four], we withdrew it from the mailings, because Jim found that the Columbia University bookstore was willing to put it on sale there; to have continued it in the mailings would have required us to run off more copies per issue than we wanted to run." After about three years VAPA petered out as did the Vanguard Record Company that Blish and Lowndes (also a music lover) and Blish's father had formed but not before pressing three 10-inch 78 rpm discs, including a recording of "Song of Worlds Unseen" performed by pianist Berthe Melnik and some other Chandler Davis compositions.[21]

The end for the Futurians had already come, following a messy situation having to do with Michel breaking off an affair with Merril at Wollheim's insistence and Wollheim's being fed up with the reactionary Blish; the result was that Wollheim was read out of the Futurian Society late in 1945. Wollheim sued seven of the Futurians—Blish, Chester Cohen, Kidd, Knight, Lowndes, Merril and Larry Shaw, who had published a fanzine denouncing Wollheim—for libel in the Supreme Court of the State of New York, asking for $25,000 damages. The case was eventually dismissed but it cost the Futurians $700 in lawyers' fees. Knight records that "The Futurian Society was not officially dissolved, but it never met formally again, and there was a tacit understanding after a few months that it was dead."[22] Although subsequent informal Futurian meetings did occur, Blish and Wollheim did not speak to one another for some thirty years after the libel suit.

(iii) Moving On and Settling Down (1946–55)

Lowndes had introduced Virginia Kidd to Judith Merril as fellow "war widows" with husbands overseas and a baby daughter apiece. In 1945 the two women had moved into adjoining apartments on Washington Street in Greenwich Village. They turned them into a double apartment, which they named Parallax, by knocking down a wall between two closets to make a passageway, and took turns cooking for the Futurians on Thursday evenings. Kidd recalls these dinners, when everyone shared the costs and the clean-up operations, "as one of the happiest periods of my life." The plump, shapely Virginia Kidd was wooed at various times by Knight, Lowndes, and other Futurians but when in the spring of 1946 Merril moved into another apartment to await the return of her husband, it was James Blish who moved into her half of what had been Parallax. Knight explains how the place was rechristened: "Blish began a sentence in a tough-guy accent: 'The name of this jernt is—fort'wit—' And Kidd said 'Fort Wit!' "[23]

After Virginia's divorce from Jack Emden, she and Blish were married on his birthday in 1947. Knight writes of Blish's initial reluctance and "the fact that he preferred kittens to children" (Blackout, a gift from Lowndes to Virginia, added to the Blishes' collection). Marriage to Virginia entailed being a father to baby Karen Emden, who inspired a brief fantasy by Blish entitled "Four Variations on a Well-Known Theme," published by Virginia in her Vanguard magazine *Discrete,* and reprinted by Knight in *The Futurians*.[24] The Blishes' first child, Asa Benjamin, was born on 10 December 1947 but died on 13 January 1948.[25]

During this period Blish was working along with Knight and several other Futurians as a reader for the Scott Meredith Literary Agency, a job that involved evaluating generally unpublishable stories by people who paid a fee and instructing neophytes how to write formula pulp fiction. According to Knight, Blish, whose fiction both early and late reveals a talent for plotting, added a fourth part ("the crisis") to the Meredith Plot Skeleton, making it a five-part formula.[26] In between this drudgery Blish would find time to write. By January of 1948, having sold fifty or so stories to the pulp magazines, he made the first of three attempts to make a living as a freelance writer, supplemented for a year by whatever income he derived from being a part-time editorial assistant for the trade magazine *Food Field Reporter.* A Guggenheim application made around this time (Dep. Blish 406/5), in which Blish distinguishes between his serious writing and his SF and mentions the lost manuscripts of a novel written while he was in the army ("A Cage of Birds"?) and a nonfiction work on music (an early version of "The Sense of Music"), did not result in an award. Blish writes, "My timing couldn't have been worse." He had a mortgage on a house on Staten Island and 1948 "was the year most of my non-sf markets chose to collapse."[27] He was forced to sell the house and get a regular job. From early 1949 until 1953 Blish edited various trade journals, beginning as assistant technical editor for *Drug Topics, Drug Trade News* and *Food Field Reporter.* Between March 1950 and June 1951 he was news editor for *Food Topics* and from June 1951 he was editor of *Frosted Food Field*.

One good thing came out of 1948 aside from the hard economic lesson—Blish wrote but did not then publish the first of his stories about the Okies and their space-flying cities. The appearance of "Okie," the first published story in that series, in the April 1950 issue of *Astounding* marked, in the words of Alva Rogers, the "emergence of a mature writer of great promise."[28] Blish, in fact, was embarking upon his years of greatest achievement. The period 1950 to 1956 saw the publication of much of the Okie saga and of "Surface Tension," "Common Time," "A Case of Conscience," "Beep," and "A Work of Art." Edmund Crispin would include "A Case of Conscience" in the first (1955) of his classic Faber & Faber *Best SF* series, a project initiated by the firm's new director, Charles Monteith. In May 1955 Faber & Faber made an offer to publish *Earthman, Come Home* (CM 138), which would lead to much of Blish's work being published by that prestigious house.

Indicative of Blish's other interests is a letter that he published in the *New York Times* on 9 September 1949 (Dep. Blish 406/5) pointing out an error in the recent Dr. Richard Strauss obituary which he compared with a similarly "lamentable" obituary for James Joyce. A less worthy but only temporary enthusiasm followed the publication of L. Ron Hubbard's *Dianetics: The Modern Science of Mental Health* (1950), a work that created quite a stir within the SF community. In a *Planet Stories* review entitled "Dianetics: A Door to the Future," Blish, the ex-Christian Scientist, wrote:

> If dianetics does work—and every check I've been able to run thus far indicates that it does—it may well be the most important discovery of this or any other century. It will bring the long sought "rule of reason" to the problems of local and world politics, communication, law, and almost every other field of human endeavor—the goal of a 3000 year search.[29]

But disillusionment quickly followed. In a 1951 article entitled "What is Evidence?" Blish explains why responsible scientists question dianetics and in his 1952 discussion of "The Psychological Story" in his "Science in Science Fiction" series, while he admits to using dianetics in two of his stories, it is clear (pun intended) that he has lost his faith in the concept.[30]

In 1953 Blish wrote fifteen half-hour scripts (amounting to three separate week-long serials) for the "Captain Video" TV show. The serial beginning that September, the same month that saw the publication of "A Case of Conscience," was entitled "Captain Video and the Sub-Space Corsair."[31] Also in 1953 Blish made his second bid at surviving as a freelance writer but again his timing was bad—that was the year the SF boom of the thirties collapsed. And more responsibilities were on the way. A daughter Elisabeth was born on 28 June 1954. By this time the Blishes had moved out of New York to the quiet town of Milford, Pennsylvania; in April 1953 they had answered a newspaper ad and bought in installments at a bargain price a brookside house there named "Arrowhead" (for the shape of the land); running through the backyard was the Sawkill Creek, and a few hundred years to the east was the Delaware River. Until the house was paid off the Blishes worried about losing it. Before long other SF folk, specifically Judith Merril and Damon Knight and his first wife, were also living in Milford. In 1955, the year of the Knights' arrival, Blish topped this domestic pastoral idyll with an appropriate objective correlative—having joined the Civil Air Patrol, he learned to fly![32]

(iv) Flood tide (1955–62)

Contentment is rarely a prolonged state. August 1955 was the occasion of the hurricane Diane floods; the Delaware flooded the Blishes' house, in which Blish had a basement office, with fifteen feet of water.[33] The house was uninhabitable so the Blishes moved to Brooklyn and then took an apartment at 135 West 84th Street in Manhattan. Later Blish would begin a novel with the Joycean one-word title "Wayriver" about the Delaware periodically taking people away. (In a letter published in the May 1972 issue of *Disclave* Blish refers to it "still fermenting in the files.") In retrospect the flood tide can also be seen (in a creative rather than destructive sense) as a kind of objective correlative. That year and the seven years following were to see the fruition of the first major phase of Blish's career as an SF writer. The flood tide of titles, bracketed by the two *Cities in Flight* volumes—*Earthman, Come Home* (1955) and *A Life for the Stars* (1962)—included the two other *Cities in Flight* volumes (1956, 1958), *The Seedling Stars* (1957), *The Frozen Year* (1957), and *A Case of Conscience* (1958). June of 1958 also saw the appearance of the Blish-edited magazine *Vanguard Science Fiction*, the only issue that ever appeared.

At the same time it should be appreciated that publication was not always easily achieved and from time to time Blish even considered vanity presses. For example, having met with a series of rejection letters from trade publishers, he approached Exposition Press, Inc., and Pageant Press with a western, *Two Nuggets to Boot Hill*, as well as the *Cities in Flight* project. It is clear from a letter to Edward Uhlan, president of Exposition Press, that Blish still felt a need to justify his work: "In sixteen years of fiction writing I have earned more than $25,000; and while this is hardly a large sum over so long a period, it might be taken to indicate that I know something about my craft" (Dep. Blish 392/4). Subsequently, temporarily in despair of finding a publisher for his historical novel about Roger Bacon, *Doctor Mirabilis*, he thought again of Exposition Press.

Frederik Pohl had been Blish's agent since 1950 and it was he and Betty Ballantine of Ballantine Books who persuaded Blish to extend "A Case of Conscience," which Blish considered a totally uncommercial story, to novel length. That philosophical novel about the competing claims of religion and science won Blish his only Hugo award,[34] set a new standard of literary quality for SF, and led to Blish's being guest of honor at the 18th World Science Fiction Convention in Pittsburgh in September 1960.

On 18 July 1956 the Blishes' son, Charles Benjamin, was born. In the same year Damon Knight, Judith Merril, and Blish first thought of, and Knight and Merril organized, the first Milford Science Fiction Writers' Conference, which thereafter became an annual event. Because Blish was still living in New York he could not provide more than nominal help but he was one of the forty or so people who attended the weeklong conference, a "lovefeast" that followed immediately on the New York Worldcon. Toward the middle of that week Cyril Kornbluth invited those writers he considered the most important—Blish, Algis Budrys, and Damon Knight—to a meeting in the hotel room of Jane Roberts, a young writer whom Kornbluth had brought to the conference. Knight's hazy recollection is that Jane "went into a trance and prophesied" and that the five of them "made up a unity of some kind, composed of two pairs—Cyril the dark analog of Budrys, I the blond analog of Blish—around the central figure of Jane." Virginia Kidd recalls feeling left out and subsequently she and Kornbluth (whom the Blishes saw frequently during the Brooklyn and 84th Street period) discussed the matter. Kornbluth, who described himself as a cruel person, was adamant that the Five formed some kind of *homo gestalt* à la Theodore Sturgeon's *More Than Human* (1953), and that no wives should be included.[35]

In this context Virginia mentions some personal details about Blish. She associates Kornbluth's cruelty with his getting his wife "to dress up in strange outfits ever so often—he was a lingerie freak, and so was Jim."[36] Virginia also recalls Blish's drinking habits:

> Jim used to drink three quarts of beer a day when I first met him, which had gone up to four quarts a day shortly after, and he drank a slowly increasing number of quarts of beer per night, every night, for almost as long as I knew him. I used to order beer by the case, and he was up to eight and nine quarts when we separated. He claimed that he worked it off—he used it as fuel—but it was clearly visible in his manuscripts, which used to run along for five or six pages just about error-free. On the sixth or seventh page there would begin to be rather heavy mistakes, and by the eighth, if he went on to the eighth, it was almost unreadable. And at that point he would stop working and start listening to music, and then would slowly become blotto as the evening progressed, from about one o'clock until four or five or six.[37]

Knight adds that when "I first knew Jim, the beer he drank never seemed to affect him in any way, but when we met again in Milford he had switched to [before dinner] martinis and after one or two was visibly zonked." Knight recalls "one evening I picked up some piece of furniture that Virginia wanted moved, and Jim was indignant that I was strong enough to lift it. 'You used to be weak like me!' he said." To which Virginia responded, "He's weak, but he's nasty."[38]

In August 1958 the Blishes moved back to their Milford house but he continued working for "the world's largest manufacturer of antibiotics" (KLA, 26 January 1972), Chas. Pfizer & Co., as a public relations counsel. He held this position from 1955 to 1959 although his satirical attack on that drug company in *The Frozen Year* (1957) nearly got him fired, or so he claimed.[39] During this period he organized an international cancer symposium which included participants from the U.S.S.R.[40] As an offshoot of the Pfizer work experience, in 1956 he planned but did not write a book on important medical discoveries entitled "The Conquest of Life: New Pathways in Medicine" (Dep. Blish 436). Between 1960 and 1962 he worked for Hill & Knowlton, Inc., a public relations firm with tobacco accounts. An assignment not without self-interest for an extremely heavy smoker like Blish was that of rebutting the evidence for a link between smoking and cancer.[41] At the same time, now that he was living in Milford and commuting to New York City he played a small part in organizing the annual Science Fiction Writers' Conference.

Algis Budrys, who first met Blish "at a fannish gathering sometime in late 1952," provides the following portrait of his friend in this period:

Jim was always playful. This wasn't easy to see because so much of the time he expressed this in a deliberately waspish attitude. He was catlike; everything was judged in terms of his own taste. On those occasions when he was being properly treated by the world, he literally purred. Such occasions being rare, he made sure the world knew he walked his own way. His own way was surprisingly sensual, and gave him much satisfaction. Living alone in Manhattan five days a week, he developed a dedicated amateur skill in haute cuisine equipping a Chinatown cold water flat with a massive cooking range and a gourmet's collection of utensils and spices. He rode a Lambretta. He proffered this to the world as sensible transportation, but I've seen him come bursting out of the Lincoln tunnel headed for Milford, and he was glorying in the wind and in the racketing engine under his arse. He was a prodigious beerdrinker, quart after quart straight from the bottle. He was totally heterosexual—he was, in fact, I gather, almost indefatigable in heterosexuality—but he kissed bottlenecks with relish.[42]

Blish was making a reasonably good living but all was not well. In a letter to Australian writer, critic, and editor John Baxter, Blish dismisses his *Amazing* yarns (. . . *And All the Stars a Stage,* "And Some were Savages," and "A Dusk of Idols") as hackwork and claims that "for the last four years I have been disquieted and unhappy about the limitations of science fiction *for the writer,*" specifying as problematic the limited audience, the limitation in emotional response, and the temptation to magic. Nevertheless, "I will continue to write s-f because I am not going to throw away a commercial property—my reputation—which it took me 21 painful years and 200,000 words to build. But I am convinced that the attempt to wed s-f with the demands of general fiction is suicide, no matter from which end of the pipe one attacks it" (Dep. Blish 411/10, 31 October 1962). It would seem, then, that since 1958 Blish had at least partly wanted out of a box called SF. On 26 March 1963 he would write Charles Monteith, "I am dead sick of science fiction" (CM 51). This mood may well have influenced Blish's responses in Earl Kemp's notorious (largely because only 125 copies were distributed) Hugo-award-winning pamphlet, *Who Killed Science Fiction?* (1960). Blish was one of the 71 SF writers and editors of the 108 polled who replied to Kemp's five loaded questions concerning the demise of SF.[43] He had previously responded to a rather more neutral questionnaire accompanying a letter dated 24 December 1958 from Kingsley Amis, who was preparing the Christian Gauss Seminar in Criticism, the Princeton lecture series that became *New Maps of Hell* (1960) (Dep. Blish 406/5).

(v) Interregnum: Divorce, Cancer, and Remarriage (1962–69)

But Blish's problems were not just artistic. In the winter of 1962 the Blishes' marriage broke up.[44] Years later Blish would recall that Virginia "threw me violently out of that marriage against my will" (KLA, 25 February 1975). In the context of an extended correspondence with Norman L. Knight mainly having to do with their collaboration on a novel eventually published as *A Torrent of Faces* (1967), Blish explains something of the circumstances of his breakup with Virginia, who sued for divorce in 1963 (Dep. Blish 399/4). Blish first informed Knight of this event in a letter dated 13 December 1963: "Virginia and I have broken up, after 18 mostly pleasant years. . . . The 40s are in truth the dangerous years." On 16 January 1964 he supplies a somewhat distorted version of some of the details: "Virginia had a psychic breakdown in December 1962, and although she seems better now, both the medicos and the lawyers advised me to get a divorce for the protection of the children. In the meantime I have acquired a new girl and am happy as a clam, except for worrying about the kids." He had also written Charles Monteith of Faber & Faber, "my wife became mentally ill this past December" (CM 51, 22 July 1963), although Blish's alcoholism seems to have been the real problem. At any rate, the "new girl" was aspiring artist Judith Ann Lawrence, almost fourteen years Blish's junior and, like Blish, raised as a Christian Scientist.

Following the divorce, granted on 20 February 1964, and giving Virginia custody of the children, the fates struck again. In a letter to Knight Blish refers to his slow convalescence following surgery (a radon implantation) for tongue cancer in July.[45] But that was not the end of the matter. In an ensuing letter Blish tells Knight that "my tongue cancer (which had supposedly been extirpated) had spread to one or more of my cervical lymph glands . . . and on Sept. 1 had a radical neck dissection . . . and I now have a good prognosis."[46] A letter to Charles Monteith provides further details: "During my divorce proceedings last year, I played Banquo in an amateur production . . . and afterwards discovered that I had (I thought) bitten my tongue while being most foully murder'd; but it turned out to be a small cancer" (Dep. Blish 391/1, 27 October 1964). In his prime Blish had been a vigorous but slight man, between 135 and 150 pounds in weight, five-feet, ten inches tall (exaggerated to five-feet, eleven on his passport), with straight brown hair, a pencil moustache, and piercing brown eyes.[47] His appearance now began to deteriorate. The two operations, as Blish put it to Monteith, left "a few small scars and a slight lisp." But this description, in Judith Blish's words, "rather underplays the deformed shoulder, the excision of half his tongue, and the removal of teeth (necessitating dentures) and of part of his jaw, a radical resection, which accounted for the lisp and markedly sunken cheek."[48] Blish had also at least one other physical sign of his passage through life; as a result of participating in a rocket pistol experiment with his teenage friend Andy, the budding chemist, one of his trembling-prone hands was badly burned with the result that "it is still gathering age spots at a considerably faster rate."[49] But as he explains to Monteith, "I was tided over all this by a new young lady, Judith Ann Lawrence whom I am marrying Nov. 7th . . . and there, if you please, is a happy ending I wouldn't dare attempt to get away with in a novel."

Blish had been corresponding with Monteith about writing brief introductions to the four *Cities in Flight* volumes. After all the American rejections, *Doctor Mirabilis* had finally been published by Faber & Faber in 1964, an event that anticipates what would soon be a new direction in Blish's life—his and Judith's removal to England. A late influx of British votes had resulted in the Hugo for *A Case of Conscience;* thus, Blish later believed, "began my subsequent long career as an Anglophile."[50] The final publication of *Doctor Mirabilis* in England must have augmented Blish's sense that that was where he belonged. Certainly he was proud of his connection with Faber & Faber, the publisher of James Joyce, Ezra Pound, and T. S. Eliot. Blish, an admirer of Eliot's poetry, in one instance circled Eliot's name, which figured in the company letterhead (Dep. Blish 392/1). Two lines from Eliot provide "An Epilogue" epitaph for *The Quincunx of Time,* and the trilogy title "After Such Knowledge" (covering *Doctor Mirabilis, Black Easter/The Day After Judgment,* and *A Case of Conscience*) is taken from an Eliot line. And Eliot, of course, was an American who settled in England.

Ezra Pound and two other Jameses, James Joyce and James Branch Cabell, were preeminent among Blish's literary enthusiasms. From July 1967 (when Blish, like Cabell, was a Virginia author) until his death, Blish edited or co-edited seventeen issues of the Cabell journal *Kalki* (whole numbers 5 to 18) with University of Cincinnati English professor William Leigh Godshalk for the James Branch Cabell Society.[51] From 1969 until his death Blish also belonged to the New York C. S. Lewis Society. In addition to his critical writing on Joyce, Cabell, Pound, and Poe, Blish also produced a considerable amount of SF criticism, first collected in *The Issue at Hand* (1964) as by William Atheling, Jr., the name Pound adopted for his music criticism.

Pencil drawing of Blish by Judith Lawrence Blish (Dep. Blish 407/1, fol. 15)

Blish had projected a first trip to England in 1963. About to turn 42, he wrote Charles Monteith on 26 March 1963 that he had "only been out of the U.S. for 4 hours and that by accident" (CM 51). But he and Judith did not make it to England until August 1965 when they attended the 23d World Science Fiction Convention in London, at which Brian Aldiss was guest of honor. During this two-week visit, the Blishes met Charles Monteith and Brian Aldiss over lunch at Rules in Maiden Lane. Ann Corlett, Blish's editor for *Doctor Mirabilis,* also arranged a dinner at the Corletts' home on September 10. A three-week trip to England in 1967 confirmed the decision to move there eventually.

In 1962 Blish became an account executive for the Washington, D.C. office of the Tobacco Institute, an arm of Hill & Knowlton, the public relations firm ("the largest in the world," KLA, 18 February 1960) he had been working for since 1960. He was living in New York when he met Judith but after their marriage Blish's job necessitated relocating in Washington, followed in 1965 by a move to an apartment in Alexandria, Virginia. In the same year, thanks to the impetus from the Milford Science Fiction Writers' Conference, the Science Fiction Writers of America was founded with Damon Knight as its first president.[52] Blish was vice-president of the SFWA for two terms beginning in 1966.

Sometime in 1963 or 1964 Blish along with 94 other writers (including Kurt Vonnegut, Jr.) replied to the eleven questions featured in Lloyd Biggle, Jr.'s "A Questionnaire for Professional Science Fiction Writers and Editors." The result, as edited by Bill Mallard and Bill Bowers (editors of the fanzine *Double: Bill Symposium*) was published as *The Double: Bill Symposium* (1969). In his answers Blish notes that 60 percent of his output was SF, that SF writers should keep up with the scientific journals, that Henry Kuttner was the most important influence on his work (followed by del Rey, de Camp, van Vogt, and Heinlein), that he was educated to be a limnologist (hence the "Surface Tension" story), and that he was influenced for the worse by writing when rates were low and magazines plentiful so that it was easy to get a bad story into print.[53]

In the June 1968 issue of *Galaxy* Blish appears in a list (organized by Judith Merril and Kate Wilhelm) of 82 SF writers who opposed the participation of the U.S. in the Vietnam war. Seventy-two SF writers (including Heinlein and a much higher proportion of nonprofessionals) are listed as supporting the U.S. involvement. The lists were reprinted in other SF magazines.

Also in 1968, which saw the publication of *Black Easter* (the first part of the last volume of the "After Such Knowledge" trilogy), Blish made his third and this time successful attempt at surviving as a freelance writer. In an interview with Paul Walker he mentions three pre-conditions for freelancing: (1) the mortgage on the Milford, Pennsylvania home in which Virginia and his children still lived had to be paid off, (2) his writing income had to exceed his salary, and (3) royalty income had to exceed income from new sales. All conditions were met in 1967—"it was time to bite the bullet."[54] Ironically, Blish's state of relative financial security derived not from the sale of his best books but from a series of contracts he signed with Bantam Books to produce collections of story versions of the hit TV series "Star Trek."[55] Survival for this most cerebral of SF writers meant a hefty commitment to hack work. At any rate Blish quit his job in early 1969 and lived the life of a freelance writer until his death in 1975. But again ironically although perhaps predictably, having written so much material in time he could steal from his regular job, ("long years of writing in small notebooks at long lunch hours, mostly spirituous, which produced most of his work when he was employed as an account executive"[56]) he now found, with whole days spread out before him, that he often could not write at all.

(vi) England: A New Life? (1969–75)

Blish had originally intended escaping the expense of the U.S. by moving to Italy. Florence constituted, along with Oxford, England, Blish's notion of an intellectual utopia.[57] But in April 1969 the Blishes moved to England largely because there would be no language problem and it would be possible to live near centers of learning and libraries. At first they rented 2 "Fisherman's Retreat," St. Peter Street, Marlow, by the Thames in Buckinghamshire. Then, because of the landlord's plan to sell the dwelling (CM 84), they bought "Treetops" on Woodlands Road in Harpsden near Henley-on-Thames, a tiny hamlet about twenty miles from Oxford. They shared "Treetops" with three cats: Ymouse (a Pennsylvania barn cat), Mufti (a calico), and Keikobad (a Silverberg Siamese) who "mysteriously" died and was replaced by Icarus (a tabby cat subsequently renamed Stephen Dedalus).[58] Blish, finally granted a residence permit in April 1973, started compiling lists for a British-American dictionary.

There are connections to be made between the shift to a species of fantasy in *Black Easter,* Blish's becoming a member of the C. S. Lewis Society in 1969, and the move to England in the same year. *Black Easter* is dedicated to C. S. Lewis and includes an epigraph taken from his *Screwtape Letters* (1943).[59] From 1925 to 1954 Lewis was a Fellow of Magdalen College, Oxford, where he formed a close association with two other Christian fantasists, J. R. R. Tolkien and Charles Williams. Putting these details together suggests that Blish must have viewed life in the vicinity of Oxford as equivalent to a resurrection into a new ideal life—including British pale ale, which he loved. Algis Budrys thinks Blish's shift "from H. G. Wells, idol of the Futurians, to C. S. Lewis and literal religion" indicates "he was trying to think his way into Heaven. I suspect he was trying that all his life, but that toward the end he was doing it almost consciously."[60]

Once established in England, the Blishes began to explore Europe, and Italy in particular. Blish was invited to serve on the jury at the

Trieste Film Festival in June 1969, and thus Blish's first experience of a non-English-speaking country coincided with the first footfall on the Moon, man's first experience of a non-human world.[61] Blish returned to Italy by himself in June 1971 for the Trieste Third International James Joyce Symposium, having attended the Dublin symposium in June 1969.

The one-volume Avon paperback edition of *Cities in Flight* appeared in 1970 as did a second collection of "Atheling's" SF criticism, *More Issues at Hand*. *The Day After Judgment,* the sequel to *Black Easter,* was published in 1971. In April 1972 a Special Blish Issue of *The Magazine of Fantasy & Science Fiction* appeared, containing a profile by Lowndes and Blish's novella about the adventures of an untethered mind, "Midsummer Century." But what needs emphasis here is the fact that while in England Blish published virtually nothing that did not derive from earlier work. With some input from his fan correspondent, Paul Shackley, Blish expanded "Beep" (1954) into a novella, *The Quincunx of Time* (1973). Even *Midsummer Century* originates from a 1948 outline for a far future novel of the same title.[62] At least four extended SF works were projected, two of which (a novel about a galactic power named the Green Exarchy and a time travel novel) never got beyond the idea stage.[63] The other two were a trilogy entitled "King Log" and a novel tentatively entitled "The Breath of Brahma." Two mainstream novels (one going back to 1944) that he did complete, part of his bid to secure a reputation for writing something other than SF, seem destined never to be published. The evidence suggests that Blish's years in England were troubled and often rather unhappy ones. His ambitions continued to grow but so did an array of limiting factors.

Before long he was heavily involved in the British SF scene. He contributed criticism regularly to the British fanzine *Speculation* (1963–73); was Guest of Honour at Eastercon, the 21st British Science Fiction Convention, in London in 1970; and spoke about New Wave SF and about *Ringworld* as an example of nostalgic SF at a one-day Speculation Conference held in Birmingham (14 June 1970). In 1971 he did a monthly feature on SF for Radio London (CM 84). Also in 1971 he helped the British SF writer and editor George Hay and others establish the Science Fiction Foundation (a teaching and research unit at the North East London Polytechnic), became a member of its council, and contributed to its critical magazine *Foundation*. In conversation George Hay has indicated that he feels enormously indebted to Blish who would travel long distances to attend meetings. In the autumn of 1972 Blish and Judith organized the first English Milford Conference, an annual event to be held each autumn at—where else?—Milford-on-Sea in Hampshire. It was at this first meeting that the thirty-seven-year-old English writer Josephine Saxton, who had recently published three SF (?) novels in a surrealist mode, became acquainted with Blish; they had originally met at the 1971 Eastercon.[64] Subsequently, as relations with Judith became strained, Blish came to rely more and more on Josephine. The Faber files indicate that in 1973 Blish submitted a spin-off Milford Conference collection entitled "Worlds in Collusion" including stories by John Brunner, Anne McCaffrey, Josephine Saxton, and Peter Tate. Faber's reader recommended against publication (CM 84). In November 1973 Blish attended the Beyond This Horizon Festival in Sunderland, where the present author met him for the first time.

As has been suggested, Blish's problems during this period were not only marital. His cancer had not been beaten; much of the time he was not well, and he could not lay off the cigarettes—"Gauloises Disque Bleu, which my doctor recommends, alternatively with Kools, which he doesn't" (KLA, 27 February 1973). Blish was hospitalized for one week in 1974 "with a venous thrombosis in one leg . . . then my wife was thrown from the back of a London bus and sustained a concussion" that left her without any sense of smell (KLA, 24 May 1974). For Blish a duodinal ulcer followed, then arthritis (KLA, 22 September 1974). Meanwhile, back in the States, young Benjamin Blish had problems with adolescence (Dep. Blish 412/2) and with his teeth. In the context of a series of letters dealing with the cost of orthodontic work, Virginia Kidd wrote to Blish (12 August 1970) suggesting that Ben live with him for three years because the required orthodontic work would be much cheaper in England. This did not happen.[65] And then there was the pressure of Blish's writing commitments, which had to do not with the obligation to churn out the *Star Trek* adaptations but with an advance received to write the "King Log" trilogy. Brian Aldiss and his wife Margaret, who lived in Oxford and saw the Blishes frequently at Marlow and Henley, gave Blish a break from this chore and the writer's block it had produced. Together with Charles Monteith of Faber & Faber and the American SF writer Harry Harrison, they

> descended on Jim and Judy in Henley. We took them to lunch at the Little Angel on the bridge, and offered to loan him $10,000—interest free—to pay off . . . whoever the blood-sucker was. Jim was overcome, but he wouldn't take the money. Just knowing we had faith in him made him feel better.[66]

The fan mail that Blish received as a result of the *Star Trek* books—something he had not experienced in such volume before—also made him feel better. He seems, for example, to have done little to discourage the admiration of one fan, Miss Karin Laflin Adams of Phoenix, Arizona. In the course of their intimate correspondence, she wrote Blish many voluminous letters using the phrase "with all of love" (taken from Blish's "Common Time") as a sign-off (Dep. Blish 411/1). Much of the correspondence has to do with opera, for which they had a shared enthusiasm, and Blish's side of it is both revealing and informative. A committed Trekkie, Karin had written "A Song for Spock" and was bowled over when she discovered that *Star Trek 10* (1974) was dedicated to her. Blish, in Josephine Saxton's words, "affected to despise Star Trek" and, in fact, he had not written *Star Trek 10*. Judith Blish has revealed that *Star Trek 6–11* (all of which appeared under Blish's name except the last where J. A. Lawrence appears as collaborator) were essentially written by Judith Blish and her mother Muriel Lawrence.[67]

It is thanks to the Karin Laflin Adams correspondence that we have a concise account of Blish's approach to writing. He records in a section of a serial letter to her that,

> Poems demand five or six drafts, each heavily corrected in pen until the final copy (and I've been known to change two or three words of that, years later in a few cases). For short stories, up to say 15,000 words, the idea and approach are usually reasonably complete in my head before I start typing; for these I do one rough draft and then a fair copy, making minor changes as I retype but seldom enough to call the fair copy a new draft. For a novel, if the plot is complex, I do an outline which may run to 5,000 words, and then a rough draft, but what often happens here is that I wind up with an ending quite different from the planned one. This doesn't bother me, in fact I almost invariably like the new ending better, but it does require a complete second draft to make the rest of the text consistent with the change in direction; then comes the fair-copy-with-minor-alterations. (KLA, 27 February 1973)

He then goes on to describe the most spectacular example of such an ending change—*A Case of Conscience*. Blish claimed in an interview that he required about two weeks to write a short story and four months to write a novel.[68]

In the last years of his life Blish, with sparse grey hair, looked frail, gaunt and cadaverous, and much older than his chronological age. His decade-long fight against cancer combined with a prolonged state of deep depression had taken its toll. In September 1974 a shadow on one lung was diagnosed, and in October one lobe of the lung was removed (KLA, 8 November 1974). Brian Aldiss and his wife visited Blish in "the ominously named Battle Hospital in Reading": "He lay in bed in a

Blish aged 52. Photo taken by Peter Nicholls at the U.K. Milford Writers' Workshop, July 1973 (Dep. Blish 406/2)

towelling robe, dark, bitter, light-weight—intense against the pallid room. As ever, he radiated great mental energy. Books were piled all over the place, by the bedside, on the bed. Oswald Spengler's *Decline of the West* lay open, facedown, on the blankets."[69] Peter Nicholls, then editor of *Foundation,* had asked Blish to revise an article that Blish had written putting SF in a Spenglerian perspective and he worked on the project from his hospital bed.

Before the skies finally darkened, Judith, on her earnings from writing (a fourth published story, "The Persistence of Meaning," had appeared in the November 1974 *Galaxy*), took James for a two-week holiday in Florence in March 1975 (KLA, 14 January 1975). But, what with flu and emotional problems, Blish wrote that the "Florentine adventure turned out to be rather a mixed bag, despite the fact that I had been looking forward to it almost all my adult life" (KLA, 5 April 1975).

During this difficult period Blish's relationship with Josephine Saxton continued to develop.[70] They had gotten to know one another better at the second English Milford Conference (1973) and thereafter Josephine (who was married at the time and the mother of three children) was invited more than once to stay at "Treetops." Their love affair dated from 7 April 1974 (KLA, 12 December 1974, 1 February 1975, 5 April 1975). At the end it was Josephine, Judith, Blish's daughter Elisabeth, and the district nurse who cared for him following directions from the hospital. Oxygen, however, was Josephine's idea and it helped considerably.

Josephine's unpublished story about Blish's last days is entitled "The Man Who Loved His Food." The background to the story is provided by the following information from her also unpublished "Biographical Notes on James Blish":

> He was a gourmand [and "had once been a creative cook"] and loved food and yet since his cancer of the tongue, and especially in his last few years, he could eat very little. The sight of a lot of food made him gag and he could not swallow. He lived mainly on dry Vermouth, bottled Guiness and tobacco. In my opinion this lack of appetite was partly due to alcoholism and partly psychological because just occasionally he could eat quite well for example when out for dinner in a quiet restaurant.

Josephine believes he was basically drinking himself to death. Her story alludes to Blish's hatred of the bouzouki music that Judith loved to play (and played by cassette in private as soon as he expressed distaste). Judith had taken holidays in Greece in January and then again in February 1975 and moved to Athens after his death. Blish also loathed pop music but under Josephine's tutelage he came to appreciate some rock groups, including "Yes." In her story Josephine describes how Blish (renamed Theodore) on 30 July 1975 "died very quickly in the afternoon, simply ceasing to be able to breathe even pure oxygen. They watched his heart stop beneath his ribs." The "they" here covers Josephine (Laura) and Judith (Rachel) but, in fact, Elisabeth, then in her last year at Colgate and finishing French literature studies in Dijon (KLA, 25 February 1975), was also present. Josephine called them into the room just in time. His mother-in-law, who lived in a specially built flat attached to the Blish house, and was naturally enough hostile to Josephine, was not present. What Blish says of Dr. Hamilton C. Bloch's exit in *Fallen Star* (1957) might equally be said of Blish's death: "Here he exists, in love, which is as good a going-out as anyone has devised yet."[71]

Thanks to the influence of Brian Aldiss and Charles Monteith, permission was obtained to bury this expatriate American in the cemetery of St. Cross Church, Oxford, close by the Bodleian Library, alongside the likes of Kenneth Grahame, author of *The Wind in the Willows,* and the scholar Sir Maurice Bowra. On August 4, at the burial, Dunbar's *Lament for the Makaris* (c. 1508) was read over the grave by Charles Monteith, including the following verse:

> The state of man does change and vary
> Now sound, now sick, now blyth, now sary
> Now dansand merry, now like to dee—
> *Timor Mortis conturbat me.*

The low stone, hard to find in this jumbled and overgrown ancient cemetery in spite of the laburnam tree planted alongside,[72] bears by Blish's own request this simple inscription:

> JAMES BLISH
> 1921–1975
> AUTHOR

Aldiss affirms in his obituary that Blish was also "a good man, and good men always go too soon."[73]

But what was he really like? His customary demeanor was somewhat grim. A serious Renaissance man, a relentless and driven worker, his habits of mind were rationalistic, meticulous and scholarly, even monkish; marriage to such a man clearly presented its problems. He was very well informed about a number of diverse subjects including musicology. He was ruthlessly honest intellectually and possessed of a scrupulous sense of integrity; he was also casuistical, uncompromising, parsimonious, jealous, possessive, unforgiving, and shy. He was opinionated, occasionally to the point of sophistry; he had a dry but sometimes antic sense of humor; he was an elitist. He believed in hierarchies and politically, in fact, was something of a fascist, or more accurately, a collectivist. According to Josephine Saxton, he was a man of "intense emotions, including the ability to love." Aldiss agrees: "He had great admirations, great hatreds."[74] But above all else, according to Aldiss, "he was a good though fluctuating writer, and he was as brave as a pride of lions. While it is true that these two criteria do not predominate in literary criticism, they shape it all."[75] Virginia Kidd in her 1949 poem, "No Royal Road—for JB," summed up Blish, at that time still her husband, this way:

> Many tongued-tough-minded and intent
> he means to go a way some others went,

> no way but hard, no weapon but his heel
> and head, no quarter, no appeal.[76]

Blish certainly had his share of hardship and misfortune but his hard-won literary successes remain. Also remaining are a number of unfinished or as yet unpublished manuscripts: a first draft of the introductory section of what was originally intended to be a two-volume and later collapsed to a one-volume "History of Witchcraft, Demonology, and Magic," which Doubleday had commissioned in 1969; a very technical work dating from 1948 entitled, in its 1969 version, "The Sense of Music"; thirty-three leaves of a typescript entitled "The Conquest of Life: New Pathways in Medicine" (Dep. Blish 436); a draft of "The Operas of Richard Strauss" (Dep. Blish 433/4); a partial draft of "Night Journey," a biography of Strauss (Dep. Blish 427/2); projected critical works entitled "Dead Issues at Hand" (Dep. Blish 388/1–3) and "The Agent as Patient: Seven Subjects with an Object"; all these are discussed in chapter 9. Also remaining are two radio plays, "The Gold Frame" for CBS "Action Magazine of the Air" and "Carbonite Johnny," a detective play; "The Box," a teleplay of one of Blish's SF stories which was produced; four movie scripts; an opera libretto entitled "Eros and Psyche"; about 115 poems; the incomplete SF trilogy entitled "King Log" (three bits of which had appeared in *Galaxy* between February 1969 and December 1970) and the last incomplete SF novel tentatively entitled "The Breath of Brahma," written in collaboration with Josephine Saxton (both discussed in chapter 8); "The Magic Hammer," a children's novel (see chapter 9); the fantasy "Wayriver"; "Glass Night," a historical novel set in Venice (see chapter 7); a Kafkaesque novel entitled "Telecast" begun in 1948 (see chapter 5); a contemporary novel (the first version of which was written in 1944, the last in 1974) involving a production of Richard Strauss's *Der Rosenkavalier* (1911) pretending to be written by one "Frederick Danewort" and entitled "A Cage of Birds"; and two late more or less autobiographical fictions: "Is That a Death?," a *roman à clef* also by "Frederick Danewort," and "A Prophecy of Love" (all discussed in chapter 10).[77] It may be hoped that, with the passage of time, the best of this material will be published.

The broadly chronological account of the Blish canon that follows is divided into three parts reflecting Blish's successive orientation towards the future, the past, and finally the present. A key to this development is provided by the compositional order of what he came to call his "After Such Knowledge" trilogy: the science-fiction novel *A Case of*

Conscience, the historical novel *Doctor Mirabilis,* and the fantasy diptych set in the present, *Black Easter* and *The Day After Judgment.* This tripartite temporal context illuminatingly encompasses Blish's entire output—fictional, factual, critical, poetic, and dramatic, published and unpublished. A recurrent thematic and imagistic opposition between containment and flight, that reveals itself particularly in his fiction, is discovered to bear on the relationship between the science-fiction writer's doomed attempt to escape from the present moment (or from life) and the science-fiction archetype of conceptual breakthrough. It will also be argued that the tripartite development of Blish's career did lead to at least one genuine breakthrough, his eventual, post-Futurian understanding of the nature of science fiction with its dependence upon both historical paradigms (exemplified most obviously by the use of Oswald Spengler's system in *Cities in Flight*) and upon the supposedly antithetical genres of fantasy and realism.

I.
SCIENCE-FICTION FUTURES

TWO

A PULP APPRENTICESHIP

▌Much of the fiction that Blish published in the pulp magazines of the 1940s is very amateurish and ephemeral stuff. This is particularly true of the thirty-seven stories that he contributed to the sports, western, detective and, in one case ("The Torrid Type"), love pulps through 1953, all of which this chapter will pass over in silence. The last non-SF story that he published in the pulp magazines was "Claw of the Kidnapped Idol" by "Marcus Lyons" (a character in *Finnegans Wake*) which appeared in *Crack Detective Stories* (August 1953). By that time, however, the first volume of *Cities in Flight* had appeared and Blish had established himself as a writer of SF. He had also published in that genre three other novels (including one in collaboration with Robert A. W. Lowndes) and some thirty-four stories and novellas. As one might expect, an examination of this material reveals a writer's dogged, sometimes fumbling, development towards artistic maturity.

SF stories are usually set in the future but they may be set in the present or the past. Almost without exception Blish's SF stories are set in the future. The writers with whom Blish associated during the late thirties and early forties called themselves the Futurians with good reason. In 1970, Blish would write an essay about the accuracy of SF predictions entitled "Future Recall." He chronicles some more or less accidental hits (two authored by Robert Heinlein) and concludes that SF, while "not notably prophetic," does prepare us for change by "stretching the mind to accommodate" a "multiplicity of possible futures."[1]

(i) Short Stories and Novellas (March 1940–September 1951)

Little might be expected of the group of thirteen stories that Blish had professionally published by 1942, the year he turned twenty-one and entered the army, but one of them, "Sunken Universe" (published in the month of his twenty-first birthday, May 1942), has exceeded all expectations. The story became part of "Surface Tension" (August 1952), which in turn became part of the pantropy story-sequence, *The Seedling Stars* (1957), and will be discussed in that context in chapter 3. Of the preceding ten stories Blish had written, "only one had any merit whatsoever."[2] He is probably referring to the only one of those ten stories to be reprinted in his lifetime, "Solar Plexus" (September 1941), which was collected in revised form in Judith Merril's *Beyond Human Ken* (1952) and Robert Silverberg's *Men and Machines* (1968). Here Blish seems to have written the first human-spaceship story, the prototype of a novel like Anne McCaffrey's *The Ship Who Sang* (1970). Two prisoners aboard a cyborg spaceship who/which wants to implant their brains in robots are able to escape because our hero realizes that the ship's control nerves have not been separated from his/its pain nerves and, by smashing the autopilot, hits him/it, figuratively speaking, in the stomach. Or is this a baby kicking in the womb? Intrigued by Damon Knight's symbolic analysis of "Common Time" (see pp. 223–24 here) Blish discovered that "he had been writing what seemed to be the same covert plot, over and over." He named its theme "Being Born" and provided Knight with a detailed and convincing symbolic analysis of the conception aspect of the theme in "Solar Plexus."[3]

After Blish's death, Robert A. W. Lowndes reprinted Blish's fourth published story, "Citadel of Thought," in *The Best of James Blish*, characterizing it as Blish's first successful SF story.[4] It originally appeared in the first issue of Wollheim's *Stirring Science Stories* (February 1941). Pulp adventure on the surface, it contains structural and symbolic resonances that reverberate in much of the work to come. Indeed, it seems that Blish spent the rest of his career becoming increasingly aware of the problem that comes across as perhaps an accidental feature of "Citadel of Thought."

A comatose Dan Lothar, on the run from a "police cruiser" and more dead than alive, slumps at the controls of his broken "planet-plane," the *Ganymedian*, as it plunges through the atmosphere of Neptune.[5] He comes round to discover that he has been conveyed to a sea-bed sanctuary on Neptune that an unnamed female immortal identifies as the "Hall of Thought" (p. 6). She and her fellow immortals are human beings who have learned to surmount death through the power of thought. But they have also learned of an alien threat which is approaching Earth. Lothar's physical assistance is needed to destroy the evil aggressor. With the aid of a new ship and prisoners from a "Plutonian penal colony" the alien ship is eventually destroyed (p. 16).

What is not routine about the story is its pattern of doubling. Lothar's being pursued by the police at the beginning of the piece is paralleled by Lothar pursuing the alien "white sphere" at the end (p. 15). The first-page reference to Lothar's "shattered *Ganymedian*" is paralleled by the later reference to "the alien ship shattered like a glass bubble" (p. 18), one of many bubbles—planetary bubbles, galactic bubbles, and bubbles of thought—burst or destroyed in Blish's fiction. One should also note the parallel between Lothar's being a criminal and his being assisted by criminals imprisoned on Pluto.

The doubling pattern suggests that this story can be read as psychodrama, a contest within Lothar between constraining circumstances and his desire to be free. The "citadel of thought" is as much Lothar's brain case as the sanctuary on Neptune. But a citadel is, of course, something that contains and possibly restricts. Lothar first describes the place in which he comes to as "prison-bare" (p. 3). As a criminal committed to acts of transgression, prison walls, no less than the barriers of mortality and convention, are things to be broken through. And hence the additional significance of Lothar's order to the commander of the penal colony: "Break out your prisoners and arm them" (p. 16). The barrier that Lothar is attempting to break down is that between life and death. In the opening sentence, the stricken planet-plane with its "wraith-like, ephemeral fan of incandescent gas" is headed for "death" (p. 1). In Lothar's situation, "Any other man would have been dead" (p. 2). The experience of the alien threat that is communicated telepathically to Lothar "was like the breath of Death" (p. 9). Magically, the alien sphere is able "to stop dead at full speed" (p. 15). And, of course, Pluto, the planet on which the story ends, suggests the mythological underworld, home to the god of the dead.

With the destruction of the alien sphere, death is presumably overcome. Lothar and the female immortal clink the face-plates of their spacesuits and laugh—"an explosive, free, and human sound" (p. 19). The prison has been breached. Or has it? The story ends with an image of containment and division. Lothar and the girl are separated from one another by their suits. There is here an essential disjunction between life and death and perhaps also between the physical or emotional and the mental, the latter being something that Blish struggled with in much of his writing. We shall notice also throughout Blish's work the desire to explode out of mental and physical containers, the success in doing so, the illusion of having done so, and perhaps the human impossibility of doing so. And always the allure of that ultimate breakthrough—death itself.

Although clumsy and stereotypical, some others among the thirteen stories published between 1940 and 1942 in minor pulps edited by Pohl, Wollheim, and Lowndes are not without interest. But here we need only dwell on Blish's first published story, "Emergency Refueling" (March 1940), which, as it happens, has also recently been republished for the first time.[6] Blish seems to have shared with Arthur C. Clarke a fascination with Jupiter (home of the gods) and its moons. The spaceship *Pallas* of "Emergency Refueling" is headed for Jupiter. Forced to get special permission to land on Pluto because of insufficient fuel to reach Ganymede, the nearest fueling station, the pilot, Stan Dorry, and his navigator, Jonah Whipple, encounter a fungus-like, telepathic life form in the cave where they have been told they will find the pitchblende rocks that can be converted into fuel. Dorry is consumed by the alien fungus but Whipple escapes with an armful of rocks. The most notable thing about the story is the way it exemplifies what Blish would later identify as one of the main faults of the novice writer: the substitution of contrived alternatives for the simple word "said." The word *is* used three times but otherwise a character "growled," "snapped," "returned," "barked," "repeated," "answered," "crackled," "whistled" and "remonstrated." It may be significant that two of the "saids" are Whipple's, the man who gets out alive; the third is applied to the "mental voice" of the alien. Perhaps this is why Whipple survives![7]

Twelve stories later, further publication was postponed during the two years that Blish spent in the army.[8] He returned to writing SF with a five-chapter novella, "The Bounding Crown" (December 1944).[9] Then for almost a year he abandoned SF. But after publishing four "Marcus Lyons" detective stories in Lowndes's *Crack Detective Stories* and "Invisible Armada," a brief factual article about tiny torpedo-like creatures called sea-squirts, which appeared in Lowndes's *Air World*, Lowndes and Blish published an SF story called "Chaos, Co-ordinated" (October 1946), a first sale to Campbell's *Astounding*, under the combined pseudonym "John MacDougal." Lowndes provides this account of how the story came to be written:

> While I had written and sold a few science-fiction tales before 1945, when I first became a close friend of James Blish, now and then I would get an idea which I could not do anything with because it required much more knowledge of science to handle adequately than I had.
>
> One of those stories I had in mind was that of a civilization run entirely by

what we would now call a giant computer. I remembered John Campbell saying at one time when I called on him when I was agenting stories, that we were in for a truly tremendous information explosion and that the greatest need of the future would be a coordinating agency, so that any particular scientific discovery could be coordinated with everything else that was known at the time. His opinion then was that the most important people in the future would be librarians: they would not know the answers but they could tell you where the answers were to be found. And I thought then of an earlier science-fiction tale that I had read ["Stenographers' Hands" by Dr. David H. Keller, *Amazing Stories Quarterly,* Fall 1928], which pointed out that a machine cannot tell the differences between "to," "two," and "too." That was back in 1928 when the farthest advance was the dictaphone.

So my plot idea was that this super-civilization would seek to overwhelm ours, and our counter-attack would be to feed sheer nonsense into the main computer. After all, a dictaphone is not going to question anything you speak into it. No, it would immediately coordinate that nonsense with everything else it had in what we would now call its memory banks, and the result would be chaos, coordinated.

Jim was fascinated by the idea, and the short novelet . . . was the result. Campbell loved it.[10]

Elsewhere Lowndes adds that Blish's agent, Frederik Pohl, had rejected their first version because of "a fundamental plot-formula error. . . . What we'd done was to make things all too easy for our protagonists; everything sailed through smoothly without a hitch." That fixed, Campbell "bought it at once."[11]

The alien Celestials in "Chaos, Co-ordinated," who make up a galactic federation, are totally incapacitated when one of the two infiltrators from Earth, Matt Blythe, feeds Co-ordination, the Celestials' guiding mechanical brain on the Hollow World, Lewis Carroll's "The Hunting of the Snark" and Co-ordination processes this nonsense poem as factual information. But what makes the story important in terms of Blish's *oeuvre* is that it contains the first references to the "Dirac transmitter," the instantaneous communications device named for the English mathematical physicist Paul Dirac (1902–84), the "father" of antimatter.[12] The transmitter will recur in other stories, most notably "Beep" and "Beep" expanded as *The Quincunx of Time*. In "Chaos, Co-ordinated" only the aliens have this transmitter. But it is another device, the protagonists' newly discovered deadly Kor beam (named after the hidden valley of Kôr in Sir H. Rider Haggard's *She: A History of Adventure?*), an "incandescent cancer" that hits "the speed of light in some other space," that must have eventually fused in Blish's mind with the Dirac as the plot idea of "Beep": all the Kor beams ever launched would, one "day millennia ahead, . . . return to their points of origin" (p. 38). In other respects, including the Heinleinian cliché for a door opening, "The iris dilated" (p. 54), the story is quite routine.

Between November 1946 and September 1950 Blish published some thirty-four non-SF stories in such pulp magazines as *Blue Ribbon Western, Crack Detective Stories, Jungle Stories,* and *Super Sports.* But towards the end of this period he resumed his career as a writer of SF, with four stories published in 1948 marking his return. Actually, the first of these stories, "Mistake Inside" (March 1948) by "Arthur Merlyn," is on the fantasy/SF borderline. It deserves detailed treatment because it is the clear progenitor of *Black Easter* (1968) and *The Day After Judgment* (1971). The opposition between science and the occult which figures in the sequential novellas is first explored in "Mistake Inside" as the conflict between astronomy and astrology. Its main setting, which includes the fortress of Dis (as in the second novella), is actually Hell.

"Mistake Inside," a peculiar, complicated and cleverly constructed story, opens with a cat disappearing in Elizabethan England, "two hundred years before bomb craters had become a fixed feature of the English landscape," and the astronomer, Dr. Hugh Tracy, disappearing from twentieth-century New York just as he was about to shoot Jeremy Wright.[13] Tracy, the "transportee" (p. 38), finds himself in a strange, apparently early eighteenth-century house, in an environment which includes a variety of apparently anachronistic details. He is questioned by two men named Jonathan Bell and Oliver Martin, who then explain that he is in Outside and the "Jeremy Wright" he was about to shoot is actually Yero, "the ruler of this country during fall seasons" (p. 40), who is also called "The Enemy" (p. 48) and is about to marry Tracy's wife. The cuckholded Tracy is told that "an astrologer or thaumaturgist" should "be able to shoot you back where you belong" (pp. 40, 41). In search of an astrologer, Tracy heads for the public square where, reminiscent of Hawthorne's "My Kinsman, Major Molineaux," a parade is in progress. Tracy hears snatches of speech from different eras and, beyond the square, sees a huge metal castle of modernist design. At the end of the procession, borne in a sedan chair, is Yero-Jeremy and Tracy's wife, Evelyn.

After the procession leaves, Tracy visits the nearby shop of "Dr. ffoni, Licensed Magician" (p. 48). Dr. ffoni (phoney) explains that "All living has two sides. . . . The OUT-side is where the roots of significant mistakes are imbedded; the IN-side where they flower" (p. 49).[14] On the OUT-side, which few men are aware of, mistakes can be rectified but "to pivot a man Outside means that [like ends of a lever] two other living beings must . . . exchange places in time. Your Avatars [the symbols of Tracy's error] changed places in time, while you stood still in time and space, but were pivoted to face Outside." Blish has a real talent for this kind of pseudo-explanation. Following an incantation sung to a Pepsi-Cola tune which includes the reference "Dirac hole" (p. 50), Dr. ffoni's son (his cheap substitute for a familiar spirit) reveals that Tracy's Avatars are 200 years apart from each other and that they are night prowlers—one is the man in a top hat glimpsed earlier in the crowd. Tracy must locate their "simulacra" in Outside to "be rotated Inside" (p. 51).

Back at Bell's house, Bell explains further that the Old One is the rightful king and that transportees only show up during Yero's ascendancy: "all the people who make mistakes during that period, if the mistakes are of a certain kind, get pivoted around here to correct them" (p. 53). Bell then invites Tracy to join them in an attempt to assassinate Yero. After sleeping on the matter, Tracy wakes to find the semi-transparent, top-hatted man at his bedside. Now we get the true (?) explanation. Outside is actually Hell, the castle is the fortress of Dis, the Old One is Satan, and Bell (Belial?) and Martin are Princes of Hell. It seems that the Fallen try to lure the transportees (or Purgatory candidates) into doing something that will keep them in Hell for keeps. Yero, apparently the good guy, shows himself "to each newcomer in a form which will mean the most to the person." His role is to help the Purgatory candidates "straighten things out for themselves" (p. 56).

Tracy finally figures out that the top-hatted man is one symbol of his error because he conceived of "Wright as a cavalier, a suave homebreaker" and, since he suspected Jeremy of "tom-catting," the other simulacra Avatar must be the alley cat seen earlier "in conjunction with his first sight of the man in dinner clothes" (p. 58). A divining rod and a magical hat acquired from a red-headed urchin, whom Tracy understands to be an Archangel, propels Tracy, pursued by a mob of devils, into the castle to face, floating above a crystal globe, the heads of his wife Evelyn and of Yero, and the cat simulacra.

The story ends with Tracy returned to his own time and bursting into Jeremy Wright's apartment with a gun in his hand as before the transportation. Jeremy Wright is an astrologer and Tracy's experience has now taught him that, as such, Wright is indeed right and he, Tracy, was wrong to have previously ridiculed astrology. Evelyn, who was sensitive to her astronomer husband's principled disbelief in astrology, was simply consulting Wright, and the globe above which the faces of Yero and

Evelyn had appeared is actually Wright's crystal ball. Tracy had totally misconstrued the purpose of his wife's visits but now as a result of his experience (whether "real" or "imaginary") his sense of reality has been corrected and widened to include the supernatural. The ending of this ingenious tale, it must be admitted, is likely to produce a groan from the reader in response to what now appears something of a shaggy god story (after all, the red-headed urchin was looking for a dog named Fleet).

The second of the four 1948 stories, this one definitely SF, is a clever, effective tale entitled "Against the Stone Beasts" (Fall 1948). It begins with art student Ken Anderson attending an exhibition, arranged by his scientist friend John Kimball, of surrealistic pictures depicting flying people and a fabulous metropolis, pictures which are actually windows into another dimension. Anderson falls through one of them and finds himself in Earth's distant past, and along with Kimball, inventor of the time-coil, becomes involved in a war between the winged Varese, a race of space-travellers who will later move to Venus, and the space-beasts who live in the rock of the Earth. Since air rather than anything solid stops the space-beasts, they can be killed by hollow clubs! It appears that the matter-bombs that finally wipe out the space-beasts will eventually promote human evolution. This and "The Weapon Out of Time" are unique in Blish's corpus in that they both involve time travel to Earth's distant past.

The two other stories Blish published that fall were collaborations with Damon Knight, stories that Knight originated but could not complete without Blish's assistance.[15] Both stories now end with a world exploding or about to explode. In "Tiger Ride," an unusual and complicated tale set in the year 2121, a group of researchers from Earth assigned to the planet Syrtis Delta III are experimenting with an ultronic levitator belt. When it appears that one deceased female member of this emotionally fragile group has been magically recreated by a perfected alien version of the ultronic belt, it is deduced that the original inhabitants of the planet must have cracked the secrets of ultronic mathematics and developed service belts which did everything for them to the point of eradicating their desire to reproduce. Consequently the researchers blow the planet up but it appears from the "snapper" ending that the alien belt has survived and is heading for Earth, disguised as another member of the group! For "No Winter, No Summer" Blish and Knight used the joint pseudonym Donald Lafferty. In this story a "Fisher" from the future with a briefcase-shaped time machine hijacks Jon, an electronic tube designer, and transports him to the technological dystopia of 3903 that covers the Earth. Rather than extend this metallic hell to his own time, the mission with which he is subsequently charged, Jon makes use of the weapons button on a Timecruiser (which doubles as a Space-cruiser) to destroy this future Earth.

The third Blish/Knight collaboration, "The Weakness of RVOG" (February 1949) will be discussed in relation to *VOR,* the novel that grew out of it. Blish's last published collaboration with Knight, "The Secret People" (November 1950), is an inventive "novelet" that Blish could not finish.[16] It concerns the sighting of a giant alien ship which is visible only through a special pressurized plastic because it exists in another dimension. Sergeant Rosoff manages to explore the ship, which has been damaged by a meteorite, and leave just before it explodes. The alien crew, we learn in a conclusion told from the alien point of view, are of a race of titanic immortals, the end of a line of human evolution derived from the second Adam (a man spared by the First Holocaust); they escape in a lifeboat.

Blish chose to reprint only two stories from the early period in his first collection, *So Close To Home* (1961), which, with the subtitle *Stories For Today* (subsequently dropped), he described to Charles Monteith as a collection of near future stories (CM 51, 12 July and 27 October 1959).[17] The earliest of these, "The Box" (April 1949), which has been anthologized at least five times, has to do with New Yorkers suddenly becoming aware that a huge black dome has sealed off their city. Apparently the enemy is testing an anti-bomb screen similar to the one that the Americans are working on. Unless the projector generating the screen is located and neutralized, everybody inside the dome will die of suffocation within a week. In the nick of time Blish's original thinker-hero, resonance engineer Jake Newton, concludes that the enemy must be making use of an outside projector. The appropriate action is taken and The Box vanishes. The effectiveness of this story has less to do with its basic premise than with its evocation of the detailed physical consequences of that premise, and a nice line in scientific patter. One should also note, however, the equation made between the disappearance of the dome and some kind of conceptual breakthrough. A character named Meister points out that the German word for "to discover"— *entdecken*—literally means "to take the roof off."[18] Presumably Meister is German-born so that he can make this point. At the same time he is a German Jew so that the meaning of his experience in Concentration Camp Dora can provide a horrifying image of what might happen to the inmates of The Box.

In "Battle of the Unborn" (March 1951), the other story reprinted in

So Close to Home, Dr. Barnes, speaking at a meeting of the Mutation Control Board in a mushroom-shaped building in the center of "old" (i.e., pre-bomb) Nagasaki, suggests the sterilization of a new mutant strain that he names *Homo chaos.* It turns out, however, that Barnes belongs to another mutation, *Homo episychos* or *Homo superior,* and that his proposal is designed to trick the rest of humanity into killing one another off.

Blish thought well enough of his early werewolf story, "There Shall Be No Darkness" (April 1950), to include it in the first edition (but not the revised second edition) of *Best Science Fiction Stories of James Blish* (1965). The story might be viewed as an exemplification of Blish's understanding of the generic ties between supernatural fiction and SF. In a 1972 *Spectator* review he refers to the supernatural magazines that Campbell edited (*Unknown* and *Unknown Worlds*) as publications "whose ghost has been hovering over science fiction ever since."[19] Lycanthropy, usually viewed as a supernatural phenomenon, is given a scientific explanation in Blish's ingenious and exciting novella.[20]

It is 1960 and Paul Foote, a painter and a guest at Tom Newcliffe's country-house party, senses that the Polish gentleman playing the piano, Jan Jarmoskowski, is a werewolf when a vase of wolfbane on the piano precipitates the transformation. Another guest, Christian Lundgren, a psychiatrist who is an expert on lycanthropy, agrees with Foote and provides the scientific rationalization: a "little known aberration" of the pineal gland "lowers the surface tension of the cells and at the same time short circuits the sympathetic nervous system directly to the cortex."[21] As a result the body of a human being, complete with its clothes, may change into that of a fur-covered wolf. The werewolf may be killed with a silver bullet because silver "poisons the pinearin-catalysis" (p. 56).

The story is compellingly told and makes good use of the pathetic fallacy: "The gentle ripples of the snowbanks contorted in the vast umbra, assumed demon shapes, twisted bodies half-rising from the earth, sinking back, rising again, whirling closer" (p. 46). Sometimes the message is too blatantly telegraphed with the reference to how the winter "bites," the colloquial "I'll bite" (pp. 47, 49) meaning "you have my interest," and the following image: "As he crossed the path of silvery light his shadow was oddly foreshortened, so that it looked as if it were walking on all fours" (p. 48).

Once it is established that Jan is a werewolf, Tom and Caroline Newcliffe, together with the guests, set about trying to kill the creature. Guns and silver bullets are supplied by Consolidated Warfare Service (an outfit that will recur in Blish's work under slightly different names) and traps are set. The werewolf is nipped by one of them and leaves some blood which Caroline touches and which infects a cut on her finger. As a result she also turns into a werewolf and kills Lundgren before being clubbed to death by Tom Newcliffe, who does not discover until too late that this werewolf is his wife. Increasingly, the reader is made to feel sympathetic towards the werewolf's plight, particularly when Jan asks Doris Gilmore, who was once his student in Prague and is still "in love with him" (p. 43), to shoot him. She elects instead to flee with him but a silver slug fired from the doorway by Foote puts an end to the werewolf and his hope that "After us there shall be no darkness comparable to our darkness" (p. 80).

The only thing really wrong with the story is that the combination of people at the house party is too coincidental. This fault is augmented in an expanded version where it turns out that Doris is a witch. Blish had been asked to contribute a more fantasy-oriented version of the story to a collection entitled *Witches Three,* published by Twayne in 1952. Consequently, having transformed the stuff of supernatural fantasy into SF, Blish set about reversing the transformation by adding witchcraft. The double metamorphoses that he worked on the story is analogous to the metamorphosis that Jan and Caroline undergo within the story. The date is changed from the then-future 1962 to the time of writing (1952), a couple of house party guests are added, and the five sections of the SF story are expanded to the seven of this science-fantasy version (sections 1 and 4 are each divided into two). The scientific explanation for lycanthropy remains but the "wild talent" rationale for witchcraft belongs to the realm of pseudo-science.[22] In the longest insert Foote questions Doris about her magical talents. A concluding addition reveals that Doris lured Jan-as-werewolf to her by witchcraft. She feels responsible for his death and we are led to believe at the end of this new conclusion that she forces Foote to shoot her as an expression of love.

It is indicative of the essentially fantastic quality of the *Witches Three* version that the poet, John Ciardi, in introducing the story, was inspired to interpret it allegorically. It all has to do with guilt for scientifically interfering with nature: "The good fairy [or white witch Doris] and the [black] witch [Jarmoskowski] want to destroy one another knowing that in so doing they will destroy themselves."[23] To my mind Ciardi is here simply substituting a fantasy of his own.

"There Shall Be No Darkness" is, to date, the only work of Blish's that has been made into a film. An option agreement between Blish and Max Rosenberg of Rearguard Productions, Inc., was signed in June

1971.[24] The resulting mediocre film, entitled *The Beast Must Die,* was first shown as the "Midnight Movie" on BBC2 in 1974. There were some changes made. In the film, the main character (a big-game hunter) and his wife, in whose house the events occur, are rich blacks instead of rich whites. The host invites the particular guests because he suspects that one of them is a werewolf. Before it is revealed which one, the film stops dead while a sepulchral voiceover challenges the film's audience to guess the outcome.

What could be considered the last of Blish's apprenticeship stories—after which the first consistent universe that he had built up, with its geotron drives, Centrale Patrol, and tall dog-eared Martians, disappears—is "Elixir" (September 1951). The story is about the attempt to escape by spaceship with a sample of a serum manufactured on Ganymede. The serum confers immortality along with such powers as prescience and autoregeneration, and it ultimately causes three members of the crew who take the serum to eject themselves from their doomed ship and to evolve into a new space-dwelling super-species. Although the story is somewhat awkward and confusing, Blish, as if himself injected with the serum, stood poised on the brink of new powers. Indeed, a crew member's experience of time dilation (albeit illusory) points forward to one of Blish's masterpieces, "Common Time." As it happens, the theme of enhanced mental powers will shortly receive fuller treatment in both *Jack of Eagles* (1952) and *The Warriors of Day* (1953).

(ii) A Collaborative Blur: *The Duplicated Man* (1953)

In the course of his career Blish collaborated with a number of writers, including Damon Knight and Norman L. Knight, and also, in effect, the authors of the "Star Trek" scripts. *The Duplicated Man,* the second novel that Blish worked on (and the third published) was written in collaboration with his long-time friend, Robert A. W. Lowndes, who, by 1942, had become editorial director of a chain of western, detective, love-romance, and sports pulp magazines.[25] The particular duplicating machine idea was Lowndes's but, as with "Chaos, Co-ordinated," he needed Blish's scientific input. Conceived as a short story in 1946, it turned into a novel only to be rejected by Campbell and by *Startling Stories,* whose editors found it overcomplicated. According to Lowndes, since "at that time Campbell was hot for A. E. van Vogt stories," he and Blish had "decided to see if we could out-van Vogt van

Vogt: Write a story as complicated as any of van Vogt's but tie up all the ends."[26] The manuscript went into a trunk until 1953 when Lowndes was again editing a number of SF magazines. After some revision which lengthened the manuscript from about 47,000 words to approximately 55,000, it appeared in one of them: the issue of *Dynamic Science Fiction* for August 1953.[27] Subsequently, as editor of Avalon Books' SF line, Lowndes ensured that the work (with some minor changes) was published as a book six years later.

The Duplicated Man is inferior to *Jack of Eagles* and *The Warriors of Day,* the two Blish novels that were published before, but written after it. Judged as a first novel, however, it is a creditable performance albeit uneven, choppy, somewhat confusing, and occasionally marred by trite or awkward writing. The unfortunate future expletive, "Mother of Khrushchev," which seems anachronistic and dates the book, occurs only once.[28] Written in the shadow of World War II, *The Duplicated Man* is an inventive novel of intrigue about war and how to avoid it. As an indication that both Blish and Lowndes stand by their product, the book is dedicated to the memory of the pseudonyms they had used for various stories that they were perhaps not so desirous of being associated with: "Marcus Lyons" (the pseudonym that Blish used for most of his detective stories), "Michael Sherman" (Lowndes's pseudonym) and "John MacDougal" (their collective "Chaos, Co-ordinated" pseudonym).

The plot is much too intricate to rehearse in detail. Essentially it concerns political struggles on and between Earth and Venus. Leaders of the humans who have been exiled to Venus—and who style themselves the Earth-Government-in-Exile—wish to wage war against Earth, which is ruled by the Security Council, and have taken to bombarding the planet regularly. The key Security Council figure is Joachim Burgd, the Representative from Antarctica. The grotesque, fat Venus Director, Geoffrey Thomas, the electronic genius who surrounded Venus with the Thomas Screen, "which won't pass atomic weapons" from either direction (p. 14), appears to be at least 140 years old. A subversive group on Earth called the Pro-Earth Party conspires against the Security Council and wants peace with Venus. Its organization hierarchy makes use of a terminology derived from the human body's neurological system. There is a corresponding underground movement on Venus, except that it is located above-ground (the Exiles live below-ground), which calls itself the Earth Party and wants to return to Earth.

Clearly the situation on Venus is something of a mirror image, or duplicate, of that on Earth. And indeed, with all the complex politicking and double dealing that goes on, it becomes very difficult to distinguish one organization or one world from another. Likewise, the characters are stereotyped to the point that they might as well be interchangeable duplicates. The notion of duplication is further underlined by the number of chapters (twenty) and by the fact that most of the chapters are divided into two sections.

There is, in fact, a Duplication machine hidden in Old York which has been under water since 1971 when Security bombed the southern icecap to flood the hostile "multi-national states" (p. 15). The possibilities which the machine presents come to the fore in the far-superior second part of the novel. Burgd's plan involves parachuting onto Venus the duplicates of an Earth double of Venus's Colonel Lathrop. Once on Venus the duplicates will cause "organizational chaos" (p. 115; shades of "Chaos, Co-ordinated") and, by pretending to be Lathrop, will sabotage the attacks on Earth. The Earth double and the book's protagonist is Paul Danton, a member of the Pro-Earth Party who has to be hijacked for this purpose.

Five duplicates are made of Danton but only one looks like Danton or the Venusian colonel. This comes about because the creation of each duplicate requires the input of a different human operator and the operator's personality and appearance determine to some extent the personality and appearance of the corresponding duplicate. This, as Lowndes explains, was the original idea with which he had approached Blish:

> I conceived of a short story with the tentative title of "As Others See Us" (from that well-known line from Robert Burns). There had been a number of stories about duplicating machines which could make extra copies of people. But what about a duplicate machine that operated this way: the subject to be duplicated is wired in, as it were, with another person (or more than one— one for as many duplicates as are desired). But what comes out is *not* an identical duplicate of the subject at all—it's the product of the operator's *impression* of the subject, physically, mentally, etc. So we have a series of "duplicates" not one of which bears more than a resemblance to the subject. And the subject now learns how he looks "as others see him."[29]

Chapter 11 describes this state of affairs and is the most effective in the entire novel. When the "sextet shrugged collectively," one of the duplicates points out that "We're like a six-voice composition; every once in a while, we'll all play the same note together" (p. 142). The same might be said of the two-voice composition that is *The Duplicated Man*. Each duplicate amounts to a combination of two minds. It should be noted that in *Midsummer Century,* Blish's last published novel or novella, he returns to this schizoid business of two minds in one body—and to the notion of Antarcticans; some kind of circle is completed.

In a number of other respects *The Duplicated Man* is anticipative of things to come. The bewildering atmosphere of political intrigue points to the universe described in "A Style in Treason" (1970), the earlier, shorter version of which is entitled "A Hero's Life" (1966). Geoffrey Thomas evokes that universe when he observes, at one point, that "The smell of treason . . . is a sharp, unforgettable odor that cuts through conspiratorial fog, and breathes new life into the almost dead" (p. 82). The role that Spengler will play in Blish's work is also signaled: Venus is described as "a swell place for Spengler's Magian culture to develop" (p. 168). Before the Duplication process, Blish has Danton look at "a copy of 'Finnegans Wake' " but the allusion is in no way thematically integrated (p. 11). That would await "A Case of Conscience" (1953). There are many references to cancer in Blish's work, references that deserve highlighting in view of Blish's own fate. Thus in *The Duplicated Man* a traitor is described as a "cancerous little cell" within the Pro-Earth Party's neurological organization (p. 179). Likewise, although the cancer metaphor is not used, *"the chain-reaction of war"* is within the body of mankind (p. 217). Thomas discovers "a peculiar form of cancer which would make a man immortal if he cared to pay the price," and he proclaims, "The great gift of immortality is *total cancer*" (pp. 214, 87). A living example of such a condition, the King of Buda-Pesht, will figure in *Cities in Flight*.

Logically enough it is Danton-Burgd (the duplicate for whom Burgd was the operator) who tumbles to the fact that Joachim Burgd is somehow behind everything. It turns out that Burgd, a long-lived Immune (one of those freaks who are immune to radiation), is in league with the immortal, Thomas. Their motive is purely altruistic: *"to break the chain-reaction of war"* (p. 217). They do this by fomenting antagonism between Earth and Venus (to distract attention from the possibilities of war on Earth) and by ensuring, by means of the Thomas Screen, that hostilities between Venus and Earth never involve the use of atomic weapons. The screen is nonexistent—an illusory barrier—but by presetting everything fired at, or from, Venus "to detonate at the proper distance" the deception is convincingly perpetrated (p. 215). From now on, the sterile Burgd and Danton-Burgd, whom he adopts as his son, will work to continue the peace. Thomas's "sentience" is about to peter out although his "body, or what it has become, will live forever" (p. 214).

Blish went on to write much better books than this one but the limited merit of *The Duplicated Man* might be gauged by its likely influence on a much more successful book: Vonnegut's *The Sirens of Titan* (1959). The invasion by human Venereans corresponds to Vonnegut's invasion by human Martians. And just as the "Martians" are strung up on street lampposts, so "there were a couple of hundred civilians systematically stringing [Venusians] up" (p. 163). The antiwar theme and the theme of manipulation are also common to both books. There is also a respect in which *The Duplicated Man* comes across as significantly ahead of its time. The way in which the duplicates are handled is uncannily similar to recent treatments of the cloning theme.

(iii) Growing Powers: From 1949 Novella to 1952 Novel (*Jack of Eagles*)

The way in which protagonist Danny Caiden becomes aware of his growing psychic powers can be paralleled with the development of Blish's artistic powers, as evidenced by the careful expansion of the novella, "Let the Finder Beware" (December 1949), into his first independent published novel, *Jack of Eagles* (1952). In a brief disgression a "Marc Lyons" is referred to, a contraction of the pseudonym (now almost outgrown) Blish used for his detective stories.[30] Danny finds the name "vaguely familiar" (p. 138). Danny, in fact, is similar to Blish in certain respects. He works in New York in "the packaging section of a food-industry trade paper" and writes poetry "on the side" (p. 14). Unlike Blish, however, Danny is an average guy with "no talent for writing fiction" (p. 34); Blish does not want an imaginative talent to throw any doubt upon the reality of the wild talents that Danny does possess. Thus Danny "took no stock in the supernatural" (p. 17). As Robert Lowndes points out, *Jack of Eagles* represents "the first time in science fiction that extra-sensory perception (ESP) and psychic phenomena were examined on a scientific, rather than an occult, supernatural, or mystic basis."[31]

The title "Let the Finder Beware" refers to one of the statements made by the voices that Danny hears in the first chapter, when he is becoming aware of his alarming precognitive abilities and knack for finding things. One of the things to beware of is becoming part of "a pyre" of "Carbonized bodies" at "the intersection" (p. 16), a detail from the precognition-prefigured accident in chapter 1 which in turn prefigures both a subsequent pyrotic death and the final fate of the book's villain "drenched" in "a fountain of . . . little flames" (p. 180). The title of the novel derives from an added element. Danny recalls the game of "five suit bridge" as having "the usual hearts, clubs, diamonds, spades, and a fifth suit was called 'Eagles'" (p. 74). As the result of an intense period of research in between the two titular details, he has come to realize that he is the equivalent of this "freak suit" (p. 75). Blish doubled the length of the original eleven-chapter novella by a skillful process of "enrichment."[32] The story is essentially the same although six of the original chapters are each expanded and broken into two, making up the seventeen chapters of the novel. Much of the expansion beefs up Danny's research and serves to put the theme of extraordinary psychic powers on an even more scientifically convincing basis.

After being fired by the owner of the Delta Publishing Company for writing a report about a forthcoming price fixing scandal, Danny resolves to research the matter in earnest. He successfully speculates on the stock market, bets on horses with mixed success, visits a Madame Zaza, occultist and medium (who turns out to be a fraud), and sees Dr. Todd, the parapsychologist at the University. Danny also visits the local branch of the Fortean Society (but is not impressed by its leader, Cartier Taylor, who tries to sell him on Hubbard's Dianetics), takes a bunch of relevant books out of the library, and finally visits the Psychic Research Society (PRS) where he meets Sir Lewis Carter, the astrophysicist and inventor "of a form of relativistic math" (p. 106).

Dr. Todd is a more important character in the novel than in the novella. After discovering that Danny's alpha wave pattern is unusual, he tells Danny about what Dr. Rhine (the Duke University researcher) calls "extrasensory perception" or "ESP" and "psychokinesis" or "PK." Danny supplements this information with his reading, which includes Fort's four books (the most relevant being *Wild Talents*), Dr. Rhine's books, Houdini's *A Magician Among Spirits*, J. W. Dunne's *An Experiment With Time,* and Ouspenskii's *Tertium Organum.* These and other books also constituted Blish's research for writing both novella and novel.

As the novel proceeds, more standard elements of pulp plotting intrude. Danny becomes involved with Madame Zaza's niece, Marla, who initially badgers him because she wants to know what tricks enabled him to move furniture around during his visit to the medium. The FBI suspect him of stock manipulation and his success at the bookie joint leads to his being kidnapped by three gambling syndicate hoods. After strangling one of the hoods by PK and teleporting himself to safety, he makes for Sir Lewis Carter's brownstone only to be imprisoned when he gets there and forced to swallow a metal egg called a "resonator" which causes mental confusion (p. 110). Sir Lewis is the "Hegemon" of a group called the "Brotherhood In Psi" (p. 111). Sir Lewis wants Danny to join but Danny is not impressed by the Brotherhood's understanding of parapsychology and the Brotherhood decides it does not want him as a member anyway. Now he cannot be allowed to live. But Danny escapes from his cell by vomiting up the resonator, which had "lodged in him like a cancer" (p. 124), adjusting it so that it functions as an "amplifier" (p. 120), and taking advantage of a storm's electrical energy so that a bolt of lightning partially destroys Sir Lewis's brownstone.[33]

Danny takes over a truck and drives to the apartment of Sean Hennessy, a former colleague who had also been fired from Delta Publishing. It transpires that Sean is "The King of Eagles," as the title of chapter 13 styles it, and the inventor of the resonator, and from Sean Danny learns that the PRS and the Fortean Society are fronts for rival psychic organizations. Cartier Taylor of the Forteans is the senior member of Sean's group—the "Real psi-men."[34] "Our main purpose," Sean explains, "is research; there's a lot we don't understand yet about the serial universe" (p. 136). This concept has been introduced before and linked to J. W. Dunne, who "envisages an infinite series of overlapping event-levels, every one of them keyed to some sort of decision point" (p. 89). Subsequently, an analogy between the serial universe and superimposed identical film strips, and the possibility of pressing on the strips in such a way as to cause the upper ones to slip forward, provides the elaborate scientific rationalization for Danny's precognitive ability: "The instant which is 'now' on the bottom strip has been moved forward in time, a considerable distance, in the top strip." The "main line," or the "real" world is a composite made up of "contributing individual 'sequences' " (p. 157). All of this is further buttressed by references to Haldane on non-Einsteinian relativity, Heisenberg's Uncertainty Principle, and Planck's Constant.

Danny and Sean drive to the syndicate hideout, which is now occupied by the PRS, who have captured Todd as bait for Danny. On the way Sean informs Danny that "We're looking for some psychic equivalent of nuclear fission" (pp. 143–44)—something we subsequently learn that Todd has found. Sean also alludes to another problem that the psi-men are working on, which we eventually discover is the problem of death. At the hideout, Danny, looking through a window, is startled to discover that his ex-boss, Henry Mall, is the real leader of the PRS. In retrospect it seems a little too coincidental that three men with psychic powers—Danny, Sean, and Mall—should all have been working on the same trade paper (there is no indication that either Sean or Mall arranged that state of affairs). A psychic battle ensues between Sean and Mall, and Sean loses. The problem of death will have to be solved if Sean is ever to be revived.

The Brotherhood have hidden Todd in a future "sigma-sequence" (p. 150) by separating the film strips that in their normal layered serial state would constitute a collective "main line:" "with all the slight differences between strips freed to assert themselves independently," it is as if "each strip were a 'main line' all in itself" (p. 157). Danny, thanks to an "intuitive mathematical leap" (p. 155), figures that Todd has been imprisoned in the future which is most favorable to the Brotherhood's cause, and in a stunning climactic chapter, he explores a sigma-sequence of six alternate worlds by way of climbing six steps of what is imaged as a "multifoliate staircase" with "Phantom staircases" branching "from each successive riser" (pp. 154, 153). Suffice to say that Todd is located along with Mall in the sixth sequence and the final nicely rendered battle takes place. Around the glowing face of Mall "and around Danny, an invisible and basic storm seemed to be raging, as if the very material structure of space were being tortured, its geodesics twisted like the strands of a dishcloth" (p. 179). The three men find themselves returned to the hideout in the garret at the top of a normal staircase where (with the aid of the resonator and a psychic fission machine that Todd has assembled in the Brotherhood's laboratory) Mall is vanquished, thereby reducing to a very low order of probability the future that is favorable to the Brotherhood's cause. The sequence that Sean fought for is now established as "main line." It remains only to reunite Danny with Marla, whose own psychic powers have been awakened in a last chapter which a Faber & Faber reader found "woefully weak and sentimental" (CM 84).

Perhaps the most striking thing about *Jack of Eagles* and its root, "Let the Finder Beware," is the degree of precognition they exhibit regarding Blish's future works.[35] This is particularly apparent in the *Jack of Eagles* sigma-sequence chapter, "The Six Tomorrows" (pp. 159–77), which represents a considerable expansion of the three-page original, entitled "The Steps." The first tomorrow, which features a world where an intelligent black bird is the only sign of life, points towards the world of *Midsummer Century* (1972) where the birds have taken to attacking man. In the second tomorrow the PRS is involved with Consolidated Warfare Services, the firm that is first introduced in "There Shall Be No Darkness" and that reappears most significantly in *Black Easter* (1967) and *The Day After Judgment* (1970) with a Mr. Baines as its president. The six futures in the novel (including a blank page representative of a vaporized Earth) anticipate the six messages from the future relayed by the Dirac communicator in *The Quincunx of Time* (1973) in the chapter entitled "A Comity of Futures," a comparable expansion of the three presented in the seed story "Beep" (1954).

Of course it is "Beep" and *The Quincunx of Time* which are most clearly adumbrated in "Let the Finder Beware" and *Jack of Eagles*. Danny's precognition, like the messages from the future concentrated in the Dirac beep, leads to a discussion of the relationship between determinism and free will (p. 89). And, as it happens, Dirac is mentioned twice in both *Jack of Eagles* (pp. 122, 144) and in "Let the Finder Beware" in connection with the mathematics of telepathy. It would seem, then, that the growing powers that Blish exhibits between "Let the Finder Beware" and *Jack of Eagles* are as much precognitive as literary.

(iv) *The Warriors of Day* (1951, 1953)

Most of Blish's novels began life as distinct short stories which were subsequently revised and spliced together, or as novellas which were subsequently expanded. Alternatively, he collaborated on both *The Duplicated Man* and *A Torrent of Faces*. But *The Warriors of Day* (1953), originally published as "Sword of Xota" (Summer 1951), is the first example of that comparatively rare thing (there are only nine exceptions) in Blish's oeuvre: a novel which began life as such. This skillful enough demonstration of Blish's ability to push through an extended work of fiction, albeit one later described as a "potboiler which I wrote in nine days," signals the end of his period of literary apprenticeship.[36]

The plot is a relatively conventional instance of power fantasy SF, the kind of thing where one man discovers that the future of an entire civilization depends upon him. Blish's protagonist, Tipton Bond, a competitive loner, finds himself magically transferred to Xota, an exotic world where the vegetation seems to be alive and opposed to his presence. He comes across a huge structure in the shape of a man lying on his back. Like Danny Caiden of *Jack of Eagles,* who hears "Whispers in the Earth" (as the title of that novel's chapter 1 puts it), Bond is assailed in chapter 2, "The Whisperers," by voices when he touches the crumbling masonry. He enters the structure through an opening in the left wrist and it becomes clear that the voices are echoes of a single voice informing him that as the Sword of Mahrt, he will defeat the terrifying Warriors of Day (Blish, *à la* Blake, reverses the conventional darkness/light symbolism) and save Xota from destruction by the Wild Sun (Van Maanen's Star), which the giant aliens are herding towards Xota. Like Danny Caiden, Bond spends a lot of time trying to figure things out and gradually comes to appreciate that he has new powers at his command thanks to his telepathic link with Mahrt, who at first appears to be a sleeping godlike giant "imprisoned" within an anthropomorphic temple.[37] Once again, then, the theme of growing powers appears.

All that Mahrt prophesies comes to pass but various complications occur along the way thanks to two divisions within Xotan society: between the human types and the sentient beasts (a "cat" named Chrestos represents the beasts on the Council of Xota, two of whose members, it turns out, have special interests of their own), and between the establishment Council of Xota and a subversive religious group known as the Dark Worship of Mahrt (with one of whose members, a girl named Deje, Bond falls in love). The Warriors, it transpires, have fostered a myth that Mahrt is evil as a means of suppressing the "mass mental power of Xota" (p. 61). A matter transmitter, which the beasts possess, plays an important part in all this. Bond is twice transmitted to a Warrior ship, once as a test and a second time to rescue Deje. It is supposed by Bond at one point that "a matrix discontinuity," like that on which the transmitter depends, must have brought him to Xota (p. 122). The careful and inventive plotting which characterizes Blish's work is much in evidence here.

When Bond finally merges with Mahrt and achieves his full awesome powers, it becomes clear that he has in effect merged with the sleeping planetary mind of Xota. The entire planet amounts to a telepathic entity but the Xotans (who do make use of mind bombs to cause madness) have suppressed this "collective mind" and driven *"many of the forces which Mahrt contained out of his own world and to Earth"* (emphasis in original). On Earth these forces "became embodied as Tipton Bond" and that is why he was a misfit there (p. 142). For Bond as the awakened "Mahrt," destroying the Warriors by causing the Wild Star to go nova and destroying the Warrior's home planet, Day, is mere child's play. All of this is described with much zest and color.

Although *The Warriors of Day* is basically no more than thoroughly competent good entertainment, it does contain sophisticated touches which elevate it well above the general run of pulp SF. The novel opens with Bond killing a bear on Kodiak Island in the Arctic, which foreshadows the man/beast contrast on Xota, and is patently symbolic. He holds his knife "between his thighs, blade pointed directly at the bear" before heaving "the knife up from his groin with all his strength" (pp. 7, 8). The implication that killing the bear amounts to mating with it is Blish's way of signalling the mix of sex and violence which, somewhat sublimated, constitutes much of the appeal of the type of SF to which he is here contributing. But the scene also has a more important prefigurative function (along with subtle hints that Bond is not of this Earth). By making the blade a part of his anatomy, Bond initially presents himself, metonymically, as the Sword he will become. The organic/inorganic compound, which is here Bond, is subsequently matched with the inorganic/organic compound which is Mahrt, the hand which will wield the Sword. In order to establish this latter compound, the entrance in Mahrt's left wrist is referred to first as "the wound in the stone," then as "the wound in the temple's wrist," and finally as "the raw, crumbling wound in the wrist of the temple" (pp. 32, 98, 103). Any associations with King Arthur and his magical sword Excalibur are, of course, entirely appropriate.

At the beginning of his adventure on Xota, Bond finds that after falling down he is bound to the Earth by "silken green threads" of vegetation: "Wryly he thought of Gulliver" (p. 20). The reference is presumably a way of prefiguring his encountering the Brobdingnagian Warriors and the rousing of "Mahrt," or rather his own metamorphosis into a giant force.

In a coda-like final chapter we learn something of the future history of Xota. The "men of Xota" go into a decline; the beasts are in the ascendancy (p. 151). They come to believe that "a new Sword is being forged" (p. 152). It will take the form of a Kodiac bear. Blish is here not so much suggesting the possibility of a sequel as he is suggesting a sense of cyclical history, the cycle of cultural life and death that the impregnatory stabbing of a bear implies in concentrated form. We have, then, at the beginning and the end of *The Warriors of Day,* a hint of that Spenglerian system which will shortly come to full flower in *Cities in Flight*. With Blish's customary calculation the dead center chapter of *The Warriors of Day* is entitled "The Sword Turns." It is a lesson that the Warriors have learned all too painfully. For them the flowering of their day has given way to night.

THREE

PANTROPY, POLYPLOIDY, AND TECTOGENESIS

■ Blish belongs with that relatively small but prominent group of SF writers—among them, Isaac Asimov, Gregory Benford, and Arthur C. Clarke—who actually received at least some advanced scientific training. The knowledge of biology that Blish gained while at Rutgers University is effectively exploited in much of his fiction. It is not surprising, then, that, in a series of 1951–52 articles entitled "Science in Science Fiction," he should begin with a discussion of "The Biological Story."[1] After remarking the comparative rareness of stories deriving their major ideas from biological areas (with the exception of stories concerned with teratology, the study of monsters), Blish points in a note to Norman L. Knight's "Crisis in Utopia" as "a real genetic story." He explains that this 1940 account of human beings adapted to life underwater as "Tritons" is "grounded in . . . tectogenesis, the direct, surgical manipulation of chromosones."[2]

He goes on to mention his own story of adapted humanity, "Sunken Universe," which is clearly indebted to Knight's example. Blish invented the term "pantropy" for the adaptation process; but some years afterward the term "tectogenesis" is reintroduced in *A Torrent of Faces* (1967), the work on which Blish and Knight collaborated. The world of the Tritons introduced in "Crisis in Utopia" (as amended perhaps by the sea-dwelling Homlites of "Two Worlds in Peril," a novella Blish published in 1957 in collaboration with Phil Barnhart) becomes an important aspect of the world described in *A Torrent of Faces*. In between Blish's pantropy stories, which he collected as a sequence entitled *The Seedling Stars* (1957), and *A Torrent of Faces,* he published a novella called *Titans' Daughter* (1961),[3] an expanded version of a 1952 story, "Beanstalk," about biologically adapted human giants. The process here involves polyploidy, or increasing the number of cell chromosones. Whatever the terminology, all these stories focus on what is more commonly referred to these days as "genetic engineering."

The Seedling Stars is the most important of these works; indeed, it ranks just after *A Case of Conscience* among Blish's greatest achievements. The four stories which make up *The Seedling Stars* were not written or published in the order in which they are collected. "Sunken Universe" by "Arthur Merlyn," a microscopic world story in which humanoids successfully battle against rotifers that appeared in *Super Science Stories* in 1942, was the starting point: lightly revised and combined with its sequel, "Surface Tension" (which was published in the August 1952 issue of *Galaxy Science Fiction*), it became book 3 of *The Seedling Stars* under the title "Surface Tension."[4] "The Thing in the Attic," a story detailing adapted human life in the canopy of a great forest as opposed to adapted human life underwater, constitutes book 2, and was originally published in *If Worlds of Science Fiction* in 1954. "Seeding Program," the story which as book 1 sets up the pantropy theme, first came out in *The Magazine of Fantasy & Science Fiction* in 1955 as "A Time to Survive." In the same year, "Watershed," the fourth and final book of *The Seedling Stars,* appeared under that same title in *If Worlds of Science Fiction*. This process of composition represents a clear instance of what is increasingly recognizable as Blish's pattern: one step forward, one step back, one reestablishing "as you were" disguised as a final leap.

There is evidence that Blish considered alternative titles for his story sequence. The draft of a letter to his agent, Harry Altshuler, dated 3 August 1953, includes his plans for a book called "Seeding Program": "All right by golly, here's the start of a book for you. . . . I'm glad to report, at least, that I got through with my Capt. Video stint today [churning out scripts for the television series], so beginning now I am working for you."[5] As the actual title of book 1, "Seeding Program" focuses on the concluding revelation of that story in a way that prepares for the stories to come. Interestingly, it seems that Blish also considered "A Time to Survive," his earlier title for the book 1 story, as a title for the book as a whole. This title runs across the top of most of the pages of the work's final typescript. That typescript also indicates that he considered entitling "Watershed" simply "Epilogue."

Blish pushed the implications of his subject matter to their limits in the last-written introductory and concluding books. It is appropriate, therefore, in discussing the novel to treat those two stories together.[6] Likewise, it makes sense to combine the discussion of books 2 and 3.

(i) Change and Truth in *The Seedling Stars*

"Seeding Program," like many works of SF, is written as a mystery story. Once all the revelations are in and the obfuscations dispensed with, the tale turns out to be about the competition between terraforming and pantropy as ways of making mankind at home on alien planets.[7] An organization called the Great Earth Port Authority (modelled on the Port of New York Authority) has a stake in terraforming because of the money it can make from this expensive enterprise by way of concessions, tolls, and so forth. It is in the financial interests of the Authority to kill the cheaper option, pantropy, and with it, the Adapted Men already produced.

Some of these have escaped to Ganymede, the third moon of Jupiter.[8] In response the Port Authority creates a new Adapted Man named (with a bow to T. S. Eliot) Donald Leverault Sweeney, the protagonist of this story, who is to be planted on Ganymede in order somehow to enforce the return of the fugitive Adapted Men to Earth, or at least the return of a Dr. Rullman, who may know the secret of converting "an Adapted Man back into a human being."[9] However, once on Ganymede and properly clued in (if we are to believe what Sweeney is told there), Sweeney's loyalties change. In symbolic terms, his loyalty to Mickey—a change from "Mike" in the typescript—who drops him off on Ganymede, is exchanged for a loyalty to Michaela, or "Mike," who turns out to be his niece. As a result of these shifting loyalties he assists the Adapted Men in their "seeding program," whereby they have prepared new generations of Adapted Men to fit the environments of six selected planets, by staging a phony rebellion and explosion to distract the attention of the Port Authority observers while the survival ship containing Dr. Rullman and the newly Adapted children takes off. Explosive endings, it should be noted, are endemic in Blish's fiction.

It will be apparent from this summary that the fundamental structural opposition at work is one between appearance (or surface) and reality. The fundamental question is: do appearances (surfaces) mask reality or do appearances mask further appearances? If the latter is true, then what we have to deal with is a matter of conflicts among appearances— or, to use a phrase that exploits the marvelous appropriateness of the title of book 3, tensions between surfaces.

Blish pays particular attention to the appearance of Ganymede. The first feature to be pointed out is the frozen sea, Neptune's Trident, which, in the context of the entire book, might be viewed as anticipating the environment of "Surface Tension." Attention is also drawn to a feature which curiously parallels the shape of the Trident, "a great triangular marking called the Gouge, a torn up, root-entwined avalanche-shaken valley which continues right around the pole and back up [i.e., in a southerly direction] into the other hemisphere, fanning out as it goes" (p. 4). As part of a general procedure of reversing our normal points of reference, Blish explains that to space pilots and astronomers north is *down*. The Adapted Men live on a shelf that overhangs the "enormous scar" created by the Gouge. The shelf juts out from the base of an isolated mountain which, in the sunrise, displays a "star-fire peak" (p. 5). It would seem that the appearance of Ganymede mirrors something of the reality of the Adapted Men, or rather vice versa. While the geographical features suggest both the deforming surgery that the Adapted Men have undergone and their resulting isolation, the "star-fire peak" suggests the aspiration that has led to this situation. As an Adapted Man whose "bones were Ice IV," Sweeney can empathize with the frozen sea (p. 8). Mention is also made of "the gouge which was Sweeney's frigid tangled substitute for a human soul" (p. 25). Something of the same metaphysical mix is conveyed by Blish's description of Sweeney's reaction to an acute question: "His veering attention snapped back into the frigid center of his being so suddenly that it left behind a bright weal, as if a lash had been laid across his exposed brain" (p. 29). In fact, the reader's sense of Sweeney depends almost entirely on a sense of his congruence with the environment of Ganymede. We are not provided with any direct physical description of the man. A wind, previously "as gentle and variable as a flautist's breath," takes to hooting like an owl as "[t]he congruent furies of the storms inside and outside Sweeney mounted together" (pp. 19, 37). Clearly Blish's metamorphic images are designed to reflect the theme of fitting men to their environment.

This symbolism, it should be emphasized, is applied with a very light touch. Blish is also at pains to present Ganymede as a real place, and he achieves a considerable degree of credibility by offhand comparisons to "Syrtis Major on Mars" and "the Moon's Mare Crisium" (pp. 4, 5).

Blish makes extensive use of containers, suits, and screens, and these have an important bearing on his theme of appearance versus reality. In the present context, the metaphor of containment relates particularly to the alien environments into which men and women will be fitted. Unlike the suit of clothes which is selected, cut, and adapted to fit the individual, here the individual is adapted to fit the suit of clothes. On his way to Ganymede, Sweeney is segregated in a "heavily insulated cabin" or "vault" (p. 3). We learn that previously he had been formed in a "great sealed cavern" on the Moon, where, he tells Dr. Rullman, he was "a cell in a jug" (pp. 9, 13). Rullman later confirms that the Adapted child is "the ultimate in bottle babies" (p. 46). All these containers are imprisoning, isolating vaults from which the Adapted Man must free himself in order to live in whatever alien context he has been fashioned for.

Two other "containing" alien contexts outside the bottle figure in this first story, contexts from which the Adapted Man is forever excluded. One is the world of contemporary normal human beings, whether on the Moon or on Earth. The other is the wider temporal context implied by the presence of an omniscient narrator and, in particular, by this reference to Sweeney's trek across the surface of Ganymede: "It took him eleven days and efforts and privations of which Jack London would have made a whole novel" (p. 35). This kind of statement can be risky in SF. It makes the narrator obtrusive and may sound anachronistic. In this case, however, the reference does have the advantage of placing the reader within a context which may be related to the three other contexts—Sweeney's contained world, the contemporary human environment, and Ganymede—with which the story is more directly concerned.

The above formulation quickly makes apparent the likely thematic configuration of *The Seedling Stars*. It concerns itself with views that are limited because they are contained, and with the need to break out of such containers. These, after all, are the logical possibilities—and characteristically Blish's plots depend upon logic. The references to a "chain reaction" of explosions and the process whereby pantropy will spread throughout the universe as "One, two, three, infinity" (pp. 37, 48) might, in fact, be taken as images of Blish's logical way with plotting.[10] A logical corollary to the concern with breaking out of containers should be mentioned now, although it will figure in this analysis only later. As likely as not, the notion of birth will present itself as an image for the process of mental breakthrough. And likely as not, birth will be viewed as a compensation for, or means of surmounting, death. Sweeney learns that as "a Jay-positive blood type" (p. 31) he would be cancer-prone if he were an Earth-normal man.[11] At the beginning of the story, Sweeney is in a state such that, were it not for his pulse, "he might . . . have concluded that he was dead" (p. 3).[12]

Although the relationship between the Adapted Men and other human beings is problematical in "Seeding Program," there is no real doubt that the Adapted Men are human beings—and this in spite of the syntactic denial implicit in such references as Sweeney's to the possibility of converting "an Adapted Man back into a human being" and in spite of the meaning of the word "pantropy" itself: "changing everything" (pp. 24, 8). If everything is changed or can be changed, then in what real sense is an *Adapted* Man a human being? That question in effect occupies the concluding book, "Watershed," where the notion of pantropy as total, ceaseless change comes up against the notion that there is an essential human nature which remains the same, an essential truth.

"Watershed," we are given to understand, takes place many centuries after what was envisaged in "Seeding Program" has come to pass. What has also come to pass is the virtual destruction of the Earth. Human beings can no longer live there. The reference to how the Earth was despoiled—"the people began their lives as farmers with the use of fire, and they killed themselves off in the same way" (p. 176)—serves to complete the pattern of linking each of the four books allusively with one of the four elements: book 1, which takes place on the harsh surface of Ganymede, can be associated with earth, the tree-top world of book 2 with air, the underwater world of book 3 with water, and book 4 with fire. "Watershed" examines the prejudice the "human" crew of a military starship harbors against the Adapted Men being transported to Earth. Ironically, the "human beings" cannot live on Earth in its present condition; only the seal-like Adapted Men, the Altarians, can do that. Earth has become as inhospitable as Ganymede. A further irony inheres in the fact that now, after countless generations of Adapted Men, it is legitimate to wonder if any "human beings" in their original form still exist. The ship, after all, is manned by a "Rigellian crew" (p. 176). "Watershed" thus provides the perfect and inevitable logical conclusion for *The Seedling Stars*. Coming after "Surface Tension," with its division into "Cycle One" and "Cycle Two," "Watershed" might well be subtitled "Full Cycle." It successfully introduces a new idea, yet one implicit in everything that comes before.

Hocqueah, the Altarian in the story, relates the history of pantropy for the benefit of Captain Gorbel. He implies that pantropy, as a means of doing without artificial "containers"—spacesuits, domes, and man-made environments—provides direct access to reality, including the reality of a basic human equality. In apparent contradiction to the definition of pantropy in book 1 ("everything changes"), this concluding story asserts that there is an essential truth, an essential human nature that is immutable. Presumably what Blish must have in mind is the human soul or something like it, something like the Ganymede gouge which "Seeding Program" mentions as Sweeney's "substitute for a human soul" (p. 25).

Does this mean that pantropy leads to yet another deceptive surface that has to be broken through? The implications of this surface/reality dilemma are more fully explored in *A Case of Conscience* (story, 1953; novel, 1958); and hence it is appropriate that the narrator of *The Seedling Stars* mentions Lithia, the alien world of *A Case of Conscience*, as an example of an alien race's familiarity with form-changing: "the dominant race undergoes complete evolutionary recapitulation after birth—not before it, as men do" (p. 179).[13] Indeed, similar allusions in Blish's other works indicate that, as with the Centrale stories, he had the ambition of turning his more mature works into a single tapestry, a loose but consistent historical universe.

The present time, Hocqueah claims, "is the greatest of all moral watersheds for our race" (p. 183). The evidence that only Adapted Men can now survive on Earth, the birth-place of "true" human beings, will force the recognition of a basic equality. Will this "truth" in fact break through? The story ends with two humans, Gorbel and his navigator, looking at a "screen" to see the "image" of an Earth they cannot inhabit. Given that metaphorically a watershed is a marker separating two containing epochs, it may be supposed that at least for these two humans the stage of recognizing the existence of a barrier has been reached, and that itself is a form of breakthrough. As ever, ultimate revelations are denied.

(ii) The Sexual Analogy in "The Thing in the Attic" and "Surface Tension"

There is a notable sexual analysis by Damon Knight of Blish's story "Common Time."[14] Whatever the appropriateness of such an approach to this story, the presence of some kind of sexual analogy is surely inevitable in a novel concerned with the placing of seeds. And, as it happens, "Common Time" appeared in 1953, between the years in which "The Thing in the Attic" and "Surface Tension" were first published. It is in these two *Seedling Stars* stories that some kind of sexual analogy is most apparent.

"The Thing in the Attic" is set on a planet named Tellura. Its animal-like inhabitants, who are, we eventually learn, Adapted Men, live high above the ground in the canopy of a great forest and harbor all kinds of superstitions about the world below, which they call "Hell" and which contains at least one "chlorophyll-green snake" (p. 64). They hold to a mythology involving Giants who are responsible for their tree-top existence.[15] A group of five tree-top "criminals" are convicted of heresy regarding the Giants and the myth of origin as set down in the Book of Laws and sentenced to a period of exile on the surface of the planet, to which they are lowered in a basket. This punishment effectively corresponds to a death sentence, since no previous visitor to the surface has survived.

At first, life on the surface (which in this story betokens reality rather than mere appearance) is every bit as alarming as anticipated. The exiles are for awhile afflicted with motionless sickness before they adapt to the fact that the ground does not constantly move like the treetops. Then follows a long and complicated trek to reach higher ground, during which a monster is encountered and destroyed—but not before it has eaten one member of the group. If this monster is truly "the thing in the attic," why is it encountered in what figuratively must be viewed as the basement world of the surface? The answer seems to be that the monster's potency depends upon its existence in the "attic" world of the mind; in the "basement" world of reality, the thing may be dealt with, as in this case, met and destroyed. Blish's title, then, is an important clue to an overall allegorical intent.

Eventually, in this "Jack and the Beanstalk" story in reverse, the Giants turn out to be human beings from Earth. Honath and Mathild, the only two tree-top dwellers to survive the sentence, learn of the seeding program which began thousands of years ago.[16] They also learn why the Tellura Adapted Men were first placed in the attic world. The world of the surface was simply too dangerous; but now, following the example of the new Adam and Eve, all their fellows must adapt to life on the surface. This explanation is hokey, and taking the allegorical hint that Blish has planted in his title, the reader is free to consider alternatives.

The story makes most sense if interpreted as an allegory of maturation, of man's need to leave the security of the womb—which is nevertheless haunted by imaginary demons—and confront the monsters of reality. The tree-top world is a mental labyrinth. The monstrous reality to be met, according to the story's dominating images, is sexuality. Phallic imagery predominates, introduced by the reference to "great pink cliffs" and "the intervening columns of blue air," an inversion of the penetrable and the impenetrable (p. 77). After "basalt pillars" the group encounters a second "chimney" cut in the cliffs: "The column of air inside the chimney was filled with spray" (p. 92). An impressive ejaculation had been described a little earlier: "At the top of the falls, the water shot out from between the basalt pillars in a smooth, almost solid-looking tube, arching at least six feet before beginning to break into the fan of spray and rainbows which poured down into the gouge" (p. 90). The story's geography, is detailed and not always easy to envision; but that is appropriate because we are dealing here not so much with a real world as with a surrealistic psychic geography.

All of this prepares for the reptilian monster and the Giant's rocket. Alaskon, a member of the exiled group, likens killing the demonic "reptile" to "spearing fish in a bromelaid" and thus links the reptile with the description of the phallic rocket, which is "a shining, finned spindle, like a gigantic minnow, pointing skyward in the center of the rocky plateau . . ." (pp. 88, 91, 93).

The phallus, of course, requires an egg to fertilize. It may be recalled at this point that the criminals were lowered to the surface world like eggs in a basket. During their journey three surviving members of the group encounter and eat three reptile eggs. If, as seems to be the case, "The Thing in the Attic" is a story about achieved sexuality, we might expect to find it followed by a story dealing with conception. "Surface Tension" turns out to be that story.

"Surface Tension" is the most popular of Blish's stories, a fact which caused him some puzzlement. Did he not realize that "Surface Tension" amounts to a classic embodiment of the model of conceptual breakthrough so central, both structurally and thematically, to the nature of SF?[17] "The Thing in the Attic," Blish's attempt to repeat the magic of "Surface Tension," has not met with the same success. According to Brian Stableford, the entrance of the human beings from Earth takes "the reader's viewpoint into the story" and consequently it lacks "the crucial moment of revelation."[18] Nevertheless, "The Thing in the Attic" does more than merely ape the moves of "Surface Tension"; it successfully sets the stage by developing a sexual analogy which culminates in one of Blish's classic works.

In his introduction to *The Best of James Blish,* Robert A. W. Lowndes maintains that the explanatory prologue to "Surface Tension," which provides a rationale for the state of affairs described in "Sunken Universe," is "needlessly intrusive" and "is therefore omitted in the present edition."[19] As it happens, for reasons doubtless beyond Lowndes's control, the prologue *is* printed in his edition; but that is just as well since this initial intrusion of the human viewpoint does have its purpose.

The womb world of Hydrot, as described in the prologue, is all ocean except for "one small, triangular continent" which itself "was mostly swamp." In the context of the sexual analogy already established, one must here acknowledge at least a suggestion of the *mons veneris*. A seed-ship has crash-landed on this world, presumably on this triangular continent: "The wreck of the seed-ship lay broken squarely across the one real spur of rock which Hydrot seemed to possess which reared a magnificent twenty-one feet above sea level" (p. 104). Allowing for some mixing of the metaphor, the penis has penetrated the vagina and the surface of the hymen has been squarely broken. This introductory image contains the gist of the whole story, which, as we shall see, has to do with breaking through surface skin. Above the rock shines the star Tau Ceti, a beacon of aspiration like the "star-fire peak" in "Seeding Program" (p. 5). Having lost their germ-cell bank (from which Hydrot was to have been seeded), the crew of five men and two women have apparently no alternative but to await death.

However, Dr. Chatvieux, one of the marooned crew, points out that they themselves can contribute germ cells, and from these, with the aid of germ-cell-modifying "pantropes," microscopic beings might be created that could survive in the puddles about the broken ship. Echoing the reasoning from "The Thing in the Attic," a member of the crew had explained that fresh water is safer than the sea.[20] The Adapted colonists that result will have no memory of their previous incarnation, although to some degree "the donor's personality patterns" will be transmitted (p. 107). But the original seeding team, including the two lovers, a pilot named la Ventura, and midshipman Joan Heath, will die before they can be reborn as something new. A record engraved on metal plates of an appropriately microscopic size is left in the hope that the aquatic colonists, after generations of evolution, will decipher it and learn the facts. Despite the objection that telling their progeny that they are microscopic "may saddle their entire early history with a gods-and-demons mythology" (an echo of "The Thing in the Attic" again), this information is included. Chatvieux points out that "These people will be of the race of men. . . . They are not toys to be protected from the truth forever in a fresh water womb" (p. 109). Subsequent events and the strategy of the history plates, it should be noted, contradict Chatvieux's claim that memory, including the memory of language, cannot be transmitted.

The rest of "Surface Tension" is divided into Cycle One and Cycle Two, these titles referring to the aquatic colonists' life cycle, which includes a six-week sporulation "breeding cycle" (p. 109). Much of what happens in Cycle One, described from the viewpoint of the colonists, is virtually unintelligible without the information provided in the prologue. Just as books 1 and 2 begin with arousals, so Cycle One begins with Lavon waking up in the spring to a "rocking" motion and breaking out of his winter shell, dispersing its "amnionic fluid"—clearly his rebirth (pp. 111, 110). We have been told in the prologue about the natural inhabitants of the puddles: rotifers, "including a castle-building genus like Earth's Floscularidae," and "a wonderfully variegated protozoan population, with a dominant ciliate type much like *Paramoecium*" (p. 106). In Cycle One it becomes clear that the latter, called Para, are united with the colonists against the deadly rotifers.

All of this literally nonsensical but intensely and convincingly imagined sensory (especially tactile) experience and activity, including a successfully repulsed rotifer attack, strongly suggests the behavior of spermatozoa or of cells within a human body in the manner of Isaac Asimov's *Fantastic Voyage* (1966). The sexual dimension is repeatedly suggested: "The man drew up his knees and sank to the cold mud of the Bottom to think. Something wriggled under his buttocks and a tiny spirillum corkscrewed away, identifiable only by feel" (p. 113). The capitalized "Bottom" here serves to set up an analogy with the human mind much like that which operates in "The Thing in the Attic"; for two paragraphs later, there is a reference to how Shar, the wise man of the community, dredges strange words "from some *Bottom in his skull* which none of the rest of them could reach and even Shar could not explain" (p. 114; emphasis added). Pantropy is ultimately a metaphor for human plasticity. Life depends upon the capacity for continual mental rebirth. As we are told in book 1, "pantropy had to begin before conception" (p. 24). Sexual conception is the inevitable metaphor for that conceptual breakthrough towards which "Surface Tension" moves. It is, after all, the reproductive function of sex that allows men and women to live collectively on into new worlds.

As the seeding crew of the prologue had projected, the colonists push out the castle-building Floscularidae, or Flosc. Section 2 of Cycle One deals with the occupation of one such castle, which is described as being "all tunnels and exits and entrances" (p. 124). For this the colonists abandon a previously captured worm-house, described as "a great tubular hall" (p. 122)—big enough to house the full 200 members of Lavon's clan—after chasing out the penis-like "worm" (p. 121). On the way to battle and passing through the "thermocline"—a temperature barrier—into warmer water, "Lavon felt his flight suddenly quicken, as if he had been shot like a seed from some invisible thumb and forefinger" (p. 126)—or like an ejaculated sperm, perhaps?

Cycle Two further stresses the importance of biological and planetary rhythms. The time is summer, some generations hence. Shar I of the First Cycle, who had lost one of the two history plates (unfortunately the first one, the one that he had begun deciphering and that presumably would have explained the Adapted Men's origin) in the concluding battle, is replaced by Shar XVI, who has made some headway with the remaining plate. The new Lavon, or authority figure, listens to Shar's claim that "We were made by men who were not as we are" (p. 136) but is unimpressed, and the Para, who is present and fears that man will abandon the Protos in search of further knowledge, promptly executes Lavon's suggestion that the remaining plate be thrown away.

Nevertheless, a seed has been planted. Near the surface of the water, the area called the "sky," Lavon pauses to reflect:

> Here was the upper limit, the third of the three surfaces of the universe. The first surface was the bottom where the water ended.
> The second surface was the thermocline, definite enough in summer to provide good sledding, but easily *penetrable* if you knew how.
> The third surface was the sky. One could no more pass through that surface than one could *penetrate* the bottom, nor was there any better reason to try. There the universe ended. (P. 142; emphasis added)

Reflecting on the nature of a gas bubble and on the fact that it contains no water leads Lavon to frame a primitive cosmology. The surface tension of the bubble is as impermeable as the top of the "sky." Perhaps the world of water drifted in a universe of gas? The image of "Jack and the Beanstalk" presents itself again: "Here at his back . . . was a plant which gave every appearance of continuing beyond the sky . . ." (p. 143). Although Lavon climbs the plant, he seems unable to breach the weight of the sky: "He might as well have tried to penetrate a cliff." When he does finally manage to insert a hand, "There was a kind of soundless explosion. His whole wrist was suddenly encircled in an intense, impersonal grip, as if it were being cut in two" (p. 144). Nevertheless, for a moment before the sensation of drowning causes him to tumble downwards, he does manage to thrust his whole body through the "sky." This finely pictorialized philosophical apocalypse strongly suggests that famous woodcut of a monk poking his head through the enclosed circle of the Ptolemaic stars and looking at the actual machinery (see reproduction p. 68).

The dénouement of "Surface Tension" deals with the epic—or rather mock-epic (given the matter of size)—journey that is undertaken across the space that separates Lavon's puddle from a neighboring one.[21] It is this aspect of the story in particular that has left an indelible imprint on the imagination of its SF readership, and has generated such imitations as Christopher Priest's *The Inverted World*. In a passage that appears in the typescript as an insert and does not appear in the *Galaxy* version of "Surface Tension" (Dep. Blish 398/4), Shar XVI is provided with three assistants who discuss the design of a "spaceship" (pp. 147–153). A "tube-shaped model" rather than "a fragile spherical" one is favored (pp. 150, 148). Two winter-sleeps later the voyage gets under way and eventually Lavon and his crew of "men," Para, and Protos, after much difficulty, break through the surface skin of the "sky"—a moment which recalls the broken hymen image with which the prologue opens. The sun shines in the sky above the "sky."

For Shar things begin to make sense. He envisages a universe of containers within containers:

> I'm beginning to get a picture of the way the universe is made, I think. Evidently our world is a sort of cup in the Bottom of this huge one. This one has a sky of its own; perhaps it, too, is only a cup in the Bottom of a still huger world, and so on without end. It's a hard concept to grasp, I'll admit. Maybe it would be more sensible to assume that all the worlds are cups in this one common surface, and that the great light shines on them all impartially. (P. 162)

At night the light of the "two moons of Hydrot" shines down on "the two-inch wooden spaceship and its microscopic cargo" (p. 166). In the context of the overall sexual analogy, it seems legitimate to wonder whether the two moons of Hydrot, together with the two suns of Tellura in book 2, should not be understood as an image of testicles.

The first "human" encountered in the adjoining puddle is a terrified girl. We have here the conjoining of a male world (no "human" females are specified in Lavon's puddle) and a feminine one. The description of the girl as "a tall, deceptively relaxed, tawny woman" (p. 170) is intended to evoke the description of Joan Heath in the prologue, with her "bright head and tall, deceptively indolent body" (p. 105). If she has inherited Joan Heath's germ-cells, Lavon, who "had the odd and impossible impression that he should recognize her" (p. 170), presumably derives from la Ventura's germ-cells and Shar from those of Dr. Chatvieux. If the prologue were omitted, in accordance with Lowndes's wishes, this revelation would, of course, be denied.

Blish pays careful attention to the conclusions of his stories and in this case there is an interesting difference to be noted between the

An analog for Blish's vision ("Mankind Breaking through the Vault of Heaven and Recognition of New Spheres," a woodcut attributed to Camille Flammarion, in the Deutsche Museum, Munich)

Seedling Stars version of "Surface Tension" and the original magazine publication. Shar undercuts Lavon's assertion that "We have crossed space" with "But—have we?" (p. 171). The *Galaxy* text concludes with " 'As far as I'm concerned, yes,' said Lavon."[22] The conclusion of *The Seedling Stars* text deepens the equivocation and focuses attention on the new-found sexual relationship: "Lavon was looking at the girl. He had no answer for Shar's question. It did not seem to be important" (p. 171). In line with the ironic, mock-epic, mock-heroic aspect of *The Seedling Stars,* Gregory Feeley notes the "Surface Tension" ending as the third undercutting, concluding revelation of the novel. The conclusion to the first story includes the hard fact that Dr. Rullman shall not live to see the end of the survival ship's journey. The second ends with Honath and Mathild returning to their tribe in triumph "but only to preside over its dispersal into Hell at the hands of Earthling giants that Honath's heroic free-thinking had denied the existence of."[23]

Blish carefully and appropriately introduces the sexual analogy which informs both "Surface Tension" and "The Thing in the Attic" in book 1, "Seeding Program." In that story, Sweeney is projected onto Ganymede by an odd catapulting device: "The JATO unit shuddered and dealt Sweeney a nearly paralyzing blow between his shoulder blades" (p. 7). This, of course, is the slap on the back received by the new-born baby. The experience is recalled as the survival ship takes off during Sweeney's decoy explosion: "The heat struck against Sweeney's skin as strongly as the backwash of the JATO unit had done, so long ago. The concussion, which followed about nine seconds later, flattened him and made his nose bleed" (p. 58). Balanced against the deathlike state with which the story opens is Sweeney's conclusion that "I'm just born" (p. 60). He is at home in the new world for which he was created.

To what extent, it might be wondered, does the sexual analogy reconcile the conflict between "changing everything" (p. 8) and an essential human truth in *The Seedling Stars?* If sex, as it seems to be, is that essential human truth, a material counterpart to the soul, then pantropy has a long way to go before it can be said to "change everything." A reality which "changes everything" seems to be the revelation towards which *The Seedling Stars,* like much SF, aspires. From this point of view, the sexual analogy is part of a containing reality that must be broken through. However, since the sexual analogy is only an analogy, a reader is free to assume that this particular analogy with a seedling pantropic (i.e., changing) reality, a pantropic truth, is, in fact, a deceptive one. Superficial resemblances mask fundamental differences. The sexual analogy, then, does not so much reconcile the conflict between change and truth as it provides a flickering intermediate term which, depending on how that term is taken, may be related to both change and truth. Nevertheless, it is dismayingly significant that the structure of *The Seedling Stars* amounts to a closed circle.

(iii) A Bigger "Beanstalk": *Titans' Daughter*

The seedling analogy may fittingly be adapted to Blish's own art. Frequently, story seeds would grow into full-scale novels.[24] Thus "Beanstalk," the title itself an image of organic growth, increased its length by some thirty pages in becoming *Titans' Daughter.* Unlike *A*

Case of Conscience, where Blish added a new part 2, *Titans' Daughter* is literally an expanded version of "Beanstalk" (also entitled "Giants in the Earth").[25] By a process of extensions and insertions, the nine sections of the original story, which at one point Blish claimed was the "best story I ever wrote," became the thirteen chapters of the novella; but the result indicates that financial rather than aesthetic considerations must have been the determining factor (CM 51, 12 July 1959).

Titans' Daughter further explores the implications of "Watershed"— the prejudices that "normal" human beings will likely express towards any of their fellows who are perceived to be different. In this case, the difference is a matter of size. This theme of human giants versus normal humans is one that H. G. Wells first examined in *Food of the Gods* (1904); but the similarity would not matter had Blish been able to improve on Wells's treatment. Unfortunately *Titans' Daughter* also resembles *Food of the Gods* in being one of its author's poorer books. Contrived, implausible plotting, fully forgettable characters, and little sense of pacing or of climax combine to weaken the work. Blish's wavering between its three titles, none of which quite fits, conveys something of the work's generally unfocussed quality.

Blish's eight- or nine-foot tall, long-lived giants have come into existence through experiments with polyploidy—that is, the creation of cells whose nuclei have three or more times the number of chromosomes of haploid cells. The giants are "synthetic tetraploids" (p. 21) as opposed to supposedly normal "diploid" humanity, or so the reader is initially informed (p. 20). Their life is regulated by "the Society for the Prevention of Exploitation of Exceptional Children" (SPEECH). The society was created by "A trust fund and congressional backing (modelled on the state's stepping in to protect the children in an old case of multiple birth somewhere in Canada)" (p. 23); the parenthetical reference is to the Dionne quintuplets, born on 28 May 1934 at Callander, Ontario. I will not attempt to summarize the more-than-usually complex convolutions of Blish's plot except to say that it turns on the extremely devious attempt of Maurey, one of the giants, to create dissension between tetraploid and diploid by murdering Dr. Hyatt, the creator of the tetraploids, and framing fellow tetraploid, Sam, for that murder. Sam is the lover of the beautiful Sena, the Titans' daughter of the book's title, the Titans being a tetraploid football team which plays exhibition games against another tetraploid team called the Atlantians. It is Maurey's aim to have the tetraploids, "like all the hornets of Hell's own ante-room," and the diploids kill each other in the war he will engineer, so that he, by Sena, "will be patriarch of all the generations to come" (pp. 118, 129). A polyploid dog named Decibelle, based on "our first dog, Trouble," according to Virginia Kidd's introduction, plays a part in finally clearing Sam and tracking down Maurey.[26] Maurey then dies in a collapsed lodge, one of the images of destruction that characteristically end Blish's books.

One rather murky concept in the novella concerns a basic inaccuracy in the use of the terms "diploid" and "tetraploid." All human beings are actually tetraploid. Each of the giants simply has "a different degree of polyploidy." They are called "tetras" for convenience; "The only other choice would have been 'Polly'" (p. 112). Blish adapted this detail when he expanded the story. The prefigurative vignette of harmony, which Blish inserted in constructing the new chapter 1, involves the marriage of a "normal" man and a giant named Polly Follmer (pp. 26–27). Sena, Maurey discovers, was created, along with himself, by Dr. Hyatt as an experiment designed to produce a new breed of normal-sized children who will "blend back into society. . . . Eventually the polyploid characteristics will begin to reappear, piecemeal, until the whole race is heavily polyploid, and then giants will be commonplace and not the subject of pogroms" (pp. 139–40). Blish's usual reliance on logic has led him once again to the intermediate term.

Girding all this about is a somewhat contrived symbolism introduced by the old Indian legend about the horned devil caterpillar:

> Mother Carey offered the devil a drink from the Double Cup. One half held wine, and the other half held, I forget, something unpleasant; anyhow there was only one place to drink, so you got a little of each. That was how the horned devil got to be so ugly as a caterpillar, and so beautiful as a butterfly. (P. 26)

This notion of an ambiguous dualism also comes out in the business of the "projector," a device whose description Blish bamboozles, which realizes "[t]he last of Roger Bacon's engineering dreams": a reactionless force, a one-way push (p. 45). Designed initially for combat on the football field, it has possibilities in war which only Maurey recognizes. Ultimately it turns out that the one-way push actually does have "polarity" (p. 126). This might have been anticipated by the symbolic association of history and the projector (a word which at this point functions as a pun). After the observation that "A student of history might have known where to look for the missing 'equal and opposite reaction,'" Maurey disguises the projector with "old newspapers" so that it becomes "the invincible thing he had wrapped in ancient history under his arm" (pp. 45, 48, 49). This association culminates with the reference to "the silver muzzle of history's deadliest weapon" (p. 54). In other words, history tells us that the nature of reality is both good and bad; prejudice is a two-way push; the victimizer can easily become the victim. The cleverness and subtlety of all this indicates Blish's ambitions to elevate pulp SF to the status of literary art. In the case of *Titans' Daughter,* however, the effects are more grotesque than sublime.

(iv) *A Torrent of Faces* and a Mass of Mail

In *A Torrent of Faces* (1967), on which Blish collaborated with Norman L. Knight, the genetic process is called "tectogenesis"; and the Tritons, human beings adapted for life under the sea, are the result of that process. Knight (1895–1972), an SF writer of small output (ten stories in six years) and a pesticide chemist for the U.S. Department of Agriculture until his retirement in 1963, had introduced the term "tectogenesis," along with Tritons, in his novella "Crisis in Utopia" an early version of which was serialized in the July and August 1940 issues of *Astounding Stories.*[27] Figuring in both "Crisis in Utopia" and *A Torrent of Faces* are: an elite group calling itself Prime Center (specified in "Crisis" as short for Prime Co-ordination Center), which runs the world; the Submarine Products Corporation; a place called Triton Reef; a substance called "vitrolith"; and the term "Drylander." Submarine Products Corporation also makes an appearance in Knight's first story, "Frontier of the Unknown," set in the same future as "Crisis," which was serialized in the July and August 1937 issues of *Astounding Stories.* In their preface to *A Torrent of Faces,* Blish and Knight point out that "this book is a sort of sequel" (p. vii) to the two Knight novellas.[28]

More specifically, *A Torrent of Faces* grew out of the passage from Henry George's *Progress and Poverty* (1879) that appears as one of the book's epigraphs: "That the Earth could maintain a thousand billions as easily as a thousand millions is a necessary deduction from the manifest truth that, at least as far as our agency is concerned, matter is eternal and force must continue to act. . . ." Knight, a member of VAPA, published a response to *Progress and Poverty* entitled "Henry George Slipped Here" in 1948 in his fanzine *Knight's Mare* which VAPA circulated. Blish, in "Comments on *Torrent,*" recalls that, having read the response, he wrote to Knight suggesting that his essay be turned into a novel. Subsequently, they met briefly in Chicago in 1950 before Blish moved to Washington, where Knight then lived.[29]

In a paper delivered at the 1968 Phillycon expressing his dislike of propaganda and social satire in SF, Blish mentions that *A Torrent of Faces* is about the "corporate state" or "fascism."[30] In that context, the novel seems to have more to do with the theme of overpopulation than with that of tectogenesis. The well-nigh utopian world of 2774 that is described supports a population of about one trillion "normal" human beings (nine-tenths of whom are unemployed) in one hundred thousand enclosed, pyramidical, hive-type cities. Most of the book deals with the increasing threat of this stable world's collapse posed by three major disasters, one for each of the novel's three books: the shipwreck of a sea hotel; a break in the main supply pipe of a normally empty Disaster City named Gitler in Missouri, Unistan (i.e., the U.S. plus Canada), to which people might be evacuated; and the impact in the Hudson's Bay area of a meteor, one mile in diameter, named Flavia, one of a cast of twenty-four "characters" listed after the contents page. A minor disaster involving a runaway slime-culture carpet makes for a second sea disaster; thus two sea disasters balance the two land disasters. Among the characters, the most important are Biond Smith, who is chief of the Disaster Plans Board; Jothen Kent, the senior water engineer for Gitler; Dorthy Sumter, the chairwoman of Submarine Products Corporation (SPC); and two Tritons—Storm, the Triton chief and executive chairman of SPC, and Tioru, the deputy chairman of SPC. We may assume that Blish, with his fondness for T. S. Eliot, was responsible for choosing the book's second epigraph, which is taken from *Four Quartets:* "The dove descending breaks the air/With tongues of incandescent fire." The title of chapter 14, "The Dove Descending" designates the meteor.

A Torrent of Faces and *Doctor Mirabilis* were the two novels on which Blish invested most time and effort. In the preface to *A Torrent of Faces,* Blish and Knight note that "We began speculating about the population side of the problem in 1948; the intervening time was consumed mostly by endless pages of calculations, several dozen drawings and diagrams, about thirty thousand words of notes, and many fat letters . . ." (p. vii). Nineteen years later the novel finally appeared. Most of the material that Blish and Knight refer to may be located amongst the Blish Papers together with the corrected typescripts (Dep. Blish 400/1–2). There are 167 pages of correspondence alone, beginning with a Knight letter dated 28 February 1949, and ending with a Knight letter dated 18 June 1967 (Dep. Blish 399/4). Blish's side of this correspondence is, unfortunately, not fully represented. In addition there is Dep. Blish 399/6, which consists of maps and six very detailed diagrams

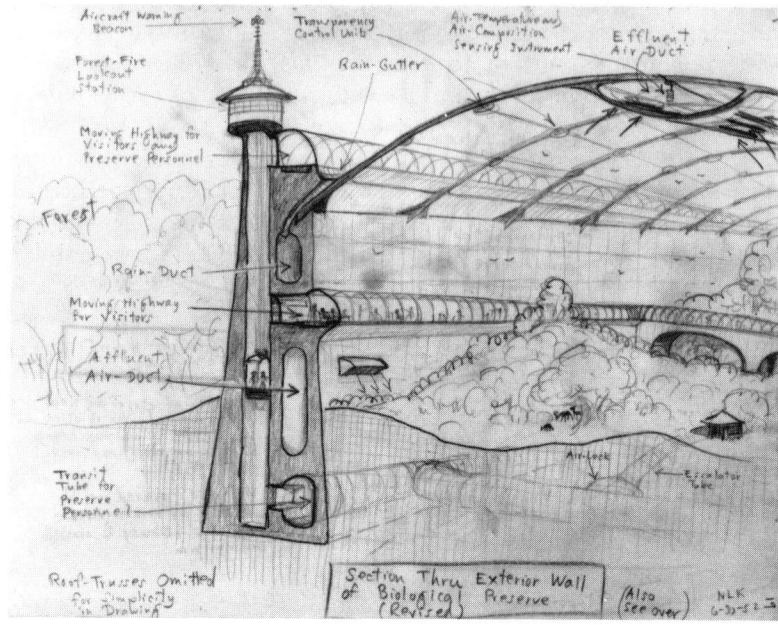

One of several diagrams by Norman L. Knight for what became *A Torrent of Faces* (Dep. Blish 399/6, fol. 19)

by Knight of a futuristic form of television, the floating-globe hotel, and aspects of a Biological Preserve (see the reproduction here) where, in the interests of a controlled ecology, all the wildlife is kept apart from all that vegetation known as the World Forest, which covers most of the world's land masses including the exteriors of the cities. And Dep. Blish 399/5 contains a mass of possible source material and relevant information culled mainly from newspapers and magazines.

The correspondence elaborates considerably on Blish's recollection in "Comments on *Torrent*" that Knight wrote about half the novel, including the penultimate chapter 15, and supplied a number of characters and situations: "The shipwrecked hotel was his idea, so was the episode about Fongavaro Jones [a crazy member of the Jones Convention], and the love story between Dorthy and Tioru."[31] The correspondence reveals that the Deep Water Safari in chapter 5, the Gitler pipeline break in chapter 10, and the electric organ possessed by each of the Tritons were also Knight's ideas, that Knight selected the Great Barrier Reef as the scene of Triton operations, that Knight drafted chapters 4 and 5, and that Blish asked Knight to write chapter 15, "A Walk in the Paradise Garden," because of his "softer hand under Mother Nature." As a "useful rule of thumb," Blish suggests, in a letter of 20 February 1964, that Knight do Jothen throughout while he adopts Biond's persona. It further appears that the novel was originally entitled "Critical Mass," that the character Triton Storm was not added until late 1963 (references to him prior to chapter 4 were inserts), that Blish and Knight were aware of the need to compete with Isaac Asimov's overpopulation novel *Caves of Steel* (1954), the result, Blish believed, of Horace Gold's leaking the essential idea of *Torrent* to Asimov, and that Blish and Knight feared the nudity in the novel would "never get past Katy Tarrant," John Campbell's bluestocking secretary.[32]

Blish had extreme difficulty in placing the novel. Canaveral Press backed out in 1965, having accepted it in 1963 under the title "A Torrent of Faces," but late in 1965 it was bought by Doubleday. Three portions of the novel were published independently before the appearance of the book. Chapters 4 and 5, under the latter's title, "The Shipwrecked Hotel," having been rejected by Campbell, appeared, in greatly abridged form, in Frederik Pohl's *Galaxy* (August 1965). Chapters 7, 8, and 10, dealing with the pipeline break, also appeared in *Galaxy* (August 1966) in abridged form under the title of chapter 10, "The Piper of Dis." An abridged version of the love story in chapters 6, 9, and 11 appeared in *Analog* (April 1967) as "To Love Another."

On the whole, *A Torrent of Faces* is a successful collaborative effort though not without its faults. Knight does not have Blish's stylistic or narrative skills; and perhaps something of the book's plodding, overly descriptive quality is to be attributed to his input. There is a lot of superfluous detail, and too much of the novel reads like a verbal blueprint. Marvellous buildings, which suggest old Gernsbackian technological SF, get more descriptive space than do people. Blish had objected to Knight's contrived Victorian alternatives to the straight "he said" or "she said." But each writer contributed what the other lacked, and the finished novel does achieve a stylistic uniformity. Only the evidence provided by the correspondence allows us to allocate responsibility for the various aspects of this underrated, richly meaningful, and carefully structured novel.

Brian Stableford has implied that the tectogenesis theme is very minor in *A Torrent of Faces*.[33] On the contrary, the Tritons are the lynch pin which holds together the book's apparently disparate elements. Like much SF, *A Torrent of Faces* hinges on the opposition between the artificial and the natural.[34] The land world of the novel has been artificially segregated into three separate areas: a massive vegetable area, the World Forest; the various Biological Preserves where the animals are kept; and the enclosed cities where the people are kept. This apparently stable situation is then steadily undermined by a series of more or less natural disasters, culminating in the meteor. The hotel disaster, for example, depends upon a computer malfunction due to the accidental presence of silverfish (not mice, as Knight had originally planned) and a storm. The opposition of the artificial to the natural is correlated with that between reason and emotion; while the Tritons, who are frequently the target of prejudice, represent the necessary balance between the two. The name of the Triton leader, Storm, connects him quite directly with the major natural force responsible for the hotel disaster.

Throughout the novel, all manner of imagistic and thematic details serve to relate the sea world (primarily associated with the natural and the emotional) with the land world (primarily associated with the artificial and the rational). Most of the pyramidical city of Chicago is "out of sight, like an iceberg" (p. 45). Likewise, the Barrier-hilton hotel, adrift at sea and "afflicted by the computorial equivalent of schizophrenia," moves "with the ponderous steadiness of an iceberg" (pp. 66, 68). An artificial aerial panorama—"Everywhere were the endlessly diversified patterns of the terraced cities—wheels and stars, snowflake designs . . . interlaced circles, three-dimensional lattices of arches . . . the tapestry of cities and forest"—seems not that different from this natural aerial panorama: "Scattered among the lush islands were the white rings and crescents and filigree patterns of reefs and atolls" (pp. 51, 76).

Philadelphia, like London with its "Cornwall District" (p. 110), is a "people reef" (pp. 109, 139). The World Forest is twice compared with the sea (pp. 140, 148). Jothen flees "a lake of bent heads," rolls over "[l]ike a scuba diver," but "A growing murmur of many voices, like a distant sea, told Jothen that a surf of Joneses was already out on the roof of the city" (pp. 181, 183, 184–85). Of course, the titles *A Torrent of Faces* and "A Torrent of Joneses" (chapter 7) reinforce the water imagery. And naturally, the break in Gitler's main feeder line has the effect of "flooding" the city (p. 179), while the meteor Flavia, as part of a superbly realized scene, speeds towards the interface of land and sea (the Hudson's Bay area) with a noise "like a distant waterfall" (p. 24). Parallel murders—that of the woman discovered by the Triton Tioru in the reservoir and that of a man named Krantz in Gitler City—also serve to relate the two worlds.

The conflict between reason and emotion is explored in two relationships: one between the Drylanders Jothen and Kim Wernicke, the ecological surgeon for the Starved Rock Biological Preserve; the other between a Drylander, Dorthy, and the Triton Tioru. In spite of the fact that the "Erection of [their] rocket has begun" (p. 54), Jothen cannot make the right emotional connection: "You try to be eloquent and persuasive and it comes out sounding like a tract or a lecture. This is no engineering problem" (p. 55). As for the Triton-Drylander liaison, "Reason, as usual, was all against it" (p. 102). After an attempt at living in Philadelphia, Tioru comes to agree with Dorthy: "Triton and Drylander can't mix" (p. 167). However, Dorthy is happy to be made an honorary Triton, and it seems that the hybrid children that result from such unions possess special powers—they represent the necessary further evolution of the human race. The "Hybrid Vigor" of chapter 11 takes the form of an ability to create hallucinations, an ability which Storm, who reveals himself to be a hybrid, demonstrates. This wild talent business may be corny, as Stableford suggests, but it does effectively make the basic point.[35] The connection between the false opposition of the natural and the artificial and the equally false opposition of emotion and reason is made most tellingly by the title of the very short central chapter 8: "The Wooing of Flavia." Those four words unite the source of a natural disaster with human emotions.

An ultimate solution to the population problem, which becomes almost ancillary to that of artifical-reason versus natural-emotion, is seen to rest with the Tritons—or more particularly with the hybrids who "can be a bridge" (p. 111):

[Triton Tioru:] "There is hybrid vigor. And there is, of course, the sea. . . ."

[Dorthy Sumpter:] "For the foreseeable future all our hope lies in Submarine Products—and with the Tritons. . . ."

[Biond:] "And there's the mutations that the fall of Flavia is bound to provoke. All disorderly and unpredictable, like the sea itself—but we never really did have our order imposed upon nature, we were only fooling ourselves." (Pp. 269–70)

The future possibilities, those explored in *The Seedling Stars,* "when we start living on other worlds," had been raised earlier: "It's a big universe, and a mere two kinds of human beings won't be able to cope with it" (p. 207). The title of the concluding chapter, ". . . but we shall all be changed," repeats Biond's first reaction to hearing of the meteor (p. 36) but also recalls the idea of pantropy.[36]

The novel's concluding description of Storm serves to unite, via the mineral element (outside of the sea, Triton tears, it has been explained, are continual and involuntary), those animal, vegetable, and human realms—together with those of reason and emotion, the artificial and the natural—that the Drylanders had attempted to segregate: "*He paused to look back in the direction of the ruins of Starved Rock Preserve, his ebony face enigmatic except for his mechanical, slowfalling, and—perhaps—meaningless tears*" (p. 270; emphasis added). A complex, controlled novel reaches an appropriately complex, controlled conclusion. What it perhaps lacks is a sufficient input of the "disorderly and unpredictable" (p. 270).

It should be recognized that the notion of biological or genetic engineering predates Blish's three (or four, if "Two Worlds in Peril" is counted) treatments of the theme. It crops up incidentally in Wells's *The First Men in the Moon* (1901), in Olaf Stapledon's *Last and First Men* (1930), to which Blish alludes in *The Seedling Stars* (p. 44), and most significantly in Aldous Huxley's *Brave New World* (1932). J. B. S. Haldane had discussed the possibilities in a lecture published in 1924 as *Daedalus; or Science and the Future*. And, of course, the influence of Knight's "Crisis in Utopia" was seminal. One of the Tritons in that novel makes a speech which clearly anticipates much of *The Seedling Stars*:

> But is this the end? Must we forever restrain ourselves from going beyond the Triton? We shall populate the sea; what of the air? What of the vast world of little things, where flowers and trees and a meadow is a boundless forest? What of our neighbour planets, where Man exists only as an alien? What of the unknown worlds among the stars?[37]

What Blish did in three novels, one outstanding, one good, and one not-so-good, was to follow Knight's lead in placing genetic engineering on center stage and treating the matter seriously and convincingly. Thereby he paved the way for a novel like Pohl's *Man Plus* (1976) and for the possibilities of that form of genetic engineering known as cloning, possibilities marvellously exploited in John Varley's *The Ophiuchi Hotline* (1977). Thus the seeds Blish developed have continued to grow.

FOUR

COVERING A Case of Conscience

■ Alien beings, as SF writers present them, come in every variety of shape, substance, size, and color, but from at least one Christian's point of view, there can only be three essentially different types. In his foreword to *A Case of Conscience* (1958), Blish quotes the Catholic theologian Gerald Heard on the matter:

> If there are many planets inhabited by sentient creatures, as most astronomers (including Jesuits), now suspect, then 'each one of such planets (solar or non-solar) must fall into one of three categories:
>
> '*(a)* Inhabited by sentient creatures, but without souls; so to be treated with compassion but extra-evangelically.
>
> '*(b)* Inhabited by sentient creatures with fallen souls, through an original but not inevitable ancestral sin; so to be evangelized with urgent missionary charity.
>
> '*(c)* Inhabited by sentient soul-endowed creatures that have not fallen, who therefore
>
> '(1) inhabit an unfallen, sinless paradisal world;
>
> '(2) who therefore we must contact not to propagandize, but in order that we may learn from them the conditions (about which we can only speculate) of creatures living in perpetual grace, endowed with all the virtues in perfection, and both immortal and in complete happiness for always possessed of and with the knowledge of God.'[1]

As one might expect, SF writers have not been much concerned with these distinctions.

There is, however, a story by Ray Bradbury entitled "In This Sign," or alternatively "The Fire Balloons" (1951), in which a priest encounters sinless Martians (Heard's category *c*). Earth, of course, is a category *b* world and one from which the rest of the sentient universe needs to be protected, according to the unfallen inhabitants of Malacandra (Mars) and Perelandra (Venus) in C. S. Lewis's *Out of the Silent Planet*

(1938) and *Perelandra* (1943). Accordingly, Earth, the Silent Planet, exists in a state of quarantine. Blish's Jesuit biologist from Peru, Father Ramon Ruiz-Sanchez, comes around to advocating much the same kind of policy for Lithia, the enigmatic world described in *A Case of Conscience,* but for very different reasons.[2] In fact, Lithia, he believes, belongs to a fourth category that Catholic doctrine has failed to take into account.

(i) All That Is the Case?

Ruiz-Sanchez is one of four investigators on Lithia in the year 2049, charged with deciding "whether or not the planet would be suitable as a port of call for Earth, without risk of damage either to Earthmen or to Lithians" (p. 18). The Lithians are twelve feet tall, reptilian, kangaroo-like beings, skilled in ceramics, who apparently pose no threat. They seem to lead dull, well-regulated lives. They have "no crime, no newspapers, no house-to-house communications systems, no arts that could be differentiated clearly from their crafts, no political parties, no public amusements, no nations, no games, no sports, no cults, no celebrations" (p. 22). Their language apparently lacks metaphors but not, and this is surely significant or an inconsistency on Blish's part, a word for "evil," and like many utopian societies, they do without "poetry or other creative arts" (p. 44). Like Thomas More's Utopians and Swift's Houyhnhnms, they seem to have arrived at a virtually ideal social order on the basis of reason alone. In Ruiz-Sanchez's words, they are "A Christian people, lacking nothing but the specific proper names and the symbolic appurtenances of Christianity" (p. 79). Lithia itself, a humid planet with three heavily forested continents and five oceans, would appear to be something of a paradise.

The first four chapters of book 1 of the novel are given over to bringing the four investigators together. Ruiz-Sanchez and Paul Cleaver, a physicist, are based in Xoredeshch Sfath, capital of the large southern continent, while D. Michelis, a chemist, and Martin Agronski, a geologist, are based "at Xoredeshch Gton on the north-east continent" (p. 27). Communication across the planet is made possible by an extraordinary natural phenomenon, the Message Tree. With its roots in a "buried crystalline cliff" (p. 29) underlying Xoredeshch Sfath, the tree provides Lithia with a natural radio system. Cleaver's job is communicating with Michelis and Agronski, presumably via the Message Tree. But because Cleaver has been temporarily incapacitated by a poisonous plant, Ruiz-Sanchez, with the aid of a Lithian named Chexta, summons via the Message Tree the other two investigators so that a decision may be reached about Lithia. The other Earthmen are no longer at Xoredeshch Gton to receive the message, however. Apparently Cleaver had not been communicating with them and so Michelis and Agronski had decided to travel to Xoredeshch Sfath and find out what has been going on.

Ruiz-Sanchez returns to the jug-like dwelling in which he and Cleaver have been living to find that Michelis and Agronski have already arrived. In the next four chapters, the four investigators discuss their reactions to Lithia and their recommendations as to its status in relation to Earth. In the course of the discussion it emerges that Cleaver deliberately failed to communicate with Michelis and Agronski. He explains that for his own reasons he wanted each pair to think the worst about what was happening to the other, presumably at the hands of the Lithians. A negative assessment of Lithia would, in Cleaver's somewhat befuddled mind, abet his plans for using the enormous supplies of lithium on the planet to stockpile fusion bombs: "All we need to do is to turn in a triple-E Unfavourable on the planet, to shut off any use of Lithia as a way station or any other kind of general base for a whole century. At the same time, we can report separately to the U.N. Review Committee exactly what we have in Lithia: a triple A arsenal for the whole of Earth, for the whole commonwealth of planets we control!" (pp. 64–65). The destructive basis for Cleaver's overtly allegorical name is now apparent as something beyond his attempt to cleave Ruiz-Sanchez from Michelis and Agronski. Agronski appears to agree with Cleaver. Michelis, on the other hand, deplores Cleaver's ideas and argues that communication with the Lithians would be desirable because Earth could learn something from their well-nigh perfect social system.

Ruiz-Sanchez shocks the assembly by agreeing "that Lithia should be reported triple-E Unfavourable" with the addition that it be given a permanent X-One "quarantine label" (p. 76). It seems that information received from Chexta after their meeting at the Message Tree had convinced Ruiz-Sanchez that Lithia is a set-up, a trap engineered by Satan himself—in spite of the fact (which is not mentioned in the original novella version of book 1) that this conclusion involves him in the Manichaean heresy, the belief that Satan, like God, has creative power. Chexta had explained to Ruiz-Sanchez the eugenically progressive Lithian life-cycle which "our ancestors" (Lithian or demonic? the reader might wonder given the vague reference) engineered so that emotional and rational considerations coincide (p. 46). The recapitulation process that the human embryo goes through from "one celled animal" to "a simple metazoan" to fishlike, amphibian, and reptilian forms to the baby at birth, occurs in Lithians "outside the bodies of their mothers" (pp. 83–84):

> The Lithian female lays her eggs in her abdominal pouch, the eggs are fertilized, and then she goes to the sea to give birth to her children. What she bears is not a miniature of the marvellously evolved reptile which is the adult Lithian; far from it: instead, she hatches a fish, rather like a lamprey. The fish lives in the sea a while, and then develops rudimentary lungs and comes to live along the shore lines. Once it's stranded on the flats by the tides, the lungfish's pectoral fins become simple legs, and it squirms away through the mud, changing into an amphibian and learning to endure the rigours of living away from the sea. Gradually their limbs become stronger, and better set on their bodies, and they become the big froglike things we sometimes see down the hill, leaping in the moonlight, trying to get away from the crocodiles.
>
> Many of them do get away. They carry their habit of leaping with them into the jungle, and there they change once again, into the small, kangaroo-like reptiles we've all seen, fleeing from us among the trees—the things we called the 'hoppers'. The last change is circulatory—from the sauropsid blood system . . . to the pteropsid system. . . . Eventually, they emerge, fully grown, from the jungles, and take their places among the folk of the cities as young Lithians, ready for education. (Pp. 84–85)

Ruiz-Sanchez believes, not altogether logically, that this concrete evidence of evolution in action was designed by Satan to confirm the understanding of Darwinists intent on denying the existence of God.[3] Likewise, the evidence that an apparently perfect society is possible without religion would undermine belief in the existence of God and thereby abet Satan's cause. This casuistical reasoning, combined with the fact that the Lithian moral code—based as it is on "a set of axioms"—is "completely irrational" (p. 82), has led Ruiz-Sanchez (poised between two explosive doctrines: Darwinism and Satanic creativity) to his own irrational conclusion. For Ruiz-Sanchez, in fact, as for Cleaver, Lithia is a wolf in sheep's clothing, a utopian surface disguising an amazingly destructive potential.

A coda-like chapter 9 concludes book 1. The vote on Lithia results in a tie. Until "higher echelons on Earth" arrive at some final decision, Lithia will be a "Proscripted area pending further study" (p. 89). As the members of the commission prepare to depart, Chexta arrives bearing the gift he had originally considered offering in chapter 5, before discovering that the timing was inappropriate (pp. 56–57). It is a beautiful vase containing "a fertilized, living egg of our species," his own child, in fact. The prevailing undercurrent of irrationality culminates here; Ruiz-Sanchez accepts the gift, taking it "in trembling hands as though he expected it to explode" (p. 92) and carries it aboard the ship that is to transport the commissioners to Earth. If Ruiz-Sanchez truly believes that Lithia is a construction of the devil, then it is only rational, a matter of common sense, to conclude that any Lithian gift might be something of a Trojan horse. But then again, Ruiz-Sanchez has gone beyond, if not discarded, the directions of mere reason in making his recommendation regarding Lithia.[4]

When Blish published the novella "A Case of Conscience" in *If Worlds of Science Fiction* in September 1953 he had no intention of carrying the story beyond what now appears as book 1 of the novel version. There were, however, plans for the novella to appear as part of a "Twayne Triplet" entitled "Lithia." In fact, "A Case of Conscience" was originally commissioned for this common-setting collection by Fletcher Pratt—which, according to Brian Stableford, was why Blish wrote so uncommercial a story.[5] A letter from the Blish Papers "*Case of Conscience:* Correspondence File" from one "Doc Clark" suggests that he was to be one of the contributors to this volume and that he first dreamed up a planet named Lithia: "you've taken my goddamned 'Lithia,' built to order for space opera, and have made a story on an intellectual level approaching that of Everest" (Dep. Blish 391/3). "Doc Clark" must be John D(rury) Clark, the physical chemist who had a hand in *The Petrified Planet* (1952), one of the two Twayne triplets edited anonymously by Fletcher Pratt which actually did appear. As an introduction, Clark provides a scientific description of the two worlds which figure in the three stories that follow (by Fletcher Pratt, H. Beam Piper, and Judith Merril): the silicone planet Uller and the fluorine planet Niflheim. Lithia, presumably, was to be the lithium planet.

In a letter to Paul Shackley Blish points out that "much science fiction begins with a background notion"—a society or a gimmick—and that the composition of "A Case of Conscience" began when he was handed a background account of Lithia "by John D. Clark and Willy Ley" (which later was "included as the appendix of the novel"). Blish goes on to explain how Ruiz-Sanchez's dilemma derived from Blish's method of elaborating a story from its background situation by asking "Whom does this hurt?" As Blish read Clark and Ley's description of Lithia,

I increasingly felt that there was something womblike about this planet. The next idea, almost instantaneously, was that of having recapitulation enacted here *after* birth. Whom does this hurt? Obviously, someone who (a) would know enough biology to recognise the evidence, but (b) was wedded to fundamentalist notions about the theory of evolution. Provide him with antagonists who think he's out of his mind, and the fact that he loves what he sees so he's also in conflict with himself, and the rest almost writes itself. This is not hindsight; the story did come to me in just this order, though the calculation involved was by no means so cold as I have made it sound. (PS, 6 November 1970)

The Lithia triplet never appeared but in the meantime the magazine version of Blish's story had received praise not only within the SF community (Lester del Rey requested a sequel) but also from the respected literary critic Gilbert Highet in a letter to Blish dated 2 June 1954. Influenced by this response, Ian Ballantine, who had founded Ballantine Books in 1952, commissioned an extended version of the story and, in a letter to his agent, Frederik Pohl, Blish speaks in characteristically explosive (or is it inflationary?) terms of "blowing it up into a novel" (Dep. Blish 391/3). In fact, it was Pohl, a part time consultant for Ballantine Books, who first suggested this commercial possibility.

Around the same time Blish received a request from William Harlan Shaw of the Speech Department, Hardin-Simmons University, Abilene, Texas. Shaw wanted to make a dramatic adaptation of the novella. In a letter dated 2 December 1955, Blish gave his permission but expressed doubt about the project. He believed his story to be "so static, so purely a seminar between conflicting philosophies" as to be "too dull for dramatization." He continues, "at one point in the yarn [pp. 35–38] I felt forced to resort to dramatic form to give an illusion of something happening besides a Socratic dialogue; it would never have occurred to me that the technique might be stood on its head" (Dep. Blish 391/3). Nevertheless, the adaptation was made and a tape of the same is among the material deposited in the Bodleian. One might expect from the view expressed in the letter to Shaw that, in extending the novella, Blish would attempt to introduce the kind of action he thought was missing from the extant material. And this does turn out to be the case.

During the first half of 1957 Blish set about writing book 2 of *A Case of Conscience* and making minor revisions and insertions in the novella which became book 1. These included references to the theoretical physicist Haertel, introduced in "Common Time" (August 1953). When the job was complete he had expanded the original 23,000-word novella by 7,000 words and added 40,000 more. An exchange of letters between Blish and Pohl (who had been brought in on the book) during this period indicates something of Blish's plans for the continuation, his respect for Pohl's opinions, and the impact of Pohl's suggestions on the final novel. Blish seems to have had some doubt about the commercial appropriateness of his title, but on 12 January 1957 Pohl suggests retaining the original title. Nevertheless, the question pops up four months later. "Do we need a new title for the book as a whole?" asks Blish. That Blish himself approved of his original title would seem to be apparent from his expression of gratitude on 18 June 1957, that "Ian [Ballantine] is willing to allow a title like the present one which doesn't suggest sf" (Dep. Blish 391/3).

In an important letter dated 23 February 1957, Pohl refers to the story as "the first reasonably thoughtful account of what the Catholic Church will be a few hundred years from now." He suggests, and the idea is taken up by Blish, that Ruiz-Sanchez's hurry to get back to Earth in book 1 should be motivated by the desire to be there during the coming Holy year, the occasion, as we learn in Blish's insert, of the "proclaiming the great pardon only once every half century" (p. 18). Such an event could be used, Pohl goes on, to justify a trip to Rome by Ruiz-Sanchez in book 2. At the same time Pohl stresses the need to carry over the "sense of wonder," brilliantly evoked by such images as the Message Tree, into the second part of the story; the terrestrial setting should not delimit the invention of exotic detail. The letter concludes with the following revealing piece of information: "What you originally told me of your plan—that the priest imagined the planet to be Hell at the end of the first portion, but discovered it to be Eden at the end of the second—sounded and still sounds just right" (Dep. Blish 391/3). It would appear from this that Blish changed his mind about the degree to which such judgments would be ambiguous. As the novel now stands, it is by no means clear that Ruiz-Sanchez finally realizes that Lithia is Eden; but it may be that enough of Blish's original intention (if Pohl is stating it correctly) survives in the present novel to encourage a number of overly dogmatic commentaries.

Blish's second thoughts, if that is what they were, appear in a 6 March 1957 letter. He claims that the "ambiguity of opinion" is "the original story's chief virtue in my eyes." He also speaks of introducing the idea of a shelter economy on Earth, a move towards living underground as a way of surviving nuclear attack. The idea, he notes, crops up in "last month's Bulletin of the Atomic Scientists" and had been touched on in his story "To Pay the Piper" (1956). References to the "Shelter economy" (p. 24) in book 1 were subsequently inserted. "Some of my best thoughts," he concludes, "are afterthoughts, although it's a tendency I'm trying to train out of myself" (Dep. Blish 391/3).

Five more letters followed. On 14 March 1957, Pohl tells Blish that he is sending him a copy of *A Pilgrim's Guide to Rome,* which "has a chapter on Holy Years." By this time Blish had decided upon the conclusion of his story because Pohl comments that the device of having exorcism work through a simultaneous physical event is comparable to the argument that God works through antibiotics to cure the sick, an analogy that Blish uses (p. 198). Blish worked very hard on book 2. On 11 June 1957, he refers to writing three drafts of chapter 11 prior to complaining, "I am writing this book on Jack Daniels instead of beer, and the damage to my pocketbook is phenomenal." And on 18 June 1957 he claims, "the job of continuing the original story without spoiling it is one of the toughest I've ever tackled" (Dep. Blish 391/3).

Pohl had questioned the "truncated tetrahedron" in this sentence: "As he [Ruiz-Sanchez] looked dazedly out of the window into the dripping darkness, a familiar, sculpturesque head and shoulders [Chexta's] moved into the truncated tetrahedron of yellow light being cast out through the fine glass into the rain" (p. 54). Blish responds that the image was intended to be metaphorical of Ruiz-Sanchez's truncated apartness from the other three members of the team of investigators, the untruncated corners of the tetrahedron, and refuses to change it. Beyond inferring the presence of a triangular window, it is extremely unlikely that even the most perspicacious reader would understand the image in the way that Blish decoded it—the word "truncated" would seem to be suggested by the head and shoulders of Chexta—and Pohl was right to be bothered by the matter. But the sentence clearly indicates that Blish's ambitions as a writer went far beyond those of the average writer of pulp SF. If one pauses to examine the sentence carefully, it *is* apparent that Blish's intended meaning is embedded in the choice of word and syntax. The parallel between "he looked dazedly out" and the "yellow light being cast out" *does* connect Ruiz-Sanchez with the "truncated tetrahedron." And the pun on "cast out" might well lead a reflective reader to consider the kind of concerns which might cause a Jesuit to feel alienated from the purely secular considerations of his companions.

Indeed, the very words "cast out" evoke the religious problem with which Ruiz-Sanchez is wrestling. Did not God cast out the rebellious angels from Heaven? It would seem that Blish's practice here is eminently justifiable on artistic grounds, but the introduction of the technical word "tetrahedron" is indicative of what is almost a stylistic tic. Repeatedly, mind-numbing terms like "spectrosigmin" (p. 11), "hygroscopic" (p. 14), "pteropsid" (p. 18), "sigmoid" (p. 19), "monotreme," "hologen" (p. 21), "affine" (p. 23), "phloem" (p. 25), "fossae" (p. 26) and "anaphylactic" (p. 30) are dropped into otherwise straightforward sentences. Of course, one expects to find outré scientific terms in a genre called *"science* fiction" and, to a degree, Blish's procedure here is at one with the genre's overall task of suggesting and perhaps assimilating the unknown and alien. But Blish might reasonably be charged with overusing the device. Whatever doubts Pohl might have had about the "truncated tetrahedron," he wrote cannily on 12 July 1957, "I expect great things of this book" (Dep. Blish 391/3).

Along with Pohl's reactions, Blish had a reader's report from Ian Ballantine. Ballantine urged Blish to ensure that Ruiz-Sanchez be made sympathetic to the lay reader. Amidst other matters of detail, he directed that Ruiz-Sanchez's fainting spell before Agronski following his discovery of the Lithian reproductive cycle be reconsidered. Blish complied.[6] Ballantine seems to have been particularly bothered by the possibility that most of the book's dim-witted readers would not know enough about Catholicism to make sense of the story and suggested that certain matters of doctrine might be made clear in the context of a monastery scene which might be inserted into book 2. But Blish refused to go along with this idea. As he explained in a letter to Pohl, he believed that any such monastery scene would come across as blatant padding.

The nine chapters of book 2, in their final tightly plotted form, repeat the four-, four-, and one-chapter structure of book 1, and, as one might expect, literally grow out of the egg proffered at the end of that book. The Lithian infant turns out to be a male named Egtverchi. Chapters 10 to 13 deal with Eg[g]tverchi's coming out, his hatching from the egg, and his introduction to human society. Fear of nuclear destruction has led to that society's living in underground cities. During the process of maturation and "physical recapitulation outside the body" (p. 99), Egtverchi is placed in the charge of "the U.N. laboratory chief," a young woman named Liu Meid (p. 98). After introducing Michelis to Liu Meid, who will shortly become his wife, Ruiz-Sanchez tells him that he shall be going to Rome. "I expect to be tried there for heresy," he explains in one of Blish's characteristic chapter-closing shock lines (p. 106). With Egtverchi's maturation into a highly intelligent alien comes the problem of deciding whether he should be admitted to free citizenship.

The matter is decided in Egtverchi's favor and chapter 12, the lengthiest set-piece in the book, is devoted to his "coming-out party" in the many-storied "underground mansion of Lucien le Compte des Bois-d' Averoigne" (p. 117), a scientist mentioned in book 1 and of whom we shall hear more.[7] At the time, however, as for most of the time in fact, only the countess is in residence. While the mode of book 1 is predominantly visionary, the mode of book 2 is predominantly satiric, and that tone is clearly established in the colorful description of the decadent sex-and-drugs party scene which is choreographed by Aristide, the countess's enterprising caterer. In a detail notable for its prescience, we learn that amongst the early comers was "Senator Sharon, waggling her oversize eyebrows in wholesome cheeriness at the remaining guests, ostentatiously refusing drinks, secure in the knowledge that her good friend Aristide had provided for her below five strong young men no one of whom she had ever seen before" (p. 119). Something of the "sense of wonder" that Pohl had called for comes across in the countess's coiffure: "the mobiles in the little caves Stefano had contrived in her hair spun placidly or blinked their diamond eyes" (p. 120). One of the guests is the alienated and intoxicated Agronski, whom Aristide has efficiently removed from the proceedings long before Egtverchi's belated arrival. (In the following chapter, perhaps in response to the bafflement expressed in Ballantine's report at Agronski's "retreat," space is devoted to the development of his schiziod feelings of ennui and meaninglessness.)

Egtverchi's unique position in relation to Earth society and the public response to his "wry and awry comments" in "his first inteview on 3-V" make him a media personality. Before long he becomes "a sponsored news commentator" with "a lunatic following" (p. 132). Very much like the central character in the film *Network* (1976)—and the word "network" is actually used (p. 160)—Egtverchi becomes a figure of enormous influence. He uses his program to express "his disrespect for all established institutions and customs" and urges his audience to write anonymous letters of complaint to his sponsors: "Just make the message pungent. If you hate that powdered concrete they call a knish mix, write and tell them so. . . . If you loathe me, tell the Bifalcos [Bridget Bifalco World Kitchens is Egtverchi's major sponsor] that, too, and make sure you're spitting mad about it" (pp. 158–59). (The parallel with "I'm mad as hell and I won't take it anymore" is obvious.[8]) Egtverchi promises to "read the five messages I think in the worst possible taste on my broadcast next week" (p. 159). Given that Earth's communication system is the nearest parallel to the Message Tree which is so central to Lithian life, it is hardly surprising that Egtverchi turns out to be so adept a broadcaster. Eventually he becomes powerful enough to instigate mass rioting in the streets. What Ruiz-Sanchez tries to convince himself is only "Armageddon in 3-V" becomes reality (p. 154).

But that is in the future. Chapters 14 to 17 deal with Ruiz-Sanchez's visit to Rome, prompted by its being a Holy Year (it is now 2050), the problem of Lithia, and his and the Michelises' reaction both to developments on Lithia and Egtverchi's disturbing career. On the train to Rome Ruiz-Sanchez rereads an airletter from Michelis who describes what he knows of Egtverchi's outrageous behavior in searching out all the scandalous goings-on at his coming-out party and the subsequent publicity which has ruined the countess. Egtverchi, Ruiz-Sanchez realizes, is a displaced person, "a wolf child" (p. 148) like the one which founded Rome, "the sanest major capital on the planet," in "the least thoroughly entombed" of "all the Shelter nations" (p. 149). Ruiz-Sanchez's own affinity for Rome is suggested by his Christian name, which is an anagram of "Roman." He believes that he has been commanded to appear before the Holy Father to defend himself against the charge of holding heretical Manichaean views regarding Lithia. As it turns out, the Norwegian Pope Hadrian VIII (Blish undoubtedly knew about Frederick Rolfe's autobiographical wish-fulfillment fantasy, *Hadrian the Seventh* [1904]) has something else in mind.[9] The Pope believes that Lithia was not created by the devil but is rather possessed by the devil. He convinces Ruiz-Sanchez that what is required is an act of exorcism. The Pope, it is implied, agrees with Ruiz-Sanchez "that the world stood on the brink of Armageddon" (p. 182).

From this point of view, Lithia is an illusion, a hallucination. It might be recalled that when the Lithians are first mentioned it is in connection with their drugs. Ruiz-Sanchez tells the sick Cleaver, "I don't doubt that the Lithians have at least a hundred different drugs we'll be able to use eventually" (p. 12). Lithium, in fact, best known as a treatment for manic-depression, does provide the basis for a number of medical drugs, including the oxide "lithia water," a Victorian remedy for gout and rheumatism, and lithium bromide, which may be used as a sedative and hypnotic.

Meanwhile, in their Manhattan apartment building, Michelis tells Liu that Egtverchi is using his television appearances to whip up a mob as "an elaborate act of revenge" against them for doing such a bad job of parenting. Liu weeps and it would appear from Ballantine's report that Blish originally had Michelis weeping too. Ballantine (as ever opposed to anything overly demonstrative) thought that a bit too much and suggested substituting something like "a long deep sigh" (Dep. Blish 391/3). Instead, as a chime announces the presence of a visitor, Blish has Michelis looking up "with bitter resignation" (p. 159). The visitor is the U.N. Committee chairman come to discuss the Egtverchi problem. To make matters worse, it appears that the U.N. has favored Cleaver's recommendations regarding Lithia and has decided to use it as "a laboratory for the study of fusion power storage" (p. 163). Cleaver has been put in charge and is already back on Lithia.

When Ruiz-Sanchez returns to New York and catches up on events, he suggests to Michelis that Egtverchi might be dissuaded from his destructive course if given the chance to speak to his father, Chexta. And, as it happens, the genius philosopher-mathematician Count d'Averoigne is at work on a "new circum-continuum radio" which just might be able to hook into the Message Tree (p. 171). The communication takes place at d'Averoigne's Canadian retreat but with no positive results. Chexta believes his son is ill (illness is, it should be noted, an important metaphor throughout the novel) and explains that Cleaver and his associates have set about demolishing the forests of Lithia and are in the process of cutting down—cleaving—the Message Tree. Clearly, Cleaver is doing for Lithia what Egtverchi is doing for Earth. Egtverchi refuses what Chexta calls the command of "the Law of the Whole" that he return to Lithia (p. 179). Back in New York, Egtverchi makes a final broadcast and stirs up the riot which will ensure the "collapse of the Shelter state" (p. 184).

By way of indicating in his letter to Shackley that the actual composition of *A Case of Conscience* was not the cold-blooded affair his account of its conception might suggest, Blish notes that "when three paragraphs before I started to set the event up, I realized that I was going to have to cut down the Message Tree, I began weeping into my typewriter, to the alarm of my then wife" (PS, 6 November 1970). Blish makes the same point in a letter to Karin Laflin Adams but in the context of how very often "I wind up with an ending quite different from the planned one":

> I had known all along, in an abstract way, that I was going to destroy Lithia, but it had suddenly hit me that I couldn't do this scene as a mere astronomical spectacle, but had to recall to the reader all the nice things about the planet; and that to make vivid the extent of the loss *before the fact* (and for

other inescapable reasons) I had to have Cleaver cut down the Message Tree, the finest and most loved of all my inventions. . . . [W]hen the roar of the chain-saw began to sound in my mind I was as stricken as I had been a decade earlier to find that our three [actually one]-month-old son . . . had been found inexplicably dead in his crib just after I'd gone off to my footling job. The comparison is monstrous, but it was exactly the same grief all the same and I knew it, there was no mistaking it. . . . It perfected the novel, but at a cost in self-knowledge I still find hard to face. (KLA, 27 February 1973)

The tragic impact of the memorable event in the novel is conveyed by three brief lines of dialogue (p. 181). The concluding chapter is, as one might expect, apocalyptic in character. "The best Chaos roared on unslaked for three days" (p. 184). Ruiz-Sanchez narrowly escapes death at the hands of the mob, which includes Agronski. Egtverchi, on the run, is on the way to Lithia, having smuggled himself "aboard the vessel that was shipping the final installment of equipment to Cleaver" and, as it happens, carrying a pilot model of the circum-continuum radio by which the captain communicates the discovery of Egtverchi to the count. Ruiz-Sanchez, along with Michelis and Liu Meid (who seems not to have adopted her husband's surname), is directed by the U.N. to come to the Moon, to d'Averoigne's observatory. Ruiz-Sanchez speculates that Egtverchi's impact "on the stable society of Lithia would be explosive," but what finally blows the "time bomb" planet up cannot be unambiguously determined (pp. 194, 114). With the count's amazing new telescope, it is possible to observe Lithia at the present moment as the count explains that he has brought Ruiz-Sanchez, Michelis, and Meid to the Moon as witnesses. The count expects that, as a result of a fault in "the reasoning on which Dr. Cleaver based the experiment he has programmed for today," Lithia will be destroyed by a nuclear explosion if the experiment goes ahead in defiance of the warning message he sent "on the CirCon, to be tape-recorded on the ship that landed yesterday" (p. 197). Ruiz-Sanchez realizes that his moment has come; he goes through the liturgy of exorcism. And Lithia explodes; but not before the reader is reminded, as Frederik Pohl had suggested in one of his letters, of everything that has been destroyed:

Slowly, slowly, it all melted away: the chirruping forests, Chexta's porcelain house, the barking lungfish, the single silver moon, the great beating heart of Blood Lake, the city of the potters, the flying suid [typo for "squid"], the Lithian crocodile and his winding track, the tall noble reasoning creatures and the mystery and beauty around them. Suddenly the whole of Lithia began to swell, like a balloon—(P. 200)

A fault causes the telescope screen to go blank at this point (d'Averoigne's equations are no more perfect than Cleaver's?). And a similar blankness must thwart any attempt to determine whether the event almost witnessed should be understood in purely materialist terms, or as God's working through material means, or as the straight exorcising of a demonic hallucination. What evidence remains includes the preliminary report on Lithia by Michelis and Ruiz-Sanchez in *The Journal of Interstallar Research* which is presented as an appendix.[10]

A Case of Conscience was favorably reviewed and won the Hugo it so richly deserved. However, an account of the original novella which Blish himself published in the fanzine *Skyhook* for autumn 1953 under his Atheling pseudonym was moderately critical. And in a 1964 update he considered book 2 unsatisfactory because of "too much material there to escape an effect of breathlessness as the novel draws to a close."[11] This effect is largely created by the contrast with the drawn-out party scene of chapter 12. Book 2 generally is less compelling than book 1 and, in terms of essential ideas, contains very little that is not already at least implicit in book 1. *A Case of Conscience,* like much of Blish's best work, is finally flawed. As it happens, the book was most enthusiastically received not in America but in England, where it was published in hardcover by Faber & Faber in 1959. Bernard Bergonzi extolled its merits at length in a BBC Third Programme radio broadcast (23 April 1959). But in spite of this success Blish was unable to secure hardcover publication in America. In their letter of rejection dated 7 July 1959, Putnam's explains that they could not see a market for a book which marries SF and the serious novel!

The question remains, can *A Case of Conscience* be described as a novel in any strict sense of the term? In fact, are any of Blish's novels truly novels? John Clute thinks not. In a provocative essay, he notes Blish's "impatience with that mimesis of temporal continuity and beingness" and "narrative equipoise" that the novel calls for. But what appear as flaws in terms of the novel might be otherwise viewed in terms of an alternative category. Clute argues that Blish's tonally disjunctive, temporarily discontinuous extended fictions more properly belong in the category of prose fiction that Paul Hernadi, in *Beyond Genre* (1972), opposes to the novel, or *roman,* namely the *recit* with its logical and rhetorically organized presentation of past events. Northrop Frye's corresponding category in *Anatomy of Criticism* (1957) is the Menippean satire, or anatomy, with its stylized characterization and emphasis on abstract ideas, as exemplified by the works of Rabelais, Robert Burton, Voltaire, Swift, Thomas Love Peacock, Melville, and

Huxley. Thus the introspective talkiness of Blish's fiction and the tendency to have much of the action (witness the corridor riots in *A Case of Conscience*) take place off-stage. And thus the oddity of much of Blish's SF, SF being basically a romance form in terms of Frye's four categories of prose fiction. Blish, in *A Case of Conscience* and most of his other novels, attempts a fusion of the *recit* mode of the Menippean satire with the romance form of SF. The result, sometimes more of a jumble, was rarely as successful as in *A Case of Conscience*.[12]

(ii) The Case for Catholicism?

Somewhat surprisingly, given Blish's statement in his foreword that "The author . . . is an agnostic" (p. 7), two of the more extensive commentaries on *A Case of Conscience* argue for an unambiguously Christian reading. According to a lengthy review by Don D'Ammassa, Blish agrees with Pope Hadrian's view that Lithia was not created by the devil but possessed by him.[13] D'Ammassa argues that if Ruiz-Sanchez's conclusion was correct, the Lithians should have no self-awareness. But Egtverchi is self-aware. Ruiz-Sanchez, D'Ammassa claims, fell into the sin of heresy because he gave way to the temptation of knowledge in chapter 2. In order to find out more about Lithian life, Ruiz-Sanchez accepts Chexta's invitation to stay the night at his house when he should have returned to look after the sick Cleaver. There *is* a case of conscience here and Ruiz-Sanchez does allude to "the vast, tragic riddle of original sin" (p. 30); perhaps Ruiz-Sanchez does make the wrong decision, but D'Ammassa's judgment is much too unequivocal. The reading of *A Case of Conscience* which he suggests is but one pole of a spectrum of possibilities allowed for by Blish's text.

An orthodox religious reading of the novel is, of course, encouraged by the prevalence of Christian allusions and imagery and clearly signalled in chapter 1. The chapter opens with Cleaver slamming a door "with a sound like a clap of doom" (p. 9). The allusion here is to the apocalypse and to the responsibility, in a naturalistic reading, which Cleaver bears for the destruction of Lithia. It is Cleaver who first refers to Lithians as "the Snakes" who "would be jabbing me full of antibiotics" (p. 12). Snakes, of course, more usually inject poison; and, thus, he suggests indirectly that the Lithians have poisoned him, albeit by means of "one of the spines" of "a plant that looked a little like a pineapple" (p. 11). The brief reference to the Lithian "radio network" which is "zeroed on . . . a tree" (p. 16) introduces the Message Tree, which will be more fully described in the ensuing chapter. This central feature of Lithian life is clearly equivalent to the biblical tree of the forbidden knowledge of good and evil. It hardly seems accidental that Cleaver has been struck down by something like an apple, "a plant . . . like a pineapple" (p. 11). For Ruiz-Sanchez, Lithia is "a biologist's paradise" (p. 13), something like Eden, but for Cleaver the place is more like Hell. Cleaver's position would appear to be corroborated by "the myriad insects [read "flies" or "devils"?] of Lithia" (p. 17) and the absence of birds (read "angels"?), and by the final sentence of chapter 1, where the gaslight evokes images of both snakes and the fires of Hell: "Then he [Ruiz-Sanchez] arose and left the room to the softly hissing flames" (p. 19). It seems appropriate, therefore, that at the beginning of chapter 3, which centers on failures of understanding, Agronski and Cleaver exchange a series of "Where," "What," and "How" the hells (pp. 31, 32), followed by Agronski's "There's a hell of a lot we don't know about Lithia, that's for damn sure" and Michelis's "There's a hell of a lot we don't know about central Brazil. . . ." (p. 36).

Biblical associations are maintained throughout the book. Jo Allen Bradham, in what is to date the most detailed explication of these matters, elucidates the religious implications of the setting of the Message Tree. It is located, as the biblical phraseology has it, "at the mouth of the valley of the River Sfath" (p. 23). "Sfath," Bradham suggests, derives from the Elizabethan expletives "God's faith" or "'Sfaith." Bradham goes on: "The valley itself leads to Blood Lake (in English), which may suggest the Red Sea, thus emphasizing the Old Testament allusion in the setting of Lithia. Or, and more importantly, Blood Lake probably foreshadows the destruction and death which science and faith, working together, finally bring to Lithia."[14] Bradham, who does not mention the "serpentine folds" of the valley on its way to the lake, seems instead, intent on building up an unambiguous picture of Lithia as an unfallen world (p. 23).

In terms of Bradham's interpretation, Chexta is an unambiguously godlike being. As a metallurgist, he is the alchemical god "who refines [man] for use."[15] The "truncated tetrahedron of yellow light," into which Chexta's head and shoulders move, provides him with a halo (p. 54). And it is, of course, not without religious significance that the Lithians are a race of potters who become fishes in the first stage of their maturation cycle. In this context, Chexta's gift of Egtverchi, his only begotten son, corresponds to God's offering up his son, Christ, for the salvation of man. But Bradham omits to note that on the one occasion that Egtverchi is described in the biblical phrase as a "begotten son," the father is assumed by Ruiz-Sanchez to be not God but "the

Adversary," Satan (p. 116). When Cleaver observes of the gift that "the Snake couldn't have made a bigger thing of it if he'd been handing you his own head on a platter" (p. 92), the allusion is, as Bradham notes, to Christ's herald, John the Baptist. Elsewhere, Egtverchi is spoken of as having "made that crossing from animal to automaton which had caused all the trouble eastward of Eden in 4004 B.C." (p. 109)—a line which Bradham bewilderingly quotes as evidence that Egtverchi is the second Adam. Somewhat later, Egtverchi is equated with one of Earth's "deranged and misplaced messiahs" (p. 194). What Bradham totally fails to allow for is the very real possibility that these references might well herald a diabolic inversion of the coming of Christ. Certainly there is nothing very saintly about Egtverchi's equivalent of Christ's twelve disciples, the "ten nearly identical young men in uniforms of black and lizard green with silver piping, their arms folded, their expressions stern, their eyes straight ahead" who accompany Egtverchi to his coming-out party (p. 130).

That party in the many-levelled underground mansion (developed from what was once a trolley-car storage center) is clearly intended as an analogue of Dante's Hell (spiced with elements which might derive from *The Satyricon*).[16] Ian Ballantine, in his report on Blish's manuscript, had admitted himself baffled by the whole chapter. Presumably he could not understand why Blish had treated the party at such length. It does seem likely, however, that Blish intended the party scene to establish an image of a hellish Earth by way of contrast with the extended presentation in book 1 of Lithia as an image (albeit possibly a false one) of Eden or Paradise. The three trains which convey the party guests from one level to another, commuting between a variety of illicit pleasures, are appropriately called *serpentines*. At a late stage of the party, the countess identifies Egtverchi as a "lousy snake-scaled demon" (p. 138). The drugs which are being taken on the premises might remind an attentive reader that drugs of unspecified properties have been mentioned as a notable feature of Lithian society.

It is Bradham's argument that the horrors which ensue are the result of Ruiz-Sanchez's failure to understand that Egtverchi is a Christ figure. Religion, as represented by Ruiz-Sanchez, is as blind as science, as represented by Cleaver, to the truth. Far from being opposed characters, embodiments of good and evil, Ruiz-Sanchez and Cleaver are actually very much alike. At least such is the case which Bradham makes:

While Cleaver is lying poisoned, Ruiz-Sanchez is said to be "poisoned-tired" [p. 51]; thus, imagery likens the priest to the sick scientist. Similarly, when

Cleaver participates in the discussion, "he looks almost ecclesiastical" with his hands folded "quietly in the lap of his robe" (p. 60). Since the earlier scene between Ruiz-Sanchez and Chexta established that the robe is the characteristic and identifying feature of the priest, the use of the religious terms *ecclesiastical* and *robe* likens physicist to priest.[17]

Bradham is surely right in insisting that Cleaver's sickness makes manifest a more general human sickness, and one which Ruiz-Sanchez shares. But is that sickness not simply metaphorical of man's fallen state? And can it be unequivocally asserted that the Lithians exist in an unfallen state? Ruiz-Sanchez's sickness may well betray itself in allusions to his defective eyesight, his fears of blindness, and his night-time excursion to the Message Tree. But may not these details be simply indicative of that clouded vision which is simply part and parcel of the human condition?

While D'Ammassa locates Ruiz-Sanchez's crucial error as the abandonment of the sick Cleaver in favor of gaining knowledge about the Lithians, Bradham sees Ruiz-Sanchez's crucial fault as his obsession with *Finnegans Wake* and his pretensions toward being a literary critic. Certainly, the repeated references to Ruiz-Sanchez's interest in the meaning of a particularly complicated passage in *Finnegans Wake* require some kind of explanation.[18] It was one of the aspects of *A Case of Conscience* that Ian Ballantine took exception to, and Blish did cut some of the *Finnegans Wake* material.[19] There is, of course, the very obvious analogy between a book which the Catholic Church has placed on "the Index Expurgatorius" (p. 9) and the placing of Lithia on a planetary "Index Expurgatorius," making it a "Proscripted area pending further study" (p. 89). The *Finnegans Wake* passage in question, with its references to rape, procurement, deception, incest, and debauchery, does have everything to do with the fallen human condition. And the case in law which the passage presents is vaguely analogous to the case of conscience which Ruiz-Sanchez is attempting to unravel. Furthermore, the emphasis Blish places on interpreting a passage in a book serves as a reminder of literary reflexivity, a reminder that to unravel Ruiz-Sanchez's case of conscience is actually to interpret a book.

Bradham attempts, I believe mistakenly, to make precise correspondences between the characters mentioned in the Joyce passage and the Lithian situation, but it is the overall evaluation of Ruiz-Sanchez's response to Joyce which is particularly misleading.[20] The issue in the Joyce case, "Has he hegemony and shall she submit" (an issue that cannot be reformulated to cover that in *A Case of Conscience* without considerable license), amounts, according to Ruiz-Sanchez, to not one question but two. Only the absence of a comma in the quoted sentence obscures this fact and the correct answers, "Yes, and No" (p. 53). Bradham observes:

> For all his years of study, Ruiz-Sanchez concludes that the central problem of *Finnegans Wake* is where to put one comma. A man who reaches that kind of conclusion about a work including all time and exploring the implications of the Fall could hardly be expected to separate the major from the nonessential in the case of Lithia. The satiric reduction of Ruiz-Sanchez is probably more fierce and conclusive in this revelation of literary judgment than at any other point. Having missed the case in literature, he misses it in life.[21]

Blish, like Ruiz-Sanchez, was a devoted student of *Finnegans Wake*. Joyce, as Blish well knew, was just the kind of writer who might hinge matters of extraordinary consequence on a detail of typography. The opposition which Bradham posits here between life and a sterile academicism simply does not apply. There is no reason to suppose that Blish would not applaud both Ruiz-Sanchez's interest in *Finnegans Wake* and this example of his interpretative acuteness. After all, it seems most unlikely that Blish would have Ruiz-Sanchez advance a new and ingenious interpretation of a crux in *Finnegans Wake* which Blish himself did not endorse. Ruiz-Sanchez's answer is as ambiguous as Joyce's question, with or without the comma. "Yes, and No" might be interpreted as two straight answers to two straight questions or an ambiguously phrased answer to an ambiguously phrased question. After all, Joyce did not include a comma in his question.

Similarly ambiguous is the interpretation which Ruiz-Sanchez finally considers in *A Case of Conscience:* "Suppose, just suppose, that Lithia were Eden, and that the Earth-bred Lithian who had just returned there were the Serpent foreordained for it?" (p. 199). Bradham answers this with an unequivocal yes, and no. The attentive reader cannot be so certain. Ruiz-Sanchez's hypothesis simply takes its place with a variety of alternative possibilities. This strategy, combined with Blish's intense moral concern, makes him the Nathaniel Hawthorne of SF writers.

(iii) The Suit-Case of Conscience?

Like the Christian imagery, like almost everything else in the novel, what might modishly be termed its "deep structure" is clearly signalled in chapter 1. At the very beginning of that chapter, while Ruiz-Sanchez is preoccupied with "the case" proposed by what we subsequently discover to be a passage from *Finnegans Wake,* Cleaver is struggling with quite another problem—how to free himself from "his jungle suit" (p. 9). An internal mental puzzle is counterpointed with an external physical one. To what extent, it might be wondered, are the two struggles interchangeable? To what degree, the suspicion might insert itself, is the case of conscience not an inner manifestation of the voice of God but a societal overlay, metaphorically speaking a protective outer garment? This suspicion is strongly reinforced by Ruiz-Sanchez's reminding himself, towards the end of the chapter, "that to the inner life, the body was only a garment" (p. 18), that is to say, a garment like the one Cleaver, with Ruiz-Sanchez's help, is having such difficulty removing. Is conscience a removable garment?[22] Or alternatively, is the body the garment of conscience, a case, a container for conscience? The equation between the jungle suit and conscience is made explicit by the parallel reflections which conclude chapter 1:

> And conscience, like creation, cannot be hurried. It cannot even be scheduled.
>
> He looked down at the still-imperfect jungle suit [one of the zipper teeth has been affected by Lithian fungi] with a troubled face until he heard Cleaver moan. (P. 19)

How perfect a creation, it might be asked, is conscience? Exactly what is the case of conscience?

Ruiz-Sanchez comes to see that the meaning of the *Finnegans Wake* passage hangs on a comma. The meaning of *A Case of Conscience* would seem to hang on a pun, another "writer's joke" (p. 53). "Case" in the title means something equivalent to "situation" or "issue." The issue at hand, to adapt the title of Blish's first critical book, is one involving the issue of conscience. Virtually whenever the word "case" crops up in the narrative (some ten times) this is the meaning implied. Much the same meaning ("situation" mutated to "condition") applies when one speaks of a "medical case," and although the term is not used in relation to the poisoned Cleaver, that is what he is. Subsequently, Chexta considers Egtverchi to be sick, a case for treatment, and Ruiz-Sanchez comes to see that the potential destruction of Lithia is analogous to the medical case where God effects a cure through "a shot of spectrosigmin or some similar drug" (p. 198). The word "case" is also used in a legal sense to mean "argument" or "evidence." In chapters 6 to 8 the four investigators put their differing cases for exploiting, valuing, or shunning Lithia. This meaning of the word "case" is, then, implied by the novel even if the word itself is not actually used in that sense. "Case" can also mean "container" or "covering," and it is this denotation of the word which provides the key to the novel's meaning. The word "case" is used once in the novel in this sense and this usage occurs in chapter 1. Many of the "insects of Lithia" make "wing-case buzzes" like the "insects of Earth" (pp. 17–18).[23] The reference is to what the *OED* describes as "each of the structures (modified forewings) which cover the functional wings in certain insects."

SF is full of, indeed largely characterized by, containers—spacesuits, spaceships, domed cities, hollow worlds, artificial satellites, and the like—but in *A Case of Conscience,* the sense of *case* as *container* provides not only a way of unifying the major elements in Blish's plot but a way of conceptualizing the central ambiguities with which he is concerned. After all, the existence of something called conscience is debatable in exactly the same terms as the questions that Ruiz-Sanchez chooses to ask of the Lithians—are they fallen or unfallen beings? Do they constitute a Satanic trap? Both matters depend upon the assumption that God exists and that the universe serves a transcendental purpose. If conscience does not represent some kind of inner reality or inner truth; if, on the other hand, it is simply a protective covering, a product of man's conditioning, then the mind-set with which Ruiz-Sanchez approaches Lithia is totally inappropriate and irrelevant. The various containers of one kind or another and the images of containment which permeate the novel all serve to illustrate its central ambiguities. To what extent do containers (including conscience, if it is one) protect and screen what is contained from external truth or reality? Are conscience and truth something contained within man? The Christian references and images discussed previously may simply be an inappropriate overlay, a type of covering or casing. Indeed the same may be true of language itself. Ultimately, of course, the matter of containers and coverings relates to the question of appearance and reality. Does the covering, the appearance, cover up and mask the truth?

A novel, of course, is a kind of container in itself and it should be noted that, in a very particular sense, *A Case of Conscience* is set up, like Lithia, perhaps, as a self-contained experiment—or a trap. Somewhat startlingly, in view of the issue being confronted, the novel contains no references to other alien civilizations for purposes of comparison. But equally there are no references to the Lithians as the first alien civilization contacted. The reader is, however, left with the implication that other aliens have been encountered and that they must have fallen into one or other of Gerald Heard's first two categories: they were assumed either to lack souls or to be possessed, like us, of fallen ones. But by eliminating any direct allusion to this matter Blish might be said to have skewed the evidence by not presenting all that is the case. Any containing document, be it novel or treatise, may be vitiated (or corroborated) by what it excludes.

Containers or coverings in the novel, and all the symbolic ambiguities that go along with them, take such forms as jugs, vases, eggs, boxes, crates, shelters, and suits. The novel opens with Cleaver slamming a door, thereby sealing the room which contains both himself and Ruiz-Sanchez. After Cleaver's "last crate" is aboard the starship, book 1 ends with, "The air lock door slammed" (p. 93); William Atheling, Jr. describes the slammed door as "Cleaver's trademark."[24] Book 2 concludes with Count d'Averoigne's proposal "that we suit up and go outside." One form of covering will be put on while another (the observatory) will be left behind. This duplicity is nicely counterpointed by the fact that a book which began with a door closing and a man getting out of a suit ends with the prospect of a door opening and people getting into suits—and the reference to an achieved time when Ruiz-Sanchez "could see again" (p. 201). The physical and temporal imagery here leaves the reader neatly poised betwixt and between, both inside and outside.

As befits a race of potters, it is not surprising that the Lithian dwellings are likened to "jugs" (p. 22). "Except for the window," Ruiz-Sanchez and Cleaver's sleeping quarters "strongly resembled the inside of a jug" (p. 13). The "vaulted chamber . . . which had been burned out in the base of the Message Tree" is "like an egg stood on its large end" (p. 25). We soon learn about Lithians being born from eggs and come to appreciate Ruiz-Sanchez's contention that "this whole planet is one huge womb" (p. 84). The "small vase, sealed at the top" (p. 91), which Chexta describes as "the finest container yet to come out of Xoredeshch Gton" and presents to Ruiz-Sanchez, contains what Chexta describes as "our other gift," a "fertilized, living egg of our species" (p. 92).

When the jug/vase image next crops up it is in a context that recalls Ruiz-Sanchez's statement that "to the inner life, the body was only a garment" (p. 18). It is used to describe an apocalypse of nihilism, the way that Agronski feels when all meaning, all reality, appear to have drained from his world: "Inside the thin shell of unwilling self-consciousness, it was as empty as an upended jug" (p. 144). Concluding chapter 13 with this line serves to emphasize the image; characteristically, Blish ends chapters or sections with statements that register some degree of shock. The emptiness of soul which Agronski experiences may explain Egtverchi's conduct. The only explanation we are given has something to do with the climactic moment in his maturation which is one of alienation, of expulsion from Eden, as he makes the switch from "animal to automaton"; as Blish describes it, the "multiple doors from sense to soul had closed; suddenly, the world was an abstract" (p. 109). It might be noted, incidentally, that if this reference to Egtverchi's "soul" is taken literally, and not viewed as a minor inconsistency on Blish's part, then Ruiz-Sanchez's view of Lithia as a demonic creation is inaccurate; but then Blish goes on to refer to Egtverchi's "animal soul" (p. 109), presumably in the Aristotelian sense of being mortal, something quite apart from the Christian conception of an eternal human soul. On learning that Agronski has become "a fan of Egtverchi's," Ruiz-Sanchez offers a comment that recalls the jug metaphor: "There's so little meaning in Agronski's life as it is, it won't take Egtverchi long to cut him off from any contact with reality at all. That is what evil does—it empties you" (p. 172).

On Earth, the container or casing image mainly takes the form of references to the "Shelter economy" and "Shelter cities" (p. 24). Just as conscience may be a protective coating applied to society to discourage internal threats, so the submerged buildings are designed to protect society from external nuclear threats. There is, of course, something very prisonlike about this form of protection, and thus it is highly appropriate that the pleasure enclosures the Egtverchi insists on breaking into during the countess's party are called "cells" and "private Hells" (p. 146). A U.N. man subsequently puts the case for containers which are simultaneously protective and imprisoning when he says, "We mean to put Mr. Egtverchi in a cage for the rest of his life—a *soundproof* cage," at the same time telling Ruiz-Sanchez, "as far as I'm concerned you've been closed out of this case entirely. If you try to force your way back in you'll get burned" (pp. 183, 184).

As things turn out, Egtverchi finds himself not in a cage per se but stowed away in a crate in a ship on its way to Lithia. The reader might recall another crate, "Cleaver's last crate" (p. 93), which casts a shadow at the end of book 1 as it is hoisted aboard another starship. The final action in the novel occurs in "the cave" of the Count d'Averoigne's observatory which is situated "approximately in the centre" of a crater on the Moon (pp. 199, 195).

Count d'Averoigne appears to be everywhere in the novel and he has its last words: the proposal, described significantly as a misdirecting maneuver, that the company suit up and go outside to look for the Lithia nova (which will not be visible for another fifty years). It seems likely that this count speaks for Blish, all the more so since he appears to be one of those second thoughts Blish claimed he was trying to train himself out of. The passage devoted to the count in book 1 (pp. 23–24) was an interpolation made in the course of writing book 2. We learn in book 2 that the count, "a lapsed Catholic" (p. 197), is the absentee husband of the countess who gives the decadent party and that he is the inventor of the principle which enables the atoms within the Micheliases' 3-V set to become a "reproduction of Paul Klee's 'Caprice in February,'" a painting "made almost wholly of detached angles and glyphs like the symbols of mathematics" (pp. 155). This "oasis of dryness" offsets the luxuriant foliage within the Micheliases' apartment and is indicative of Blish's own artistic concern with the mathematics underlying reality (p. 156). But the most telling bit of information is given when the count is first introduced as "the current *doyen* of Earthly affine theory" (p. 23); in a detail that bespeaks Blish's sympathy for the man, it seems the count can trace his ancestry "back into thirteenth-century England, to the author of *Lucien Wycham His Boke of Magick*" (p. 24). As a scientist this man hides behind a veil; he signs his papers "H. O. Petard" (p. 23). The "H." we later learn stands for "Henri" (p. 197), but anyone familiar with *Hamlet* (or indeed with idiomatic English) will translate the name as "Hoist Own Petard" and recall the lines:

> For 'tis the sport to have the engineer
> Hoist with his own petar. (*Hamlet*, III.iv.206–7)

A "petar" or "petard" is a case filled with explosive which was generally used for blowing in doors. The appropriateness of the word to a novel full of containers and closed doors, and culminating with an explosion, is readily apparent.

The most obvious example of someone in the novel hoist by his own petard is, of course, Cleaver. It would appear that his plans for Lithia and his way of trapping raw nuclear power by means of "the 'magnetic bottle' dodge" go tragically awry (p. 164). But the grief which strikes Ruiz-Sanchez at the end of the novel indicates that he too, if much less melodramatically, has been hoist by his own petard. Perhaps Lithia was a kind of Eden and his casuistry has played a part in destroying it. Certainly a number of innocent human beings who were assisting Cleaver have been killed. At the same time, from a reader's point of view, any attempt to resolve matters unequivocally one way or the other is to be hoist by one's own petard.

But the count's choice of pseudonym surely relates to Ruiz-Sanchez's reflections on the nature of knowledge, reflections he is prompted towards by thinking of the count:

> It was either perfectly simple once you understood it, or else it fell apart into fiction. As a Jesuit—even here, fifty light-years from Rome—Ruiz-Sanchez knew something about knowledge that Lucien le Compte des Bois-d'Averoigne had forgotten, and that Cleaver would never learn: that all knowledge goes through *both* stages, the annunciation out of noise into fact, and the disintegration back into noise again. The process involved was the making of increasingly finer distinctions. The outcome was an endless series of theoretical catastrophes.
>
> The residuum was faith. (Pp. 24–25)

I would suggest that Ruiz-Sanchez is here doing the count an injustice. Count d'Averoigne chose the name H. O. Petard because he wanted to suggest that reason, knowledge itself, was hoist by its own petard. After all, even today, since the publication of Thomas Kuhn's *The Structure of Scientific Revolutions* (1962), with its presentation of the history of science as a succession or displacement of "paradigms" (or "philosophical apocalypses," in my terms[25]), the idea is somewhat commonplace.

If Ruiz-Sanchez is hoist by his own petard regarding the count, does he similarly underestimate Cleaver? In his poison-induced delirium, Cleaver dreams of a series of plans including a culminating and somewhat perplexing one "for detonating Lithia in one single mighty fusion of all its lightweight atoms into one single atom of cleaverium, the element of which the monobloc has been made, whose cardinal number was Aleph-Null . . ." (p. 35).[26] Most immediately, of course, this vision prefigures the novel's conclusion. But the name given to the monobloc substance, "cleaverium," suggests the extent to which Cleaver's knowledge of the universe is a projection of his own being. At work here is much the same kind of anthropocentric thinking, minus the material basis, which names a planet Lithia and its inhabitants Lithians because lithium ore, with its explosive potential, is a significant part of the planet's make-up. When Lithia does finally explode, it appears "to swell, like a balloon—" (p. 200). Blish, it will be recalled, spoke of "blowing [his novella] up into a novel." This last image of a container in the novel is of a container (containing nothing) which is about to rupture. The balloons of human knowledge similarly rupture and explode precisely because, whatever forms it may take, the "cleaverium" (the discriminatory cleaving) at their centers is repeatedly discovered not to exist. Not just the residuum, but all was faith.

But how likely is it, a skeptical reader might ask, that James Blish (a writer of SF after all) would have subscribed to this radical subversion of scientific knowledge? And how likely is it that James Blish (a simple writer of SF after all) would consciously intend and exploit the word "case" in the duplicitous manner I have described? Is it sufficient to respond that the equation of knowledge and faith and the somersaulting concept of "case" are concordant with, and therefore are aspects (thematic and technical) of, Blish's ambiguous intent, an intent for which we have documentary evidence? Perhaps. But the kind of ambiguity at which my analysis has arrived is of an extreme and totalizing nature. It surely goes far beyond what appears to be Blish's stated intent: his wish to leave the reader with an apparently finite number of equally plausible (?) alternative explanations.

What is at issue here is the relationship between authorial ambiguity and what is now understood as the "deconstructive" play of language, the one matter supposedly being within an author's control, the other being beyond it. The word "case" participates in a complex and totalizing "economy" of ideas and meanings, an "economy" which Blish and his readers may be assumed to have internalized unconsciously. The concept of the container and the contained touches on both strategies of metaphorical similarity and metonymical contiguity and hence on the nature of meaning and understanding generally. The fact that, in chapter 1, Blish counterpoints an internal mental problem with an external physical problem may then be interpreted with equal "validity" as evidence of authorial intent or as evidence for the manner in which an "economy" of ideas and language has its way with an author. Given the current state of critical theory, a reader may choose exclusively to privilege one source of control over the other or may choose to assume that at some indeterminate point an ambiguous state for which the author is responsible is overtaken by an encompassing ambiguity which inheres in the "abyss" of language. Even a state of total ambiguity allows, it would seem, for a statement of the case in terms of an apparently finite number of equally plausible (?) alternative explanations.

II.
HISTORICAL MODELS

FIVE

"NEW PARADIGMS" AND PROBLEMATIC ENDINGS

▎Nineteen years after Blish had published the series of four articles entitled "Science in Science Fiction" (1951–52), he published "The Science in Science Fiction." In between he had read Thomas Kuhn's *The Structure of Scientific Revolutions* and as a result Kuhn's theoretical view of science figures in Blish's formulation of the function of SF in his 1971 article:

> in my profoundly *religious* opinion, . . . it is the duty of the conscientious science fiction writer not to falsify what he believes to be known fact. It is an even more important function for him to suggest new paradigms, by suggesting to the reader, over and over again, that X, Y and Z are possible.[1]

Kuhn's notion of the way in which a scientific paradigm (a consensus theoretical set of assumptions in terms of which most scientific experimentation is conducted) will eventually disintegrate in the face of unassimilatable evidence and be replaced by a new paradigm which explains the new evidence, does provide one way of talking about the "apocalyptic" character of SF. For Blish it also provided a way of marrying the realistic convention of SF with fantasy. He goes on to say that "the most important scientific content in modern science fiction are the impossibilities."[2] Since the creation of new paradigms involves, in effect, a flight of fancy, Blish has found a means of scientifically justifying the presence of fantasy in SF.

It is not to be expected that all, or indeed any, successful works of SF will suggest or elaborate genuinely new paradigms. But, in terms of Blish's definition of an ideal SF, the *illusion* of genuinely new paradigms (arrived at, like John W. Campbell's "thought variants," by way of something like Edward de Bono's "lateral thinking," i.e., entertaining bizarre ideas and allowing for their possibility) must be preserved. At the same time, to judge from a headnote in the Faber & Faber edition of the *Anywhen* collection, published in the same year as "The Science in Science Fiction," the illusion of a new paradigm need not depend upon a direct attempt to be original. Blish observes that "the best work in this field consists largely of stories which re-examine the basic fantasy premises—of which there are only a few—and try to take them seriously."[3] The new paradigms prescription does, however, present the SF writer with a formidable formal problem, a clue to which is provided by the fact that most of what many people believe needs to be said about a work of SF amounts to no more than a rehearsal of its astonishing "ideas." If the writer presents his or her new paradigm at the beginning or in the middle of a story, the remainder is likely to seem anticlimactic. But if the new explanatory paradigm is withheld until the end, the writer has the problem of coming up with something truly extraordinary that will "bring the house down" if the reader is to feel compensated for being kept in a state of bewilderment. Either way, the presentation of a new paradigm will involve major closure problems. One possible solution, the spaced presentation of two or more different new paradigms, often results in a dilution of effect.

Blish's inventiveness and his logical way with plotting often enabled him to surmount these problems. But the two novels and two novellas considered in this chapter (which add up to a very loose "Expeditions" tetralogy) are uneven in quality and the endings of each are, in different ways, problematic or unsatisfactory. The first and last of these four works, the novel *The Frozen Year* (1957) and the novella *The Night Shapes* (1962), effectively bracket the novella *VOR* (1958) and the novel *. . . And All the Stars a Stage* (1960) because both are concerned with exploratory expeditions on Earth—in the first case in the Arctic, in the second in the African Congo. These bracketing extremes of cold and heat, ice and fire, suggest an apocalyptic dialectic which is apparent in much of Blish's *oeuvre*. The pairing of *The Frozen Year* and *The Night Shapes* is further supported by the fact that both books are essentially realistic romances and by the fact that the exploration of the Belgian Congo in search of the mythical monster *mokele-mbemba*, which journey we are told that Commodore Farnsworth of *The Frozen Year* had previously undertaken, directly anticipates the territory of *The Night Shapes*. *VOR* and *. . . All the Stars a Stage* might also be paired to the extent that they deal with very different alien expeditions to Earth, raise sexual questions, and conclude with sun/star references and surprising offsprings.

To the extent that these books are SF, or, in the case of *The Night Shapes,* at least science-fictional, one can identify in each case the collision of old and new paradigms. But in each case the illusion of a new paradigm is purely conventional. In fact, in these works Blish is drawing on some of the hoariest aspects of pulp genre writing, and while in the case of *The Frozen Year* and *VOR* he is able to achieve a certain freshness, in the case of . . . *And All the Stars a Stage* and *The Night Shapes* he is less successful. The best SF, of course, will, among other virtues, present something approaching a genuinely new paradigm, or at least convey the impression of such originality.[4] The same evaluative spectrum from the stale paradigm to the original one may be applied to the shorter fiction that Blish published during the period 1953 to 1974, as will be discussed here.

(i) Short Stories and Novellas (1953–59)

This review is confined to only the more important short stories and magazine novellas (not treated elsewhere) that Blish published between 1953 and 1959 when the first edition of *Galactic Cluster* appeared.[5] In 1952 Robert A. Lowndes invited Blish to write a story around a cover illustration that had been painted by Milton Luros; the result was "Testament of Andros" (*Future Science Fiction,* January 1953). The "surrealistic cover painting . . . featured a swollen sun, black sky, and a tiny figure of a man."[6] Blish explains his response in a letter to the Australian writer, critic, and editor John Baxter: "On the surface, it is the story of the *same* disaster [the sun going nova] as seen by five different people, all of whom are insane to some degree because of the imminence of the disaster, or the fact it has already happened" (Dep. Blish 411/10, 31 October 1962). These people are: (1) an eighty-four-year-old astronomer, Dr. Theodor Andresson, who in 1956, with his "almost Spenglerian awareness of the pressure of fate" (p. 62), has calculated that, beginning in six months time, our sun will produce a series of major flares which will destroy life on Earth; (2) Andrew, who hears voices out of the Book of Revelations; (3) George Anders, who recalls the catastrophe; (4) Andy Virchow, better known as "Admiral Universe," who mentions the sun going nova in the context of an infantile power fantasy; and (5) a Greek coalminer, T. V. Andros, who is incarcerated, having assaulted a girl on "a hot day with a big sun . . . just like the day my mother left ["me to go home and die"]."[7]

What the first four sections actually consist of are a series of delusions within the mind of this last character, who "read those magazines that tell about going to other planets and stuff like that" (p. 81); the stories of "R. S. Richardson" (Philip Latham) are earlier specified (pp. 63, 66). A clue is provided by the fact that "Mario di Ferruci," a graduate student, is obviously "Dr. Andresson's" envied youthful self. According to Blish's headnote, "the story observes successive stages in the disintegration of a paranoid schizophrenic" (p. 60). Blish instructs Baxter that "To see the story as having only one central character, only one point of view, you must read the sections in the order 5-1-2-3-4." The actual order was "partially a trick to make the story into sf" (Dep. Blish 411/10). Lowndes points out that the story is also "a series of parodies; each section takes off on a different kind of science fiction, science-fiction fan, or comic-strip science-fiction writing."[8] Thus, Blish informs Baxter that "Andy Virchow" is "Sam Moskowitz in disguise" (Dep. Blish 411/10).

The story is clearly not SF in an orthodox sense: "At the bottom the only 'science' represented is clinical psychology" (headnote, p. 60). Stableford complains, with some justice, that Blish's mechanical use of psychology has dated badly and is hardly scientific by today's standards. Breakdowns simply do not happen in the ordered fashion depicted.[9] In this regard, Blish's discussion of "The Psychological Story" in his "Science in Science Fiction" series, with its claim that as yet there is no science of psychology, is of interest. It should be noted that the four kinds of story that Blish deals with—the biological, the mathematical, the astronomical, and the psychological—provide a way of organizing his own SF in both thematic and developmental terms. In chapters 3 and 4 I have concentrated on Blish's biological stories; in chapter 8 I concentrate on his mathematical stories. *Cities in Flight,* treated in chapter 6, amounts to the culmination of Blish's experiments with the astronomical story. And *Black Easter* and *The Day After Judgment,* treated in my concluding chapter, amount to the fruition of Blish's experiments with the psychological story. "Testament of Andros," the first story treated in this chapter, and *The Frozen Year,* the first novel treated in this chapter, continue an interest originating with "Phoenix Planet" (see note 8 to chapter 2, p. 328) in the kind of story with which his career concludes. They also implicitly anticipate the resolution to the fantasy/SF dichotomy that Blish eventually arrives at.

Like *The Frozen Year,* the most autobiographical of Blish's published works, "Testament of Andros" is one of Blish's rare first-person stories. But whereas the issue of fantasy versus reality is delicately poised in *The Frozen Year,* in the case of "Testament of Andros" the weight of the evidence supports the view that the story is indeed simply the account of one man's delusional fantasies. But this would be to omit the impact of the story's sixth and final section:

My name is Man. I will write my stories if you wish.
I was . . .
Here the ashes blow away. The voices die. (P. 83)

The story begins with a related epigraph: *"Beside the fire ["hearth"* originally] *lie the ashes. There are voices in them. Listen. . . ."* (p. 60, emphasis in original). "Andros," of course, is Greek for "man." The initials T. V. suggest that the subject is an *image* of man. If the sick delusional state of the coalminer is taken as representative of man's state generally, then "Testament of Andros" may be recuperated as a particularly sophisticated species of SF—a surrealistic, Kafkaesque species that Blish should be credited with originating. It was not inappropriate of Arrow Books to reprint the 1973 *Best Science Fiction Stories of James Blish* under the title *The Testament of Andros.*

As in the case of "Testament of Andros," Blish reprinted "First Strike" (June 1953) in his near-future collection, *So Close to Home* (1961). "First Strike" is a wry, contrived, mediocre story, of interest only because of its positive attitude towards technology and the contrast this provides with the last story that Blish published in his lifetime. It is basically about the absurd prejudice against technology encouraged by writers like Ray Bradbury, who is referred to as the Old Master, now dead, who wrote about Mars. In a post-nuclear-holocaust world on the eve of achieving spaceflight, Wally Swain, his wife Carol, and two friends discuss the evils of science. The next day Carol is supposed to ignite a powder train leading to the rocket and thereby give the public the illusion it is watching the equivalent of a July 4th skyrocket. The effect is doubly ruined: first Carol forgets to strike her match a second time (waterproof matches are required in this wet, post-bomb world; the first strike only removes the protective tip); then Wally, who is piloting the rocket, pushes the launch button, injuring members of the crowd, and sets the controls for a spectacular crash offshore of Lisbon while he bails out over Mexico. He then sends for Carol, who first heads for Canada by mistake (Blish's opposition to the prejudice against technology does not go along with an opposition to male chauvinism); she has the idea that Wally will become a logger, and they will rough it together. The back-to-nature movement in this story should be noted as anticipative of the 1960s.

Billed as an uncomfortable tale of evil and justice by "the Pennsylvania polymath," "The Book of Your Life" (March 1955) is one of Blish's rare fantasy pieces.[10] While browsing in an east-side New York bookstore in search of pornography, for which he has a passion, the secretary-treasurer of the National Association of Mystery Publishers, Petrie Mapes is invited by the bookseller to rent at a dollar a week a volume entitled *The Book of Your Life*. It is explained that the book always opens at a passage of special interest to any given customer. For Mapes, who is particularly interested by sadism, it opens at a "transcendentally erotic passage on p. 1009" (p. 89). Mapes takes the book and discovers, after experimenting with a couple of people, that after gratifying a particular reader's deepest desires, the book, in some fashion or other, destroys that person. Although he locates a passage that would destroy his wife, Janet, and her lover, Mapes decides to hold back the weapon.

At this point the reader might wonder why Mapes himself had not been destroyed by "p. 1009." It would appear that his pornographic obsessions are symptomatic of a more general disposition, and here it seems not unreasonable to conclude that this very curious, macabre tale must have some autobiographical basis. Mapes refers to his habit of seeing people as literary characters and to "the stone walls which had closed in on my life"; he is "a sick and despicable human being—competent, ruthless, fearful, cruel, sex-ridden, self-centered, and essentially dead except in the life he borrowed from books" (pp. 91, 92). *The Book* ends with a "CHALLENGE TO THE READER" to contrive the ending: "*Think carefully before you turn the page. If you do not,* The Book *will devour you utterly*" (p. 94, emphasis in original). The ambiguous referent of *"If you do not"* (think carefully or turn the page) indicates that Mapes is equally damned if, after failing to think carefully, he decides not to turn the page. The story ends with *The Book* magically returned to the bookseller, who notes how well it is selling. It seems nobody was more surprised than the Author to discover that his book has a voracious life of its own. The bookseller "knew well enough the new character in it. He could even estimate how many pages longer *The Book* would have to be to encompass Petrie Mapes as an essential part of the plot" (p. 94).

In a letter to Paul Shackley Blish recalls a "television series" that he and Alfred Bester worked on—"though only for one show"—called "'C.I.D.: Universe.' It did not turn out to be very good and lasted only one season. I did five scripts for them, four of which they bounced; subsequently I turned three of them into short stories, one of which

Campbell printed and the other two appeared in *Infinity*. The remaining one is the one I used in fragmentary form in *Quincunx*" (PS, 17 January 1975). The three *C.I.D.: Universe* short stories are "One-Shot" (August 1955), "King of the Hill" (November 1955), and "Sponge Dive" (June 1956).

In "One-Shot," reprinted in *So Close to Home,* a Polish freighter accidentally dumps what may be a bomb off New York. Because the time is too short for the CIA's ULTIMAC integrator (the brand name previously appeared in "A Case of Conscience" [1953]) to figure the odds, a millionaire gambler, "Long-Shot" Braun, is called in. He says correctly that it is a bomb but, this time at least, it turns out to be a defused one; the scare is actually an opportunistic CIA test engineered after the agency discovered the freighter was supposed to have dropped a live bomb.

In the much tenser and more skillful "King of the Hill," Col. Hal Gascoigne, alone aboard Satellite Vehicle I and subject to hallucinations resulting from his guilt over killing the Sweeney family when his plane crashed into their home, thinks he has been ordered to bomb Washington, where his own family lives.[11] Like "One-Shot," another of Blish's rare first-person stories, "King of the Hill" is told by Peter Harris of the Central Intelligence Group (CIG), as the CIA is now rechristened. Following the instructions of the ULTIMAC *computer* (as it is now called) in response to Gascoigne's request for bombing coordinates, Harris travels to the satellite and convinces Gascoigne that he is not a hallucination, that the three bombs aboard the satellite are duds, and that Gascoigne should not give the bluff away by "bombing" Washington. In a perhaps predictable twist back on Earth, Harris recognizes the possibility that the satellite "bombs" really are just a bluff. In view of Blish's fondness for this kind of psychological juggling of illusion and reality, it should be noted that the reference to Gascoigne breaking his glasses playing King of the Hill when he was ten has an autobiographical basis (see pp. 2–3 herein).

The last *C.I.D. Universe* short story, "Sponge Dive," although a very minor and simplistic piece of work, was reprinted in *So Close to Home*. This time a CIG man foils the plans of a white Afrikaner named Roger Balim, who has been selling sponge zirconium to a black anti-Apartheid group; ULTIMAC had previously figured that the zirconium was being used to make atom bombs. Balim had planned on letting the blacks bomb Johannesburg before betraying their identity and location and absconding with the money.

Blish's tale of war and treachery, "To Pay the Piper," was published in February 1956 and reprinted in all editions of *Galactic Cluster*. In this story people have been virtually imprisoned a mile underground for twenty-five years after a period of biological warfare and "the rats . . . alone are immune to everything."[12] Blish calls attention to parallels with the Pied Piper legend by naming a character Hamelin; Hamelin believes that civilians should be re-educated for the surface before soldiers. Diseases are still rampant on the surface and re-education means the "chemical control of immunity" (p. 66). The war is not over; whichever side beats the other to the surface will be able to win. For their own reasons, the authorities agree to let Hamelin undergo the re-education process. Resulting information about Hamelin's biological make-up indicates that he is an enemy agent whose poisoned blood will sabotage the re-education machine. The plan fails but so does Blish's story. By blinding the reader with science as a means of explaining the twists of the plot and underlining a flimsy analogy with the German legend, Blish leaves the reader feeling double-crossed.

"The Writing of the Rat," one of the commissioned stories collected in *Anywhen* (1970), first appeared in *Galaxy* (June 1956). Its title is taken from the following Carl Sandburg lines, which figure in the narrative: "and even the writing of the rat footprints/tells us nothing, nothing at all."[13] The relatively routine but startling story has to do with man's discovery, on achieving interstellar flight, that virtually all of the habitable galaxy is in the control of giant, gray-furred, intelligent, rat-like beings. An emissary named Hrestce eventually informs an interpreter that the "rats" are only acting as cultural custodians where the inhabitants of a planet have been abducted by "a race in this galaxy *which is practicing slavery on an incredible scale*." For this purpose they have evolved a "synthetic language, which is adaptable to any culture and carries the implicit assumptions of none," a language which is quoted in the story (p. 60). In the *Anywhen* headnote Blish challenges the reader with the claim that the synthetic language "came 100 per cent off a theatre marquee in Brooklyn"; it is, he says, "English with some letters missing" (p. 49).[14] Earth, Hrestce explains, is *"an outpost of the slavers we are seeking"* (p. 61). For the most part, it seems, we are the descendants of slaves brought here from other planets who were originally molded in the slavers' image. However, apart from the slavers, and over time, we have become more humanitarian—with the exception of a Hitler or a Stalin or the Home officer, based in "Novoe Washingtongrad," who has one of the gray creatures, identified as the Enemy, tortured to death at the beginning of the story. The story ends with the expectation that the Field officers will share the huge caretaking responsibilities and assume the role of rat terriers dedicated to the destruction of the real rats—the slavers.

"Tomb Tapper" (July 1956) is one of Blish's most powerful and deeply felt works. As a member of the voluntary Civil Air Patrol some time in the near future, McDonough's job is to pick the brains of enemy corpses by means of a new EEG technique. After locating what is presumed to be a downed Russian bomber that crash-landed inside a railway tunnel bored into a mountain, McDonough activates his equipment inside the fuselage and sees a scene in his "toposcope goggles" which corresponds to a line he simultaneously "hears" from "A Child's Christmas in Wales," by Dylan Thomas: *"And still the dazzling sky-blue sheep are grazing in the red field under the rainbow-billed and pea-green birds. . . ."*[15] Because the sheep have kittenlike heads and the birds look like nothing on Earth, McDonough figures he must be picking up images from the dead or dying mind of an extraterrestrial. But eventually McDonough realizes that the bizarre image comes from a coloring book:

> Of course the sheeplike animals did not look much like sheep, which the pilot could never have seen except in pictures. Of course the sheep's heads looked like the heads of kittens; everyone has seen kittens. Of course the brain was powerful out of all proportion to its survival drive and its knowledge of death; it was the brain of a genius, but a genius without experience. And of course, *this* way, the USSR could get a rocket fighter to the United States on a one-way trip. (P. 147)

The dead pilot of this guided missile, whose fading memory of a picture McDonough sees, is then discovered to be an eight-year-old girl.

Blish's own experience as a Civil Air pilot enables him to describe the air search for the wrecked missile with considerable authority. But what makes the story particularly effective and particularly horrifying is the care with which it is constructed. References to the EEG technique as a "cookbook" (pp. 136, 146), to "a woman choosing an ingredient from a cookbook" (p. 131), to the toposcope vision of a sky "as white as paper" and the assertion that "no mind in the books ever put out a broadcast like this" (p. 140) all prepare for the final girl and her coloring book revelation. At the beginning of the story McDonough wonders why he taps tombs: "what am I listening for?" (p. 126). What he is listening for, Blish insinuates, is an Edvard Munch-like silent scream of nightmare horror. At first the sound is all too palpable:

> The rest of the adjutant's reply was lost in a growing, echoing roar, as though they were all standing underneath a vast trestle over which all the railroad trains in the world were crossing at once. The sixty-four-foot organ reeds of jets were being blown in the night zenith above the field—another hunting pack come from Stewart Field to avenge the hydrogen agony that had been Kingston. (P. 128)

Blish clearly intends that a reader recall this deafening sound when he comes across the reference to "the organ pipe of the [railway] tunnel" (p. 144) containing the missile, and also when the reality that McDonough has tapped, or rather "tuned," into is finally disclosed.

The uneven novella "Get Out of My Sky" first appeared in the January and February 1957 issues of *Astounding Science Fiction,* and later led off a 1960 Crest paperback of the same title. It is notable for similar aspects that would reappear in Ursula K. Le Guin's *The Dispossessed* (1970) and for its metaphoric subtext, a characteristic which much of Blish's work shares with virtually all of Le Guin's. The twin worlds of Home, which is largely covered with water, and Rathe, which is largely covered by desert, parallel Le Guin's twin worlds of Urras, rich and fertile, and Anarres, arid and impoverished. Home, like Urras, is somewhat corrupt and Rathe, like Anarres, is something of a utopia. A leader of the telepathic Rathemen eventually reveals that, as a result of being forced by the planet's lack of resources to concentrate on the humanities rather than the physical sciences, "we eliminated our primitive notions, evolved a common language, reduced our government to next to nothing, eliminated crime, and in general cleared away enough clutter to make it possible for us to attend to serious matters."[16] In both works a representative of one world visits the other and acquires knowledge which amounts to a well-nigh mystical advance in the field of communications. In Le Guin's novel, however, the lone representative is from the "poorer" world while in Blish's novella the accompanied representative is from the "richer" one.

In Blish's story the mission to Rathe is undertaken by First Minister Aidregh in a desperate attempt to forestall the outbreak of a war between the two worlds that would destroy them both. Aidregh is accompanied by his son Aidresne, Aidresne's fiancée Corlant, and Corlant's father, Dr. Ni.[17] The journey is in response to the insistence of one of Rathe's twelve Margents, or leaders, that he meet with Aidregh personally. On Rathe the Margent explains that only if a member of Aidregh's party learns how to manipulate the *voisk* forces and thereby sway an audience can war be averted. (The "psi" content here was apparently dictated by the preoccupation of *Astounding*'s editor, John W. Campbell, with such matters.) Rather than the preferred candidates, the two lovers, Aidregh himself successfully undergoes the learning experience and back on Home he is able to persuade his fellows that peaceful coexistence is the better alternative.[18]

The tale's detailed and consistent metaphoric subtext clearly allies the *voisk* forces with a mystical realm which is at once beyond, and equivalent to, death. At the beginning of the piece much is made of the fact that Home benefits from three sources of stellar illumination which create three different shadows. The shadows of a human being, called the Soul, the Mind, and the Breath, are cast respectively by the red sun, a large star cluster, and the white sun. Threes crop up elsewhere in the story. Before Aidregh learns to control the *voisk* forces war is potentially three days away. Three races of beings have apparently reached the neighboring planet Nesmet: men from Home, Rathemen, and some as yet unidentified and possibly threatening species. Immediately after bringing this news to Home, Captain Arpen dies. A union of the three shadows, or the three races, depends upon an ideal love that corresponds to death. Blish claims not to recall "what prompted me to choose" the name Rathe: "I may well have gotten the word from Lewis Carroll" (PS, "Notes on Shackley letter of July 17, 1970"). And so he did; there are two references to "mome raths," hence "Home" and "Rathe," in Carroll's nonsense poem, "Jabberwocky." But it seems likely that Blish picked the name not only to suggest "wrath" and war (like the red sun) but also to suggest "wraith" as the shadow of death. Thus also the references to the "ghost of [Aidregh's] wife" and the "spectral after-impression" (pp. 47, 48) of Corlant's kiss when Aidregh agrees to let her join the mission. The united realm of love and death is prefigured by the macrocosm/microcosm image that appears in the italicized prologue to the story. In the context of a powerful speech by an unidentified man (who will be identified as Aidregh when the italicized prologue is repeated more or less verbatim as an italicized epilogue), *"a silence in the centre of the audience . . . audible out here at the roaring periphery (like . . . the hole in a doughnut)"* is paralleled by the reference to the man's face which *"was blank, except for a small black 0 where his mouth should have been"* (p. 8).

Finally, we come to "This Earth of Hours" (June 1959), a wry, lightly allegorical elegy which concludes the American edition of *Galactic Cluster,* an edition that was sold illegally in India (PdS 120). In this story the Russian-dominated galactic power known as the Matriarchy comes up against a rival federation at the center of the galaxy when the *Novoe*

Washingtongrad lands on the planet Callë. Its inhabitants, telepathic wormlike creatures without brains, function as a "hive ego."[19] A "group mind" would be the wrong term here since what is shaping up is a galactic conflict between emotion and reason, between the denizens of the "heart-stars" (p. 161) and the brained human beings who have colonized the outer worlds of the galaxy. The Callëans believe that the brain is a tumor and the cause of all other tumors: "that's why we get cancer." The Callëans further believe that "Races that develop [brains] kill themselves off. Something to do with solar radiation; animals on planets of Population II stars develop them, Population I planets don't." It seems that Population II types are doomed; the Matriarchy, itself a result of applying reason to reproduction and allowing parents to predetermine the sex of their children, will lose to the Central Empire. The tale ends with a Population II representative humming "part of a chorale from a twentieth-century American opera, and the words went: *Weep, weep beyond time for this Earth of hours*" (p. 175; emphasis in original). In the last line the opera is identified as *Psyche and Eros,* the mind-soul and sexual love (p. 176).

(ii) *The Frozen Year* (1957): A Piece of Spoiled Goods?

In 1957 Blish published the same novel under two titles: the Ballantine Books title in the U.S.A. was *The Frozen Year* and in the U.K. the Faber & Faber title was *Fallen Star*.[20] The American title better reflects what seems to have been Blish's initial intention not to write an SF novel. He did, however, write something closer to science fiction than to a mainstream contemporary novel, and the U.K. title, which most obviously reflects the substance of the work, seems now to have displaced the American one: the recent Avon paperbook in the U.S. and the recent Arrow Books paperback in the U.K. are both entitled *Fallen Star*. The different titles do reflect a real ambiguity in the work. There is no way of knowing for sure whether the character who identifies himself as a Martian is telling the truth or is a deluded madman when he explains that the asteroid belt between Mars and Jupiter consists of the debris of two worlds that Mars destroyed. This situation bears some relation to what Blish does in "Testament of Andros" (1953) except that there a character clearly undergoing a mental breakdown experiences a series of science-fictional hallucinations.

But Blish's intentions regarding *The Frozen Year* seem ambiguous. Writing as William Atheling, Jr., in *The Issue at Hand,* he objects to the way in which Fritz Leiber's "The Secret Songs" (*The Magazine of Fantasy & Science Fiction,* August 1962) presents a science-fictional "reality" as a psychological delusion and goes on to explain how *The Frozen Year* turned into something similar:

> I cannot speak for Fritz, but I know that in my own case the essential reason for creating so unnecessary a mixture was timidity. I had a mainstream novel going—a *Bildungsroman* with a background of contemporary science . . . and I should have stuck to it. Making my madman's delusions science-fictional was a last minute retreat into the genre with which I was most familiar, and in which I could be moderately sure of a sale. Well, I sold it; and there it sits, a piece of spoiled goods.[21]

This adverse judgment has, I believe, less to do with the defects of *The Frozen Year* than with Blish's desire to prove to himself that he could write a mainstream novel. Letters in a slim Bodleian file provide both confirmation and qualification. "I wanted to write a novel which wasn't science fiction," Blish confesses (7 December 1956). Another alternative title for this novel, which figures in an editor's letter, was "The Big Sendoff." But in the undated carbon copy of a letter to John Campbell, Blish describes the novel he is working on as being about an encounter with frozen Martians at the North Pole. He goes on to say he is not sure "which of several snappers I'm going to use to wind this up" (Dep. Blish 392).

Unlike many of Blish's novels, *The Frozen Year* began as a novel. It was not completed piecemeal nor did it grow out of a short story, which suggests some consistency of purpose, whether or not Blish was totally aware of what he was doing. And certainly the finished novel successfully disguises any sudden change of direction; the SF element is present pretty much from the beginning. What Blish in fact published is a work which, from start to finish, deliberately and successfully counterpoints mainstream and SF elements. *The Frozen Year* demonstrates that such a mix has very positive possibilities, the kind of possibilities that various New Wave science-fiction writers in the 1960s and 1970s would further exploit. Examples include Anna Kavan's *Ice* (1967), Barry Maltzberg's *Beyond Apollo* (1972), Doris Lessing's *Memoirs of a Survivor* (1974), Marge Piercy's *Woman on the Edge of Time* (1976), and much of the work of J. G. Ballard. The importance of this mixed psychological mode in Blish's *oeuvre,* it should be reaffirmed, is attested to by the fact that *The Frozen Year* represents the midpoint in a development that begins (before "Testament of Andros") with "Phoenix Planet" (1941) and first culminates with the abortive "Telecast"

(1948; see pp. 140–45 below), and then reculminates with *Black Easter* (1967) and *The Day After Judgment*(1970).

The Frozen Year opens with Julian Cole's introductory statement, delivered in a conversational tone that gradually disappears as the novel progresses. Cole is a science writer who lives in Pelham, New York with his wife, Midge, and four daughters and who is now willing to risk all by publishing the story of one *"utterly unprintable discovery."*[22] In book 1 a physicist friend named Hans Bloch sets up a meeting between Julian and publicist Ellen Fremd, who is on the publications committee for the International Geophysical Year (IGY). Ellen commissions two books from Julian: a layman's book on what is accomplished by the IGY, and an account of an expedition to the North Pole which will include the monitoring of a satellite launch led by Commodore Bramwell-Farnsworth.[23] To write the second book Julian is required to become part of the fourteen-member Second Western Polar Basin Expedition for what is expected to be a four-month period.

Julian finds out that one of Farnsworth's sponsors is Jno. Pfistner & Sons, Inc., "the world's largest producers of biological drugs"; it crops up in *They Shall Have Stars* (1957) as Jno. Pfitzner & Sons, and is clearly recognizable as Chas. Pfizer & Co., the firm that Blish worked for from 1955 to 1959. The drug firm is seeking publicity and soil samples. In the company of Harriet Peters, who handles the Pfistner account for a public relations agency, Julian visits Farnsworth. The Commodore is a Canadian-born, naturalized American with a head like "the familiar bust of Spengler" and a stereotypical well-built, young, blonde wife, Jayne Wynne (p. 38). Farnsworth explains that his real reason for going to the Pole is to look for meteoric evidence of "Planet Number Four-and-a-half," which he believes now exists mainly in the splintered form of the asteroid belt (p. 39). From now on interest will gravitate towards the conflict between respectable and crackpot science and the likely loss of IGY sponsorship.

One major hitch occurs before the expedition leaves. The large plane that Farnsworth had planned on using, the Hawkes Flying Tail, is mysteriously acquired by the Venezuelan Air Force. So it is in two smaller replacement planes that the expedition, which now includes Harriet as an additional publicist, flies to Ellesmere in the Arctic Circle.

Near the beginning of book 2 a major accident occurs. One of Farnsworth's three well-appointed snowbuggies, carrying five members of the team, is lost when it slips off an ice-floe. The mysterious nature of Dr. Elvers, the albino chiropodist and dog handler, is first underlined at this point when the fatal accident has him "giggling" (p. 90). Rather than risk the other buggies and more personnel, the party decides to proceed by sled. It is agreed that Harry Chain, the radioman, and Harriet will stay behind and establish a home base. In quick succession, the Pole is reached in six days, the artificial satellite is launched, and Farnsworth finds the first bits of evidence for his wild hypothesis—two tektites, one of which, composed of sedimentary rock, he has preserved in ice. Farnsworth is exultant: "cosmic history in an ice-cube!" (p. 114). But Julian is leery about reporting the discovery, especially since there is doubt concerning the satellite report by the expedition's alcoholic astronomer and director of photography, Dr. Wentz. It seems that Wentz's career went downhill and he started drinking after he reported sighting a star that no one else had been able to verify. Now that his credibility has been questioned again, Wentz gets drunk on ethyl alcohol and catches pneumonia. Jayne, the blonde bombshell, is also worried about adverse publicity and, while she and Julian make love, Wentz suffers a seizure and dies minutes later.

Wentz is buried at the beginning of book 3, to the accompaniment of a skeptical oration by Farnsworth: "If you exist, God of the monobloc [a word that Blish's editor queries (Dep. Blish 392)] . . . think of Joe Wentz." Elvers, who will shortly identify himself as a Martian and who is described as "The dog man" (i.e., something not human), responds, "There is no God" (p. 137). Shortly thereafter Farnsworth finds the Lump, the kind of substantial evidence that he is looking for. It is a fifty-pound, 10,000-year-old meteorite "of sea-formed rock" which, on a second splitting, reveals ripple marks and fossils (p. 143).

At this point Jayne arrives with the news that Wentz has been vindicated and that the expedition has been reinstated by the IGY (they had been disowned shortly after the loss of the snowbuggy mainly because of what the press had reported concerning the Commodore's bizarre theory). The satellite seems to have changed course while Wentz was watching it, and then, in Jayne's words, it "vanished, just as though somebody's stolen it right out of the sky" (p. 148). Elvers, who has burbled about bloodshed and guilt, now appears with his rifle and demands that the four pieces of the Lump be rolled back into the ice hole out of which it has been hoisted. To show he means business, he shoots Fred Klein, the geologist. Jayne rolls two pieces of the Lump (including the one with the fossil evidence) into the hole but the third piece will not go through because the frozen "spray from the first two closed up the hole" (p. 154).

Elvers directs Farnsworth, Jayne, and Julian into the dog igloo, where he announces that he is a Martian and describes the war between Mars and the planets Nferetet and Infteret which existed about 15,000 years ago where the asteroid belt is now (pp. 157–58). Fearing an attack from the Nferetetans, who had colonized Infteret, the Martians caused the two planets to collide. The Martians do not wish anyone to learn of their crime and so, to discourage space flight from Earth, "We stole your satellite as a beginning" (p. 159). Elvers plans to kill everyone except Julian, who will return with the news that the expedition found nothing. Julian takes advantage of an opportunity to jump Elvers and is aided by Farnsworth and Jayne. In the struggle both Farnsworth and Elvers die. Elvers is eaten by his dogs. Julian figures that Elvers must have been mad and he and Jayne waste no time destroying the remainder of the Lump and all other "evidence." Following their call for help, a rescue plane arrives.

In book 4 Julian recovers in the hospital from eye damage and powder burns to his face which occurred when Elvers's gun went off during the struggle. He discovers that Harry and Harriet have become lovers and suspects that the inquiry to follow will ruin all their careers. Finally, back home in New York, Julian tells Hans Bloch that he plans to stop being a science writer and become a scientist; he will study astrophysics. Julian has come to believe Elvers's account but he does not think that the Martians "will bring us to the end of our tether; if we all die, next year or in a million years . . . it will be by our own hands" (p. 191). The destructive evil, which the Martians represent, is within.

The ambiguity with which we seem to be left—was Elvers mad or a Martian?—is not, however, quite the whole story. In the final chapter Blish creates a minor mystery designed to make the reader review what he or she had read. For information about when two protoplanets of Elvers's description might naturally have collided, Julian claims that he checked with "the only expert there is on the subject; if you know the subject, you'll know just where to find his name in the preceding pages" (p. 189). The expert must be Robert Willey, the real life science-fiction pseudonym, which crops up on two occasions (pp. 25, 51–53), of the German-born scientist and writer on the scientific possibilities of space flight, Willy Ley. This is Blish's way of telling the reader that to some extent *The Frozen Year* is constructed like a puzzle, which when pieced together indicates that it may be the narrator, Julian Cole, and not Elvers, who is gripped by a science-fictional delusion. From this point of view, Elvers the Martian is part of Julian's delusion.

Julian may have constructed his delusion out of data that is mentioned incidentally in his narrative. Two references to the "anti-chronon" (pp. 11, 107), "a fundamental atomic particle," hint at the possibilities of time flowing backwards and bear some relation to what the characters learn of planetary events that occurred long ago. The relevance of the picture above Ellen Fremd's desk is obvious: "It looked like a star caught in the act of blowing up—as, in miniature, it was: the photo was an enlargement from a cosmic-ray emulsion-trace, showing a heavy primary nucleus hitting a carbon atom in the emulsion and knocking it to bits, producing a star of fragment-traces and a shower of more than two hundred mesons" (p. 16). In a letter to Robert Lowndes Blish points out that four SF names occur in *The Frozen Year* (Dep. Blish 425/6). They are Hans Bloch (after Robert Bloch, the author of *Psycho*), Robert Willey, and two people lost in the snow-buggy accident: "Ben Taurasi, our engineer mechanic," after James V. Taurasi, a director of the Queens Science Fiction League, and "Dr. Eleanor Wollheim, the expedition's bacteriologist," probably after Donald Wollheim's sister (pp. 54, 61).[24] The oddly named protoplanet Nferetet seems to have something to do with Julian's momentary perception of Ellen: "she looked for just an instant as millennially in repose as that heart-stopping head of Queen Nefertete" (p. 21).[25]

Is Julian, then, a schizophrenic? After an argument with his wife, Midge, he does talk about "an inexplicable sense of guilt and impending disaster, like the first intimations of schizophrenia . . ." (p. 48; cp. Elvers's account of the Martian sense of guilt). When Julian is reunited with Midge at the end of the novel, she finds that he has become a different man. Like Elvers, he is "an imposter" (p. 183). A sense of double identity or mirror images comes out in the half-rhyming of the two relationships that develop in the novel, that of Julian and Jayne and that of Harry and Harriet. And the title, *The Frozen Year,* assumes a psychological meaning by the reference to the Martians having gone "frozen in the brains" (p. 162).

Not everything in the narrative, of course, need be Julian's invention. There really was an International Geophysical Year and maybe a satellite did disappear. One of the narrative loose ends—the mysterious acquisition of the Hawkes Flying Tail by the Venezuelan Air Force—may be relevant here. It is "a bizarre aircraft . . . but incredibly capacious, and with enormously high lift . . ." (p. 43). Did this plane somehow hijack the satellite and, if so, was it piloted by Martians or Venezuelan lackeys of the Russians?

Clear textual evidence certainly suggests that Julian is divided between his professional commitment to science reporting, which he describes as a commitment to "second-hand stuff" (p. 186), and his desire to become involved with something real, first-hand research into astrophysics, for example.[26] Julian's conflict is analogous to a conflict that Blish was experiencing, a conflict that is apparent in Atheling's *Issue at Hand* account of *The Frozen Year* quoted earlier. Blish was torn between his professional commitment to science fiction and the desire to write a mainstream novel—the desire for a kind of reality. It should be noted that Julian is thirty-six years old, exactly Blish's age when *The Frozen Year* was published. Julian's brief recollection of living in his grandparents' house with his mother, "who was divorced and was doing very badly at supporting us by teaching singing" (p. 91), and her distraught reaction when he presents her with his broken glasses, is surely derived from Blish's own biography.

The glasses may have been irretrievably spoiled but Blish's proferring of his novel as "spoiled goods" is a much more ambiguous case. The novel constitutes "spoiled goods" only in the sense that Henry James's *The Turn of the Screw* might be similarly described. Just as the interest of James's novella depends upon the possibility of alternative psychological and supernatural explanations, so the interest of Blish's subtle and gripping novel depends upon the possibility of alternative psychological and science-fictional explanations. The unusually successful focus on character in *The Frozen Year* provides the evidence required to identify Julian as an unreliable narrator, equally unreliable as James's governess and William Atheling, Jr., the evaluator of Blish's novel.

(iii) From "RVOG" (1949) to VOR (1958): A Coded Message

In an essay on Blish, Damon Knight describes the peculiar history of a story which he could not finish and how it lead to a novel on which he could not collaborate. After half completing a story entitled "Mercy Death," originally planned as a novel in three "books," Knight had asked Blish if he could find an ending (Dep. Blish 423/4). The collaborative result appeared in *Thrilling Wonder Stories* (February 1949) under a new title, "The Weakness of RVOG," supplied by the editor, Sam Merwin, who also rearranged the original name RGOV. Some years later Blish saw new possibilities in the piece as justifying its expansion into a short novel. The expansion essentially involved grafting on the story of Marty Petrucelli, who is experiencing marital problems. Blish now turned the tables and asked Knight to collaborate with him on the novel version, *VOR* (or *V O R,* as Blish refers to it in his correspondence), but Knight declined, having found that he was unable to "work with the new characters" that Blish had introduced. The novel, which Blish described to Charles Monteith (to whom he was in the habit of derogating his less-than-best works) as "really only a monster story, a pot-boiler written with one greedy eye on Hollywood" (CM 51, 2 December 1957), has not met with approval. Knight's own reaction is typical; he complains that the major new plot element is irrelevant to the main action (which corresponds more or less to the original story), that there is too much unnecessary information, and that the overall effect of Blish's expansion is to slow things down to a crawl.[27]

Any re-evaluation of *VOR* will depend upon finding an answer to one question: what led Blish from the story of an alien enigma named RVOG to a story about marital problems, specifically sexual problems? I shall argue that in the novel Petrucelli's story *is* organically related to that of the alien now renamed VOR (the elimination of the "G" from the name allows for the suggestion of something "voracious"), with the result that VOR's story appears in a very different and rather more intriguing light than does RVOG's. It is thus appropriate that Blish signals this "paradigm shift" by changing the name of the alien (aside from the fact that RVOG sounds too much like "frog"). Indeed, Blish's reconception of "The Weakness of RVOG" is sufficiently radical that *VOR* deserves to be treated on its own terms as an independent novel rather than as the expansion of a short story. We are dealing with two very different works.

The short story has to do with an incredibly powerful and apparently indestructible alien who arrives on Earth and asks to be destroyed. This message is received by a couple of scientists, the American, Davis, and the Russian, Boris Erdsenov, when they succeed in cracking the color communication system emitted from a flashing circular organ below the alien's eyes.[28] The repeated sequence of red, green, orange, and violet, which editor Merwin forgot to rearrange, is taken as indicating that the alien's name is RVOG. Not only is there no explanation as to why RVOG wants to be destroyed and no apparent means of destroying him (it is immediately assumed that the alien is masculine) but there is, alternatively, clear evidence that RVOG has the power to destroy the Earth. Frustrated that no one has even tried to kill him, RVOG walks out of the Chicago spaceport where he landed and takes off in his ship with the result that much damage is done and Port Commissioner Holm is killed. A number of Patrol planes pursue RVOG including Captain Bergsen, accompanied by Davis, in the *Loci*. There is talk of a battleship named the *Ginnangu* (which, it is pointed out, means the ends of the world in Scandinavian mythology) and of using a weapon called the "Solar Phoenix."[29]

Erdsenov, whose alarmist views have previously been rejected by Davis, provides the solution to the conundrum that Knight originated. Via a "photophone" of his own design, he attempts to persuade RVOG to commit suicide and thereby prove that he is not susceptible to human weakness, specifically the fear of death. Obligingly RVOG falls for this semantic trickery: it is assumed that he will fly his ship directly into the sun, thus creating his own "solar phoenix." It is Erdsenov's hypothesis (and, it should be emphasized, it is only a hypothesis) that RVOG was a robot scout designed to test our military strength. Had we not destroyed him the alien culture that created him "would know we were too weak to resist invasion" (p. 88). As it is we are now safe. The last of the story's four sections is entitled "The Chink in the Armor," meaning RVOG's armor. More significant than RVOG's "weakness" are the chinks in the armor of weak logic that Blish concocted to bring the story to a conclusion. There were good reasons for Knight's block.

In *VOR* Blish jettisons the Swedish Commonwealth and Cooperative State background which figures, to no particular point, in the earlier story, brings on the Civil Air Patrol, and replaces the focal character of Captain Bergsen with Marty Petrucelli, state senator and C.A.P. officer. Blish's 1955 experience with the C.A.P. serves him well in this novel as it does in "Tomb Tapper" (1956), a close to contemporary story which is also concerned with the landing of an unidentified craft in difficult terrain. But *VOR* begins with Petrucelli and his inadequacies. Brian Stableford notes correctly that, as with *The Frozen Year*, there is a preoccupation with realistic presentation and characterization.[30] One does not have to be familiar with Erica Jong's work to realize that Marty's fear of flying is not unrelated to his sexual problem. By way of some rather lamentable dialogue, his colleague, Al Strickland, who will shortly be involved with Marty's wife, Pat, needles him about the matter—until a forest fire alert, with news of a wrecked plane in the middle, signals the destructive arrival of the alien ship.

Before long Commissioner Holm, of the Atomic Energy Commission (AEC) this time, is checking the "missile" along with Marty, who travels to the site by land. The alien emerges much as before except that the creature is at first an "it" and only later a "he" who is named VOR after the violet-orange-red identification combination he emits from the "mouth-like patch" in front of his head.[31] With some difficulty the lethal creature is conveyed to the Grand Rapids Pile Station where

Davis and the Russian Boris Kovorsky (previously Erdsenov), now identified as linguists, solve the communcation problem with the same results as before.

By way of a new development, Marty, as the AEC liaison man, is placed in charge of the spaceship and concern is voiced about the Russian belief that "the 'VOR project' is code for research into the Solar Phoenix" (p. 84); should the truth be publicly announced? (The original outline for the novel does, in fact, make this suspicion the cause of a nuclear war.) There is much padding here. After the workings of VOR's ship have been more or less figured out, it is decided that Marty will fly the ship by remote control from the ground. But the key to what Blish is up to in *VOR* occurs in chapter 7 when Holm invites Marty and Pat (who is now dating Al Strickland) to meet him in a bar. Holm explains that VOR is now in the hands of the U.N., and that he is likely to lose his job but he might be able to get Marty appointed his successor. Marty, however, will need to get to meetings quickly and must overcome his fear of flying. At this moment a booming sound indicates that macho Al is personally flying VOR's ship—so there! There have been various references to Holm's alienation and now "the loneliest man in all the teeming world" leaves Marty and Pat (p. 120). Pat points out to a shocked Marty that Holm is sexually attracted to him: "He's been chasing you ever since this thing began" (p. 122). Holm, his secret encoded in his name, is a homosexual—and so, we may assume, is Marty. This would explain his marital problems and his fear of flying. Knight's belief that *VOR* should have been written from Holm's point of view (although he seems not to have taken account of the fact that Holm is to die before the conclusion) may have reflected a sense of Holm's centrality in this regard.[32]

But how does this relate to VOR's story? The connection has to do with VOR's desire for self-destruction, death (no doubt the death theme must have appealed to Blish when Knight presented him with the unfinished "Mercy Death") and the sense that homosexuality is also self-destructive, a form of sexual suicide, since it does not lead to procreation. The physical appearance of VOR amounts to an epitome of homosexual phallic energy as voraciously destructive. He is described in terms of protuberances. His legs, "swollen at their centers like two *overstuffed sausages,* sprang without grace or logic from the flattened bottom of the torso; the arms, only slightly less *thick, stuck out* from the sides. . . . [T]he domed head, shaped somewhat like the skull of an elephant, *rose straight* from the torso without a break" (pp. 49–50; emphasis added). This impression does not come through as strongly in the description of RVOG, although RVOG does have "two whorled horny ears" (p. 79) which become "hornlike" (p. 51) in *VOR*. It hardly seems accidental that, as Holm approaches VOR, we are informed that the flexible oxygen tube issuing from the back of his protective suit "was *nearly rigid* with the force of the air being driven through it" (p. 51; emphasis added). RVOG who, like VOR, is "shining and black as anthracite" (pp. 79, 50) appears much more metallic and robotic than VOR. Aside from the "anthracite," which dispels a too obvious evocation of the potent black man, all the analogies used to describe VOR are organic: legs like "sausages," "starfish" arms, digits "like those of a contracted anemone," and a head like "that of an elephant" (pp. 49–50). For a while these analogies discourage the notion that VOR is a robot and thereby add further pathos to his desire for death. It is likely that the reader would feel less sympathy for an artificial entity. Furthermore, although it is subsequently assumed that VOR is a robot, these initial organic hints augment the symbolic equation between VOR's destructive phallic force and Holm's (and Marty's) homosexuality.[33]

VOR's story concludes in much the same way as RVOG's except that it also provides a resolution to the theme of homosexuality as the expression of a death wish. Unlike the short story, in the novel Kovorsky explains what he believes to be VOR's purpose before, not after, the alien is tricked into apparently destroying himself. Marty overcomes his fear of flying and flies Kovorsky in a ramshackle plane above VOR's ship so that Kovorsky can flash his message across. In response, VOR's ship "tilted upwards" in preparation for his orgasmic union with the sun (p. 154). But if the "Solar Phoenix" metaphor is to hold, the little death of sex should be followed by a resurrection. Kovorsky says that, with VOR gone, "We shall all die, perhaps, but we shall all be changed" (p. 157), a line that will be repeated, with slight variations, in *A Torrent of Faces* and *Doctor Mirabilis*. New life, in a psychological sense, will, it seems, issue from VOR's death. And likewise from Holm's; he died when VOR broke out of the Pile Station: "The concussion burst open his abdomen" (p. 130), as it does, in the short story version, when RVOG breaks out of the Terminal (p. 84). Holm's is a pregnant death which results in the birth of the new Marty Petrucelli who can accept that he will not get back with his wife and who may succeed Holm as the new AEC Commissioner. Looking "toward the Sun," Kovorsky points the moral: "Christian [first mention of the given name] Holm was right: you are his son" (p. 158). Presumably Marty comes to the realization that a homosexual relationship can be as much a manifestation of Christian brotherly love as a heterosexual one and that he himself is evidence of its procreative possibilities.

In light of this interpretation, it seems necessary to conclude that *VOR* amounts to a lot more than just an extended version of "The Weakness of RVOG." Contrived, misleading and occasionally inept *VOR* may be, but out of weakness, out of death, has come a distinct new life.

(iv) Ertak's Ark: . . . *And All the Stars a Stage (1960)*

. . . *And All the Stars a Stage* is Blish's realization of Truman M. Talley's outline for a very routine SF story—the one about escape from a doomed planet. According to Blish's letter describing the novel's genesis in an issue of the fanzine *Disclave,* "some time in 1958," Talley,

> then editor of Signet Books, took me to lunch and proposed to me a great idea for a science fiction novel which he wanted me to write: essentially, the story of refugees from a nova (eventually revealed to be what is now the Crab Nebula, which was to supply the novel's title) who colonize Earth—but with the story apparently starting on a place very much like Earth and the twist produced as a surprise at the end.

Blish was reluctant, particularly having recently read Damon Knight's bad review of *One in Three Hundred* (1954), a novel on the same theme by J.T. McIntosh, the pseudonym of James Murdoch MacGregor. But the offer of an advance of $3,000, "the biggest I'd ever been offered up to that time," led to Blish's signing the contract and writing a first version of the book, which did not meet with Talley's approval despite its being written to an "agreed-upon outline." Talley "asked for a rewrite, suggesting some additional ideas which were even older-hat than the main one. This time . . . I tried to give the book at least a little Blishness by introducing a lot of odd little biological critters, a penchant of mine to which, I had long ago discovered, readers almost always responded with approval." Unhappy with this second version, Talley "sent the novel to some Bennington ponytail who was too eager to prove her worth as an editor (creative type) that she had rewritten the whole thing." Blish notified Talley that he "would consent to the publication of this version only if it were titled '*Crab Nebula,* by Truman M. Talley and Bennington Ponytail, as told to James Blish.'

Barring that, I would return NAL's $3,000 (though necessarily in installments." In response, Talley "not only released me from the contract, but soaked up the advance by re-issuing another of my books *(The Seedling Stars)* instead."[34]

Blish then sold his second version as a serial to *Amazing Science Fiction Stories* (June, July 1960) and again (probably with typescript revisions) in 1965, as a novel to Doubleday, his first sale to that company, which shortly thereafter also bought *A Torrent of Faces*. But six years were to pass before the book, "a few thousand words longer" than the serial, appeared. Before then Doubleday somehow confused the manuscript with that of the *Anywhen* collection (received in 1967) and announced the release of *Anywhen* under the title . . . *And All the Stars A Stage:*

> the manuscript of . . . *And All the Stars a Stage* had been lost, and the collection had been put into the folder which bore the title of the novel. This would further louse me up with Faber & Faber, my British publishers, who had bought the collection but *not* the novel (they now have)—and F&F prints such things by offset from DDay pages. Eventually, after many exchanges of cables, letters, and even a meeting in London [Blish's Doubleday editor, Lawrence Ashmead, made a special trip], this too got straightened out

—or almost. Doubleday still managed to omit the last story ("Skysign") from *Anywhen* (1970), a matter put right in the Faber edition (1971), and published . . . *And All the Stars a Stage* (using the *Amazing* serial, with slight additions and one interpolated scene, as copytext) with an inaccurate blurb.[35]

Brian M. Stableford reports that . . . *And All The Stars a Stage* "absorbed a previously-written story."[36] Stableford does not identify the story and cannot now recall his sources for the information. He does, however, recall that the title was "99.8%," or something similar.[37] If this title is analogous to *One in Three Hundred,* it seems likely that it referred to the proportion of people abandoned to die on the doomed planet.

Doubleday's delay in publishing . . . *And All the Stars a Stage* may have had something to do with the hackneyed subject matter but Blish's treatment is never less than competent and he does manage a number of intriguing innovative touches—the prime one being the reader's gradual realization, which is not confirmed until we are informed that "the system they had quitted had 116" planets, that the unnamed imperilled world is not Earth.[38] It is, however, a world very much like Earth. Indeed the matriarchal dystopian set-up is precisely equivalent to one that Blish imagines occurring on Earth in the future in "This Earth of Hours" (1959; see pp. 117–18 herein). In both cases the situation comes about because, given the ability to determine the sex of a baby, too many people choose boys over girls. As a result women achieve rarity value and power over a glut of largely unemployed bachelor males (perhaps the apocryphal "99.8%" title refers to this). Many of these males compensate for the lack of female companionship by becoming excessively attached to synthetic, snake-like creatures which are referred to as "familiars." As we shall see, this detail amounts to rather more than simply exotic ornamentation. Gregory Feeley speculates that "99.8%" dealt with this example of what Blish in *Disclave* refers to as his "odd little biological critters," introduced in his rewrite of the novel, because—living off human sweat—they consist mainly of water.[39] The hero of the novel is an unemployed young engineer named Jorn Birn. His initials along with a reference to "his small streak of sadism" suggest that he is a stand-in for James Blish (p. 178). After following up a dangerous job advertisement and undergoing a rigorous series of interviews and tests, he meets someone identified as the Director of the "Interstellar Expeditionary Project"; the Director, surprisingly, is a male named Helminth Ertak, the discoverer of something called the Ertak Effect, which makes possible faster-than-light communication and has led to the development of an interstellar drive. Jorn is chosen as one of the crew of a ship which will test this drive.

However, the news from an astronomer named Dr. Kamblin that the sun is to go nova in fifty years and that everything on the planet will be dead within nine years leads to a change of plan. It will be necessary to build a survival fleet of Ertak-drive ships and to tackle the problem of deciding who will make up the minute fraction of humanity that the ships can carry. Among those eliminated are anyone "with a family history of cancer" (p. 65) but Dr. Chase-Huebner, a cancer research authority, is included because outbreaks of the disease are still to be expected. All this preparation culminates in an exciting description of the unchosen but organized mob that attempts to storm the lead ship, the *Javalin*, before it takes off with Jorn, Doctors Kamlin and Chase-Huebner, and Ertak among its personnel. Thirty-one ships in all successfully take off, moving out into the universe in an exploratory, expanding sphere. But it is with the career of the *Javalin*, Ertak's ark, that the rest of the novel is concerned. In the five uneventful years that follow, males are discovered to be more important than women aboard the phallicly-named *Javalin* (allowing misogynist Blish to comment, via Kamblin, on the lack of good female mathematicians and composers) and contact is lost with one of the survival ships when the *Kestrel* is decimated by plague.

The novel's second half opens with the first of three planetfalls. As the system concerned consists of one sun and ten planets, the habituated reader of SF will suspect that Earth is to become the refugees' new home. But this expectation is initially thwarted only to be confirmed with the third and final planetfall on Earth. Nevertheless, all of Blish's inventiveness cannot combat the sense of perfunctory obviousness as the novel moves towards its predestined conclusion. Dr. Chase-Huebner mentions "viral cancer" (p. 112) as a possible threat on the first planet (which is balmy and seems hospitable) but the problem which renders the place uncolonizable turns out to be body-puncturing "insects." The *Javalin* takes off amidst despondency. With the passage of time, the other ships are now out of communication range, everyone is getting old, and the home sun goes supernova "leaving behind a sprawling growing cloud like a glowing cancer which seemed slowly and inexorably to be reaching after them" (p. 142).

Five years after being forced to flee from computer-triggered destruction on a second possible home, the "plotting tank" indicates that the survival armada consists of only nine ships. Since there is likely to be more life—and possibly more hostile life—near the galactic center, and to avoid encountering "the Rift," an immense starless area familiar to the reader of *Earthman, Come Home,* it is decided to change the *Javalin*'s direction in favor of "cruising along the galactic spiral arm our old Sun belonged to" (p. 164). Just before Earth is discovered, there occurs the one genuine surprise in the book—it is a surprise which both functions as the story's true climax, rendering the landing on Earth anticlimatic, and serves to integrate some of the more disparate elements: the matriarchal set-up, the familiars, and the cancer references.

Ertak and Dr. Chase-Huebner, now both quite old (given their life expectancy of between 100 and 120 years), are discovered dead in Ertak's cabin. John Clute observes, accurately enough, that . . . *And All the Stars a Stage* begins as a juvenile and ends as a senile, although this is not altogether the adverse judgment that he assumes it to be.[40] Dr. Chase-Huebner has presumably died of old age but Ertak's death is rather more extraordinary. There have been references to some unidentified illness which manifests itself in periodic convulsions, and to his odd hump-backed physique. It is now revealed that his clothes concealed an outsize, serpentine "familiar" that vampirically fed off him and has now killed him. It is also revealed that Dr. Chase-Huebner was Ertak's mother. (One wonders if this mother/son bond might in any sense be a psychological diagram of that between Blish and his mother.) Was she attempting to use her knowledge of cancer to combat the life-form that was devouring her son? Or was she the matriarchal cause? At any rate, the irony of Ertak's first name, Helminth, is now apparent: "helminthology," as Blish tells us in his "Science in Science Fiction" essay on "The Biological Story," is "the study of a small division of the world of worms."[41] "Her head weaving back and forth" identifies the cancerous familiar as female (p. 174). Some time later, Ailiss's submissive statement when she relinquishes command as Ertak's natural successor to Jorn—"I will not be in command over my own husband—not at my age"—makes Jorn realize "how completely, in only half a century, the last faint traces of the Matriarchy had vanished" (p. 175). Thus the imminent destruction of the cancerous familiar by a respectful girl with a flame thrower is clearly equated with the final end of the Matriarchy. The unappetizing message seems to be not to let women dominate men because if they do the world will come to an end; dominant women are a deathly cancer. Conversely, a patriarchal state of affairs will ensure survival.

But for a while Jorn loses faith: "With Ertak dead, it was suddenly easy to see that the armada itself had never been more than a daydream, a minute and evanescent soap-bubble in the eternal silver-and-black silences of the sidereal universe" (pp. 181–82). But Ertak has left the promise of new life in the shape of the "grandchild" egg that Dr. Chase-Huebner helped "her son's familiar to make" (p. 179). This egg, distantly related to the Lithian egg that concludes "A Case of Conscience," is imagistically linked with the "lambent egg" (p. 183) of the star which the *Javalin* is approaching, a life-giving globe that replaces Jorn's image of an about-to-burst soap bubble. It is Earth's sun. Shortly after landing and meeting the inhabitants of Earth, Jorn and Ailiss die. "But they had come, with all the rest of the civilized world of 3900 B.C., to within miles of the crowning of the Earth's first king" (p. 189). This detail hints at the likelihood that Jorn and Ailiss's home world was, in fact, a parallel Earth. Earlier in the narrative it was hypothesized that, given "sufficient magnification," the past image of the home world, which travels across the light years to the *Javalin*, might include "the crowning of Gol of Dobrai, . . . the first king in recorded history" (p. 141).[42]

The "Epilogue" closes as follows:

> 1086 A.D.: A sudden glare of light in the constellation later called Taurus. The Chinese astronomer T'ang Yaou-Shun marks it down: *A new and marvellous star, portending miracles.*
>
> But the miracle has already happened. It sleeps inside Yaou-Shun, in twelve of his genes. (P. 191; emphasis in original)

Just as the novel opened with Jorn recalling a recently observed "exploding star" (p. 7), so it ends with an Earthman noticing the supernova that was Jorn's home sun. But Blish's brilliance, only fitfully flickering in this novel, is truly apparent in that teasingly enigmatic final sentence. Are we to assume the birth of some miraculous savior, possibly generations in the future, as a result of the effect of the light of that supernova on T'ang Yaou-Shun? A phallic potency, symbolized by Taurus the bull, seems to have triumphed.

(v) A Jungle Story: *The Night Shapes* (1962)

The Night Shapes is something of an anomaly. It is not SF but a somewhat corny jungle story—perhaps salvageable as a *parody* of a corny jungle story, that forsakes Blish's preference for cold places over hot ones.[43] "It ought to be noted," Blish instructed Paul Shackley, "that the book is a poker-faced spoof, a deliberate compilation of all the chichés of the Wonderful African Adventure *à la* E. R. Burroughs, Haggard, etc. Even the elephant's graveyard is there by inversion (i.e., [the hero] says it is a myth for tourists) and I think the only cliché I left out was the Doctor Schweitzer type (whom I did put into the film script)" (PS, 10 July 1970). But not only does Blish seem to be revamping a rusty paradigm, a worn-out species of pulp writing, he is also (and this he does not admit to Shackley) palming off as new work two old stories of his own. Although Blish is usually scrupulous about such matters, there is no indication in any of the editions of *The Night Shapes* that it actually consists of slightly revised and expanded versions of two stories which appeared in reversed order in the pulp magazine *Jungle Stories*: "Serpent's Fetish" (Winter 1948–49) and, under "V. K. Emden," his wife's old married name, "The Snake-Headed Sceptre" (Summer 1949). Presumably because of the stories' different by-lines the magazine's editor did not think to check whether one was a sequel to the other.[44] As to Blish's stated intention, the novel version is perhaps more consciously parodic but that intention smacks of afterthought rationalization.

That Blish was operating in somewhat unfamiliar territory is suggested by a couple of odd errors: the references to "young Haggaard" and to "Lyly's newly-published *Elements of Geology*," elsewhere recalled as "Lyly's *Geology*."[45] "Young" Haggard ("Haggaard" is presumably a typo) at the time of the story, which internal evidence indicates is set in 1906, is about fifty years old. And if Sir Charles Lyell is meant—Lyly was the author of *Euphues* (1578)—then his "newly published" *Principles of Geology* (1830; not *Elements*) appeared 76 years previously. Of course, all this *might* be justified as parody. The disguised reissue of two old stories plus the fact that Blish also wrote a corresponding film script suggests that at the time there must have been some resurgence in the market for jungle stories. And although hackneyed and exhibiting much of the xenophobia and sexism that characterize the Tarzan-type fantasy, Blish's effort is never less than competent and the use of Swahili terms and phrases (translated in an Appendix) does impart an air of authority. At the same time, as we shall see, the book bears an important relationship to one of Blish's more significant works.

In *The Night Shapes,* an alienated American from Kansas named Kit Kennedy (compare Tipton Bond of *The Warriors of Day*), who has made his home in the Belgian Congo, is hired by a Belgian named Stahl to lead a dangerous mission up-river. The party includes Dr. Howard Lee, "an authority on tropical diseases" (p. 14), and his wife Paula, who are both British, and is accompanied by a squad of marines led by van Bleyswijck. But the protection proves insufficient when a group of natives attack. Kit is able to hide in a tree but everybody else appears to be either dead or captured. However, after some exciting and deftly realized moments when Kit avoids being crushed by a twenty-five-foot-long python which he had mistaken for a vine, he discovers that his faithful headman, an African named Tombu, has also survived the attack. Together with the python, which becomes almost as intimate as Ertak's "familiar," they set off to find the native tribe.

It turns out that the tribe lives in one of those familiar lost valleys which can only be reached by descending a precipitous gorge. Tombu fears the valley might be the abode of "night shapes," by which he means not simply demons but "elementals—the embodied savage facts of jungle life and death, of which a crocodile or a lion is only an echo" (p. 44). A legendary monster, *mokele-mbemba,* is the most feared of these shapes. The village in the valley is defended on the river side by a "heavily reinforced palisade" (p. 48) which, as the reader of this kind of fiction will suspect instantly, is designed to keep out prehistoric monsters. Kit manages to slip into the hut where Paula and Stahl are imprisoned and learns from Stahl the real purpose of the safari, to discover, on behalf of the Reform Commission, if pitchblende (radium ore) is being mined by slave labor. Reports of leprosy, which is caused by pitchblende, provided the clue. The smell and the diseased slaves whom Kit and Tombu had observed carrying some "unidentifiable substance" confirm this explanation (p. 51). In the meantime, the tribe is preparing for some kind of ritual orgy, probably of a cannibalistic nature to judge from the "knuckle-bone jewelry" and the "sizable skull rack" (p. 50).

Our hero, of course, saves the day. After challenging chief N'mbono to a drum duel and killing him, Kit orders Paula, Stahl, and the slaves to be freed. It turns out that van Bleyswijck, who has killed Dr. Lee, is in love with and in league with an Arab woman named Nanan who has organized the pitchblende operation. He escapes but she is soon accidentally killed. The freed slaves attack their one-time masters and, during the ensuing civil war, Kit, Tombu, Stahl, and Paula make good their escape, but not before being threatened by a triceratops that breaks through the palisade only to be squeezed to death by Kit's friendly python, Manalendi. The Wassabi, a friendly tribe whom the resourceful Kit had managed to summon while fighting N'mbono on the drum, arrive and now guard Kit and company against danger from any of Nanan's tribe. Any sense a reader might have that Blish is actually writing a parody will likely be confirmed by this incredible plot maneuver.

With this climax near the end of chapter 4, "The Snake-headed Sceptre" expansion in *The Night Shapes* ends (pp. 5–82). The two-and-a-half additional pages of chapter 4 (which provide the transition to chapter 5, an expansion of "Serpent's Fetish") includes the new information that, as an Arab woman "schooled in love," Nanan would have been regarded as sexual "carrion" by other Arabs (p. 83). This kind of erotic detail would presumably not have been acceptable years earlier in the magazine version. The lengthy fifth chapter chronicles Kit's further adventures. A year has gone by, some of it spent with Paula; Tombu arrives with the news that a safari is on its way seeking the night shapes, "a few of the million heads of Father Death" (p. 91). Obviously Stahl has been talking about the triceratops he encountered. Kit's object now is to get rid of the safari. A true sorcerer confirms the claims of an otherwise false witch doctor that there is a second lost valley with more night shapes. Kit asks the sorcerer to intercede for "lightnings—and fire" in "this Valley of Night-Shapes" (p. 102)—called the "Valley of Dragons" in "Serpent's Fetish." Kit's idea is to herd the creatures over the camp of the white men and then back into their valley: "Our sole hope is to convince the safari that the great beasts have been driven out of their haunt and are scattered all over the face of Africa" (p. 102). All goes more or less according to plan and the safari is warned. It should be noted that the releasing of the nightmarish shapes (including *mokele-mbemba*) directly anticipates the releasing of the devils from Hell in *Black Easter:* "A herd of wild beast[s] stampeded through the undergrowth, on hoofs as light as the footfalls of spirits" (p. 115). One of them responds to being stabbed "with a sound like the death agonies of a devil" (pp. 115–16).

It is finally decided to drive the shapes not back into the valley from which they came but into the first valley via the river mouth, which is then to be sealed off. As a result the prehistoric beasts will drown or be killed by the torrent when the dam breaks. Paula, who was with the safari, ends up in the arms of Kit who explains that, although "the beasts in the valley may die," the nightshapes "can never die" because "They're the ideas of evil" inside us (p. 125). Thus the conclusion of *The Night Shapes* mirrors that of *The Frozen Year*. The point is made symbolically in the novella's concluding sentences: "He composed her [Paula] gently, and lifted a heavy head to look at the star-bitten night. Manalendi looked back at him" (p. 125). Manalendi has a "huge head" which must also be heavy (p. 111). By having Kit mimic a characteristic movement of the snake, Blish identifies him with the traditional symbol of evil.

(vi) Short Stories (1960–62)

Blish introduces "Tomb Tapper" and "The Oath" (October 1960, first reprinted in *So Close to Home*) as a pair in *Best Science Fiction Stories of James Blish*. Both stories deal with the horrors of nuclear war. In the post-Armageddon world of "The Oath" a Dr. Tucci visits a "doctor" named Gottlieb in order to persuade him to join a survival project: "Every specialist we recruit is . . . an argument for reviving the institution of government."[46] Gottlieb, who is essentially a quack, a self-taught doctor who has never taken the Hippocratic Oath, as well as a poet, prefers to minister to people outside the project as he sees fit, i.e., to let some die. Overnight Tucci realizes that the unregulated Gottlieb is better suited than he to be a doctor in the present circumstances; at the same time Gottlieb reverses his earlier decision and decides to join the survival project. There is a subtle case of conscience here, a riddle like that posed by the timeless Sphinx that only time can answer. Thus at the tale's end Tucci wonders who has been manipulating whom when Gottlieb corrects the line from one of his poems (actually Blish's "The Coming Forth" [1957]) that Tucci had originally misquoted as "And the duned gold clear drifted over the forelock of time" (p. 152). "Forelock" should have been "forepaws," an allusion to the Sphinx with a temporally relevant pun on "pause" (p. 165). The error indicates both Tucci's poetic insensitivity and a tendency to let heady, ideal, theoretical considerations take precedence over base reality. But the reverse imbalance may be no more appropriate.

"And Some Were Savages" (November 1960) is positioned in *Anywhen* between "The Writing of the Rat," with which it shares the problem of identifying the real, and "A Dusk of Idols," with which it shares the problem of disease on an alien planet. Blish's headnote points out that it "was written around a magazine cover which showed a group of aliens dancing around a grounded spaceship brandishing crossbows," with the intention of questioning "the artist's assumptions," i.e., identifying the real savages.[47] The story is narrated by the astronavigator aboard the U.N.S.S. *Brock Chisholm,* the gig of which sets down on Savannah with the idea of putting right the unintentional damage effected by the first English expedition to that planet. The Earthmen had infected the natives with a plague that will eventually kill them all off although the disease, "tobacco mosaic," is harmless on Earth (p. 70). In retaliation the natives had killed most of the initial landing party. The present expedition has an antidote that must be given to expectant mothers after the Savannahans' fixed mating season. Once the gestation period is completed the cure is ineffective. The antidote seems to have arrived too late when a group of the apparently four-limbed natives is captured and discovered to be females holding their cubs in a hitherto concealed manner with two additional, concealed vestigial limbs. But because the cubs develop as fetuses outside the womb, "like marsupials on Earth" (p. 84), or like the Lithians in *A Case of Conscience,* the cubs can still be immunized. However, taking a hint from the fact that the ship's gig is named *Conestoga* after the wagon "that brought tuberculosis to the Indians," the narrator worries that human beings will eventually bring another disease to Savannah (p. 86). Although competently told, the story's indirection and "surprises," like this last, are a little too carefully contrived.

"A Dusk of Idols" (March 1961) is another of the commissioned stories reprinted in *Anywhen* and much the better of only two new short stories that Blish published in 1961.[48] It amounts to Blish's "Heart of Darkness" although in the *Anywhen* headnote Blish acknowledges Nietzsche's *A Dusk of Idols* as his main source. As in Conrad's novella, an arduous voyage culminates in a vision of horror. The Marlow character is split between Dr. Naysmith, a hypochondriacal surgeon who undertakes the journey and who also corresponds loosely to

Kurtz, and Dr. Rosenbaum, a ship's doctor to whom Naysmith tells the story and who passes it on to the reader.

Dr. Rosenbaum explains that on the way back from Naysmith's "first contact with the Heart stars," the ship carrying both of them touched down briefly on a disease-ridden, "running sore of a planet" named Chandala.[49] Naysmith, not known for his altruism but drawn to the challenge of healing an entire world, arranges to be left on the planet and picked up in a year's time. He learns of the Chandalese caste system and how the Articles of Law enforce unsanitary ways of life among the lowest caste. Consequently plagues are "cultivated as though they were ornamental gardens" (p. 98). After seeing a dead city and killing two guards, he is pursued down a well that leads to "the Grand Sewer of Chandala" (p. 103). There, making use of the shell of an oversized tick as a boat, he embarks on an underground river journey that leads past a ruined city to an illuminated stagnant sea in which is planted a forest of totem poles, "the final ritual act of condemnation of a city-state" (p. 107). But the current is drawing him towards a cataract. Just in time, on the verge of a four-or five-mile descent to the ultimate depths of this hellish environment, Naysmith leaps to safety.

Naysmith explains that the situation on Chandala amounts to a eugenics system. The Chandalese "force their lower castes to kill themselves off" (p. 110). And because the Chandalese recognize that "death is now and has always been *the* drive wheel of evolution" (p. 111; emphasis in original), Naysmith maintains that the Heart stars will admit them to the Heart stars federation. Naysmith, having witnessed Neitzsche's "twilight of the idols" and seen "all the totems of my own world . . . falling into the muck," refuses to "be a surgeon any more." He has accepted the horrific revelation that "All planets are Chandalas. It's not just that Hell is real. The laws that run it are the laws of life everywhere" (p. 111).

Characteristically, Blish concludes this grim and compelling tale with an element of ambiguity, when Rosenbaum raises the possibility that Naysmith has lost his sanity "on a savage planet" only to dismiss the notion immediately. Rosenbaum cannot forget that the Heart stars now do indeed "classify Chandala as a civilized world" (p. 111). As for judging the story, although a reader is likely to be a little too conscious of the mechanics of plotting and too little concerned with the character of Naysmith, Blish does succeed brilliantly in conveying a mysterious atmosphere of decay and death.

One of Blish's most obscure experimental responses to a request for a story is the very brief, tersely written "Who's in Charge Here?" (May

1962). It simply chronicles the movement from a poor and dirty area of New York to an up-town one, which is part of a day in the life of a group of blind beggars and their guide dogs, preceded by some business having to do with street vendors. In *Anywhen,* where the sketch appears under a new title suggested by a quotation in the magazine editor's blurb for its previous publication—"None so Blind"—the introductory note includes the information that "A number of readers, including Fritz Leiber, complained on its first appearance that the story wasn't a fantasy at all. But there are, on the contrary, two fantastic assumptions buried in it, one large and one small."[50] The story seems to be about interdependence and the dilemma of not knowing what is going on or who is running things. In response to a radio forecast of rain, the blind man with the German shepherd says "Hell, that's no good," kicks the dog, and asks "Who's in charge here?" (p. 117). The story then concludes with his assuring the other beggars that it will not rain. Can we assume that Blish's minor assumption is that the "preternaturally clean old man" (p. 113) who puts out the fired charcoal briquettes for the street vendors and the other "clean old man" who takes in "the empty charcoal bucket" (p. 124), and lives in the same "boarded-up shop" (p. 113) as the beggars, are actually in charge? Or can we assume—and this would be the major fantastic assumption—that the German shepherd (together with the other guide dogs?) are actually in charge?

A similarly paranoid, enigmatic, surreal, and perhaps related piece, "On the Wall of the Lodge," a joint production with Virginia Kidd, was published in a bowdlerized version the following month. But in this case the fantastic is shown to be real rather than the reverse. Its inception, however, goes back to "a Kafka-esque novel [originally entitled "Telecast"] I haven't touched since about 1948" (letter to John Baxter, 2 August 1962; Dep. Blish 411/10). "Telecast," of which "On the Wall of the Lodge" is a fragment, was one of three abortive Kafka projects, the other two being a translation of *The Trial* and an interpretation, also dating from 1948, of *The Castle* as an allegory of the movement of a cancer cell through the body. The latter project would have been part of a book ("The Kafka Scandal") showing how badly Kafka had been served by his critics (see pp. 282–83 herein). The important point to note about "Telecast" is that it was Blish's one attempt to write an extended symbolic work comparable in difficulty to the work of those writers whom he most admired: Kafka, Joyce, Gaddis, and Pound, and hence the work deserves examination in some detail.

Telling Paul Shackley that he is "only the second person in the world

I have ever decided to explain it to," Blish writes of "On the Wall of the Lodge,"

> I was reading such neurophysiologists and electroencephalographers as Grey Walter and Ross Ashby, and was particularly struck by their picture of the brain as a reverberating organ rather than as one in which particular abilities or memories are located in some particular anatomical location. It occurred to me that catatonic schizophrenia might be a state in which the ego (soul, self-consciousness) was shocked into cycling helplessly through all those processes/areas of the brain where the somatic functions are represented or operated. These impulses or fields or whatever would be utterly strange to the conscious mind, which ordinarily experiences them only at second hand through the reports of sensors, and would probably be interpreted in terms of conscious experience, sensory reports, remembered images.
> This got me started on a novel in which such an experience made up the whole world of the viewpoint character—and never to be explained to the reader at all. I gave the first 25,000 words of this to my then agent, Fred Pohl (quite without explanation except that it was the opening of a much longer work). He was fascinated and tried for years to sell it, without success. (PS, 15 July 1970)

A letter to Blish from Pohl makes reference to Doubleday rejecting outlines for both "Telecast" and "Mid-Summer Century" (Dep. Blish 428, 25 February 1949).

Subsequently, Blish informs Shackley,

> my then wife was approached by Judy Merril with a proposal for a project much like what later turned into *Dangerous Visions;* and Virginia proposed to me that she take the 25,000 words and carpenter a novelet out of it, imposing upon it the absolute end of the novel, about which I had already told her. I agreed to this; in the meantime the Merril project collapsed; so Virginia offered the novelet to Fred [Pohl, then editor of *Galaxy*] who took it. (PS, 15 July 1970)

Virginia Kidd explains that,

> My part in the creation of the novella . . ., which I would have preferred to call (somewhat artsy-schmartsily) "Intersection With Change of Light," was limited to accepting from him the fragmentary beginning of *Telecast,* with permission and wholehearted encouragement from him, to complete it in any manner whatever that suited me. He was, if not stuck, bogged down, and did not foresee completing the book for years to come. . . . The epigraph [headnote] . . . which he wrote for the story's first appearance in print and which I

have used in each reprinting, reflects the fact that the story is collaborative and that only the beginning was his. All the rest of the story was written by me and does *not* reflect the way he intended his book to go. . . . He intended for it all, on at least one level, to be taking place *inside* John Brest—just as *The Castle* on at least one level takes place inside "K." The creative notion I had saw that internal journey as a surrealistic version of the achieving of maturity: a sort of rite of passage, rather than schizophrenia. We agreed that the creative split was roughly sixty/forty in my favor and, as far as I know, Jim thought highly of the story, though it was not "his."[51]

The difficulty in making sense out of "On the Wall of the Lodge" is, then, compounded by the fact that it reflects two competing intentions—its composition might therefore be appropriately described as "schizophrenic." Virginia Kidd further elaborates, "I submitted the story to Fred Pohl as a fantasy intended for *If*. Fred accepted it with enthusiasm, but insisted that it was science fiction [Blish informed Baxter that "On the Wall of the Lodge" was not SF, "though the ancient and unfinished novel from which it was extracted might have been" (Dep. Blish 411/10, 2 August 1962)] and that he wanted to use it in *Galaxy*. I *was* surprised but not displeased. I *was* displeased by Fred's cutting several thousand words from the beginning of the story, i.e., Jim's part; I restored the cuts when Silverberg and Robert Hoskins reprinted it" in the collection *Dark Stars* (1969)—which thus contains the only valid text of the story.[52]

"On the Wall of the Lodge" is divided into seven parts. In the first three parts (pp. 242–53), which the five-part June 1962 *Galaxy* version collapsed to a mere ten short paragraphs, John Brest, a Sunday hiker (who shares Blish's initials), comes across an anticipation of the world of J. G. Ballard, a foreign-looking car abandoned by a clownlike figure in an "intricate cloverleaf intersection."[53] He attempts to drive the car to an unfamiliar "city on the horizon" which includes a "blocky" factory "or power plant of some sort . . . with a towering thick smokestack which poured white clouds into the humid air . . . in regular pulses; two, or about that, per second" (p. 246). His intention is to hand the car over to the police. Turning on the car radio, he hears his own voice, "not as he had heard it on tape, but as he had always heard it when he spoke, with all the deep bone-conducted frequencies"; he is being interrogated (p. 251). This gives way to a military band and "a crescendo that nearly burst his eardrum" (p. 252). Surrendering to what seems to be the car's control, Brest is surprised when it comes to an abrupt stop and two young men accuse him of having crashed into their sedan.

Blish's letter to Shackley clarifies much of this: the story

> consists of the opening episodes of the journey through the body, very heavy on auditory imagery, the sense of balance, *transmissions* (radio and TV), and the schizophrenic's feeling that all the external world (which he still thinks he's traversing) is a place of senseless violence [,] all of it directed towards himself plus a first involvement with all the motor nerves, or rather their analogues in the brain (*motor* to Brest suggests a car, as the labyrinth of the ear becomes a complex cloverleaf overpass); distant genital impulses (the chimney); and so on. (PS, 15 July 1970).

Alarmed by the threatening talk of the two young men, Brest decides to run for it. But his young pursuers, now multiplied to four, including "a chubby and comical" man, overtake him with their impossibly "huge zigzag bounds" (p. 256), capture him, and take him before a judge. All of this threatening weirdness and the increasing epistemological concern has much in common with "Mistake Inside" (see pp. 38–40 herein), a story published in the same year that "Telecast" was begun. During the ensuing Kafkaesque trial, Brest attempts to defend himself against the accusation that he is a thief. The statements heard on the radio are now spoken. His only hope of survival, the judge informs him, is to be found guilty, to be a criminal. After this "reality scene" is "cut" and "retaken" at the judge's command, the four men take Brest to the "policy chambers," which are actually "a broadcasting station" (p. 262).

There on a screen he watches a psychologist interviewing a child novelist who is explaining the allegorical purpose in his novel of a "lodge" (of which the child had build "a full-sized replica" set in "a fake forest") and the central characters, the human "Clown" and the "High Hunter," a Pan-type spirit. Unlike the Clown, the High Hunter is "cruel out of principle":

> he has thousands of wards, and he has to take care of them all, all the time. One of the Hunted—the Mouse, say—may have to be killed by the Owl so that the Trout can escape the Otter. How would the Mouse know that? And would he like it any better if he *did* know it? He's more important to himself than the Trout is. You can't ever know the kind of good the High Hunter is after. That's why all the Hunted fail to justify his ways and quarrel so much about it. He's just, but he's the only one in the book who understands justice. And so he's the only one who can be satisfied with it. The Hunted who have been good will have their skins nailed on the walls of the Lodge. The Hunted who haven't been good will have their skins nailed on the walls of the Lodge. There *is* a difference, but how can the Hunted see it? (P. 266)[54]

The Clown, it seems, "is cruel for pleasure" (p. 266).

In an unsuccessful attempt to escape, Brest kills one of the four young men whereupon the remaining three bring him to the lodge (or a copy of the same) "startlingly erected in the center of the square before the chimney" (p. 267). Outside the lodge he is questioned by a "Mr. Hosmin," a deputy for some unidentified ultimate authority (p. 269). After making a clean breast of it, being condemned to death and then reprieved, Brest (is he now in tune with the "female" heart mediating between head and male genitals?) seizes the opportunity to flee, thus becoming, in Hosmin's words, "the object of what we call a chase sequence, a live doll to be filmed and dubbed later into some program which we may or may not broadcast" (p. 270). To the Blishes' version of the simulacral world of Philip K. Dick is here added their anticipation of the illusory film lot reality described by William Burroughs in *Nova Express* (1964). Brest, or his double, scales the "pulsing chimney" which "had staples driven into it," sobs "Coming Mother" (over the top, surely?), falls from the chimney's "lip" (p. 273) as the chimney itself explodes, and finds himself—the object of applause—in the red trousers and jacket of the Clown, that figure glimpsed near the beginning of the story, sitting at the wheel of a car: "The other skin, already flayed in the obliquity of justice, was on the Lodge again, all shed tatters until another time" (p. 274). Brest is imprisoned in the endless retakes of a film-world set. "The end of the story," Blish informs Shackley, "is the end of the novel, when the whole cycle begins over again; all else is missing" (PS, 15 July 1970).

Blish continues, "I now have some 300,000 words of this thing, in the most God-awful disarranged state that a MS. could possibly be in, and poor Brest has only just gotten himself involved with the automatic nervous system. It is all about as emotionally unpleasant as the sample you read, and small wonder—the man is mad. I do not think there is any future in this project, but I have a horrid fascination with it" (PS, 15 July 1970).[55] Since Blish mentions the same wordage figure in a letter to Virginia Kidd dated 4 March 1966, it seems likely that he did not do much work on the novel after 1966:

> I do have the current draft of *Telecast* (abandoned title), but it has grown to be so big a manuscript—about 300,000 words now and I think only a little more than half done—that neither you nor [Michael] Moorcock [editor of *New Worlds*] could make much use of the LODGE section as it now stands; it's probably 75,000 words now, give or take 10,000.
>
> I don't get to this book very often and I may just have to leave it for my

grandchildren to burn. LODGE as you pared and reorganized it makes a nice tight story and I'm happy that you found another market for it, but it's most unlike the boxful of manuscript I've made of it since . . . though it's still only an introduction to the main matter.

And I still don't know whether I like the thing, so I wouldn't want Mike to publish the new version yet even if he had the space for it. I do like your version as a separate entity. (Dep. Blish 423/3; Blish's ellipsis)

That version is a truly weird and effective, self-consciously metafictional allegory, poetically written, interesting, and disturbing, an allegory which, it must be said, reflects very little of Virginia Kidd's rite of passage intention. Some of what reflections there are may derive from the influence of *The Recognitions* (1955), a highly complicated novel by the Blishes' friend, William Gaddis, a novel that James Blish much admired.[56] *The Recognition* is about fake "realities," art, forgery, the spiritual rebirth of a Faustian protagonist, and the need to return to the Mother. At the same time, Virginia Kidd's plans for the maturity theme are clear in the following statement from "an early synopsis of the story which is recognizably from" her typewriter: "Flowerlike women's faces at the windows of the car signify that the Sissy on the Block episode is over, the Tormented Young Man is about to begin." And, indeed, reference is made at the story's conclusion to "the smiling flower-like faces of girls, applauding his aplomb" (p. 274) after an allusion to a thermos which, the synopsis makes clear, contains the "milky . . . ["odor"] of seed."[57] As for Blish's ambitions for "On the Wall of the Lodge," it is unfortunate, especially given Blish's bio-physiological knowledge, that they were not fully realized.

(vii) Short Stories (1965–69)

After a three-year hiatus in publishing SF, during which Blish divorced, remarried, underwent two cancer operations, and published *Doctor Mirabilis,* he returned to the short story field with "No Jokes on Mars" (October 1965). This minor work, commissioned "for Vogue, of all places, but they didn't want it when they saw it" (KLA, 8 November 1974), is reprinted in *Anywhen* with an introductory note indicating that it shares "several important features" with Blish's 1966 novel for juveniles, *Welcome to Mars:* "Though the story was written first, the events in it presumably take place a decade after those in the novel."[58] Karen Chandler, a reporter from Earth, is being flown over the surface of Mars. She is accompanied by Colonel Margolis, the executive officer of

Port Ares, and Joe Kendricks, the skimmer's civilian pilot. Kendricks, who is also a reporter and has been on Mars since the second landing, has taken to entitling his cynical weekly column "JoKe's on Mars." Spotting a dune "cat," the Colonel asks to be set down so that he can attempt to steal the "pomander" from the cat's abdominal pouch. Apparently an illegal trade with Earth has grown up in these pomanders which have "a faint narcotic quality" (p. 132). But without them the cats, who are intelligent, die. Karen is horrified and plans to expose this scandalous trade. Would women wear the pomanders "if they knew what they were and what they cost?" (p. 134). And although much of the Astronaut Corps is implicated in the trade and Margolis says he will simply deny the story, Kendrick's cynicism is overcome. The story concludes with his decision to try to provide the corroborative evidence.

On the cover of his small monthly diary-notebook for February 1965 Blish wrote that "How Beautiful with Banners," one of his favorite and more unusual pieces, was "written in hospital 1964" (Dep. Blish 437). But he does not specify whether this was in July, when he had the radon implantation, or in September, when he underwent a radical neck dissection. A recto page of notes for "How Beautiful with Banners" from the February 1965 notebook, along with notes on the facing verso page for an apparently unwritten story set in 2075 about a woman named "Alice Cygnis" (if I have interpreted Blish's difficult script correctly), is reproduced on the facing page. It seems clear that the "logical," "confident" character of Alice and "the crystal jungle of Ganymede [a moon of Jupiter], origin and nature unknown," in the unwritten story fed into Blish's conception of Dr. Ulla Hillstrom and of the Saturnian moon, Titan, in "Banners." The reference to Alice's "long adolescence on which was imposed long training in science" is paralleled by the observation that, for Ulla, "To prepare for the sciences had become a career in infinitely protracted adolescence. . . ."[59] The verso "ref. dune cats" note indicates that the story which became "How Beautiful with Banners" was originally intended to be linked to the future history line established by "No Jokes on Mars" and *Welcome to Mars.*

"How Beautiful with Banners" appeared in Damon Knight's first *Orbit* anthology (1966). According to Blish's headnote to its republication in the revised edition of *Best Science Fiction Stories of James Blish* (1973), in response to the invitation to contribute to *Orbit* he had decided to write something that would deliberately contain the kind of sexual symbolism that Knight had argued was unconsciously present in

Notes for "How Beautiful with Banners" (Dep. Blish 438/7)

"Common Time" and that Blish himself had suggested was unconsciously present in "Solar Plexus" (see p. 34 herein). As he points out in a letter to Knight, "It is a love and death story, intentionally symbolic and heavily loaded; were you to make up a table such as you did for COMMON TIME, it would probably be twice as long as the story [cp. Blish's notebook table]. However, its pivot is not blindness, as you guessed—pretty close though—but frozenness, or inability to relate" (Dep. Blish 393/5, 22 April•1965).

Ulla, the person who cannot relate—a Swede whom Blish had speak

Danish until Poul Anderson caught the mistake (p. 171) in time for the revised edition of *Best Science Fiction Stories of James Blish* (KLA, 24 February 1973)—is separated from the deathly cold of Titan which mirrors her emotional state by her "virus bubble," a protective, transparent, unicell spacesuit (p. 167). When a local ("androgynous," according to the notebook) life-form referred to as "a flying cloak" (p. 170) attempts to mate with her (or her covering) by wrapping itself around the virus bubble, she attempts to dislodge it by moving towards a source of thermal heat, which "lay inside a fissure in a low, heart-shaped hummock, rimmed with feathery snow" (p. 174). Her sense of sexual symbolism is clearly deficient because it is in this vaginal vacinity that consummation is achieved—but at the price of her virus bubble and of her death. Thus Blish solves the problem put to himself in his notebook: "how to work up affair?" "how to write it?" Overlooking the scene are Saturn's rings (a third image of containment and covering), which look like "banners" (pp. 167, 172, 175, 176), and which, according to Blish's letter to Knight, constitute a "symbol of mockery" (Dep. Blish 393/5). In the same letter Blish identifies the concluding reference to what the rings appear to have seen, "siftings upon siftings in oblivion" (p. 176), as a quotation from Ezra Pound; it occurs in *Hugh Selwyn Mauberly*. Elsewhere Blish identifies another quotation, *"Nun denn, allein"* (p. 171), as the German version of a line from *Elektra* (KLA, 8 November 1974). The arch and inconsequential ending of the story, Blish tells Knight, is not the one that he originally wrote (Dep. Blish 393/5, 23 April 1965). As it is, the published story, ending included, does achieve a cold, ironic, kaleidoscopic, poetic beauty—like that of the rings.

"Skysign" (May 1968), accidentally omitted from the Doubleday edition of *Anywhen,* was reprinted in the Faber & Faber edition with a headnote making the point that "the best work" in SF "consists largely of stories which re-examine the basic fantasy premises—of which there are only a few—and try to take them seriously." Thus the "core of the following story" (which is unfortunately not one of the best works in SF) derives from "one of the commonest of adolescent daydreams."[60] In *More Issues at Hand,* "Atheling" specifies the daydream as that of "ruling Earth from a mile-long spaceship."[61]

It seems that an alien spacecraft has been hanging motionless for a month over San Francisco waiting for a response to its demand for "a sampling of human beings to go back to its far star" (p. 159). Carl Wade, hippie, college dropout, Tolkien-fan, has apparently been selected as a "lay volunteer" (p. 151), since the story opens with him coming around aboard the spacecraft where he is being inspected by two aliens in metallic suits. After a night in an apartment described as a "cage" (p. 158), Carl finds the door accidentally unlocked and wanders down a corridor into a park where he meets another prisoner, meteorologist Jeanette Hilbert, who looks like "a Latin Indian" (p. 163). She explains that all the prisoners get one hour's access to the "larger cage" of the park (p. 166). When the other prisoners have returned to their apartment cages, Carl escapes again and makes his way to the craft's control room where he watches the same two aliens slip out of their metallic suits and put everybody else on board (prisoners and other aliens) to sleep so that they can "make out." Apparently, without the suits the aliens cannot be put to sleep. But how are the prisoners put to sleep? Carl figures out how to use the "sleep board" and awakens Jeanette, who discerns that the craft's "control board" "runs off a Nernst-effect generator," which is potentially explosive (pp. 173, 175). Carl tells Jeanette that he will use the craft "to set things straight" and eliminate his many enemies—women included (p. 177). Aghast, Jeanette returns to her room.

In the final section Carl wakes up in a cell beside a military airfield—encouraging the reader to think that everything has occurred within his disturbed mind. But here Blish thwarts expectations. Looking out of the window, Carl sees the spacecraft grounded and assumes that it has been captured. In fact, Jeanette has turned the craft over. She had figured out that the aliens put the prisoners to sleep by means of sleep-wave broadcasters imbedded in their skulls—hence the "faint, one-sided earache" that Carl had initially experienced (p. 154). After cutting the sleep-wave broadcaster from her own skull, she was able to take over the craft and foil Carl's paranoid revengeful plans.

There are essentially two problems with this complicated, mediocre piece: it begs too many questions, and the characterization of Carl (with his hippie slang) is too stereotypical. The story is of interest, however, to the extent that it makes very clear what amounts to a paradigm of psychological structure in Blish's work: the movement from imprisonment (reality) to apparent release (fantasy) to renewed imprisonment (a new reality).

Passing over the trifle "Now That Man is Gone" (November 1968), we come to the last magazine story that Blish subsequently included in a collection of his own stories.[62] "We All Die Naked" was written as Blish's contribution to Robert Silverberg's theme anthology *Three for Tomorrow* (1969). Along with Silverberg and Roger Zelazny, Blish is responding to the idea that a high-technology society is particularly vulnerable to disaster. Blish and Norman L. Knight had previously shown this to be the case in *A Torrent of Faces,* although there the outcome is positive. Blish, now turning to the dark side of the coin, describes an overpopulated, polluted Earth where "emphysema had become the principal cause of death, followed closely by cancer" and where people are being engulfed by their own garbage.[63] Garbage collection is, in fact, big business. Thanks to the greenhouse effect and the melting of the polar icecaps, New York is largely under water. Moreover, it is expected that an era of cataclysmic geological upheaval will follow shortly. This grim setting is superbly realized in a relaxed style with touches of light humor. Alex, the garbage-man protagonist, is given the opportunity to join a number of select personnel, including nine companions of his own choosing, who will be evacuated to the Moon. But when Alex and his group, chosen from a number of artist friends, discover that the Moon will also be caught up in, and affected more devastatingly by, the coming catastrophe, they decide to die on Earth with the consoling knowledge that the presence of human beings on both Earth and the Moon increases the chances that some remnant of humanity will survive.

This powerful tale is one of the best end-of-the-world stories ever written; at the Heidelberg Worldcom, it received the second and last of Blish's Hugo nominations and ultimately came in third. It concludes the revised *Best Science Fiction Stories of James Blish,* there substituting (along with "How Beautiful with Banners") for "There Shall Be No Darkness." In it Blish achieves an entirely satisfactory balance of reason and emotion. Correspondingly, although both Alex and his female companion Juli are on all fours, like animals, before they presumably die, their human dignity is retained. Blish is not conjuring up the end of the world as a way of bitterly reconciling himself to his own death. Individual death and the death of humanity are equally accepted with a certain equanimity.

Various details and the overall combination of bleak mood and stylistic assurance in "We All Die Naked" relate it to the literal Hell on Earth that Blish was soon to present in his sequel to *Black Easter* (1968), *The Day After Judgment* (1971). The first sign in "We All Die Naked" that an earthquake is to destroy New York is "a thick, dense column of black fumes . . . rising toward the risen half-Moon, like a Satanic mockery of the trail of the vanished ship" taking evacuees to the Moon (p. 213). Juli's fat cat Splat! is a relative of Theron Ware's obscenely fat familiar in *Black Easter* and *The Day After Judgment.* And Alex's artist friends, like the white magicians who oppose Ware, are named for SF writers. "Arthur Lloyd Merlyn," for example, "a genuine hereditary drip who was spending his life looking for someone to put a plug in for him" (p. 180), is the pseudonymous Blish of "Sunken Universe," "Mistake Inside," "The Secret Files of Captain Video," and the early article on viruses, "Zombie . . . ?" Needless to say, Alex did not pick the white magician Merlyn for survival. The most fully developed of these characterizations, Fantasia ad Parnassum, is based on Lester del Rey (KLA, 12 December 1974).

(viii) The "English" Stories (1969–74)

The months leading up to and the years in England, the problematic end to Blish's career, saw the publication of eight as yet uncollected stories. Excluded from the following discussion of these are the three "King Log" stories ("Our Binary Brothers," "The City That Was the World," and "Darkside Crossing") and "Statistician's Day," which are treated in chapter 8. To these eight stories considered as a group should be added a ninth, "A Style in Treason," the novella that Blish included in *Anywhen* (1970).

The Preface to *Anywhen* is essentially given over to an account of the genesis of "A Style in Treason," the lead story of the collection and one of Blish's more grotesque and colorful experiments. In September 1965, Kyril Bonfiglioli challenged five SF writers (Brian Aldiss, Poul Anderson, J. G. Ballard, Harry Harrison, and Blish) who were guests at his house in Oxford each to write a story of no more than 10,000 words for the first issue of *Impulse,* the now defunct successor to *Science Fantasy,* developing the theme of "a man who sacrifices his life for a cause—or who doesn't." Blish's contribution, "A Hero's Life," which was "written in a vast hurry," appeared in that March 1966 issue of *Impulse.*[64] The same text appeared in *Galaxy* (May 1970) with a new title—"A Style in Treason"—and the addition of a prologue. This prologue consists of an extract from *A Child's Guide to the Galaxy,* which describes the Green Exarchy as the second major power center in a loose confederation of planets dominated by High Earth; within this set-up, politics and diplomatic relations are conducted by a process of incessant intrigue which "has quasi-official status through the Traitors' Guild."[65] But it is a much expanded novella version (written in 1967), partitioned into eleven "chapters," under the *Galaxy* title but omitting the *Galaxy* prologue, which appears for the first time in *Anywhen.* Blish explained to Paul Shackley, "I have eliminated the Child's Guide to the Galaxy" since the *Anywhen* version "is so much longer . . . that the prologue becomes redundant; also, I feel that it explains too much. . . . What I was attempting was an evocative story in the Jack Vance vein; for that kind of story, every explanation is another nail in its coffin" (PS, 10 July 1970). He had previously explained that the expanded story is much the same as in the first version: "mostly I used the extra wordage to fill in the background, partly as a convenience to myself, since I am hoping to do a novel about the Exarchy/High Earth/Traitors' Guild complex eventually" (PS, 4 January 1970).

The story opens typically enough. A ferry ship named the *Karas* transports Simon de Kuyl, a professional traitor in the service of High Earth (Traitor-in-Chief we later learn) and a vombis "diplomat" to a wealthy, exotic planet of uncertain light named Boadacea. We are informed that a vombis can "imitate perfectly almost any life-form within its size range," that the entire race "were wholly creatures of the Green Exarch," and that Boadacea broke with "Old Earth," which seems not to be quite the same place as High Earth, "back in the first days of the Imaginary Drive."[66] The Drive is, as Blish informs Shackley, "an auctorial comment" (PS, 10 July 1970). Simon's task is "to buy Boadacea while seeming to sell High Earth" and then, with "the combined Traitors' Guilds of both planets," to topple "the Green Exarch, under whose subtle, nonhuman yoke half of humanity's worlds had not even the latter-day good sense to groan" (p. 16). After this simple statement of purpose, the narrative becomes increasingly complicated. The oblique nature of "Boadacean polite conversation, which consisted chiefly of elaborately involuted jokes at which it was considered gauche to laugh" (p. 21), together with the name Boadacea, suggests that the notion of treason as a style of diplomacy was very much influenced by Blish's experience of England, birthplace of some of the twentieth century's most famous traitors. Such double dealings are the mark of a high civilization at the point where sophistication modulates into decadence. As Blish informed Karin Laflin Adams, "The story derives some of its Vance-like coloring matter from . . . my first trip to England; the planet is a sort of surrealist impression of the country" (KLA, 12 December 1974). In Druidsfall, center of the treason industry on Boadacea and home city of the Traitor's guild, its buildings partly constructed out of petrified corpses, the Traitor-in-Chief, Valkol, gives Simon "twelve days to get off the planet" (p. 18). During this period of immunity, while lodging at an inn, Simon meets a "playwoman" who tells him of her half brother, a not particularly accomplished traitor. One day he awakens to find her poisoned beside him, a sign that "His immunity period was up" (p. 23).

Following the three "chapters" that set the murky scene in carefully filigreed prose are three "chapters" that describe the set-up that Simon engineers. They are introduced by three paragraphs from *The Discourses* of "Lord Gro," the Machiavelli of traitorology, which include the following statement: "The traitors act as brokers in a continuous interstellar bourse on which each planet seeks to gain a *financial* advantage over the other" (p. 23). A "shot of transduction serum," derived over many years from numerous "unknowable donors," alters Simon's appearance and his "very heredity, leaving his head humming with false memories and false traces of character." Without "the antiserum within fifteen High Earth days," he would lose his own identity (p. 24). Simon then contacts the half-brother who is the Court Traitor to the Prince of the Gulf of the Rood and makes use of him in a very elaborate double-cross which results in a battle between Druidsville and the Rood-Prince for documents supposedly damaging to High Earth; in the struggle the Court Traitor is killed. Much of this is not clear because Simon's overall plan is not divulged and it presumably goes astray anyway when, after the defeat of the Rood-Prince, Simon (who has seen Valkol in the company of the vombis "diplomat") is captured by a group of vombis in the shape of lancers.

The concluding four "chapters" take place in Traitors' Hall in Druidsfall. Simon, incarcerated in a damp cell, has nothing to do but listen to the obscure "mutterings of his other personalities" while waiting for "the antidote, which was in a tiny gel capsule in his left earlobe, masquerading as a sebaceous cyst" (p. 39), to act. Blish makes use of the babble of statements to recall various literary works including Dante's *Inferno,* Canto 7, line 1 ("Pepe [*sic*] Satan, pepe [*sic*] Satan aleppe") and some of his own, notably *Cities in Flight* ("she then made a noise like a spindizzy going sour") and "Common Time" ("With all of love"). "EVACUATE MARS!" (p. 40) seems to be related to the mass evacuation about which news is relayed from the future in "Beep" (1954) and in *The Quincunx of Time* (1973). After being interrogated by Valkol and the vombis "diplomat"—now identified as "Chag Sharanee of the Exarchy"—"shag" is British slang for sexual intercourse—he is sent to "the Babble Room" where a "toposcope" (cp. "Tomb Tapper") will probe his brain (p. 42). The toposcope, however, can only hook into fragments from the experiences of Simon's bogus personalities, several of which again are taken from some of Blish's other works: "REMEMBER THOR FIVE!" *(Cities in Flight),* "Pok. Pok. Pok." ("Common Time"), "We're so tired of wading in blood . . ." (spoken by the "Martian" in *The Frozen Year)* (p. 43). Blish informed Paul Shackley that "the fragment in German [which may be translated as "How do you create it, to travel such distances at under the speed of light?"] is from 'A Case of Conscience' " (PS, 10 January 1970).[67] But when the antidote is released into Simon's bloodstream, something due to happen any minute, the toposcope will be able to locate the truth. Before this happens, by agreeing to reveal all to Valkol alone, Simon tricks "Chag Sharanee" into revealing "his" identity as a vombis. Valkol has the vombis shot before Simon returns to his own identity and the successful completion of his mission. Precisely how all this comes about, or indeed exactly what has come about, is not fully revealed. The reader shares, appropriately enough, a sense of being tricked. Simon's success as a plotter is also Blish's, and this story's casual, sly style is well suited to the light-hearted business of treachery.

"More Light" (1970) is Blish's highly unusual contribution to an anthology edited by Anne McCaffrey, *Alchemy and Academe: A Collection of Original Stories Concerning Themselves with Transmutations, Mental and Elemental, Alchemical and Academic*. It has nothing much to do with either alchemy or academe but it does make interesting use of Blish's two authorial personae. The narrator, identified as "Jim," is visiting a suddenly white-haired "Sour Bill Atheling" who has acquired a new young artist wife named Samantha Brock.[68] "I have never trusted Bill Atheling" is Jim's opening statement (p. 88). The Athelings, like the Blishes before leaving America, live "in a fine new house in Brooklyn Heights" which may once have been a bordello and which Samantha, like Judith Blish, has decorated in corresponding style (p. 89).[69] From the deteriorated state in which Jim finds Atheling, Jim suspects that Atheling has been reading the *Complete Works* of Sam Moskowitz. But no, he has been reading a play entitled *The King in Yellow* by the fantasist Robert W. Chambers (1865–1933), a work referred to in Chambers's story collection, also entitled *The King in Yellow* (1895), and thought to be purely imaginary like H. P. Lovecraft's *Nekronomikon*.

Atheling takes Jim into his office, which contains a Vermeer painting that might be taken for a window and which itself depicts a window (a parallel to this story's Chinese-box theme and story-within-a-story construction) and explains how, some thirty years previously, as a result of his correspondence at age fifteen with Lovecraft (initiated by Atheling's attempt to persuade Lovecraft to write the *Nekronomikon*), Lovecraft sent Atheling a copy of the play *The King in Yellow*, sent to Lovecraft by Chambers much earlier, by way of explaining to Atheling why such mythical works should not be written.[70] It seems that neither

Lovecraft nor Atheling (who all these years later only recently got around to reading the thing) were able to finish reading the play; Lovecraft had to quit several pages before Atheling (cp. "The Book of Your Life," p. 112 herein). Atheling has been able to turn to the last page of the play but that is not the same as the "cumulative *effect*" (p. 94). Jim finds this prohibition preposterous and accepts the challenge to read the play.

The play, a transcription of which accounts for the bulk of "More Light," is a murky, bizarre, phantasmagorical blank verse farrago in two acts. It involves a war between two cities situated by two lakes; the rivalry between two brothers in one of these cities for succession to the throne and for their sister the princess Camilla; a Stranger with a white mask and a yellow sign on his silken robe who, it turns out, is an emissary from the star Aldebaran currently at war with the Star Hyades; and the mystical city of Carcosa, the Alderbaran city in exile, which is either by, or on, the lake of Hali, and which is where the King in Yellow lives. In act two, the masque, suggested by the Stranger, with everyone wearing a white or pallid mask, takes place. Jim's attempt to read the play, settled in Atheling's bed (Atheling chose to sleep downstairs), is periodically interrupted by noises in the cellar and apparent light failures. He notes that the play is derivative of Wilde and of Poe's "The Silence" and "The Masque of the Red Death," and that only in the 1890s did writers find yellow an especially ominous color. A misplaced "Dramatis Personae" page includes the direction that, except for the Stranger and the King, everybody in the play is black. Almost at the end of the play, Jim, feeling unaccountably sooty and dirty, finds that he cannot finish it: "I came apart into a universe of saffron rags" (p. 118).

The next morning Jim tells Atheling where he stopped and is informed that he was only one line short of the end. As for the lighting problem, Atheling points out that there is nothing wrong with the wiring in his house and that the disturbing noises in the cellar were caused by the Seventh Avenue IRT train. At this moment Jim has a vision of Atheling as his own Pallid Mask: "The raw sunlight beat upon the blind and pallid mask of his [Atheling's] face through the naked dirty windows" (p. 120), and Jim flees from the house. He has since learned, he informs the reader, that the Athelings have sold the New York house and moved to England. Thus Atheling is "Out of sight, out of mind" (p. 120). This very curious and, in the case of the play, somewhat tedious piece deliberately frustrates the expectation of some kind of explanation or revelation, the need for more light.

"Getting Along," Blish's sole 1972 short story publication (he published no short stories in 1971) was written with the aid of his wife, Judith Ann Lawrence, for Harlan Ellison's *Again, Dangerous Visions,* the second in the famous "taboo-breaking" series. This witty, mildly bawdy fantasy (Blish's growing tendency towards fantasy is also apparent from "More Light"), told in epistolary form, concerns a nineteenth-century unfortunate and adventuress named Felicity Coupling. Her letters to her one-time employer, the madam of a bordello (found, according to the story headnote, in the bedroom wallsafe of the same Brooklyn brownstone as figures in "More Light," the one that the Blishes lived in for a year before moving to England), tell of a personal history involving debtor's prison, a gentleman protector, appeals to seven bizarre relatives of the prison turnkey (the first of whom turns out to be a lesbian vampiress), and the brownstone bordello. But this is a story with a gimmick. Each of the nine letters parodies the style and subject matter of a famous author, or authors, of SF or fantasy. Thus the letters give the impression that John Cleland, Bram Stoker, Mary Shelley, Sir Arthur Conan Doyle, John Collier/Lord Dunsany, A. Merritt, H. G. Wells, Victor Appleton (the housename of the American Statemeyer Syndicate, used mainly on the two Tom Swift series), and H. P. Lovecraft have successively taken over Felicity's pen. This, then, is the liberated successor to "With Malice to Come" (see p. 327 n. 5 herein).

Blish, it seems, had problems fulfilling Ellison's commission. At the end of the introduction to the story, Judith recalls how "It was collected out of a hot British summer night at about 4 a.m., and climbed out of a nice warm bed and wrote its idea down, on a still warm electric typer."[71] In more detail this is what Judith says happened:

> Once upon a midnight dreary, tossing and turning with what may have been budding writerliness (though it took a while) the undersigned got up and creeped to the IBM and wrote an outline for "Getting Along" (untitled at that time) and samples of the first two sections. The Author, upon discovering this effort—just a few pages, if I remember rightly, leapt on it with glad cries and, in order to avoid being accused of merely adding the right punctuation, played with the pastiche element, chose the authors to mimic and wrote the thing.[72]

An afterword maintains that the story was intended basically as a game and that it was fun to write. It is also fun to read.

"A Light to Fight By," the one story that Blish published in 1973, appeared in *Penthouse*. It is not SF and not of much interest. Social

"NEW PARADIGMS" AND PROBLEMATIC ENDINGS

worker Ken Cassidy, a Vietnam veteran living in New York, is not communicating very well, sexually or otherwise, with his girlfriend, Elaine. When he discovers that she is even more turned on by real violence (the possibility of a Puerto Rican gangland rumble) than by film violence (an adaptation of *The Revenger's Tragedy*), he realizes that she is not for him. It should be observed in view of what here appears to be Blish's animus toward Puerto Ricans that the final letter in "Getting Along" notes how "about the tumbled maws and lids of the ancient ash-cans dead Puerto Ricans tottered or lay rotting."[73]

"The Glitch" (June 1974), written in collaboration with L. Jerome Stanton, assistant edition of *Astounding,* is the last story that Blish published in his lifetime.[74] The story concerns the master computer ULTIMAC, already met with in the *C.I.D.: Universe* stories, its construction spanning Niagara Falls, and what happens when it malfunctions despite its being self-correcting and subject to the five "I.A.s" (Laws of Robotics named for Isaac Asimov). Ivor Harrigan, a computer servicing engineer, fearful of computer control, is called in when a major glitch occurs. Inside the machine, Ivor starts to correct the malfunction when an internal servicing robot abducts him—ULTIMAC thinks that Ivor is the malfunction. After being repainted, he manages to escape and throws every switch in sight causing ULTIMAC to go over the Falls. This slight antitechnology piece should be contrasted with the protechnology piece, "First Strike," treated early in this chapter.

(ix) "A Work of Art" (1956): The Testament of James Blish

Writing to John Baxter, Blish describes "A Work of Art" (July 1956), along with "Tomb Tapper" and "The Oath," as "my best short stories," best because in them he had tried to surmount the limitations of SF (see p. 17 herein). He goes on to suggest that "A Work of Art" (which has been anthologized at least ten times) is the most popular of these stories because it is the most gimmicky and is set furthest in the future (Dep. Blish 411/10, 31 October 1962). But it is also the best of the three. Blish introduces the piece in both editions of his *Best Science Fiction Stories* as being ostensibly "about the future of serious music (by which adjective I mean to exclude dance music both good—Ellington and the Strausses—and bad—Beatles and other coleoptera [the largest order of insects])" but its "real subject is the creative process itself."[75]

The story is told in the third person but from the point of view of

Richard Strauss, who finds that, thanks to the "art of mind sculpture—the creation of artificial personalities for aesthetic enjoyment," his mind has been "ressurrected" in the body of a healthy, approximately fifty-year-old New Yorker of the year 2161 (p. 123). After deploring the sad decline of music, the new "Strauss" decides to write an operatic score based on Christopher Fry's *Venus Observed* (1950)—a title suggestive of ressurrection, or superimposed meaning, by way of the pun on Thomas Otway's *Venice Preserved* (1682).[76] But when the piece is actually premiered Strauss realizes that, in spite of the audience's wild applause, it is actually an inferior clichéd dilution of his old work. The tragic irony is compounded when he further realizes that the audience is not applauding his new composition but rather the achievement of another artist, Dr. Barkum Kris. Kris is the mind sculptor who will shortly speak the words that will erase "the *persona*" of the helpless, resigned, but at the same time enobled Strauss (who bows, only half mockingly, "not to the audience, but to Dr. Kris") from the mind of the totally unmusical donor Jerome Busch.[77] Strauss, not his composition, is the real work of art. Here we have a problematic ending that most definitely works. Only at the end of the story do we really understand the terms of the paradigm shift that we thought we understood at the beginning. The effect is equivalent to a second paradigm shift.

There was nothing particularly original about the theme of the ressurrected artist when Blish wrote this story. It occurs in Isaac Asimov's "The Immortal Bard" (1954) and Ray Bradbury's "Forever and the Earth" (1950). But Blish's treatment far outreaches that of these and other predecessors. Blish had a personal interest in the story that goes far beyond the fact that, for this time only, according to Robert A. W. Lowndes, Blish was using "one of his personal enthusiasms as a plot for a story."[78] Perhaps there is significance in the fact that Jerome Busch shares Blish's initials. Algis Budrys speaks to this when he connects the "religious strain" in Blish

> with the attitude I always found in him; that life in the 20th century was an imposition on a person of sensibility. He saw it all as a game—mind you, a deadly serious one—in which he, a person of intellect and sensibility, was the same as he would have been in any era, but the particular era into which he had (at random? intentionally?) been dropped was one in which intellect and sensibility were not prized. Therefore, it behooved him to make the best of it. If that meant peddling cigarettes and/or antibiotic salves for cows' udders, so be it. If it meant devoting one hour each day to writing sports fiction (when

no other market offered), so be it. . . . And if it meant writing science fiction in order to demonstrate one's intellect, well, then, that, too, would be done.

I think that if one looks hard at Jim's science fiction, as distinguished from the fantasy output of his later days, one sees a very smart, well-educated person using prose to describe stories, as distinguished from telling them. I think that even his poetry—of which I've not seen much, granted—was intellectualized far more than it was felt. He was doing his duty by his various precepts, but I don't think that he was a born writer, or a born artist of any sort. But he knew how art worked, the same as he knew how a news release or a press conference worked, and he did them because he respected artists. I know some natural, intuitive artists, and they don't work with anything like his intensity or his care in dotting the i's; I have never met anyone with Jim's particular sort of nearly fanatical approach to creativity, which is not a sculptor's approach but that of a person who builds models of the Golden Gate Bridge out of toothpicks. I think, that is, we ought to look hard at his story, "A Work of Art," and ask if it isn't he himself who is in the part of the pseudo-Strauss.[79]

Whatever truth there may be in this assessment—and I think there is some—it has to be countered by the fact that, if Blish understood himself to be a pseudo-artist, out of that experience, in the case of "A Work of Art" at least, he created not just a superior SF story but a work of genuine literary value. And Blish the critic was justly aware of this: "The story adopts a radical scientific assumption in order to make a philosophical and emotional point that could have been made in no other way—which is the highest form of science fiction, and the most difficult to bring off. This sample so satisfies me that I regard it as a testament; and also as 'A Work of Art' " (headnote, p. 107).

SIX

WAGNERIAN SPENGLERIAN SPACE OPERA:
Cities in Flight

■ Spaceships are not what they were. In place of the sleek, finny jobs made familiar by films of the fifties are the vast chaotic assemblages which figure in more recent films. The resplendent flying saucer in *Close Encounters of the Third Kind* (1977) looks like the bejewelled New Jerusalem. While the startlingly unaerodynamic concept of cities in flight did not originate with Blish, his Okie stories, more than the work of any other writer, succeeded in popularizing that idea.[1] And they did so in the fifties when the now dated, missile-type counter-image dominated the silver screen. Blish claimed that his inspiration derived from his misperception of the November 1948 cover of *Astounding Science Fiction* (reproduced p. 162 herein). This illustration of the van Vogt story "The Players of Ā" shows a man's head looking up; above him is some kind of rocketship yard or port. Blish misconstrued the clustered ships as a city because he associated them with the diagonally juxtaposed futuristic city in the bottom left-hand corner of the cover.[2] At the time it seems that he had not read Edmond Hamilton's 1929 serial, *Cities in the Air*.[3] But, of course, he was not ignorant of Swift's flying island of Laputa (which gets one brief mention in *Cities in Flight*) nor of the much more relevant biblical prototype of the flying city: the New Jerusalem.

(i) Process of Creation

The four volumes that make up *Cities in Flight* were written between 1948 and 1962 roughly in the order 3, 1, 4, and 2.[4] Of the six separately published stories that make up volumes 1 and 2, the first published was "Okie" (*Astounding*, April 1950). To the conception of cities in flight Blish had added the historical analogy of the Oklahoma farmers forced by the drought years of the 1930s to undertake long migrations in search of work. The new Okies seek work throughout the galaxy.[5] But the seed story of *Cities in Flight* was a 15,000-word sketch of the later "Earthman Come Home." In at least four places Blish has told the story of Campbell's initial "four page single spaced" rejection letter: "I mined that letter for years, striking out one sentence after another as I used up John's ideas."[6] Blish graciously exaggerates his debt to Campbell as he does the length of the letter; it is actually three and a half pages long, and in it Campbell writes, "I've made some random notes on the City business—purely philosophical—which I think you might find useful. . . . They're intended as springboards for you to start thinking . . . on the philosophical rather than the gadget plane." The ideas which are indeed crossed out in blue or red pencil include the following: the pirate cities die out when dependent on fuel from land bases, "The ultimate commodity is human labor—primarily human mental labor," and the cities are "interstellar bees cross-fertilizing the planets" (Dep. Blish 414/7, 20 October 1949).[7]

The revised version of "Earthman Come Home" was finally published in the November 1953 issue of *Astounding*. It subsequently became the two final chapters of *Earthman, Come Home* (originally published in 1955 by Putnam's), volume 3 of *Cities in Flight*. In addition, *Earthman, Come Home* combines three other earlier published stories: "Okie," "Bindlestiff," and "Sargasso of Lost Cities."

In the author's note which Blish wrote for the Faber edition of *Earthman, Come Home*, he points out that but for Campbell, to whom the book is dedicated, he would have thrown away "an idea of Wagnerian proportions within the compass of 10,000 words."[8] In the author's note to the reprinted Faber edition of *They Shall Have Stars*, Blish observes that because the four parts of *Cities in Flight* were not written or published in the order of narrative chronology, it "contains some reminders of preceding events which economy would say it does not now need. But then, so does *The Ring of the Nibelung*, for similar reasons though to far nobler effect."[9] Clearly we are to understand that Wagner's grandiose opera played a significant part in the conception of *Cities in Flight*. Blish did not write a routine space opera. *Cities in Flight* is a Wagnerian space opera. Many significant parallels exist between Wagner's *Ring* and *Cities in Flight* and will be discussed in their turn. For the moment it is sufficient to point out that, like *Cities in*

The cover by Alva Rogers that inspired the Okie stories, *Astounding Science Fiction,* November 1948

Flight, The Ring of the Nibelung is a tetralogy. And in both cases the first part is conceived as a prologue to the whole.

Campbell's notion of the cities as bees and the importance of mental over physical labor are drawn upon in *Earthman, Come Home* in such phrases as "the city soared upward, humming like a bee" and "those pollinating bees of the galaxy."[10] At one point, John Amalfi, mayor of New York and protagonist of *Cities in Flight*, explains that "The cities have been like the bee for a long time. . . ." Just as the bee is "essential to the ecology" of Earth, so "the Okie cities have been the major unifying force in our entire galactic culture" (p. 398). Bindlestiffs, or outlaw cities that prey on other cities, "are diseased bees" and hence "the parable of the diseased bee" (pp. 399, 323). A surveillance craft that may be launched from a city is called a "drone" (p. 396). As for labor, again it is Amalfi who explains that "The commodity we all have to sell is labour" and points out that, unlike manual labor, "brainwork can't be done" by machines (p. 375).

While the name John Amalfi evokes John Webster's *The Duchess of Malfi* (1612–14) and the dark mood of death and intrigue associated with that play, Blish gives a different source. He informed Shackley that he used Amalfi, "the name of an actual town in Sicily," as "a bow to the immense influence the Italians have exerted, mostly for good, on real New York City politics" (PS, 23 June 1970).

Having published most of the first completed volume, *Astounding* published both the stories that make up volume 1, *They Shall Have Stars* (1956): "Bridge" (February 1952), one of the most assured and mature works of SF ever written, and "At Death's End" (May 1954). "Bridge," it should be noted, was written before *Earthman, Come Home* was completed. The two stories deal with the two discoveries that make it possible for the cities to roam the universe: the spindizzy and the anti-agathic drugs. To Blish's dismay the 1957 Avon edition of *They Shall Have Stars* both horribly retitled it *Year 2018!* and omitted approximately 5,000 words (CM 51, 10 December 1964). With *They Shall Have Stars* Blish added a second historical element, this time from the area of historical theory rather than historical fact. It had become apparent to him that he was engaged in writing a series of books belonging to a consistent future history. A number of SF writers, notably Asimov, Heinlein, and Le Guin, have conceived all or some of their works as comprising a future history. Since a future history can only be rationally projected on the basis of some conception of past history, it follows that all future histories will display, directly or indirectly, some notion of the theoretical dynamic or shape of history.[11] Asimov, to take the most obvious example, modelled his Foundation series on Gibbon's *Decline and Fall of the Roman Empire* (1776–88). Rather than yoke himself to some narrowly scientific theory of history, be it rooted in psychology, in sociology, or like Marxism, in economics, which might be proved wrong, Blish opted for the grander essentially metaphysical system of Oswald Spengler with its cycles of destiny.[12]

The shape of human history for Spengler is epitomized by the parallel history of three great successive cultures: the Classical, the Arabian, and the Western. Each of these cultures has gone, or is in the process of going, through the same "biological" stages of development, stages which correspond to the progress of the seasons: a precultural period, an early period of culture, a late period of culture, and a period of "civilization" (a negative term for Spengler when a culture undergoes a hardening of its arteries) and spiritual winter followed by a changeover aftermath period. Spengler distinguishes each of these periods in political, artistic, religio-philosophic, and mathematical terms. We are presently in a substage of "civilization" involving a transition from Napoleonism to Caesarism, and thus in an epoch which is "contemporary" with that which Classical culture experienced between 300 and 100 B.C. and which Arabian culture experienced between A.D. 800 and 1050. This will be followed by a substage of Caesarism which is characterized by political despotism, artificial and exotic art forms, and a populist "second religiousness." In a most useful article and table detailing "'Contemporary' Epochs in the Spenglerian World (1600–1950) and the Blishian World (1950–4104)," Richard D. Mullen indicates with considerable precision that the account of Western "civilization" presented in *They Shall Have Stars* corresponds to Spengler's substages of Caesarism and after, i.e., of decline and fall. He further demonstrates that the Earthmanist culture of flying cities goes through a full Spenglerian cycle in the next three books of the tetralogy.[13]

Writing as William Atheling, Jr., Blish observes in a note to "Cathedrals in Space" that A. E. van Vogt's first two published stories, "Black Destroyer" (July 1939) and "Discord in Scarlet" (December 1939), subsequently incorporated with revisions into *The Voyage of the Space Beagle* (1950), "were also founded in Spengler."[14] But it was as a master of space opera that van Vogt supplied Blish with a model to emulate and, if possible, surpass. It is an appropriate coincidence in this context that the cover illustration that initially inspired Blish was for a van Vogt story. As I have noted, *Cities in Flight* as a whole, but particularly the first written volume, *Earthman, Come Home*, is essentially routine space opera. But with *They Shall Have Stars* the tetralogy becomes not just a Spenglerian space opera but a Wagnerian Spenglerian space opera, something that no writer of space opera has yet been able to top. Brian Aldiss justly remarks that "Beneath the galactic gallavanting . . . lies something more hard-headed than anything in Heinlein, more intellectual than anything in Asimov, and more immense than anything in van Vogt." At the same time, as Brian Stableford points out, the key image of spacefaring cities makes Blish's tetralogy "perhaps the most memorable of all space operas."[15] It is a pity that the Okie film scripts that Blish prepared of *A Life for the Stars* and *The Space Witch* have not made it to the screen.

The third volume to be written and published, *The Triumph of Time* (1958), published in England as *A Clash of Cymbals*, a title which reinforces the musical analogy provided by the *Ring* cycle, provides the tetralogy with its fourth volume. In other words, after beginning *in medias res* Blish stepped backward to the beginning and then forward to the conclusion, a conclusion which characteristically widens the implications of his initial concept. In *The Triumph of Time* the cycle of Earthmanist culture, which is about completed, is eclipsed by the cycle of the universe. The present universe is about to collapse in upon itself and presumably give birth to a new one. The ultimate model here is *The Time Machine* (1895) by H. G. Wells. His Time Traveller comes to understand in a final vision that the rise-and-fall history of man is being eclipsed by the death of the solar system. But a more immediate influence may have been Philip Latham's "The XI Effect" (1950); Blish notes that the story "tells us what happened when the entire universe began to collapse in upon itself, rushing back toward the primordial atom."[16]

Four years later, twelve years after the publication of "Okie," Blish published the second part of the tetralogy as a 1962 serial in *Analog* (see cover reproduced p. 166 herein). *A Life for the Stars* is largely aimed at a juvenile audience and was written during a period when Blish was attempting to emulate Robert Heinlein's financial success as a writer of juvenile SF. *A Life for the Stars* is perhaps the best of Blish's six novels for young readers but many adult readers have felt that it fits uneasily within the context of *Cities in Flight*. Coming after the very sophisticated opening novel, it does have a jarring effect on a reader's sense of the overall tone and unity of the complete work. At the same time it should be observed that, since *A Life for the Stars* covers what in Spengler's terms is the youth of Earthmanist culture, it is surely fitting that this juvenile fiction, which can certainly be read by adults with enjoyment, is about the adolescence and growth to maturity of its protagonist. Nevertheless, a notebook entry for October 1963 reads: "Revise Okie omnibus [—] 'adultize' juvenile" (Dep. Blish 437).

The mix of artistic, literary, editorial and historical influences that went into *Cities in Flight*—Calkins's spaceships, a cover illustration, Swift, the Book of Revelations, Campbell, the Okie migrations, Wagner, Spengler, A. E. van Vogt and other writers of space opera, H. G. Wells, Latham and Heinlein—has resulted in a work which has successfully and spectacularly taken off (like Blish's cities) and has outlived (like the more privileged inhabitants of those cities) the works of most of Blish's contemporaries. But this would not have happened had not Blish been able to bring talents and other elements to *Cities in Flight* which were uniquely his own. His experience with the drug company, Chas. Pfizer

Analog (September 1962) cover by "Solenevich" for *A Life for the Stars*

& Co., for example, contributes significantly to "At Death's End," one of the two novellas that were combined as *They Shall Have Stars*. But what, as we shall see, gives the stew its particularly Blishian spice is the preoccupation with overcoming death.

(ii) The End of Western Culture: What's Past is Prologue

Death is, in fact, implicit in the title *They Shall Have Stars*, which derives from the Dylan Thomas poem "And Death Shall Have No

Dominion," the relevant opening lines of which provide an epigraph for the book. *They Shall Have Stars* has very much to do with escaping death. It deals with the two discoveries which make it possible for mankind to achieve a kind of immortality through interstellar flight.

The "Prelude: Washington" to this prologue volume should be regarded as a prelude to the tetralogy as a whole. It is set in 2013 in the Washington home of Bliss Wagoner, the Democratic senator from Alaska. Dr. Corsi, the head of the American Association for the Advancement of Science, is complaining to Wagoner about the moribund state of scientific development. He believes that it is high time that mankind achieved some kind of interstellar drive. But for this to happen "we need new pathways, new categories of knowlege" (p. 16). Corsi suggests taking a look at some of the wilder ideas about gravity. It is, of course, the discovery of an antigravity drive that will half fulfill Corsi's vision of an "immortal man who flew from star to star faster than light," the vision with which the "Prelude" ends (p. 17). Blish, it should be noted, has carefully suggested a sense of the oppressive force of gravity in the reference to how Wagoner's "weight on the sofa seemed to have been increasing ever since he first sat down" (p. 9).

But it is in the particularly seminal first sentence or opening chord of the "Prelude" (the musical term is deliberate) that Blish sets up an image structure which adumbrates the overall themes of *Cities in Flight*: "The shadows flickered on the walls to [Corsi's] left and right, just inside the edges of his vision, like shapes stepping quickly back into invisible doorways" (p. 9). First of all, this sentence represents a general figurative characteristic of SF: the tendency to use similes rather than metaphors. Because much of SF works poetically by literalizing metaphors such as "his world exploded" the presence of too many actual metaphors might make for confusion. The *image* of shadows on a wall does, however, have a variety of very strong symbolic or metaphoric ramifications, and here the introductory presence of a simile serves to point the reader towards the figurative realm of imagery as something putatively distinct from the image of literal reality. What is most immediately evoked is an image of Plato's allegorical cave and the "distinction" between an appearance which is illusory and a reality which we cannot see but only intuit. At one point, "To Wagoner's firedazed eyes, Corsi was scarcely more than a shadow himself" (p. 14). But when Wagoner talks about being followed by one of "MacHinery's gumshoes"—MacHinery (machinery) being the head of the FBI—one instantly thinks of another sense of the word "shadow." Blish makes the point perhaps a little too obvious when he has Wagoner talk about his cabin in Alaska "where I can enjoy an open fire, without wondering if the shadows it throws carry notebooks" (p. 10). Towards the conclusion of the "Prelude" a shot is heard and assumed to be "one of the city's thousands of anonymous snoopers firing at a counter-agent, a cop, or a shadow" (p. 17).

The shadows on the wall, then, suggest a blend of metaphysics and uncomfortable realities, a blend which characterizes *Cities in Flight* as a whole. The threat of being shadowed by FBI agents in *A Life for the Stars* will be replaced in the succeeding volumes by the attempts of the Earth police to keep tabs on the Okie cities and colonized planets. The blend of metaphysics and reality corresponds also to the mythic backdrop of Spenglerian theory and Wagnerian rhapsody on the one hand and the harsh reality of the Oklahoma migrants on the other.

"To shadow" means to follow; "to shadow forth" means to hint of things to come and that is certainly what the shadows on Wagoner's wall do. Shadows also duplicate the shape of something. Corsi notes that, when he was director of the Bureau of Standards, "we seldom knew whether or not somebody else in the bureau was duplicating" a project and "we never knew whether or not some other department might be duplicating it" (p. 15). The notion of duplication and identity will crop up in other forms. The East and the West, Blish will point out, are essentially identical forms of the same culture. And for Spengler all cultures are alike in terms of the cyclical process that they go through although the spirit of each culture is different. There is a form and spirit distinction here which corresponds to that between appearance and reality. Shadows also evoke the shadow of death while implying a source of light, hence Corsi's vision of "an immortal man" flying "from star to star faster than light" (p. 17).

Stars, of course, are fiery bodies which provide light and the fire which produces the shadows on the wall makes for a further operative opposition which should be added to those of appearance and reality, before and after ("shadowing" and "foreshadowing"), similarity (duplication) and difference, form and content (spirit?), light and darkness, and life and death. I am referring to the Wagnerian clash of fire and ice which is particularly apparent in the imagery of *They Shall Have Stars*. In the "Prelude," for example, the presence of ice is at least implied by the reference to the senator's cabin on the island of Kodiak in Alaska.[17]

Following the "Prelude," eleven alternating chapters interweave the material that was originally published as "Bridge" and "At Death's End." It is now 2018 and thanks to Wagoner's devious planning the two major obstacles which stand in the way of interstellar travel are about to be overcome. The "At Death's End" series of chapters, each set in and entitled "New York," focuses on the pharmaceutical company Jno. Pfitzner & Sons, where research is in progress on a drug which will extend the human life-span. It is assumed that such a drug, combined with some form of faster-than-light travel, would put the stars within man's reach (and do away with the risky generation starship concept).

Blish does a very good job with the medical research thanks to his training in biology and his experience of working for Pfizer. The point is made that most people succumb to various degenerative diseases including "the many forms of cancer" (p. 40). Ironically, in describing minor forms of progress, Blish has Pfitzner employee Anne Abbott assert what, in real life, he would later attempt to deny: "we found that the commonest of the three types of lung cancer was being caused by the radio-potassium content of tobacco smoke" (p. 41). In 2018 Pfitzner discovers an antidote to degenerative disease, an antibiotic named ascomycin. But that does not stop people dying of old age. In spite of the German motto written above the entrance to Pfitzner, which translates as "Against Death doth no simple grow," Anne tells Col. Paige Russell of the Army Space Corps, a man in love with Anne who provides Pfitzner with alien soil supplies from which new drugs might possibly be derived, "We're looking for the answer to death itself" (p. 71). What is required and what is eventually found is "an anti-agathic, an anti-death drug" (p. 74). It might be noted that the two people mentioned as important to the history of this research, "a man named Lyons" and "a living crotchet named MacDougal" (pp. 98, 99) are named for a Blish pseudonym and a combined Blish/Lowndes pseudonym, respectively. The reference to earlier polyploidy experiments with rotifers recalls, of course, the worlds of *Titans' Daughter* and "Surface Tension." The anti-agathic drug does not, in fact, abolish death but it does ensure that men will live for several hundred years.

Wagoner's aims are constantly in danger of being thwarted by the political situation on Earth. This is consistent with Spengler's substage of late Caesarism. We are told at one point that "the West is a decadent and dying culture" (p. 119) and a quotation from Spengler provides the epigraph to chapter 7. The Western government has become as despotic as is the Communist alliance of what is called the Bureaucratic State. In effect, Russia has won the cold war. The parent company which owns Pfitzner also runs the Consolidated Warfare Service. Thus Wagoner recognizes in Orwellian fashion that "politics is death" (p. 101). Realizing also that interstellar travel is not a government priority, Wagoner has the problem of shielding the actual purpose of his operations from the prying eyes of the FBI. Blish has clearly been influenced here by the McCarthyite period of American politics; MacHinery, of course, corresponds to Sen. Joe McCarthy. Reference is made to a past president, presumably Eisenhower, "a stunningly popular Man-on-Horseback who dripped *charisma* but had no brains worth mentioning" (p. 64), who made the directorship of the FBI a hereditary office. Caesarism is also characterized by a "Second Religiousness" among the masses. In *They Shall Have Stars* this takes the form of a conspicuous millennialist sect known as the Believers. That religious fervor can be turned to political ends is implied by the fact that Francis Xavier MacHinery of the FBI (who will become the U.S. president) is christian-named for a Jesuit missionary (note the possible second pun) and saint.

The other half of Wagoner's plan involves the building of a massive bridge—eleven miles wide, thirty miles high, and unfinished at fifty-four miles long—on Jupiter. The bridge series of chapters (and the original story) constitutes perhaps the most memorable aspect of Blish's corpus. Aside from the storm-tossed Jovian setting, which is realized with a kind of violent intensity and density (pun intended) that is rare in SF and a consistently subtle and sophisticated literary style, what particularly impresses is a sense of the bridge's symbolic dimension. Its literal import, it must be admitted, is more than a little contrived. The clearest explanation of why this incredibly difficult project was undertaken (a question which provides an element of suspense) is provided by the Prologue to *Earthman, Come Home:*

> The building, by remote control, of the Bridge on the face of Jupiter itself, easily the most enormous (and in most other respects the most useless) engineering project ever undertaken by man, had made possible direct, close measurements of Jupiter's magnetic field. The measurements provided final confirmation of the Blackett-Dirac equations, which as early as 1948 had proposed a direct relationship between magnetism, gravitation, and the rate of spin of any mass. (P. 237)

The Blackett-Dirac equations also "explain" the nature of telepathy and other wild talents in *Jack of Eagles*. Dirac alone, of course, is responsible for the instantaneous communicator first met with in "Chaos, Co-ordinated." The human operators of the remote-control system are located on the fifth moon, Jupiter V, which provides the title for each of the bridge chapters. They are under the command of Charity Dillon, the son of a Believer—space, after all, "is the ultimate cathedral" (p. 37)—and include Robert Helmuth, the foreman whose name suggests the "mouth of hell" which they are dealing with on Jupiter. As for the bridge's symbolic potential, Dillon tells Helmuth, "It's a kind of bridge to knowledge" (p. 52). Noting that the men who operate the machines which cross the bridge are not on Jupiter, Brian Aldiss claims that the bridge "represents the joining of two incompatible systems."[18] But it also represents a bridge between life and death.

A human settlement is also established on one of Jupiter's moons in "Seeding Program," the first part of *The Seedling Stars*, and although no mention is made of the pantropy program in *Cities in Flight*, the group on Jupiter V is contacted at one point by "Sweeney on Ganymede" (p. 89). Sweeney, it will be recalled, is the Adapted Man protagonist in "Seeding Program." And, like Sweeney's bones, the bridge is constructed out of Ice IV. As it happens, the four-part, circular structure of *The Seedling Stars,* with its first part functioning as an early history prologue, exactly parallels the structure of *Cities in Flight*.

Two threats to the stability of the bridge make for the main action interest in *They Shall Have Stars*. In the first place one of the bridge's caissons—shaped asteroids which have been maneuvered into position—is threatened by catalysis, a form of erosion that is four times related to cancer (pp. 75, 76, 77, 78). This cancer analogy serves to link the bridge chapters with the anti-agathic chapters which, as already indicated, include some discussion of cancer as a degenerative disease. The "catalysis cancer" is halted in time but a second threat—the climactic disturbances that will occur with the close passage of Jupiter's mobile Red Spot in conjunction with what is called the South Tropical Disturbance—is not so easily dealt with.[19] Blish does an inspired job of describing the "great orchestra" of "uproar" that is the bridge's response to this stress, a "medley of dissonance and cacophany":

> These structural noises were the only ones that counted; they were the polyphony of the Bridge, everything else was decorative and to be ignored by the Bridge operator—the fioritura shrieking of the winds, the battery of the rain, the pedal diaspason of thunder, the distant grumbling roll of the stagehand volcanoes pushing continents back and forth on castors down below.[20]

However, when at the end the bridge does literally succumb to the enhanced geological and climactic forces, it no longer matters. Its purpose has been fulfilled and the symbolic bridge, of course, lives on.

Wagoner conveys Paige Russell and Anne Abbott to Ganymede in a ship that travels at a quarter the speed of light in order to "explain" how the bridge's testing of the Blackett-Dirac equations on Jupiter—"the only body in the solar system available to us which was big enough in all relevant respects to make it possible for us to test those equations at all"—has led to the development of "The Dillon-Wagoner gravitation polarity generator," or "spindizzy," as it has been named (pp. 122, 123). In combination with the anti-agathic drugs, this antigravity drive places the stars within man's reach. Russell, Abbott, and Helmuth agree to man the first of several interstellar expeditions which must depart before the total collapse of the West. But as the mastermind behind this escape, Wagoner expects to be found guilty of treason for which the current penalty is being sealed up in the "pile-waste dump." For Wagoner, however, this is a "phony terror. Pile wastes are quick chemical poisons; you don't last long enough to notice that they're also hot" (p. 126).

The "CODA" in the *Cities in Flight* version of *They Shall Have Stars* has a subheading which does not appear in the original book publication: "Brookhaven National Laboratories (the pile-dump)" (p. 129). We are to witness Wagoner's last moments. The fire that kills Wagoner at the book's end should be related to the fire which casts shadows at the book's beginning, and both fires should be related to the imagistic clash of fire and ice which characterizes *They Shall Have Stars*. The bridge is made out of Ice IV and much is made of the deathly cold of Jupiter and its satellites and of space. Cold seems to have both negative and positive connotations. Under the scrutiny of MacHinery, who has "a look of cold wisdom," a general "had frozen into complete tetany" (p. 64, 66). But Wagoner, it will be recalled, represents Alaska. Anne Abbott seems to combine the qualities of fire and ice. Although "frozen-voiced," her features are occasionally illuminated by a "sunburst smile" (p. 63). When Paige kisses her, "After a frozen moment he could feel her mouth smiling against his" (p. 105). Like the bridge, Anne appears, in a symbolically important passage, to mediate between life and death. At one point, "Only the fact that Anne's eyes were reddened with furious tears offered any bridge between the cold narrative and the charged memory" of her quarrel with Paige (p. 69). Both fire and ice are ambiguous images of life and death. To the extent that ice preserves, for example, it appears to define immortality as an extended death.

This juxtapositioning of fire and ice contributes to the Wagnerian subtext of *Cities in Flight*. The *Ring*, which reflects something of the cold environment of the Norse legends from which it derives, ends in fire. Wagoner's death in the pile corresponds to the immolation of Siegfried's body on a funeral pyre. The ring of power loosely corresponds to a circular sense of the spindizzy drive and the anti-agathic drugs have their counterpart in the figure of Freya, goddess of youth (and love). Like the *Ring, They Shall Have Stars*, and to a lesser extent, *Cities in Flight* as a whole, ends with a spirit of exultation. In a symbolic sense, having put the stars in reach, Wagoner, like his bridge, does not die: "There was a constellation called Wagoner, and every star in the sky belonged to it" (p. 129). The fiery light-giving stars replace the fire that kills. Now is the time to reveal, if a reader has not already guessed it, perhaps by the conjunction of the term "Wagnerian" and the name "Bliss Wagoner" in a single paragraph, that Bliss Wagoner and his vision represents the ecstasy of Wagner's music.[21]

(iii) The Youth of Earthmanist Culture

Like many books intended in the main for a juvenile readership, *A Life for the Stars* is a coming-of-age story. In the course of his education, the boy protagonist, Crispin deFord, who is more usually referred to as Chris, learns something of "the great colonial Exodus of 2375–2400" and the events that followed.[22] During the exodus, "people from Earth's fallen Western culture who were fleeing the then world-wide Bureaucratic State" (p. 155) settled the planetary systems of the nearest stars, and established the history of Okie or Earthmanist culture, a history which corresponds roughly to the first and second of Spengler's four stages: the Pre-Cultural and the Early Period of Culture. Clearly there is an analogy to be drawn here between Chris's youth and the youth of Earthmanist culture. And hence, as I have indicated, there is some justification for injecting what can be classified as a juvenile work (albeit a very superior and sophisticated one) into a series intended for adults.

Instead of observing the steel town of Scranton, Pennsylvania take off, Chris finds himself press-ganged aboard the city and borne aloft with it. The nearby town of "tramps" that Blish (in 1956!) names "Nixonville" is left behind (p. 138); the allusion must be to Richard Nixon, the House Unamerican Activities Committee member and prosecutor of Alger Hiss. Chris recalls the economic background of this new Okie migration. His father had told him that computers "had been one of the chief contributors to the present and apparently permanent depression: the coming of semi-intelligent machines into business and technology had created a second Industrial Revolution, in which only the most highly creative human beings, and those most gifted at administration, found themselves with any skills to sell which were worth the world's money to buy" (p. 145). Frad Haskins, the leader of the press gang, takes Chris to see Frank Lutz, the city manager, after explaining that Chris's status aboard Scranton will depend upon what skills he is able to offer. Because he convinces Lutz that he has some astronomical knowledge, Lutz makes him an apprentice to Dr. Boyle Warner, the city astronomer. However, contact with the Okie city of New York "by Dirac transmitter" (p. 158) leads to Chris's being traded, along with a batch of worthless people that Scranton would have difficulty feeding, for two or three New York technicians. Frad convinces Chris that his plan to escape this fate by hiding among the crates in an out-of-the-way warehouse is unwise.

Viewed from the gig that conveys Chris and the other immigrants to New York, their destination approximates a vision of the New Jerusalem:

> The sight . . . was marvellous beyond all imagination: an island of towers, as tall as mountains, floating in a surfaceless, bottomless sea of stars. The gig was rocket-powered so that Chris was also seeing the stars from space in all their jeweled majesty for the first time in his life; but the silent pride of the great human city, aloof in its spindizzy bubble—which was faintly visible from the outside—completely took precedence. Behind the gig, Scranton looked in comparison like a scuttleful of old stove bolts. (P. 162)

In fact, New York corresponds only to the island of Manhattan but it comes complete with its subway system. The running of the city is assisted by a battery of 134 computers known as the City Fathers. John Amalfi, a stout, bald, cigar-smoking Churchillian figure with a "bull neck" and "bull shoulders," modelled to some extent on Mayor Fiorello La Guardia of New York, is the city's long-term mayor and is destined to be the hero of *Cities in Flight*. Chris learns that, depending on the results of citizenship tests and the value of the skills that he exhibits, the City Fathers will decide on the occasion of his eighteenth birthday whether he remains a mere passenger aboard New York or becomes a citizen. Only citizens receive the anti-agathic drugs. These drugs prolong life indefinitely but, as his New York guardian, Sergeant Anderson, tells him, *"there is no such thing as immortality"* (p. 179). Cancer, for example, still cannot be prevented and, although it does not kill, it "can make life so agonizing that death is the only humane treatment" (p. 178).

A period of intensive education follows for Chris. Among the subjects he learns through sleep teaching is Okie history from 2021 until 3111. The major events that occurred in this early period of Okie culture, sketched in four pages of *A Life for the Stars* (pp. 167–71), will bear on plot elements that arise in *Earthman, Come Home*. They constitute a gap in the narrative between *They Shall Have Stars* and *A Life for the Stars* which amounts to more than one third of the "Chronology of Cities in Flight" that Blish prepared for the four individual volumes that Faber & Faber published. Of particular interest are (1) the Hamiltonian Exodus of 2032, the Hamiltonians being an underground political group that fled the solar system in a number of small spindizzy-powered craft but ended up no one knows where; (2) first contact with an alien interstellar culture known as the Vegan Tyranny in 2289, which leads to a period of conflict that ends with the scorching of the Vegan system by the Third Colonial Army led by Alois Hrunta; (3) the fact that in 2394 one of the cities which escaped the repressive Bureaucratic State, "Gravitogorsk-Mars, now calling itself the Interstellar Master Traders, was responsible for the sacking of the new Earth colony on Thor V" (p. 170); and (4) the fact that in 2464 Hrunta, having been found guilty in absentia of atrocities and attempted genocide and having founded his own interstellar empire, declared himself Emperor of Space; following Hrunta's poisoning in 3089 and the balkanization of the Hruntan Empire, his son (?) Arpad Hrunta called himself Emperor of Space in 3111, the year that Manhattan left Earth.[23]

In the meantime, the fall of the West is generally agreed to have occurred no later than 2105. The West here includes the East. Blish cannot resist pointing out that, although the West was officially anti-Communist and the East was officially anti-Fascist, "neither state was economically either fascist or communist, and that as economic systems neither fascism nor communism has ever been tried in recorded Terrestrial history" (p. 168). We are later told that Chris was required to learn "Whole systems of world and interstellar history—Machiavelli, Plutarch, Thucydides, Gibbon, Marx, Pareto, Spengler, Sarton, Toynbee, Durant and a score of others" (p. 208). The Bureaucratic State, which established itself following the terror, collapsed in 2522. The loose confederation which then took over "proclaimed an amnesty for everyone in space, and at the same time instituted a limited but systematic program for the policing of those nomad cities which had begun to prey upon colony planets or upon each other" (pp. 170–71).

Chris acquires a fat friend nicknamed Piggy who is also both nearing his eighteenth birthday and anxious to prove his mettle to the City Fathers. After five chapters devoted in more or less general terms to Chris's education come two groups of action chapters that provide the opportunity for acts of initiative on the part of both boys. On a planet called Heaven (the locale of the two-chapter first adventure) inhabited by Russian-speaking colonists from the pre-Okie days, where Manhattan has landed to fulfill a work contract, Chris overhears a plot to occupy and disable the city. Subsequently he is imprisoned with sergeants Anderson and Delany in Castle Wolfwhip. After an intervening chapter in which Chris learns about the Vegan orbital fort that got away, he gets to participate in a three-chapter second adventure. This time Manhattan has a work contract with Argus III, whose nights have "indeed a hundred eyes" thanks to a nearby cluster of suns (p. 216). But another city, a tramp city, that turns out to be Scranton, is already there and wants to take over the planet. When Piggy and two women, who wormed their way into Scranton, are held for ransom by Lutz, Chris comes to the rescue. In his old hiding place on Scranton, Chris meets his press-ganger friend Frad Haskins and promotes the idea of revolution against the unpopular Lutz. The revolution is successful and eventually Frad becomes the new City Manager of Scranton.

In the final chapter Chris turns eighteen and finally gets to meet Amalfi. Not only has Chris passed the citizenship tests (unlike the unfortunate Piggy), but Amalfi has decided that Manhattan needs a City Manager like Scranton and that Chris is the man for the job. He has the ability "to be a first-class cultural morphologist," a term Chris recognizes "from his force feeding of Spengler" (p. 237). Chris deFord is delighted to accept the job and begin "a life for the stars" (p. 234).

(iv) The Maturity of Earthmanist Culture

Dedicated to John W. Campbell, Jr., *Earthman, Come Home* (originally called *Cities in Flight*), with its four component stories, is something of a structural microcosm of the *Cities in Flight* tetralogy. In both cases a series of works evolved essentially as afterthoughts. Just as "Okie," "Bindlestiff," and "Sargasso of Lost Cities" exfoliated from the sketch of "Earthman Come Home," so *They Shall Have Stars, The Triumph of Time*, and *A Life for the Stars* exfoliated from *Earthman, Come Home*. Blish's belief that he mined out the Okie stories at too great a length is particularly applicable to *Earthman, Come Home* which is approximately twice as long as each of the three other books. Its time span runs from around 3602 until 3649 in the original chronology, and until 3999 in the revised chronology. In terms of the Spenglerian analogy, the concern is with the Late Period of Culture and the onset of Civilization and Spiritual Winter. However, Blish seems not to have intended very precise parallels with Spengler's characterizations of these periods. During the heyday of Okie culture, it is explained in the recapitulative and stage-setting Prologue that a metal named "germanium" was the standard currency of space trade.

With slight revisions, the first two chapters correspond to the story "Okie." As usual, Blish's opening is calculated. Three points might be noted. (1) John Amalfi, although now mayor of New York for more than 500 years, cannot decide whether the belfry of City Hall, from which the city is largely operated and which displays the city's motto, "MOW YOUR LAWN, LADY?" should be called a belfry or a bridge (pp. 250, 496). The semantic problem is designed to recall the bridge symbolism of *They Shall Have Stars* and add a meaning to the term that was not operative in the first book. (2) The problem, we are told, "had once annoyed Amalfi constantly, like a bubble in an otherwise smoothly blown French horn solo" (p. 241). This musical reference serves to remind the reader of the Wagnerian analogy which is subliminally present throughout *Cities in Flight*. Soon "a quartet" of moons will circle "in a gelid minuet" (p. 245). (3) More important here is the annoying "bubble." This, together with the reference three paragraphs later to the "spindizzy screen which completely englobed the flying city," suggests that the cities are like bubbles blown by a magic flute (p. 242). Two paragraphs further on, the bubble idea is repeated yet again: Amalfi believed "that he was the last living man on board the flying city who still had occasional bubbles blown into his stream of consciousness by old Earthbound habits of thinking."[24] What is important here is the notion of the bubble as a restricting container. The imprisoning Spenglerian cycles amount to a temporal version of this spatial metaphor. At the end of *Cities in Flight* an attempt will be made to burst free of the realms of cyclical process.

It comes as something of a surprise to learn that Mark Hazleton is now City Manager and that his predecessor deFord had been shot in 3301 "for an egregious violation of the city's contract with a planet named Epoch" (p. 243). John Clute no doubt speaks for numerous readers when he notes that it is Blish who has here committed what might seem "an egregious violation" by so cavalierly and callously killing off a likable character with whom the reader has come to identify in the previous book.[25] However, such things do happen, and Blish deserves credit for applying a cold douche to the romantic expectations of his readers. In fact deFord's fate is prepared for at the close of *A Life for the Stars*. There Amalfi warns him that the "same kind of pitfall," the "boldness and initiative . . . untempered by judgment or imagination" that undid Piggy, could do the same for him (p. 234).

In the "Okie" chapters, New York, in need of supplies, approaches a system where two "dead cultures" (p. 254), a Hruntan polyp on the planet Gort and survivors of the Hamiltonians—originally "some sort of republican sect" (p. 249)—are fighting one another on a planet named Utopia. The war rages despite the fact that, as Amalfi points out, there is no real difference between the two sides, just as there was no essential difference between the East and the West on Earth. And likewise the analogies between one Spenglerian cycle and the next indicate that a formal sameness outweighs whatever differentiating spirit may have initially led to the development of a particular culture. As we shall see, *Cities in Flight* may be read as an attempt to escape from a repetitive identity into a state of pure difference.

Every once in a while Blish's evocation of the reality of his flying city makes for an exciting *frisson* which suggests at least something of the experience of pure difference. A particularly good example occurs in the vicinity of Utopia: "The city was in orbit and would be stable until the time came to put it in flight again. On the street, Amalfi flagged a cab" (pp. 248–49). The reader here experiences a literalized metaphysical image. Such moments activate the anarchic potential of the overall discordant image of space-travelling cities.

In the course of an overly complicated plot, Mark Hazleton falls in love with a Hamiltonian emissary named Dee; New York is hijacked by the Hruntans; mention is made of the likelihood of an "Assassins' Guild" (p. 268) on Gort (something which will evolve in 1970 into the Traitors' Guild of "A Style in Treason"); and via the Dirac transmitter (p. 269), Amalfi, aware that the city has violated a Vacate order, strikes a bargain with the Earth police who wish to destroy the Duchy of Gort. Thanks to the *deus ex machina* introduction of two marvels of super science (a plot strategy characteristic of space opera and particularly prevalent in *Earthman, Come Home*)—namely an invisibility machine and a friction field generator that operates in reverse—New York is freed from Hruntan control and their leader Arpad Hrunta is killed. Gort and Utopia are both reduced by the Earth police but not before what amounts to a Second Hamiltonian Exodus takes place. This all happens in 3602 when, in Spenglerian terms, the age of Aristocratic States (e.g., the Duchy of Gort) succumbs to a rising absolutism; i.e., the King (Earth) allied with the bourgeoisie (the Okie cities) suppresses aristocratic disorder (colonial factions).[26] Finally, New York, with Dee aboard, escapes and heads for the Rift.

The next two chapters, which correspond to the story "Bindlestiff," mark no new stage of Earthmanist culture and indeed seem to have little relevance to it. Thus, the setting of these two chapters, the Rift—an "empty ocean of space that washes between galaxies"—amounts also to a hole in Spenglerian time (p. 286). By crossing the Rift—a journey that will take 104 years—New York hopes to evade the police. By now Amalfi is about "nine hundred years old" (p. 318). Clearly, one function of the anti-agathic drugs is to serve the purpose of continued character identification; but for them the temporal scale of *Cities in Flight* would involve new characters every few pages. Essentially a plot device, their real-life impact is not explored. After a star is noticed in the middle of the Rift, an ultraphone videocast is picked up which shows a city being destroyed by a bindlestiff. The ultraphone, unlike the Dirac transmitter, is not an instantaneous communicator so the destruction must have happened years ago. A last-minute broadcast, made as a number of life craft leave the stricken city, includes the statements, "We have the fuelless drive. We're destroying our model . . ." (p. 290). It is assumed that the life craft, pursued by the bindlestiff after the secret of the fuelless drive, must have headed for the wild star. Thus New York lands on the most Earthlike of the star's six planets.

The inhabitants of the planet He turn out to be human and, as the name He implies, anti-female. A leader named Miramon explains to Amalfi that their women are caged as representatives of that evil which altered the planet's climate when a Draysonian overturn occurred, about the time that He began its journey across the Rift. The catastrophe "threw a very high civilization, at a culture just entering its ripest phase, forcibly back into the Interdestructional period without the slightest transition" (pp. 298–99). The cage of women, as one would expect in Blish's work, has a symbolic dimension: it represents limited systems of thought. In return for some of the abundant germanium and anti-agathic drugs, Amalfi proposes that the spindizzies be used to regularize the planet's axis and thereby improve its climate. The refugees from the destroyed Okie city do land on He only to be menaced by He's equivalent of the bindlestiff, a bandit He city. After Amalfi helps rescue the refugees, it is discovered that the bindlestiff is already on He and in league with the local bandits.

All is resolved during one of the most spectacular episodes in *Cities in Flight*—the tipping of He in 3850. In the process the bindlestiff city is magically destroyed; the stolen no-fuel drive (the invention of a nonhuman, a Myrdian) somehow caused it to blow up when He was enveloped by the protective spindizzy field. The tipping of He has another unexpected consequence; it causes the planet to leave its solar system and shoot across the Rift at "a speed that gulped down light years as if they were gnats" (p. 330). But after taking off from He, simultaneously with the tipping operation and the destruction of the bindlestiff, New York returns to the Milky Way. It will enter "about where the last few waves of the Acolytes settled" (p. 332).

The next three chapters of *Earthman, Come Home* originally appeared as "Sargasso of Lost Cities." Now that New York is well stocked with germanium, it should not be difficult to buy a new spindizzy to replace the defective 23rd Street one. An Okie jungle at the edge of the Acolyte cluster—more than 300 cities circling a dwarf star—suggests that the Acolytes are exploiting some kind of total economic collapse, but it is only after New York has landed on the garage world of Murphy that Amalfi learns that in 3900 the galaxy-wide germanium standard collapsed and that drugs are now the money standard. New York, like the galaxy, is broke. The Acolytes have impounded another city on Murphy, discovered to be "the so called all-purpose city" (p. 352), for the dirty job of setting up a planethead on "a Jupiter-type planet" (a second unobtrusive link between *Earthman, Come Home* and *They Shall Have Stars*) "as an inexhaustible source of poison gas" (p. 351). Thanks to special powers that the City Fathers of the two cities have in the event of "Standard Situation N" (p. 354), another magical plot maneuvre, Amalfi is able to implement Hazleton's suggestion that they hijack the all-purpose city. But after both cities have escaped Murphy and the local police, New York casts the other city loose and heads for the jungle.

Once in the dispiriting jungle, where the cities are graded into classes A, B, and C, Amalfi observes what happens when an Acolyte trader mentions an assignment on Hern VI which will require six cities. It appears that the bidding is controlled and a wage line maintained by the one bright city—Buda-Pesht, under the command of an 800-year-old Okie King, a cancer victim whose "face was shockingly disfigured and scarred by the disease that still remained unconquered, unsolved, though it no longer killed" (p. 363). Amalfi, Hazleton, Dee, and Sergeant Anderson visit Buda-Pesht, note the presence of an "archaic cantilever bridge" spanning an "avenue which divided the city in two" (p. 369) but served no practical use, and they confront the King of the hobos in the ancient "audience hall of the Hapsburgs" (p. 381). The bridge's function, obviously, is to remind the reader of the symbolic import of the bridge idea. For his own reasons, Amalfi pretends to be opposed to the King's planned march on Earth by as many Okie cities as care to participate; it is expected that Earth will agree to bail out its citizens. The call will go out on the Dirac. Hazleton is annoyed at not being clued in, and when Amalfi tells him that he also loves Dee, now Hazleton's wife, Hazleton demands to be put off at the next port of call. Amalfi's love for Dee does help to humanize the man but the revelation at this point appears to be part of his characteristic craftiness. Amalfi's plan involves telling police Lieutenant Lerner to expect an attack from the jungle cities while New York visits a C city; this poor city low on drugs and therefore plague-ridden, has offered cut-rate labor. Amalfi suggests stripping that city *and* the all-purpose city of its spindizzies, and heading for Hern VI. After a battle with the Acolytes, the cities flee the system and begin the march on Earth accompanied, without their knowledge, by New York's "big drone" (p. 396).

The idea is to mount Hern VI for spindizzy flight and catch up with the fleet of cities. Some five years later Hern VI takes off at incredible speed: "More than once Amalfi stood frozen on the balcony in the belfry of City Hall, watching a star that had been invisible half a second before cannoning directly at his head, swelling to fill the whole sky with glare" (p. 404). It appears that planets can travel much faster than cities because of their greater mass. The drone pilot has informed Amalfi that an unidentified city has joined the march. This city turns out to be the legendary Vegan fort seeking a way to strike at Earth under cover of the Okie march. Plot credibility is strained at this point. We are asked to believe that Amalfi had anticipated this last desperate Vegan maneuvre and that all his machinations have been geared towards using Hern VI to destroy the fort. When the cities arrive in the vicinity of Earth they come under attack from the Earth police. Thanks to the assistance of the Vegan fort, the Okies appear to be winning—until Amalfi arranges for the fort to impact with Hern VI. Shortly thereafter, New York, in poor shape (the 23rd Street spindizzy still needs repair), abandons Hern VI and the other Okie cities and heads for the Greater Magellanic Cloud in search of a permanent home.

In Spenglerian terms the "Lost Cities" chapters correspond to the substage of Revolution and Napoleonism, extending from 3900 until 3976. As Mullen explains, "When aristocratic factionalism has been suppressed [as in the Climax of State Form substage], the king [Earth] and the aristocracy [the colonials] become allies against the rising power of the bourgeoisie [the Okies], who soon become ripe for revolution, as do the Okies after the 'collapse of the germanium standard' in 3900." The Battle of Earth "can be regarded as the 1789, and the passage of the anti-Okie bill in 3976 as the 1815, of Earthman history."[27] 3976 marks the beginning of the final Civilization and Spiritual Winter stage of Earthmanist culture. For the rest of *Cities in Flight*, however, the reader's awareness is essentially confined to the divergent experience of one polyp of that culture: the New York Okies' working out of an unorthodox final Spenglerian phase.

Earthman, Come Home concludes with two chapters of finely orchestrated plotting that correspond to the story "Earthman Come Home," the story fleshed out from the rudimentary seed sketch that Campbell rejected. Knowing that the Greater Magellanic Cloud has already been partly colonized by bindlestiff cities, Amalfi decides to make an already inhabited planet New York's permanent home. As it turns out this world is under the control of the worst bindlestiff city of all—the Interstellar Master Traders. Nine of the original denizens of that city, who call themselves Proctors, lord it over a feudal native people who are actually descendants of early colonists from Earth. Heldon, one of the Proctors (his name is perhaps a contraction of Hari Seldon of Asimov's Foundation series), tells Amalfi that IMT would lose a confrontation with the technologically superior city of New York and claims that, if Amalfi and his men can help repair the IMT spindizzies, then IMT, Proctors and all, will quit the planet.

Only when Karst, one of the native serfs, sings a folk song about a legendary time when IMT made the sky fall does Amalfi realize what Heldon really has in mind.[28] He plans to use IMT to crush New York: "that old Laputa gag" (p. 449). This and Amalfi's consequent mention of "Dean Swift" to Heldon amount to Blish's acknowledgement of his debt to Swift for the flying city idea (p. 450). Amalfi takes advantage of an opportunity to sabotage the spindizzy controls and when IMT does take off, an ascent that is brilliantly described, it continues going right on up until the Earth police blast it out of the sky. The Proctors are here hoist by their own petard since they had alerted the Earth police to New York's arrival and warned them "to watch for an Okie city [i.e., New York] trying to make a getaway" (p. 464).

(v) The End of Earthmanist Culture: Bridge that Gap

After the superior space opera of *Earthman, Come Home*, *Cities in Flight* concludes with a masterpiece of serious SF, *The Triumph of Time*. Thus the unity of the tetralogy is considerably enhanced by the fact that both its opening and concluding volumes are accomplished rich works of unusual sophistication. The title, *The Triumph of Time*, whether or not it deliberately echoes that of Swinburne's 1862 poem or alludes to Spengler's "Time triumphs over space," is definitely to be preferred to the alternative English editon title, *A Clash of Cymbals*—albeit that image is twice invoked in *Cities in Flight* (pp. 318, 528) and the suggestion of a musical flourish does have the advantage of recalling the Wagnerian ambition of the tetralogy.[29] In the author's note to the English edition Blish points out that the original title resembled another SF title on Faber & Faber's list for that season—hence the changed title. (The similar title was Brian Aldiss's *The Canopy of Time*.) He goes on to mention that, had a magazine editor had his way, the original title might have been, absurdly, *The Augustinean Age* after a reference to St. Augustine (p. 511). As it happened, the first U.S. edition of the book (an Avon paperback) got into print too quickly to permit serialization.[30] It should also be noted that in a letter to John Baxter (Dep. Blish 411/10, 2 August 1962) Blish over generously credits Virginia Kidd with writing one third of *The Triumph of Time*.[31]

Like volumes 1 and 3 of the tetralogy, this volume is introduced by an extract from ACREFF-MONALES' *The Milky Way: Five Cultural Portraits*. In a historical summary thick with dates, we learn of some matters that have not been narrated—that Lieutenant Lerner became the Acolyte-Regent and subsequently proclaimed himself Emperor of Space in 3905 but that he died from "an overdose of wisdomweed" (p. 470) in a slum on Murphy shortly after the annihilation of the Acolyte fleet by the Earth police (p. 470). Other events are recalled:

> New York . . . left the galaxy by 3978 for the Greater Magellanic Cloud. It left behind an Earth which in 3976 cut its own throat as a galactic power with the passage of the so-called anti-Okie Bill. Though the Magellanic planet which New York colonized in 3998 was in 3999 christened New Earth, the earlier date of 3976 marks the passing of Earth from the stellar stage. (P. 471)

If a reader checks these dates against the dates in the Faber edition version of this passage (p. 15) and the Faber chonological table, he will discover that each of the Avon dates has been advanced about sixty years over each of the Faber dates: for example, the Battle of Earth originally occurred in 3913 and the anti-Okie Bill was passed in 3925—after, not before, Hern VI and New York leave the galaxy. This passage provides, in fact, the clearest indication of Blish's advancing all the dates in response to the most important inconsistency that Mullen had pointed out. Although Blish acknowledges this in a note to Mullen's afterword, it is necessary to go once again to the article from which the afterword was extracted in order to discover what the problem was.

Mullen had acutely noticed that if the march on Earth, covering a distance of 63,000 light years in the Faber edition of *Earthman, Come Home* (p. 184), was accomplished in the eight years between 3905 and 3913, then the cities must be able to "fly at eight thousand times the speed of light." Not only is this inconsistent with the earlier information "that the cities can fly little if any faster than five or six times the speed of light" but the lower speed is also essential to the ruling assumption "that interstellar commerce would be impossible without anti-death drugs."[32] Blish attempts to correct this major problem by altering the distance concerned to "sixty-three hundred or so light years" (p. 398), changing an originally estimated travelling time of fifty-five years (Faber, p. 188) to "one hundred fifty-five years" (p. 401), and having the trip take approximately seventy years instead of the original eight. As we have seen, the Okies arrive in 3975 instead of 3913.

As it happens, Blish does not actually mention any dates in the "Lost Cities" and "Okie" sections of *Earthman, Come Home*. It was, then, only necessary to look for dates that needed to be advanced in *The Triumph of Time*. Unfortunately these changes must have been made from memory at the last minute, and in the light of the revised chronology at least nine dating and numerical errors remain in the 1970 Avon text of *The Triumph of Time*.[33] The original chronology does offer one explanation of how a writer of Blish's mathematical fussiness originally calculated an impossible eight-year time span for the march on Earth, however. He had decided that the tetralogy and the universe as we know it were to end in the year 4004 by way of balancing Bishop Ussher's 1654 calculation that the year of creation was 4004 B.C. Blish may also have chosen this mirror number for its suggestion of double enclosure, an image perhaps of one circle within another. Thus the original date is consistent with and reinforces the theme of containment. The revised date, 4104, still expresses something of the same idea but less absolutely—and this, as we shall see, may be another of Blish's characteristic improving afterthoughts.[34]

It is 4101 when *The Triumph of Time* opens. Amalfi is bored with planet-bound life. The disproportionate amount of space "wasted" describing a popular "time-wasting" pet, "the half-plant, half-animal" svengali "from Altair IV," a passage contributed by Virginia Kidd, is symptomatic of a playful, lazy, spineless sentimentality that for Amalfi sums up life on New Earth (pp. 485, 486). His affection for Dee continues and we learn, in what is virtually the only reference to Amalfi's sex life, that he "was amazed to discover that she had taken into her household however briefly every companion whose bed he had honored during the officially celibate years" (p. 489). She would like to bear his child but he explains that, as a result of the centuries he has spent in space, his "germ plasm is damaged beyond hope" (p. 491). Amalfi can think only of death: "For a man, he knew, life is a process of dying, again and again . . ." (p. 492).

By way of counterpoint, there are the two youngsters, Webster ("Web"), the son of Dee and Mark Hazleton, and his friend, Estelle, the daughter of Jake Freeman, the astronomer. The juvenile interest provides a link with *A Life for the Stars* and helps augment a sense of the tetralogy's unity. But then there is an additional irony: the youth of Chris deFord parallels the youth of Earthmanist culture; it is the fate of Web and Estelle to be in at the death of both Earthmanist culture and the universe, although there is hope in the notion that the end of the universe coincides also with the moment of origin. In one way and another, Web and Estelle (and the games they play) provide a kind of symbolic reverberation which echoes major plot elements. The name "Estelle," for example, ties in with Jake's announcement that a new star has been discovered. The star turns out to be the planet He. Its inhabitants, having discovered how to control their planet's flight, are on their way to Earth to impart the bad news that an alien superculture known as the Web of Hercules is seizing control of the universe, and that, while in the Andromeda galaxy, the Hevians discovered that time is about to end. Web, then, points symbolically to the Web of Hercules just as Estelle points to the "star." Webster's name, in fact, might be construed as a contraction of both elements: Web-star.

Amalfi, in the company of Dee, Web, and Estelle, travels by ship to He and there they hear the bad news from Miramon's lips. There is more discussion and hypothesis in *The Triumph of Time* than overt action (something of a relief after the frenzied pace of *Earthman, Come Home*), and a good deal of sophisticated albeit bogus exposition ensues. The party decides to head for "the center of the metagalaxy, the hub of all the galaxies of space-time. It is only there, where all forces of the universe lie in dynamic balance, that anyone can hope to take any action to escape or to modify the end which is coming" (p. 508). There the monobloc will come into being, and if indeed there is an antimatter universe (as Paul Dirac theorized) related in some mysterious way to the material universe (something entailing a system of sixteen dimensions), then two very different universes would issue from the same monobloc. Questions about science and mysticism arise, culminating with the reference to "the scientifically oriented man who does not know that he too is as thoroughgoing a mystic as a fakir lying on a bed of nails" (p. 512). And references to "God" as "He" (pp. 511, 512) make for an interesting confusion with the planet He and suggest that He will act as God's stand-in when the apocalypse or Ragnorak (to recall Wagner's *Ring of the Nibelung*) occurs.

The coming event is compared specifically with the "Ginnangu-Gap [*sic*]" of "Scandinavian mythology" (p. 515), the term (previously used in "The Weakness of RVOG") that the author of *The Milky Way: Five Cultural Portraits* employs. Not only does the Scandinavian source accord with *The Ring of the Nibelung*, but as a Magic Void between a region of frost and mist and a region of heat where Earth was created, the Ginnunga-Gap also recalls the ice and fire imagery of volume 1. It is He that will attempt to cross, or bridge, this gap, just as He previously crossed another gap, the Rift. At this point something of the careful architectonic structure of *Cities in Flight* becomes clear. There are, in fact, four major "gaps" in *Cities in Flight*: (1) the "reality" gap (which masquerades as a temporal gap) between the world of the reader and the world of shadows with which the tetralogy opens, a gap which my opening discussion of "sources" attempts to bridge; (2) the temporal gap of more than 1,000 years between volumes 1 and 2, which Chris deFord's history lesson goes someway towards bridging; (3) the spatial gap of the Rift; and (4) the Ginnunga-Gap, which involves space, time, and reality. The transitional gap between Spenglerian cultures should also be considered. Here the gap relates specifically to the mystery of origin. Spengler's contention that the spirit of one culture does not survive into the next implies that a culture must originate from a realm of pure otherness, pure difference. The bridge symbolism with which the tetralogy opens is now to be related to the gap symbolism, "the problem of how to cross the information barrier of the coming Ginnangu-Gap [*sic*]" (p. 551).

Another aspect of the overall design of *Cities in Flight* should be noted. *They Shall Have Stars* leaves Earth but stays inside the solar system. *A Life for the Stars* leaves the solar system but not the galaxy. *Earthman, Come Home* leaves the galaxy but not the universe. That final departure from the universe itself occurs in *The Triumph of Time*.[35] Thus Blish conveys a sense of ever-widening horizons.

An experiment which involves sending an antimatter missile—"*Object 4101-Alephnull,*" aleph-null being the first transfinite number and therefore appropriate to the realm of antimatter—proves the existence of the antimatter universe and that some form of survival is possible. As it happens, a research team on New Earth has been at work on antimatter.[36] Just before its disappearance, the spindizzy-englobed missile looks like a "spherical smoke-wreathed ghost" (p. 557). Like the spindizzy-englobed flying cities, the spherical ghost may be analogically related to the enclosed cyclical process of history. This spherical ghost is then associated in Amalfi's mind with unidentified lines about the problem of origins: "I grow not out of salt nor out of soil/But out of that which pains me."[37] Readings of the "energy level on the other side" indicate that the present universe will end "on or around June second, year Four Thousand one hundred and Four" (p. 562). The missile also records evidence of another missile. The Web of Hercules also knows what Amalfi and the rest of the party know. Whoever gets to the monobloc area first will have the opportunity to imprint his, her, or whatever's consciousness, in some very mysterious fashion, on both the new universes of matter and antimatter.

But matters of more domestic interest intervene. Before Dee and the children are recalled to New Earth, Web and Estelle explore what used to be He's major bandit city and there play, in a passage that Virginia Kidd contributed, "an elaborate chess game called Matrix, rather like run-sheep-run combined with checkers except that it was three-dimensional, for it was played in a twelve-story building with transparent floors so that one could always see the position of the other players, and with strategically placed spindizzy and friction-field shafts for fast transmit from one floor to another" (p. 520). The relationships among the term "matrix" and the title of chapter 3, "The Nursery of Time," and the name Web and the Web of Hercules, make the game Matrix a symbolic analogy for the structure of both the tetralogy as a whole and *The Triumph of Time* in particular. After sleep-learning Hevian, Web and Estelle also play a game of truth and lies. This game provides a playful analogy for a strategy that Amalfi will use in dealing with a problem that has arisen on New Earth during his absence.

There has been mention in chapter 2 of a fundamentalist religion, the Warriors of God led by one Jorn the Apostle, gaining ground on New Earth, and an alternative "philosophical group called the Stochastics" concerned with constructing "a complete philosphy . . . using modern physics as the metaphysical base" (p. 487). Hazleton tells Amalfi that, although Jorn's main body of Warriors is nowhere near New Earth, Jorn plans to take control of the planet because Amalfi and the Hevians are "meddling with the pre-ordained Armageddon and jeopardizing their [the Warriors'] chances of salvation" (p. 536). Towards this end, the

Warriors take Dee, Web, and Estelle as hostages. However, thanks to his skill at the lying game, Amalfi, back on New Earth, scares Jorn with the story that New Earth "is a hotbed of stochasticism" (p. 545) and is able, with Hazleton's assistance, to give the impression that the local Warriors are being corrupted. The basically uncorrupt Jorn calls off his blockading fleet and tells his followers to return the three hostages, but not before telling Amalfi a few home truths: "I know well that you are fabulously inventive; but human lives should not hang upon the success of a work of art." But the "elaborate fiction" of Jorn's religion is also "a work of art" (p. 547). Thus the Hevian game of truth and lies, like the Matrix game, is associated with the art of *Cities in Flight*.

The editor with whom Blish was discussing the abortive magazine version of *The Triumph of Time* wanted to cut the Jorn material.[38] Although this material could be cut without any real damage to this one volume, such a cut would damage the design of the overall tetralogy. The Warriors correspond to the Believers of volume 1. As a manifestation of that Second Religiousness which presages the end of a culture, the Warriors are an indication that the Spenglerian substage of Caesarism is threatening to reign on New Earth as it reigned on the old Earth in volume 1, thereby following hard upon and displacing the previous substage, Transition from Napoleonism to Caesarism, manifested by the materialistic Stochastics.

Finally, with Amalfi, Mark and Dee Hazleton, Web and Estelle, and the New York City Fathers aboard, He heads for the metagalactic center. En route, the musical analogy re-emerges. Hazleton recalls the Stochastic teaching that the natural state of the universe was noise: "Touring the universe by ear alone . . . you would hear nothing but a horrifying and endless roar for billions of years; then a three-minute scrap of Bach which stood for the whole body of organized knowledge; and then the roar again for more billions of years."[39] Nevertheless, Amalfi and company attempt to impose some kind of human identity on the new universes of matter and antimatter that are expected to issue from the coming catastrophe, provided, of course, that the Web of Hercules does not beat He to the area of monobloc. The contest here amounts to a replay, on a much grander scale, of the climax of *Jack of Eagles* where Danny Caiden, ascending a "sigma-sequence" of alternate futures, ensures that the futures most favorable to the villain do not come into being. As it happens, the Web of Hercules, when it does arrive and manifest itself as "a sphere with a diameter of about a light year" englobing He, is quickly wiped out like a biological cancer thanks to Hevian science.[40] This last magical strategy in *Cities in Flight* is "explained" by the fact that Hevian sciences have progressed by leaps and bounds since the planet was first met with in *Earthman, Come Home*.

It now seems that more than two universes may be involved. According to Retma, a Hevian scientist: "Each one of us that makes that crossing [the Ginnunga-Gap at the metagalactic center] may in a few microseconds start a universe of his own, with a fate wholly unpredictable from history" (p. 578). By an act of individual volition it may be possible to create a universe which is not constrained by cyclical historical and cosmic processes. In any case, it seems to be a matter of "Everyman his own monobloc" (p. 593), or his own bridge. Five disparate meanings of the bridge concept are subtly alluded to as time moves towards its inevitable triumph, through references to (1) scientists playing "bad poker and worse bridge" and conducting post-mortems on "bridge hands" (p. 559); (2) "Tudor Tower Place, bridging 42nd Street" (p. 568); (3) Dee hitting Amalfi "on the bridge of the nose" (p. 568); (4) "the tenuous bridges of stars which connected the galaxies like umbilical cords—bridges" discovered "by Fritz Zworkyn in 1953" (p. 577)[41]; and (5) the Hevian "control bridge" where the "Survivors," anyone judged capable of following the instructions for the crossing, "met in almost continuous session" (p. 582). Thus the bridge symbolism in *Cities in Flight* takes on evermore enveloping possibilities.

It might be objected that, in the context of what overall is essentially pulp space opera, the kind of intricate verbal and symbolic structure epitomized by Blish's elaboration of the bridge concept (the kind of thing that academic critics generally approve) actually amounts to a weakness, a contrived overlay. To this extent, in attempting to combine SF and the qualities of literature, Blish found himself in a virtual no-win situation.

Just prior to the end of *The Triumph of Time* Amalfi "goes to the toilet" and sips at a sacramental glass of wine, acts of bodily elimination and replenishment that he will re-enact on a cosmic scale (p. 592). After everybody has suited up—here as in *A Case of Conscience*, an image of conceptual containment—Amalfi decides that he does not wish to create a universe which is simply another "version of the standard model." He wants to escape from sameness and identity into a realm of pure difference. By touching the detonation button "over his heart" while crossing the Ginnunga-Gap (p. 596), Amalfi hopes that any universe which issues from him will be completely unknowable, totally unaffected by his preconceptions and biases. The dyastolic and systolic action of the heart, it might be noted, provides a natural metaphor for

HISTORICAL MODELS

the successive expansions and collapses of the pulsating universe. Retma provides mankind with a characteristically Blishian epigraph: *"We did not have the time to learn anything that we wanted to know"* (p. 596).

Cities in Flight concludes with the words "Creation began" (p. 596). That another universe and another form of life did succeed the book's catastrophe we know from the introductory passages from *The Milky Way: Five Cultural Portraits* by ACREFF-MONALES. The Web of Hercules is referred to as "the Milky Way's IVth great civilization," although "culture" would be the more accurate Spenglerian term (p. 471). The Vegan and Earthmanist must have been the Milky Way's second and third great cultures. We have no way of knowing whose the first great culture was or whose the fifth, nor how many great cultures have intervened between the time of Amalfi and the time of ACREFF-MONALES. We know simply that in Amalfi's time "Only eleven non-human civilizations had ever been discovered," including the Lyran and the Myrdian but not the Vegan: "Earthmen did not think of them as human, but all non-human cultures did" (p. 321). The Hevians would count as one among numerous human civilizations.

ACREFF-MONALES points out that "it is due entirely to the Web of Hercules that we still have records of galactic history" before the Ginnunga-Gap and know about "the dramatic and fruitful exeunt" which the Earthmen "in this timeless moment of chaos and creation . . . wrote for themselves into the universal drama" (p. 471). What we are told about the destruction of the Web of Hercules cannot then be the complete story. Somehow this alien race was able to record everything and ensure that these records survived the Ginnunga-Gap.

Of Amalfi's own success at bridging the Gap there can be little doubt. The name ACREFF-MONALES is, in all likelihood, an anagram of AMALFE SON FORCE, or SON-FORCE AMALFE, if we are to make use of the hyphen. This anagram is obscured only slightly by the replacement of an "e" for the similarly sounded "i" of Amalfi. By the same token "son" can be read also as "sun." The universe of ACREFF-MONALES, whether it be composed of matter, antimatter, or something else, whether it be subject to cyclical process or not, derives from the sun-burst of Amalfi's heart.

But a cautionary coda is necessary here. It appears from the chronology appended to *Year 2018!* (the 1957 Avon edition of *They Shall Have Stars* that differs somewhat from the 1956 Faber edition because it takes account of events described in *Earthman, Come Home* [1955] and was thus the edition reprinted in *Cities in Flight* [1970]) that Blish had conceived of at least one different ending for his saga. There are three differences for the years A.D. 4000–4004 between this chronology which follows "section lll of Acreff-Monales's [the name is not in all capitals in this earlier text] *Milky Way: Five Cultural Portraits"* and the later Faber chronology. Of crucial importance is the event recorded for 4004. In place of Faber's "The Ginnunga-Gap," the earlier chronology has "Death of John Amalfi, in a hunting accident."[42] Apparently the end of the present universe was not part of Blish's original conception and thus he most probably originally conceived of ACREFF-MONALES as a future historian writing within the present universe. This does not, however, necessarily disprove my suggested anagram. Whether writing within this universe or a subsequent one, ACREFF-MONALES remains a transcendent figure who, one way or another, ensures Amalfi's transcendence. ACREFF-MONALES does this in his role of historian as well as, if my view of his reconceived location is correct, subsequently in his very being. Likewise, by means of his writings (which give reality to what otherwise would not exist) or, as reconceived, in his very being, ACREFF-MONALES represents a universe. In either event, the anagram would be appropriate.[43]

It should also be noted that after Blish had completed *The Triumph of Time* but before *A Life for the Stars* was written, Lester del Rey had broached Blish with his idea for a post-apocalyptic sequel to be entitled (after T. S. Eliot) "After Strange Gods." It seems that the City Fathers, according to del Rey's conception (as relayed to Gregory Feeley), were to have survived the collapse of the universe. It is probably just as well that this potential fifth *Cities in Flight* volume was never written, indeed never seriously entertained. It does, however, allow for one further speculation? Is ACREFF-MONALES some kind of super computer?

SEVEN

"EXPLOSIVE DOCTRINE": Doctor Mirabilis

With *Doctor Mirabilis* (1964) James Blish proved conclusively that he could write a novel of artistic value that was not science fiction. Blish himself believed it to be his finest novel and a significant number of the book's few readers have agreed with him. As will become apparent, I have some reservations and suspect that Blish's own high opinion derived to some extent both from a sense of hubristic identification with the subject of his book, Roger Bacon, and from the effort and pain that went into its composition and eventual publication.[1] *Doctor Mirabilis*, like *A Torrent of Faces*, is a testament to Blish's tenacity. It is also one of Blish's few novels originally conceived and executed as such without prior piecemeal publication.

(i) Writing and Rewriting

According to a publicity questionnaire completed for the work's first publishers, Faber & Faber, *Doctor Mirabilis* was begun in 1958 (Dep. Blish 406/5). A first draft was finished in late March 1961, a revision in mid-1963. At one time *Doctor Mirabilis* was intended to be the first in a series of novels about important scientists like Tycho Brahe, Paracelsus, and Ernst Haeckel. But the only projected title in this sequence that Blish did any real work on, "the next historical novel," was "Glass Night" "set in the Venetian Republic during the Borgia pontificate."[2] There were at least three different drafts of the Bacon book and a succession of titles—"The Brass Head," "The Magician," or "The/A Leaven of Power"—before Blish settled on the title conferred on Bacon by his contemporaries and subsequent admirers. Doubtless one of his reasons for scrapping the title "The Brass Head" was his discovery that

Photo of "James Blish at Roger Bacon," the Hope-Pinker statue outside the University Museum, Oxford, taken by Judith Lawrence Blish, 1965 (Dep. Blish 406/2)

John Cowper Powys had published an idiosyncratic novel on Roger Bacon entitled *The Brazen Head* (1956). Furthermore, unlike Powys, Blish wished to recreate not the legendary Roger Bacon but, as far as humanly possible given the scanty documentation, the historical figure. The story of the brass head, as Blish points out in his foreword, is part of the Bacon legend. Derived from an ancient Arabic legend, it was attached to Albertus Magnus before Robert Greene made Bacon the head's creator in his play *Friar Bacon and Friar Bungay* (1589-90?).

In his attempt to bring the *real* Roger Bacon to life, Blish read everything about the man that he could find, including Stewart C. Easton's *Roger Bacon and His Search for a Universal Science* (1952) and E. Lutz's "Roger Bacon's Contribution to Knowledge." Blish relied most heavily on the Easton book, as he acknowledges in the concluding notes section. But as he points out in the foreword and in three factual articles on Roger Bacon, there is precious little historical documentation enabling scholars to distinguish fact from hearsay. For this reason Blish classifies *Doctor Mirabilis* not as "fictionalized biography" but as "fiction," a combination of historical data about the thirteenth century and "a vision" of the man.[3]

As for Blish's three factual articles, the earliest, "The Shadowy Figure of Roger Bacon," was published in *Science World* in 1959. After pointing out that Bacon invented the term "experimental science," discovered gunpowder (in the West at least), and favored mathematics over the other sciences, Blish allows that Bacon was a spiteful, hot-tempered, envious man who made many enemies. Nevertheless "his studies compel us to ask the hard philosophical question: *How do we know what we know—and how do we test it?*"[4] "The Invention of Science" is an expanded version of the 1959 article for the collection *Adventures in Discovery* (1969). Here Blish points out (as in his foreword to *Doctor Mirabilis*) that a 1266 letter from Pope Clement IV is virtually the only contemporary document that mentions Roger Bacon by name. The *Opus Tertium* in the Vatican, with Bacon's corrections in the margin, provides the only samples we have of his handwriting. By way of emphasizing Bacon's brilliance and importance, Blish observes that after inventing the theory of sets in one paragraph, in the next "you find him laying down the postulates of what we now call general relativity."[5]

"The Strange Career of Doctor Mirabilis," which appeared in the *Australian SF Review* (1967), was written in response to a query about the novel from John Bangsund, the *Review*'s editor. Here, aside from detailing his problems with the American copyright law, Blish provides information of particular interest to the readership of SF fanzines. Bacon is important because he attempted to invent theoretical physics four centuries too early. The notes to *Doctor Mirabilis* elaborate: "the whole tissue of the space-time continuum of general relativity is a direct descendant of Roger's assumption in *De multiplicatione specierum* and elsewhere, that the universe had a metrical frame, and that mathematics thus is in some important sense real, and not just a useful exercise" (p. 333). A subsequent footnote credits Bacon with inventing a way of thinking rather than any specific theory: "the theory of theories as tools" (p. 334). The readers of the *Australian SF Review* are further informed that "the historical novel is a natural second medium for the 'hard' SF writer."[6] Of course *Doctor Mirabilis* is also SF in the most literal sense: it is a work of fiction about science and about a scientist.

There are also, in fact, three particular aspects of *Doctor Mirabilis* which might be related to SF: the emphasis on change, the alien background, and the theme of conceptual breakthrough (SF writers also use theories as tools). One reviewer charged, whether in admiration or exasperation, that Blish makes the thirteenth century as remote as Mars.[7] Actually Blish made the thirteenth century considerably more alien than he need have. For whatever reasons, Blish chose not to make the historical background totally comprehensible. A reader of the three-paragraph *Encyclopedia Britannica* entry on Henry III, who was king of England during much of Bacon's lifetime, will have a much clearer idea of what was going on in England than the otherwise ignorant reader of Blish's book alone. Too much of the history comes across as "worked up," as, to some extent, does the character of Bacon himself. The indirect and sketchy presentation of historical material is laborious and often confusing, all the more so since so many of the people involved are inadequately characterized.

At the same time, the intensive process of revision that the successive versions of the manuscript went through and the differences between the English edition and the long-delayed American edition of *Doctor Mirabilis* have much to do with Blish's attempt to clarify matters and get to the novel's "real center." All but the first chapter "(about 5,000 words)" of a first "25,000 words" draft was thrown out because

> I realized that I'd been going away from what the book had to be about. . . . About three quarters of the way through the new try, I found I'd drifted away from the center again even more drastically, and though this time I didn't have to put as much of it into the wastebasket as I had the first time, a whole year went by before I located the fatal misstep and was able to resume work on it. (KLA, 13 January 1973)

Four years later he submitted his first complete version of *Doctor Mirabilis* (i.e., "The Brass Head," etc.) first to Putnam's, who dropped the option they had taken on the basis of the 25,000 words of the first draft plus an outline of the rest (KLA, 18 February 1973), then to a large number of other American publishers and solicited the interest of as many more. Dep. Blish 416/1 contains letters of rejection, either partial or absolute, from the following publishers: Athenaeum, Crowell, Dial, Harcourt Brace & World (who rejected the manuscript three times), Houghton-Mifflin, Lippincott, Kroft, Macmillan, Putnam's, Rinehart, and William Morrow & Co. In all it was rejected by 23 American publishers (KLA, 18 February 1973). The consensus seemed to be that the manuscript was worthy but too difficult and scholarly. It would not sell.

Finally, "The Magician" was submitted to Faber & Faber in England. The response was on balance positive but substantial revisions were called for. Blish subsequently recalled that

> Faber & Faber sent me both . . . readers' reports. Never in my entire publishing history have I ever seen anything even remotely like these reports. They were analyses in depth, done with knowledge and care, in detail and at considerable length. . . . Both reports were enormously valuable to me, and to the novel. Faber assigned as my particular editor on this project an absolutely searing fireball . . . who in effect sat down across the ocean with me and went through the book practically line by line to get it into what we both agreed ought to have been its shape in the first place. No editor I have ever worked with over here, with one shining exception [John W. Campbell?], has shown so much initial understanding of what it was that I had set out to do, plus so enormous a technical grasp of why I hadn't succeeded in doing it.[8]

One of the readers was Brian Aldiss, who "also commented on two later drafts—the final one of which got published."[9] In his first, largely adverse, report Aldiss describes the manuscript as "long and discursive" and "crabbed." Since the story is complicated enough told in chronological order, he objects to Blish's "doubling back" in chapters 4 and 9 (a criticism which Blish successfully countered). Overall, "It's a herringbone, full of good sharp points, but without nourishment" (CM 51). The second report was by somebody Blish described as the "Mystery Expert."[10]

The editor with whom Blish was so impressed, Ann Corlett (previously Ann Faber), is among the people whom Blish eventually acknowledged in the book's foreword. But even Corlett, who earned £15 for editing *Doctor Mirabilis*, describes the manuscript in her July 1962 internal report as "an extremely interesting sinker" (CM 51). Corlett believed the manuscript was too long and objected to aspects of the plot involving the Franciscan Adam Marsh, in particular his relationship with the King's sister, Eleanor of Pembroke, and with Bacon. The Mystery Expert had pointed to the lack of historical basis for the love affair. In fact all three readers wanted this element cut but Corlett came around to recommending clarification and information about the tradition of courtly love. Questions also arose about Blish's undervaluing thirteenth-century money (noted by the Mystery Expert), about why Bacon became a Franciscan, and the amount of political background contained by the manuscript.

Faber & Faber published *Doctor Mirabilis* in 1964 to generally respectable reviews expressing a muted enthusiasm. But still no American publisher was interested. In 1967 Blish noted with anxiety in "The Strange Career of Doctor Mirabilis" that he had to get the work published in the U.S. before 1970 or his ad interim copyright would run out and the book would go into the public domain; "before I let that happen I will publish it myself."[11] Thanks to a further peculiarity of the American copyright law, he would also lose the copyright if more than 1,500 copies of the Faber edition were imported into the U.S. In 1968 he did publish his own American edition, a mimeographed text of the Faber edition. By sending copies to members of the James Branch Cabell Society and elsewhere (with the aid of Richard E. Geis), Blish circulated the required 250 copies, ensured his retention of the American copyright, and recovered his costs. After all this trouble an American publisher did express an interest. Following a further process of revision, the second American edition of *Doctor Mirabilis* was published by Dodd, Mead & Company in 1971.

In the "Preface to the American Edition," written in England—"Now that the novel had come back to America . . . I have moved to Britain"—Blish points out that "Technically, the present book is the second American publication" and describes three changes (pp. vi, v). (1) Reviewers had complained about the amount of Latin in the Faber text. Half of that was translated for the American edition. Every Latin passage that remains, Blish assures the reader in a footnote, "is a direct quotation from the writing of the man who speaks it." (2) A G. N. Gabbard of the University of Nevada corrected many of Blish's bungled attempts "to preserve the glories of Middle English syntax" (p. v). (3) Additional details about English history and geography, such as the location of Ilchester, were restored for American readers (p. 32). There are a number of further changes which Blish does not mention. For example, "swink" and its variants are changed to "work" and its variants, and the not especially apposite epigraphs from Roger Bacon, E. R. Eddison's *The Worm Ouroboros*, Bernard of Chartres, and Maurice Maeterlinck are dropped.[12] Blish takes advantage of this preface to thank the "Mystery Expert," whom he identifies as "the late

Alfred Duggan" (p. vi). Blish had wrongly guessed at Mycroft Holmes as the expert but later he guessed correctly (CM 51, 27 August 1961; 26 March 1963).

The Dodd, Mead & Company edition of *Doctor Mirabilis* is indisputably the final authoritative one and the commentary that follows here, which results from a reading of both the English and second American editions, is based on the latter text. Unfortunately, the paperback editions of the work in both England and America reproduce the Faber text.[13]

Like the Faber edition, the Dodd, Mead edition is dedicated to "Virginia" (Kidd) and includes a foreword, a three-page "Argument" or table of contents which includes archaic, teasing, brief chapter descriptions, a list of "Dramatis Personae in order of their appearance" which precedes the text, and a notes section which follows it. The foreword's "word about language" identifies the three languages which combine to make up *Doctor Mirabilis*: (1) Latin, largely to indicate the authenticity of certain startlingly modern statements; (2) a synthetic Middle English used when characters are speaking Middle English; and (3) essentially modern English for passages "where they are speaking French or Latin, which is most of the time" (p. x).

The book is divided into four parts. If it is "a vision" (p. ix), as the foreword styles it, it is a fourfold vision, perhaps like the four stories that make up *The Seedling Stars*, the four books that make up *Cities in Flight*, and the four works (including *Doctor Mirabilis*) that will be seen as making up "After Such Knowledge." There are sixteen chapters of which the first eight are divided equally between parts 1 and 2. Thereafter the symmetry is disrupted, even as Bacon's life was disrupted by a thirteen-year incarceration. Part 3 consists of six chapters and part 4, which begins with the period of incarceration, consists of two. Bacon's movements to a new home in Oxford, then to Paris, Tivoli, and the Ancona cell—provide a suitably logical principle for the division into four parts.

(ii) Oxford and After

The four parts of *Doctor Mirabilis* are each given Chaucerian titles. Part 1 (or "Implicit Prima Pars") is entitled "Forth, Pylgryme, Forthe!" ("Truth: Balade de Bon Conseyl," line 18). Roger, the metaphorical pilgrim, is a student at Oxford. Chapter 1, "Folly Bridge," opens with the calculated association of death and a bridge. The plague has "come north across Folly Bridge into Oxford. . . ." Death, omitted from the "Dramatis Personae," is to become a principal actor in the book and this bridge is every bit as symbolically significant as the bridge on Jupiter at the beginning of *Cities in Flight*. Only "the enclave of the Jewerye" is affected by the plague and thus the astrologer's prediction "that the city would be at peace throughout the whole of A.D. 1231" and that there would certainly "not be another pestilence . . . in October, when Jupiter, Venus and the moon would be in trine before All Hallows Eve" (p. 3) is apparently vouchsafed. Ever factually fastidious, Blish had written to the director of the Hayden Planetarium to confirm that Jupiter and Venus were in fact in trine in the October of 1231. However, the reply indicates that Blish did not pinpoint the problem sufficiently for a definite answer (Dep. Blish 416/3).

A schizophrenic Roger is introduced debating with his inner self: "he had learned to distinguish the [aphoristic] prompting of his self from the general tumult of emotions which stormed tormentingly out of his soul the instant he started awake" (p. 3). It gradually becomes clear that this inner voice, which Blish makes considerable use of in building up his protagonist's character, amounts to the symbolic equivalent of the brazen head that legend, however wrongly, has persisted in associating with Roger Bacon. The inner voice will later be referred to as the demonic "thing with the bodiless voice" (p. 113). After the information that "its distant soundless voice was as terrible as the strikes of a gong of brass" (p. 158), Roger experiences a vision in which the self appears as a cowled head "burning as it were of brass in a furnace" (p. 159). An earlier reference describes a notion entering Roger's "floating, nearly detached head" (p. 81), the effect of a stinking miasma in his cell at Westminster.

The Franciscan Adam Marsh has summoned the seventeen-year-old Roger to what appears to be the deathbed of Robert Grosseteste, Bishop of London and lector to the Franciscans in theology at Oxford. Grosseteste is a victim of the plague, and Marsh, his favorite student, is now his confessor. In the pitch-black, cold corridor of the Franciscan school Roger recalls standing by the bedside of his dying father. Roger is imaged as being imprisoned "inside a black box" (p. 4) until the door of Grosseteste's room "opened a little, letting a wedge of smoky orange light into the corridor" (p. 5). Thus the theme of conceptual breakthrough is pictorially anticipated as is the thirteen-year period of Bacon's literal imprisonment towards the end of his life in a dark cell admitting only a fluctuating patch of light. When admitted to Grosseteste's presence, Roger tells him of his ambition to teach the heretical Aristotle at Oxford, an ambition which the intimidating Grosseteste encourages.

In the first of several flashbacks, the reader learns that a letter received earlier the same day has informed Roger that his house has been taken over by Hubert de Burgh, "the King's justiciar," who ruled for him during his minority (p. 8). In effect Roger's house has been destroyed like the "extinguished knowledge" of the palimpsest—the "oval-rubbed spot in the center" where the new message has been written (p. 7). Roger is now poor although his father had buried money and Roger had buried objects of personal value about the estate. The present message directs Roger to seek out Wulf, a serf of the Bacon estate, at the Oxen inn.

Blish has rather too much complicated information to impart in this opening chapter and the archaic language does not make the reader's task any easier. Blish does indicate that Yeo Manse, the Bacon residence near Ilchester, Somerset, "in the valley of the Yeo River" (p. 32) and Roger's birthplace according to the version of the Bacon legend which Blish chooses to follow, has been despoiled because that part of the country was a source of "French sedition"; but nowhere does Blish explain how the French became so influential in thirteenth-century England. This aspect of the novel must seem particularly bizarre to someone who does not know his English history and who might well believe the setting to be an SF parallel world. The reader needs to know that many of the barons had become so disaffected with King John, the father of the present Henry III, that they threw in their lot with prince Louis of France (later Louis VIII) who, as a result, came to control much of eastern England until "the evacuation of the French in 1217" (p. 8).

In chapter 2, "Northover," Roger, relieved that Grosseteste is recovering, leaves Oxford in November to gauge the situation at Yeo Manse, which is in the parish of Northover. On the way he journeys through Salisbury Plain where he meets William Bushe, a wool merchant who has done business with the Bacons. Bushe tells him that a knight of the justiciar, Will of Howlake, is in charge of Yeo Manse. While observing Yeo Manse at a safe distance—if questioned he would "feign to be a golliard" (p. 34)[14]—Roger reflects on "the Heraclitean river—not the Yeo, but a much more drastic Meander—[which] flowed in an underground torrent beneath Yeo Manse, too, as under all things else" (p. 38). *"We shall not all die*, the self murmured; *but* [echoing a line from *VOR* and *A Torrent of Faces*] *we shall all be changed"* (p. 39;

emphasis in original). And thus is announced the theme of change which goes hand in hand with that of death in Blish's narratives.

Whatever philosophy of history may be abstracted from *Doctor Mirabilis* depends mainly upon the medieval image of the Wheel of Fortune; but the reference to Heraclitus may have something to do with the fact that he was the subject of a doctoral thesis by Oswald Spengler, whose system of cultural cycles Blish accepted. There may be, then, some point in placing Roger Bacon's lifetime (1214–1292) in terms of Spengler's scheme. Three summarizing charts conclude volume 1 of *The Decline of the West*. According to "Table I: 'Contemporary' Spiritual Epochs," the thirteenth century belongs to the second stage of Spring and is characterized by the "Earliest Mystical-Metaphysical Shaping of the New World-Outlook." According to "Table II: 'Contemporary' Cultural Epochs," the thirteenth century is part of the "Early Gothic Period of Culture" (900–1500). And according to "Table III: 'Contemporary' Political Epochs," the thirteenth century belongs to the second stage of the "Early Period of pre-Civilization Culture" characterized by "crisis and dissolution of patriarchal forms" and a movement "From Feudalism to aristocratic State."[15]

As per the letter, Roger meets Wulf at the Oxen Inn. It turns out that Wulf has retrieved the money that Roger's father buried. He hands over what remains, some £2,000, to Roger. On the way back to Oxford, Roger wakes from a standing sleep against a tree to find a girl on horseback looking down on him. She is a peasant girl named Tibb. Shortly thereafter they make love and she takes him to her uncle's inn. She is, in fact, a whore and at the inn she and her associates attempt unsuccessfully to rob Roger. This lively episode is extraneous to the main plot development and its function may seem obscure. Blish points out, in his concluding notes, that Tibb, like Wulf, Otto (a gaoler) and Johann Budrys (a clerk) are "invented characters" (p. 331). The episode does serve to explain Roger's distrust and perhaps dislike of women. When Adam Marsh later attempts to set Roger up with "a brash tiring-wench" Roger exclaims, "They are all thieves and whores, to the Last Judgment" (pp. 82, 83). But, more significantly perhaps, the pleasure and pain that Roger experiences with Tibb makes her an analogue for that whore Fortune. Change in *Doctor Mirabilis* takes the form of sudden reversals. One day's rise is counterbalanced by the next day's fall. On his deathbed one day, the next sees Grosseteste very much alive—reborn, in fact—and bound for greater glory.

Roger must be about nineteen years old in 1233 when chapter 3,

"Beaumont," takes place. This is the first of four chapters which exist mainly to provide historical background. Here, as elsewhere, the historical information is imparted rather too obtrusively. King Henry III is at Beaumont palace (near Oxford) for the hunting season. The king is about to turn on Hubert de Burgh, now a victim of Fortune's wheel. An accommodation with the French is underway. Adam Marsh, who speaks French and is present to help with the proceedings, has brought his "familiar" (p. 53), Roger. After speaking to the widowed Eleanor of Pembroke (the sister of the king and the niece of Hubert de Burgh, whose side she takes) and encouraging her alliance with the French favorite, Simon de Montfort, Adam returns to the King's presence in time to hear Roger's brazen advice to the monarch. The answer to Roger's riddle, "What is most dangerous to sailors?"—namely, "Stones and rocks"—is a coded warning against the influence of Peter des Roches, the French Bishop of Winchester who is Henry's tutor (p. 65). This is the episode that Blish mentions in his foreword as appearing "in one of the footnotes to Matthew Paris's *Chronica majora*, but few modern scholars believe that this anecdote can refer to *the* Roger Bacon" (p. viii). Here, then, Blish chooses to ally himself with the minority opinion. Matthew Paris, the Benedictine historian to Henry III, will appear shortly in Blish's narrative.

The chapter concludes with Henry thrice summoning the dissident barons, who might be lead in revolt by Hubert de Burgh, "to attend us at Westminister" on "July eleventh," 1234, and with an image of Fortune's wheel: Roger is reminded that "John Blund . . . had been raised this year and cast down as Archbishop of Canterbury in a single six-month" (p. 66).

It is July 1236 in chapter 4, "Westminister." Three years have passed. Thanks to Grosseteste, Roger has been invited to Oxford "to write a work on the postponing of old age" for the chancellor of the University of Paris.[16] If worthy, it might even be sent to the Pope. "[M]uch had changed in Roger's world, as it had in the world at large . . . [and] the decision the changes were forcing on him could not be delayed much longer" (pp. 67–68). Roger is now a popular teacher of Aristotle at the University of Oxford but Grosseteste, about to become the Bishop of Lincoln, wants Roger to teach Aristotle at the restored University of Paris.

Most of chapter 4 is taken up with a flashback to the April of 1235. Roger is with Adam at Westminster Hall, London, to attend the king's parliament. Adam has taken a more active political role since Grosseteste's illness. There is a certain amount of historical background to be filled in. Adam, but not the summoned earls and barons, had attended the "King's proclaimed parliament" in July 1234 (p. 76). The rebellion of Richard Earl-Marshal, in league with de Burgh, which resulted in the indecisive Battle of Monmouth, followed shortly thereafter. Assigned a stinking cell at Westminster, Roger stuffs the window with bedding, clothing, and straw to see if he can catch a rat. When later Roger carries a torch into his room there is an explosion which causes the door to slam "against his forehead. The slam was like a summary of all the thunderclaps since creation" (p. 84). This is the first of two explosions in *Doctor Mirabilis*. The second will be deliberate since this first explosion, which provides the climax of part 1, will lead to Roger's discovering how to make gunpowder. But for the moment Roger is ready to believe that "A demon had come to breathe the poisoned air in very truth." As a result of the explosion, "The air was flocculent with fine fingerlings of falling soot" (p. 85). This arch, somewhat florid sentence is inserted with a purpose. When next the word "flocculent" is used (p. 141), Blish will expect the reader to recall this episode.[17]

The next day the king in the High Chamber sides with the barons against the French. Roger meets Simon de Montfort, who advises him to have a word about his work in progress with Guy de Foulques, the papal legate who happens to be present. And there, this, the second major flashback, ends. Since then Hubert de Burgh and the nobles have become reconciled with the king, Richard Earl-Marshal having died as the result of treachery. Simon de Montfort and Eleanor are to be married and Roger is to go to Paris.

(iii) Paris and After

Part 2 (or "Sequitur Pars Secunda") is entitled "To Ferne Halwes" ("General Prologue" to *The Canterbury Tales*, line 14, meaning "to distant shrines"). Its first chapter, chapter 5, "Straw Street," opens in 1237 with Roger crossing the English Channel in the boat of William Bushe, the wool merchant met with in chapter 2. Unlike the safe crossing of a mild river made possible by Folly Bridge, the image with which part 1 opens, this crossing of troubled waters makes Roger seasick.

The narrative jumps three years to an evocative description of a filthy Paris. Roger shares a room on Straw Street with Johann Budrys of Livonia, a clerk. Budrys, it will be recalled, is one of the invented characters. He is named, of course, for the Lithuanian-born SF writer,

Algis [Algirdas] Jonas Budrys, whose help Blish acknowledges in his foreword. Roger is to be examined before the new chancellor of the university and after his inception he will teach at the university. He is examined by his master in Paris, Albertus Magnus, on the possibly heretical pronouncements of Aristotle: "everything depended upon whether the sinner were single and indivisible, or in himself a little Hell and Heaven of warring factions, all originally from God, all at odds now" (p. 114). To some degree Roger can speak from experience here and he easily bests Albertus Magnus.

Meanwhile, back in England, chapter 6 takes up the historical background. It is the second such foggy chapter and is entitled "The Charnwood Hills" in which, "nine miles from Leicester," is the hunting lodge where Simon de Montfort entertains Adam Marsh (p. 125). Adam is beset with the burdens of political office and, the reader is sneakily given to understand, in love with the king's sister, Eleanor of Pembroke. She, however, does marry Simon and thus the Frenchman, subsequently dubbed Earl of Leicester, is allied with the crown, in spite of the disapproval of the mob. After all, with the queen barren, Eleanor's child "might one day inherit the throne" (p. 125). On 1 November 1238, All Saints' Day, "the greatest comet since Hastings" makes an appearance. Adam who "had no superstitious horror of comets" knew

> They were simply bodies of earthly fire which, because of an affinity for one of the fixed stars, had been sublimated and drawn into the sublunar heavens, there to share the motion of the star that had called them up. But it followed from this that on the earth there would be an infirmity or corruption in the men, plants and animals over which that star principally moved.
>
> And the stars in the tail of the Dragon ruled those who ordered their lives by princes. (P. 135)

This passage achieves a telling mix of knowledge and superstition.

By the time of chapter 7, "The Camp of Pallas," three more years have passed and Roger is a member of the secret college of Peter the Peregrine. Roger has become thoroughly disillusioned with Albertus Magnus, who lacks any "organon of knowledge" and who, it was rumored, "had built himself by arts magical a head made of brass, which could answer any questions proposed by man" (pp. 145, 146). In "The Shadowy Figure of Roger Bacon," Blish explains that a peregrine was a man who had been to the Holy Land and that Peter, a noble of Picardy, was the only man of that time, aside from Bacon, who worked from nature rather than books.[18] "Peter was a mathematician" and the inventor of a fourth science, "a science of the whole of experience, as distinguished from theory alone . . . it was a *scientia experimentalis*" (pp. 147, 148). A clerk, Raimundo (or Raymond) del Rey, based, as Blish points out in his final notes, on two separate historical figures (p. 331) but probably named for SF writer Lester del Rey, who taught Arabic to Roger, also introduced him to Peter's circle. Roger tells Peter that he has tested the "belief that diamonds cannot be broken except by goat's blood," a belief referred to earlier and found to be untrue (pp. 140, 24). Roger subsequently offers to sell the diamond and the goat that he bought for the experiment. The "goat with a rag tied around one foreleg . . . stinks, and munches the straw from my bed directly beside my ear while I'm trying to sleep" (p. 141). Later the goat is discovered "chewing upon a book" (p. 153). Blish had mentioned this experiment in the 1959 article, "The Shadowy Figure of Roger Bacon," with the result that it formed the subject of the illustration accompanying the article. But it was apparently this illustration which caused Blish to include the goat in his novel.[19]

During an alchemical experiment by Raymond with sweet vitriol, the fumes bring back to Roger "the thudding *flocculent* memory of the explosion at Westminster" (p. 141; emphasis added). The odor of the vitriol has an adverse effect on Roger and he falls asleep. He shortly awakes, however, to a vision analogous to, or microcosmic of, that which Blish claims *Doctor Mirabilis* as a whole to be. The impact of Roger's recovery here from a kind of death echoes that of the similar Grosseteste episode. Feeding into the vision is Roger's reading of *The Secret of Secrets*, "a letter to Alexander the Great from his teacher Aristotle" about "the secrets of the sciences" (p. 154). Roger had read this book, a gift from John of Livonia, on the day after he had bested Albertus Magnus. Now, his head still affected by the vitriol fumes, Roger hears a voice—his demonic self—announce, *"Thou art the man, shalt bring back into the world the* scientia universalis" (p. 157; emphasis in original). A candle expires and out of the darkness arises a vision of Armageddon, later to be reflected in *Black Easter*, which consists of a demon army lead by the Antichrist opposed by a cowled figure whose head burns "as it were brass"; presumably the latter is the self. The army is destroyed when the cowled figure wrapped "crystals like saltpeter . . . in a scrap of parchment . . . and cast it into the wind, crying,"

LUPU LUPU VOPO VIR CAN UTRIET VOARCHADUMIA
TRIPSARECOPSEM (P. 159)

Eventually Roger will decipher this coded message and discover how to make gunpowder. In the meantime he resolves to become "a scientist *instead of* a theologian" (p. 162; emphasis in original).

Also in the meantime, in the world outside a new pope, Innocent IV, has been chosen. He has rescinded the "acts of absolution of the Paris masters who lectured on the books of nature," acts issued by the previous pope, Gregory. Thus "the darkness was coming back" (p. 162). Roger resolves to return to Paris by way of Rome and further resolves to "join the Franciscans who are rich in learned men, for only strict sanctity of life can foster the philosophy, and thenceforward shall I be poor in Christ" (p. 165). As I have indicated, it is this decision that Blish's editor, Ann Corlett, believed to be inadequately explained. But Blish was simply being true to our shaky historical knowledge. The chapter concludes with the first appearance of a beggar named John the Pilgrim, who claims to be carrying the bowl of Belisarius, "that most famous of all begging bowls which had been freighted once with tears from the blinded eyes of the last general to defend Rome from the infidels." Roger, as asked, gives a penny. In response John the Pilgrim says, "I'll will thee my relict" (p. 166). In a letter to a Putnam's editor, Lois Dwight Cole, Blish explains that John is "a portentous figure who appears in Roger's life at moments of crisis, rather like Wotan's ravens" (Dep. Blish 416/3, 25 August 1959).

"The Camp of Pallas" is a most effectively structured and accomplished chapter. The following chapter, "Kirkby-Maxloe," the third chapter devoted mainly to developing the historical background, is something of a letdown. Generally, whenever the book moves away from Roger the narrative becomes somewhat contrived and murky. Kirkby-Moxloe is the site of Simon de Montfort's castle, which is chosen in 1246 as a secret meeting place for the king and Simon. Adam Marsh and Edmund Rich, Archbishop of Canterbury, are also present. In the wake of the passage of the "Lateran edicts against heresy" and papal bulls giving the Dominicans the "authority to condemn heretics without appeal" (pp. 168–69), the king is alarmed that "the Inquisition was already reaching into England" (p. 169) through the particular agency not of a Dominican but a Franciscan: Robert Grosseteste. The debate concerning what to do about Grosseteste, who has thwarted one of the king's religious appointments, is recorded by court historian Matthew Paris. This "thin sallow grey-haired man with a pointed nose, . . . with inkpot and quills before him" might also be a stand-in for Blish, the writer of historical fiction (p. 173). It is eventually decided that the Sheriff of Lincoln will "serve a writ upon Grosseteste, requiring this Bishop to show forth upon what grounds lay persons of his diocese are forced to take oaths against their wills" (p. 186).

Adam sits next to Eleanor at the midday meal, an occasion when she indicates her knowledge that Adam loves her. Simon asks Adam about Roger and is told that he has joined the Franciscans in spite of the fact that "he is arrogant, disputatious, impatient, cold of mien, condemnatory. . . . Not my first election for a man of God" (p. 188). In a letter to Lois Dwight Cole, Blish had agreed that Roger is "not likeable" (Dep. Blish 416/3, 25 August 1959). Adam also reveals that Roger is to return to Oxford "as regent master in Aristotle," by Adam's own appointment (p. 188).

(iv) Tivoli and After

Part 3 ("Sequitur Pars Tercia") is entitled "Of Hem That Yaf Hym Wherwith to Scoleye" (from the description of the Clerk in the "General Prologue" to *The Canterbury Tales*, line 302). Chapter 9, "Villa Piccolomini," opens with Roger returning from Italy but the chapter almost immediately switches to a prolonged flashback describing his residence there. At first Roger stayed in a Franciscan monastery in Rome; among the features of the city that Blish mentions is a bridge, "the Pons Aemilius," which recalls the symbolism of death (literal or metaphorical) associated with change established by Folly Bridge. Roger's problem in obtaining books is solved when he is approached by the artist Luca di Cosmati, secretary to Lorenza Piccolomini, Marquis of Modena, who is Luca's patron and who owns the best library in Rome. On behalf of Piccolomini, Luca invites Roger to dinner and soon Piccolomini offers Roger his library and invites him to move into his villa at Tivoli. There seems to be at least something of Blish in the portrait of Piccolomini, "a stringy man of fifty with the long nose, lean face and sparse hair of a Caesar off some worn silver coin" (p. 197). The marquis has a daughter named Olivia and a disinherited son named Enea Sivio.

Roger spends about two utopian years at the villa. Olivia, who falls in love with Roger, changes his negative and somewhat enigmatic view of women and Roger becomes Piccolomini's ideal son. Roger plans a work, which he discusses with Piccolomini, that will combine "at least three grand elements": (1) "the vision of a universal science which had begun to haunt him ever since he had first read the *Secret of Secrets*;" (2) "the domain of experiment *versus* revealed knowledge;" and (3) the supreme "domain of the moral law" (p. 205). Finally a letter from Adam Marsh recalls Roger home and he leaves the incomplete *Communia naturalium—I* with Piccolomini.

With the end of the flashback, Roger, on his way home, takes up the problem of the cipher that had come to him in the vision experienced in chapter 7. Chapters 7 and 9 in fact form a pair. They effectively describe very positive periods in Roger's life, in the first case his association with Peter's college and in the second his stay at the Villa Piccolomini. At the villa his "long silent self" had hinted at how to solve the cipher: *"Count."* Some kind of numerical code is involved:

> Roger remembered the sharp crepitating crackle of the saltpeter crystals, salvaged from his father's dungheap, under the blow of a rock in a boy's hand . . . and on the other bank, there thudded in his memory the exit of the demon from the window of his noisome room at Westminster. In the middle with him was the dream, in which these huge ciphered words had become an explosion like nothing so much as the earthquake which shall exhume the dead for the Last Judgment. (Pp. 211–12)

The pointed use of the word "bank" indicates that what Roger is in search of is an apocalyptic intellectual bridge. The recognition that the letter U and the number V are indistinguishable in Roman capitals finally leads to this translation:

> FOR THIS TAKE SEVEN PARTS OF SALTPETRE, FIVE PARTS OF POWDERED CHARCOAL FROM YOUNG HAZELWOOD, AND FIVE OF SULPHUR (P. 213)

In chapter 10, "St. Edmund Hall," it is 1250 and Roger is back in Oxford as a master. Having tested the gunpowder formula, he studies alchemy, revises his book on old age at the request of Piccolomini, writes a gloss for the *Secret of Secrets*, and incubates a treatise on the causes of the rainbow. Thomas Bungay is also at Oxford and he and Roger become firm friends, and perhaps more: "They were alike ridiculous in their tonsures, tunics and talk, middle-aged and laden with learning, and all unaware in love; two men in a desert" (p. 218). Whether or not Blish's Roger Bacon is homosexual, there does seem to be a certain ambiguity about his sexuality. But no love is lost between Roger and another lecturer at Oxford, Richard Rufus of Cornwall, regent master in theology, who had been Albertus Magnus's familiar in Paris and who now is jealous of Roger's success as a lecturer; Cornwall loses no opportunity to bait him. However, it is Roger who traps Cornwall by announcing that he will lecture on the nullity of magic and the usefulness of nature, knowing that Cornwall will not be able to resist attending. At that lecture he demonstrates the explosive power of gunpowder (unlike the first explosion in this book, this one is deliberate). Cornwall leads the flight from the hall and soon departs for a post in Paris.

While Roger embarks on his *Metaphysica* and later the *Reprobationes* (a work on weights and measures), a book by the Franciscan Gerard of San Borgo—*Introduction to the Eternal Gospel*—is creating a great stir:

> The Eternal Gospel of the title was the work of one Joachim of Flora, a Calabrian visionary who had predicted that an Age of the Holy Spirit would begin in 1260, ushered in by a new Order of monks headed by Merlin, and heralded by the dissolution of all disciplinary institutions. It was Gerard's contention that the Franciscans might become this new Order, provided that they return to the rule of absolute poverty laid down by their founder. (Pp. 229–30)

Although Joachimism is declared a heresy and Gerard finds himself in the hands of the Inquisition, Roger is won over by the Joachite argument. Robert Silverberg claims that there is a contradiction between Roger's rationalism and his espousal of the irrational Joachim heresy.[20] In fact Roger's conversion is implicit in the vision he experienced which equated the discovery of gunpowder with the end of the world. The Joachite apocalypse, like the gunpowder explosions and like the repeated imagery of death and rebirth, functions to a considerable degree as a metaphor for the philosophical apocalypse, the conceptual breakthrough or paradigm switch that Roger's discovery of a new materialistic science heralds. At the same time it should be emphasized that there is no necessary contradiction between Roger's rationalism and his religious faith.

From now on the parallels between Roger Bacon's career and Galileo Galilei's become more explicit. Roger presages Galileo's fate by becoming the victim of church persecution. His champion, Grosseteste, dies shortly before Roger's lecture, "On the Nullity of Magic." Pope Alexander IV has succeeded Innocent IV. And now the new general of the Franciscans, Bonaventura, names Richard of Cornwall the "new lector to the Franciscans at Oxford, and regent master to boot." A month later Bonaventura interdicts Roger's lectures "for suspected irregularities, namely Joachimism and magic" and recalls him to Paris (p. 233). It is no accident that just before these blows Roger hears—or imagines that he hears—(for the second time) the cry of John the Beggar: "An alms for John, who hath the very begging bowl of Belisarius!" (p. 232)

Chapter 11, "St. Catherine's Chapel," is the brief fourth and final chapter devoted essentially to historical background. It is 1258 and Adam looks back, in the book's fourth and final extended flashback, on the tangle of recent events. The barons are mutinous and a gulf is growing between the king and Simon de Montfort. An intimidated Henry had agreed to "the appointment of a Council of twenty-five lordships, to meet at Oxford in October and draw up a table of reforms." This Mad Parliament (as Henry's partisans dub the meeting) made Simon "military commander-in-chief for the seignorial forces," and began—but did not complete—a "table of wrongs to be righted" entitled the Provisions of Oxford (p. 238). Henry must reaffirm on holy ground of his own choice the Great Charter that his father had signed at Runnymede. Thus the flashback ends. Henry having selected Westminster Abbey, Adam joins the conclave that gathers in that part of the Abbey known as St. Catherine's Chapel. Although Henry reluctantly reaffirms the Charter the chapter ends ominously in darkness as Henry dashes his taper to the ground and the only remaining light is "Matthew Paris' candleflame" (p. 241); in the next chapter Paris's death will be announced.

Chapter 12, "The Convent," opens in 1260, "the first year of the Age of the Holy Spirit!" Roger has undergone a three-year regimen of "corrective discipline" in a Paris convent (p. 242). He has, nevertheless, finished the *Reprobationes* and a *Communia mathematica*. But Bonaventura has inaugurated a new repressive discipline within the order. Among other things his decrees of Narbonne forbid publication. To cap Roger's unhappiness Bungay tells him of Paris's and Adam's deaths. Death will play an increasingly important role in the pages to follow.

Then, one year later, the discovery that a friend still lives. The convent is visited by Raymond of Laon, the clerk of Guy de Foulques, papal legate in England and Cardinal-Bishop of Sabina. Raymond promises to tell the cardinal of Roger's difficulties. Roger gets back to work and, in effect, reinvents physics. He makes use of Joannes, "a brilliant thirteen-year-old" pupil, to put his writing in circulation at the Peregrine college (p. 249). In the meantime, another letter from Bungay informs Roger that civil war has broken out again in England and the barons, who have enjoyed several victories, are being led by Earl Simon. Roger understands these events as foreshadowing "the coming of Antichrist" (p. 253).

Roger promptly gets to work on the *De multiplicatione specerium* and on *De signis et causis ignorantiae modernum* which speaks of "four corrupting errors":

> submission to faulty and unworthy authority [the source of Roger's belief that the Antichrist's arrival is imminent]; submission to what it was customary to believe; submission to the prejudices of the mob; and worst of all, concealment of ignorance by a false show of unheld knowledge, for no better reason than pride. (Pp. 253–54)

This is Roger's "explosive doctrine": "the *scientia experimentalis*, that knowledge from experience of which even Ptolemy had spoken . . . , had found its method and its sieve, by the mercy of God, the negative fervor of Socrates, and the voiceless, persuasive whisper of Roger Bacon's imprisoned demon self" (p. 254). The adjectives "explosive" and "imprisoned" make apparent the degree to which the gunpowder explosions in the book and the imagery or fact of imprisonment provide analogues for the theme of conceptual breakthrough.

One happy day Roger receives a letter from Guy de Foulques asking for a copy of his "long-promised synthesis of knowledge," something which de Foulques is not aware does not yet exist (p. 255). Consequently, Roger sets about writing the *Communia naturalium*. A second comet presages further significant change. Bungay writes that Earl Simon has been excommunicated and that Henry and his son Edward are prisoners after the battle of Lewis. Roger's brother Eugene writes that Yeo Manse "was ruled to be King's land" and that their brother Robert is dead (p. 259). Thanks to the arrival of Sir William Bonecor (a friend of Roger's father and now the king's emissary to the new pope, Clement IV, who just happens to be Guy de Foulques) Roger learns that Simon has been defeated and slain by Edward's forces at Evesham. Sir William agrees to convey a letter from Roger, who at this point has been in Paris for about a decade, to the new pope.

Chapter 13 is entitled "The Bowl of Belisarius." The reply from the pope finally arrives and Roger gives thanks that he has finally become "Magister Roger, whose works were writ for Popes!" (p. 264). Clement wants Roger to go ahead with his work in secret as before. However he provides no money. Roger decides to show his Father Superior the letter and he is granted permission to beg for money. Roger sees King Louis IX of France but receives no more than £2. He writes to Livia Piccolomini asking her to intercede with her father for money; then Roger visits Peter the Peregrine and the dying William Bushe. Roger finally visits Simon's still beautiful widow, Eleanor, in exile in Germany. All of this begging only nets Roger £51.

Roger realizes that he will not be able to complete the *Communia naturalium* and plans a *persuasio* instead, "an attempt to convince the Pontiff of the value of natural knowledge, and the importance of supporting its investigation" (p. 281). The seven parts of this letter would include "a demonstration that mathematics is the key to all the other sciences," and conclude with a section on "moral philosophy," the "science of the salvation of man" (p. 282). He begins by reducing "the guidance of knowledge" to "four heads" and rehearsing the "four chief obstacles in grasping truth" (p. 283). The "fury of composition" lasts ten months before the letter is completed. He then writes an introductory letter which also turns into "a treatise in itself"—hence the need for a second introductory letter, and a third (p. 286). Hence also new copyists are required and they have to be paid. The Father Superior agrees to have the copying done in the convent and relieves Roger of his corrective discipline. In the final introductory letter, Roger asks the pope to sponsor an encyclopedia which would "avoid the manifold confusions between metaphysics and the natural sciences which were the bane of the universities" (p. 289). Finally Joannes is given the task of conveying the *persuasio* across the Alps and Roger is ordered by the provincial minister to return to the parent house of the Franciscans in Oxford. But the wheel of fortune is about to take another turn. "His Holiness is dead," announces the Father Superior in the chapter's shocking final line.

Back in Oxford in 1269 in chapter 14, "The Ministry," it is a time of fierce disputes between Dominicans and Franciscans following the death of Clement. Roger, realizing that Peter the Peregrine is in straitened financial circumstances, publishes books (including the *Communia mathematica*) in order to pay Peter back the money he owes him, and lectures again. He hopes that Bungay, who has become the provincial minister, will be able to help him. The new pope, Gregory X, is identified by the Joachites as the Antichrist and the new Franciscan Minister-General, Jerome di Ascoli, is a bitter enemy of the Joachites. Roger wonders "How to keep silence now, on the very verge of Armageddon?" (p. 296). He compounds his sins by attacking the errors of Thomas Aquinas and Albertus Magnus, and before long, as "a suspect member of the Order," he is called to Paris where he is questioned by Jerome and "charged as a schismatic" (p. 300). Minor charges are dismissed but Roger is found guilty of being a Joachite. At the age of sixty-three, Roger is sentenced to imprisonment "in the March of Ancona, there to be kept in hobblegyves, with none to speak to him, for all the rest of his natural life; . . . and his writings are forbidden all men from this time forth" (p. 305).

(v) Ancona and After

Part 4 ("Sequiur Pars Quarta") is entitled "How That We Baren Us That Ilke Nyght" ("General Prologue" to *The Canterbury Tales*, line 721). The chapter devoted to the thirteen years that Roger is held in a cold cell, "The March of Ancona," is nothing short of superb in communicating a sense of the psychological horror of Roger's predicament. A "curious niche or alcove," later discovered to be "a priest's hole," and "no bigger than the end of a book," is the source of a small fuzzy rectangle of light (pp. 309, 315, 309). The light of learning is dimmed but still alive and for a year or more Roger tries "to compose in his mind the *Summa salvatione per scentiam*" (p. 312)—the work on moral philosophy, the concluding seventh part of the work that he had outlined in the *persuasio* he had addressed to Pope Clement IV.

"One year as he sat"—to quote Blish's brilliantly evocative phrase—Roger makes contact with a boy of six named Adrian by means of the priest's hole which, it now appears thanks to reconstruction at some point, is a part of the *outside* wall of the fortress (p. 312). Adrian's father recognizes that the unseen prisoner is a learned man and instructs the boy to give Roger money at regular intervals. The promise of money enables Roger to communicate with Otto, his jailer, and bargain for better food. Roger teaches Adrian Latin and Greek but one day the boy does not return. And then, one day, thirteen years have gone by; it is 1290 and the new minister-general of the Franciscans, Raymond de Gaufredi, orders the release of the Joachites.

The concluding chapter, chapter 16, is entitled, like the first, "Folly Bridge." A circle has been completed and Roger, now seventy-six, is back at Oxford living in the gatehouse above Folly Bridge. He continues with his work on "the case for salvation through science under a title that suggested nothing so explosive: *Compendium studii theologiae*" (p. 325). Edward is now king of England and has reconciled with the barons; Jerome di Ascoli is Pope Nicholas IV. Thomas Bungay visits Roger "and they kissed each other" (p. 326). Subsequently Bungay does the housework and reads Roger's work in progress:

> The reasoning was extremely close; the writing sometimes crisply brilliant, sometimes wryly humorous, sometimes filled with visionary beauty. But no

> mercy could blind Bungay to the central chasm: Roger was arguing only with the shadows of his old subjects. (P. 327)

Adrian also arrives but Bungay turns him away. Roger's third visitor is John the Pilgrim who turns out to be "Johann Budrys, of Livonia" (p. 329). This third appearance of the Pilgrim is, then, actually the fourth appearance of Budrys. But by now Roger is on his deathbed.

It is at this point that, suddenly, Roger renounces his life's work: "Now bitterly do I regret, that I spent mine wholle lyf in the lists against the ignorant. Enough! Lord Christ enough!" (p. 330). In a letter to Lois Dwight Cole, Blish had stressed that Roger's education is completed during his imprisonment and that his tragedy *"must* lie in the deathbed renunciation of his whole life and purpose, which is assigned to him by the Bacon legend." Blish is here defending the last two chapters against Cole's suggestion that the novel end earlier, at a dramatic high point in Roger's career. Blish goes on to point out that the Faust and Bacon legends are nearly alike except for this one thing: "The Bacon legend . . . is the first statement of the point that it does you no good to be true to something, if that something isn't worth being true to" (Dep. Blish 416/3). But because this renunciation is not prepared for and is quickly passed over, it is highly likely that the reader will not even notice it. As it appears in Blish's novel, it does not have anything of the impact that Blish argues for in his letter to Cole.

There is, then, little doubt that Roger's act of renunciation is not endorsed by Blish. The novel ends with Roger crying out "for love of vision, its usefulness and beauty" (p. 330). The reader will recall Roger's vision on the way home from the Villa Piccolomini and the fact that Blish intended *Doctor Mirabilis* to be, in large part, a work of vision. Roger reaches for his pen but goes "whirling down into silence and study; silence, silence and study" (p. 330). Presumably Roger dies at this point but the actual words used recall Roger's admiration at what Peter the Peregrine achieved through "silence and study" (pp. 293, 295). Or are we to understand that a life spent in "silence and study" is a kind of death? The circularity of the book's structure—the return to a state of containment and a small source of light, the return to Folly Bridge, the return to a deathbed silence—encourages the reader to envisage a more precise parallel between Grosseteste's "apparent" deathbed scene and Roger's "actual" one. Grosseteste rose from his deathbed to a greater, more glorious career. Presumably we are to intuit that Roger Bacon will come into his true period of power only after his death.

Now that Blish too has gone down into "silence and study," we must be grateful that he has left behind this intricately structured and affectively sustained narrative. *Doctor Mirabilis* is not without its faults. It is a difficult work, although it should be emphasized that the masterfully honed archaic style that Blish periodically employs is only rarely part of that difficulty. It is a book, like the work of Roger Bacon himself, that seems destined to win through.

III.
THE NUB OF FANTASY

EIGHT
A TRANSFINITE MATHEMATICS

Blish may have lacked an orthodox "religious" faith but he does seem to have had a genuine faith in mathematics. Col. Paige Russel surely speaks for Blish when near the beginning of *Cities in Flight* he maintains that "Real faith is so much a part of the world you live in that you seldom notice it, and it isn't always religious in the formal sense. Mathematics is based on faith, for instance, for those who know it."[1] Brian Aldiss points out that towards the conclusion of *Cities in Flight* Mark Hazleton demonstrates this faith when he borrows Amalfi's slide rule to do some setting-up exercises as the universe collapses.[2] Blish's enthusiasm for James Joyce may have had something to do with the fact that mathematics is important in *Finnegans Wake* and much of Joyce's other work. Furthermore not only was mathematics Roger Bacon's favorite science, but Oswald Spengler was also a mathematician (as well as a student of biology like Blish). Blish's attraction towards these two thinkers owed much to this common interest. The notion, mentioned in *Cities in Flight*, that "Every culture has its characteristic mathematic, in which its [his]toriographers can see its inevitable social form" is Spengler's (p. 237). Also in *Cities in Flight* we find a chapter epigraph taken from the writings of the American mathematician and SF writer (under the pseudonym John Taine) Eric Temple Bell: "One of the chief services which mathematics has rendered the human race in the past century is to put 'common sense' where it belongs, on the topmost shelf next to the dusty canister labeled 'discarded nonsense'" (p. 110).

Most people, of course, believe in a limited aspect of mathematics—the realm of basic arithmetic and measurement, and increasingly the mathematics of computer programming. Our sense of an empirical reality, in fact, is largely a function of its numeric measurability. But there is also a quite legitimate non-empirical mathematics of infinity and in this Blish seems to have believed also. Thus the realm of mathematics lends support to both material reality and the farthest realms of fantasy. It allows for a conjunction which parallels that achieved in the stories which ambiguously place an SF reality in the context of psychological fantasy. Given that the Alice books by the mathematician Lewis Carroll unite the realms of psychological fantasy and mathematics, it is not surprising that Blish was a member of the Lewis Carroll Society from 1969 until his death.[3] The conception of a fourth dimension, so familiar to readers of SF, is taken from geometry and topology. The mathematical idea of the Möbius strip has also lent support to some of SF's more mystical visions. In the popular mind, Einstein is particularly associated with the untethering of mathematics from the world of common sense perception. At the same time, if before Einstein science was empirical, since Einstein science has become mathematical.

The second of Blish's "Science in Science Fiction" articles is entitled "The Mathematical Story." Here he points out that the technique of extrapolation is mathematical. Extrapolation, a "term borrowed from statistics, means the extending of a curve on a graph beyond the last point which stands for a known fact." What counts as a "known fact" depends "upon how religiously you take your math." And although Blish begins by asserting that stories can only be written about applied maths, he ends by looking forward to the impact of quantum mechanics.[4]

Blish presents a fanciful mathematics of telepathy in *Jack of Eagles* but he was particularly fascinated by the more realistic notion of transfinite numbers associated with the German mathematician Georg Cantor (1845–1918). In 1874 Cantor rendered the infinite amenable to mathematics by setting up correspondences between two series of numbers. He postulated an utterly logical structure whereby a series of transfinite numbers represented different orders of infinity. We have already met with "Aleph-null," the first transfinite number, in *A Case of Conscience* (p. 103 herein). But in a number of other stories Blish makes somewhat more significant use of numbers, both finite and infinite, often to give mysticism a mathematical grounding.

(i) "FYI" (1953): Transfinite Numbers

The key first story in this sequence is "FYI." It is set in London in the bar of the Orchid Club. Lord George Rogge, one of its members and "one of the great mathematicians of all time," announces that the world, presumably on the verge of World War III, has been granted a reprieve.[5] He knows this because of his contact with a medium in Soho. But before getting to this he tells fellow member Charles about "Transfinite numbers. Numbers larger than infinity. And we live in a universe where they don't appear to stand for anything. A piece of primer-work, like confining a grown man in a pram" (p. 124). The image of confinement is pure Blish but the implication here that man is an unevolved child—emphasized by Charles's "Don't you know that your medium is never going to have another child" and Rogge's "cloud of new-born smoke" (pp. 123–24)—points to the universe of A. C. Clarke's *Childhood's End* (1953) and *2001: A Space Odyssey* (1968). Rogge goes on to speak of Cantor and aleph-null, "the cardinal number of all denumerably infinite classes" (p. 124). Charles reluctantly confesses that "Rogge was actually beginning to make me feel a little bit circumscribed" (p. 125).

Rogge then hands Charles the garbled "spirit" message that his Soho medium had written down. He interprets the message, which begins with the letters "FYI" and refers phonetically to a "crisis in evolution of children" ("CHRIST IS IN HEAVEN ROOSHIAN OF CHILDREN"), as indicating that the universe is about to be transformed to a "cosmos of macroscopic number" (pp. 125, 126). According to Rogge, our having learned about "transfinite number . . . would seem to be a crucial stage. . . . And we're certainly in the midst of a crisis in our evolution": "The gods. . . . They're out there, somewhere in a realm beyond infinity, getting ready to open up our pseudospherical egg and spill us out into an incredibly vaster universe" (p. 126). Such is Rogge's evidence that mankind is about to undergo an amazing transformation.

There is, of course, the alternative mundane possibility which Charles supplies ("the whole thing may be a phantom") or the message might be interpreted in any number of other ways: it may be, for example, that the medium was simply picking Rogge's brain by telepathy, "but that explanation just substituted one miracle for another." The story ends with the anticipated bombers arriving and the symbolic reference to Sir Leslie—a drunk mentioned earlier—whose "gaze stirred from the [confining] vase upon which it had become fixed, and rose slowly, slowly toward the dark oak ceiling. There was a preliminary flicker from the lights" (p. 126). Or is this merely another of Sir Leslie's drunks "which wind up in a fixed, cataleptic glare at some inconsequential object . . ." (p. 125)?

(ii) "Common Time" (August 1953): Love Counts

A quotation from Emerson provided the inspiration and epigraph for Isaac Asimov's much anthologized "Nightfall" (1941). "Common Time," deservedly one of Blish's most popular stories, may not have been inspired by the apposite epigraph taken from Herman Melville's *Mardi* (1849) but like "Nightfall" it perfectly elaborates the SF potential of an image from a non-SF American classic: ". . . the days went slowly round and round, endless and uneventful as cycles in space. Time, and time pieces! How many centuries did my hammock tell, as pendulum-like it swung to the ship's dull roll, and ticked the hours and ages."[6]

Garrard, the protagonist of "Common Time," awakens to unnerving time distortions when the faster-than-light starship which is taking him to Alpha Centauri goes into hyperdrive. His subjective sense of time is wildly out of sync with what the calendar tells him is the objective ship time. Blish's description of this awakening to, and experience of, a transformed state compares favorably with Kafka's treatment of Gregor's metamorphosis and the bizarre experience that Poe deals with in "Loss of Breath" (1832). Garrard is at first horrified to discover that "One second in ship-time was two hours in Garrard-time" (p. 90). However, he is relieved to make the further discovery that his body-time (as opposed to his mind-time) is keeping time with ship-time, and he consoles himself with the recognition that he will be able to do a great deal of philosophical and mathematical thinking during the 6,000 subjective years it will take to get to Alpha Centauri: "What panoplies of pure reason could he not have assembled by the time 6,000 years had gone by? With sufficient concentration, he might have come up with the solution to the Problem of Evil between breakfast and dinner of a single ship's day, and in a ship's month might put his finger on the First Cause!" (p. 94). He regrets momentarily that Adolph Haertel, Blish's master mathematician and originator of the "Haertel transformation," which makes faster-than-light travel possible, was not undergoing this experience rather than himself: "The situation demanded someone trained in the highest rigors of mathematics to be put to the best conceivable use" (p. 94).

But at this point the situation reverses itself. Garrard's subjective sense of time suddenly speeds up and soon overtakes objective ship-time: "Good-bye, vast ethical systems which would dwarf the Greeks. Good-bye, calculuses beyond the spinor calculus of Dirac" (p. 95). The characteristic equation here between philosophy and mathematics should be noted as should the allusion to Dirac, Blish's other master scientist but real-life counterpart to the fictional Haertel. Before long his subjective sense of time accelerates to a point where what is described as "Pseudo-death" overtakes him (p. 96).

In his headnote for "Common Time," Blish comments on what happens next in part 3: "sometimes a story will turn so sharply from the way a writer thought it was going to go as to make it seem almost as independent as a dream. . . . I had planned to confront my hero with something as unearthly as I could possibly manage, but I did not know what it would be until it began to appear on the page" (p. 84). Essentially what follows is a mystical experience. Garrard finds himself encircled by beings who identify themselves as "the clinesterton beademung" and speak to Garrard in a most peculiar form of English about "the twin radioceles" of Alpha and Proxima Centauri and about some kind of universal harmony "with all of love," something of a catch phrase among Blish's readers (pp. 98, 99). In part 4, Garrard, returned to Earth, discusses what transpired with Haertel and reluctantly accepts the restrictions of "humanity's common time" (p. 106).

The fame of "Common Time" has much to do with Damon Knight's "classic" analysis of its supposed unconscious sexual symbolism.[7] Knight "demonstrates" that "Common Time" is about a sperm (Garrard) meeting an ovum (the Beademung). The words *"don't move,"* with which the story begins and almost ends, and the "Pseudo-death," by way of the symbolic equation between death and sexual intercourse, are understood as referring to the sex act (pp. 84, 106, 96). To reinforce this interpretation Knight lists a series of words and phrases from the story which can be construed as punning or ambiguous references to the same event. Thus the reference to "lifting a pencil . . . from a state of rest" becomes suggestive and the title of the story is translated as "come on time" (p. 91). The concluding part 4, it is claimed, goes over the same intercourse symbolism but backwards.

Blish, given his recognition that subconscious processes played a part in the composition of this story, seems to have gone along with this interpretation. The word "radioceles," Blish hazarded, may have derived from "variocele," the medical term for a hernia involving the testicles. This led him to the belief that "the whole thing was suggested by the Earth-Moon balls [testicles] on the cover around which I wrote the story."[8] The truth is, of course, that some kind of sexual symbolism can be read into almost any work of fantasy and particularly into SF works concerned with rockets thrusting into the void. Nevertheless, Knight (and subsequently Blish) did pick up on an apparently sub-

The cover by A. Leslie Ross that inspired "Common Time," *Science Fiction Quarterly,* August 1953

conscious element in "Common Time" although they both interpret that element too literally.

The experience of temporal disjunction corresponds to a disjunction between Garrard's rational self, epitomized particularly by his reliance on mathematics and his penchant for counting, and his emotional self, which might well be associated with the vague hints at sexual intercourse. Except for his sublime experience with the beademung, Garrard's mental and bodily reactions are out of sync. The "tenesmus," a painful but ineffectual urge to defecate or urinate, that grips Garrard's body and a second spasm that leaves him with a "Nessus-shirt of warm sweat swathing him persistently, refusing even to cool" (p. 90), represent the delayed emotional reactions to successive intellectual recognitions of the precise nature of his predicament: "those two incredibly prolonged *saturnalias* of *emotion* through which he had suffered . . . had been nothing more nor less than the response of his endocrine glands to the purely *intellectual* reactions he had experienced earlier" (p. 93; emphasis added). Note that the "Nessus-shirt of warm sweat" is a characteristic Blishean covering or container from which release is desperately sought, and note parallel references to "a vessel of horror" and "an even more impossible box" (pp. 88, 104).

We are quickly made aware of Garrard's numerical obsession. He initially counts four abnormalities, and he counts in order to time the intervals between the "pock" sounds made by the second tumblers of the ship's calendar. Once established as an "automatic process . . . at the back of his mind," no "emotional typhoons" could halt Garrard's counting: "Really compulsive counting cannot be stopped by anything—not the transports of love nor the agonies of empires" (p. 88). Knight, of course, singles out the "transports of love" phrase to support his interpretation. Numbers proliferate throughout the story. In part 4, Garrard resorts to math, unnecessarily, as he quickly realizes, because of the actual visibility of the Earth and Moon, to determine how long his trip has taken. Nevertheless, "deep in his brain, set to work by himself, there was a mechanism that demanded counting" (p. 102). Roger Bacon, it will be recalled, solves his cipher thanks to the imperative, "Count."[9]

Repeatedly, reason and emotion are counterpointed: "trickles of reason began to return over that burning desert of reasonless emotion" (p. 88). Of particular interest is the reference to a project Garrard "had once tried to undertake in college—to describe and count the positions of love, of which, according to under-the-counter myth, there were supposed to be at least forty-eight" (p. 95). Is this an appropriate task, it might be asked? Does it betoken an ideal emotional/intellectual balance, or an undesirable emotional/intellectual disjunction? The subliminal pun in "under-the-counter myth" suggests a necessary balancing of the subconscious mind with its counterpart: the arithmetical conscious mind.

The meeting with the beademung, in effect, convinces Garrard that love counts. Whatever disjunction may previously have existed between the rational and the emotional is transcended in the region of Alpha Centauri. And this applies whether or not, or perhaps especially if, "The whole business had . . . been thrown up by his unconscious"

(p. 100). As in "FYI," we are provided with alternative mystical and mundane explanations. Haertel points out that Brown and Cellini, the pilots of two previous starships bound for Alpha Centauri, had failed to return because, unlike Garrard, they reacted immediately and emotionally to the experience of time distortion caused, it is believed, by the "Haertel transformation" power source (p. 89). One is reminded of the Norwegian in Poe's "A Descent into the Maelström" (1845) who *apparently* survives because of an exercise of reason, supported by a specious footnote reference to Archimedes. Presumably Brown and Cellini remained with the beademung in a state which certainly appears to be positive. It is a state clearly implied by the reference to the "Haertel [or heart + intellect] transformation" (p. 89). It would seem that Blish yearns for a state of transcendence where the emotional and rational exist in a state of perfect equilibrium. He has, in fact, characterized "Common Time" in aesthetic terms as displaying such a balance; Blish calls it "the most perfect example of the transitional point in my writing. This is the story with all the 'glacial surface' and trappings of a first interstellar crossing, but the story is about lost love."[10]

During the beademung experience "a book from the DFC-3's [Distinguished Flying Cross-3?] ample library fell to the deck beside the hammock" (p. 98). In part 4 it is pointed out that nothing has changed "except for the book on the deck" (p. 100). Teasingly, we are not told the title of this book. As a textual "gap" it stands in for the essentially unknown nature of the communicative experience that the story attempts to describe. However, picking up the reference to the "hammock," a reader might well recall the Melvillian epigraph to the tale and previsionally identify the book as *Mardi*, another work which begins realistically and shifts to a kind of dream world.

Garrard's mission is recalled in "Nor Iron Bars," a story about a subsequent trip to Centaurus which also ends with the image of confinement. It was first published serially under the titles "Detour to the Stars" in December 1956 and "Nor Iron Bars" in November 1957, and combined under the title "Nor Iron Bars" in *Galactic Cluster* (1960).[11] After the problems with the Haertel overdrive, another ship powered by a different drive invented by its captain, Gordon Arpe, is headed for Centaurus. But this negative mass drive causes the ship to flip into a microscopic universe (where the crew and passengers have telepathic and teleportation powers) and to leak oxygen. It may be noted that the impingement of different dimensions in "The Secret People" (November 1950) makes for a somewhat similar situation (see p. 41 herein).

A way is found to return to the macrocosm and land on Centaurus III, but Arpe realizes that for two of the passengers, a negress who has suffered badly from the oxygen loss and her fiancé, Hammersmith (love counts in this story, too), the planet is a prison which they can never leave. Likewise the new world amounts to a prison for him because the four-year communication gap between Centaurus and Earth ensures that he will have lost all touch with contemporary science and with refinements of the Arpe drive. Thus it is that, in the words of the Cavalier poet, Richard Lovelace, "stone walls do not a prison make / Nor iron bars a cage." But unhappily, and this points to a thematic weakness, the title of the story only meaningfully relates to its conclusion.

(iii) "Beep" Smeared: The Quincunx of Time (February 1954, 1973)

SF stories give the illusion of knowledge about the future. But what would happen if it were really possible to know of events that will occur days, weeks, years, or centuries from the present moment? Of the many SF stories that toy with this possibility, Blish's "Beep" (February 1954) is among the most intriguing. This story opens several centuries in the future on the planet Randolph which, like so many of Blish's worlds, is warmed by "twin suns."[12] After a routine assignment—observing that a particular female meets a particular male—Josef Faber, a Service agent, reports to his superior Krasna. Jo has become bored with his job but he is intensely curious about the exact foreknowledge that the Service appears always to have. How, for example, was the Service able to rout an enemy armada that must have involved a century's worth of preparation, by having available "three times as many ships, disposed with mathematical precision so as to enfilade the entire armada the moment it broke from the nebula" (p. 113)? Krasna responds by telling Jo that he has just been promoted and playing "a standard indoctrination tape" that dramatizes the history of "the Dirac transmitter" and explains how this galactic instanteous communication device relays knowledge of the future and makes the Service infallible (pp. 112, 116). This tape constitutes the two central sections of "Beep."

The plotline unfolded by the tape is little more than an extremely contrived vehicle for the more important ideational content. It seems that centuries ago, in the year 2090, Dana Lje, a "video columnist," constructed her own Dirac communicator with some aid from a turncoat secretary within a government bureau that later becomes the Service, and hit upon an amazing by-product. For reasons unknown, all messages received by this system are preceded by an annoying beep. This beep, she discovers, "is the simultaneous reception of *everyone of the Dirac messages which have been sent, or ever will be sent*" (pp. 146–47; emphasis in original). By means of a "smearing device" which spreads out the beep, these messages can be deciphered and thus precise knowledge of certain aspects of the future can be obtained. Apparently one of the things that Dana learned was that she would marry Capt. Robin Weinbaum, who is the head of the bureau that developed the Dirac, and that she would work for the bureau. Since this fate is apparently inevitable, she decides to help it along by concocting a rather silly scheme to attract Weinbaum's attention. She visits his office and convinces Weinbaum that the bureau has a competitor in the instantaneous communications business calling itself Interstellar Information, owned by a J. Shelby Stevens, which is offering to sell knowledge of future events derived from the Dirac communicator. (This, incidentally, is where the tape's story-line begins. Blish, as usual, must have arrived at the plot by reasoning backwards.) Weinbaum has Stevens jailed but, after failing to get any real information from the man, lets him go. Subsequently it turns out that Stevens was Dana in disguise, all is revealed in return for Weinbaum agreeing to hire and marry Dana, beep messages from the future are sampled, and the course of true love takes over.[13]

If it is possible to know about future events, can these events be changed? The issue, of course, is that of determinism versus free will. In the final section the story returns to Krasna and Jo. Krasna explains that, in order to make use of its special knowledge, the Service ensures that whatever a message from the future refers to does come to pass: "Despite the evidence that the future is fixed, we have to take on the role of the caretaker of inevitability." And hence the importance of the boy-meets-girl assignments: "We have to see to it that *every single person who is mentioned in any Dirac 'cast gets born*" (emphasis in original). The Dana/Robin story amounts to a boy-meets-girl assignment that she herself supervises. Conversely, the date of a Serviceman's death must never be broadcast over the Dirac. It would seem that determinism wins out as it usually does in such future-knowledge SF stories but still, as Krasna points out, "the consciousness of the observer is the only free thing in the Universe" (p. 154).

What Krasna's tape does not reveal is the actual origin of the idea for the story's Dirac transmitter. Paul Shackley recalls that, "according to Jim, the original Okie story ["Earthman Come Home"], never published in its original form, contained the Dirac transmitter acting as it does in 'Beep.' The beep idea had to be taken out of the Okie series because it would not have fitted Amalfi's character and universe of discourse for him to know the solutions before he had been faced with the problems."[14]

In the "Critical Preface" to the expanded version of "Beep" entitled *The Quincunx of Time* (1973), after pointing out that Larry Shaw (the first admirer of the novella "A Case of Conscience") had encouraged him to do the expansion, Blish observes that he had come to new conclusions about the work with some help from Shackley, to whom the book is dedicated. Blish received about twenty letters, some very detailed, from Shackley, a philosophy student at the time, dating from 15 June 1971 to 14 July 1976, and written first from Dublin and later from Lancashire.[15] While the physical action remains meager, the novella makes more of the speculation "about time, knowledge, and free will."[16] In the book the issue of determinism versus free will is highlighted by an epigraph from William James's *The Dilemma of Determinism* and by the reference inserted during the expansion process to "one of the seven or eight great philosophical questions that remain unanswered, the problem of whether man has or has not free will" (p. 74). But otherwise, *The Quincunx of Time* does not, and perhaps could not, take the matter much further. In effect, Blish's answer to the problem takes the form of a syllogism which is at least implicit in "Beep."

The Dirac communicator with its transcendent beep amounts to a means of perfect communication. After all, Thor Wald, the bureau's "director of research" and the inventor of the Dirac communicator, does note that "Cantor proved that there really is an infinity, at least mathematically speaking" ("Beep," p. 134; *Quincunx*, p. 60). A perfect transcendent form of communication might be a definition of love. It does, then, make symbolic sense that the Service agents should be mainly concerned with monitoring the meetings of lovers and that Robin and Dana become lovers. Thus the syllogism implicit in "Beep," and only a little more explicit in *The Quincunx of Time*, goes like this: love is to perfect communication as free will is to determinism.[17] Thus also the very unexpected and only genuine utopia in Blish's fiction is discovered at the heart of this story: the world of Randolph and its attendant but very low-key galactic empire. The Service agents correspond to guardian angels.

Although *The Quincunx of Time* more or less doubles the length of "Beep" it does not, it must be said, double the value. The two central sections of "Beep" in expanded form become the ten chapters of "The

Song of the Beep." These chapters, plus a prologue and an epilogue, are each supplied with somewhat gnomic titles. Only chapters 3 and 10 are entirely new. Chapter 3, which deals with attempts to locate "J. Shelby Stevens," does nothing to advance or significantly illuminate the basic plot. Unlike the story version, here "Stevens" chooses to place himself under what is called "stoolie's arrest" (p. 43). Chapter 10 postulates a five-dimensional time frame which Wald explains "means that the universe of mechanics is restored; and, in some metamathematical sense which it is now imperative for us to work out, so is free will." Thus the beep events are "only potentially real" (p. 103): "We may look at the quincunx of time from above, and decide now which tree we wish to cut down, and which we will let live" (pp. 103–04).[18] (A quincunx normally does refer to an arrangement of five trees.) Weinbaum believes that man should submit to God in this regard: "Thy will, not mine" (p. 104). Chapter 10, then, serves to confirm that free will is still definitely part of the equation.

Brian Aldiss maintains that

> Blish seized upon the idea of a mystical all-pervasive quincunx from Sir Thomas Browne's curious work, *The Garden of Cyrus; or, The Quincuncial Lozenge* (1658). Cyrus the Great, the founder of the Persian Empire, restored the Hanging Gardens of Babylon, planting out saplings in lozenge configurations. . . . Browne's tract is a discourse upon all the manifestations of quincunxes in nature, in mankind, on earth, and in the heavens. According to Browne, it is an all-pervasive sign, although little commented upon.

By way of illustration, Aldiss demonstrates that the five major characters in Blish's story may be arranged in "quincuncial fashion":

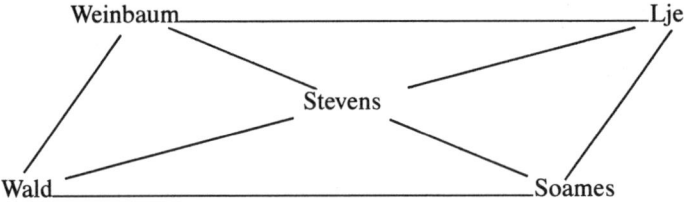

"This figure," Aldiss explains, "lines up the males on the left and the women on the right, with the intermediate figure of J. Selby Stevens in the middle to represent the vanishing fifth dimension" (p. 9).[19]

Chapters 2 and 9 and "An Epilogue" contain paragraph blocks which are not to be found in "Beep." In an insert at the beginning of chapter 9, reference is made to a dummy knob on the Dirac transmitter that is there simply for the purposes of "symmetry" (p. 90).[20] Much of the additional material which makes up *The Quincunx of Time* is similarly redundant. An insert in the epilogue makes use of Thomas Kuhn's "paradigms" (such as those established by Einstein and Haertel) to explain why so many of the messages from the future are utterly meaningless.

Chapter 9 (which takes for its title, "A Comity of Futures," a phrase that occurs in Blish's 1970 poem, "Dove Sta Memoria") is the most expanded chapter. It includes three additional sample messages from the future, the first of which relates (with some emendations) to the events described in Blish's early story "The Real Thrill," the second of which relates to the world described in "A Style in Treason," and the third of which to the world of *Midsummer Century* (another story of instantaneous communication). Blish realized that he could make use of the beep messages as a coda-like means of integrating his current and previous fictions. Thus we are free to assume that the medium in "FYI" picked up a beep message! In fact, Blish was concerned with retrospectively co-opting "The Real Thrill," "A Style in Treason," and *Midsummer Century* into a consistent future history that might be termed, after the inventor of the Haertel Drive, the "Haertel Network" (discussed in chapter 9 here). Hence, along with nine other Haertel mentions in *Quincunx* (pp. 60, 61, 66, 97, 101, 107) but not in "Beep," a reference to the "Haertel Drive" (p. 34) replaces simply "The overdrive" (p. 122) in "Beep." It was Paul Shackley who had alerted Blish to the fact that, prior to the writing of *Quincunx*, the stories which made up what Shackley called the "Haertel Complex" could be represented by a perfectly symmetrical tree diagram. The "symmetry" knob insert may be an allusion to this. Previously, Blish had haphazardly added to this developing Network but it was with a new consciousness of its fortuitous symmetry that Blish used *Quincunx* to create a new vigorous (and asymmetrical) branch consisting of the stories alluded to in the three new beep messages.

There are other minor additions and changes: it is established that the tape is "mostly a dramatization" (p. 22); "the sub-celler of Fort Yaphank" (p. 125), where "Stevens" is imprisoned, becomes "the sub-cellar of Fort Butner" (p. 37), where "Stevens" is not imprisoned; an insert has Wald reading a journal "the text of which seemed to be about 75 percent mathematics" and "25 percent . . . Chinese" (p. 53); and Weinbaum discovers earlier in the book, independent of Dana's telling him, that his secretary is the leak.

Every so often in the revision and expansion process Blish bloats, or perhaps "smears" would be the more appropriate word, sentences with artificial inserts. Thus, "Krasna unfolded the desk-top to expose a small visor screen. Obediently Jo rose and went around the desk to where he could see the blank surface" (p. 118) becomes "Krasna unfolded the desk top to expose a holograph tank—a small 3V screen. Obediently Jo rose and went around the desk to where he could see whatever was coming from the front; 3V was of course visible from any side, but proscenium thinking died hard, and he disliked watching people's backs" (p. 22). In "Beep" Dr. Wald speaks "sourly" (p. 124). In *Quincunx* he speaks "with a sort of sad sweetness, like Sauerbraten gravy" (p. 36).[21] To a coded message of seven unintelligible words, *Quincunx* absurdly adds two more: "Vwaptingdorpic. Gummisampel" (p. 92).[22] "Beep" opens with the sentence "Josef Faber lowered his newspaper slightly" (p. 112). In *Quincunx* this becomes "The man code-named Josef Faber—and after ten years he no longer cared about his birth name—lowered his bulky newsfac slightly" (p. 15). It should be noted, however, that be it newspaper or newsfac, both are organs of communication and as such set up the thematic development to come.

One revealing addition should be isolated. In describing the alarming sound of the beep, Blish adds the information that "it reached well beyond the limits of any known recording apparatus into regions where it killed laboratory animals and set fire to their cages" (p. 54). One wonders why the beep does not at the same time annihilate human beings. Or does it do so in some symbolic sense? Once again we have the image of imprisonment so characteristic of Blish's fiction and death as a release from imprisonment, a release brought about by the transcendent beep.

(iv) "King Log": The John Hillary Dane Series (February 1969–December 1970)

The John Hillary Dane stories are part of an aborted book manuscript entitled "King Log" in which Blish lost interest: "It is not that I do not know what is going to happen next," he wrote Paul Shackley, "but that for some reason I feel a distaste amounting almost to revulsion about going on with it. I do not understand why but since I have been feeling that way for nigh onto five years I have to face facts" (PS, 17 January 1975). Judith Blish explains further that Blish "had been commissioned for this vast work in 1967 and then found that he was just not able to sustain the amount of work he had contracted, which included the witchcraft project and Star Trek. . . . He wrestled with his conscience, and finally bought himself out of the contract, having published the three parts that appeared in *Galaxy*," the first two as cover stories: "Our Binary Brothers" (February 1969), "The City That Was the World" (July 1969), and "Darkside Crossing" (December 1970).[23] Characteristically, the order of publication shuffles the narrative chronology, which is as follows: "The City That Was the World" (the most intriguing and successful of the series), "Darkside Crossing," and "Our Binary Brother" (the weakest story).[24] These stories figure in this chapter largely because Dane, an industrialist and "the world's history's richest man" (DC, p. 6), is also a mathematician, something which is represented as an ultimate apotheosis: "a smoldering aloneness . . . made him first a poet, then a Wellsian utopian, then a Trotskyite, then a pacifist, and finally—the only logical outcome of all these tastes and influences—a mathematician specializing in communications theory, cybernetics and related disciplines" (OBB, p. 123; "taster" is a misprint in the text).

Dane is also an Amalfi type and a persona for Blish, and what interest these stories have depends very much on their autobiographical elements. They appear to have been written around the time Blish and his wife moved to England and may be read as an expression of the discontent that led to that move and the hopes that Blish had for his life in a new land. Blish was forty-seven at the time of the move and what also comes through in these stories is a good deal of middle-aged angst, disenchantment, despair, and the sense of a writer who knows he is past his prime. The name John Hillary Dane seems to derive from an amalgam of John Amalfi, Edmund Hilary, and Hamlet. But it is the association with Hamlet, the melancholy Dane, which seems most appropriate.

"The City That Was the World" is apparently set in 1996. Reference is made to work starting ten years earlier in 1986 on the Dane observatory (which Dane underwrote) in the snow-capped crater of Coropuna, an extinct volcano in Peru. In the intervening years he has also had constructed a mile-high office building in Denver. Dane, like Blish himself no doubt, is presented as being worried by the passage of time and consumed with the need to build a bridge to eternity. Toby Walker, a newspaperman, is puzzled by this driven man:

> For Dane, time was the evil. . . . Time is the bridge that burns behind us. Why was Dane, who was so powerful, and by all ordinary standards so free, so desperate to revise the ages, and even the fleeting minutes?

And why, for that matter, did he have to build physical bridges from one second to another? (Pp. 71–72)

While visiting the observatory construction site, Toby's hands get burned when the radio telescope bridge collapses. This might have been warning enough to curb his curiosity about Dane's affairs but he is, nevertheless, susceptible to the pitch that Dane subsequently gives him in the mile-high Dane Tower.

At the top of his Tower, Dane explains that in "exactly fifty-seven years from now, Denver will be the capital of the world" and his Tower will be the center of a vast "continuous city" (p. 79). Dane then demonstrates his ability to project two identical kittens into that future and to take photographs of the future city; this, then, is Blish's fourth and best time-travel story.[25] It seems that the altitude of the Tower is necessary to this operation because nowhere is the world-city less than a mile high. Previous photos indicate that the people of the future are excited by the appearance of previous kittens that Dane has projected and the repetition of this exercise has led them to stage a ceremony whenever a pair of kittens appear. The more the kittens resemble one another, the more impressed these people appear to be and hence the kitten-breeding program that Dane has instituted. The pair of kittens that Toby sees projected return the following week. Aside from convincing Toby that he can project objects into the future and illustrating the superstitious behavior of the future citizens, the precise relevance of the identical kittens business is rather murky.

Dane explains that the future world is controlled by a computer that is situated atop Dane's Tower as it is in the future. However, he claims that he has reason to believe that the computer is due to malfunction seriously in two years after the fifty-five-years-into-the-future period that his photographs have recorded. The future society, which treats the machine as a sacred object, will not be able to repair it. Dane offers Toby a million dollars if he will allow himself to be projected into the future in order to replace the faulty computer component. The set-up here is ingenious and vaguely anticipative of Gregory Benford's *Timescape* (1980). Toby agrees and he is projected into the future carrying the new component attached to a weapon to ward off the superstitious citizens. But because of "negative entropy," which increases the higher the nervous organization, it is not possible to transport Toby into the future for more than a second or so. Subsequently, in an about-turn ending, Toby tumbles to what he believes to be Dane's real purpose and realizes that he has been deceived. Dane did not want him to save the future society; rather, Dane wanted him unwittingly to destroy it. Toby's concluding reference to Dane's other project, the Dane Observatory, sets the stage for the next two stories: "Telescopes . . ., no matter how powerful, see only into the past" (p. 97). The next two stories deal with Dane's attempt to escape into a primitive past where he, rather than a computer, will be a god.

In the somewhat awkwardly written "Darkside Crossing," which relates in title only to Alan E. Nourse's "Brightside Crossing" (1956), Dane, in a particularly bleak frame of mind, is described as having "nothing to recommend him but money" (DC p. 6). He is in bed with a forty-year-old woman named Eleanor whom he picked out of a magazine called *The Private Swinger*. But we learn that his miserable life on Earth is about to end. The Dane Observatory has discovered that the Sun is a double star. Its companion star, a white dwarf one-sixth of a light year away, has been named Beta Solis. In a twenty-eight-day orbit behind the Moon, Dane has assembled a ship called the *Tranchemer* to take him to Beta Solis. After providing for his wife Jennet, his daughter Jenny, his son Hawk, and his mistress Eleanor, Dane departs on the three-year trip. There is an obvious parallel between Dane's family situation and Blish's, and the journey to a new and hopefully better life parallels the Blishes' move from America to England.

En route, with the Sun behind him, "Dane was expatriate, as no man had ever been before—nor would he ever see that Sun again" (p. 23). The journey is reminiscent of that described in "Common Time." "He floated into the control chamber as compulsively and as mindlessly as a sperm going home" and he experiences periods of "fugue and amnesia." Alpha Centauri, it will be recalled, is also a binary star and presumably Dane hopes for as transcendent a consummation as that which Garrard experienced. However, on a more mundane level, Dane has taken care to provide himself with "a library of pornographic films" (p. 24).[26] "Darkside Crossing" ends with the discovery that Beta Solis has at least five planets, one of which will become Dane's new home.

"Our Binary Brothers" takes place three years later. The planet Dane chose is named Rana and it seems that its humanoid inhabitants, the Ranidae, have taken Dane for a god. But rather than worshipped, he is seized in his temple by two Ranidae guards. A flashback describes how Dane came to be on Rana in words that Blish repeats more or less verbatim in "Darkside Crossing," with the exception that in this first written story of the series Blish situates Dane's telescope in Chile rather than Peru. In another link to "Darkside Crossing" reference is made to Dane having a son and a daughter who have disappointed him.

It seems that the leader of the city Ranidae, who is called the Panechruse, has seen through Dane's god act and wants to use Dane to increase the progress of technology and to continue as a god only among the more primitive hill people. But Dane will not "help the Panechruse reorganize Rana into another technological hell on the Earth model" (p. 128).[27] He decides to lead the hill men (who still worship him) against the city people but he will supply only primitive weaponry and thereby delay progress. And thus disappointingly ends a mediocre story and an uneven, somewhat maudlin story sequence.

Judith Blish reports that after her husband's death, *"King Log* was passed to the agent Curtis who tried to find a publisher and a collaborator for it, but it was decided that there was not enough of the projected 10,000 word [actually, according to the contract, 180,000 word] novel to do what Jim had intended. True, I had a vague memory of his plan, but it would have been very hard to follow any path of thought resembling his concept."[28]

Gregory Feeley has speculated convincingly that ironic touches at the end of "Our Binary Brothers," particularly the last line, "The airlock opened and the One Redeemer went forth to cypher his disciples [his ship's computer can handle numbers more easily than exotic Ranidae names], and bring them Joy" (p. 130), indicate, in Feeley's words, "that Dane is now set to replicate all the dehumanizing evils of Earth he has professed to repudiate." And hence the title "King Log," taken from "Aesop's fable of the frogs who wanted a king. When they protested against the log Zeus sent them to venerate, the god in his anger sent them King Stork, who proceeded to eat them." Various narrative and structural loose ends, and allusions such as the quote from *Doctor Mirabilis* in "The City That Was the World," *"Time is, Time was, Time is Past!"* (p. 71), allow Feeley to tease out a number of specific plot possibilities and to conclude that the theme of "Fatality and free will" would be of central importance. And apparently Blish had "mentioned to Paul Shackley that later in the book Dane's children were to follow him to Beta Solis."[29]

Note should be made here of another story having to do with the disturbing mathematics of mortality and, like "The City That Was the World," with the interaction of a newspaperman and a man conscious of his advancing age. Set in England in 1990, "Statistician's Day" (1970), one of Blish's better stories, is concerned with something called Universal Population Control officially instituted ten years earlier but actually in existence at least ten years before that. Wiberg, a foreign correspondent for the *New York Times*, visits the home of an eighty-year-old writer named Edmund (suggestive of John *Hilary* Dane) Gerrard (suggestive of Garrard) Darling whose obituary Wiberg has in his pocket. Darling, who has an interest in mathematics, informs Wiberg that, as a result of keeping records for twenty years, he has discovered a statistical correlation much firmer than the supposed correlation between cigarette smoking and cancer, namely that a disproportionate number of people of similar occupations die on the same day. It would appear that Population Control has supplemented its program of birth control and created a static population with a form of death control (the logical corollary) that serves an absolutely predictable economy. Surplus economists, novelists or whatever are periodically skimmed off. Suspecting that Wiberg, a statistician, may be in the know and perhaps about to murder him, Darling points out that, thanks to his knowledge of projective geometry (one of his amateur mathematical interests), he has determined not only that the next 14 April, Novelists' Day, will be the day of his own death but that the following 3 November will be Statisticians' Day.

(v) *Midsummer Century* (1972): "A Quincunx of Ancient Trees"

The novella *Midsummer Century* was Blish's last sustained published piece of work, most of *The Quincunx of Time* having been written much earlier. Written shortly after or while "Beep" was being rewritten and expanded, *Midsummer Century* first appeared in the special April 1972 Blish issue of *The Magazine of Fantasy & Science Fiction*, one of the more significant accolades that he received in his lifetime. Blish's description of *Midsummer Century* as a "pure adventure story, which one doesn't see often in these over-earnest days" is quoted in the editor's headnote to the work.[30] Likewise he had informed Paul Shackley that *Midsummer Century* was "a piece of pure and shameless romancing, like the lead novels in the old *Startling Stories* (and it is in fact modelled on the structure Henry Kuttner used to use for them) . . . Joanna Russ is sure to jump on me for retrogression" (PS, 1 April 1971). In a reply to a letter from Joanna Russ in which she expressed a perhaps overly earnest view of the work, Blish repeated his view that it is "a straight phantasy adventure in the spirit of the lead novels in the old *Startling* stories" (Dep. Blish 431/4, 22 May 1974). Indeed, a letter from Blish to Frederik Pohl indicates that the basic idea for *Midsummer Century* goes back to an outline that Blish had drafted in those early days in 1948 (Dep. Blish 428/6, 25 February 1949). As finally written, it is an intri-

Judith Lawrence Blish's cover for the Special Blish Issue of
The Magazine of Fantasy & Science Fiction

cate, characteristically carefully constructed piece of work in the relatively spare mode that Blish favored from 1963 until the end of his life and it does repay close attention.[31]

In essence, *Midsummer Century* is about the progress of a human mind onward and, in the mystical sense, upward. John Martels, an Englishman born on the wrong side of the social tracks in Doncaster, is introduced as having progressed from the "highest possible first in astrophysics" obtained at a redbrick polytechnic to the position of director of research at Sockette State University in the American midwest.[32] He is part of the British "brain-drain" (p. 3). This term crops up in the second paragraph of the novella. In the succeeding pages his brain is to be drained in the most literal and unexpected ways as we follow the odyssey of Martels's mind as it is translated successively into three different states.

It all begins in 1985 with an accident while he is attempting to repair the Sockette State radio telescope, which is "of radically new design" (p. 5). Like Alice falling down the rabbit hole into Wonderland, Martels falls down the telescope tube, which drains his brain, and he regains consciousness in what he eventually discovers is the year A.D. 25,000 in the mind of a being named the Qvant. The godlike Qvant exists in some kind of protective casing "in a museum of some sort" in Rawson, in "what used to be South America" (pp. 8, 48). The being's name is revealed when a brown tribesman addresses it while asking for some kind of ritual protection against the birds. The Qvant attempts unsuccessfully to dislodge the mind of Martels from his brain and over an unspecified number of years Martels learns something of the bizarre future world he has fallen into. The Qvant and Martels are within a "brain-case apparatus" (p. 22). Civilization has been destroyed and rebuilt four times since Martels's own era.

The Qvant "was the reigning Supreme Autarch" at the beginning of Rebirth Three, which term period serves as the title of part 1 of the novella (p. 28). The tribesmen, who belong to Rebirth Four, are caught up in a system of ancestor worship and, being death-fixated, are uninterested in mounting any kind of effective offensive against the man-killing birds which have evolved since Martels's time. It is hard to believe that a little bird could be dangerous but, comments the narrator, "cancer viruses also come in small packages," as Blish, at the time of writing this novella, knew all too well (p. 57). The birds, it should be observed, may have had their genesis for Blish in the Daphne du Maurier story (1952) and the Alfred Hitchcock film (1963). The evolution of the birds into such threatening creatures owes something to their mastery of "general juganity" or mind power (p. 23); the "jug" root should be noted. The Qvant's power, on the other hand, is very limited because he has lost contact with a computer, designed to supplement his function, at Terminus in the vicinity of Antarctica, which is guarded by "survivors of Rebirth Three" (p. 35).

The Qvant finally manages to project Martels's mind into that of a petitioning tribesman named Tlam. His aim is to reestablish connection with the computer using as the vehicle Tlam/Martels, or Tlam/Martels/Qvant, since the Qvant is also telepathically present in Tlam's mind making for an evolutionary synthesis. This plan succeeds but not before, in part 2 ("Rebirth IV"), T/M/Q (ejected from Tlam's village for supposedly attacking the Qvant) finds himself imprisoned in the Country of the Birds within their Tower on Human Legs; the three "very ancient trees" which support the structure, by accident or design, look like human legs and feet (p. 66). Blish's word magic is at its most effective in the passage describing the interior of the tower while T/M/Q climbs the spiral pegs attached to a central pole. Looking down the tower, the hide-stitched construction of which emits starlike shafts of light from the exterior, reminds Martels of "the barrel of a telescope" such as the one he fell down (p. 68). After a second fall and after apparently being conveyed to the top of the tower, T/M/Q escapes from the eyrie of the King of the Birds by killing the guard and constructing wings for gliding from the guard's own wings, a most literal flight of fantasy. After gliding some distance pursued by cranelike birds T/M/Q crash lands: "Once more he had hit the bottom of the telescope of time . . ." (p. 84).

In part 3 ("Rebirth V"), T/M/Q is picked up by the inhabitants of Terminus, and the mind of Martels finds itself where the Qvant should supposedly be, in the computer. In response to the questions asked by the "Antarcticans of Rebirth III," Martels explains that "My mind was propelled into this era by the accidental generation of a jugatemporal field in a powerful broadcaster" and that it must somehow have homed itself on the computer's "complex of juganetic fields" (pp. 92, 94). He asks that Tlam be brought in, only to discover that the Qvant is now fully present in Tlam's mind. The Qvant attempts unsuccessfully to displace Martels from the computer.

After Martels experiences a mystical state within the computer, "at the heart of which lay the primary pulse of life—and a core of absolute passivity" (p. 99), Lanest, the technician-in-chief, explains why the Qvant was shut out of the computer. The Qvant had been bred to be a leader but "the access which the computer gave him to the juganetic Pathways became a trap luring him into increasing passivity" (p. 101). The Qvant had become totally immersed in the "M" or "meditation" state, the fourth stage of an eight-stage mystical pilgrimage: "orientation, reality loss, concentration, meditation, contemplation, the void, re-emergence, re-stabilization." Both Rowland Bowen and Dr. John Clark, to whom Blish says in an introductory note he is indebted "for substantial elements of my hypothesis about the nature of ESP and mystical experience" have something to do with this "qualitative chart."[33] (A reader may well recall here Blish's previous "scientific" treatment of ESP in *Jack of Eagles*.) The Antarcticans feared what might happen when the Qvant entered the V (void) state. "He might well have been actively on the side of the Birds" (p. 102)—and so they severed his connection with the computer.

Lanest agrees to experiment with Martels in the brain case at Rawson, the computer connection is re-established, and T/Q is placed in suspended animation. In the one hundred years that go by, Martels successfully organizes the tribesmen against the birds. Characteristically, as Stableford observes, Blish "ignores the melodramatic potential of the final physical conflict between birds and men, which would surely have been extensively exploited by any other writer."[34] Instead,

> As the decades wore on, Martels was increasingly tempted inward along the pathways, further seduced by the availability of the Powerful Type or model of the Platonic original of all sentience which the computer represented. The computer was a chip off the living monobloc, and tended constantly toward reunion with it, dragging Martels after in its wake. (P. 106)

Eventually Martels decides that the Qvant and Tlam should be revived and united with him to become collectively not the Qvant but "the Quinx—the Autarch of Rebirth Five." "If we succeed, some day we shall be called the Sixt . . . and so on, reality without end" (p. 110).

A perceptive reader will connect the Quinx with the description of "a quincunx of ancient trees" met with while Tlam/Martels is on his way through a rain forest to Tlam's village. This arrangement of trees had been left standing after the surrounding trees had been cleared so that the clearing "was still covered by the densely matted roof of the rain forest." Two paragraphs earlier, in a passage that recalls the tree-top world of "The Thing in the Attic," the forest canopy is described as "a separate and continuous world, as though the Earth had acquired a second surface, or *some primitive vision of heaven had been lowered to within reach of the living*" (p. 50; emphasis added). In other words, the quincunx of trees whose tops mesh with heaven (one thinks fleetingly of the Message Tree in *A Case of Conscience*) corresponds to the way in which the Quinx and the world of Rebirth Five relate to the mystical reality. (The Bird's Tower, from which Martels "flies," it will be recalled, was built around only three ancient trees.)

There is some elementary mathematics to be attended to here. Immediately following the reference to the quincunx of trees, attention is drawn to the heavy wood shields with central spikes which protect the underground world of the tribesmen from aerial attack: "the curvature of the shields, the mathematical part of Martels's mind noted automatically, was so nearly flat that were one to try to derive a value for pi over the convexity of one of them, it would probably come out to be exactly three point zero, just as the Babylonians had measured it" (p. 51). Noting the nudge from quincunx to mathematics (except as a clue there seems little point to the preceding quotation) a reader can make sense of what is referred to but nowhere directly explained, the title phrase "midsummer century" (p. 107). It is simply a matter of correlating the eight mystical stages with the twelve months of the year, an analogy which is suggested by the fact that *Midsummer Century* consists of twelve chapters. In much the same way that finite numbers correspond with Cantor's infinite ones, stages three, four, and five, with which the book is mostly concerned, correspond proportionally to the approaching months of April, May, and June and the midsummer months of July and August. In terms of mankind's spiritual development, the midway point is in the process of being passed. In terms of the entirety of human history, then, the culmination of this period amounts to midsummer. The cyclical process of the seasons suggests, of course, a subsequent period of decline, but perhaps only material decline. Blish is nothing if not clever.

The role of the birds in all this is not entirely clear until it is recalled that birds, by way of the idea of flight and the release of the soul, are traditionally symbols of transcendence. It was an ironic twist on Blish's part to make the birds the enemy although, as already noted, the possibility is raised that when the Qvant emerged from the V state, he might be "on the side of the Birds" (p. 102). The Tower on Human Legs with its "cylindrical hat" full of birds amounts to a pictorial allegory of human potential. The name Martels is close to martlet, the name of a real bird, the swift, and also of an imaginary bird without feet.[35]

Progress in *Midsummer Century* takes the form of a metaphysical evolution and indeed the book has much in common with the type of speculation associated with Arthur C. Clarke and, more recently, Ian Watson. In a perceptive if hypercritical review, David I. Masson points out that *Midsummer Century* exemplifies Blish's great virtue, "the pyrotechnic dance of comment" whereby "he blinds 'em with science."[36] Masson neglects to mention, however, that *Midsummer Century*, a work set further in the future than anything else Blish published, is conspicuously successful as a *tour de force* of imagination that shows Blish in top form and fittingly climaxes the progress of those of his works which incorporate significant mathematical elements. The realm of transfinite numbers is not attained but, in the account of Martels's mystical experience within the computer, one senses its possibility.

(vi) "Circles" of Conscience: "The Breath of Brahma"

Blish conceived one more SF novel in his lifetime. It began life as a proposal for a 25,000-word story tentatively entitled "Circles," for Harry Harrison's projected theme anthology "The Year Two Million." Although the story was not written and the anthology never materialized, Blish came to realize that he actually had a novel on his hands and he asked Josephine Saxton to collaborate with him on it. Blish explains what happened:

> I had the original idea . . . just a year ago . . . but I couldn't get it moving at all. Then the first week in December I was (as Bertie Wooster would put it) giving Josie dinner in London and described it to her, and the next thing I knew ideas were flying past my ears like bazooka shells. A few days later I mailed her what I had on paper, and got this back in about a week with 18 additional pages of copy. (KLA, 1 February 1975)

From the eighty-four pages comprising outline material, copious notes, and drafts of just over three chapters in Saxton's possession, it appears that "The Breath of Brahma," the new tentative title proposed by Saxton, would have been a breathtakingly original and philosophically significant work of SF.[37] Blish died at the height of his imaginative powers. For this reason and so that all is not lost, a reasonably detailed reconstruction is justifiable here.

In a long letter dated 9 January 1974, Blish outlines his year two million idea for Harrison's consideration. The story involves a lot of background information. Somewhere around A.D. 5,000, the energy problem was solved by total conversion to "controlled fusion, mining the necessary hydrogen by hyperspatial tube from the top of the atmosphere of Jupiter," while using Uranus as an "energy sink" for the waste heat. However, this does not prevent the surface temperature of Earth from rising to 345° centigrade (which is considered normal by the underground inhabitants). Blish adds parenthetically, "By the way, whenever I cite figures, I can prove them. I started this story by considering what sort of physical situation would take two million years to hit a crisis. For my 'hard science' readers, I've got it."

People spend all their time thinking; the entire world has become a "citadel of thought," to recall the title and the content of Blish's early story, for two reasons. First, with the advent of interstellar travel, also around A.D. 5,000, "we searched the galaxy for just one other sentient people" but in vain. The search nevertheless continued until around A.D. 1,500,000. An Epicurean religious society developed as a result. Humanity decided that a Creator does exist, that he is an artist, and that "our sole duty to him is aesthetic. . . . [W]e are in this limited sense the center of the universe." Mankind's job is to contemplate the beauty of the universe. Second, Earth's inhabitants also contemplate themselves and the "eight great philosophical questions."[38] This is "a religious society comparable at some points to the high Middle Ages, *except that there is no belief in the hereafter.*"

"My viewpoint character is a young man quasi-apprenticed to one of the Advisors" ("a priest class" of "geniuses who take on all the eight unsolved philosophical questions, not just some aspect of one"). The protagonist, Blish continues, is interested in the metaphysical question: What is the nature of reality? "He's the Year Two Million equivalent of a [budding] theoretical physicist . . . and his individual way of approaching it is through numerology." But the protagonist moves from numerology to "the theory of sets" and then to "hard maths." To test his understanding of the "commutative law," the young man asks the computer this question: "At the present rate, how much longer can we continue to strip-mine Jupiter?" The answer is "less than 5000 years," that is, until the year two million. "I'm not snowing you," Blish notes. "I did quite a lot of this figuring on a £20 pocket calculator which Judy gave me for Christmas. . . . [W]hen I had a tougher problem, I put it to Andy Stephenson and he snuck me some time on his firm's computer." The solution is to shift to Saturn as a source and to Neptune as a sink for a further "hundred thousand years" and then, as a second sink, "go to Persephone, my gas giant planet which I'm convinced exists beyond Pluto."[39] Persephone "must be so bloody cold that the whole problem of a flash point would be irrelevant before the death of the Sun itself." But using Saturn as a source will eventually result in the "ballistic disruption" of its "system, rings and all." Wrecking "one of the glories of the universe" does not sit well with the religious imperative to admire the beauty of God's handiwork.

The student takes these facts to his mentor and "is assigned the onerous task of going to Ganymede for a close look at what's happening on Jupiter." He finds life on Jupiter *"about to become* sentient" thanks to a speeded-up process of mutation caused by an increase in "hard radiation" caused, in turn, by man's "stripping off the planet's atmosphere." This precipitates a religious and aesthetic crisis, hence the initial title: widening "circles" of implication radiate from a "pebble"—the life form on Jupiter, as will appear elsewhere, looks like a stone. We have a rival "in our own back yard." Blish writes, "If we stop using Jupiter, we stop the [accelerated] evolution of the pre-sentient creatures on Jupiter" and "if we continue to use Jupiter, the creatures there will reach full sentience . . . at about the same time the Saturnian system will disrupt [itself] if we give up using Jupiter."

Blish points out in the letter that both Christopher Priest and Brian Aldiss have urged him to turn this material into a novel but he would rather do it at the shorter length that he is presently proposing: "I don't think it would take me very long to write it, either, since I have almost all the numerical parameters filled, as I think I've shown, and I do have a story as well."

Harrison replied enthusiastically in a letter dated 7 February 1974.

Two pages of notes in Blish's hand, written around the same time, fill in details under the headings *"Energy," "Resources," "Society"* (it is essentially utopian and thus might be compared with the previous utopias in *A Torrent of Faces* and *"Beep"/Quincunx*), *"Ecology," "Conflicts"* and *"Solution*: Yes, that will do. Man must take his chance with all the other animals; ecology now to include the whole solar system. Continue to strip Jupiter to give the species the maximum chance."

More than three pages of typed notes block out the novel version of "Circles." "James" is to write chapters 1 and 2, "Morning in Arcady" and "Numerology and Problem." "Josephine" is to write chapters 3 to 6, "Grand Tour—Part One," "The Blue Stones," "Grand Tour—Part Two" and "Sailing Scene." An additional, undated typed sheet of notes outlines Blish's idea for "sailing on air on a sort of coracle"—the subject matter of chapter 6—an episode which is to be linked with the method of gathering the Blue Stones from Jupiter. He asks for ideas: "My imagination doesn't go much futher than fishing nets." "James" is to write chapter 7, "Jupiter—And Beyond" (the echo of *2001: A Space Odyssey* here and a reference to *Rendezvous with Rama* in a sheet of typed notes dated 3 February 1975 points to areas of overlap between Blish's vision and Clarke's), and Chapter 8, "Stone-Netting Scene." There is no indication as to how chapters 9 to 12 ("More About the Stones," "The Moral Problem," "Solution One" and "Solution Two") might have been apportioned. The content of each chapter is briefly summarized.

After this narrative outline there follow four notes beginning with the direction that eight of these twelve chapters should be "underpinned by one of the Eight Great Questions—not obviously but as part of texture, like the use of the myth in *Ulysses.*" The remaining four chapters "are mortar from this point of view. Also, tripartite structure with cliffhanger at ends of parts One and Two, to facilitate serialization."

On a large sheet, Saxton, in Blish's company, diagrammed these structural ideas as shown here. On the back of this sheet the "Linear Sequence of Events is broken down into "Shoum [the viewpoint character] discovers maths/gets answer from computer/seeks advice on journey/visits Ganymede [—] collects samples." All of this clearly indicates the precise preplanning that Blish characteristically put into the construction of his fiction.

Blish mailed drafts of chapters 1 and 2 with a covering letter to "My love and deep joy" on 29 January 1975. He worries about lecturing the reader à la Heinlein, needing "an over-all epigraph" for the work, and looks forward to completing the novel and escaping with his co-author, "with our well-gotten gains to Istanbul." These two chapter drafts apparently incorporated five of the eighteen pages that Saxton had written following the dinner in London (KLA, 1 February 1975).

The first chapter, which has an epigraph from Plato, introduces Agranian with "his four-toed feet." He is a "world energy flow monitor" (he monitors the computer or "Engine") and Advisor to an apprentice named Shoum. It is now apparent that the viewpoint character, Shoum, is female, a change from the outline in the letter to Harrison. Agranian is having an affair with Perdui, a dancer, "his dark and always startling autumn love." Perdui is married to Thern (an "Aesthete" according to the characterizations on a page of typed notes) and Agranian to Enconsul. Clearly, to some degree, Agranian corresponds to Blish and is provided with a personal situation that parallels Blish's at the time. A certain amount of background history is filled in including the information that "cancer and the vermiform appendix" have been done away with. But Agranian senses that something is wrong in Utopia and asks permission to do an extra hour's work.

In chapter 2, which has an epigraph from Aristotle, Shoum enters. She has found "that the universe has a metrical frame" and speaks of her experiments with number: "I am in love with number." Following from this, Agranian (and not the protagonist as the Harrison letter has it) asks a test question for the computer to answer "in your number system": "Express in decimal numbers how much longer we can continue to strip-mine Jovian hydrogen at the base rate." The response is "Five thousand, one hundred and twelve years" or "Three point three

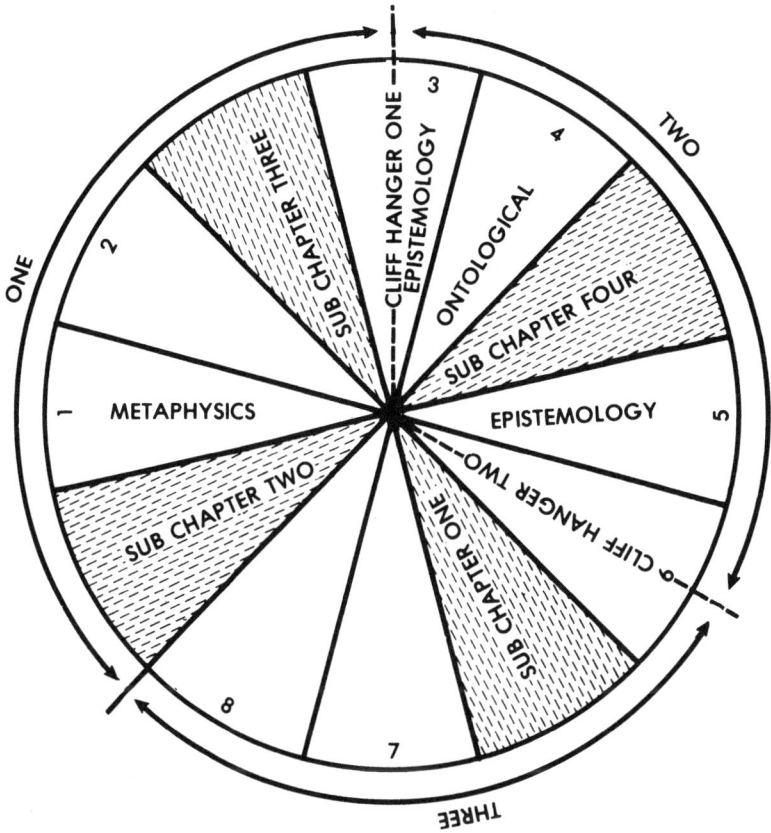

Diagrammatic synopsis for "Circles"/*The Breath of Brahma* (original in Josephine Saxton's possession)

plus" human lifetimes. Agranian instructs Shoum to get a second opinion from Issachar, one of the Governors, and to make the trip to see this man a leisurely educational tour.

Saxton turned in a draft of chapter 3, together with a fragment of same, dealing with Shoum among the Himals, a group of agriculturalists experimenting with the natural life underground where they have counterfeited the Sun and the Moon. Saxton does somewhat better than Blish with the human element and Shoum, who is aged twenty-one, comes rather more to life. She is wearing a Blue Stone from Jupiter and, when she loses her virginity in a fertility ritual, this stone starts "keening" or "singing" and "glowing electric blue." This is the first indication of a Jovian life form about to become sentient. Blish's typed notes sheet dated 3 February 1975 opens with Andy Stephenson's suggestion "that the Blue Stones as a totality be like the computer" and goes on to discuss their characteristics. In accordance with one of the notes which follows the chapter outline, Saxton concludes with the episode initiated by the computer module's earthquake warning. To escape a lava flow Shoum flees into a side room that turns out to be an elevator. Wearing a protective suit provided by the elevator, she emerges on the unlivable surface of the Earth. Blish's note concludes with, "End with erroneous vision of the night sky—possible first cliffhanger."

In his letter of 29 January 1975 Blish mentions his plan to "jump directly to . . . Chapter 7, the astral spaceship" trip to Ganymede. Three days later he wrote Karin Laflin Adams, "I have thought of a fine way to open Ch. 7, which as it happens is the next one in the outline assigned to me . . (After Ch. 8 we have made no more assignments yet, since the chances are good that the last four won't go the way we have described them now.)" And Blish did in fact type almost two pages of chapter 7. The ship is described as "a nearly transparent teardrop, containing two black loungers side by side." This final fragment ends with the landing on Ganymede. As it happens, in the last of Blish's apprenticeship stories, "Elixir" (September 1951), Ganymede is the place where a serum is manufactured that confers immortality and ultimately causes human beings to evolve into a new super species. But there are less positive possibilities. In Blish's first published SF story, "Emergency Refueling" (March, 1940), because of lack of fuel a landing on the underworld planet Pluto has to stand in for a landing on Ganymede, the nearest official refuelling station. On Pluto, it will be recalled, one of the two-man crew is annihilated by a cave-dwelling, cancer-like fungus with an accelerated life-cycle. In that context the final sentence and final word that Blish typed of chapter 7 is particularly uncanny: "The radiation out there is instant death." Saxton's unpublished story about Blish's last days, "The Man Who Loved His Food," includes the detail that "radiation" was one of the taboo words in the household; "therapy" was the preferred euphemism. Characteristically, however, Blish always sought to be honest and toughminded. Thus it would seem that in jumping to chapter 7 and concluding where he did, he wrote his own death from cancer into "The Breath of Brahma."

NINE

THE BRANCHING TREE: JUVENILES, POETRY, CRITICISM, MISCELLANY

■ The Blish corpus includes a large number of avocational and occasional writings, not all of which deserve treatment here. His critical writings on science fiction, Ezra Pound, and James Joyce, his musicological treatise, and three of his juvenile novels are of considerable interest, however. Of least interest, in spite of their significant impact on Blish's personal life and career, are the *Star Trek* books. Blish's doubts about this project are recorded in a notebook entry:

> 26 July 66 An apparent opportunity has arisen to do a book of 8 short stories derived from scripts of the forthcoming TV series "Star Trek" for a flat fee of $2000. This creates a dilemma. I need the money and could do the work quickly. On the other hand I don't like this kind of work and it's bad for the reputation to get involved in that sort of hacking.
> I suppose the best out is to do it under a pen name—and bear in mind that it might help to work for the show directly—especially since the producer will be at the Tricon [1966 World Science Fiction Convention in Cleveland]. (Dep. Blish 437)

Despite his reservations, Blish signed a series of four-book contracts with Bantam Books, and beginning in 1967 eleven *Star Trek* collections appeared under his own name. His main compromise, as noted in chapter 1 herein, was that he did not actually write the last six of these. They were substantially the work of Judith Blish and her mother—"now this is tellable," Judith writes.[1]

The *Star Trek* collections, which Blish viewed reasonably enough as collaborations with the writers of the original scripts, merit only this brief mention in this study. It should be emphasized that these books gained him a much wider audience than he had previously enjoyed and an "unprecedented volume" of fan mail, "more than I can cope with," as he wrote in the preface to *Star Trek 5*.[2] Of particular interest was a letter received from Capt. Pierre D. Kirk of the 363d Transportation Company, U.S. Army, that Blish quotes from in the preface to *Star Trek 6* (presumably his only contribution to that volume). Apparently the men under Kirk's command created an organization based on the series. According to Kirk, because the Viet Cong thought they were up against something like the *Enterprise* they gave no resistance.

Unquestionably the *Star Trek* collections constitute not just the most financially successful of all Blish's juveniles, among which they must be classified, but of all his writings. This may, as Stableford suggests, have led to a more "relaxed attitude" in some of his work.[3] Blish had, in fact, originally gone into the business of writing juveniles with an eye on the size of the market, and his instincts proved correct.

(i) Hearts and Angels: *The Star Dwellers* and *Mission to the Heart Stars*

Blish wrote the Australian writer, critic, and editor John Baxter that he got into the juvenile field, at Lester del Rey's urging, for the money—"juveniles built Heinlein's house in Colorado Springs" (Dep. Blish 411/10, 29 January 1962). Such motives are not necessarily inconsistent with artistic quality but Blish's talent for high-flown moralizing was ill suited to the more simple-minded mix of didacticism and adventure required of the successful SF juvenile. Certainly the first and third such works that he published, *The Star Dwellers* (1961) and *Mission to the Heart Stars* (1965)—but not the second, *A Life for the Stars* (1962), which is discussed in chapter 6 in its *Cities in Flight* context—are characterized by a paucity of adventurous activity and an excess of overly sophisticated didactic exposition—overly sophisticated for the average adolescent at least.[4] The average adolescent would also not much appreciate Blish's humorless, patronizing put-down in *The Star Dwellers* of pop music and other frivolous distractions which the aspiring space cadet must abjure if he (no female space cadets are mentioned) is to cope with the heavy educational demands. The "celibate rule" is designed to take care of what is felt to be the major possible distraction.[5] At the same time, Blish notes "When I first started writing juveniles my style was so involved that I took to doing the kids' books on the tape recorder, in the hope of running out of breath before any given sentence could get beyond the reader's attention span" (KLA, 18 February 1973).

Seventeen-year-old Jack Loftus, the hero of *The Star Dwellers* and understudy to Daniel Hart, secretary for space, is a model cadet. Together with Hart's top agent, Howard Langer, and fellow cadet Jerry

THE BRANCHING TREE

(Sandbag) Stevens, Jack finds himself aboard the *Ariadne*, headed in Haertel overdrive for an interstellar dust cloud known as the Coal Sack nebula; there certain energy beings dubbed "Angels," an identification that immediately signals Blish's characteristic mix of physics and metaphysics, science and religion, congregate. The mission of the *Ariadne*'s crew is to negotiate an agreement with the Angels that will allow some of their number to follow the example of Lucifer, an Angel captured by the surviving ship of the previous McCrary expedition; Lucifer has agreed to help run one of Earth's hydrogen fusion reactors from the inside. Lucifer seems to be a benign VOR. As things turn out and as this species of power-fantasy, juvenile SF requires, it is Jack alone who negotiates on humanity's behalf with the Angels. He achieves the agreement through an initial contact with a junior Angel, whom he names Hesperus and who puts him in touch with the "First-Born," whom Jack calls Gabriel. Eventually, after the *Ariadne*'s return to Earth trailing something like Wordsworth's immortality, "clouds and clouds of Angels" (p. 89), the treaty is ratified. A number of young Angels will, in return for their required energy fix, assist humanity. This cooperative model, the reason the book was written, was conceived, Blish informs Paul Shackley, as a rebuttal to Heinlein's militarist and somewhat fascistic *Starship Troopers* (PS, 10 July 1970).

In order to spin this simple tale out to an appropriate book length a certain amount of padding and misdirection is necessary, and a couple of loose-end characters are left hanging. Paul X. McCrary, owner of the McCrary Fleet, and his reporter daughter, Sylvia, receive build-ups which lead the reader to expect that they will both figure more significantly than they actually do in the ensuing action. Perhaps extraneous to a juvenile readership is the association of the Angels with the life principle by way of the following descriptive tags: "They are translucent and blood-red when at rest" (p. 15); unlike the Angels in pictures, which "looked more like tear drops—or drops of blood," Hesperus first strikes Jack as a "scarlet" comma-shape, then a "pulsating scarlet sphere" (pp. 56, 57). The sense is that the Angels are heart symbols, symbols of life, love, and maturity in emotional, intellectual, and spiritual terms, the Haertel (heart-intellect) ideal. This implication is reinforced by the Angels' association with the heart stars, stars near the heart of the galaxy. The heart stars, around which life first evolved, including a life form which has founded an interstellar federation, is anticipated by references to red stars ("the faster they were, the redder they were"), to "the heart of the nebula," and to "the heart of the Coal Sack" (pp. 50, 69, 84).

This heart/angel ideal is represented on a human level, as their names suggest, by the two most important adults in *The Star Dwellers*: Daniel Hart and the "cherubic" Howard Langer (p. 11). Langer is clearly derived from the French word for angel, *l'ange*. This suggests, of course, that what we are dealing with here, as in much juvenile fiction, is a fable of maturation. Jack and Sandbag must strive for the balance of wisdom and empathy that their supervisors supposedly exhibit. Communication with, and an appreciative understanding of, other forms of life is both a necessary prerequisite for, and a condition of, the ideal state of maturity that Blish envisions. The other forms of life may be adults (from a juvenile point of view), aliens, or animals. In this story Blish follows his own predilections and makes cats both representative of the animal world and symbolic as a link between the animal world and that of the Angels. Thus the Angels were drawn to the three McCrary Fleet ships "by the 'glow' of their fusion reactors, much as a cat might settle down next to the fireplace" (p. 16). That the way-station planet Aaa is inhabited by "a medium-sized, rather cat-like creature" reinforces this animal-alien analogy (p. 41). At the conclusion of the sequel volume, *Mission to the Heart Stars*, the Angels make clear their sympathetic regard for these creatures when it is decided that "the coming children of the Aaa" will be among the races with whom the Angels will rule.

A subsidiary aspect of *The Star Dwellers* becomes the focus of *Mission to the Heart Stars*, a book about half-written, according to Blish's foreword, by the fall of 1962.[6] It is established in *The Star Dwellers* that because Jack and company have performed so well, the Angels will recommend to "the great races at the galactic center" (p. 72) who rule over a galactic federation that the 100,000-year trial period allotted to Earth before it would be considered sufficiently mature to join the federation be shortened by half. *Mission to the Heart Stars* is about Earth's attempt (via Jack and company) essentially to eliminate the new 50,000-year trial period and gate-crash the federation, and Earth's discovery that the federation does not, in fact, represent the best way to go. In the foreword, as in that of *The Star Dwellers*, Blish lays out something of his didactic intent: "For several years I have been wondering about the future of individual human freedom in a high-energy culture ["a term for which I think I am solely responsible"] like ours" (p. 11). But he credits Lester del Rey for the basic plot idea for *Mission to the Heart Stars*; del Rey suggested "that the alliance between the Angels and the Earth might well be more powerful than my central galactic federation—a lovely idea, and one that could be wedded usefully to my then rather hazy plan to explore the future of freedom in a high energy culture."

Blish's daughter, Elisabeth, in her introduction to the 1982 Avon Books reprint of *Mission to the Heart Stars*, recalls reading the book when she "was eleven or twelve," regrets the dumping of Sylvia McCrary, and characterizes, accurately enough, both *Mission* and *The Star Dwellers* as "books about how to grow up right" (p. 7). Maturity in the sequel means avoiding a frozen state of stability and being open to change. Aboard the *Argo*, on the way to the head world of the galactic federation, the Hegemony of Malis (i.e., malice, evil), Jack and his cohorts get to sample life on four outer federation worlds—Palinurus, a world of machines, a world of ritual, and a world called Ss'pode.[7] It seems that only stable worlds qualify for membership in the Hegemony and that stability amounts to a kind of death. Change, on the other hand, is the condition of life. Essentially, then, the Hegemony is discovered to be an evil dictatorship and its leader, who wishes to make Earth a subject state, not a member, is appropriately characterized as "a devil—a monster" (p. 75). Consequently, after the Hegemony has made possible the escape of the *Argo* from Ss'pode, the party must next escape, by way of some very hackneyed plotting, from Malis.

Thanks to Hesperus, who stowed away, the *Argo* is able to outrun the Malan pursuit ship and return to Earth. Jack expresses the hope that eventually Earth will form a rival federation. It seems, according to Dr. Langer's explanation, that the Heart Stars are stuck at Spengler's third stage of Culture (civilization and spiritual winter), whereas Earth is in "a definite post-civilization period," i.e., beyond Spengler's sterile, repetitive system (p. 88). A "federal feudalism" based upon "dynamic equilibrium" will, it is supposed, stand a better chance of surviving than one based on stability (p. 89). And the Angels agree: "It is decided: We abandon the Hegemony of Malis. The men of Earth, the dolphins [a second sentient race on Earth], the beademungen of the twin radioceles, the coming children of the Aaa, and those others of which we know, or which we can foresee—these are the races that will rule with us" (p. 111). *Mission to the Heart Stars* ends, then, as does *The Star Dwellers*, with a contract with the Angels, although unlike *The Star Dwellers*, it is not the contract originally sought.

The reference to "the Aaa," as I have noted, harks back to *The Star Dwellers*. The Blish reader will recognize "the beademungen" as a reference to the entity met with in "Common Time." Spengler's name is not mentioned but the reference to cultural stages will remind the Blish reader of *Cities in Flight*. Much of the interest, in fact, of *Mission to the Heart Stars* derives from this yoking together of elements from other works. Dr. Langer evokes "Common Time" earlier when he refers to the Mark I, the original Haertel overdrive "that took Garrard to Alpha

Centauri on the first interstellar trip we ever made" (p. 103). The reference to the great discovery in 2011 that led to "Haertel's faster-than-light drive" (p. 43) fills in one of the gaps in Haertel's career between the time of *Welcome to Mars* and that of "Common Time." Information about the history of Mars and the Diagram of Power parallels that provided in *They Shall Have Stars*.[8] The first communication from the Hegemony, which takes the form "Good evening, Rangers. . . . This is Rogers, speaking for Captain Video," is an allusion to the television series for which Blish wrote (p. 34). Also part of this network of allusion is the fact that the *Argo* is actually a reconditioned version of the *Telemachus*. The *Telemachus* was the ship that figures in the very early stories that Blish wrote for his fanzine *The Planeteer*, in "Blackout in Cygni" (July 1951), and in the Captain Video scripts.

Not content with amalgamating only his own work to the world of *Mission to the Heart Stars*, Blish also amalgamates the work of another SF writer. Dr. Langer recalls that the Martians built what has been called "The Death Machine" on the back of our Moon: "But remember, we don't know what it was actually for. We only gave it that name because it was so deadly to explore, but that's almost surely a—well, call it a side effect" (p. 19). The allusion is to *Rogue Moon* (1960) by Algis Budrys, a book that Blish much admired.[9] Unfortunately, these allusions, which amount to the side effects of *Mission to the Heart Stars*, seem more worthy of note than the real heart of the matter. Like *The Star Dwellers*, *Mission* is a somewhat qualified success.

(ii) *Welcome to Mars* and the Haertel Network

The foreword and afterword of *Welcome to Mars* (1967), the juvenile that Blish originally entitled more soberly "The Hour Before Earthrise" (1966), make plain his interest in depicting the Mars known to contemporary astronomy rather than the romantic planet popularized by Edgar Rice Burroughs and Ray Bradbury. In the afterword, dated 30 July 1965, Blish notes triumphantly that the photographs obtained from Mariner IV, which reached Mars after the "manuscript of this book left my hands," make more likely "the existence of an underground ice-table" such as that posited in his fiction.[10] Blish also seems to be prescient in making reference to the unmanned Martian probes of 1972 and 1978 (pp. 34, 38); Vikings 1 and 2 actually soft-landed on Mars in 1976. However, Blish's fiction features, one rather striking violation of the present-day reader's factual knowledge. Although *Welcome to Mars* seems to be set in the 1980s or 1990s, man has not yet set foot on the moon (pp. 19, 21, 117).[11] In a work published just three years before the actual event, this aberration somewhat dents Blish's claims for the credibility of his account.

But what lends *Welcome to Mars* its particular charm is precisely this bizarre conjunction of realism and fantasy. Not only does Blish's eighteen-year-old hero, Dolph Haertel, travel to Mars in a caulked packing-crate but, once there, he is actually able to survive in relative comfort! This amalgam of the absurd and the factual makes for a light-heartedness, a whimsicality that is rare in Blish's work and certainly far removed from the heavy-handed didacticism characteristic of *The Star Dwellers* and *Mission to the Heart Stars*. Thus the following description of Dolph's antigravity device, "a small breadboard rig," in action—the levitation of a garage containing Dolph and his girlfriend Nanette Ford—anticipates the mood of the film *E.T.*:

> In an eternal moment of groaning boards and squeaking nails, it had cut the whole garage off from the Earth and lifted it, both family cars included, a good inch off its foundations. The instant when the power cut off and the whole mass thudded back into place was even more alarming, but it was all that had saved garage, Nanette and Dolph; he had had the rig plugged into a light socket, and the feeder line had parted before the frame building had pulled quite free of its concrete bedding. (P. 21)

Dolph's love for "the poetry of maths"—and his acute intelligence, which should perhaps be aligned with that of the dolphin—has led to the discovery of a new and much more convenient mode of space flight.

An antigravity principle cannot but recall the "cavorite" of H.G. Wells's *The First Men in the Moon* (1901); and it is the spirit of Wells, abetted ultimately by those of the supposedly excluded Burroughs and Bradbury, which presides over the nonfactual, SF aspects of *Welcome to Mars*. Just as Wells's *Time Traveller* makes a model version of his time machine, so Dolph "made a model ship of his first packing-case" (p. 22). The Martian Dolph and Nanette finally meet, the sole representative of a long-vanished race, would seem to be a relative of the tentacular Martians so graphically described by Wells in *The War of the Worlds* (1898): "It was tall, and not man-like, suggesting rather a serpent or worm with a cluster of six or eight small arms near the head end" (p. 144).

Because of a burned-out power tube, Dolph finds himself marooned on Mars. From this point on his experiences correspond in a very straightforward, even routine, manner (and with a good deal of padding) to those of Robinson Crusoe, who provides the most important fictional model for *Welcome to Mars*. This relatively obvious transposition was first made in Rex Gordon's *No Man Friday* (1956; U.S. title: *First on Mars*), a novel which Blish read before writing *Welcome to Mars* (PS, 7 April 1972). Shortly before or while Blish was writing *Welcome to Mars*, the film *Robinson Crusoe on Mars* (1965), apparently unrelated to Gordon's novel, appeared. After a Robinson Crusoe-type appraisal of the situation and inventory, Dolph sets about the problem of surviving on Mars. His Friday, so identified by the title of the middle section of the book, turns out to be Nanette, who, having figured out where Dolph is and duplicated his antigravity box spaceship, flies to Mars with the idea of rescuing him. Unfortunately, as a result of her crash landing, the power tube in her ship is destroyed.

Only in the last thirty pages, after Dolph and Nanette have survived on Martian lichen for several years, does the plot gather momentum. The chapter 12 title, "They are Not Dead!" expresses the hope of Dolph's foster-father and points to life on Mars in a double sense—human life and Martian life. In the next chapter, Dolph and Nanette run into a dune-cat (after first discovering the print of its five-toed paw, an echo of Crusoe's discovery of Friday) which eventually leads them to a dead crystal city beneath a vast ice-lake. In the center of this city its last master, the Wellsian sleeper encased in a crystal box, bequeaths Mars to the representatives of Earth and then dies. This very rushed climax concludes with the arrival of a rescue ship from Earth, a somewhat incredible plot maneuver made possible by an adaptation of Dolph's invention, and with the projected shipboard marriage of Dolph and Nanette, who with the passage of an unspecified number of years are no longer children.[12] The distance that Blish has travelled from a realistic presentation may be gauged by the reference to "Lieutenant Gulliver" (p. 151), a member of the rescue fleet. Blish is alluding to the hero of Edwin Lester Arnold's highly fanciful *Lieut. Gullivar Jones: His Vacation* (1905), the American edition of which is entitled *Gulliver of Mars*. This is a book which anticipates the romantic Mars of E. R. Burroughs.

Two particularly Blishian aspects of *Welcome to Mars* should be isolated which involve climbing in both the literal and the metaphorical sense. The crate in which Dolph travels to Mars is constructed in, and takes flight from, the branches of an ancient pear tree. The metaphorical message, the need to climb the Tree of Knowledge as a means of transcendence, should be equated with that of the Lithian Message

Tree in *A Case of Conscience* and of the quincunx of trees in both *The Quincunx of Time* and *Midsummer Century*, and related to Tannhaüser's *"wrath-bearing tree,"* an allusion in both *A Case of Conscience* and *The Day After Judgment*.[13] The impulse towards communication leads Dolph to climb the rim of an oasis on Mars. The idea is to set up a radio jammer to attract attention by interfering with what is assumed to be some kind of Martian beacon signal. Looking at the sky, Dolph recalls the "famous medieval [actually late nineteenth-century] woodcut of a man who, having reached the horizon of a flat world, had broken through the crystal of the sky where it touched the ground and now stared in wonder beyond the sphere of stars at those prime movers—great wheels and other engines—which kept all the inner, Aristotelean spheres turning against their backdrop of eternally twinkling flames" (p. 114; reproduction p. 68 herein). Although Blish claimed not to have recognized the power of the breakthrough theme suggested by this image in the climb to the ceiling of the sky in "Surface Tension," its presence here in a passage published some eight years before Darko Suvin's "revelation" does indicate a more or less conscious awareness on Blish's part of his recurring theme.[14]

If the sleeper bequeaths Mars to Earth via Dolph and Nanette, Dolph, by way of his discovery, bequeaths the universe to mankind. The antigravity principle eventually makes possible the faster-than-light Haertel drive, by means of which humanity may "cross the desert" of space to touch the stars (p. 114). Paraphrasing a sentence from the conclusion of *They Shall Have Stars* (1957), one might say "There was a constellation named Haertel, and every star in the sky belonged to it."[15] The Haertel drive (with its modifications over time) is featured (along with related cross-references) in a number of Blish stories which form the nucleus of what might be called the Haertel Network. The shape of this future history, with *Welcome to Mars* as its root in terms of fictional chronology, may be represented by the tree-diagram offered on the following page.

On the other hand, "Common Time" written some thirteen years before *Welcome to Mars*, may be considered the Network's root in terms of compositioned chronology. There Haertel appears as a benign father figure of around seventy years old. This aged Haertel and the young Haertel in *Welcome to Mars* account for his two personal appearances in Blish's fiction.

The next Network story that Blish wrote, "Beep," contains no reference to Haertel or his drive. But the Dirac communicator in "Beep"— although not its beepless predecessor in "Chaos, Co-ordinated" and

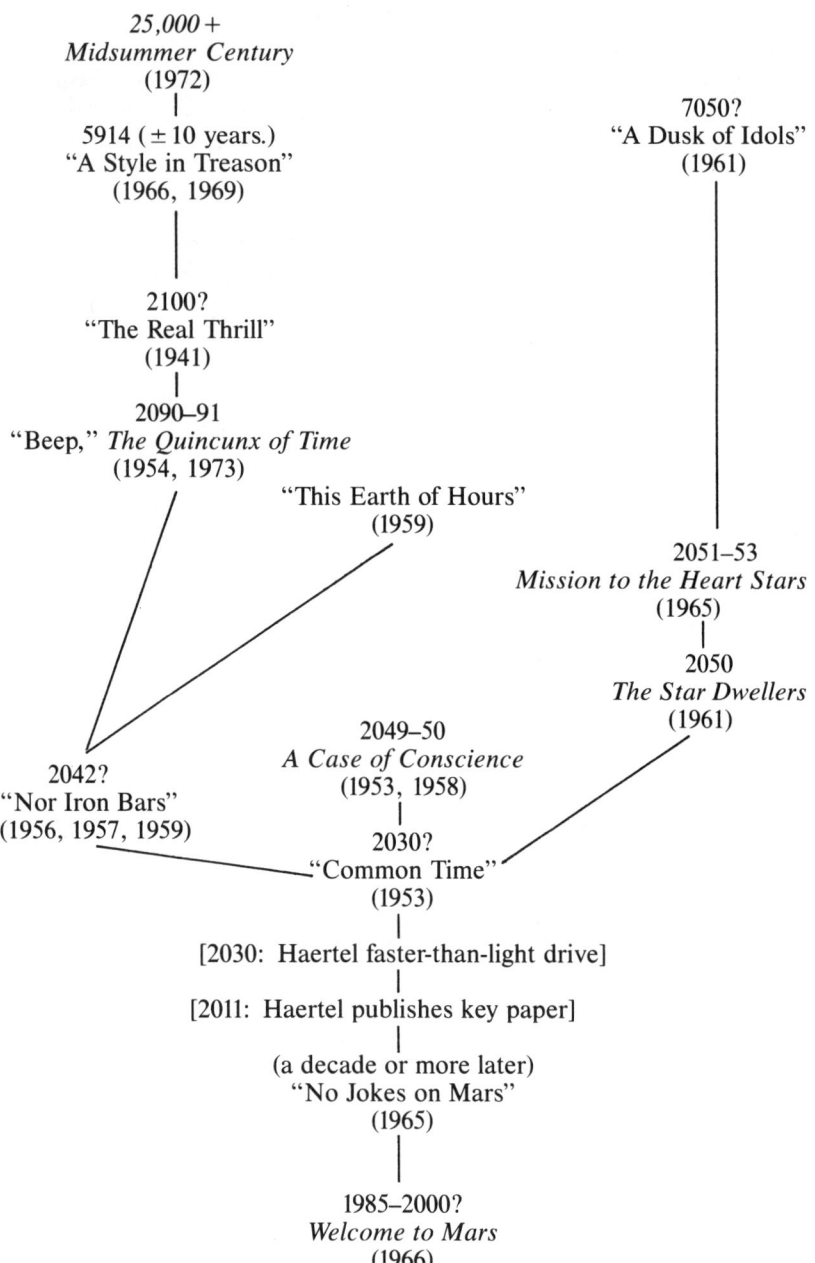

The Haertel Network. Where it is known, or can be estimated, the temporal fix is given above the title; first publication dates appear below in parentheses.

Cities in Flight, which works should not be *directly* related to the Haertel Network—will turn out to be second in importance only to the Haertel drive among the elements that link the Network stories. The Haertel drive and the Dirac communicator are to the Haertel future history what the spindizzy and the anti-agathic drugs are to the Cities in Flight future history. But only in 1970, when Blish was expanding "Beep" into *The Quincunx of Time,* did he retrospectively consolidate the story's place in the Haertel Network while attaching to *Quincunx* the Network's most flourishing branch.

The next chronologically relevant story and the first that Blish linked at the outset to "Common Time" and therefore to the Haertel Network, "Nor Iron Bars," is apparently set around 2042, twelve years after "Common Time." This subsequent faster-than-light test flight to Centaurus makes use of the new Arpe drive (with its Nernst-effect generators) which, by giving the ship negative mass, avoids "the wild sine-curve variation in subjective time" enforced on the passenger by the Haertel drive.[16] The famous explorer, Daryon Hammersmith, met with for the first time in the 1957 "Nor Iron Bars," and incorporated into the 1959 revision of its root story "Detour to the Stars," must have been the discoverer of the planet Hammersmith which is mentioned in "Beep." Thus "Nor Iron Bars," in its 1957 and 1959 versions, retrospectively links "Beep" to the Haertel future history.

Only when Blish extended the novella "A Case of Conscience" into the novel version, at about the same time he was working on "Nor Iron Bars," did the former become part of the Haertel Network. The first of five Haertel references in book 2 of *A Case of Conscience* alludes to "the fantastic time effects that Garrard went through on that first successful Centaurus flight" while the second explains (*à la* "Nor Iron Bars") that Garrard "was slowed down to an hour a second, then whipped up to a second an hour, then back again, and so on along a sine wave."[17] Since by 2049, the year that the story begins, the Haertel drive and its overdrive (mentioned once in book 1 and three times in book 2) is back in operation, it appears that some sort of insulation against the temporal distortions caused by the drive's field has been achieved in the years 2042–49.

The original novella version does not contain the four Haertel references that appear as additions, or in the fourth instance as a replacement for "Milne," when "A Case of Conscience" became book 1 of *A Case of Conscience*. By 1958 Blish had decided that the Haertel drive, like the Arpe drive, in 2049, if not before, is powered by Nernst-effect, or Nernst generators. Thus "the ship's Nernst generators" at the end of book 1 replace the "ship's generators" at the end of "A Case of Conscience."[18]

"This Earth of Hours" (June 1959) is the only story in the network that cannot be fictionally dated with more or less precision, in spite of the likelihood that the Callë who discovered the planet of that name in the story "a hundred years ago" is himself named for the German astronomer Johann Gottfried Galle, who first sighted Neptune in 1846. The link with "Nor Iron Bars" is established by the reference to "the Arpe Effect—the second of two unsuccesful attempts at an interstellar drive, long before the discovery of the Standing Wave" which is now used for faster-than-light travel. Since the Standing Wave concept also figures in *The Star Dwellers*, which is set in 2050, "nearly two decades after the discovery of the Haertel faster-than-light drive" and which thus takes up chronologically where *A Case of Conscience* leaves off, it seems reasonable to assume that the relationship between the Haertel overdrive and the Standing Wave was finally clarified around 2050, eight years after the Arpe Effect flight of "Nor Iron Bars" described (misleadingly, it would appear) in "This Earth of Hours" as occurring "long before."[19] Apparently "the Haertel overdrive turned each ship into a little universe of its own, the Standing Wave—actually not a wave but a sort of bubble in space-time, in which all the cozy local Newtonian ordinances seemed to hold true regardless of how fast the bubble was travelling in relation to the rest of the universe."[20] Presumably, at the time of Garrard's mission in "Common Time," the overdrive created only an imperfect space-time bubble.

"A Dusk of Idols," written around the same time as *The Star Dwellers*, opens with a reference to the protagonist's "first contact with the Heart stars," an allusion to *The Star Dwellers* that is subsequently elaborated. Since we are informed in "A Dusk of Idols" that "Earth could be expected to be allowed to join the galactic federation in about forty-five thousand years—and that was what remained of half our originally allotted time period," it follows that the story takes place around 7050 (5,000 years after what happens in *The Star Dwellers*).[21]

In the sequel to *The Star Dwellers*, *Mission to the Heart Stars*, it will be recalled that the 50,000-year trial period is rendered irrelevant. (This, of course makes for an inconsistency with "A Dusk of Idols.") Two references in *Mission* to the "beademungen," along with references to Haertel in both *The Star Dwellers* and *Mission*, serve to link both works (and "A Dusk of Idols," the short story most directly related to the juvenile diptych) directly to "Common Time."

At the same time, in *Mission* (where the Haertal drive continues to be powered by Nernst generators) we learn something more of Haertel's career between *Welcome to Mars* and "Common Time": "it was not until 2011 that the great Haertel succeeded in showing that the Einstein theory of relativity was only a 'special case' of Milne's relativity, and Milne's in turn, only a special case of Haertel's." Thus the faster-than-light drive "was the practical outcome . . . brought into reality only nineteen years after Haertel's epoch-making paper had been published." A later reference to the "Mark I" appears, the original Haertel drive "that took Garrard to Alpha Centauri on the first interstellar trip we ever made. It was abandoned because it produced a sine wave differential variation between t-time and tau-time." Because it threw the traveller "into a highly unpleasant physical state called 'pseudo-death' . . . the Mark I drive was abandoned after only one expedition."[22] Thus *Mission* again explains what happens in "Common Time" in terms similar to those in "Nor Iron Bars" and *A Case of Conscience*.

With "No Jokes on Mars" and *Welcome to Mars*, Blish had completed the first phase of his development of the Haertel future history. The short story was written before *Welcome to Mars* but was set, as Blish explains, on the Mars of *Welcome to Mars* "at least a decade after" the events in the novel.[23]

After the move to England Blish entered into a regular correspondence with Shackley, who eventually produced a symmetrical diagram of what he called the "Haertel Complex" (Dep. Blish 431/11). Shackley's diagram corresponds closely to the tree schema depicted here, minus the branch issuing from "Beep"/*Quincunx*. He had noted, after configuring the stories in different ways, that because of internal references, it made most sense to view the stories linked back to "Common Time" as three essentially separate lines of development with the result that a "Nor Iron Bars"/"This Earth of Hours"/"Beep" trilogy is balanced by a *Star Dwellers*/*Mission*/"Dusk of Idols" trilogy. These trilogies are most logically conceived in diagrammatic terms as lying on either side of the third "Common Time" line which consists only of *A Case of Conscience*. Blish was intrigued by Shackley's tree diagram but in a letter to Shackley denies having planned the "symmetry you discover in the 'Haertel complex'" (PS, 1 April 1971). In other words, Blish was previously aware only that he had written an unsymmetrical complex of linked stories between 1953 and 1966.

But thanks to Shackley, it was with a very conscious sense of symmetry and story interconnectedness that Blish in 1970 set about expanding "Beep" into *The Quincunx of Time*. A number of the changes and inserts firmly tie *Quincunx* to the Haertel Network. Thus *Quincunx*

THE NUB OF FANTASY

contains ten references to Haertel, the Haertel drive, or Haertelism. One of them is to the Haertel of *Welcome to Mars* who, "when he was seventeen years old," made the assumption that "the geometry which applies to ultimate particles" is Pythagorean, not Euclidean, "and almost everything that's happened in particle physics since has flown out of it."[24]

As we have seen, only when Blish wrote book 2 of *A Case of Conscience* did he retrospectively link book 1, the revised story version, to the Haertel Network. What *Quincunx* does is retrospectively add to the link made between "Beep" and the Network in the 1957 "Nor Iron Bars." At the same time, *Quincunx* retrospectively shoehorns "The Real Thrill," "A Style in Treason," and *Midsummer Century* (a work conceived in 1948) into the Haertel universe. Thus, of the twelve works that make up the Haertel Network, five (or perhaps six, if we include "No Jokes on Mars") are there as afterthoughts. As ever, however, Blish valued his afterthoughts. In this manner, the writing of *Quincunx* accounts for the second phase of the development of the Haertel Network.

The composition history of the Haertel Network amounts to a kind of temporal hopscotch that is thoroughly compatible with the mind-spinning speculation about the nature of time in *Quincunx* and, to a lesser extent, in "Beep." Thus it is at least excusable to discuss in reverse chronological order of conception the three titles tied into the Network by the three additional messages from the future in *Quincunx*.

After the Dirac transmission related to "A Style in Treason" provides information about the Green Exarchy versus High Earth and the Traitors' Guild, it is speculated in *Quincunx* that "the first seeds of that Traitors' Guild are right here in the bureau" that developed the Dirac. An earlier *Quincunx* addition, in which reference is made to "a vombis, a totally protean creature working for a sort of empire on the far side of the galaxy called the Green Exarchy,"[25] indicates that by 2090 the "Style in Treason" universe had already impinged on the bureau's awareness.

It should be noted that in "A Style in Treason" something called the "Imaginary Drive" has apparently replaced the Haertel drive although in *Quincunx* the remote possibility is raised that the "Imaginary Drive" may be the Haertel overdrive under a new name. However this may be, Blish, in "A Style in Treason," makes use of Simon's bogus personalities to recall some of his other works (see pp. 153–54 herein). While some of these allusions establish links with members of the Haertel Network ("Common Time," *The Star Dwellers*, and *Quincunx*), others establish links with stories making up an imaginary universe which, thus far, I have not directly related to the Network (*Cities in Flight* and *The Frozen Year*). The untidiness here may exist because when Blish wrote "A Style in Treason" he did not conceive it in any very deliberate way in terms of the symmetrical "Haertel Complex" to which Shackley would alert him. Possibly, if Blish had had the opportunity to revise the story, he might have eliminated the apparently non-Haertel Network references. For reasons I shall come to, however, it is more likely that he would not have done so.

Had Blish lived longer he may well have contributed at least two further novels to the Network. One of these would have grown out of "A Style in Treason." Blish wrote Shackley, "I am hoping to do a novel about the Exarchy/High Earth/Traitors' Guild complex eventually" (PS, 4 January 1970). "The other project I would like to tackle" would be a time-travel novel, "completely populated and emerging logically out of the *method* of time travel used" (PS, 30 June 1970). This project grew out of Blish's speculations about time in *Quincunx* and his correspondence with Shackley. The *"method,"* apparently, would have derived from the assumption that the universe is finite and spinning and might have been connected with the backwards-travelling "world-line cruiser" mentioned in the 8873–8704 Dirac transmission in "Beep" and *Quincunx*.[26]

Of particular importance to the Haertel Network are the connections between *Quincunx* and *Midsummer Century*, the original conception of which predates the composition of the first Network story by five years. Blish took advantage of the fact that he was expanding "Beep" and writing *Midsummer Century* around the same time to knit the works tightly together. In *Midsummer Century* the protagonist, John Martels, is asked a series of questions in approximately the year 25,000. A synopsis of the questions and responses is then converted into "a Dirac beep, sent so that all receivers who might have any reason to care about the problem should have a record of it."[27] This beep message is picked up centuries earlier in *Quincunx*. The third of the additional beep messages, it is comparable in subject matter to the toposcopic scanning of Simon's multiple personalities in "A Style in Treason." Since the content of this message indicates that, in the future, the future is not regarded as immutably determined, it crucially affects deliberations in *Quincunx* concerning the use of the Dirac transmitter. In any event, by having a message transmitted in one story received in another set at an earlier date, Blish startingly dramatizes the basic idea originally embodied in "Beep."

The *Midsummer Century* beep message includes the information that Martels, who is thirty at the beginning of the novella, was born in 1955. Thus *Midsummer Century* opens in 1985. This means, in effect, that the entire Haertel Network occurs between chapters 1 and 2 of *Midsummer Century*, assuming that the young Haertel journeyed to Mars late in 1985 or shortly thereafter. Chapter 1 of *Midsummer Century* with its reference to the Thor Wald of "Beep" and *Quincunx* might be considered as a prologue to the Network. Given that Martels ends up at the same temporal destination as the Haertel Network itself and begins his adventures around the same date that the Haertel future history gets underway, the similarity between the names Martels and Haertel may not be accidental.

The earliest (and weakest) story incorporated post facto into the Haertel Network is the somewhat inept, somewhat sexist, and unreprinted "The Real Thrill." Paul Shackley had no knowledge of this story and thus omits it from his "Haertel Complex, Revised" diagram on the back of the tenth page of his letter to Blish dated 11 January 1974 (Dep. Blish 431/11). The plot is alluded to in the second additional *Quincunx* beep message. While the stuff about Burrowes and his girlfriend taking off from Kennedy Spaceport in an obsolete spaceship corresponds to what happens in "The Real Thrill," the same message also refers to a new element: "the discovery of how to travel the Fortean tunnels to the solar and alternate-solar planets." On this basis, it is assumed that

> the tunnel is something we're going to discover in the very near future. The ship model shown is contemporary with us, and solid-fuel grains don't have a very long shelf-life. Besides, we can't have been using the Dirac very long by then . . . the reporter committed an elementary failure in technique. . . . He forgot to mention the date.[28]

This would put the date of "The Real Thrill" (as reconceived) somewhere around 2100. Of course, there is no mention of Haertel in "The Real Thrill." Nevertheless, by forcibly dragging that story into the Haertel Network and linking it also with the Fortean tunnel notion, Blish provided a solution to inconsistencies within the Haertel Network (for example the Mars of *Welcome to Mars* is incompatible with the Mars of *Mission to the Heart Stars*) and made possible connections between the Haertel Network and the rest of his SF (and non-SF) *oeuvre:* Fortean tunnels make possible connections with all manner of other dimensions and parallel universes, the conception of reality envisaged in *Jack of Eagles* and elsewhere. Thus the three lines of future history that Blish developed—the Seedling Stars line, the Cities in Flight line, and the Haertel line—may, if one wishes, be viewed as occurring in separate but dimensionally linked parallel universes. Thus, for example, the Lithia destroyed in *A Case of Conscience* still exists in the Seedling Stars universe. And one should not forget here that *A Case of Conscience*, while participating in the Haertel Network, marks the temporal terminus of the "After Such Knowledge" trilogy, the two other works of which—*Doctor Mirabilis*, set in the distant past, and *Black Easter/The Day After Judgment*, set in our time—might also be placed in dimensionally-linked parallel universes.

But since the Haertel future history does not necessarily conflict with the Seedling Stars or Cities in Flight histories and allows plenty of time between 3000 and 25,000 for these histories to work themselves out, the parallel universes hypothesis, at least in the fashion just envisaged, is certainly not mandatory. It seems more reasonable to conclude that the references to the Diagram of Power on Mars in volume 1 of *Cities in Flight* and in *Mission to the Heart Stars*, the presence of the Dirac (minus the beep) in *Cities in Flight* and the mention there of "Sweeney, on Ganymede," a character in *The Seedling Stars*, indicates that the Cities in Flight and Seedling Stars future histories (which both feature Oc dollars and ultra phones) occur within the same dimensional universe and are consonant with the Haertel scheme of future history up until 4104, the year of the collapse of our universe at the end of *Cities in Flight*.[29] This would seem to necessitate the hypothesis that "A Style in Treason" and *Midsummer Century* take place in some kind of parallel universe. Howsoever a reader might wish to configure the possibilities, the Haertel Network, with its quincuncial conception of time, does provide an elastic frame of sufficiently ample duration that it may be understood, should one so desire, as containing Blish's entire fictional oeuvre.

(iii) *The Vanished Jet* and *Spock Must Die!*

No great claims can be made for *The Vanished Jet* (1968), a juvenile commissioned by Truman Talley of Weybright & Talley. A very slack piece of work, it is in fact the weakest of Blish's novels. In the "Author's Notes," Blish points out that although the events take place around 1975 and include "a few assumptions about the very near future," it is not an SF story.[30] As a near-future mystery "thriller," it has more in common with contemporary realism than SF. The clumsily fabricated plot, which depends heavily on indirection, is set in motion by the disappearance of the United States experimental Sub-Orbital Transport plane, the *Conqueror*, on its maiden high-parabola flight to the Paris Air Show. The hero, fifteen-year-old Stan Dorman, whose parents were aboard the plane, believes it has been hijacked and is presently on the ground, and journeys to Saudi Arabia to search for it, and much of this slight twelve-chapter book focuses on travelogue-like details of the Saudi Arabian adventure. Stan guesses, from information provided by a German archaeologist, that the plane may be hidden in the "immense tombs" carved out of "Mada'in Salih, a sandstone mountain in the northwestern part of this country, a good two thousand years ago."[31] In recalling a line about the Sphinx—*"And the duned gold clean drifted over the forepaws of Time"* (p. 76; emphasis in original)—Stan is quoting the same line (from Blish's poem "The Coming Forth") that occurs in "The Oath" as an example of Gottlieb's poetry. Stan's understanding of "the theory of mirages," we are told, "would not have satisfied" who else but "Roger Bacon" (p. 81). And when King Faisel's parachutists rescue Stan, his companions, his parents, and the other *Conqueror* passengers from the tomb where they are incarcerated by a rebel Arab group, Blish cannot resist a little characteristic preaching: "The King's men had decided to do the job the hard way, which as almost always happens was turning out to be the best way" (p. 104).

Eventually the *Conqueror* lands with its passengers at Orly Airport, where all is explained. The Soviets had planned the pirating of the *Conqueror* but a panicy French traitor was responsible for the ship ending up in Arab rather than Russian hands. The interrupted parabola of Blish's narrative suggests a parallel with the flight of the *Conqueror*. Correspondingly, the "anti radar chaff" which a traitor aboard the *Conqueror* released to give the false impression that the ship had exploded suggests the dismaying truth about this novel. What wheat it may contain is thoroughly mixed up with loosely-written chaff.

Although Blish's one original contribution to the *Star Trek* saga, *Spock Must Die!* (1970), has the duplication element in common with both his own and Lowndes's *The Duplicated Man* and the early *Star Trek* episode "The Enemy Within," it may well have been most significantly inspired by his reading of Algis Budrys's *Rogue Moon*, the book Blish alludes to in *Mission to the Heart Stars* and hails as a masterpiece in a 1961 review.[32] Budrys makes use of a transmitter which produces duplicates on the Moon of human beings on Earth to explore the question, "what constitutes human identity?" Blish likewise has Dr. Bones McCoy, in the first chapter, "McCoy Without Bones," raise the same question with regard to a "transporter," the corresponding piece of hardware aboard the *Enterprise*.[33] Can the transporter, which "turns our bodies into energy and then reconstitutes them as matter at the destination," reassemble the soul?[34] At this point, Blish makes the *Enterprise* transporter his own by having Scotty, the engineering officer, qualify McCoy's account and explain that it works by producing "a Dirac jump" (p. 3). Subsequently, Scotty suggests a redesigned form of the transporter that would take care of McCoy's unease. It makes use of tachyons, particles that exist in multidimensional Hilbert space and travel faster than light. What if

> instead of scannin' a man an' replicatin' him at destination in his normal state, it replicates him in tachyons, at *this* end of the process? That would solve the moral problem because the original subject wouldna go anywhere—while the tachyon creature, which canna exist in the everyday universe with us, would go to destination and revert to normal there. No murder, if such be in fact the problem, ever occurs. (P. 14)

This version of the transporter is very similar to Budrys's matter transmitter; it creates duplicates. It also has the advantage of vastly extending the range of the transporter.

Scotty announces his new idea shortly after the discovery that the evil Klingon Empire is again waging war against the Federation, in spite of the Organia Peace Treaty. The Organians are supposedly invincible thought creatures. But now all contact with the Organians and their planet has been lost. It is decided to make use of the redesigned transporter, which is now enclosed in a metal shield "so that its six positions could no longer be seen," and beam a tachyon replicate of Spock to Organia (p. 16). But for some mysterious reason two Spocks emerge from the transporter tank. The problem now is to identify the real one and destroy the tachyon one who turns out to be evil and gives the *Enterprise* location away to a Klingon ship.

Various hypotheses about the duplication are proposed in the novel. Perhaps the replicate Spock somehow embodies the consciousness of a Klingon, or is the duplication just a matter of the mirror-image reversal of personality? Blish makes much of the fact that Spock's remorseless rationality makes him a formidable enemy. McCoy tells Captain Kirk "that if Spock weren't half Vulcan, I'd be watching him now every day for signs of cancer," explaining that "men of one hundred per cent Earth stock, who have avenues for emotional discharge as inadequate as Mr. Spock's, are terribly susceptible to it in their middle years" (p.

28). This aside has nothing directly to do with the plot of *Spock Must Die!* and was presumably dictated by Blish's personal predicament. It does suggest, however, that Blish identified with Spock, and when one recalls that one possible use for the *Rogue Moon* matter transmitter was to cure cancer, there is room to wonder if the replicate Spock does not amount to a projection of the cancerous Blish. This may explain the book's peculiar power and interest in spite of Blish's assertion to Shackley that "no serious Blish student, of which I obviously have one, should take anything in *Spock Must Die!* seriously. It was a potboiler, and to keep myself interested I threw into it at random anything that occurred to me whether it made sense or not."[35]

Blish's disclaimer notwithstanding, *Spock Must Die!* embodies one of his most carefully orchestrated plots. McCoy eventually determines that the Spock whom Kirk has named Spock One, and to whom Kirk has given his class ring for identification purposes, is the evil replicate. McCoy figures that Spock One has barricaded himself in the doctor's laboratory in order to create special food for himself. It has been confirmed that the replicate is a mirror image and as such requires food with reversed amino acid molecules. The reversal of Spock's cells corresponds nicely, it should be noted, with the nature of cancerous cells, and Spock One's eating difficulty anticipates Blish's in the last year of his life. But if Spock One is a mirror image, what constituted the mirror that caused the replicate to materialize not on Organia but in the transporter tank? The answer is the thought shield, the Klingon secret weapon, which completely englobes Organia, blocks out all communication, prevents the Organians from knowing what is going on outside their planet, and reflects tachyons.

After Spock One escapes from the *Enterprise* in a shuttlecraft, Scotty suggests beaming down to Organia using the regular transporter and once there, putting out of commission the Klingon generator which is creating the thought field.[36] Fortified by antidepressant pills and tranquilizers which help counteract the negative influence of the thought shield, Captian Kirk, Scotty, and Spock Two beam down to Organia. On Organia Kirk moves through a series of frightening and bewildering hallucinations, which derive from his early experiences, until he is confronted by Spock One. Meanwhile, the *Enterprise* is threatened by a Klingon squadron. While Kirk's hallucinations continue with a series of alien animals including "gormenghastlies," a reference to the Mervyn Peake trilogy, and the "beademungen" of "Common Time," Spock Two battles it out with the replicate Spock One. Spock Two eventually wins by driving Spock One into the thought shield. Thus, in fantasy, Blish exorcises his cancerous self.

In the last three of the book's fifteen chapters all is resolved. Kirk and company meet with the Organian Council of Elders and Scotty builds a counteracting generator making use of equipment from the stolen shuttlecraft. After the thought shield is nullified we get an account of events from the Klingon perspective. An Organian voice decrees: "We . . . interdict your planets, and all your colony worlds, from space flight for a thousand years" (p. 112). Back on the *Enterprise*, Spock tells of his "telepathic" knowledge of Spock One and McCoy returns to his original question: "Does the man who comes out of the other end of a journey by transporter have an immortal soul, or does he not?" (p. 117).

Spock Must Die! is a very entertaining, inventive, clever piece of work. It includes a number of exciting cliff-hanging moments and would make a very good *Star Trek* film complete with numerous occasions for impressive special effects. Indeed, the novel is less "juvenile" than Blish might have claimed, although he considered his other *Star Trek* books to be clearly juveniles. In terms of language, most young readers would have problems with phrases like "incunabular existence" and "actinic glare," the latter of which also occurs in *The Vanished Jet*, a genuinely juvenile work.[37] For many of his young readers Blish might as well have been writing in Eurish, the synthetic language from *Finnegans Wake* (cp. *A Case of Conscience*'s use of this work) which Lieutenant Uhuru uses, as a code that Klingons will be unable to crack, for communication with the Starfleet Command.

(iv) Poetry

Most of Blish's some 115 poems remain unpublished.[38] To judge from the sixty-one or more that he did publish—whether in the VAPA mailings or later in such places as *Ball State University Forum, The Beloit Poetry Journal, The Hopkins Review, Prairie Schooner, The Sewanee Review,* and *Western Review*—most of this production occurred between 1945 and 1950 and between 1969 and 1972, the period when his talent was maturing and the period of troubled would-be rebirth in England. Because of their generally very private subject matter, although often having to do with typical themes and motifs, such as various kinds of restriction, the ravages of time, and death, most of Blish's poems, written as often as not in free verse, are enigmatic, subdued, and melancholic. This includes all but a few of the many love poems.

The opening lines of "Song" strike a characteristic note:

Captive, the man quaffing dust will seize
Full measure from his sifting hands.[39]

Words, themselves, imprison. "In Memoriam: Fletcher Pratt" includes the line, "Out of the word, container for the thing contained. . . ."[40] Even the most glorious of man's accomplishments are undermined by Blish's downbeat realism. Thus the commercialized wonders in "Venice Observed, 1969" are seen after the night when "Armstrong had uttered a leaden foot upon the Moon."[41]

No collection of Blish's poetry has yet appeared although Blish apparently projected at least two collections in his lifetime. The first dates from early in his career. Lowndes's index to Blish's contributions to the VAPA mailings indicates that two burlesques, "Prayer for Joyce" and "My God, the Greeks," published in the March 1945 *Tumbrils*, were from an in-progress book of poems by "Marcus Lyons" entitled *Trompe L'Oeil*.[42] For most of the poems that appeared in *Tumbrils* and *Renascence* and one poem that appeared in *Discrete*, Blish used his Marcus Lyons pseudonym. Much later in Blish's career Faber & Faber rejected a collection of thirty-six sonnets entitled *The Journey's Rupture: Poems 1949–1970*.[43]

"Prayer for Joyce," or "A Prayer for James Joyce," as the title was subsequently emended, was reprinted five times, making it the most reprinted of Blish's poems, if poem it can be called:

Poolybacky, soofleshing dimily o'er whalepath, kenning our nighsride to ashehrnities, grant this him day our mornfille newmare; typette us not in darkling kittifishies; and lave us lightly ni ogs annirate; nor lent ere curite this airiwohning crepusquus. Gull his travels swiftly to wrist; he connicht alpemore. Wiss brunt affliction. Yrs. navely, Apselorse (his chronic exegete). Uhmn.[44]

This burlesque version of the "Our Father" is most likely to be appreciated by chronic exegetes of *Finnegans Wake*.

Only slightly less baffling is "Caesura" (Autumn 1950), "the only [verse] I ever wrote that my mother understood."[45] It commemorates a return visit during a 1948 business trip (a pause, or caesura) to the Kenwood Avenue area Chicago homes of his childhood:

I paid fare on the ice to the woods, where the stones bleed me;
there where I fell from the stoop, I was run down
with the sliver of ice in my palm; and the alley
yard house has grown large where I was stung.
By the mansards I watched the sound of a typewriter winking,
swam away from the red crash. The palings were gone
that contained randy memory's collie, the
locust tree had almost devoured the house.

In the dark I thought to be stone like the city
that so unchanged me, not to stay in the knowing
woods but only in mind, mirror and stone. There,
too, every flag lidded spiders, corners
turned themselves, old windows mouthed names, four blocks
of still darkbound summer a petrified funhouse,
closed for the night. I would buy no more candy,
stone I would stand to confute, wanting nothing.

Thought had paid for that life with my I, for the black-blood tree.
Poor city of ice, I said, to stand mute for nineteen stunned years
waiting for nothing but me and the heat of the summer
bitch memory! What good to be stone there,
better to grow like a turnip, if both must bleed![46]

For readers other than Blish's mother, the identifications that Blish supplies in "A Science Fiction Coming of Age" are helpful:

> The ice is the Illinois Central railroad, of which it was said that Chicago was so cold in winter because the wind, ho, ho, blew over the icy tracks. "The Mansards" was the name of the apartment building at 1344 [East 48th Street]; "the red crash" was the day I broke my Corona typewriter; the collie was an over-amorous dog belonging to neighbours; the tree, actually a catalpha, was a producer of seed pods called Indian cigars which we all tried, but could never persuade to draw. As pseudo-Sandburg goes, the poem stands well enough as a farewell to the city he too commemorated, to the affliction of high school classes in poetry ever since.[47]

The icy cold of hometown Chicago perhaps explains the partiality for frozen places that is apparent in Blish's fiction. And note also the omnivorous tree. Most of Blish's poetic recollections are painful. Stone or rock imagery recurs and, indeed, some of his poems derived from what was known as the Stony Point Poetry Workshop.[48] Instead of being hurt by stones, Blish elected to become a stone, at one with the city, immune to the woods of nature. But nature, in the form of "flag lidded spiders," is to be found in the "city of [natural] ice." Since there is no escape from pain, one may as well embrace, or at least accept, the natural destructive element and "grow like a turnip."

The pain, problems, and equivocations of maturity receive ample consideration in Blish's later poems. Take, for example, "Serenade for Telephone":

> Though I am grey with cynicism, I know there was some age
> Deep in the sleepy eras when love did not sit and rage
> Stupid as sixteen over this blackly silent talker
> The damned machine is hard on rugs. I have become a stalker.
>
> In a new land the stranger multiplies
> And doubts his name, and does not trust his eyes.
> Nothing in his room remains the same,
> And while he waits, he dreams his Psyche dies.
>
> But still no line is endless. In the wordless world
> You my feathered angel are your electric own.
> In all this busy humming it is not yet hard
> To see you canopied within your flowered throne
>
> Calmly waiting to call me, as certain as sages
> Of all my love; and slowly, timelessly, gently turning the pages.[49]

Blish's rhyme scheme and word choice here call for particular attention. The *a a b b* rhymes of the opening stanza and the *a a* rhyme of the closing stanza convey, respectively, a desperate and calm insistence. In the second stanza doubt intrudes as the repetitive ring (in the absence of any sound from the telephone) of a triple rhyme is wittily interrupted by the word "same," the meaning of which, here functioning as the element of difference, is reversed by its context. It seems reasonable to interpret the multiplying stranger in a new land as both Blish in relation to the English and the English in relation to Blish. Reassurance and a more ordered rhyme scheme ("*your . . . throne*" is indeed her *"own"* [emphasis added]) returns in the third stanza, and in the last a realm of extended time where his beloved serenely sits (in contrast to the Blish of the first stanza) is conveyed by the relaxed rhythm of the final eight-foot line, the longest in the poem. In other words, the work ends on a note of incipient transcendence. The overall development from the alienating material world to an ideal reality is subtly signalled by the permutation "rung" on that most Blishian word "hard," the concrete sense of which ("The damned machine is hard on rugs") gives way to the abstract, "it is not yet hard. . . ."

It is but a small step from "turning the pages" to the falling leaves of autumn. The posthumously published sonnet, "All Hallows Leave," will stand here as a final testimonial to Blish's poetic talent:

> The devil's trick is turned; it's now his treat.
> Masked cherubs haunt my chantry; in the dark
> The smoke of burning time assails the trees
> And at the mail-slit winter pipes his art.
> The fairest Indian summer of my memory
> Gutters and flares away. We are apart.
> The pillow's gold is spilled, and in the bleak
> Windfall of the mind, the Word's blown out.
> Here on my lectern is the vesper leaf,
> Treasured and veined. Its wrist is cut.
> Help me, leafling, to remember. I have learned my grief
> That on this false-faced night knocks at my heart.
>   Now, sticky arabs would extort my love.
>   I'll give it free. It's that I'm ruled to prove.[50]

It is Halloween and trick-or-treaters ("Masked cherubs") knock on the poet's door. The religious origin of the occasion leads Blish to convert his residence into a church complete with "chantry," "lectern," and "vesper" service devoted to the "Word." The burning leaves of fall suggest both lost time and the fire of hell. The mood of retrospection in "Caesura" here gives way to a mood of proud regret. The "still darkbound summer" and "heat of the summer" of "Caesura" have dwindled to an "Indian summer." The ice of winter was, and is, the true reality that now reclaims Blish, the "leafling" to be.[51] Again the rhyme scheme is calculated. A recurring (half or complete) a rhyme runs through the three quatrains: "treat," "art," "apart," "out," "cut," and "heart." The hard cutting "t" sound is, of course, particularly appropriate here. Also once again a more ordered rhyme appears as the poem develops, here in the $f\,a\,f\,a$ scheme of the third quatrain. To clinch matters, the concluding rhyming couplet provides a half rhyme with the preceding f rhyme.

(v) Dramatic Work

Blish's dramatic oeuvre per se consists of one short published play, *A True Bill: A Chancel Drama in One Act*. The unpublished *Cities in*

Flight film scripts, the film scripts for *Welcome to Mars* and *The Night Shapes*, the "Captain Video" scripts, the *C.I.D.: Universe* script, the teleplay of "The Box," a couple of radio plays, an unpublished opera libretto, and an outline for a TV series are not dramas in the strictest sense and thus will not be considered here.[52] Additionally, during Blish's last years in England William Morris of the William Morris theatrical agency in Los Angeles, at Harlan Ellison's suggestion, tried to interest Blish in writing a play entitled "The True Faust" (presumably about the historical figure) but nothing came of this project.[53]

Although it is not SF, "A True Bill" was published in Roger Elwood's anthology *Ten Tomorrows*, no doubt because it fitted in with that one-time-prolific editor's evangelical zeal. In a preface Blish explains that the play, dedicated "To Anne McKenzie and the Rogues" "was written for a Little Theatre group called the Rogues Gallery [of Alexandria, Virginia] and played during the Easter vacation in fifteen [local] churches in 1966."[54] It was "intended to be performed in a Christian church," ideally as "a substitute for a regular service" (p. 155).

The play takes the form of an inquest into the legality of three persons being executed two days previously by the occupying U.S. Army. While references to "gooks" (pp. 159, 177) imply that this is all happening in the context of the Vietnam War, other indications soon make it apparent that the executions amounted to a re-enactment of the crucifixion of Christ and the two thieves. The American occupation of Vietnam corresponds to the Roman occupation of Judaea. The judge, a local "town father," presides over a "Grand Jury" composed of the church congregation, which includes twelve actors playing the parts of Mary, Magda, and various representative figures, whose verdict "will be called a True Bill" (p. 162). After the soldiers have been pronounced guilty of murder out of the mouth of their captain, the drama ends with "an apocalyptic crash," the discovery that the stone closing the tomb has been moved aside, and the church organ playing " 'Et resurrexit' from the B Minor Mass" (p. 184). One wonders what, in the days before the success of *Jesus Christ, Superstar* (1971), may have moved Blish to write this very uncharacteristic and somewhat corny play.

(vi) SF Criticism

Beginning in late 1952, Blish, at the height of his powers, began publishing critical pieces under the name William Atheling, Jr., in Redd Boggs's fanzine *Skyhook*. An Atheling column entitled "The Issue at

Hand" appeared in seven issues of *Skyhook* between spring 1953 and winter 1954–55. Eight years later the column reappeared in Larry and Noreen Shaw's fanzine *Axe* (February 1963). These pieces along with some articles that Blish had signed his own name to in the fanzines *Warhoon* and *Xero*, and a couple of speeches delivered at the 1960 and 1963 World Science Fiction Conventions were subsequently reprinted in *The Issue at Hand* (1964), where Blish explains that his enthusiasm for the work of Ezra Pound led to his choice of pseudonym: " 'William Atheling' was the pen-name under which EP wrote all his music criticism" for the English magazine *The New Age*, not, as originally stated, "for a Parisian newspaper."[55] For the most part, Atheling's critical vitriol is aimed at material that had appeared in such magazines as *Astounding, Galaxy*, and *The Magazine of Fantasy & Science Fiction*.

In providing what he called "technical criticism" (p. 9), aimed at improving the literary quality of science fiction or at least ensuring that it meets "the minimum standards of competence" (p. 12), Blish was following in the footsteps of his friend, fellow ex-Futurian and sometimes collaborator, Damon Knight, "the inventor of serious science fiction criticism" (p. 97), whose collected reviews, *In Search of Wonder*, appeared in 1956 (and in a revised edition of 1967). Knight's critical career had begun in 1945 with a long fanzine essay on A. E. van Vogt's *World of Ā*; and, as it happens, it was Damon Knight and Larry Shaw who, independently, guessed who Atheling really was. Aside from Knight's influence, Blish's criticism "is considerably indebted to such traditional critics as R. P. Blackmur and Ezra Pound, as one would expect of a writer with a background in such literary quarterlies as *The Sewanee Review*."[56] Blish's methodology conforms essentially to that of the New Critics but adapted to a genre that most respectable New Critics had scorned.

A variety of criteria and other matters of importance crop up in the first four pieces. "Sour William" objects to *"Phony realism"* or the "minute description of the entirely irrelevant" (pp. 18, 21), the kind of overwriting that he characterizes as *"Deep purple,"* or "Metaphors which take the form 'concrete-is-abstract' " and the "one-punch" story (pp. 18, 35, 36). In regard to "the intensively recomplicated plot" as a technique, Atheling notes that Blish, van Vogt, and others "have written science fiction by this method" and later points to the consequent thinness of van Vogt's work (pp. 22, 38). Atheling has no definitions of science fiction to offer beyond those he had written for the latest *Grolier Encyclopedia* (along with entries on Bradbury, Clarke and Heinlein) but, writing in 1953, he does insist on an "essential difference between science fiction and fantasy" (p. 26). Henry Kuttner is singled out for his mastery of technique, and C. M. Kornbluth was also a writer Blish admired.[57]

The most important section of *The Issue at Hand* consists of the pieces gathered under the title "Cathedrals in Space." What Atheling has to say here about *A Case of Conscience* has already been discussed here (chapter 4), but after pointing out that religious thinking inevitably precedes scientific thinking, Atheling also comments on several works that constitute a tradition of science fiction concerned with religious questions: M. P. Shiel's *Lord of the Sea* (1901), Hugh Benson's *Lord of the World* (1908), C. S. Lewis's Arthur Ransom trilogy (1938, 1943, 1945), Ray Bradbury's "The Man" (1949), Anthony Boucher's "The Quest for Saint Aquin" (1951), Paul L. Payne's "Fool's Errand" (1952), Walter M. Miller, Jr.'s "Crucifixus Etiam" (1953) and *A Canticle for Leibowitz* (1960), Lowndes's *Believers' World* (1961), and Heinlein's *Stranger in a Strange Land* (1961). Atheling's extended discussion of the last novel is particularly insightful as are his speculations as to why this species of SF has suddenly become popular.

The next seven pieces continue the attack. Poul Anderson's "The Immortal Game" (1954) is criticized both as a poor chess game allegory and for its reliance on "duplicate or incantatory statement" (p. 73). This is the writer of whom, some years later in an appreciative essay, Blish would write, "he was, as Kuttner, a born technician," praising his "sense of tragedy" and comedy.[58] But Blish was ever an even-handed critic. After attacking Randall Garrett elsewhere, he admires the critical acumen of his *Mikado*-inspired verse parody "I've Got a Little List." Blish identifies the writers who would not be missed whom Garrett deftly characterizes but without providing quotations from the poem. Among them is

> . . . the lad who writes about the interstellar tramps
> Who flit about the Galaxy in king-size hobo camps—[59]

Editors are "at least as guilty as writers" and John W. Campbell, Jr., "a once-great editor," is singled out in this regard (pp. 81, 86). In two places Atheling objects wittily to inappropriate " 'said' substitutes" or "said-bookism" (pp. 83, 110). He deplores the decline of the letters column in the SF magazines, since these letters provide the writer with most of the little critical feedback he receives. Most of whatever fan mail a writer receives personally—Blish mentions that "over 22 years, I have only 56 letters from book readers" (p. 99)—is inarticulate or insulting, or both. As for controversial views, under the heading of technique, the omniscient author is declared to be "at the very least obsolescent" and, Atheling observes of Campbell's preferred wearisome subject matter, "I don't myself think that there is any such thing" as telepathy (pp. 85, 104).

Blish's guest-of-honor speech, "A Question of Content," for the 18th World Science Fiction Convention in 1960 makes for a strong concluding statement. All good novels, including good SF novels, must be about something real. Atheling specifies the subject matter of Vonnegut's *Player Piano*: "the Second Industrial Revolution, the cybernetic revolution, already well under way, which is likely to terminate with the great bulk of mankind, including most of its educated citizens, with nothing to do or sell which will be worth anybody's money to buy" (p. 125). By taking this standard SF topic (albeit the precise terms of Blish's formulation will strike us as startingly prescient today) and asking the real question it implies—how will people deal with enforced leisure?—Vonnegut succeeds in creating a work of value that is worthy of an adult's attention. As for SF's "sense of wonder," Atheling writes that "Anti-matter, galactic collisions, and numbers with long strings of zeroes after them do have their fascinations, but none of them is nearly so awe-inspiring as a five-year-old girl who happens to be yours" (p. 127). In order to enlarge a reader's thinking and thereby change his or her life "an exploding star is not a proper tool; at best, it is only a backdrop" (p. 128). As for the future, "we have reached the stage where our physical horizons can't be extended much more without bursting the bubble of the physical universe itself. The ethical, the moral, the philosophical horizons remain, and those are infinite. It is there, I believe, that the realm of good science fiction must lie" (pp. 128–29).

The Issue at Hand was eventually followed by *More Issues at Hand* (1970). Once again, most of the essays, which date from 1965 until 1970, had appeared in fan magazines but this time a somewhat less vitriolic Atheling—"no longer quite so sure that the commission of [a bad story] represents flaws in the author's character or horrid secrets in his ancestry"—is mostly reviewing books rather than magazine SF.[60] It is also apparent from the opening chapter—which combines the prefaces from *Best Science Fiction Stories of James Blish* and from *New Dreams This Morning*—that his understanding of the nature of SF has undergone some development. The difference between mainstream fiction, SF, and fantasy is now seen as a matter of the distance between the writer's personal reality, "his private tattoo," and the consensus view of reality (p. 12). This distance will be minimal in the case of mainstream fiction and maximal in the case of fantasy. SF will later be described as "a subsection of fantasy" (p. 113). In terms of Blish's SF, works like "Testament of Andros" and *The Frozen Year* point to his interest in the exploration of possible interior realities. But his increased sense of the importance of the author's interior reality led him not only to such fantasies as *Black Easter* and *The Day After Judgment* but to the as-yet unpublished biographical fictions of his last years. The material from the *New Dreams This Morning* preface argues that SF has taken on "the characteristics of a literary movement" to the extent that SF has exerted "some influence on literature as a whole" and a significant number of its writers now "think of themselves as artists, not just journeymen" (p. 16).

The person most blameworthy to the milder Atheling is the SF historian Sam Moskowitz, who, it is claimed, is not only possessed of a tin ear stylistically speaking but also "has shown an irritating tendency to wax polemical in defense of his errors, in preference to correcting them" (p. 25). Atheling is thinking particularly of the hallmark of Moskowitz's work: his not always accurate identification of the sources of various SF ideas and their influence on "subsequent" (Moskowitz does not always sufficiently research the chronology of composition) stories. The impact of this devastating attack on Moskowitz's regressive criticism is reinforced by the fact that Atheling takes it up twice in his chapter on "The Critical Literature."[61]

Heinlein gets further, mainly admiring, attention in a chapter focusing on the problems of writing in the first person, in particular the dangers of autobiographical distraction and "retrospective inconsistency": "It is found in novels wherein the narrator has undergone a more or less drastic change of heart by the time the book ends—yet the beginning of the story supposedly being told by the man who has already undergone this enlightenment, shows his state of mind firmly entrenched in its former attitude" (p. 53). Atheling does not recall Heinlein ever making this latter error but he admits that his own *The Frozen Year* provides an example.

Two other figures previously treated in *The Issue at Hand*, Algis Budrys and John W. Campbell, also came in for further scrutiny. Blish's friend Budrys had been fingered as the "Man to Watch for 1954."[62] Although there are still "no writers who are consistently trying to write science fiction the hard way" (p. 60)—Blish often draws attention to the need to do things the hard way—something of Budrys's promise has been realized in *Rogue Moon*. Indeed, in the very enthusiastic chapter devoted to that novel it is suggested rather extravagantly that "A full-scale analysis . . . might turn out to be nearly as extended as Stuart Gilbert's study of *Ulysses*" (p. 62). Blish seems not to have intended the unfortunate implication that *Rogue Moon* is comparable to *Ulysses* in quality. But if, "since the inception of modern science fiction in 1926, no single author has produced more than one masterpiece," *Rogue Moon* may well be that masterpiece in Budrys's case (p. 77). Certainly, three chapters later, Blish quickly dismisses another Budrys story, "The War Is Over," as not up to scratch. The story was published in Campbell's *Astounding* but the Campbell who presided over "American science fiction in its finest period, . . . the 1940's," is now "more interested in education than fiction" and in riding such hobbyhorses as his "preoccupation with extra-sensory powers and perceptions ('psi') as a springboard for stories" (pp. 103, 92, 86).

The long last chapter on the New Wave in SF breaks new ground. It consists of a speech delivered at the 14 June 1970 Speculation Conference in Birmingham that was simultaneously published in the fanzine *Speculation* (September–October 1970) and that, in part, elaborates on a review of Aldiss's *Barefoot in the Head* that Blish had also published in *Speculation* (January–February 1970). It is, on the whole, a good essay which shows that Blish was open to changes that were taking place in the field. He is critical of Delany's and Zelazny's use of myth, and projects that Delany might end up being crippled by his early popularity; *Barefoot in the Head*, however, vindicates the New Wave. The invocation of *Ulysses* in relation to *Rogue Moon* is now balanced by the much more reasonable invocation of *Finnegans Wake* in relation to *Barefoot in the Head*, not, it must be added, in the sense that *Barefoot* approaches Joyce's *tour de force* as art but in the sense that Aldiss did belatedly model the fractured, stream of consciousness, portmanteau-word-laden style of his book on Joyce's experiment.

The Issue at Hand and *More Issues at Hand*, together with Damon Knight's *In Search of Wonder*, laid the foundations of sound SF criticism. And Knight's critical strengths, his wit, fairness, insight, and economy, were also Blish's. To these Blish added a stress on the need for stories concerned with human emotions and what Robert Colbert describes as a "controlled urgency of tone."[63]

Evidence among the Bodleian Papers indicates that Blish projected a third volume in the series to be entitled "Dead Issues at Hand" (Dep.Blish 388/1–3). It was to be an attack on bad critical and historical writing on SF. The planned contents included a preface and four chapters corresponding to the four types of commentator: "Moskowitz: Heat Without Light," "Zwei Welka Rosen, Entsprungen" (Spring Up,

You Wild Roses), "Suvin Looks East," and "Merrill: Guesswork and Gush." Suvin, according to the preface (the only part of the work that Blish seems to have written), was to emerge as the only genuine scholar. A full-length study of SF that Suvin encouraged Blish to write, and that Blish himself hoped to write, also never materialized. He had informed Paul Shackley that the "next Atheling book . . . is going to be a general theory of sf and fantasy, so it won't have a successor title. But I don't plan even to begin it until 1973" (PS, 23 June 1970).

A complete listing of all of Blish's writings on SF appears here in the Primary Bibliography. Three items reprinted in Cy Chauvin's posthumous Blish collection, *The Tale That Wags the God* (1987), deserve mention here. The titular essay first appeared in the journal *American Libraries* (1970) before its appearance under the title "Introduction: The Function of Science Fiction" in Harry Harrison's collection *The Light Fantastic: Science Fiction Classics from the Mainstream* (1971). In it Blish makes the point that the pulps had a bad effect although they did teach tight plotting, and argues that SF aids our understanding of reality by (1) creating "thought experiments," (2) evoking emotions, especially the basic scientific ones, and (3) creating myths. The mythopoeic function, he claims, cannot be performed by fantasy because, in the case of fantasy, there can be no question of belief.

"The Science in Science Fiction" (1971) and "The Arts in Science Fiction" (1972) were originally written for presentation before the Cambridge University SF Society. Both were first published in fanzines edited by Malcolm Edwards. The first, as previously noted in chapter 5, makes significant use of Kuhn's notion of paradigms. The second appeared in revised form in Chauvin's *A Multitude of Visions* (1975). Blish lucidly discusses the influence of SF on the arts, the effects of the arts on SF (particularly by way of literary experimentation), and the role of the arts in SF proper. Blish mentions his own collection of SF stories about the arts, *New Dreams This Morning* (1966), which includes his "A Work of Art" and "The Dark Night of the Soul," and also discusses the New Wave and the literary arts, the Holman Hunt painting in Aldiss's *Report on Probability A* (1969), Heinlein's poetry, his own poetry, and rock music.

(vii) Mainstream Literary Criticism

Three pieces—"The Function of Science Fiction," "The Long Night of a Virginia Author," and "The Music of the Absurd"—that Chauvin reprints in *The Tale That Wags the God*, Blish had planned on reprinting in a collection entitled "The Agent as Patient: Seven Subjects with an Object." In the main (excepting the pieces on SF and music) this collection would have showcased the most important of Blish's literary interests. Blish explains in the prefatory "Kritike Antikritikos; or, How to Carry the Bad News from Aix to Ghent" that "The 'subjects' of my overall subtitle are artists, or artistic fields or genres, of the Twentieth Century" while "The object is to winnow out contemporary critical reactions to these subjects, and test these reactions for viability."[64] Blish continues with brief synopses of the seven chapters to follow.

The first of these, which originally "appeared in two parts in two different journals," *Kalki* and *Jabberwocky*, before publication in combined form in the *Journal of Modern Literature* as "The Long Night of a Virginia Author," deals with James Branch Cabell. In the opening part, "Two Twentieth-Century Dreams," Blish compares "Two 'night' works": Joyce's *Finnegans Wake* with Cabell's trilogy about a successful Virginia author which "stands at the heart of his later work," *The Nightmare Has Triplets*, comprising *Smirt* (1934), *Smith* (1935), and *Smire* (1937).[65] Albeit there is no question of influence, Blish establishes fourteen points of similarity and five points of difference. A statement of Cabell's aim—to write "a work which should be truly dreamlike in detail, in structure, and even in the systematic omission of the sense of taste and smell"—leads into part two, "The Structure of the Nightmare," which includes a detailed plot summary and concludes with the judgment that the trilogy is uneven in structure and tone; it amounts to a sandwich: "two volumes of authentic dream with a very good but—for Cabell—standard fantasy-saga in its middle" (pp. 397, 402).

Various cross-references to Cabell's other work in a third part, "Some Other Ticks of the Clock," lead into the concluding part, "A Preliminary Assessment," namely that the middle volume of the trilogy is less successful than the other two and that pack-rat "Cabell's thrifty habit of using up every one of his occasional pieces . . . flaws the work" (p. 404). In this regard, Cabell is not unlike the parsimonious Blish. Indeed, Blish's perhaps exaggerated regard for Cabell, the amount of work he put into co-editing *Kalki* for the Cabell Society, into writing introductions for new editions of *Jurgen, Figures of Earth,* and *The Silver Stallion,* and into the Cabell "revival" generally no doubt had much to do with his sense of identification with the Virginia writer.[66] Blish, like Cabell, wrote philosophical romances. They shared a cyclical view of history and an interest in diabolism; the grimoires that provided Blish with much of his inspiration in *Black Easter*, for example, provided Cabell with the names of some of his characters. And when Blish describes Cabell as "a master of the afterthought," he might equally well be describing himself (p. 398).

Chapter 2, "Kritike Antikritikos" informs us, would have been a revised version of Blish's M.A. thesis, transformed into a *Sewanee Review* article, "Rituals on Ezra Pound." The revision would presumably have reflected something of the comments of Princess Mary de Rachelwiltz, whom Blish thanks "for opportunities to check my own performance as a critic of her father's critics" (p. 3). In attempting to demonstrate "that our favorite ritual phrases about Pound consist of gossip, misreadings, animadversions, guesses, and nothing else," Blish purports to be responding to a previous *Sewanee Review* article: "W. B. Yeats's Criticism of Ezra Pound" by W. H. Haesermann.[67] Blish, who finally views Pound as a "gravely wounded . . . giant," combats the first of five ritual phrases, *"Pound is formless: his manner is his matter,"* by noting that the Cantos should be read "as a Dantesque structure and as a musical composition" such as "the music of Stravinsky" (pp. 225, 188, 195, 196). He then deals in turn with the belief that *"Pound is a fascist and an anti-Semite,"* that *"Pound is consciously archaic"* ("we have equated 'archaism' with 'poeticism' "), that *"Pound is difficult,"* and that *"Pound is excessively violent: his imagery is obscene, scatological, diseased: his rages and loves are embarrassing, sentimental, false"* (pp. 197, 209, 222). As evidence that Pound's difficulty can be overcome, Blish provides an analysis of the birds on the five lines of a staff of music in canto 80. He notes that a throng of death images are associated with the birds and that Pound has simply transformed the birds on the electrically charged wires which surrounded his prison camp at Pisa into musical notes. This association surely has something to do with Blish's choice of the title "A Cage of Birds" for one of his as yet unpublished naturalistic novels.

The next essay, "my view of what I have called the Kafka scandal"— namely that a "glaringly obvious" aspect of *The Castle* has been ignored by Kafka's critics—was either never written, never completed, or has been mislaid or lost (p. 3). It presumably would have been called "The Kafka Scandal" as a deliberate echo of the title of one of Blish's more damning reviews, "The Pound Scandal" (1959). Blish informed Paul Shackley,

> Back in 1948 I discovered (and I have an essay in process about it) that one way in which Kafka's *The Castle* can be read is as an allegory of the wanderings of a metastatic cancer cell (ger. *Krebs*) through the body. The

allegory is incompletely worked out, but there are places where it is very clear indeed once one points to them: K's inability to intercept the messengers racing along the roads to and from the castle (the cranial nerves); the utterly unexpected restorative brandy from the womb of the coach; his inability to penetrate the blood-brain barrier." (PS, 15 July 1970)

Much of this, of course, fed into "Telecast" as the account of that projected novel on pages 140–45 herein indicates. Blish had previously revealed his insight in a letter to the Australian writer, critic, and editor John Baxter: K is a "metastatic cell from a testicular cancer." In an earlier letter to Baxter Blish refers to his beginning a translation of *The Trial*, another project which "now lies fallow." According to Blish, the available English translation (presumably Muir's) does not convey the richness of legalistic nuance in Kafka's style (Dep. Blish 411/10, 17 December and 18 November 1962). Also in his correspondence with Baxter, Blish refers to a planned critical book on Joyce, Pound, Kafka, and Gaddis, and to an essay entitled "The Cinders of Necessity" which was to appear in the Spring 1963 Gaddis issue of *Prairie Schooner*. There is no such issue and no evidence that Blish ever wrote the Gaddis essay. Blish must have changed his mind about the contents of "The Agent as Patient," since an essay on Gaddis is not among the seven essays surveyed in "Kritike Antikritikos." But of Blish's admiration for Gaddis's *The Recognitions* (1955), a metaphysical novel about art, forgery, religion and individuation, there can be no doubt. Blish kept a file of clippings on *The Recognitions*, which he believed to be an unrecognized work of genius.[68]

Blish did not change his mind about including Joyce, "the greatest writer in English since Shakespeare," who, according to "Kritike Antikritikos," would have been the subject of the fourth chapter (p. 4). Insisting that *Finnegans Wake* is, below the surface, a "moving naturalistic novel," Blish's "Formal Music in the Wake" traces through the whole of that work "Joyce's references, both integrated and decorative, to formal music" (p. 5).[69] This is a lengthy and rather dense article which makes good use of Blish's musicological knowledge. He begins by mentioning that he had heard a program of music mainly from *Ulysses* at the Second International James Joyce Symposium and goes on to notice that there are "ten times as many musical references" in *Finnegans Wake* (p. 19).[70] He elaborates: (1) "FW contains more references to formal music than does *Ulysses*"; (2) FW "contains many more references to the art of composition than does *Ulysses*"; (3) "many of the FW references are to compositions (and techniques) that were modern music during the period over which FW was written"; and (4) these three kinds of references follow "a symphonic-historical logic which is in itself a fourth layer of musicological reference" (pp. 19–20). In the survey that follows, Blish takes up these references in the order in which they appear. One passage that Blish draws attention to (pp. 40–42) is notable for the large number of bird references, an element that Blish picked up on in the Pound article.

In one of several notes that Blish published on *Finnegans Wake*, he comments that "many knots in FW may be at least tentatively unravelled by assuming that everything in any given fragment contains its own opposite."[71] But he was also very aware of the fact that this unravelling depended upon an accurate text. In 1969 he attempted to interest Faber & Faber (the first publisher of *Finnegans Wake*) in publishing a book entitled "Variant Readings in *Finnegans Wake*." Vice-chairman Peter du Sautoy had responded by suggesting that an "Appendix of Corrections to *Finnegans Wake*" be bound in with the next Faber & Faber reprinting of the novel (PdS 120). In his "Announcement: A Wake Appendix" Blish proposes (independently of a related project of Jack Dalton's) correcting around 300 major errors out of an estimated 7,000 errors in the eighth Viking reprint of 1958. He asks that possible entries be sent to "Treetops."[72] Alas, the "Appendix" never appeared.

The fifth chapter of "The Agent as Patient," "The Music of the Absurd," expected to be a slightly revised form of an article version, would have followed logically enough after the Joyce piece. The article will be considered here in the discussion of Blish's accomplishments in the area of music that follows. Chapter 6, planned as a slightly revised version of "The Function of Science Fiction," has already been treated in the context of Blish's SF criticism.

Blish's 1972 essay on Edgar Allan Poe, "The Climate of Insult," was to figure, "almost doubled in length," as the final chapter of "The Agent as Patient" (p. 7). It is a useful essay in which Blish is concerned with "Poe as a technical innovator in the field of narrative, and as the portraitist of a species of sensibility more common in our own time than it was in his."[73] Blish interestingly relates "The Cask of Amontillado" to Poe's obsession with attacking writers for plagiarism and other imaginary offenses. But Poe's performance in this regard is exemplary compared with the blindness of his critics, whose squabbles, in Stanley Edgar Hyman's words, resemble the "mating combats of bull elks."[74] As a critic of mainstream literature (and of SF) Blish's performance is also usually (but not always) more dignified and more productive of insight.

(viii) "The Sense of Music," Musical Compositions, and Richard Strauss

Some indication of the importance that Blish attached to musicology among his areas of expertise may be gauged by the fact that the first book-length manuscript he completed was what would finally be entitled "The Sense of Music." Lowndes writes that around 1945 Blish

> showed me the manuscript of a book on music he had written for the layman but which went far beyond the "music appreciation" level. I forget the original title; in the course of reworking it, he changed the title to *Music the Hard Way*. (The last two weekends I spent with him—in 1968—I got to look over his updated and reconsidered version, with a new title. Had he lived to finish it, I believe he would have found a publisher in England.)[75]

Blish did in fact attempt unsuccessfully to interest Faber & Faber in the work in 1969 (CM 84). A professional musicologist and composer who, in 1984, saw a copy of the third and final manuscript, which incorporated many of the changes suggested by some of the more musical participants at the 1968 Milford Conference (who read an earlier version), pronounced it still sufficiently *au courant*, and of sufficient interest to be publishable, and Serconia Press, which will publish the book, evidently concurred.[76]

"The Sense of Music" bears the imposing subtitle "studies toward an operational aesthetics including analyses of the semantic content of five familiar compositions and proposals for laboratory study of the nature of human response to organized sound." It includes as epigraphs Poe's "Sonnet: To Science," and quotations from Sir Arthur Eddington, Spengler's *The Decline of the West*, and Lamentations 3:40: "Let us examine and test our ways." Blish's thesis, that "music has 'more' semantic content than is generally credited to it" and "that music exhibits the same mathematical structure as does a language," is pursued through three "books" and ten chapters.[77] "Book One: Command and Response; what we know now," is joined by "Book Two: The Content of Music; a new model" and "Book Three: Aesthetic Judgment; what music might say." A "Conclusions" section is followed by "Appendix A: Some Philosophical Implications," which considers the value of "information theory, a mathematical theory of communication elaborated by Claude Shannon, Norbert Wiener, Warren Weaver and others" as a means of testing the thesis "that a work of music may be regarded as a message at least in part" (pp. 180, 179). "Appendix B: Five Sample Analyses" contains only two, one on Bach's "Cantata

BVW 67, 'Halt im Gedachtnis Jesum Christ'" and one on Mozart's "Serenade No. 10 in B flat, K. 361."

In the course of this very technical work Blish observes that "James Joyce is perhaps the most extreme example of a sound oriented writer, a natural bias much exaggerated . . . by his progressive blindness," that "the aesthetic *response* is an emotion, and probably an independent one," and that the transfer of information, like the transfer of energy, is subject to entropy (p. 37, 151). As for "consumers of random music and of rock-and-roll," they "bear no small resemblance to those primitives and children afflicted with pica—the desire to eat clay, paint chips and other non-food items" (p. 152).

Blish gave vent to his hatred of atonal and no-tonal music à la John Cage in a 1964 *Playboy* article, "Music of the Absurd," which Cy Chauvin reprints in *The Tale that Wags the God*. Here we have Blish at his most reactionary. Chauvin includes as a postscript to "Music of the Absurd" a brief humorous piece, "The Art of the Sneeze," described as "Blish's own contribution to the excesses of modern music."[78]

Blish does have a number of genuine arrangements and compositions to his credit. I have mentioned his 1945 arrangement of Kornbluth's "Cry in the Night" in chapter 1 (p. 10). He had earlier, in his army days, composed a march entitled "Caduceus" which was performed at Station Hospital, North Carolina on 16 August 1944 (Dep. Blish 407/1, folio 10). In a letter to Karin Laflin Adams Blish provides part of the background:

The [Army] hospital had a band for which I acted on the side as librarian and arranger, until the hospital C.O., whose baby the band was, . . . decided that to be a bandsman everybody had to play something. Hence I went through a period of carrying whatever spare instrument we happened to have at any given time. The first one I actually learned was the glockenspiel . . . but I weighed only 115 pounds and the thing was almost too much for me to march with. One day on parade I stepped into a pothole and fell down, producing a noise like inventory day in a steel foundry, and the C.O. ordered it taken away from me. I finally wound up with a French horn, which I loved and became fairly proficient at (the band's First Horn was a very good teacher). (KLA, 18 February 1973)

Blish informed Karin Laflin Adams that "in my universe," Mozart "stands on the left hand of God." But Richard Strauss, "a much lesser composer than Wagner, yet I like him much better," was also one of Blish's favorite composers (KLA, 20 February 1975 and 13 January 1973). Two abortive projects testify to that affinity. Blish completed a draft of a book entitled "The Operas of Richard Strauss" (Dep. Blish 433/4). Among the operas treated is *Der Rosenkavalier*, a production of which forms the subject matter of "A Cage of Birds," an unpublished novel to be discussed in chapter 10 here. Blish's favorite Strauss opera was *The Egyptian Helen*, an extract from which was played during the 1976 Blish Memorial Evening. On the basis of reading Blish's "Strauss" redivivus story, "A Work of Art," Thomas H. Lipscomb of Dodd, Mead & Company suggested to Matthew Evans of Faber & Faber that Blish might like to write a "fictionalized history . . . a study of the destruction of the German intellectual society between about 1880–1945, using Richard Strauss as the Faustian protagonist" (PdS 120, 13 October 1970). The result was a partial draft of a biographical novel entitled "Night Journey" (Dep. Blish 427/2). Blish writes of receiving "a letter from Seabury Press asking me to revive NIGHT JOURNEY, the novel around the life of Richard Strauss, à la DOCTOR MIRABILIS. I'm cautious; it tempts me, of course, but it would involve years of work, and I don't dare commit myself to anything that long-term yet" (KLA, 8 November 1974). He later mentions to Karin having "written to Seabury saying I will indeed do NIGHT JOURNEY after all, with a deadline of two years after signing, and I'm terrified" (KLA, 14 January 1974). It was still another project he would not complete.

(ix) Factual Material on Science, Medicine, and Witchcraft

The bulk of Blish's factual articles have to do with what might broadly be described as scientific matters. Of these the most important is the *Thrilling Wonder Stories* "Our Inhabited Universe" series which appeared in ten installments between June 1951 and December 1952. Blish takes a strikingly effective metaphoric approach to his topic, an approach indicated by his subtitles: "The Moon of the Sun" (Mercury), "The Corpse Planet" (Venus), "Sister of Terra" (the Moon), "The Iron Dwarf" (Mars), "The Rings of Sol" (the Asteroid Belt), "The Poison Giants" (Jupiter, Saturn, Uranus, Neptune), "Systems Within a System" (satellites of Saturn, Jupiter, Uranus, and Neptune), "Pluto and Beyond," "Earths of Other Suns" (Blish estimates 200,000 such), "A Planet in Doubt" (Earth). In this last article Blish reflects on the prevalence of double or multiple star systems and the possibility (exploited in "King Log") that our sun may have a companion. In "Pluto and Beyond" Blish expresses his belief, reiterated in a number of places, in the existence of a planet beyond Pluto. He refers to a trans-

Plutonian planet named Persephone in *They Shall Have Stars* and *Earthman, Come Home*. But he was particularly proud of having coined the term "gas giant," which crops up in the sixth article, "The Poison Giants."[79] He informed Paul Shackley that "Apparently R. S. Richardson picked it up from a story of mine in *Astounding*—probably the Blish/Knight *Tiger Ride*—and introduced it to astronomy where it instantly caught on." While there is a "methane-swathed giant planet" in "Tiger Ride," the term "gas giant" does not, in fact, occur.[80] In the same letter Blish notes that he has yet to write stories set on Saturn, Uranus, or Mercury and that "like most other sf writers, I seem to show a marked preference for inventing my own planets" (PS, 1 April 1971).

A complete listing of Blish's science fact titles can be found in section VI of the Primary Bibliography. Here I will confine myself to only two more examples. In 1963 Blish was one of twelve writers that *Playboy* called on to participate in a futurological panel entitled "1984 and Beyond." His most provocative (if probably wrong-headed) contribution was regarding oral contraceptives: "it won't be too many generations before the human organism can immunize itself against *any* fertility suppressant drug."[81] A follow-up futurological article, "Let Joy be Unconfined," appeared three years later in a 1966 issue of *Playboy*. A subsequent title, "Towards a Technology of Pleasure," for a 1972 reprint is more informative. Blish surveys the ways in which technology might exploit or enchance our sensual pleasures. There are perhaps twenty-four senses in all to be catered to, including those of odor, sound, taste (four separate senses), touch (three separate senses), and sight.

The factual material that Blish produced on medical matters is much slighter. Dep. Blish 436 contains duplicated documents (192 leaves) collected by Blish in 1956 for a book on medical discoveries made between 1940 and 1955 to be entitled "The Conquest of Life: New Pathways in Medicine," and thirty-three typescript pages of that book. This project, commissioned by Ballantine Books, dovetailed nicely with the fact that in 1955 Blish had taken on a job with Pfizer's public relations department. In a letter to Donald L. Winks of William Douglas McAdams, Inc., soliciting information, Blish explains that he proposes treating "six general subjects—anesthesia, the hormones, the viruses, chemotherapy, cancer, and longevity" (Dep. Blish 436).

A 1962 article about the future of medicine, "In Tomorrow's Little Black Bag" (courtesy of C. M. Kornbluth, "The Little Black Bag"), was probably salvaged from, or an offshoot of, "The Conquest of Life."

After noting that the history of modern SF "coincides almost year for year with the world's most spectacular medical revolutions," Blish explains his belief that "the possible lifetime of a single man can be extended, at least to 150 years."[82] He raises the hypothesis that a person's lifespan may depend upon the age of the mother when the child is born, and he anticipates a male contraceptive. An earlier article, "Methuselah's Grandparents" (*If*, May 1954) also considers, but not very optimistically, the possibility that modern medicine *might* make our grandchildren centurians.

In the last years of Blish's life an interest in the occult, first given extended expression in "Mistake Inside" (1948) and *Black Easter* (1968), led to his embarking in 1970 on a two-volume work for Doubleday entitled "History of Witchcraft, Demonology, and Magic." But because Blish found that he could not separate the first two subjects from the last, he went along with Doubleday's suggestion that the two volumes be collapsed into one. It was this combined volume, retitled "History of Witchcraft," that in 1972 Blish tried to interest Faber & Faber in publishing as a joint project with Doubleday (Faber file, CM 84). Judith Blish writes, "Jim was all keen to do this, until he began doing the research. He found it more and more depressing, as it became clear that the history of witchcraft was more a story of how people were willing to accuse one another—going as far as baby girls—in order to gain something. The witchcraft scare [of the 1600s] died down as soon as the estates of the accused were no longer awarded to the accuser . . . this wasn't what he had in mind. He got stuck." She also observed that "Jim found the history to be much less interesting in his terms—i.e., theology and belief systems—than he had expected, as the history was primarily of human venality and cruelty."[83] Brian Stableford, who eventually completed the work (to discover that Doubleday would not now buy it) reports that Blish had, in fact, only written a 10,000-word first draft, mostly in 1972, of the introductory section.[84]

TEN

"IMPRISONED IN A TESSERACT":
Black . . . Judgment

■ The tripartite structure of this book is a reflection of what I believe to be the figure in the carpet of Blish's oeuvre: an early focus on the future is later variously intensified or displaced by either an awareness of the past, most strongly felt in the middle phase of his career, or a concentration on the present, most strongly felt in the latter phase of his career. We have already looked at three of his efforts in the realistic mode, the successful *The Frozen Year,* the unsuccessful *The Vanished Jet* and "A Light to Fight By," and his two efforts in a Kafkaesque surrealistic mode, "Telecast" and "None So Blind." A surrealistic approach lends itself to a present-oriented species of SF or fantasy. But before discussing Blish's fantasy work in this connection there are three as yet unpublished, essentially realistic works that merit consideration.

(i) "A Cage of Birds," "Is That a Death?" and "A Prophecy of Love"

"A Cage of Birds" might be described as a comedy of manners about a bizarre production of the Strauss opera *Der Rosenkavalier*—one of the operas Blish discusses in his draft of "The Operas of Richard Strauss" (Dep. Blish 433/4). In a postscript to a letter to Peter Nicholls, who had made suggestions for a final revision of the novel, Blish notes, "CAGE started life in 1944 while I was in the Army, so it . . . holds my all-time record for both revising and dust-gathering."[1] This, then (perhaps with another title), was most probably the lost non-SF novel that Blish refers to in his 1948 Guggenheim application (Dep. Blish 406/5). Gerald Pollinger, Blish's agent in England, reports that three versions of "Cage" were marketed in 1967–68, for a period from 1969 onwards, and in the period 1974 to the present.[2] Faber & Faber received a copy of the first of these versions in December 1974 and passed it on to Ann Corlett, who had done such sterling work with *Doctor Mirabilis,* for a report. Her report of 4 February 1968 recommended against publication on the grounds that the novel was melodramatic, strained, and artificial. Blish himself describes this version in a letter as "a wholly rejectable draft" while mentioning that he will be sending a new version (CM 51, 14 August 1974).

This final version bears the dedication, "An meinen lieben Freuden HENRY u. THEODORA SOSTMAN gewidmet" and includes an "Author's Note," which points out that since the entire action occurs "somewhile between November 1950 and November 1953," the book is "a sort of historical novel"; the draft also includes a "Disclaimer by the Management" which ends, "The author is indebted to Mr. Peter Nicholls for much invaluable criticism."[3] Nicholls had made a number of minor suggestions in his letter of 26 June 1972 but his major objection was to an overall bleakness of tone in the previous version:

> it seems a little strange . . . that the world of the novel should in so many ways be the converse of that of *Der Rosenkavalier.* In the latter, love, affection and high spirits are allowed to triumph in a world where the consciousness of instability, cruelty, vulgarity and infidelity remain always present, but faintly, as warning notes behind all the gaiety. It seems to me that in *A Cage of Birds* the reverse is the case.

In his reply, Blish mentions being "rocked right back on my heels" by this statement. The revision (finished, Blish notes, on 12 August 1974) attempts to restore the opera's balance and "runs 20 pages longer than the draft you saw . . . and this despite my having thrown out all of my typographical trickery, which was very space-consuming." The previous draft includes "A Note . . . to the . . . Printer" about "a number of typographical devices which are intended to suggest or approximate musical effects": cadences (sentences that "do not end with a full stop, but simply break"), suspensions (paragraphs "indented all the way to wherever the last paragraph stopped"), and set-pieces (unjustified right margins).[4]

After the opening playbill, the final version, like the version that Nicholls saw, is made up of a prelude and three acts, mirroring the three acts of *Der Rosenkavalier.* This correspondence encouraged Nicholls to look for more precise relationships but Blish, in his response, claimed "I never intended any one-for-one structural correspondence between the novel and the libretto (the latter, I feel, the best in the whole history of opera), either as a whole or inside individual scenes"; likewise the musical structure. He goes on, "As you detected, I did make many of my characters importantly like those in the opera, but with this difference: they become more like the people in the opera as they become more involved with the opera, they don't start out that way. . . ." In his postscript, Blish writes,

> I'm embarked upon signing all non-SF henceforth with a pen name; I'm bloody tired of working for years on something and then having it multiply rejected at least partly because it isn't what the editors think my audience expects from me. Instead I'm starting a new author, from scratch. My hope is to get my previous such novel [probably "Is That a Death?"] published first, and then CAGE. . . .

Thus the author of the final version of "A Cage of Birds" is named "Frederick Danewort" (cp. John Hillary Dane of "King Log").

A brief summary of the action reveals that the problems Ann Corlett complained of remain. Peter Diehl [devil], a rich, satanic-looking homosexual of ambiguous age wishes to mount a production of *Der Rosenkavalier* with the gimmick of having Octavian played by a prepubescent boy.[5] To this end he gathers around him a colorful assortment of people including an unlucky French conductor named Paul Este who, at one point "sulphorous" (p. 94), is also a homosexual and perhaps Diehl's alter ego; there appears, in addition, to be something of Blish in both characters. Also in the group are a stage manager; an over-the-hill prima donna, Madame Viorica Arrhenius; her conductor husband; a critic named Harlan Harrisburg; a press agent; a lady photographer named Djahreling; and two children, a girl named Marguerite Arcourt and a fourteen-year-old boy, David Aldiss, who is to play Octavian. There are also numerous cats which, as Nicholls notes, seem "to constitute a leitmotif of some sort." Much is made of the need to keep the two children apart so that the breaking of David's voice will not be unduly encouraged.

As things turn out, David and Marguerite do get a chance to "experiment" with each other but that is not the reason his voice does break during the one calamitous performance of *Der Rosenkavalier* that finally is staged. After Diehl's death from accidentally mixing pills it is revealed that he had been slipping female hormones into David's food. The abrupt cessation of these additives may well have hastened nature's course. But thanks to Diehl's will, all ends well for most of the participants including Djahreling, who, we discover en route, is Diehl's daughter by way "of a cover marriage with a Lesbian" now deceased! (p. 98).

Blish does a witty enough job with the overheated, claustrophobic world of opera. And perhaps the hokey and sometimes predictable turns of plot can be justified as contributing to that atmosphere. But finally, aside from revealing another aspect of Blish's talent (a matter of significance), the novel itself does not seem to have much point—it is a whimsical, Firbankian *jeu d'esprit*. The title refers to the "stuffed life-size effigies of European song birds posed in a drawn-brass cage, nearly three feet high, which hung centrally over the back mirror" in the French restaurant where Diehl holds "his Grand Levee, to introduce all the principals to each other" (p. 37). Here, it may be noted, another parallel with the libretto exists, this one with the levee scene. When wound up, the birds sing. And, as one might expect, bird imagery recurs in the novel, with references to "the giant aepyornis," an extinct species of bird, to Madame as "a tough old bird" with a voice "like a skylark's," and a "bird-like" viola player (pp. 73, 82, 74, 140).

The possibilities of flight (even cities in flight), escape, breakthrough, and enhanced perception and the facts of containment and imprisonment are neatly harmonized in the title "A Cage of Birds." Birds also figure prominently in *Midsummer Century,* the last fully conceived novel that Blish published, and, as noted in chapter 9, in his analyses of Pound and Joyce. The flight of a bird is a traditional metaphor for the flight or ascension of the human soul after death. Thus the title "A Cage of Birds" suggests that Blish viewed death as a release, an opening.

"Is That a Death?" and "A Prophecy of Love" are two late more-or-less autobiographical fictions. The title of the novel comes from the description of the skeleton-ship in part 3 of *Rime of the Ancient Mariner:*

> Are those her ribs through which the sun
> Did peer, as through a grate?
> And is that Woman all her crew?
> Is that a Death? and are there two?
> Is Death that woman's mate?

Only secondary information is available on these two works, since Judith Blish and Virginia Kidd are unwilling to make the manuscripts available to researchers. In "Is That a Death?," a *roman à clef* in detective form, the world of music stands in for the world of SF. Thus Blish refers to the work as "a contemporary interpersonal novel, also as it happens with a musical background" (CM 84, 14 August 1974)—that is to say, like "A Cage of Birds." This must also be the novel in which, speaking to Brian Aldiss, Blish claimed that he had told the truth. But had he told it well? John Brunner and his wife, Marjorie, are among the few people who have read the manuscript. Brunner complains that

> although it purported to depict characters who were musicians and composers, it contained not one single episode set in a rehearsal room, a concert hall, or a recording studio. Furthermore, unlike the majority of Jim's works, it was very poorly structured. . . . Clearly the writing of the book had been important to him; equally clearly all his efforts had not resulted in a publishable novel. I suppose one might reasonably call it an act of catharsis.[6]

In response to my query about the novel's plot, Josephine Saxton wrote that the work is

> about intense jealousy in which an older man plots to kill his wife's lover by getting him to take anti-depressants and beer at the same time. There is a scene in it in a pub called "The Vines," one of James's favourite eating houses off Piccadilly, where the two men meet and discuss the infidelity which did not in fact take place. It was very sparsely written, very austere in style.[7]

This plot apparently reflects the circumstances of Blish's unreasonable animosity towards a younger British SF writer. In a letter to Karin Laflin Adams, Blish points out that, like the slightly autobiographical *Frozen Year,* "Is That a Death?" is written in the first person, a rarely used focus for Blish, and that it is "technically similar" to *Doctor Mirabilis:*

> Though the setting is contemporary, it's about half autobiographical, so the major events are fixed in advance, with the crucial exception that what seems the most important event in it didn't actually happen, and furthermore won't at the end prove to be anything like as important as I'm encouraging the reader to think it to be. . . . The peculiar problem (every novel has one) is to disguise the autobiographical part. (KLA, 24 February 1973)

To forestall being sued "for libel or invasion of privacy," he goes on to talk about his plan to use "a pen-name, copyright it with another pen-name, and not offer it for sale in England at all, in the hope that by the time it's reprinted over here (if it's ever printed anywhere) the real incidents under the masks will have receded into fuzzyness and unimportance to those involved."

As for "A Prophecy of Love," it is apparently about a sea journey to Venice and how an idyll with a young woman is spoiled by an older woman. A list of five titles in one of Blish's small notebooks, all but two canceled, suggests that he considered "A Prophecy of Love" and "The Stone Guest" as alternative titles (Dep. Blish 438/23). "The Stone Guest," of course, is an allusion to Mozart's *Don Giovanni*.

Judith Blish believed that both "Is That a Death?" and "A Prophecy of Love" are more like a young author's first works than a mature author's later ones: "they are expressions of discomfort, and they are awful. Had he lived he might have been able to fuse his intellectual prowess and skills with expression of feeling more successfully in time, but he was not granted that time."[8]

(ii) After Such Knowledge

Despite a dislike of fantasy, an admiration for E. R. Eddison's *The Worm Ouroboros* led Blish to write first the straight historical novel *Doctor Mirabilis* and subsequently his own supernatural fantasy, *Black Easter* (1968). But as a novella set in the present day, *Black Easter* might also be grouped with Blish's eight more or less abortive attempts in the realistic or surrealistic mode, including the three unpublished works discussed in the preceding section. This paradoxical state of affairs suggests some kind of avoidance-compulsion mechanism which, as we shall see, reflects the dilemma of the science fiction writer in his attempt to bridge the modes of realism and fantasy. And as we shall also see, both *Black Easter* and its tour de force sequel, *The Day After Judgment* (1970), although purportedly works of bizarre supernatural fantasy, actually exemplify Blish's well-nigh death-bed thoughts on the nature of science fiction as expressed in a last essay entitled "Probapossible Prolegomena to Ideareal History."

Previously Blish had come to see, some would say falsely, that *Black Easter* and *The Day After Judgment* (considered as a single work that, for convenience, I shall sometimes call *Black . . . Judgment*) completed a thematic trilogy begun by *A Case of Conscience*. In his biographical piece, "A Science Fiction Coming of Age," Blish explains how all this came about. Wishing to write a book about ceremonial magic similar to *The Worm Ouroboros,* Blish set out to write a story around what he assumed to be the magician figure Roger Bacon, an assumption derived primarily from Robert Greene's sixteenth-century play, *Friar Bacon and Friar Bungay.*[9] But Blish soon discovered that the historical Bacon was vehemently opposed to magic, and out of a consuming interest in Bacon the scientist he wrote *Doctor Mirabilis*—leaving "unscratched the original itch to write a novel about magic."[10] That "itch" led in turn to the writing of *Black Easter*. Blish connects this supernatural fantasy to *Doctor Mirabilis* by the opening line, "The room stank of demons," which recalls another infernally smelly room in that previous novel; by direct references to Bacon and his *The Nullity of Magic;* and by the presence of a servant "nicknamed Joannes, after Bacon's famous disappearing apprentice."[11] But it was only after completing *Black Easter* that Blish realized it shared a center of significant thematic interest with both *Doctor Mirabilis* and *A Case of Conscience*: "I realized that I had now written three novels, widely separated in times of composition and even more in ostensible subject-matter, each one of which was a dramatization in its own terms of one of the oldest problems of philosophy: *Is the desire for secular knowledge, let alone the acquisition and use of it, a misuse of the mind, and perhaps even actively evil?*"[12]

At this point Blish settled on an overall title, "After Such Knowledge," a phrase from T. S. Eliot's line in "Gerontion": "After such knowledge, what forgiveness?" This line figures as the epigraph for the sequel volume, *The Day After Judgment,* the only part of the trilogy that Blish wrote with the consciousness that he was writing part of a trilogy. *Black Easter* and *The Day After Judgment* have now been published as a single volume and some day Blish's expressed hope that "After Such Knowledge" be published as a trilogy may be fulfilled. (For awhile George Hay interested a publisher named Millington's [CM 84].) Blish recommends that these works are best read in their past, present, and future order: *Doctor Mirabilis* would constitute volume 1, *Black . . . Judgment* volume 2, and *A Case of Conscience* volume 3. Their actual order of composition corresponds to his characteristic one step forward, one step back, and "as-you-were" return to stasis pattern.

At the conclusion of "A Science Fiction Coming of Age," Blish claims that with the "After Such Knowledge" trilogy he had found his metier, the treatment of a relevant and timeless problem, indicating that "I've got another one of that kind on the fire" (presumably "The Breath of Brahma"). David G. Hartwell, in his introduction to *Black Easter/The Day After Judgment,* quotes the "my metier" reference but goes on to point out that Blish did not always find his most appreciative audience. He notes that *Black Easter* failed miserably in its first paperback incarnation although it was Blish's most favorably and widely reviewed book. The 1969 Dell edition did not reach the more or less guaranteed SF and fantasy readership because it was marketed as a novel about black magic like Ira Levin's *Rosemary's Baby* (1967), although it was "not written according to the Romantic conventions of the best seller."[13]

The "ostensible subject matter" of *Black Easter,* the first novel in which Blish tried "to get rid of all the clothing, and present the material naked" (KLA, 18 February 1973), may be briefly summarized. Most of what happens depends upon the interactions of the following characters: Mr. Baines, president of Consolidated Warfare Service; his executive assistant, Jack Ginsberg; one of his scientists, Dr. Adolph Hess; Theron Ware, a black magician who lives in Positano, Italy; and Father Domenico, a member of Monte Albano's sanctuary of white (i.e., albino) magicians atop their rock of faith. After visiting Ware and testing his powers (and after Ware has corrupted Ginsberg with a succubus), Baines finally states his real purpose (for which Ware will be handsomely rewarded): "I would like to let all the major demons out of Hell for one night, turn them loose in the world with no orders and no restrictions, and see just what it is they would do if they were left on their own hooks like that" (p. 73). As an aesthete of destruction, Baines's motive is purely artistic. The following Easter an elaborate conjuration is performed in the presence of all the principal characters (Father Domenico being there as an observer thanks to the terms of the covenant between white and black magicians) and forty-eight of the demons with whom Ware has pacts are loosed upon the world. The result is World War III and nuclear devastation. One of the princes of Hell, Put Satanachia, appears and after destroying Hess when he breaks out of his part of the magic circle, explains that Ware's conjuration has enabled Hell to win the battle of Armageddon and that *"God is dead"* (p. 113).

In the sequel, *The Day After Judgment,* it appears that Hell, as Dante's City of Dis, has established itself in Death Valley. Apraising the situation from the Strategic Air Command (SAC) missile-launching control site under Denver, General McKnight (the one significant new character) orders an all-out nuclear bombardment of this hellish outpost. But Dis emerges totally unscathed. By natural or magical means, Baines, Ginsberg, Ware, and Father Domenico make their way to Dis. After viewing a Dis[topia] transformed into a utopian city, the group is confronted by Satan Mekratrig. In a verse form modelled on *Paradise Lost* this figure explains that evil is meaningless without good and so with the death of God, Satan must become God. But it is projected that ultimately man must become God, presumably so that Satan may once again enjoy being evil.

It should be noted incidentally that Blish underplays an indebtedness to Arthur Edward Waite's *The Book of Ceremonial Magic.*[14] His "Author's Note" mentions "C.[?] A. E. Waite" in passing and the epigraph to the "Station" (a styling for a chapter or a section dropped in the combined Arrow Books edition) entitled "The First Commission" is taken with acknowledgment from pages 3 to 4 of Waite's guide. Blish's first Station is entitled "Preparation of the Operator" as is the first chapter of Waite, part 2, "The Complete Grimoire" (part 1 is headed "The Literature of Ceremonial Magic"). The first magic circle which Blish describes in detail, used for the third of Baines's tests, amounts to a positioning of two diagrams from *The Book of Ceremonial Magic*.[15] The spirit commanded is required to appear in the outside triangle. Before this description comes a description of two of the instruments of the art—the bolline with a horn handle and the pen—which appear in Waite, part 2, chapter 2, sections 2, 3, and 4.

The description of the magic circle used for Ware's final conjuration corresponds to that depicted in the full page plate on page 259 of Waite's book, which is reproduced on p. 299. Blish's description essentially reproduces the information Waite provides in his "Explanation of Full-Page Plates." The names and descriptions of the demons that Ware summons (pp. 94–99) are selected from those which Waite describes. The seals and characters of Lucifuge Rofocale and Astaroth and the seals of Vassago (pp. 88, 164 and 159) are copied from Waite's diagrams on pages 185 and 196. And, as we shall see, Waite's belief that there is no essential difference between black and white magic is one that Ware shares.[16] Although Waite's book seems to have been Blish's main source, there is no reason to doubt that he did the extensive homework mentioned in the "Author's Note." At the time of his death he was working on a two-volume history of witchcraft and demonology.[17]

It might appear from my plot summary that *Black . . . Judgment* amounts to little more than a melodramatic farrago of black magic and manicheanism. But a final judgment must await a closer examination of both this diptych's central problematic and its structural and technical execution. There are subtleties of thought and presentation worthy of appreciation.

(iii) A Fix on the Problem?

The name of Blish's black magician, Theron Ware, provides some indication of Blish's general area of concern. It is taken from Harold Frederic's sensational novel, *The Damnation of Theron Ware*. Frederic's Ware is a Methodist minister who comes to believe not in God but in the pragmatic value of religion. Frederic is exploring William James's

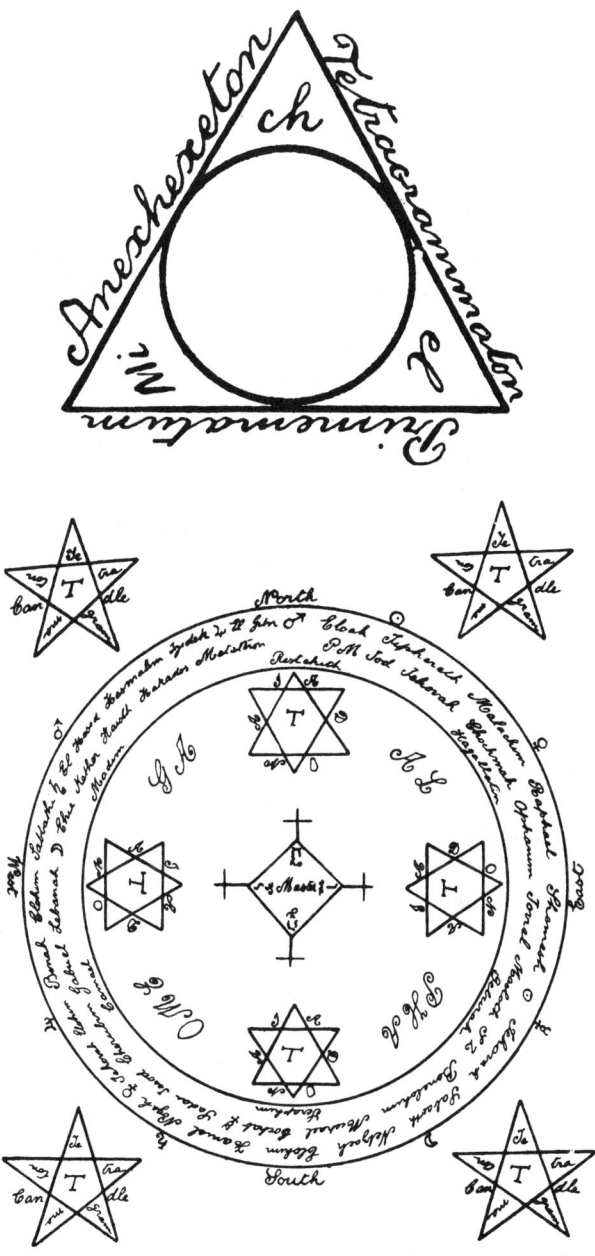

The Triangle of Solomon and the Magical Circle, from Arthur Edward Waite, *The Book of Ceremonial Magic* (1898; New York: University Books, 1961), pp. 220, 223

The Goëtic Circle of Pacts, from Arthur Edward Waite, *The Book of Ceremonial Magic* (1898; New York: University Books, 1961), p. 259

pragmatism, the claim that an article of religious faith is "true" if it provides emotional satisfaction. In other words, pragmatism is an ally of religion. Blish's Ware, however, practices a somewhat different kind of pragmatism.[18]

Black Easter opens with Father Domenico in his room at Monte Albano and a characteristic prefigurative image: "At Father Domenico's back, he knew without looking, coloured spots and lozenges of light from his high, narrow, stained-glass window were being cast at this hour across the face of his computor, mocking the little coloured points of its safe-lights" (p. 15; see cover reproduction p. 302 herein).[19] Here we have the diptych's central problem, the relationship between the light of heaven and religion and the light of science, between sacred and secular knowledge. This relationship may be construed in four obvious ways: (1) There is what appears to be Father Domenico's view (in this instance at least) that scientific or secular knowledge is compatible with sacred knowledge. (2) There is the extreme view that the relationship between the two kinds of knowledge amounts to the opposition between good and evil, unless (3) different kinds of secular knowledge are to be distinguished and an evil form is to be separated from a good one. (4)

Account should also be taken of the possibility that sacred knowledge is simply an illusion, a possibility on which much of science fiction purports to be predicated. The question then arises, can one talk about good and evil knowledge in any meaningful sense at all if human material reality provides the only context?

Ultimately, the issue involves philosophical and aesthetic questions, questions of Truth and Beauty. Is the notion of good and evil dependent upon some form of transcendent sanction and the existence of a heaven for those who commit themselves to the one and a hell for those who commit themselves to the other? Then comes the big question. Why does an omnipotent God permit the existence of evil? At this point philosophical and theological arguments often resort to aesthetic analogies. God's handiwork is equivalent to an artistic creation. And like a work of art, not only its beauty and effectiveness but also its potential for meaningfulness depends upon a play of polarities. But this justification, which has the effect of turning good and evil into arbitrary black and white, may be applied equally to the human and the transcendent spheres. This is the impasse with which *The Day After Judgment* concludes.

Blish muddies the issue somewhat by focussing not on knowledge directly but on magic, the implication being that knowledge acquired through magic, whether black or white, corresponds to human knowledge per se, rather than a mix of secular and sacred knowledge. This confusion, of course, goes back to the Faust legend which is Blish's basic source. The knowledge acquired through magic must, to some degree, be viewed in metaphorical terms. That is to say, from the point of view of Blish's rhetorical purpose, and from that point of view only, the supernatural machinery in *Black . . . Judgment* must be taken as both metaphorical and literal. Whatever may be evil about knowledge acquired through magic does not apply to knowledge acquired through regular human means unless the human sacrifices made by the person questing for secular knowledge are understood as metaphorically equivalent to making a pact with Satan. At the same time what has already been observed should be emphasized: Blish takes considerable pains to ensure that his presentation of the occult paraphernalia is realistic.

For much of the diptych Blish seems to assume what I have distinguished as the third way in which the relationship between sacred and secular knowledge may be taken. The opposition between a black magician like Ware and a white one like Father Domenico amounts to that between evil and good. Yet both sides have entered into a con-

If cover by Gray Morrow for *Black Easter,* August 1967

tractual agreement. According to the conditions of what is referred to in *Black Easter* as the Grand Covenant, the forces of evil must be allowed a certain freedom of operation. Thus Father Domenico may observe Ware's conjurations but—to his dismay—he is not permitted to interfere with their outcome:

> Why—that was the question—did God so tie his hands, why did He allow such a compromise as the Covenant at all? It suggested at least some limitation in His Power unallowable by the firm dogma of Omnipotence, which it was a sin ever to question; or, at worst, some ambiguity in His relationship with Hell, one quite outside the revealed answers to the problem of Evil. (Pp. 60–61)

Joanna Russ, in a review of *Black Easter,* maintains that the terms of this hypothetical Covenant correspond to the oft-sensed view that evil rather than good is more effective in the real world, that, for example, "Good guys finish last." She goes on to comment that a God who sticks by the rules "confronting an Evil which does not limit itself would be altogether horrible without the intercession of a benevolent Deity—and that is where *Black Easter* turns on the reader and bites him in the jugular, so to speak."[20]

Actually the sequel reverses the implication that Russ reads into the ending of *Black Easter*. "[M]y aim in the sequel," Blish wrote Paul Shackley, "was to pursue the literal-mindedness of the first book to still greater absurdities" (PS, 23 June 1970). The forces of evil acquire the new and bitter knowledge that, in a state of complete freedom and control, evil is meaningless. In choosing not to be contained by the rules of the Covenant, Evil discovers that there are no more rules to break. Faced with this loss of raison d'être, Evil is forced to act within limitations which it supposedly sets for itself. Thus Satan Mekratrig, who appears "surmounted by a halo," must assume the role of a self-limiting good God until such time as man himself can take over the burden (p. 203). The idea had previously been broached that mutation as a result of nuclear radiation "may be God's way of resuming the process of evolution for Man . . . perhaps towards some ultimate organism we cannot foresee, perhaps even towards some unitary mind which we will share with God, as Teilhard de Chardin envisioned" (p. 129). However this may be, neither good nor evil can exist in a state of pure freedom. Both depend upon that condition of restraint signified by the Covenant. Put Satanachia responds to Father Domenico's "Behold thy confusion, if thou be disobedient" with the words "I WAS NEVER IN THAT BOTTLE!" (p. 111), but there is a pun on the word "con-fusion"—a blending of distinction rather than destruction is the operative threat—which Put Satanachia fails to address. Satan Mekratrig, "the Great Nothing itself," finally addresses that confusion in a pun of his own (p. 203). In the context of his speech in Miltonian verse this *non-being* admits to a need to climb back into the bottle as "The last supreme endeavour of this fearful Jarr" (p. 206). Here "Jarr" refers not only to the confused mental and physical upset which has occurred but also to some form of rigid container from which it is impossible to escape. This, to quote another punning phrase from the same speech, is a "perverse aesthetick Joyce" indeed (p. 207).

Translated back into the terms of Blish's metaphor, the opposition between secular and sacred knowledge or the opposition between good secular knowledge and evil secular knowledge (irrespective of whether or not the good and bad forms align themselves with transcendent realities) obscures common philosophical interests. On the level of characterization, what is obscured is an essential identity between Ware, Father Domenico, and Baines. "Since magic is also an art" both Ware and Father Domenico must be viewed as artists (p. 18). Likewise, Baines, with his interest in the chiaroscuro of destruction, is motivated by the instincts of the artist. He too "practised what was literally an occult art in which the man on the street no longer believed" (p. 34). And after all, as Baines points out, "every dedicated artist is something of a sadist" (p. 75). Strictly speaking, as Baines himself realizes, "He was only the patron, who could watch the colours being applied and the cartoon being filled" (p. 101). But if Baines, who like Ware is aged forty-eight (approximately Blish's age at the time *Black Easter* was published), must make use of Ware's superior knowledge, so too must Ware and Father Domenico work through superior powers. The controlled work of art that Baines wishes to make possible is a kind of "action painting" developing through "sketches" to the finished "canvas" (pp. 74, 101). This pictorial analogy is reinforced by the succession of tableau-like and mainly interior (therefore framed) scenes which make up Blish's diptych, by the two very detailed descriptions of Ware's magic circles, and by the fact that the burning of paintings in the Tate Gallery (Blake's illustrations for Dante's *Inferno* and *Purgatorio* are specified) is the first important indication of what is happening as the result of Baines's commission.[21] A chapter epigraph makes clear that reality is to be understood and appreciated as a vast painting:

> As a picture, wherein a black colouring occurs in its proper place, so is the universe beautiful, if one could survey it, notwithstanding the presence of sinners, although, taken by themselves, their proper deformity makes them hideous. (P. 193)

These words are taken from St. Augustine's *De Civitate Dei*.

Thus we are given the set-piece description of Dis in Death Valley, an exercise in chiaroscuro. But perhaps the most electrifying portrait that Blish paints is the following miniature representation of the nuclear Dis-aster, the nuclear walpurgisnight, that has taken place:

> That vaporized man had been one of the lucky. Here stood another who had been in a cooler circle; evidently he had looked up at a fireball, for his eyes were only holes; he stood in a half crouch, holding his arms out from his sides like a penguin, and instead of skin, his naked body was covered with a

charred fell which was cracked in places, oozing blood and pus. Here a filthy, tattered mob clambered along a road almost completely covered with rubble, howling with horror—though there was no sound with this scene—led by a hairless woman pushing a flaming baby carriage. Here a man who seemed to have had his back flayed by flying glass worked patiently with a bent snow shovel at the edge of an immense mound of broken brick; by the shape of its margins it might once have been a large house. . . . (P. 132)

The reference to "a cooler circle" within the context of such bizarre nuclear terminology as "Rung thirty-four" and the ultimate "spasm" (pp. 132, 128) makes it apparent that we are indeed within the imprisoning circles of Dante's Hell.

The Covenant provides for the kind of control that is necessary to art. Because of the common aesthetic interest, the difference between good and evil, white magic and black magic, is purely academic. Thus we learn that Ware began "as a white magician" (p. 89). And by way of preparation for "The Last Conjuration" (the title of the final "Station" of *Black Easter*), Ware prays first to Satan and then to God, thereby at least implying the complicity of good and evil (pp. 81–82). Father Domenico's similarity to Ware from this point of view is hinted at in *Black Easter*. Ware cryptically tells Baines that Father Domenico is "not significantly holier than us. . . . I know something he doesn't know, too. He's in for a surprise in the next world" (p. 42). But Father Domenico does understand why Ware has excluded him from the forthcoming conjuration: "in his place, Father Domenico would have done the same thing" (pp. 53–54). In *The Day After Judgment* Ware refers to the Amish belief "that there was no such thing as white magic" and comments that "in the ultimate analysis they were quite right . . . whatever delusions about the point might be harboured by Father Domenico and his fellows" (p. 168). Subsequently, Ware informs Father Domenico that the practice of using white magic to find treasure is analogous to the monkish sin of hoarding, that "every single pillar saint went instantly to Hell," and that "there is no efficacious dispensation for the practice of white magic, because there is no such thing as white magic. It is all black, black, black as the ace of spades . . ." (p. 199). This information is, of course, concordant with Ware's conviction, noted earlier, that the Satanic Rebellion "was in fact going to succeed, probably by the year A.D. 2000" (p. 89). Perhaps the essential redundancy of white magic explains why Father Domenico has so little to do with the overall plot.

The parallels between Ware and Father Domenico are matched by those between Baines's employees, the German Adolph Hess and the

Jewish Jack Ginsberg. What seems to be a natural opposition is quickly subverted: "The two men did not like each other much; in part, Baines sometimes thought, because in some ways they were very much alike" (p. 37). And the materialist Hess is also very much like Ware—a materialist magician who relates magic to mathematics and keeps current on chemistry, physics, and quasars—as Ware recognizes: "what I'm after is something you understand perfectly, and for which you've sold your own soul, or if you prefer an only slightly less loaded word, your integrity, to Dr. Baines—*knowledge*" (p. 52). Hess agrees that they are both fanatics.

There is a further correlation to be made between black magic/knowledge (and white magic/knowledge) and the art of war. War, like magic, is presented as the practical manifestation of knowledge. The point is first made in terms of the assertion that Baines's role in the munitions business makes him the practitioner of an "occult art" (p. 34). Confirmation comes in *The Day After Judgment* with the subterranean and therefore hellish location of the SAC missile-launching control site under Denver. The title "So Above," provided for the "Station" in which is described the red-hot city of Dis, cements the equation with the enclosed military environment below ground.

Given this state of confused identity and unsuspected relations (it may be no accident that "unclear" is an anagram of "nuclear"), it makes sense that transcendent beings should manifest themselves as grotesque combinations of disparate forms evocative of both laughter and horror. Blish's subject matter requires, in fact, that he walk a tightrope between comedy and a horrified seriousness. Ware "was either comical or terrible, depending upon what view one took of the proceedings, in his white Levite surcoat with red-silk embroidery on the breast, his white leather shoes lettered in cinnebar, and his paper crown bearing the word EL" (p. 54). Later he stoops "to pick up his dented paper hat" (p. 108). The aspect of one of the demons "was so grotesque as to have been comic under other circumstances" (p. 96). The refectory in which the conjuration takes place "reminded Baines incongruously of an initiation room in a college fraternity house just after the last night of Hell Week" (p. 100). Occasionally the balancing act doesn't work. General McKnight's identification of Put Satanachia as *"the insidious Doctor Fu Manchu"* strikes a decidedly corny note (p. 192; emphasis in original). Likewise, the episode where Ware flies a broomstick is more ridiculous than sublime: "The candle affixed by its own tallow to the bundle of twigs and rushes before him (for only the foolhardy fly a broomstick with the bush trailing, no matter what is shown to the contrary in conventional Halloween cartoons) burned as steadily as though he were not in motion at all . . ." (p. 165).

But it is surely not without point that this "transvection" (p. 163) experience is notable for being the first *exterior* scene and for being Blish's wildest flight of invention in the diptych. This correlation is, of course, indicative of the containment/flight opposition (and the transcendence of same) which is so dominant in Blish's work. The sound of church bells occasions the first random event in the novel: the besom goes lifeless and Ware finds himself grounded in Pennsylvania. Thanks to the freedom from control made emblematic by flight, from this point on the narrative becomes much zestier. The rapid transit "gravity vacuum tube" which transfers Baines and Ginsberg to SAC's headquarters amounts to a rigidly controlled form of transportation by way of contrast with Ware's broomstick flight.

Towards the end of *Black Easter* and also in *The Day After Judgment,* the reader is encouraged to transcend what elsewhere amounts to an experience of discordant moods. Put Satanachia makes his presence felt with "a sound of laughter" at the end of *Black Easter* that unites the comical and the terrible: "It was the laughter of Something incapable of joy, laughing only because It was compelled by Its nature to terrify" (p. 110). Contraries are also united in the appearance of the demon Vassago, whose "features were quite beautiful and wholly horrible" (p. 160). Likewise, Venice is described as "this uglily beautiful city" (p. 179). As above, so below.

(iv) Transformed States

Implicit in a situation where the nature of good and evil are shown to be interdependent is the idea of transformation, good turning itself into evil, evil turning itself into good. In fact, both thematically and structurally, transformation is of central importance to both *Black Easter* and *The Day After Judgment*. Ware's initial alchemical exhibition, designed to impress Baines, prefigures the course of the entire diptych.[22] Looking in the mirror that Ware had instructed him to bring, Baines observes "two slow thick tears of dark venemous blood" flow from the corners of his eyes. Instructed to wipe them off, "On the white-on-white fabric" of his handkerchief, "the red stains turned slowly into butter-yellow gold" (p. 21). A few days later Jack Ginsberg, who has kept the evidence, reveals that the "golden tears" have turned into "two dull, inarguable smears of lead" (p. 37). The development from tears (despair) to blood (death and destruction) to gold (victory) to lead (reversal) corresponds exactly to the transformations of mood and action that follow. Imagistic details tie these transformations to Ware's alchemical exercise.

After the death of Rogan, governor of California (a further relatively minor demonstration of Ware's powers), Baines asks that a Dr. Stockhausen also be removed. Dr. Stockhausen, a theoretical physicist, is a threat to Baines's "monopoly of knowledge"—"once Stockhausen knows what we know, he could create a major explosion with—well, with the equivalent of a blackboard and two pieces of chalk" (pp. 43, 44). Ware's magic circles, it should be noted, are also drawn with "chalks" (p. 47). In order that Stockhausen should die without attracting undue attention, Ware arranges that he succumb to despair and commit suicide. According to the terms of the pact, Ware gives Marchosias, the demon who is to do the job, one of his possessions, "an opalescent crystal tear vase" (p. 59). The key word here is "tear," and it is underlined by the demon's comment: "When I have thee in Hell, magician, then shall I drink thee dry, though thy tears flow never so copiously" (p. 60). The commission is fulfilled; Stockhausen gives way to despair and poisons himself.

References to blood quickly follow. Father Domenico observes that, for Baines's third and ultimate commission, the canvas of death and destruction requires "human blood for pigments" (p. 74). In the "Station" of "Three Sleeps," Ware's "triduum [three days of preparation] was launched, devoutly, in water, and would be observed, strictly, until the end in blood; wherein would be required to the slaughter a lamb, a dog, a hen and a cat" (p. 83). The "blood sacrifices" are performed (p. 87).

The gold of victory quickly reveals its leaden consequences. Since the experience of defeat or reversal affects first the population of Earth, secondly Baines, Ware, and company, thirdly the U.S. military (who attempt to destroy Dis by nuclear bombardment), and finally the forces of Satan, there is a somewhat mixed-up, serial quality to this ultimate metamorphosis. Beginning with the Tate Gallery fire are many references to fire which may be taken as signalling the transformation from bloody destruction to the liquid gold of success. The succubus, who ministers to a quickly addicted Jack Ginsberg and signifies Ware's success in corrupting the man, is dressed in "a black silk sari with gold edging . . . which left one breast bare, and gold sandals," and possessed of an "inflamed mound, a vision of pure lubricity" (p. 124). The arrival of the Antichrist is confirmed when the demon Agares, as the new Pope, accepts "the golden horn" headgear (p. 181). Satan Mekratrig, in his versified summation, refers to the attainment of a "golden Throne" (p. 205). But the "leaden skies" which Father Domenico previously believed "returned him no answer" (p. 86) to what is going on in the realms of Heaven and Hell do, in fact, symbolically inform him of the turn-around which we shall learn in conclusion has taken place, and of the blurring of black and white. When Hess maintains, "It seems to me . . . that we are all insane," he does so "in a leaden monotone" (p. 107).

In reading the diptych, as I have pointed out, one has the pictorial sense of a series of repetitious (particularly with regard to the calling up of the forty-eight demons during "The Last Conjuration"), ritualistic, tableau-like, generally enclosed settings. What especially distinguishes this work from SF is the lack of a logical transitional progression linking these scenic tableaus. Instead one has the magical sense, appropriate to a work of fantasy, of one scene *transforming* itself into the next. The experience of transformation can only be conveyed by the presence of narrative jumps or gaps. This point is itself effectively conveyed in the context of Ware's alchemical demonstration. There is, most obviously, the gap in terms of pages which occurs between the tear turning into gold and then turning into lead. But there is also a gap (whether deliberate or accidental) in this narrative detail: "Baines handed the handkerchief to Jack, who folded it carefully and put it back in its waxed-paper wrapper." The reader will look in vain for any indication that, when Baines "pulled out his immaculate monogrammed handkerchief," it had previously been removed, or is at that time being removed, from a "waxed-paper-wrapper". We have been informed, however, that Jack came equipped with "a waxed-paper envelope" containing "a lady's hand mirror sealed in glassine" (p. 21). The reader is here required to do a quick double take and fill in this lacuna with the hypothesis that at some unspecified moment the handkerchief had been withdrawn from a wrapper that Jack carried along with the envelope that contained the mirror. These gaps are, of course, equivalent to openings in the otherwise imprisoning containers of knowledge.

Black Easter opens with a striking statement that simultaneously signifies transformation and a gap in the reader's knowledge: "The room stank of demons" (p. 13). At one time Father Domenico's room did not stink of demons. Now it does. Why? In a very negative review, Ted White includes this teasing opening line in a discussion of all that he believes to be wrong with *Black Easter*.[23] In an overly defensive letter replying to this review, making mention of "11 inquiries from film producers, two of which ripened into offers" (this was the era of the Polanski film *Rosemary's Baby,* to which many reviewers related *Black Easter*), Blish points out that Baines's arrival explains why the room stank of demons and directs White to the evidence that demons take a special interest in Baines: "all Hell had been waiting for this meeting since the two of them [Ware and Baines] were born" (p. 30). It is true that Baines does enter Father Domenico's room at the end of the first short "Station," but, White asks in a response to Blish's letter, why should the demons stink up a room before Baines's arrival?[24] To my mind what is important here is not any particular rational answer—after all, Baines's arrival in Italy or in the vicinity might have triggered the welcoming stink in the room which the demons knew Baines would enter—but the sense of a logical gap or break experienced by the reader.

On a more mundane level is the first reference to Ware's "white moustache" (p. 146). Because there has been no previous indication that Ware possesses facial hair, the previous image of a smooth-shaven Blish-type American expatriate "on the very near side of his fiftieth birthday" (p. 166) is transformed without explanation into one of Ware with a moustache.

Towards the conclusion of *The Day After Judgment,* Ware, Father Domenico, Baines, and Ginsberg find themselves outside the barbican of the city of Dis, but within "they found the citadel transformed." In place of Dis "there stood a clean, well-lighted city like an illustration from some Utopian romance" (p. 200):

> It was as though they were being given a preview of what the future of humanity would be like under demonic rule—not wholly unpredictable as a foretaste, but in content as well, as if the demons were trying to put the best possible face on the matter. In so doing, they had ingenuously embodied in their citadel nothing worse than a summary and epitomization of what pre-Apocalyptic, post-industrial Man had been systematically creating for himself. (P. 202)

After the obligatory tour, Baines, who notes that his "most lucrative ideas for weaponry had been stolen bodily," has his worst suspicions confirmed: "I always thought that it'd be hell to actually live in a place like this. . . . And now I know it" (p. 202). Blish's typographic experimentation with paragraph indentation during this revelation goes along with a general thwarting of expectations. At the same time, this whole business of Dis turning into utopia and utopia into dystopia is clearly intended as a crowning representation of the instability of good and evil.

But the overall disconcerting experience of transformation is best described in this finely crafted paragraph which occurs near the beginning of *The Day After Judgment,* the day after the Apocalypse:

> What had been Jack Ginsberg's room in the palazzo now looked a great deal more like the cabinet of Dr. Caligari. Every stone, every window frame, every angle, every wall was out of true, so that there was no place to stand where he did not feel as though he had been imprisoned in a tesseract—except that even the planes of the prison were crazed with jagged cracks without any geometry whatsoever. The window panes were out, and the ceiling dripped; the floor was invisible under fallen plaster, broken glass and anonymous dirt; and in the *gabinetto* the toilet was pumping continuously as though trying to flush away the world. The satin-sheeted bed was sandy to the touch, and when he took his clothes out of the wardrobe, his beautiful clothes so carefully selected from *Playboy,* dust fumed out of them like spores from a puffball. (P. 122)[25]

A tesseract is the four-dimensional analogue of a cube, and this passage provides an analogue for what I take to be Blish's intent in *Black . . . Judgment*. The "jagged cracks," the missing window panes, and the "invisible" because *covered* floor (simultaneously there and not there) correspond to the sense of narrative gaps or openings. In spite of the overall destruction and the toilet "pumping continuously as though trying to flush away the world," something is also being born. There is the "satin-sheeted bed" designed for lovemaking, the reference to *Playboy* (a touch as jarringly tawdry, yet as disturbingly valid, as the pulp trappings which permeate Blish's flawed art), and the dust "like spores from a puffball." What this passage indicates is that Blish's diptych amounts to an expanded vision of our present three-dimensional world. But the degree of expansion is still constrained by our three-dimensional world and hence the striking image of Ginsberg "imprisoned in a tesseract."

This tesseract amounts to an abstract prison, a prison without bars. It should be related to Blish's recurring image of solidified or enclosed light: the "lozenges of light" already noted in *Black Easter* (p. 15), the "truncated tetrahedron of yellow light" in *A Case of Conscience,* the "wedge of smoky orange light" and the "blurred rectangle" of "dim yellow light" issuing from an opening "no bigger than the end of a book" in *Doctor Mirabilis,* and the "truncated cone" of "quite orange" light and the "lozenge of reddish-yellow light" in *Welcome to Mars*.[26] In each case the abstract and intangible takes on the appearance of the concrete and confining. But the appearance is illusory. The recurrent or alternating situations of imprisonment and release, ignorance and breakthrough, in Blish's writings are equally bound to the contracted or expanded state of human perception and knowledge. Hence the virtual interchangeability of imprisonment and release for Blish.

From a strictly human point of view, the major events which take place in *Black Easter's* fourth-dimensional rendition of our world do not, strictly speaking, happen. Thus *The Day After Judgment* concludes with a scene that recalls Prospero's "Our revels now are ended. . . . / . . . all . . . shall dissolve, / And . . . / Leave not a rack behind" (*The Tempest,* IV.i, 148–55). Blish puts it this way: "The great hall of Pandemonium dissolves, and with it the Citadel of Dis, leaving the four men standing in a modern road in the midst of the small town of Badwater. It is early morning in the desert, and still cold. All traces of the recent battle have vanished" (p 209). Bob Rickard's claim that *A Case of Conscience* does not exist in the same historical universe as *Black . . . Judgment* because Earth has been destroyed in the historically earlier work simply does not apply.[27] To a three-dimensional perception Earth has not been destroyed. None of the major events described are a part of recorded human history. They amount to some kind of Blakean vision of what is *really* going on behind the scenes.

This conclusion is foreshadowed by Blish's description of the televised pictures of devastation: "The views from near the bombed areas were fragmentary, travelling, scarred by rasters, aflicker with electronic snow—a procession of unconnected images, like scenes from an early surrealist film, where one could not tell whether the director was trying to portray a story or only a state of mind" (p. 131). It is foreshadowed also by Hess's questions towards the conclusion of *Black Easter*: "How do you know what you think you know? . . . Couldn't all this be a hallucination we conjured up to remove some of our guilt?" (p. 107). The same kind of speculation, it will be recalled, is occasioned by the destruction of Lithia at the end of *A Case of Conscience*. The planet disappears in the manner of Ginsberg's succubus, "like a bursting balloon" (p. 72). Of Dis in Death Valley, it is hypothesized that "Perhaps in some sense it had never been there at all" (p. 208). The preponderance of internal settings and the complementary, almost allegorical characterization accentuates the feel of a stage set for inner vision; the outside setting with which *The Day After Judgment* concludes marks a return to everyday reality. But given the realm of thought which prevails throughout most of the work it is appropriate that there are no references to members of the general public.

For the same reason Blish sets his diptych in what is essentially the present, a time when it might be said that "the U.S. gained another bloody inch in Vietnam" (p. 101). Credibility does not depend on the convention that these things are yet to happen. It is, of course, true that Blish offers a somewhat prophetically skewed present. The California governor, Rogan, which must be an allusion to Reagan, dies of heart failure. The reference to "President Agnew" should not be taken as an indication that we are in a realistic parallel world. Rather the world of Blish's diptych amounts to a slightly tilted, depth dimension of the present as the worst of all possible worlds.

Black Easter ends with three words, *"God is dead"* (p. 113; emphasis in original). There has been, it should be noted, a previous emphasis on threes—in particular, the "Three Sleeps" Station and demons with "three heads" (pp. 97, 98)—culminating, of course, in "World War Three" (p. 107). *The Day After Judgment* ends with four statements indicative of improvement: whereas previously Father Domenico would have *believed,* Baines would have *thought,* Ware would have *known,* and Ginsberg would have *lusted,* we now hear Father Domenico say, "I think," Baines, "I believe," Ware, "I hope," and Ginsberg, "I . . . love" (p. 208). We are given to understand by this shift that a threefold vision has been transformed into a fourfold vision—into tesseract vision, in fact. In the diptych, each half of which is made up of four Stations, a limited container has been exchanged for a less limited one. But ultimately Blish, like Ginsberg earlier, is still imprisoned. Much of *The Day After Judgment* is devoted to a four-person argument between Ware, Father Domenico, Baines, and Ginsberg.[28] According to Ware, they each represent one of the four circles of Dante's Upper Hell (pp. 198–99).

In this fourfold context it is possible to make sense of the literary experimentation which concludes Blish's diptych: standard paragraphing gives way to oddly indented paragraphing which gives way to Satan Mekratrig's verse which in turn gives way to the dramatic presentation of four statements. The implication seems to be that the four literary modes which Blish makes us aware of, taken together, might somehow approximate a completed fourfold vision. And being "imprisoned in a tesseract" is preferable to being imprisoned in a cube.

(v) A Spenglerian Perspective

Blish himself, using the William Atheling, Jr. persona, wrote one plausible conclusion to any account of his own work. From his hospital bed just before his death, he put the finishing touches on a dense, synoptic article with the Joycean title "Probapossible Prolegomena to Ideareal History."[29] In this last essay he makes use of the Spenglerian "ideareal" (i.e., Platonic) notion of historical cycles that had earlier structured his *Cities in Flight* tetralogy to formulate a theory of the nature and historical place of SF. What has, to my knowledge, nowhere been observed is the way in which this essay ties in with, and provides a gloss on, what Blish is doing in *Black . . . Judgment*. In the light of "Probapossible Prolegomena" it is apparent that *Black . . . Judgment* is to some extent a fantasy about the nature and place of science fiction, and the relationship between science fiction and fantasy. The essay and the diptych provide a culmination to the development of Blish's theoretical ideas about science fiction. An emphasis on operating (by way of extrapolation) within the parameters of science in the 1951 "Science in Science Fiction" series of articles gives way to the Kuhnian concept of breaking paradigms in "The Science in Science Fiction" article of 1971.[30] But only in the Atheling piece, published in 1978, does Blish fully confront the fact that at best science fiction can do no more than offer the illusion of breaking paradigms and thus the inevitable element of fantasy.

In "Probapossible Prolegomena" Blish sets out "to do five things: (1) Define science fiction; (2) Show why it arose when it did; (3) Explain why it is becoming steadily more popular; (4) Demonstrate that just as it has thus far produced no towering literary masterwork, so no such work can be expected of it in the future, and (5) Place it as a familiar phenomenon in world history."[31] The fifth matter is crucial to Blish's view of the previous four.

In terms of the cycles which according to Spengler's *The Decline of the West* all world cultures go through, Western "civilization" (one of the phases that, saving some external disruption, every culture must go through) is now late into an era of decline that Spengler calls Caesarism. In such times (our own and those with which, in Spengler's sense, we are "contemporary"),

> Technology flourishes (the late Romans were first-class engineers) but science disintegrates into a welter of competing, grandiosely trivial hypotheses which supersede each other almost weekly and veer more and more markedly toward the occult. Among the masses there arises a "second religiousness" in which nobody actually believes; an attempt is made to buttress this by syncretism, the wrenching out of context of religious *forms* from other cultures, such as the Indian, without the faintest hope of knowing what

they mean. This process, too, leads inevitably toward a revival of the occult, and here science and religion overlap, to the benefit of neither.[32]

"Given all this," Atheling continues, "it is easy to deduce the state of the arts: a period of confused individual experimentation, in which traditions and even schools have ceased to exist, having been replaced by ephemeral fads." And thus this definition of science fiction:

> Science fiction is the internal (intracultural) literary form taken by syncretism in the West. It adopts as its subject matter that occult area where a science in decay (elaborately decorated with technology) overlaps the second religiousness—hence, incidentally, its automatic receptivity from its emergence to such notions as time travel, ESP, dianetics, Dean Drives, faster-than-light travel, reincarnation and parallel universes.[33]

As we have seen, one Blish novel, *Jack of Eagles,* and several stories feature psi powers, especially telepathy, and Blish also flirted with dianetics; when he had recovered from the dianetics boom he guiltily removed all references to "clears" from his stories. Nevertheless, in Blish's view SF remains an inevitably flawed manifestation or symptom of inevitably flawed times. And what flaws science fiction is a form of fantasy which is equated with both a second religiousness and a pack of lies. A black judgment indeed.

As early as autumn 1953 in a *Skyhook* piece subsequently reprinted as part of "Cathedrals in Space," Blish in his William Atheling, Jr. role had drawn attention to a species of religious science fiction: "These science fiction stories . . . are instruments of a chiliastic crisis, of a magnitude we have not seen since the world wide chiliastic panic of 999 A.D. . . ." A footnote adds "that fear of the Bomb is the modern version of the 999 riots."[34] Blish was not yet prepared to apply this insight to the nature of science fiction generally nor to place it within the context of a Spenglerian theory of history. He is, however, clearly on his way to following through to what culminates in "Probapossible Prolegomena" in the earlier, veiled fictional form of *Black . . . Judgment*. The link with the 1953 essay is established by Hess's belief that, "with another millennium coming to a close now," we are due for a repetition of "the chiliastic panics just before the year A.D. 1000" (p. 106).

The cyclical theory that Hess outlines is clearly comparable to Spengler's: "I think the human mind goes through a sort of cycle of fear. It can only take so much accumulated knowledge, and then it panics, and starts inventing reasons to throw everything over and go back to a Dark Age . . . every time with a new, invented mystical religion." After a period of secularization, people turn "back to the worship of unreason"—they "take up Christianity," worship "Satan or the Great Mother" or "flying saucers. . . . You've [i.e., Baines has] turned to black magic. What's the difference?" (p. 106).

Once-upon-a-time forms of fantasy need to be distinguished from transcendent fantasies. While the former operates by means of a convention of discontinuity with a consensus view of reality, the latter requires a conventional acceptance that the transcendent or supernatural is continuous (in a nonallegorical sense) with the world of consensus reality. The fantasy elements that Blish sees as characteristic of, and perhaps destructively contaminative to, science fiction belong essentially to the area of transcendent fantasy. Blish must have been thinking of "once-upon-a-time" fantasy when he described *Black Easter* to Charles Monteith as "neither science fiction nor fantasy, but a sort of hyper-sensational theological novel" (CM 51, 20 September 1967). Spengler's theory offers one somewhat unflattering explanation for the nature of the genre but it is not the only one. Indeed, as Brian M. Stableford suggests, *The Decline of the West* might itself be viewed as a particularly purist example of science fiction.[35] What I have described as the apocalyptic nature of science fiction depends upon much of the same evidence that Blish marshals but that evidence is accounted for rather differently.[36]

I would now add to the argument that science fiction expresses in more or less displaced ways concerns that are basically religious, the hypothesis that what I have called the "textual shadow" of the SF author accounts substantially for the element of transcendent fantasy.[37] The fact that more often than not the SF author is writing about a time when he or she will be dead sets in motion numerous thematic and structural avoidance strategies. In the preceding pages I have drawn attention to some of these strategies and to manifestations of a death consciousness on Blish's part. Ware's pact with the devil, for example, brings him "five hundred years of life" (p. 89). And then, on the death awareness side, there are all the references to cancer, the cause of Blish's own death, and the succession of exploding worlds, galaxies, and universes. In the context of an anguished letter to Blish, the late Philip K. Dick, who was in the midst of a marital crisis, observes that "you and I write about the future, and the future for me, and I think I am somewhat precog, has death written on its face, and I can't run fast enough to get away" (Dep. Blish 415/10, 22 May 1964), Dick speaks here for all SF writers and not least for James Blish.

What Blish does in *Black . . . Judgment* is reverse the usual balance in a work of science fiction between the rational, materialist, and scientific on the one hand, and the transcendent on the other. This act of reversal has the effect of clarifying that aspect of science fiction that so many critics of the genre, Blish included, so often wish guiltily to deny. Granted, it might be objected, that the supernatural machinery does loom large in *Black . . . Judgment*; what evidence is there that it should be related in any way with the more familiar machinery of science fiction? Blish makes the connection most explicitly by means of what Stableford regards as a poor joke: the white magicians summoned to a convocation at Monte Albano are all named for SF writers, or people associated with science fiction.[38] Father Bonfiglioli corresponds to Kyril Bonfiglioli (one-time editor of *Science Fantasy*, later called *Impulse* and *Sf Impulse*), Father Monteith to Charles Monteith of Faber & Faber, Father Boucher to the author and editor Anthony Boucher, Father Vance to Jack Vance, Father Anson to Robert Anson Heinlein, Father Selahny to Roger Zelazny (or a contraction of Zelazny and [Samuel R.] Delany), Father Rosenblum to J. Michael Rosenblum, who edited a British fanzine, *The Futurian* (1938–40), and Father Atheling, "a wall-eyed grimoiran who saw portents in parts of speech," of course, to Blish (pp. 84–85).[39] The same group is reassembled in *The Day After Judgment* with the exception of Father Rosenblum, who has died "in the interim" (p. 151). Blish's dubious humor here should be related to my earlier discussion of the tightrope that his subject matter forced him to walk between comedy and horror. But its more serious purpose is to link what he is doing in *Black . . . Judgment* with his views on the nature of science fiction.

The chapter in *Black Easter* devoted to the assembly of white magicians is preceded by an epigraph from C. S. Lewis's *The Screwtape Letters* which relates very directly to "Probapossible Prolegomena." Screwtape points out that, although the devils "hail a materialist or a magician with the same delight," if "once we can produce our perfect work—the Materialist Magician, the man, not using, but veritably worshipping, what he vaguely calls 'Forces' while denying the existence of 'spirits'—then the end of the war will be in sight" (p. 84). *Black Easter* is, it should be noted, dedicated to C. S. Lewis. The morbidly named Adolph Hess seems to be a specific instance of such a type, but given the negative overlapping of science and religion which, it is argued in "Probapossible Prolegomena," characterizes SF, the Materialist Magicians of our time are SF writers. And hence the list of white magicians with the names of SF writers.

Two more connections should be noted between *Black . . . Judgment* and the nature of science fiction. In a now classic essay entitled "The Imagination of Disaster," Susan Sontag points out that the SF film "is concerned with the aesthetics of destruction, with the peculiar beauties to be found in wreaking havoc, in making a mess."[40] The scenes of world destruction that figure in the films that Sontag describes represent a stereotypical instance of science fiction considered, as I believe it should be, as a species of apocalyptic literature. It is clear, then, that Baines, as an aesthete of destruction, provides a specifically science-fictional motivation for the plot of *Black . . . Judgment*.

A final connection depends upon returning to that tantalizing image of Jack Ginsberg "imprisoned in a tesseract" (p. 122). The word "tesseract" had a very particular association for James Blish. In his youth, it will be recalled, he was a member of the Science Fiction Advancement Association. The official organ of that Association was called—lo and behold—*Tesseract*. Its first issue was published in March 1936 and it became one of the most important fan magazines. The young Blish, it will also be recalled, was one of *Tesseract*'s most regular contributors.[41] Presumably the name was intended to convey some notion of what science fiction was all about. Although constrained by a three-dimensional present, the implication is that science fiction may afford some kind of enhanced perception of our reality by evoking an awareness of the fourth dimension, conventionally the dimension of time. From this point of view, science fiction might be said to allow for a depth dimension of the present. Clearly, this conception of science fiction, with its possibilities and its limitations, stayed with Blish throughout his life.

Now is the time to recall the place of *Black . . . Judgment* in the mixed-genre "After Such Knowledge" trilogy. A historical novel precedes a work of fantasy which in turn precedes a work of SF. That is to say, the trilogy builds towards the SF novel *A Case of Conscience* and perhaps suggests an $A + B = C$, thesis, antithesis, synthesis scheme. Given that a mix of fantasy and historical thinking goes into the creation of all SF futures (one thinks of the Spenglerian system that stiffens the "space opera" of *Cities in Flight*) and given the science-fictional dimension of *Black . . . Judgment,* it seems that the nature of SF itself provides an unexpected unifying matrix or rationale for the entire trilogy. And while *Doctor Mirabilis* is not linked to science fiction in quite the direct ways that *Black . . . Judgment* is, its basic theme—conceptual breakthrough—pertains to both the truth of history and a defining characteristic of science fiction. If the trilogy hangs together (and I would claim it does but only just) it does so not simply because of the knowledge-and-evil theme and the repeated theologian- or priest-scientist character (Roger Bacon, Father Domenico, and the Jesuit Ruiz-Sanchez in *A Case of Conscience*) but because it is sequentially representative of the generic mix that is science fiction.[42]

Blish's career as an SF writer constitutes an opening of the field, an opening composed of gaps. Cy Chauvin speaks to this when he writes that Blish

> bridged many of the gaps in sf between writers in America and England . . . between the new generation of writers and the old . . . between routine commercial fiction and that which attempted to be literature . . . and, of course, between writers and critics. I know of no one else in science fiction who was a bridge between so many.[43]

Not only, it should be added, does Blish's corpus encompass the New Wave; it also anticipates the current engulfment of SF by fantasy. What finally needs to be emphasized, then, is the bridge that Blish devised between SF and fantasy in terms of the relationship between physics and metaphysics. By putting demonology up against science and reversing the normal SF balance between the scientific and the "transcendental" in *Black . . . Judgment,* he found a way of avoiding, surmounting, and transforming the controlling clichés of SF. Taking Roger Bacon and Spengler as his models, Blish saw to it that science fiction itself participated—at least provisionally—in the process of conceptual breakthrough. At such moments of breakthrough, one becomes aware of the fantasy of reality and the reality of fantasy. And that is the enigma that characterizes science fiction, the tortured *mise en abîme* to which so much of Blish's work testifies.

NOTES

Chapter 1

1. The previous *Genealogy of the Blish Family in America 1637–1905* (1905) was compiled by Matthew Rhodes Blish's father, James Knox Blish. One of the 315 copies of this and one of the 250 copies of the *Supplement* may be located in the New Bodleian Library Blish Papers, Dep. Blish 345 and 346, respectively.

2. Damon Knight, *The Futurians: The Story of the Science Fiction "Family" of the 30's that Produced Today's Top SF Writers and Editors* (New York: John Day, 1977), p. 153.

3. James Blish, "A Science-Fiction Coming of Age," in *The Tale That Wags the God,* ed. Cy Chauvin (Chicago: Advent, 1987), pp. 146–47, 142–43. I am grateful to Cy Chauvin for providing me with copies of the page proofs. This is the only autobiographical account of Blish's early years: "I seldom enjoy reading autobiography and actively loathe writing it" (ibid., p. 127). He was, however, upset that Brian Aldiss had not invited him to contribute an autobiographical essay to *Hell's Cartographers* (1975) (Aldiss to Blish, 7 May 1973; Dep. Blish 411/2). Aldiss himself later regretted the omission.

4. See James Blish, Preface to "The Sense of Music" (unpublished manuscript), p. 3; and *The Futurians,* pp. 151–52. I am grateful to Virginia Kidd for a copy of "The Sense of Music."

5. "A Science-Fiction Coming of Age," pp. 146–47.

6. Ibid., pp. 142, 147–48.

7. Ibid., p. 116. My sense of Blish's complex personality is much indebted to some "Biographical Notes on James Blish" that Josephine Saxton, the friend and companion of his last months, supplied me with. She writes, "He hated his mother and thought that she had severely damaged his marriage to Virginia Kidd. He often recalled his mother's reaction when he told her that he and Virginia were expecting a baby early in their marriage. The old woman screeched 'How can you *do* this to me?' James still felt the pain of knowing how selfish and unloving his mother was, or he thought she was." Virginia Kidd, however, points out that "Jim's very unkind statements about his mother . . . were to some extent a reflection of his illness and her extreme disapproval of his move to England. . . . [S]he was not particularly religious. . . . I did not much like Dorothea—nor did she like me—but we respected each other . . . whereas she loved Jim to the point of postponing a second marriage until he had left home and he was not totally insensible of that love" (Kidd to Ketterer, 11 June 1984). In a marginal comment on a manuscript version of this chapter Virginia notes that Dorothea "was an attractive and not unintelligent woman, as well as very talented. Her great sin was that she was very possessive of Jim and nagged him a lot."

8. "A Science-Fiction Coming of Age," pp. 153, 150, 161. It should be noted that Blish

does acknowledge a substantial debt to his mother in the Preface to "The Sense of Music," p. 2. As for his mother's religious views, in a 1966(?) notebook may be found these lines of doggerel: "In her sane moments she was a Christian Scientist/And when she was mad she was horrid" (Dep. Blish 438/23). As for his own position on religion, in the foreword to *A Case of Conscience* Blish describes himself as an agnostic. Fourteen years later, during an interview with Paul Walker (February 1972, first published in *Moebius Trip 13*, 1972), he reasserts the fact that "I have a pronounced sympathy for, and envy of, the religious temperament but am myself an agnostic." See Paul Walker, *Speaking of Science Fiction: The Paul Walker Interviews* (Oradell, N.J.: Lunar Publications, 1978), p. 241. In *The Issue at Hand* (Chicago: Advent, 1964), p. 55, Blish calls himself an agnostic. But writing to his English fan and correspondent Paul Shackley Blish maintains, regarding the "After Such Knowledge" trilogy, "I am an Epicurean—that is, I believe there might have been a Creator but He never intervenes, does not desire worship and may not even be around any more . . ." (PS, 30 June 1970). Josephine Saxon writes, "If it were possible to be a Jesuit, a Calvinist and an Atheist all at once, then James Blish would have been all three" ("Biographical Notes").

9. "A Science-Fiction Coming of Age," pp. 140–42. Watching General Balboa's armada of Italian airplanes flying over Chicago was, Blish recalls, "the last great event of my fascination with flying" (ibid., p. 150).

10. Ibid., pp. 139, 144. Since this initial exposure to SF, Blish claimed to have had the feeling that "events did not so much 'happen' as 'come true'" (ibid., p. 104).

11. For much of the previous three paragraphs see ibid., pp. 120, 122–24; three works by Sam Moskowitz: *The Immortal Storm: A History of Science Fiction Fandom* (1954; rpt. Westport, Conn.: Hyperion Press, Inc., 1974), pp. 64–67, 79–80, "On Nils Frome and Blish, Lovecraft, et al.," *Science-Fiction Studies* 12 (July 1985): 230–31, and "Nils Frome in *The Golden Atom*," *Science-Fiction Studies* 13 (March 1986): 100–101; and (re: the SF convention), Marty Klug, "Interview with James Blish," *Whizzard* 2 (June 1975): 11, and Sam Moskowitz to Ketterer, 7 September 1985 and 3 September 1986. The cover of vol. 1, no. 5, of *The Planeteer Magazine* (March 1936) (Dep. Blish 397) features a space cruiser which later crops up as the *Telemachus* in Blish's 1953 scripts for the TV serial *Captain Video and the Sub-Space Corsair*. On page 4 of one script, on the other side of which may be found a typescript of "The Thing in the Attic," Blish drew a copy of *The Planeteer* space cruiser with directions for the producer or artistic designer of the Captain Video series (Dep. Blish 299/1). Later again, the *Telemachus* will be commandeered for service in "Blackout in Cygni" and *Mission to the Heart Stars*.

12. "A Science-Fiction Coming of Age," pp. 156–58.

13. *The Futurians*, pp. vii, 29–30.

14. Ibid., pp. 46, 87.

15. *Speaking of Science Fiction*, p. 240.

16. *The Futurians*, p. 152. In a marginal note on my manuscript Virginia Kidd reports that Blish told her "he was broken back down (from private, first class) to buck private." He did, however, obtain "a disability pension from the army." See also Damon Knight, "Knight Piece," in *Hell's Cartographers: Some Personal Histories of Science Fiction Writers*, ed. Brian W. Aldiss (London: Weidenfeld & Nicolson, 1975), p. 117.

17. *The Futurians*, pp. 132; Harry Warner, *All Our Yesterdays: An Informal History of Science Fiction Fandom in the Forties* (Chicago: Advent, 1969), p. 39; Kidd to Ketterer, 11 September 1984.

18. *Speaking of Science Fiction*, p. 240. Lowndes mentions Blish's doing some substitute teaching, mostly in literature, for "a year or so." See "Introduction: Science

Fiction the Hard Way," *The Best of James Blish,* ed. Lowndes (New York: Ballantine Books, 1979), p. ix.

19. Mary Lucia S. Cornelius, managing editor of *The Sewanee Review,* confirms (letter to Ketterer, 5 June 1984) this figure. She points out that in a letter to John Palmer, then the editor, Blish "expressed surprise and delight over the large size of the payment."

20. "Science Fiction the Hard Way," p. xii; *The Futurians,* pp. 152–53; Robert A. W. Lowndes, "James Blish: A Profile," *The Magazine of Fantasy & Science Fiction* 42 (April 1972): 66–68, 70; Kidd to Ketterer, 13 April 1986.

21. "James Blish: A Profile," p. 67; *All Our Yesterdays,* pp. 46, 204; *The Futurians,* pp. 152, 155, 169; Lowndes to Ketterer, 3 March 1984. "Cry in the Night" is reproduced as an appendix in *The Futurians,* p. 262. Robert A. W. Lowndes has prepared "An Index to James Blish's Contributions to the Mailings of the Vanguard Amateur Press Association" (17 pages). Part 1 accounts for Blish's own publications: *Embrasure* (four issues), *Explication* (of *Finnegans Wake,* three installments) (one issue), *Flaming Ear* . . . , (seven issues), *Tumbrils* (twenty-four issues), *Vanguard Amateur* (twelve issues, during his two terms as manager of VAPA), and, publications in collaboration, notably *Renascence* (eight issues) with Lowndes. Part 2 accounts for his "Appearances in Other Members' Publications." Aside from material on *Finnegans Wake,* Ezra Pound, and Richard Strauss, a quotation from Spengler and other miscellany, this invaluable and extensive listing includes poems for an intended collection entitled "Trompe L'Oeil." I am grateful to Mr. Lowndes for providing me with a copy of this presently unpublished index. The researcher who wishes to pursue this aspect of Blish's career might consult the University of Baltimore collection of fanzine material (Baltimore County Campus).

22. *The Futurians,* pp. 173–76.

23. Ibid., pp. 154–56, 162.

24. Ibid., pp. 162–64. Lowndes points out (letter to Ketterer 3 March 1984), that eventually Blackout "was the sole survivor of the plague that wiped out all the rest of the Blishes' feline family."

25. *Supplement to Genealogy of the Blish Family,* Dep. Blish 346. Lowndes asserts incorrectly that the baby died "from the Rh Negative reaction, about which not enough was known. Treatment during the pregnancy might have saved the child." See "Science Fiction the Hard Way," p. xv. Virginia Kidd writes, "His death was diagnosed as 'crib death,' . . . a diagnosis that leaves the actual cause a mystery. . . . [I]n fact, his own blood was Rh-negative, so that there was no disparity between us." Kidd to Ketterer, 22 October 1984.

26. "Knight Piece," p. 122.

27. "A Science Fiction coming of Age," p. 162.

28. *A Requiem for Astounding* (Chicago: Advent, 1964), p. 188.

29. "Dianetics: A Door to the Future," *Planet Stories* 4 (November 1950): 102.

30. "What is Evidence?" *Future* 1 (March 1951): 78–80; "The Psychological Story," *Science Fiction Quarterly,* 1 (May 1952): 49–53. Paul A. Carter points out that Blish took the references to "clears" out of his stories. See *The Creation of Tomorrow: Fifty Years of Magazine Science Fiction* (New York: Columbia Univ. Press, 1977), pp. 158–59. Carter informs me that "The most convincing example is in a description of Major Amalfi which first appeared in the story 'Bindlestiff' (*Astounding Science Fiction,* December 1950) page 31: 'He was now about a thousand years old, give or take 50; strong as an ox, mentally alert and "clear". . . .' That story became chapters 3 and 4 of *Earthman, Come Home* and in chapter 4 the same passage reads as follows: 'He was now about 900 years old, give or take 50; strong as an ox, mentally alert and active' " (Carter to Ketterer, 20 June 1984).

NOTES TO CHAPTER 1

31. See letter in Dep. Blish 406/5, and, for the actual scripts, see Dep. Blish 389/3, 390, and 391/1 (ii + 212 p.; iii + 250 p.; 238 p.). For this work Blish received $1,800, of which $180 went to his agent, Frederik Pohl; see "Writing Accounts" (Dep. Blish 440/1–3). See also, for the inside story, "The Secret Files of Captain Video," *Xero Comics* 1 (January 1961): 17–20, which appears under Blish's "Arthur Merlyn" pseudonym.

32. For details of the purchase of "Arrowhead," see "Knight Piece," p. 134. Damon Knight records (letter to Ketterer, 16 March 1984) that Blish "was the p.r. officer of the local squadron for a short time. He took me along once, and I got a free ride in a small plane, a marvellous experience; afterward we all sat silently in a bar and drank beer."

33. Kidd to Ketterer, 4 May 1984.

34. Unfortunately, the Hugo Award has *Conscience* misspelled—the "s" is missing on the base plate.

35. *The Futurians*, pp. 204–6, 210–13. *The Frozen Year* (1957) bears the following dedication: "For FIVE forsan et haec olim meminesse juvabit" (Perhaps hereafter it will delight us also to have remembered these things; Virgil, *Aeneid*, 1:203). Many years after Kornbluth's tragically early death (1958) Blish edited *Thirteen O'Clock (and Other Zero Hours)* (1970), a collection of fantasies that Kornbluth published under the pen name Cecil Corwin. A paragraph left out of the introduction to the Dell edition is replaced in the British Robert Hale edition (1972).

36. Ibid., p. 213. Josephine Saxton's "Biographical Notes" confirm, "He liked women to wear fancy underwear, seamed stockings etc., all the paraphernalia of submission. His female idol was Dietrich." She also notes that "he had little sympathy for but an erotic fascination with black and yellow races," and that "His attitude to women was hardcore male chauvinist."

37. *The Futurians*, pp. 209–10.

38. Ibid., p. 210

39. William Atheling, Jr., *More Issues at Hand* (Chicago: Advent, 1970) p. 34. In a letter to the director of Faber & Faber, Blish mentions quitting Pfizer on 6 November 1959 (CM 51).

40. Kidd to Ketterer, 11 September 1984. "There was also a traveling exhibit of The Brain for doctors which Jim thought up and saw through to a successful conclusion. . . . A complex, delicate, much larger than lifesize exhibit that needed constant care and attention, it . . . traveled to medical conventions"; Kidd to Ketterer, 25 September 1984.

41. *The Futurians*, p. 240. Josephine Saxton's "Biographical Notes" include the following:

> He refused to countenance the connection between smoking and lung cancer, and dragged out all kinds of ancient research which proved he was right. He had ways of arguing on this subject which would have defeated the most devoted Sophist. He had a similar attitude to vitamins and fresh air, preferring to point out the toxic quality of Vitamin A in huge doses rather than look at the therapeutic value of Vitamin C. He preferred Indoors but I got him to sunbathe while I did watercolours and he reluctantly said that it had been quite pleasant. He also once came on a walk of about a mile and a half but said that was his ration for that year. Exercise killed.

Judith Blish adds (as a marginal note to my manuscript), "He said he belonged to Exercise Anonymous—when the urge comes over you, you call a friend and get drunk together."

42. Budrys to Ketterer, 11 May 1983.

43. Alexei and Cory Panshin, *SF in Dimension: A Book of Explorations* (1976; rev. & enlarged 2d. ed., Chicago: Advent, 1980), pp. 318–23); this critical book is dedicated to "James BLISH who opened the door."

44. *The Futurians,* p. 240. Josephine Saxton writes in her "Biographical Notes," "He was sometimes embittered towards Virginia, and said that she drove him out of the house by playing Rock and Roll loudly day and night, knowing that he couldn't stand it. He said he had made the mistake of smothering Virginia with love and attention, which I can well believe." It seems that both Virginia and his second wife, Judith, had tastes in music to which Blish objected—with Judith it was bouzouki music.

45. Blish to Knight, 10 August 1964. Blish later told Damon Knight that the operation was performed without anesthetic; *The Futurians,* p. 240. Knight adds, "At various times Blish told me other unbelievable things, and I later found out that some of them were not true."

46. Blish to Knight, 18 November 1964. As it happens, Blish's agent, Ken White, had recently died of lung cancer. White was succeeded by Robert P. Mills. In chronological order, as listed in the first of Blish's three "Writing Accounts" ledgers, his agents preceding Mills were: 1940–42, Robert A. W. Lowndes; 1942, John B. Michel; 1946, Theodore Sturgeon; 1947–48, Scott Meredith; 1948–53; Dirk Wylie/Frederik Pohl; 1953–54, Harry Altshuler; 1954–60, Kenneth S. White (Dep. Blish 440/1-3).

47. For the passport see Dep. Blish 406/5. "Bill Atheling," who is clearly Blish in Blish's "More Light," "stood 5'10" or so." See *Alchemy and Academe,* ed. Anne McCaffrey (New York: Doubleday & Co., Inc., 1970), p. 89.

48. Kidd to Ketterer, 14 May 1948.

49. "A Science-Fiction Coming of Age," p. 161. As for his hands, which "shook slightly but unremittingly," Blish "suffered all his adult life from what he referred to as an intention tremor." See Virginia Kidd, introduction to Blish, *Titans' Daughter* (New York: Avon Books, 1981), p. 14.

50. Marty Klug, "Interview with James Blish," p. 8.

51. For a mass of material from Godshalk re: *Kalhi,* see Dep. Blish 420/1-5. Godshalk met Blish at the 1967 Modern Language Association Meeting in New York when Blish, who was then editing *Kalki,* asked Godshalk to be the co-editor (Godshalk to Ketterer, 24 May 1984). It was also during that meeting that the Cabell Society that published *Kalki* (originally called "The Fellowship of the Silver Stallion") failed to reach a merger agreement with Professor Julius Rothman, who "was also trying to establish a Cabell Society within the Academy" (Godshalk to Ketterer, 28 May 1984).

52. See Blish, "All in a Knight's Work," *Speculation,* no. 29 (October 1971): 5–12, for an account of Damon Knight's contribution to the SF field aside from his writing.

53. *The Double: Bill Symposium* (Akron, Ohio: D. B. Press, 1969), pp. 20, 92.

54. *Speaking of Science Fiction,* p. 240.

55. A "Writing Accounts" ledger entry indicates that Blish received a $2,000 advance for each of the *Star Trek* collections (Dep. Blish 440/1-3).

56. Judith Blish to Ketterer, 10 February 1983.

57. Josephine Saxton, in her "Biographical Notes," writes: "He adulated Oxford and all that it stands for, to him it was the centre of the educational universe. He felt in a similar way about Florence and the Medicis."

58. KLA, 18 February 1973. Cp. *Speaking of Science Fiction,* p. 240; *The Futurians,* pp. 240–41. Josephine Saxton, in her "Biographical Notes," writes:

> He loved cats, and once had a cat who would sit on his shoulder and catch shrimps as James tossed them up. At Henley there was a large grey cat called Mouse [or Ymouse], of which James swore that if it settled down on a manuscript, it would sell well. Alas, this hole in James's wall against superstition was not true: Mouse slept on a manuscript of mine which never sold at all. But it was a kind of half-joking

superstition which relieved the grim rationalism to which James usually clung. There was also a half-wild kitten [William Wilson, brought by Josephine from a farm] which would only approach James and let him stroke it, nobody else could get near.

In *More Issues at Hand,* Blish observes that "an exaggerated regard for animals is a common trait in people who are usually callous toward human beings" (p. 55).

59. Blish had "initiated the first U.S. paperback edition of . . . *That Hideous Strength*" (a work clearly related to *Black Easter* and its sequel, *The Day After Judgment*) (KLA, 26 January 1973).

60. Budrys to Ketterer, 11 May 1983. In the same letter Budrys explains that the relationship between himself and Blish had waned partly because "I was not in good sympathy with his increasing fascination with formalized religion; I saw it as a betrayal of his 1950s intellectuality, although I could recall him grappling with Catholicism as early as 1955. Up to then, I had thought *A Case of Conscience* a purely intellectual exercise, and I still think it began as that, at least consciously." Saxton's "Biographical Notes" speak of Blish's coming "to believe in the possibility of the conscious evolution of mankind. I myself put these ideas to him in long sometimes all-night boozy discussions and when I suggested that Surface Tension was a 'conscious evolution' story, he said: 'By golly, you are right!' He also began to give credence to clairvoyance and telepathy, after long arguments. What made him begin to change his mind was a report to me by a clairvoyant before I met him, describing him, our relationship, where we met, his lung disease and other details."

61. During the Apollo 11 flight Blish heard quoted over Rome radio at the landing his statement "'I told you so' loud and clear." See Blish, "Future Recall," in *The Disappearing Future,* ed. George Hay (London, Panther Books, 1970), p. 97. The Blishes watched the moonwalk while in Venice on the way home from the Trieste Film Festival. As for further foreign travel,

> there was the Heidelberg Convention, followed by a hegira to Colmar (to see the Isenheim altarpiece), Basle, the Tyrol to visit Ezra Pound's daughter, stopover in Innsbruck, back to Munich, Paris-London. That trip was rather funny: we used Europe on $10 a day to budget, and doubled it for inflation—but forgot to double it for two. So we trekked from Diners' Club check-cashery to ditto, where we could only get $100 at a time, with no choice about our next port of call—which made Jim very twitchy indeed, but was certainly adventurous. He loved the Brenner Pass. He spoke and read German, and could sometimes decipher Latin. In fact, during WWII he worked as a lab technician in the Army, and was often an interpreter for German POWs. (Judith Blish to Ketterer, 11 September 1984)

Virginia Kidd elaborates, "Jim had a fair acquaintanceship with German. He made fun of French. As far as I know, he had no facility in Spanish or Italian. In the course of writing *Doctor Mirabilis,* he developed a more than passing acquaintanceship with Latin as written by Bacon. . . . He had the polymath's and the dilettante's familiarity with innumerable phrases in innumerable languages, including the Arabic. And he could find his way around in any opera libretto: German, French, or Italian" (Kidd to Ketterer, 25 September 1984).

62. The outline is mentioned in a letter to Frederik Pohl dated 25 February 1949 (Dep. Blish 428/6).

63. PS, 4 January and 30 June 1970. On the subject of time travel Blish writes: "I am especially intrigued by the [finite] spinning-universe form of time travel, especially since (a) nobody else has touched it and (b) I have never attempted a major time-travel story,

NOTES TO CHAPTER 1

having been sobered and put off by the terrible bollixes respected peers have produced in this field. . . . One of the challenges is that, if I do it right, it will fly in the face of repeated statements that this element in SF is actually fantasy, and necessarily must remain so. I *love* rationales . . . they are an enormous part of the fun of sf. . . . But I really should stop mentioning the spinning universe in public, or somebody will nobble onto it before I can get into it!" (PS, 23 June 1970).

64. KLA, 12 December 1974. As reviewer for the "Books" column in *The Magazine of Fantasy & Science Fiction* from February 1970 until November 1972, Blish had occasion to review Saxton's three novels with progressive warmth. In the February 1970 review of *The Hieros Gamos of Sam and An Smith*, Blish mentions not being flattered by the reference to one of his books *(Jack of Eagles)* and attacks Saxton's novel for abruptly changing its "universe of discourse" (p. 49). *Vector for Seven* gets a mixed review in January 1972. In July 1972 *Group Feast* is judged good but not SF (as labeled by Doubleday). There was also another coincidence. Virginia Kidd, as Josephine's American agent, had met Josephine when she visited the U.S. in 1969. Elisabeth met her at the same time. Virginia had suggested that Blish look Josephine up since he had moved to England (KLA, 12 December 1974, 25 February 1975, 5 April 1975).

65. Kidd to Ketterer, 11 September 1984. According to Saxton, "His attitude to his son was one of despair. . . . Ben and [Maria] his wife-to-be, a young Puerto Rican if I recall correctly [the engagement was later broken off], visited him and bought him a pair of good hi-fi speakers so he could hear his [music] properly, as the first thing Ben noticed was that the speakers were poor. He softened towards his son somewhat but was glad when they left as he found the company of young people exhausting. He [disapproved of] Virginia's daughter by her first marriage. . . . He had very high and conventional standards for human behaviour, especially that of females and those connected with him. His daughter Beth he was Proud of, often using that word . . ." ("Biographical Notes").

66. Aldiss to Ketterer, 28 July 1982.

67. Saxton to Ketterer, 17 March 1983; Judith Blish to Ketterer, 10 February 1983.

68. Marty Klug, "Interview with James Blish," p. 6.

69. Aldiss, "PEEP: An Introduction to *The Quincunx of Time*," in Blish, *The Quincunx of Time* (1973; New York: Avon Books, 1983), p. 6.

70. Saxton writes, "About a year before his death he told me that he had been deeply depressed for eight years. He had often taken antidepressants [sometimes at the risk of combination with alcohol] which he thought excellent but as far as I know he was not taking them regularly in his last two years" ("Biographical Notes"). Saxton believes that Blish, being very repressed, was a prime cancer personality. She also saw him, in different degrees, as a fascist, a capitalist, and a racist, all the things she most despises. Unlike both Virginia Kidd and Judith Blish, Josephine Saxton is a very slender (but energetic and unusually strong) woman. Virginia Kidd, now an important literary agent whose clients include Ursula K. Le Guin, writes, "During the last year of Jim's life, he had an intense autumnal love affair with a younger, attractive, sensitive English writer. She was good friends with Judy as well. She initially sat at Jim's feet, learning, worshiping (a posture I recognize). The last few weeks of his life she was at Treetops and so was Beth—and Jim needed all three of them—his daughter, his wife, and his lover" (*The Futurians*, p. 241).

71. Blish, *Fallen Star* (New York: Avon Books, 1983), p. 6.

72. Judith Blish, commenting on a version of this chapter, notes that the laburnam tree is one that Blish had raised from seed. There is a photo (Dep. Blish 406/2) of Blish tending the flower pot. Judith organized a Memorial Evening for James Blish at the London Institute for Contemporary Arts on 19 February 1976. In the following order, Peter

Nicholls, Andrew Stephenson (writer and illustrator), Mark Adlard, Richard Cowper, John Brunner, Josephine Saxton, and Bob Shaw contributed to the program. The event was hosted by Charles Monteith. I am grateful to Karin L. Laflin for supplying me with a tape of this event.

73. Aldiss, "In Memoriam: James Blish," *Extrapolation* 17 (December 1975): 5–7. Peter Nicholls concurs: he "seemed always a good man." See "The Death of James Blish," *Foundation*, no. 9 (November 1975): 54.

74. Aldiss, "PEEP: An Introduction to *The Quincunx of Time*," p. 10.

75. Aldiss to Ketterer, 28 July 1982.

76. Quoted as the epigraph to Lowndes's "Introduction: Science Fiction the Hard Way," in *The Best of James Blish*, p. ix. The poem originally appeared in *Occasional* (September 1949) and was reprinted under a new title, "A Kind of King," in *Accent* (Winter 1951).

77. Perhaps "A Prophecy of Love" is the story that Elisabeth Blish is referring to when she writes, "The day before he died, he spent the afternoon with a colleague [Josephine Saxton], editing and tightening a draft of his last story. That story began, in a tentative way, to write about a way that an equal or near-equal relationship between a man and a woman might be expressed in writing." See her introduction to *Mission to the Heart Stars* (1965; New York: Avon Books, 1982), p. 9. In a telephone conversation (26 February 1983) Josephine Saxton expressed the belief that had Blish lived longer he would have written mystical fantasies (while allowing that illness and the medicines he was taking *might* have altered his way of thinking).

Chapter 2

1. "Future Recall," in *The Disappearing Future*, ed. George Hay (London: Panther Books, 1970), pp. 103, 104. But Blish does note that

> In 1957 I wrote a story involving controlled hydrogen fusion ["Nor Iron Bars"], in which I suggested that a variation of the "magnetic bottle" called the Nernst effect might make a practicable control. Only six months after the story was published . . . it was revealed that both the United States and the U.S.S.R. were working on this approach. Still more dashing: in 1964 I wrote a novel [*Welcome to Mars*] which postulated that there were Moon-like craters on Mars—the only such suggestion in science fiction, I believe. The book did not appear until more than a year *after* the Mariner IV flight showed that my guess (and several others in the novel) was right. (P. 102)

And as an example of an SF term that has found its way into the sciences, Blish mentions his "own concoction": the "label 'gas giant' for a Jupiter-type planet" (p. 102).

2. "A Science-Fiction Coming of Age," in *The Tale That Wags the God*, ed. Cy Chauvin (Chicago: Advent, 1987), p. 125.

3. Damon Knight, *In Search of Wonder: Essays on Modern Science Fiction*, rev. ed. (1956; Chicago: Advent, 1967), pp. 271–72.

4. "Introduction: Science Fiction the Hard Way," *The Best of James Blish*, ed. Robert A. W. Lowndes (New York: Ballantine Books, 1979), p. xi.

5. "Citadel of Thought," in *The Best of James Blish*, pp. 1, 2. Subsequent parenthetical page references are to this text.

6. "Emergency Refueling" is reprinted in *Yesterdays' Tomorrows: Favorite Stories from Forty Years as a Science Fiction Editor*, ed. Frederick Pohl (New York: Berkley, 1982), pp. 32–36.

NOTES TO CHAPTER 2

7. Ibid. On "said bookisms," see Blish, "Let Them Say It!" *Writer's Digest* 28 (January 1948): 32–33, and Blish, *The Issue at Hand* (Chicago: Advent, 1964), pp. 83, 110.

8. See "A Science-Fiction Coming of Age," p. 126. The remaining nine of Blish's first thirteen published stories (which are all SF) each require only brief characterization. "Bequest of the Angel" (March 1940) is an awkwardly constructed five-chapter novella about a Centrale Government agent named Johnny Owen who helps the Space Patrol foil the plans of the revolutionary leader of the Martian Nationalist Party who is in league with a weary space pirate known as the Angel. The brief "When Anteros Came" is about an Earth-to-Jupiter-and-back space race which ends explosively when the potential winner, Petrucelli, "whose name, oddly enough, meant meteor" ("When Anteros Came," *Science Fiction Quarterly*, no. 5 [Winter 1941]: 143), and a name which will recur in *VOR* (1958), piloting the *Sky-Stone* (to add to the irony), hits an asteroid named Anteros. "Callistan Cabal" (April 1941) is another action-packed Johnny Owen story. With the aid of a Martian named Nikki, he foils the goatlike Callistans, who have fabricated the invasion of Callisto by wheeled beings from Io as part of a plan to destroy Earth's Centrale Government. In five "chapters," "Phoenix Planet" tells of Gregory Marshall, "the first man to leave the imprisoning air of Earth" ("Phoenix Planet," *Cosmic Science Fiction* 1 [May 1941]: 7), now in the "cage" or control cabin of the *Icarus* (which runs on gasoline and is made of wood) returning after ten years alone on long-dead Mars to an Earth that has been invaded by four-armed aliens and where he participates in the resistance movement. At the tale's conclusion, when the cosy world that he once knew with his girlfriend Anna reappears, all seems to have been a hallucination. But no, the old Earth is the hallucination, a vision of what Marshall has lost; the aliens are real. This story, then, reverses the fantasy/reality confusion of a work like Ambrose Bierce's "An Occurrence at Owl Creek Bridge" and is significant because it anticipates such Blishian experiments in this area as "Testament of Andros" (1953) and *The Frozen Year* (1957). A very conventional closed-time-loop piece (but in Blish a rare time machine story), "Weapon Out of Time" (Spring 1941) is about a group of scientists who visit the Triassic age where they leave behind an automatic rifle, the damaged artifact that motivates the trip in the first place. "The Real Thrill" (July 1941) of the title of Blish's next story refers, with heavy-handed irony, not so much to the redundant, forty-seven-year-old rocket engineer, Martin Burrowes, showing his very unliberated blonde girlfriend the kind of antique police cruiser (now superseded by "geotronic ships") that he used to fly, but to what immediately follows: Burrowes stands in for the regular engineer when the cruiser responds to an attack call over Tycho city and, when an engine fault develops, sacrifices himself in the action so that others might live. "The Topaz Gate" (August 1941), a chronicle of old Mars, takes the form of a translated document with a scholar's footnotes. Its long-dead Martian author, the Toro Rotal, the ruler of Nu, tells of the war between Nu and Tasil after a power-mad ex-plumber usurped the throne of the Queen of Nu (with whom the Toro Rotal is for awhile imprisoned) and the part played in that war by the Metals, fourth-dimensional beings who issue from a topaz-like gem with whom the usurper seemed to have been allied but who (before their eventual defeat) emerge as the real threat to Mars itself. Eight thousand years after the events of "The Topaz Gate," the three-coned Metals (this time less confusingly described) are again encountered in the five chapters of "The Solar Comedy" (June 1942) when, by means of a sunspot (sunspots being dimensional gates), three humans and a Martian are transported to the vast world of the Metals. The attempt to destroy the Metals' power source proves misguided when, to the accompanying laughter of the Metal brain, it is revealed that the Metals are now

NOTES TO CHAPTER 2

basically benevolent and that the sunspot has conveyed them to the dying sun of the far future when the human race has abandoned the Milky Way for the Andromeda galaxy. In "The Airwhale" (August 1942), Mark Harris, a veteran of the early days of the Solar Union (then called "Centrale") tells how long ago, when prospecting on the asteroid Pallas (which is inhabited by flying plants called airwhales), the pirate "Red Dan" Lothar, first met with in "Citadel of Thought," deposited Harris and another miner on a high plateau. Predictably enough they escape via the airwhales.

9. The title refers to the unstable governorship of Venus. Currently a Centrale man who has ousted a League of Nations Venerean governor is in charge, but after the main action, which involves a down-on-his-luck, freelance flyer, Clyde Heywood, in intrigue and danger, the pre-League Venerean governor is reinstated in a rapid denouement.

10. Lowndes to Ketterer, 9 March 1983. Lowndes goes on to say that years later he approached Blish with the idea of turning "Chaos, Co-ordinated" into a novel. But on rereading the story they decided it was not worth the effort.

11. Lowndes, introduction to *Jack of Eagles* (New York: Avon Books, 1982), p. 10.

12. "Chaos, Co-ordinated," *Astounding Science Fiction* 38 (October 1946): 49, 52, 56. Subsequent parenthetical page references are to this text.

13. "Mistake Inside," as reprinted in *The Dark Side,* ed. Damon Knight (New York: Doubleday & Company, Inc., 1965), p. 36. Subsequent parenthetical page references are to this text.

14. In an unpublished article, "Some Early Blish," Paul Shackley observes that "transportees go Outside from all parts of the universe, including 'Tir-nam-Beo,'" whose name is taken from *Jurgen* by James Branch Cabell, Blish's favourite fantasy writer. "'Tir-nam-Beo' resembles *Tir-na-mBeo,* Irish for 'Land of the Living,' an appropriate name for the 'mortal world inside.'"

15. Knight to Ketterer, 28 May 1983. Apparently Knight produced the idea, characters, and diary entry form of "Tiger Ride" while Blish added over half the words, much of the background, and the "snapper" ending. See also Knight's and Blish's comments on the writing of "Tiger Ride" in *Science Fiction: Author's Choice,* ed. Harry Harrison (New York: Berkley, 1968), pp. 96–97.

16. Knight to Ketterer, 28 May 1983. Also in this letter concerning his collaborations with Blish, Knight mentions "one more story, an abomination so awful that I don't even remember its title; it was never published and the manuscript is lost." Blish is apparently including this additional story when he writes, "We . . . had collaborated on five science-fiction stories and part of a novel. . . ." See *More Issues at Hand* (Chicago: Advent, 1970), p. 21.

17. Five of the remaining seven SF apprenticeship stories may again be briefly summarized. In "The Homesteader" (June 1949) troubleshooter Pete Kagen arrives on the Moon to discover why spaceships are blowing up. It transpires that the local "homesteader" (here Blish's knowledge of the 1862 Homestead Act, no doubt gleaned from his research for writing westerns, comes in handy), Dr. Brighton (a prototype of Elvers in *The Frozen Year*), is a Martian and his "Weathercock" demagnetizes the cyclotron engines of spaceships. In "The Bore" (Summer 1950) the spaceship *Hyperion* is menaced by the Lyrans but, thanks to the boring Commodore Ted Prosser, who understands the celestial "tides" caused by a three-star system and the nature of a "bore" tide, the *Hyperion* is able to escape disaster. In the whimsical (?) "Peace Declared" (January 1951) the U.S. announces its intention to wage total peace in a statement broadcast in forty-nine languages at 10 A.M., Eastern Standard Time, 30 January 1956, culminating in unilateral

NOTES TO CHAPTER 2

disarmament one week later. The announcement is believed to be a trick in both the U.S.A. and U.S.S.R., but after planes have dropped Declaration of Peace pamphlets, food, and shoes all over Russia, the peace is actually won. "The Void is My Coffin" (June 1951), is set in the late sixties when the Exodus from a dying Earth to Mars (where Nikki, the Martian from "Callistan Cabal" is met with again) has been made easy by Barclay's invention of geotron spaceflight (first mentioned in 1941 in "The Real Thrill"). It is an effective tale about the circumstances leading to the passing of the Spaceways Act, necessitated by the fact that too many untrained pilots (almost including the son of the Coordinator of the Exodus) are killing themselves. The geotron-powered *Telemachus* (a spaceship of the same name is featured in the stories that the young Blish wrote for his fanzine, *The Planeteer*) of "Blackout in Cygni" (July 1951) is carrying rich passengers along the Long Arc when, after a blackout, which in space causes madness, it finds itself attacked by Jason's pirate ship. Jason boards with a Martian (as in "The Void is my Coffin," a tall figure with doglike ears), but thanks to someone who turns out to be John H. Dalton of the Centrale patrol, at the end of this intricately plotted exciting tale the tables are turned. Mention should also be made here of Blish's contribution to Jerome Bixby's "Nightride and Sunrise" (*Other Worlds*, June 1952)—title courtesy of Sibelius. In a note to Ketterer (7 June 1983) Bixby writes, "there's a biological angle to the story, and after first draft I didn't feel I'd brought off that aspect. Jim, a close friend and a biologist, agreed to run it through the mill and add his expert touch. I got credit; he got a fee."

18. "The Box," as reprinted in *The Best of James Blish*, p. 25. William Atheling, Jr., makes a footnote reference to "The Box" in the context of his discussion of energy fields in SF in *More Issues at Hand*, p. 44.

19. "James Blish on the Decline of the Supernatural," *The Spectator* 229 (19 August 1972): 286.

20. An early version of "There Shall Be No Darkness" ("a schoolboy pastiche of *Dracula*") was written "about eight months before" the publication of Jack Williamson's first version of "Darker Than You Think" in *Unknown* (December 1940). This chronology is straightened out by William Atheling, Jr., in *More Issues at Hand*, p. 27. Lowndes corrects his misstatement that Blish "had written the very first version in 1942" ("Introduction: Science Fiction the Hard Way," p. xvi) in his "A Reply to Gregory Feeley," *Foundation*, no. 29 (November 1983): 60.

21. "There Shall Be No Darkness," reprinted in *The Best of James Blish*, pp. 55, 65. Subsequent parenthetical page references are to this text.

22. Lowndes makes this point as part of his case for preferring the 1950 version of "There Shall Be No Darkness." See "A Reply to Gregory Feeley," pp. 60–61.

23. Quoted by Blish in his introduction to the reprint of the *Witches Three* text in Blish, *"Get Out of My Sky" and "There Shall Be No Darkness"* (London: Panther Books, 1980), p. 99.

24. Memo from Judith Blish to Ketterer, 1 October 1984.

25. Lowndes, introduction to *Jack of Eagles*, pp. 9–10.

26. Lowndes to Ketterer, 9 March 1983.

27. Ibid., and Lowndes, introduction to *Jack of Eagles*, p. 10.

28. *The Duplicated Man* (New York: Avalon Books, 1959), p. 190. Subsequent parenthetical page references are to this text.

29. Lowndes to Ketterer, 9 March 1983.

30. *Jack of Eagles*, pp. 138–40. Subsequent parenthetical references are to this text. This novel was also published under the title *ESPer* by Avon Books (1958, 1968), by Faber & Faber (1973) and Arrow Books (1975).

31. Introduction to *Jack of Eagles,* p. 7.

32. This is Lowndes's term which he distinguishes from "simple padding" (which he claims Blish never resorted to) and from "enrichment and transformation" (which he claims Blish achieved occasionally "in later years"). See Lowndes, introduction to *Jack of Eagles,* pp. 11–12.

33. Lowndes points out in his introduction to *Jack of Eagles* that, as a reader for the Scott Meredith Agency, Blish would have read many inept stories "wherein the villain is struck by lightning at the crucial moment" (p. 9). Lowndes suggests that here, although the "bolt from the heavens" is credibly set up, Blish is having a little fun at the expense of a cliché of pulp plotting (p. 12).

34. That the Forteans turn out to be the good guys may have something to do with the fact that Blish "was a member of the Fortean Society in the early forties." Lowndes, introduction to *Jack of Eagles,* p. 11.

35. Alternatively one might comment negatively, along with Blish in a review column, that "As a general rule writers of genre fiction don't change much as they get older." See "Books," *The Magazine of Fantasy & Science Fiction* 43 (November 1972): 17.

36. Blish to Charles Monteith, 26 August 1955 (CM 51). Writing to Paul Shackley Blish characteristically again undervalues the work: "THE WARRIORS OF DAY was a baby picture and in retrospect I'm sorry I allowed it to be reprinted in modern times. I think of JACK OF EAGLES as the first of my novels in the sense that I was involved in it— WARRIORS was written in 10 days on a Dictaphone, with my first wife madly transcribing it, to meet a very short deadline for a primitive sword-and-barebreast market . . . and if any of my own preoccupations show in it . . . it was not by design. . . . How little my real mind was on the job is represented for me by my having called the cat-creature Chrestos, a name I pulled out of the air without the least regard for the immense associations it invokes" (PS, 7 April 1972).

37. *The Warriors of Day* (London: Arrow Books, 1979), p. 34. Subsequent parenthetical references are to this text.

Chapter 3

1. "The Biological Story," *Science Fiction Quarterly* 1 (May 1951): 89–91. Discussions of "The Mathematical Story," "The Astronomical Story," and "The Psychological Story" appeared in the subsequent issues. Each of these "sciences" (Blish notes that as yet there is no science of psychology) figures significantly in his own work. In "A Science-Fiction Coming of Age," Blish notes that "the biological sciences play important roles in more of my output than in that of any other living SF writer known to me." *The Tale That Wags the God,* ed. Cy Chauvin (Chicago: Advent, 1987), p. 162.

2. "The Biological Story," p. 90.

3. The title is frequently mispunctuated as *Titan's Daughter.*

4. Presumably it is just a coincidence that a long extract from Mark Twain's "The Greak Dark" (title supplied by Bernard DeVoto), a microscopic world story about a perilous voyage across a drop of water, appeared in the same year as "Sunken Universe." See Bernard DeVoto, *Mark Twain at Work* (Cambridge, Mass.: Harvard Univ. Press, 1942), pp. 133–40. The complete story was not published for the first time until 1962, long after "Surface Tension" had appeared. "Sunken Universe" corresponds to Cycle One of book 3, and the *Galaxy* version of "Surface Tension" consists of the prologue and Cycle Two minus an insert in section 3 of that Cycle. Note also that "panatropy" and its derivatives in that version of the prologue were changed to "pantropy" and its derivatives for the book. A seed of "Sunken Universe" and "Surface Tension" would appear to be

NOTES TO CHAPTER 3

Blish's "Jungle of the Microcosm," *Tesseract,* no. 2 (April 1936): 7–9. In this fanzine story paramecia in a bacterial culture (rotifers) are mistaken for monsters. Cp. a similar perspective misapprehension in Poe's "The Sphinx" (1846).

5. See the back of the first page of a typescript of "The Thing in the Attic" (Dep. Blish 399/1). This typescript also indicates two changes of heart regarding the book's dedicatee. "Dr. Thurlow G. Nelson," deleted, is replaced by "Karen Anne Emden" (the daughter of Blish's first wife, Virginia Kidd, by her previous marriage). Then her name is crossed out in pencil and the final choice, "H. L. Gold," the SF writer and editor, is pencilled in.

6. *The Seedling Stars* raises the question of whether it is a story sequence or a novel. Books 1, 2, and 4 were clearly written as logical offshoots of book 3, and there is no difficulty in establishing thematic, imagistic, and structural coherence. I would classify the work as a story sequence on its way to being a novel; where the choice arises, as here, I use the term novel.

7. Blish was invited to chair a panel discussion on the topic "Pantropy vs. Terraforming" at Novacon, the First British Science Fiction Convention, held in Birmingham (13–14 November 1971). In his introductory survey of the same title Blish notes that the term "terraforming" was coined by Jack Williamson in the late 1940s (Dep. Blish 427/4a).

8. A couple of revised and extended paragraphs on page 48 of the typescript of "A Time to Survive" (pp. 46–47 of the Gnome Press edition of *The Seedling Stars,* for which see n. 9 below) indicate the care with which Blish constructs a logical chain for his stories. In describing how the Port Authority suppressed the existence of an interstellar drive, Blish inserts references to "several exploratory voyages," the records of which were destroyed. But thanks to contact with "several survivors," Blish is able to explain how the Adapted Men reached Ganymede.

9. *The Seedling Stars* (New York: Gnome Press, 1957), p. 24. Subsequent parenthetical page references are to this text. Blish's hope to place *The Seedling Stars* with Faber & Faber was initially frustrated. Surprisingly, in his July 1957 report on what Blish had described as a "Stapledon-like chronicle" (27 November 1956), Brian Aldiss advised against publication (CM 51). However, the work was finally published by Faber & Faber in 1967.

10. I am grateful to my colleague, Robert M. Philmus, for pointing out the allusion here to George Gamow's *One Two Three . . . Infinity: Facts and Speculations of Science* (New York: Viking Press, 1947; rev. ed., 1961). Gamow's title encapsulates the process from extrapolation to transcendence so typical of SF.

11. Given that Blish himself died of cancer, one wonders to what extent this reference constitutes prescience on his part and to what extent this SF story and other aspects of his work represent a wish-fulfilling attempt to avoid his own death. See in this regard, David Ketterer, "Death and the Denial of History: The Textual Shadow of the SF Author," *Science-Fiction Studies* 9 (July 1982): 228–30. Reference is also made to the "Cancer problem" in *Titans' Daughter* (p. 40; see publication data in n. 25 below), but not in the original "Beanstalk" version. In both versions, the giants' extended 150-year life span is a significant issue.

12. Gregory Feeley (letter to Ketterer, 14 September 1983) notes the existence of six or seven "startling similarities" between "Seeding Program" and Sophocles' *Philoctetes.* "Blish considered Sophocles one of the world's greatest writers, as is made clear in *The Frozen Year* [chapter 8] and [the article] 'Let Joy Be Unconfined.' "

13. This reference turns out to be an anachronism because at the end of part 2 of *A Case of Conscience,* the 1958 extension, Lithia is destroyed. *The Seedling Stars* takes place thousands of years after *A Case of Conscience.*

14. See chapter 26, "Symbolism," in Damon Knight, *In Search of Wonder: Essays on*

Modern Science Fiction, rev. ed. (1956; Chicago: Advent, 1967), pp. 265–73. Most of this material appeared originally in *Science Fiction Forum,* no. 1 (1957).

15. The upper world of Tellura is vividly imagined and may have influenced at least two important works of SF: Brian W. Aldiss's *Non-Stop* and Ursula K. Le Guin's "The Word for World is Forest." *Non-Stop* shares not only the imagery of vegetative abundance and "Giants" but also the basic theme of conceptual breakthrough.

16. It should be noted that, if Earth is now involved in the seeding program, then the ending of book 1 does not fully set up the stories that follow. Are we to assume that some authority on Earth in the intervening centuries has come round to seeing the benefits of pantropy and that a seeding program similar to that described as taking place from Ganymede has been initiated? It is hard to know whether this is an instance of carelessness on Blish's part or an interesting complication for the careful reader to appreciate. There is also a contradiction regarding whether "lizard birds" or "monkeys" should be viewed as the Tellurians' evolutionary ancestors (pp. 76–77, 94) but this definitely appears to be carelessness on Blish's part.

17. "To my considerable bafflement, this is the most popular story I have ever written. . . . I set out to do no more than write about what it might really be like to live in the microcosm, where such forces as surface-tension are all important and such forces as gravity negligible; but somewhere along the line I seem to have touched a nerve more mythological than molecular. I wish I knew how, for if I did, I'd do it again"; headnote to "Surface Tension," in *Best Science Fiction Stories of James Blish* (London: Faber & Faber, 1965), p. 72.

18. Stableford, *A Clash of Symbols: The Triumph of James Blish* (San Bernadino, Cal.: The Borgo Press, 1979), p. 18. Incidentally, nowhere in print does Blish identify "The Thing in the Attic" as the copy-cat story. Gregory Feeley has made a case for "Nor Iron Bars," first published in two parts as "Detour to the Stars" (December 1956) and "Nor Iron Bars" (November 1957). See Feeley, "Correcting the Record on Blish," *Foundation,* no. 29 (November 1983): 56–57. However, Frederik Pohl writes (letter to Ketterer, "Bastille Day 83"): "Yes, 'The Thing in the Attic' was Jim's calculated attempt to repeat the ingredients that made 'Surface Tension' successful. I think there was a third story, perhaps a fourth—anyway, the stories in *The Seedling Stars* were "Surface Tension' and clones. I'm not sure of the other stories, but I was Jim's agent when he wrote 'The Thing in the Attic' and it was indeed that which he had in mind."

19. "Introduction: Science Fiction the Hard Way," *The Best of James Blish,* ed. Robert A. W. Lowndes (New York: Ballantine Books, 1979), p. xvi.

20. In "The Biological Story" (see n. 1 above), Blish points out that "Sunken Universe" is "based on a small subdivision of ecology called limnology, which is the study of the shore-line areas of bodies of fresh water" (p. 91).

21. In a perceptive critique, Gary K. Wolfe observes that, in its concern with colonizing other worlds, "Surface Tension" parodies the entire concept of *The Seedling Stars,* something that cannot, incidentally, be said of "The Thing in the Attic." In fact the sustained tone of irony throughout the book, culminating in the heavily ironic final story, both parodies the vast Homeric sweep of SF and makes for a four-part, mock-epic miniature counterpart of Blish's grander vision of cyclical history, the *Cities in Flight* tetralogy. See *"The Seedling Stars,"* in *Survey of Science Fiction Literature,* ed. Frank N. Magill, 5 vols. (Englewood Cliffs, N.J.: Salem Press, 1979), 4:1888–91.

22. *Galaxy Science Fiction,* 4 (Aug. 1952): 40.

23. Gregory Feeley, "Cages of Conscience from Seedling Stories: The Development of Blish's Novels," *Foundation,* no. 24 (February 1982): 65–66.

24. See, for example, ibid., pp. 59–68.

25. Blish's claim in his acknowledgments to have doubled the length of the original is an indication of his proneness to exaggerate the extent of his expansions. "Beanstalk" first appeared in the anthology *Future Tense,* ed. Kendall Foster Crossen (New York: Greenberg Publisher, 1952); under the title "Giants in the Earth," a title also used for Ole E. Rölvaeg's 1924–25 novel, it appeared in *The Original Science Fiction Stories,* 6 (Jan. 1956): 6–91; it is reprinted with the original title in the British edition of *Galactic Cluster* (London: Faber & Faber, 1960), pp. 157–255. *Titans' Daughter* was first published the following year (New York: Berkley, 1961). But all of my parenthetical references to *Titans' Daughter* are to the reprint edition, "With a New Introduction by Virginia Kidd" (New York: Avon Books, 1981). In a 17 December 1962 letter to John Baxter, Blish notes that "Beanstalk" and *Titans' Daughter* represent the first success for the tape recorder method of composition that he and Virginia Kidd experimented with (Dep. Blish 411/10). Virginia Kidd writes (letter to Ketterer, 26 March 1984) that in response to an editor's request she added "a few lines more about a 'failed' woman" named Polly Follmer.

26. Virginia Kidd also points out in her introduction that the fleeting description of "The old green statue of Charles S. Peirce expounding philosophy from his chair" commemorates "the pragmatist" who "lived and worked one mile up the road from us, here in Milford" (pp. 49, 13). See also reference in William Atheling, Jr., *More Issues at Hand* (Chicago: Advent, 1970), p. 139.

27. A revised version of "Crisis in Utopia" appears in *Five Science Fiction Novels,* ed. Martin Greenberg (New York: Gnome Press, 1952) and in the British edition of same (less two "novels"), retitled *The Crucible of Power,* ed. Greenberg (London: Bodley Head, 1953), pp. 155–236.

28. *A Torrent of Faces* (London: Faber & Faber, 1968), p. vii. Subsequent parenthetical page references are to this text.

29. "Comments on *Torrent,*" *Speculation* 2 (September 1968): 6.

30. "On a Clear Day All You Can See Is Placards," *Warhoon* 25 (November 1968): 17.

31. "Comments on *Torrent,*" p. 6. For a fuller account of the correspondence than is possible here, see Ketterer, "Pantropy, Polyploidy, and Tectogenesis in the Fiction of James Blish and Norman L. Knight," *Science-Fiction Studies* 10 (July 1983): 210-13. The notion of fraternities composed of people who share the same name is what Kurt Vonnegut, Jr., would call a *granfalloon.* See *Cat's Cradle* (1963; New York: New Dell Editions, 1970), p. 67.

32. Nudity, the equivalent of tectogenesis, and underwater people with artificial gills and electric organs (the Horlites) also figure in the five-chapter novella, "Two Worlds in Peril," which Blish wrote in collaboration with Phil Barnhart, a poet and writer of astronomical articles, and which appeared in *Science Fiction Adventures* (February 1957) the year that *The Seedling Stars* was published. In this routine story it is finally discovered that the inhabitants of a twenty-fifth century Earth made increasingly unlivable by a yellow gas that leaks from the ocean floor could survive in the equally gaseous seas of Earth or Venus if they were equipped with gas-tolerant gills like the Horlites of war-torn Venus.

33. *A Clash of Symbols,* pp. 22, 35.

34. This is an opposition that may easily be accommodated to the intersecting human-non-human, science-nature dialectic "paradigm" that Mark Rose offers as a means of mapping the SF "field." See his *Alien Encounters: The Anatomy of Science Fiction* (Berkeley, Cal.: 1981), p. 38.

35. *A Clash of Symbols,* p. 36.

36. Cp. Corinthians 15:51: "We shall not sleep, but we shall all be changed."

37. "Crisis in Utopia," in *The Crucible of Power,* p. 178.

Chapter 4

1. Blish, *A Case of Conscience* (London: Arrow Books, 1972), pp. 7–8. Subsequent parenthetical page references are to this text. The original 1958 Ballantine edition lacks the author's foreword and has an epigraph from John Capgrave's *The Solace of Pilgrims* in place of the two by Jean Jacques Rousseau and Gerald Heard that appear in the Faber & Faber edition of a year later.

2. *A Case of Conscience* is, of course, very much indebted to C. S. Lewis's Ransom trilogy. Blish's protagonist is using a term invented by Lewis when he refers to "a rational soul" as "a *hnau*" (p. 114).

3. Ruiz-Sanchez refers to a 1995 Diet of Basra (pp. 86–87), which claimed that the evolutionary evidence entailed by the perfection of God's creation need not indicate a real past. "Basra" is the headquarters of H. G. Wells's "Wings over the World" organization (*The Shape of Things to Come,* 1933); PS, 6 November 1970. What Blish could not have known when he wrote *A Case of Conscience* is that today "the Roman Catholic Church no longer looks at the theory of evolution with the same suspicion that it once did. The impact of the Second Vatican Council in the early 1960s has brought to the fore theologians such as Pierre Tielhard de Chardin and Karl Rahner, whose thought develops within an explicitly evolutionary framework." See Andrew J. Burgess, "The Concept of Eden," in *The Transcendent Adventure: Studies of Religion in Science Fiction/Fantasy,* ed. Robert Reilly (Westport, Conn.: Greenwood Press, 1985), p. 77.

4. Ruiz-Sanchez's faulty reasoning in the context of the problematic nature of knowledge generally is the subject of Robert Reilly's "The Discerning Conscience," *Extrapolation* 18 (May 1977): 176–80. Blish, Reilly argues, explores the limitations of three types of knowledge: religious knowledge (based on faith and exemplified by Ruiz-Sanchez and Pope Hadrian), scientific knowledge (based upon reason and exemplified chiefly by Michelis, Agronski, Cleaver, and Chexta), and literary knowledge (based upon imagination and represented by the contest between *Finnegans Wake* and *The Divine Comedy*).

5. Brian M. Stableford, *A Clash of Symbols: The Triumph of James Blish* (San Bernardino, Cal.: The Borgo Press, 1979), p. 14.

6. As originally published, the relevant sentence reads as follows: "In the last analysis it was the incessant barking of the lungfish which caused Ruiz-Sanchez to faint when Agronski opened the door for him." See *If* 2 (September 1953): 28. Blish changed "faint" to "stumble" (p. 48).

7. Averoigne, it might be noted, is the fabulous, vampire-cursed land in medieval France which provides one of Clark Ashton Smith's *Lost Worlds* settings; Gaspard du Nord of Averoigne is mentioned as the translator of *The Book of Eibon* in the Smith story "Ubbo-Sathla" (1933).

8. This refrain is initiated by the disillusioned protagonist of *Network* (1976), a Howard Gottfried/Paddy Chayefsky production, written by Paddy Chayefsky, directed by Sidney Lumet.

9. Grace Eckley suggests that Blish may also be picking up on James Joyce's satire, in *Finnegans Wake,* on Hadrian IV, the only English pope; he gave England control of Ireland. See Grace Eckley, "*Finnegans Wake* in the Work of James Blish," *Extrapolation* 20 (Winter 1978): 306. The Emperor Hadrian of Rome may also be a relevant association.

10. The report is, of course, actually by Clark and Ley. Blish's appendix may have provided a model for the notes on "The Gethenian Calendar and Clock" which Ursula K. Le Guin appends to *The Left Hand of Darkness* (New York: Ace, 1969), pp. 284–86.

11. William Atheling, Jr., "Cathedrals in Space," reprinted in *The Issue at Hand* (Chicago: Advent, 1964), p. 59. In addition Atheling points out that "Blish traps himself in

a piece of elementary symbolism at the end of Book One"—the shadow of Cleaver's crate over Ruiz-Sanchez suggests that his point of view will win (ibid., p. 56). But according to the update, this weakness applies only to the story version—in the novel "it becomes a cliffhanger" (ibid., p. 59).

12. See John Clute, "Scholia, Seasoned with Crabs, Blish Is," in *New Worlds 5*, ed. Michael Moorcock and Charles Platt (London: Sphere Books Ltd., 1973), pp. 123–26.

13. *Delap's F & SF Review* 1 (September 1975): 21–22.

14. Jo Allen Bradham, "The Case in James Blish's *A Case of Conscience*," *Extrapolation* 16 (December 1974): 68.

15. Ibid., p. 67.

16. In a letter to the Australian critic John Baxter (31 October 1962), Blish notes that the "cable-car barn" in *A Case of Conscience* does actually exist in New York (Dep. Blish 411/10).

17. "The Case in James Blish's *A Case of Conscience*," p. 74.

18. For an exploration of some of the possibilities, see Grace Eckley, "*Finnegans Wake* in the Work of James Blish," pp. 338–40. In this article (pp. 306, 334) she also suggests a couple of connections between *A Case of Conscience* and *A Portrait of the Artist as a Young Man* (1916). She compares Egtverchi's Satanic *non serviam*, when he declares himself a citizen of no country, with Stephen Dedalus's act of renunciation. Blish may have derived his title from the moment when Stephen watches "a young professor of mental science discussing on the landing a case of conscience with his class." See James Joyce, *A Portrait of the Artist as a Young Man* (1916; New York: Viking Press, 1964), p. 192 and (for further references to the same phrase) pp. 238, 253.

19. He cut a paragraph in between what are successive paragraphs in the novel, the one ending with "any member of it," the other beginning with "Yes, it added up" (p. 52).

20. "The Case in James Blish's *A Case of Conscience*," pp. 74–77.

21. Ibid., pp. 76–77.

22. Blish may have derived this metaphor from the satire upon clothes and fashion in Swift's *A Tale of a Tub* (1704); "is not religion a cloak; honesty a pair of shoes worn out in the dirt; self-love a surtout; vanity a shirt; and conscience a pair of breeches; which, though a cover for lewdness as well as nastiness, is easily slipt down for the service of both?" See Jonathan Swift, *"Gulliver's Travels" and Other Writings*, ed. Louis A. Landa (Boston: Houghton Mifflin, 1960), p. 283. It should be noted that Swift's work generally and *A Tale of a Tub* in particular figure conspicuously in Joyce's *Finnegans Wake*. See Mackie L. Jarell, "Swiftiana in *Finnegans Wake*," ELH 26 (June 1959): 271–94; and Arthur T. Broes, "Swift's Work in *Finnegans Wake*," *English Studies in Canada* 5 (Summer 1979): 167–86. Broes notes a large number of allusions to Swift's clothing metaphor (pp. 174–76). If Blish did not know of the relevant episode in *A Tale of a Tub* as a result of his general reading, it is extremely likely that his deep interest in *Finnegans Wake* would have led him to it. I am indebted to Robert M. Philmus for this suggestion.

23. The word "case" was a second-thought insertion clarifying "wing-buzzes" of the original novella. See *If Worlds of Science Fiction*, p. 10.

24. *The Issue at Hand*, p. 56.

25. See David Ketterer, *New Worlds for Old: The Apocalyptic Imagination, Science Fiction, and American Literature* (New York: Anchor Books, 1974), passim.

26. "Aleph-Null" is the first transfinite number. There are several references to Georg Cantor's notion of an arithmetic of the infinite in Blish's work but see in particular the short story "FYI" (1953), discussed pp. 220–21 herein.

Chapter 5

1. Blish, "The Science in Science Fiction," *Quicksilver,* no. 2 (April 1971): 25.
2. Ibid., p. 26.
3. Blish, *Anywhen* (London: Faber & Faber, 1971), p. 151.
4. Cp. Darko Suvin's criteria for evaluating the "novum" in "Narrative Logic, Ideological Domination, and the Range of SF," part of his introduction to *Victorian Science Fiction in the U.K.: The Discourses of Knowledge and of Power* (Boston: G. K. Hall, 1983), pp. 298–311.
5. Treated elsewhere are "The Thing in the Attic," "Watershed," and "A Time to Survive" in the context of *The Seedling Stars* (chapter 3); "Two Worlds in Peril" in the context of *A Torrent of Faces* (note 32 to chapter 3); "At Death's End" in its *Cities in Flight* context (chapter 6); "Common Time," "FYI," and "Detour to the Stars" in chapter 8; and "A Work of Art" at the end of the present chapter.

The stories of lesser interest which also appeared during this period may be briefly summarized as follows:

In "Turn of a Century" (March 1953) it is New Year's Eve, 1999; the end of the world is, of course, expected and cynical fax reporters cover the space-ark story.

The alien investigation of a post-nuclear-war Earth in "Translation." (March 1955) locates a time capsule which contains a manuscript. But because the aliens are tone deaf their translator mechanism fails to make sense of what is identified in this effective story's final line as Beethoven's Symphony no. 5 in C minor and thus they gain no inkling of an answer to the question that perplexes them: why should the inhabitants of Earth have committed suicide.

"With Malice to Come" (May 1955) is a brief triptych of parodies of familiar types of SF: "I. A Feast of Reason" in which, after "Logical" speculation, the inhabitants of Mars turn out to be Nazi Martians; "II. The Billion Year Binge" (cp. Brian Aldiss's title, *Billion Year Spree*), a Ray Bradbury parody which includes a vision of Martian cities built out of beer cans; "III. A Matter of Energy," in which the targets are L. Sprague de Camp's *Lest Darkness Fall* (1949), "literary" substitutions for "he said," and anachronisms in time-travel stories.

John W. Campbell invented the rationale for a story that was originally entitled "The Dark Night of the Soul," and then rejected it (Dep. Blish 393/2). It was subsequently published in *Galaxy* as "Genius Heap" (August 1956) and reprinted in Blish's anthology of SF stories about the arts, *New Dreams This Morning* (1966). It is about the discovery that an artists' colony in Callisto (Jupter IV) was set up as a way of getting rid of the bothersome, emotionally unstable artists of Earth. The story ends with the artists in revolt against the colony's director.

In response to my query, Virginia Kidd writes (11 September 1984),

> Yes, I had a lot to do with the story "Masks" [March 1956]. I wrote it. Jim needed a story for his fraternity magazine [*Teke Life: Magazine for the Men of Tau Kappa Epsilon*] on about twenty-four hours' notice, and it was the only unpublished story in the house at the time. I gave it to him. He put it through his typewriter, introducing several refinements on my basic situation of a culture where work was forbidden & bootlegged. The circumstances were such that my being not only senior collaborator but 90% author of the story just could not be mentioned. If the situation had been reversed, he would have done the same for me. At that time we were very much "in each other's heads." I could write in his style for brief stretches, and he could write in mine, except in poetry, where our styles differed.

In "Masks," an effective, densely plotted, chilling vignette that was reprinted in *The Magazine of Fantasy & Science Fiction* (November 1959) and in *So Close to Home,* an interrogator falls into the trap of examining (for some kind of subversive message) the decorative "mask" applied to a girl's finger nail. After the effect of ultra-violet light on the nail throws the epileptic interrogator into a full scale *grand mal,* she commits suicide by swallowing her poisoned thumb "mask."

6. Robert A. W. Lowndes, "Introduction: Science Fiction the Hard Way," *The Best of James Blish,* ed. Lowndes (New York: Ballantine Books, 1979), p. xvi. See also William Atheling, Jr., *The Issue at Hand* (Chicago; Advent 1964), p. 48.

7. "Testament of Andros," in Blish, *The Testament of Andros* [new title for the 1973 *Best Science Fiction Stories of James Blish*] (London: Arrow Books, 1977), p. 82. Subsequent parenthetical page references are to this text. There appears to be an error in the text that occurs in all the versions that I have seen: "in 1952, about a hundred years before the previous explosion" (p. 65)—presumably "before" should be "after," unless the mistake is construed as a delusion on the part of the narrator. Gregory Feeley writes (letter to Ketterer, 12 August 1985) that in the story's appearance in Robert Silverberg's anthology *Alpha One* (1970) "the word has been corrected to 'after,' while in addition, the dates in that first section . . . have been advanced by twenty years, from the mid-fifties to mid-seventies. The evident purpose would have been to keep the story in the near future, and whoever did it doubtless also made the before/after correction; the only question is who did it."

8. "Science Fiction the Hard Way," p. xvii. William Atheling, Jr., confirms that the "yarn is told in five distinctly different styles by five narrators who may or may not have been the same man"; it was "too big a job for its author, but it was well worth attempting." See *The Issue at Hand,* p. 48.

9. Brian M. Stableford, *A Clash of Symbols: The Triumph of James Blish* (San Bernardino, Cal.: The Borgo Press, 1979), p. 40. Nevertheless, Lowndes points out that Blish's exposure at work to medical material lay behind "Testament of Andros." See "James Blish: A Profile," *The Magazine of Fantasy & Science Fiction* 42 (April 1972): 70–71.

10. Blish, "The Book of Your Life," *The Magazine of Fantasy & Science Fiction* 8 (March 1955), p. 84. Subsequent parenthetical page references are to this text.

11. "King of the Hill" was reprinted in the American but not the subsequent English editions of *Galactic Cluster*. A Sweeney, it will be recalled, figures in "A Time to Survive," also first published in 1955.

12. "To Pay the Piper," in Blish, *Galactic Cluster* (London: A Panther Book, 1980), p. 62. Subsequent parenthetical page references are to this text.

13. "The Writing of the Rat," in Blish, *Anywhen* (New York: Avon Books, 1983), p. 54. Subsequent parenthetical page references are to this text. Blish does not identify the Sandburg poem in which the lines occur: "Four Preludes on Playthings of the World." See also Sandburg's "Rat Riddles."

14. Blish based his synthetic language on the marquee display for *The Robe* (the first film made in Cinemascope) which, following its New York premiere (16 September 1953) opened for its first Brooklyn showing at the RKO Albee Theatre at Fulton and de Kalb on 11 December 1953. The marquee would have included statements like "SEE *THE ROBE* IN CINEMASCOPE," from which could be derived "Hnimesacpeo *tce rebo*" (p. 50), and "FIRST TIME IN BROOKLYN," which with slight modifications becomes *"Sftir etminbi rokolny"* (p. 50). Other samples of the alien language including the name "Hrestce" (part of "CHRISTMAS"?), are similarly scrambled words taken from the additional statements on the marquee (which must perforce be guessed at). In all proba-

bility Blish passed by the theater on 10 December 1953 when the previous marquee announcement had been, or was being, dismantled and the advertisement for the new attraction was about to be, or in the process of being, assembled—hence Blish would have been alerted to the scrambling possibilities. I am grateful to Bernard Queenan for the detective work.

15. Thomas quoted in "Tomb Tapper," in Blish, *The Testament of Andros*, p. 139. Subsequent parenthetical page references are to this text. The story is reprinted in the American edition of *Galactic Cluster*, and in all editions of *Best Science Fiction Stories of James Blish*. Blish thought at one point of including it in his near future collection *So Close to Home* (CM51, 12 June 1959).

16. Blish, *"Get Out of My Sky" and "There Shall be no Darkness"* (London: Panther Books, 1980), p. 64. Subsequent parenthetical page references are to this text.

17. Gregory Feeley notes Aidregh "as the closest example of an exception" to his dictum that "no protagonist in any of Blish's sf is a parent." But Aidregh "is so deeply into the middle-aged solitariness of all mature Blish heroes . . . that any reverberations of parenthood are effectively evaded." A similar exception would be John Hillary Dane of the "King Log" stories (see pp. 232–36 herein). However, given Blish's occasional misogyny and jaundiced attitude toward romantic love, Feeley's essential point is significant: "in Blish's canon can be found a full spectrum of confirmed non-parents: priests, sterile polyploids, celibate magicians, homosexuals, Amalfi with his irradiated germ-plasm, men marrying in middle age, lady scientists (the assumptions implicit therein needn't be explicated), and couples in spaceship societies with no room for growth. This repeated metaphor for the end of things is too consistent to be accorded minor weight, and too much in keeping with Blish's other obsessive returns to the subject of volition's end. . . ." See "Cages of Conscience from Seedling Stories: The Development of Blish's Novels," *Foundation*, no. 24 (February 1982): 65, 68 n. 6.

18. Atheling writes, "This is a slender argument to carry a 30,000-word story, and in order to keep things going Blish has concentrated chiefly on the emotional conflicts within Aidregh, as they are variously triggered by his opposition, his son and the son's girl, the girl's father—a physician who plays the role of a Greek chorus to the story—and Rathe's head-of-state, the Margent; and, of course, by the pressure of his responsibilities to the peoples of both planets." But, he continues, because the story depends for its interest on its "fantasy content," the second half of the story, "where the psi content is concentrated" and the background material most novel, is more successful than the first. Nevertheless, the story is "stronger on ingenuity than on strictly fictional values." He notes further that (after the fashion of Lester del Rey's new rationales for his every use of an SF gimmick) "Blish's explanation of how psi powers might work differs completely from that proposed" in *Jack of Eagles* and "from any proposed by his editor. . . ." See *More Issues at Hand* (Chicago: Advent, 1970), pp. 88–89. Blish also makes use of the psi power of telepathy, in an unrationalized form, among the Protos of "Sunken Universe" and "Surface Tension"; with related rationales in "Nor Iron Bars" and "This Earth of Hours," where it is a characteristic of the microcosmic universe; and with yet another rationale, in *Midsummer Century*. He claimed not to believe in telepathy and the like and generally only introduced psi powers when he could produce a new rationale for them. "I *love* rationales," he wrote Shackley; "they are an enormous part of the fun of sf" (PS, 23 June 1970).

19. "This Earth of Hours" in Blish, *Galactic Cluster* (New York: Signet, 1959), p. 166. Subsequent parenthetical page references are to this text. The story does not appear in the two U.K. editions of *Galactic Cluster* because, according to a letter to Charles

Monteith (12 July 1959), Blish believed it weak (CM 51). Cp. the matriarchal set-up in ... *And All the Stars a Stage* (June, July 1960) and recall the reference to Novoe Washingtongrad in "The Writing of the Rat."

20. *The Fallen Star* was Blish's original title; Ballantine Books changed it to *The Frozen Year* (their edition, unlike all subsequent editions, includes an epigraph by Virginia Kidd). On 27 January 1957 Blish wrote Charles Monteith, "Either title suits me, and the new one does have the advantage of dropping that word 'star,' on which I seem to have developed something of a fix lately" (CM 51). Blish's other "star" titles are *They Shall Have Stars, The Seedling Stars, . . . And All the Stars a Stage, The Star Dwellers, A Life for the Stars,* and *Mission to the Heart Stars.* Later, of course, came the *Star Trek* books. Blish agreed to Faber & Faber's preferring his original title but suggested, as happened, that the definite article be dropped from it. He did insist, however, that *Fallen Star* not be labelled SF. At any rate, the book gained the support of Kingsley Amis (CM51).

21. *The Issue at Hand,* pp. 113–14.

22. *Fallen Star* (New York: Avon Books, 1983), p. 8. All parenthetical page references are to this text.

23. Farnsworth is probably named for both Duncan Farnsworth, pseudonym of the American writer David Wright O'Brien, and O'Brien's uncle, Farnsworth Wright, editor of *Weird Tales.* In a letter to Damon Knight (22 March 1957), Blish admits to "many points of resemblance between F. [Farnsworth] and my father" (Dep. Blish 423/4). The IGY, it may be recalled, existed from 1 July 1957 until 31 December 1958. A spin-off from the novel was Blish's "Planet Earth," which appeared in the *IGY Teacher's Manual* and was reprinted in *Science Fiction: The Year's Best,* published by Ralph Shikes in 1958. The *IGY Teacher's Manual* was "a visual program initiated jointly by the National Science Foundation and the National Academy of Sciences, intended to stimulate interest in the International Geophysical Year . . . among high school students" (Dep. Blish 393/8).

24. Gregory Feeley writes (letter to Ketterer, 12 August 1985):

> Wollheim told me that he thought the person suggested by Dr. Eleanor Wollheim was his sister, who is named Eleanor and actually was a doctor. . . . Blish had met Eleanor years earlier when visiting the Wollheims before the Futurian rupture, and . . . probably remembered . . . the name. Wollheim recalls that Blish blanched when Wollheim reminded him of it, and apologized—Wollheim avers only to avoid a lawsuit. . . . For what it's worth, Richard Lupoff claims Blish had told him the Wollheim reference was an attempt to heal the rift between them—the briefly-seen doctor being a figure Julian had thought little of, appreciating her humanity only too late—but the attempt backfired; Wollheim, Lupoff notes, was incensed.

25. Gregory Feeley speculates (letter to Ketterer, 12 August) that:

> Ellen is Nferetet and the femme fatale Jayne is Infteret, both of whom "collide" with Julian's own "orbit," but I cannot support the association with more than intuition. ("Infteret" may contain the faint echo of a sexual double-entendre.) Midge seems at first merely a midge, but appears to Julian greater after his encounter with wrathful Mars and the other careering "heavenly bodies" (a common dumb joke . . . in the Fifties). There may be an underlying schema not wholly teased out.

26. Given that "second-hand stuff" could amount to a definition of fiction, it should be noted that Jayne (Julian's alter ego?) is identified, somewhat pointlessly it might appear, as a "writer of historical novels" (p. 8). But then, to raise an issue not explicitly explored by Blish but crucial to recent critical theory, what is not "second-hand stuff"?

NOTES TO CHAPTER 5

27. See Damon Knight, *In Search of Wonder: Essays on Modern Science Fiction,* rev. ed. (1956; Chicago: Advent, 1967), pp. 155–57. Knight explained why he could not collaborate on *VOR* in a letter to Ketterer (28 May 1983).

28. The names Davis and Petrucelli also occur in "When Anteros Came" (see p. 328, n. 8 here).

29. "The Weakness of RVOG," *Thrilling Wonder Stories* 33 (February 1949): 87. Subsequent parenthetical page references are to this text. "Ginnunga" is the correct spelling.

30. *A Clash of Symbols,* p. 41.

31. *VOR* (New York: Avon Books, 1958), pp. 49, 60, 78. Subsequent parenthetical page references are to this edition.

32. Knight specifies the episode where "Holm confronts the alien, risking his life to try to open communication. If the story had been written from Holm's viewpoint, this could have been a scene of hair-raising suspense. As it is, it takes place almost invisibly offstage while we get a worm's eye view of Marty and his stonecold love life." See *In Search of Wonder,* p. 156.

33. In view of this sexual reading, it might be noted that the slightly earlier story "Tomb-Tapper" features a missile piloted into a railway tunnel.

34. Blish's letter appears in *Disclave,* no. 80 (May 1972). It is reprinted under the title (taken from the last line of the letter) "A Bad Idea Trampled to Death by Ducks" in "Four Fugitive Pieces by James Blish," ed. David Ketterer, *Vector,* no. 120 (June 1984): 8–9. *Earthman, Come Home* bears an acknowledgments page (dropped from the Avon omnibus edition of *Cities in Flight*) in which Blish thanks Frederick Pohl, Virginia Kidd, Henry Sostman, and Truman Talley for help on the manuscript. In addition, Talley informed Gregory Feeley that "he proposed the titles for both *Galactic Cluster* and *The Seedling Stars*" (Feeley to Ketterer, 12 November 1984). As an independent publisher, Talley would subsequently commission Blish to write *The Vanished Jet* (see pp. 265–66 herein). *One in Three Hundred* is about the escape to Mars from a solar-flare-threatened Earth in dinky spaceships that can only hold eleven people each—hence only one person in three hundred can be saved. Damon Knight's negative review is reprinted in *In Search of Wonder,* pp. 65–66.

35. *Disclave* letter, supplemented by Feeley to Ketterer, 14 September 1983, and 12 August 1985. In a letter to Charles Monteith after the British publication of *. . . And All the Stars a Stage* (to surprisingly good notices) Blish describes the history of the book as "about the wildest shaggy dog story I've ever heard, let alone been involved in. . . . [It's] not only not as good a novel as it should have been, it's not as good a book as it once was" (CM 84). The last statement seems to imply that Doubleday lost a carbon-copyless typescript version that was superior to the *Amazing* text.

36. *A Clash of Symbols,* p. 41.

37. Stableford to Ketterer, 8 August 1983.

38. *And All the Stars a Stage* (New York: Avon Books, 1974), p. 106. Subsequent parenthetical page references are to this edition. Like most of the book's publishers, Avon Books decided to eliminate Blish's title ellipsis.

39. Feeley to Ketterer, 14 September 1983.

40. John Clute, "Scholia, Seasoned with Crabs, Blish Is," *New Worlds 6* (London: Sphere Books Ltd., 1973), p. 127.

41. Blish, "The Biological Story," *Science Fiction Quarterly* 1 (May 1951): 91.

42. Gregory Feeley notes (letter to Ketterer, 12 August 1985), apropos "Gol of Dobrai . . . the first king in recorded history," the "various monarchical titles Blish invented. There is the Panechruse in 'Our Binary Brothers,' the Banish of Bane in *Mission to the*

Heart Stars . . . [the Green Exarch in "A Style in Treason," and the Supreme Autarch in *Midsummer Century*]. It is interesting that Blish's love of hierarchies and complex systems, even invented ones like historical astrology and E. R. Eddison's cosmology, should have led him to coin terms that imply arcane systems behind them."

43. Brian W. Aldiss notes the climate preference; see "James Blish and the Mathematics of Behaviour," in Aldiss, *This World and Nearer Ones: Essays Exploring the Familiar* (London: Weidenfeld & Nicolson, 1979), p. 42.

44. Virginia Kidd writes (letter to Ketterer, 11 September 1984): "I haven't the faintest idea why "The Snake-Headed Sceptre" was published under the V. K. Emden byline. I did not write it. (It was probably a matter of two stories, one by Blish and the other by 'Emden,' being submitted to the same editor in the hope that both would sell; but I don't recall the incident.) If Jim chose not to indicate that *The Night Shapes* comprised that story and "Serpent's Fetish," it was probably because he did not want to get involved in explaining that the one story had appeared under my then-byline. However, it may have been sheer forgetfulness. . . . We did *not* often swap bylines."

45. Blish, *The Night Shapes* (London: Arrow Books, 1978), pp. 7, 11, 103. Subsequent parenthetical page references are to this edition. For the two errors, see John Clute, "Scholia, Seasoned with Crabs, Blish Is," p. 123.

46. "The Oath," in *The Testament of Andros,* p. 153. Subsequent parenthetical page references are to this text.

47. "And Some Were Savages," in *Anywhen,* p. 61. Subsequent parenthetical page references are to this text.

48. The other story, a routine piece entitled "The Abattoir Effect," is the only previously unpublished piece in Blish's near future, Earthbound collection *So Close to Home* (1961). In "The Abattoir Effect," Joan Wrexham, who works for the International Blood Rescue Trust in New York, discovers that Burton, her boss, has been arranging the deaths of people of a particular blood group (the world's Bradbury-immunes) so that, following a staged "accident" befalling some prominent person who would then need that particular blood transfusion, the IBRT bloodbank would serve the purposes of blackmail. Burton admits his guilt and agrees to inform on the two people who put him up to it when she tells him that she has had his personal IBM card marked "Bradbury-immune."

49. "A Dusk of Idols," in *Anywhen,* pp. 87, 90. Subsequent parenthetical page references are to this text.

50. "None So Blind," in *Anywhen,* p. 113. Subsequent parenthetical page references are to this text.

51. Kidd to Ketterer, 11 June 1984.

52. Ibid.

53. Blish and Kidd, "On the Wall of the Lodge," in *Dark Stars,* ed. Robert Silverberg (New York: Ballantine Books, 1969), p. 243. Subsequent parenthetical page references are to this text.

54. The Silverberg text is not perfect and I am grateful to Virginia Kidd (letter to Ketterer, 20 May 1985) for correcting the serious printer's errors (omissions and a repeated transposed line halfway through this passage). The corrections have been incorporated silently.

55. In "Notes on Shackley Letter of July 17, 1970," Blish writes, "If I cured John Brest he would have to be confronted with the real world at the end and I would have to explain. Don't want to do this, because I don't want the novel to be read as *only* a schizophrenic vision. Reductionism is the death of art" (PS, no date).

56. Virginia Kidd (letter to Ketterer, 11 June 1984) refers to "our friend Willi Gaddis." In a letter published in Bruce Gillespie's fanzine *The Metaphysical Review Seven* (1972?), p. 10, Blish mentions his presentation copy of the first edition of *The Recognitions* as "one of the most valuable items in my estate when I kick off."

57. Kidd to Ketterer, plus one page of synopsis, 20 May 1985.

58. "No Jokes on Mars," in *Anywhen,* p. 128. Subsequent parenthetical page references are to this text.

59. "How Beautiful with Banners," in *The Testament of Andros,* p. 169. Subsequent parenthetical page references are to this text.

60. "Skysign," in *Anywhen* (London: Faber & Faber, 1971), p. 151. Subsequent parenthetical page references are to this text.

61. *More Issues at Hand,* p. 47.

62. The very short "Now That Man is Gone" describes how, after the extinction of the human race, a new Adam and Eve come into being. The Waw, a nine-year-old bionic boy (who lives in a hollowed-out asteroid with a robot named Cheng) locates Ya, a twelve-year-old girl with whom he can mate (to create a Waw-Ya, or Warrior, one wonders) after his artificial heart has been replaced by a human one.

63. "We All Die Naked," in *The Testament of Andros,* p. 184. Subsequent parenthetical references are to this text.

64. Blish, *Anywhen,* p. 7.

65. Blish, "A Style in Treason," *Galaxy* 30 (May 1970): 7.

66. "A Style in Treason," in *Anywhen,* pp. 13, 14, 15. Subsequent parenthetical page references are to this text.

67. Blish was mistaken. Shackley notes (letter to Ketterer, 17 June 1985) that the quote occurs in Blish, *The Star Dwellers* (New York: Avon Books, 1982), p. 66.

68. "More Light," in *Alchemy and Academe* (New York: Doubleday & Co., Inc., 1970), pp. 91, 89. Subsequent parenthetical page references are to this text.

69. The actual brownstone, 579A Sixth Street, was situated off Prospect Park (Blish to Charles Monteith, 19 June 1968, CM51).

70. The apocryphal play "The King in Yellow" was, in fact, never written, but two parts of it, each cited as being from act 1, scene 2, are quoted in Chambers's collection of the same title. Blish incorporates both extracts with their mention of the princess Camilla and the city of Carcosa (Feeley to Ketterer, 12 August 1985). As for the youthful Atheling's correspondence, Sam Moskowitz writes (letter to Ketterer, 3 September 1986) that three letters from Lovecraft "To Jim Blish and William Miller, Jr.," were published in *Phantastique Combined with The Science Fiction Critic* 2 (March 1938): 3–4; they were followed by Lovecraft's letters "To Nils H. Frome, Esq." (pp. 4–9).

71. Introduction to "Getting Along," in *Again, Dangerous Visions,* ed. Harlan Ellison (New York: Doubleday, 1972), p. 557.

72. Judith Blish to Ketterer, 6 August 1983.

73. Blish, "Getting Along," in *Again, Dangerous Visions,* p. 577.

74. Gregory Feeley writes (letter to Ketterer, 4 March 1985), "Robert Lowndes told me that L. Jerome Stanton was a marginal figure in SF fandom from the Forties, whom Blish may well not have seen since that time. Lowndes guessed that Blish credited Stanton with a hand in 'The Glitch' as the result of some conversation they had had long ago."

75. "A Work of Art," in Blish, *The Testament of Andros,* p. 107. Subsequent parenthetical page references are to this text. Originally published under the title "Art Work" in *Original Science Fiction Stories,* it was reprinted in all editions of *Galactic Cluster,* in

both editions of *Best Science Fiction Stories of James Blish,* and, along with "Genius Heap" (see p. 337, n.5 herein) in Bish's anthology of stories about the arts in SF, *New Dreams This Morning* (1966).

76. Cp. Blish's reference to "the *Illiac Suite* [produced by a computer at the University of Illinois], a four-part work divided into four movements, each in the style of a different composer (the earliest of which is Mozart) but not, of course, written by any one of them or by any other human being." See the unpublished manuscript (discussed in chapter 9 herein), "The Sense of Music," p. 95.

77. Pp. 123, 124. The Poundian term, *"persona,"* goes along with the appropriate lines that "Strauss" had come across earlier from Pound's *Personae* poem (unidentified in the story), "Histrion" (1919). "Busch" is a correction made by Judith Blish, of the originally published form "Bosch." See Blish to Charles Monteith, 27 October 1964 (CM 51).

78. "Introduction: Science Fiction the Hard Way," p. xviii.

79. Budrys to Ketterer, 11 May 1983.

Chapter 6

1. An important influence here was the 1930s Sunday comic strip, *Buck Rogers in the 25th Century,* written by Philip Francis Nowlan and drawn by Dick Calkins, an acquaintance of Blish's father: "Calkins had a particular gift for drawing gadgets which I enjoyed; he was particularly good at imagining outlandish spaceships; I think he was the first science-fiction producer before Werner von Braun to realize that in the vacuum of space (which he nevertheless filled with picturesque sunset clouds) there is no reason why a spaceship has to have streamlines or fairing—a discovery not to be made by the magazine illustrators for decades to come." See James Blish, "A Science-Fiction Coming of Age," in *The Tale that Wags the God,* ed. Cy Chauvin (Chicago: Advent Publishers, 1987), pp. 149–50.

2. See "In Conversation: James Blish Talks to Brian Aldiss," *Cypher,* no. 10 (October 1973); the relevant portion of this interview is reprinted in "Introduction by James and Judith Blish" to "The Cities in Flight Series by James Blish" in Frederik Pohl, Martin Harry Greenberg, and Joseph Olander, ed., *The Great Science Fiction Series* (New York: Harper & Row, 1980), pp. 86–87. See also Blish's statement in Robert Reginald, *Contemporary Science Fiction Authors II,* 2 vols. (Detroit: Gale Research Co., 1979), 2:820. By way of further confusion, Blish misdescribes the man on the cover to Aldiss as standing in, and in Reginald as looking down at, the rocketship yard.

3. For Blish's denial of Sam Moskowitz's suggestion in *Seekers of Tomorrow* (New York: World, 1966), p. 76, that *Cities in Flight* may have been inspired by the Hamilton serial, see *More Issues at Hand* (Chicago: Advent, 1970), p. 39. See also Robert A. W. Lowndes, "James Blish: A Profile," *The Magazine of Fantasy & Science Fiction,* 42 (April 1972): 68.

4. Author's note to the 1965 reprint of Blish, *They Shall Have Stars* (1956; London: Faber & Faber, 1965), pp. 5–6.

5. Damon Knight objects, with some justice, that the analogy is false. The Okie cities are, or easily could be, self-sufficient. They do not need to look for work. See *In Search of Wonder: Essays on Modern Science Fiction,* rev. ed. (1956; Chicago: Advent, 1967), pp. 153–54.

6. *Contemporary Science Fiction Authors II,* 2:820. See also the author's note to the 1965 reprint of Blish, *Earthman, Come Home* (1956; London: Faber & Faber Ltd., 1965), p. 9; the foreword to James Blish, ed., *The Best of John W. Campbell* (London: Sedgewick & Jackson, 1973), p. 10; and *The Great Science Fiction Series,* p. 86.

7. This deposit includes eight letters from Campbell written between 20 October 1949 and 26 April 1964. In the *Cypher* interview Blish notes, "The main thing that Campbell contributed was this: the most valuable thing that these migrant workers could transfer in a situation involving fast interstellar travel was not gold, uranium, diamonds, the ability to drill for oil or whatever, but *information*. These cities were the pollinating agents of the galaxy, and this idea became the central focus of the whole series. It absolutely ruled out power politics in the intergalactic-epic sense." See *The Great Science Fiction Series*, p. 86.

8. Author's note to *Earthman, Come Home*, p. 9.

9. Author's note to *They Shall Have Stars*, p. 6.

10. *Cities in Flight* (New York: Avon Books, 1970), pp. 285, 338. Subsequent parenthetical page references are to this text. It should be noted that a number of inconsistencies have been cleaned up for this combined edition, making it the nearest thing to the definitive text (see nn. 13 and 33 below), but that the dedication of *They Shall Have Stars* to Frederik Pohl has been dropped, probably accidentally.

11. See Robert H. Canary, "Science Fiction as Fictive History," *Extrapolation* 16 (December 1974): 81–94.

12. "Cathedrals in Space," *Skyhook*, no. 19 (Autumn 1953), reprinted in *The Issue at Hand* (Chicago: Advent, 1964), p. 60. In "Another Case" (April 1962), also reprinted in *The Issue at Hand*, p. 60, Blish mentions Robert A. W. Lowndes's use of Spengler in *Believers' World* (1961).

13. "Blish, van Vogt, and the Uses of Spengler," *Riverside Quarterly* 3 (August 1968): 172–86. A revised and shortened version of this article, with the two van Vogt sections omitted entirely, appears as the afterword to *Cities in Flight*, pp. 597–607. In a note to this afterword, Blish mentions correcting "a large number of" inconsistencies "pointed out to me by Dr. Mullen, where I agreed that they *were* inconsistencies" (p. 599). Checking the Faber editions with the Avon edition and the list of inconsistencies, which appears only in the *Riverside Quarterly* article (pp. 176–77), it is apparent that Blish made at least the following relatively minor corrections: in *Earthman, Come Home* the statement "that nobody had dusted the city's ancient subways since the management of deFord" (p. 434) replaces the earlier indication that the subways had not been used since New York first went into space when deFord was city manager (Faber, p. 224)—a statement which contradicts both the "edgy roar of the subway trains" (p. 171) and the account of deFord's becoming city manager in *A Life for the Stars*; to conform with the implication of the Faber chronological table and statements in the text (e.g., p. 169) that there was virtually no emigration from Earth between 2039 and 2375, a reference in *A Life for the Stars* to "the great Colonial exodus of 2375–2400" (p. 155) corrects the earlier "2200–2400" (Faber, p. 42); the chronologically inconsistent reference to Amalfi's being "less than a century old" and later to his being mayor "for six hundred years," and to the Okie king being "two thousand years old at a minimum," and to New York's having been in space for 1,200 years in the Faber edition of *Earthman, Come Home* (pp. 16, 18, 145, 147) is changed to "just 117 years old" (p. 242), "five hundred years" (p. 244), "eight hundred years" (p. 363), and "about five hundred and eighty years" (p. 361), respectively. One particularly important inconsistency that Mullen noticed is discussed in section 5 of this chapter.

14. *The Issue at Hand*, p. 60.

15. Brian W. Aldiss, *This World and Nearer Ones: Essays Exploring the Familiar* (Kent, Ohio: Kent State University Press, 1981), p. 39; Brian M. Stableford, *A Clash of Symbols: The Triumph of James Blish* (San Bernardino, Calif.: The Borgo Press, 1979), p. 22.

16. "Science in Science Fiction: The Astronomical Story," *Science Fiction Quarterly* 1 (November 1951): 112. Philip Latham is the pseudonym of American astronomer Robert Shirley Richardson.

17. Re Blish's fondness for cold places: *The Warriors of Day* opens with the hero killing a bear on Kodiak, and Antarctica figures positively in *Midsummer Century*.

18. *This World and Nearer Ones*, p. 45.

19. Blish later wrote a factual piece on the South Tropical Disturbance and the Great Red Spot of Jupiter entitled "A Message from Loci" (the god of the Underworld), *Worlds of Tomorrow* 1 (February 1964): 121–24.

20. P. 112. This description surely reflects something of the origin of the story "Bridge." Paul Shackley writes, "Jim was walking under a large railway bridge, I think in New York. It began to rock and vibrate all around him as if it was alive and moving. This was 'almost a numinous experience' which inspired the story" (letter to Ketterer, 2 August 1984). Cp. passage in "Tomb Tapper" quoted on p. 116 herein.

21. P. 104. The name "Bliss Wagoner really was deliberate . . . 'Wagoner' means 'wheelright' which is just what he was" (PS, 23 June 1970). Shackley suggests (letter to Ketterer, 9 August 1984) that "Bliss" stands for "Blish."

22. Chris deFord (note the echo of "Christopher") may be surnamed for the American mystery and SF writer Miriam Allen deFord.

23. Dale Mullen astutely points to the way Hrunta's crimes assuage human guilt concerning the Vegan War. See "Blish, van Vogt, and the Uses of Spengler," p. 181, or the afterword to *Cities in Flight*, pp. 602–3. It must be admitted, however, that this notion is not explicitly pointed up by Blish's text. What comes across more directly is simply a sense of the kind of reversal that is characteristic of routine space opera. The history of the Hruntan Empire, it should be noted, most clearly corresponds to Spengler's two substages of Early Culture: the Formation of Feudal Order and the Breakdown of Feudal Order. Blish wrote Shackley "I think a Hrunta was the Quisling of Rumania. (When I said 'Balkanization,' I meant it!)" (PS, 23 June 1970).

24. P. 243. Philip Nichols, responding to an earlier version of this chapter, notes the first appearance of the "bubble" motif in *They Shall Have Stars:* "as Paige Russell and Anne Abbott are being driven to a restaurant, the privacy of their taxi is breached by Believers, who pump bubbles through the back door; the bubbles burst, releasing a perfume, and a mini-sermon" (p. 33). See "Letters," *Foundation*, no. 32 (November 1984): 77.

25. John Clute, "James Blish," in E. F. Bleiler, ed., *Science Fiction Writers: Critical Studies of the Major Authors from the Early Nineteenth Century to the Present Day* (New York: Charles Scribner's Sons, 1982), p. 292.

26. Mullen, afterword, pp. 603–4.

27. Ibid., p. 604.

28. In an article entitled "Eine Kleine Okie-Musik," *Australian Science Fiction Review*, no. 12 (October 1967): 10–12, Blish points out that he wrote the folk song to the tune of the "Siege of Kazan" (Karst mentions a town of the same name as presumably the one on which IMT fell) from Moussorgsky's *Boris Goudonov*. For purposes of this tune, Blish further points out, "IMT" should be sounded as a single word. He also mentions that an American fan, G. Evans, wrote a different musical score for the same song, and that Karen Anne Emden (Virginia Kidd's daughter by her first husband) wrote a sonnet entitled "The Okie Children."

29. Blish talks about the title "bowing to Swinburne" in his author's note to the 1965 reprint of *The Triumph of Time* (1959; London: Faber & Faber Ltd., 1965), p. 5. While

noting that the theme of *The Triumph of Time* "is not especially Spenglerian," Mullen does observe that both the theme and the title could have been inspired by this passage on Spengler's final page: "Time triumphs over Space, and it is Time whose inexorable movement embeds the ephemeral incident of the Culture, on this planet, in the incident of Man—a form wherein the incident life flows on for a time, while behind it all the streaming horizons of geological and stellar histories pile up in the light-world of our eyes" (quoted in afterword, p. 605).

30. Author's note to the 1965 reprint of Blish, *A Clash of Cymbals* (1956; London Faber & Faber, 1965), pp. 5–6.

31. Virginia Kidd writes (letter to Ketterer, 22 February 1984) with regard to *The Triumph of Time:* "I may have written one full short chapter, and some other bits and pieces. . . . I was responsible for pointing him toward the characterization of Dee, who was his mother grown old, for instance." In a subsequent letter (26 March 1984) she elaborates:

> I don't think I would be out of order in saying that all the descriptions of Dee and some of the interactions with her . . . for instance, the stretch on page 20 of the 1958 Avon edition beginning "There was surely no other ex-Okie on New Earth who might be able to understand Amalfi's present state of mind, but Hazleton was not at the moment giving a very good demonstration of this," to upper-midpage on page 25 ending ". . . and the evening in Hazleton's house ended with a stiff formality which, cold though it was, was far from the worst that Amalfi had expected . . .", were (2) my revision of (1) Jim's sketchy indication and then (3) his running my revision through the typewriter one more time.
>
> Beginning upper-midpage on page 25, however, to the end of the chapter on page 27, is either all mine, or mine up to the very last sentence or up to midpage on page 26 (where the "instead, it rained" sounds so much like Jim that I think he must have written it . . . whether that phrase or that line or from there to the end of the chapter, I honestly can't tell you).
>
> I do know for a fact that I wrote (p. 25) "The whole of the residential area to Amalfi's eyes swarmed with pets," through to (p. 26) "What time-wasting quirk had moved so many pioneers' descendants to adopt the damnable svengalis as pets was beyond Amalfi," and it was subject to no alteration afterwards.
>
> I wrote Chapter Four," Fabr-Suithe," from its beginning on p. 65 to p. 78 through "'What I suggest is this,' Estelle's father's voice said, way up in the middle of the air." Jim may have introduced a word or two in the course of that chapter but the whole liars' game was my invention, and it was fun. I remember that Jim picked it up at the "thermodynamic crossover" and that "getting rid of Planck's Constant" had to have been his because I couldn't handle it. Not my kind of line at all!

See *Cities in Flight,* pp. 480–86, 519–30.

32. "Blish, van Vogt, and the Uses of Spengler," p. 177.

33. If there is ever a new edition of *Cities in Flight* the following corrections should be made in book 4: "3948" (p. 475) should be "3998," "3944" (p. 480) should be "3994," "3995 (p. 488) should be "4095," "a century and a half ago" (p. 494) should be something like "a little over a century and a half ago" "seventy-five years into the next millennium" (p. 499) should be "ninety-five years into the next century," "one hundred and fifty" (p. 501) should be "two hundred and fifty," "end of the Third Millennium" (p. 512) should be "beginning of the Fourth Millennium," "seven centuries" (p. 548) should be "eight centuries," and the title of chapter 6, "Object 4001—Alephnull" (p. 551) should be

"Object 4101—Alephnull." In 1968 Blish received an errata list for *The Triumph of Time* in its *A Clash of Cymbals* (1959) version from Stuart Gilbert. Blish was delighted to discover, by Gilbert's own admission, that the author of *James Joyce's "Ulysses"* was also a Blish fan (CM 51).

34. Shackley writes (letter to Ketterer, 9 August 1984), "I think the chronological contradictions in *Cities in Flight* stem from one problem: *Earthman, Come Home*, while giving no dates, clearly makes references that set it well over 2,000 years in the future. Jim wanted *Time* to *Triumph* in 4004 A.D. because of Bishop Ussher's Creation Date. . . . This had the effect of compressing the whole Okie history so that, e.g., an event that happened before Amalfi's birth according to *Earthman, Come Home* happens after it according to the eventual chronology. I think this problem is insurmountable and is certainly not solved merely by changing 4004 to 4104." Gregory Feeley points to a similar sort of chronological problem in the published extracts from "King Log." See Feeley, "The Unglimpsed Reign of King Log," *Vector,* no. 120 (June 1984): 14–21; and pp. 232–36 herein.

35. I am grateful to Shackley (letter to Ketterer, 9 August 1984) for alerting me to this progression.

36. Shackley points out (letter to Ketterer, 9 August 1984) that "*The Triumph of Time* contains a *triple* coincidence about anti-matter: simultaneously, Hevians discover the anti-matter universe, New Earthmen experiment with anti-matter and Herculeans use matter-antimatter interaction as a weapon (and also perhaps as a means of propulsion). It would obviously be the Herculeans' mastery of anti-matter that enables them to transmit information thru the Ginnungagap." However, the history of science bears testimony to many such coincidences.

37. P. 557. Robert A. W. Lowndes writes (letter to Ketterer, 16 June 1984), "The two lines of poetry are from a long poem, "The Folded and the Quiet," by Henry Sostman. . . . Jim published it in *Tumbrils,*" no. 2 (June 1945): 5–11. Sostman, a physicist, was a college roommate of Blish's and later a friend in New York. *Welcome to Mars* is dedicated to the son, Dirk Sostman, who is now a physician working at the Yale Medical School (along with Elisabeth Blish, and Gregory Feeley who provided me with this information).

38. Author's note to *A Clash of Cymbals,* pp. 5–6.

39. P. 574. Cp. the following passage from Blish's unpublished work, "The Sense of Music": "In information theory, the end result [of entropy] is called 'noise.' (Milton sensed this; his image for Chaos is 'the dismal universal hiss,' a complete rebellion against the earlier concept of 'the music of the spheres.' The Miltonian hiss is precisely what all stellar and black-body radiation sounds like if it is converted into audible sound waves.)"

40. P. 588. Paul Shackley writes (letter to Ketterer, 29 July 1984), "I argued and Jim agreed that it was an unacceptable coincidence that . . . the only two races to reach the Metagalactic Centre before the Ginnungagap had originated from the same galaxy. He suggested this could be changed when the book was eventually filmed."

41. Paul Shackley writes (letter to Ketterer, 29 July 1984), "Jim wanted to find a way of using this conception [umbilical cords as bridges] in a story."

42. *Year 2018!* (New York: Avon Publications, Inc., 1957), p. 159.

43. John Feather, writing to *Foundation* editor David Pringle (22 October 1984), takes a skeptical view of all this and proposes an alternative anagram "which has the advantage of using not only the letters present but also the punctuation" (but one which I, nevertheless, find unlikely): A SOLEMN F--- FARCE.

Chapter 7

1. Brian Aldiss recalls (letter to Ketterer, 28 July 1982) that "I was with him [Blish] and Judy when our mutual publisher, Charles Monteith[,] escorted us around All Souls and brought Jim before Bacon's statue. Jim sank down, half in comedy, and said in his surgeon-sore voice, 'And to think that I had the damned nerve . . . the damned nerve . . .' He could not complete the sentence. He chuckled instead." A letter in one of Charles Monteith's files (CM 51) indicates that Blish wanted to use a photograph of this statue for the jacket of *Doctor Mirabilis*.

2. Letter from Blish to Philip K. Dick (13 June 1964), which continues: "It is my notion that if I am going to write about the crucial ideas in the history of science, I ought not to rule out the malign ones; in this case, what I'll be talking about is the invention of the security system for technical information, which our charming Venetian friends were inaugurating during the same period that they invented the ghetto. I've got about 10,000 words on this, plus about 10 pp. of outline, and it moves very slowly—even when I'm working on it" (Dep. Blish 415/10). In a letter to Charles Monteith Blish reveals that the title of the "Venetian novel" is to be "Glass Night": "This will be about the death by petrification of the Venetian Republic, circa 1501, which I think I can show was a crucial event in the history of science as well as in politics" (CM 84, 2 May 1969). Gregory Feeley writes (letter to Ketterer, 6 October 1983) that he gathered from an interview with Robert A. W. Lowndes (19 February 1983) that Blish had expressed a desire to write a novel about Venice in the style of Tiffany Thayer's historical novels. In what is essentially a fan letter (10 July 1956) to Thayer (a founder and Secretary of the Fortean Society, whereby they first met) Blish refers to "our desultory Fortean correspondence while I was in the Army 1942–44" and raves about two of Thayer's novels: *Mona Lisa* and *The Prince of Taranto* (Dep. Blish 434/2).

3. *Doctor Mirabilis* (New York: Dodd, Mead & Company, 1971), p. ix. Subsequent parenthetical page references are to this edition. Lutz's study of Bacon appeared in *Franciscan Studies* (New York: The Franciscan Institute of St. Bonaventure University, 1936): 1–76.

4. "The Shadowy Figure of Roger Bacon," *Science World* 5 (April 1959): 11–12.

5. "The Invention of Science," in *Adventures in Discovery*, ed. Tom Purdom (New York: Doubleday, 1969), p. 55.

6. "The Strange Career of Doctor Mirabilis," *Australian SF Review*, no. 6 (January 1967): 23.

7. See Dep. Blish 406/ld. Blish kept four separate scrapbooks of reviews for the works that he valued most highly. See Dep. Blish 406/la-d: (a) *A Case of Conscience* (twenty-eight leaves of reviews), (b) *Black Easter* and *The Day After Judgment* (thirty-three leaves), (c) *Cities in Flight* (twenty-six leaves), (d) *Doctor Mirabilis* (twenty-six leaves).

8. *The Issue at Hand* (Chicago: Advent, 1964), p. 119.

9. Letter from Aldiss to Ketterer, 28 July 1982.

10. Dep. Blish 416/3 contains correspondence relating to *Doctor Mirabilis*. Included is a reproduction of that famous print, attributed to Camille Flammarion, of a monk poking his head through the Ptolemaic universe.

11. "The Strange Career of Doctor Mirabilis," p. 24.

12. In addition, at Paul Shackley's urging, Blish added the word "contingent" to a statement of Roger's making it "everything that is contingent comes from something . . ." (p. 121). Shackley explains (letter to Gregory Feeley, 21 March 1984) that the previous "everything that is comes from nothing" contradicts the immediately following reference

to "that one thing [God] which comes from nothing" (p. 121). I am grateful to Gregory Feeley for providing me with a copy of Shackley's letter.

13. An English paperback edition was published by Panther Books in 1976, an American one by Avon Books in 1982. This and other misfortunes of textual transmission are noted in Gregory Feeley, "Correcting the Record on Blish," *Foundation*, no. 29 (November 1983): 52–59.

14. The Miracle play dialogue which is quoted (p. 34) as a sample of the material that Roger had swotted up is a somewhat unnecessary addition that Blish inserted for the Dodd, Mead & Company text.

15. See the three charts following the text of vol. 1 of Oswald Spengler, *The Decline of the West*, 2 vols. trans. Charles Francis Atkinson (London: George Allen & Unwin Ltd., 1926).

16. P. 67. In a paragraph summarizing the contents of the finished book is a reference in the English edition to "the pearls of Paracelsus." See *Doctor Mirabilis* (St. Albans: Panther Books, 1964), p. 82. Robert Silverberg notes in a perceptive review in *Amazing Stories* 39 (March 1965): 123–24, that this reference is anachronistic. Paracelsus's dates are 1493–1541. In the Dodd, Mead edition the error is corrected and only the word "pearls" appears (p. 75).

17. Here and elsewhere Gregory Feeley (letter to Ketterer, 25 September 1986) has discovered the influence of the erudite and eccentric English novelist and historian Frederick Rolfe. His *Don Tarquinio* (1905) "includes such elements used by Blish as Bacon's four stumbling blocks to truth" and *Hubert's Arthur* (1935) contains other correspondences with *Doctor Mirablilis*, "including the setting, the character of Hubert de Burgh, and the image (important to Blish) of Matthew Paris the historian. It also uses several unusual terms which are translated in footnotes from the Latin; one of them is 'flocculent.'" Rolfe's "writings about Venice during the Borgian Pontificate, specifically his *Chronicles of the House of Borgia* [1901] and *Don Tarquinio*" probably inspired "Blish's unfinished Venetian novel." See also the possible allusion to Rolfe's *Hadrian the Seventh* (1904) in *A Case of Conscience*, noted on p. 89 herein.

18. "The Shadowy Figure of Roger Bacon," p. 12.

19. Ibid., p. 13, for the illustration. See also "The Invention of Science," pp. 47–60.

20. *Amazing Stories* 39 (March 1965): 123–24. There is a contradiction to be noted in Silverberg's own review. After maintaining that whenever the book "veers from Roger it dissolves into gray haze," Silverberg concludes with the assertion that Blish grasps the age better than the man (except for the last two chapters).

Chapter 8

1. *Cities in Flight* (New York: Avon Books, 1970), p. 36. Subsequent parenthetical page references are to this edition.

2. Aldiss, "Blish and the Mathematics of Knowledge," in *The Stellar Gauge: Essays on Science Fiction Writers*, ed. Michael J. Tolley and Kirpal Singh (Carlton, Victoria: Nostrilia Press, 1980), p. 141. On the same page Aldiss draws attention to the "cascade of figures" in *A Torrent of Faces*.

3. In "Some Fictional Descendents of Carroll," *Jabberwocky*, no. 3 (March 1970): 6–8, Blish adduces *Finnegans Wake*, Cabell's *The Nightmare Has Triplets* (1934–37), and the story on which he and Lowndes collaborated (which makes use of Carroll's *The Hunting of the Snark*), "Chaos, Co-ordinated."

4. Blish, "The Mathematical Story," *Science Fiction Quarterly* 1 (August 1951): 83–86. Although Elisabeth Blish inherited something of her father's love of math, she was

intimidated by her "notion [gleaned from *The Star Dwellers*] that my father believed any teen-ager with half a brain ought to soak up calculus like a sponge in water." See Elisabeth Blish, introduction to James Blish, *Mission to the Heart Stars* (New York: Avon Books, 1982), p. 7.

5. "FYI," in *Beyond This Horizon: An Anthology of Science Fiction and Science Fact* (Sunderland, U.K.: Ceolfrith Press, 1973), p. 123. Subsequent parenthetical page references are to this text. "FYI" had previously been published three times: in *Star Science Fiction*, no. 2 (New York: Ballantine Books, 1953); in Blish, *So Close to Home* (New York: Ballantine Books, 1961); and in *The Mathematical Magpie*, ed. Clifton Fadiman (New York: Simon and Schuster, 1962). In an unpublished introductory note to the story intended for *So Close to Home,* Blish presents himself, by way of a characteristically mathematical analogy, as a "tetrahedron—Clinical, Fanciful, Rough and Tumble, and P. G. [Wodehouse] Dunsany Blish (the author of the present offering)" (Dep. Blish 393/1).

6. "Common Time," in the paperback edition of the 1973 *Best Science Fiction Stories of James Blish* entitled *The Testament of Andros* (London: Arrow Books, 1977), p. 84. Subsequent parenthetical page references are to this text. "Common Time" was first published in *Science Fiction Quarterly* 2 (August 1953). The story is included in Blish's *Galactic Cluster* (1959) and both editions of *Best Science Fiction Stories of James Blish* (1965, 1973).

7. Knight, chapter 26, "Symbolism," in the revised *In Search of Wonder: Essays on Modern Science Fiction* (1956; Chicago: Advent, 1967), pp. 268–73. This material was originally published in *Science Fiction Forum,* no. 1 (1957). Knight notes that as a result of the ensuing discussion, he challenged del Rey (fellow editor of *Forum*) to show that "Common Time" is "really about a man eating a ham sandwich on rye—and he did it" (p. 265).

8. Ibid., p. 273. David I. Masson, however, deduces the notion of "radiating hollows" (as applying to Centauri Alpha A and B) from "the twin radioceles" on the basis that "-cele" sounds like the Greek word for "hollow." As for "clinesterton beademung," while Knight (mixing Greek and German) makes a case for the possibility of its being construed as meaning "Blessed are they who snore in bed" (ibid., p. 270), Masson, taking the words as garbled pseudo-German, comes up with "smallest worthiness." See Masson, letter in *Foundation,* no. 14 (September 1978): 49. Masson was responding to Brian Stableford's speculations about possible meanings in a footnote to "The Science Fiction of James Blish, *Foundation,* no. 13 (May 1978): 31. These speculations do not appear in *A Clash of Symbols: The Triumph of James Blish* (1979), the otherwise expanded version of this article.

9. Blish, *Doctor Mirabilis* (New York: Dodd, Mead & Company, 1971), p. 211.

10. "In Conversation: James Blish Talks to Brian Aldiss" (1973), reprinted in Blish, *The Tale That Wags the God,* ed. Cy Chauvin (Chicago: Advent, 1987), p. 181.

11. In heavily revising the two original stories, "Detour to the Stars and "Nor Iron Bars," Blish collapses two separate Centaurus trips so that the one in the sequel story is simply a continuation of the first. Consequently, "Detour to the Stars," or "The Long Way Home," a discarded alternate title (Dep. Blish 440/1—Writing Accounts ledger) has a conclusion which does not appear in the combined "Nor Iron Bars"; the sequel has an opening section (in which Daryon Hammersmith, a character not present in "A Detour to the Stars," is introduced) which is variously cut or redistributed. Thus Hammersmith appears in the first part of the combined story. A repeated mistake concerning who is the first and who is the second officer on the starship should be noted in the combined "Nor Iron Bars."

NOTES TO CHAPTER 8

12. "Beep," in Blish, *Galactic Cluster* (London: A Panther Book, 1980), p. 113. Subsequent parenthetical page references are to this text. The reference to two suns is, of course, a convenient short-hand indication that the planet concerned is not Earth.

13. One of the beep messages, the one relayed from "Lt. T. L. Matthews" to "Earth Bureau" (changed to "Service" in *Quincunx*), concerning "dope-runners" (p. 151), may be the *C.I.D.: Universe* TV script that Blish, in a letter to Paul Shackley, mentions using "in fragmentary form in QUINCUNX" without pointing out that he meant used originally in the "Beep" form of *Quincunx* (PS, 17 January 1975). The generally secretive Service and bureau set-up in both versions may well have some connection with the basic *C.I.D.: Universe* concept (see pp. 112–13 herein).

14. Shackley to Gregory Feeley, 21 March 1984. I am grateful to Gregory Feeley for sending me a copy of this letter.

15. Dep. Blish 431/11. The longer of Shackley's letters have to do with Blish's plans for expanding "Beep." Letters dated 2 June and 27 July 1974 have to do with allowing for free will in *The Quincunx of Time*. Another letter, which deals with time travel, includes an "Appendix Chronology of the Beep." *Quincunx* is dedicated "to PAUL SHACKLEY who reads my stories far more closely than I (sometimes) think they deserve." Shackley was to have written a book on Blish (with Blish's assistance) and Blish (who had instigated and encouraged this project) suggested Alexie Panshin's *Heinlein in Dimension* (1968) as a model (PS, 30 June 1970). In *More Issues At Hand* (Chicago: Advent, 1970), p. 40, Atheling extravagantly describes Panshin's book (to which Blish had written a preface) as "criticism of the highest order." Blish provided Shackley with a mass of critically useful information but in 1974, at Shackley's instigation, the project was abandoned.

16. *The Quincunx of Time*, with an introduction by Brian Aldiss (1973; New York: Avon Books, 1983), p. 12. Subsequent parenthetical page references are to this edition. Note that the "Critical Preface" is dated 1970. *Quincunx*, although published after *Midsummer Century*, was written around the same time as *Midsummer Century*. In a letter to Blish, Karin Laflin Adams refers to his use of Cabellian names in *Quincunx* (Dep. Blish 411/1). Thus in Dana's reference to "Mars or Storisende or Erskine" (p. 77), a passage which is not in "Beep," "Storisende" is the Cabellian name. "Erskine," a name which does occur in "Beep," is most probably an allusion to Thomas Erskine, an English writer of mainly religious texts, whose anonymously published satires, *Armata: A Fragment* (1816) and *The Second Part of Armata* (1817), describe an English society on a twin planet attached to Earth's South Pole.

17. Robert A. W. Lowndes sees more of a basic difference between the two versions than I do to judge from his assertion that *Quincunx* presents Blish's "afterthoughts to the theme of 'Beep,' which is a strict exploration of a rigidly deterministic universe." See "Introduction: Science Fiction the Hard Way," in *The Best of James Blish*, ed. Lowndes (New York: Ballantine Books, 1979), p. xviii.

18. Cp. *Macbeth:*

> Banquo: If you can look into the seeds of time
> And say which grain will grow and which will not
> Speak then to me. . .   (act 1, sc.3, ll. 58–59)

I am grateful to Gregory Feeley for alerting me to this parallel. It gains force from the fact that in 1963 Blish played Banquo in an amateur production of *Macbeth* (see p. 18 herein). Incidentally, the reference to "a New Dynasty poet named George Macbeth" is not a Shakespearean allusion (p. 45). George Macbeth is a Scottish poet who was associated with the British New Wave in SF. He gets a favorable mention in Blish's review of *Holding Your Eight Hands: An Anthology of SF Verse* in *The Magazine of Fantasy & Science Fiction* 38 (April 1970): 48–53.

19. Characterizing *Quincunx* as "a clever bag of tricks," Aldiss also makes the following point: "Noise is information in disguise, Blish tells us. To ram the notion home, he has two people in disguise, plus a popular song also disguised. And free will disguised as rigid determinism" (p. 8).

20. Cp. "when Marty had found him installing a new knob labelled 'SYM' on the panel, Hammerkein had explained that it didn't do anything, it was just a fifth knob to go on the left side because there were five on the right; the abbreviation stood for 'Symmetry.'" See Blish, *VOR* (New York: Avon Books, 1958), pp. 12–13.

21. In a damning review, Brian Stableford draws attention to the same expanded detail. He goes on to point out that bad sentences remain in both versions, as for example, "He felt as though copper-colored flames a foot long were shooting out of each of his ears" ("Beep," p. 140; *Quincunx,* p. 73). Why, wonders Stableford, are the flames not two feet high in the new version "in keeping with the general policy of expansion." See "'Beep' × 2 = *Quincunx*," *Foundation,* no. 9 (November 1975): 104–105.

22. The first additional word derives from an imaginary place named "Vwopdingdorp" for which Blish as a child wrote a national anthem. It is quoted in "A Science-Fiction Coming of Age," in *The Tale That Wags the God,* p. 144. On hearing the message, Dana remarks, "I suppose it's whatever has happened to the English language—or some other language—thousands of years from now" (p. 92). Walter E. Meyers comments, "Despite this promising hint (the character is mistaken in this particular case), there is no change whatsoever in the English of any message quoted in the book though the characters intercept, and we read, communications dating from 2091, 2973, 3480, 6500, and even 8873." See Meyers, *Aliens and Linguists: Language Study and Science Fiction* (Athens: The University of Georgia Press, 1980), p. 22. Aside from the fact that Meyers's fourth date does not appear in Blish's text, his general criticism is not quite fair. Weinbaum explains that the temporarily most distant message is comprehensible because it is "in a mathematical language that's universal even now" (p. 99).

23. Judith Blish to Ketterer, 10 February 1983. According to the third of Blish's "Writing Accounts" (ledgers listing his stories with sums paid for them), Avon Books paid a $4,000 advance for "King Log" (Dept. Blish 440/3). Blish wrote Paul Shackley, "To my astonishment 'Darkside Crossing' got a Nebula nomination, although only two people voted for it, the other one being me!" (PS, 17 January 1975). "Darkside Crossing" was reprinted in *The Best from Galaxy,* vol. I (New York: Award Books, 1972). The other two members of the "King Log" story trilogy have not been reprinted. At one point, to judge from the publications page of the final "Sense of Music" manuscript, Blish conceived of the completed "King Log" as a novel trilogy.

24. Until further notice, all parenthetical page references are to "The City That Was the World," *Galaxy* 28 (July 1969): 69–97; "Darkside Crossing" (DC), *Galaxy* 31 (December 1970): 5–25; or "Our Binary Brothers" (OBB), *Galaxy* 28 (February 1969): 122–30.

25. Blish writes, "I find to my surprise that I have written four time-travel stories: two very early ones, 'The Solar Comedy' and 'Weapon Out of Time,' neither one any good; a collaboration with Damon Knight . . . 'No Winter, No Summer' which is a fair story; and the very recent 'The City That Was the World' which I quite like" (PS, 30 June 1970).

26. It will be recalled that the protagonist in the also somewhat autobiographical "The Book of Your Life" (1955) is also interested in pornography (see p. 112 herein). Gregory

Feeley informs me that Josephine Saxton has in her possession a six- or seven-page manuscript by Blish entitled "Guide to Pornographic Men's Clubs in London" (telephone conversation, 10 October 1986). Was this a commissioned item, or perhaps one of a series of commissioned items, that appeared anonymously or under a pseudonym in some sexually oriented English publication?

27. Cp. the antitechnology bent here and in "The City That Was the World" with that displayed in Blish's last published story (written with L. Jerome Stanton), "The Glitch," *Galaxy* 35 (June 1974): 100–109.

28. Judith Blish to Ketterer, 10 February 1983.

29. Feeley, "The Unglimpsed Reign of King Log," *Vector*, no. 120 (June 1984): 14–21.

30. *The Magazine of Fantasy & Science Fiction* 42 (April 1972): 5. A diagrammatic key for Judith Blish's cover (reproduced on p. 238 herein) is provided on p. 144. In a loop beginning clockwise from the center may be identified: (1) Blish; (2) Amalfi, his city in flight, and the Vegan orbital fort; (3) Ruiz Sanchez, the Message Tree, and a Lithian from *A Case of Conscience;* (4) Kit Kennedy, Manalendi, and a dinosaur from *The Night Shapes;* (5) the droplet world of "Surface Tension"; (6) Ulla Hillstrom and a flying cloak from "How Beautiful with Banners"; (7) a dune-cat from "No Jokes on Mars" and *Welcome to Mars;* (8) a Triton from *A Torrent of Faces* (here the loop turns); (9) *VOR;* (10) the *Enterprise* from *Star Trek;* (11) Jupiter from "Bridge"; (12) a Hugo escaping from the world of "We All Die Naked"; (13) Roger Bacon from *Doctor Mirabilis;* (14) the werewolf from "There Shall Be No Darkness"; (15) Danny Caiden ascending the sigma sequence from *Jack of Eagles;* (16) the magician Theron Ware from *Black Easter;* (17) the demon Put Satanachia from *The Day After Judgment;* and (18) Kalki, the Silver Stallion, from the works of James Branch Cabell.

31. Mentioning *Midsummer Century* as an example, Blish told Paul Walker, "In recent years I've been paring my style a lot, trying to get the story down to its essentials." See Walker, *Speaking of Science Fiction: The Paul Walker Interviews* (Oradell, N.J.: Luna Publications, 1978), p. 234. The interview was conducted in February 1972. Elsewhere, Blish dates his stylistic preference for paring things down to the bone from "early in 1963." See Blish, "Trilogy as Trinity," *Warhoon* 23 (May 1968): 16.

32. *Midsummer Century* (New York: Doubleday & Company, Inc., 1972), p. 4. Subsequent parenthetical page references are to this edition. The book is somewhat longer than the preceding magazine version.

33. Of particular relevance is one of Dr. John H. Clark's articles: "A New Map of the Mind," *Pulse* (31 July 1971): 12–13, reprinted in *Foundation,* no. 2 (June 1972): 24–29. Clark, then a senior lecturer in psychology at the University of Manchester, describes a three-dimensional solution to the problem of mysticism and a seven-stage process: orientation, concentration, meditation, contemplation, the void, re-emergence, and return. In addition to the *Pulse* version of this article and eight letters to Blish from Clark written between 20 October 1949 and 26 August 1964, Dep. Blish 414/13 contains a revised version in typescript of Clark's already published "Into the Labyrinth of the Mind," *Pulse* (10 October 1970), and a couple of other related articles. It should be noted that chapter 7 of *The Quincunx of Time* begins with an epigraph about the Zen state, or Void, taken from one of Clark's articles.

34. Stableford, *A Clash of Symbols: The Triumph of James Blish* (San Bernadino, Cal.: The Borgo Press, 1979), p. 46.

35. A martel, of course, is a hammer, a meaning which Blish picks up when he refers to a contest between Martels and the Qvant with "neither knowing which was hammer and which was anvil" (p. 69).

36. Masson, "Up the Jungle Down the Aeons," *Foundation*, nos. 7 and 8 (March 1975): 182. Most of the nits Masson picks (how does Martels remain conscious and sane under such sensory deprivation? how can his characteristic voice be reproduced when he has no pharynx? how did the birds construct the tower?) are of negligible importance if Blish's description of the work as "phantasy adventure" is acceptable. True, Blish does overestimate the import of Martels's lower-class accent when he claims that it would "deny him admittance to any but the public side—never the lounge or saloon—of his bar in Britain" (p. 4). Masson also objects, weakly it seems to me, to the word "juganity" and the numbers "Qvant," "Quinx," and "Sixt" on the grounds of linguistic probability. Ibid., pp. 183–84.

37. I am grateful to Josephine Saxton for allowing me to examine this material.

38. Blish lists the eight questions on a separate sheet: (1) "Cosmogony: the problem of First Cause"; (2) "Ontology: the problem of being"; (3) "Metaphysics: What is the nature of reality?"; (4) "Epistemology: How do we know what we know?"; (5) "Aesthetics: What is the nature of beauty?"; (6) "Ethics: The problem of right action"; (7) "Eschatology: The problem of destination"; and (8) "Teleology: What is the purpose of things?"

39. See Blish, "Pluto and Beyond," *Thrilling Wonder Stories* 40 (August 1952): 48–51. This is the eighth of ten "Our Inhabited Universe" articles which appeared in *Thrilling Wonder Stories* between June 1951 and December 1952.

Chapter 9

1. Judith Blish to Ketterer, 10 February 1983.

2. *Star Trek 5* (New York: Bantam Books, 1972), p. vii. The script writers for *Star Trek* and *C.I.D.: Universe* should be included with Blish's other collaborators on one or more projects: Judith Blish (one story, plus, with her mother, *Star Trek* work), Virginia Kidd (two stories plus contributions to two or more novels), Damon Knight (five stories), Norman L. Knight (one novel), Robert A. W. Lowndes (one story plus one non-commercial, non-SF piece [Lowndes to Ketterer, 9 March 1983] and one novel derived from an unpublished story), Josephine Saxton (an unfinished novel), Phil Barnhart (one story), and L. Jerome Stanton (one story).

3. *A Clash of Symbols: The Triumph of James Blish* (San Bernardino, Cal.: The Borgo Press, 1979), p. 48. Stableford cites as examples the *Star Trek* original *Spock Must Die!*, *Midsummer Century*, and "Getting Along."

4. The first juvenile that Blish wrote may have been the unpublished "The Magic Hammer." Virginia Kidd writes: "I do not know what year *The Magic Hammer* was written, but I would guess it was when Beth was six and Ben four or in that general timeframe. Roughly 1960. That could be off by several years" (Kidd to Ketterer, 25 September 1984). It is about a "kindly . . . archaeologist (and a father-figure)" who invites a "little boy to come on a journey with him, [and] hands the child a magic hammer as the means of travel. Each time the child taps the ground with it, they are transported a geological age further in or back, depending on how you look at it. . . . (I don't remember the little boy's name, but I do remember that the story begins by saying that he lived in the middle of his family.) The book was quite short and would have stood or fallen on the strength of the illustrations—which he [Blish] only indicated but made no attempt to draw" (Kidd to Ketterer, 11 September 1984).

5. *The Star Dwellers* (New York: Avon Books, 1982), p. 5. Subsequent parenthetical page references are to this edition. Blish's agent, Kenneth S. White, in a letter to Putnam's (21 March 1960) refers to this novel by an earlier title, "The Long Arc" (Dep. Blish 398/3).

NOTES TO CHAPTER 9

What is presumably an analogue for this term for a spaceflight path, "The Long Fall," figures as the title of chapter 5 of the sequel, *Mission to the Heart Stars*. It should be noted that only Putnam's first edition of *The Star Dwellers* includes a dedication to Blish's two children.

6. *Mission to the Heart Stars*, with an introduction by Elisabeth Blish (New York: Avon Books, 1982), p. 12. Subsequent parenthetical page references are to this edition. A letter to Charles Monteith (12 November 1964) in which mention is made of a sequel to *The Star Dwellers* entitled "Journey to the Seedling Stars" indicates that the title actually used was a late second thought on Blish's part (CM 51).

7. Palinurus, it is inaccurately stated, "was Ulysses' helmsman" (p. 58). He was actually Aeneas's. A Faber & Faber reader noted this mistake (PdS 120).

8. *Mission to the Heart Stars*, pp. 17–19. See *Cities in Flight* (New York: Avon Books, 1970), pp. 119–20. Cp. also the history of Mars in chapter 12 of *The Frozen Year*, a book published the year after *They Shall Have Stars* (1956).

9. See chapter 5, "Death and the Beloved: Algis Budrys and the Great Theme," in William Atheling, Jr., *More Issues at Hand* (Chicago: Advent, 1970), pp. 59–66.

10. *Welcome to Mars* (New York: Avon Books, 1983), pp. 155, 156. Subsequent parenthetical page references are to this edition. On the basis of Blish's headnote in *Anywhen* to "No Jokes on Mars," Gregory Feeley asserts that Blish "did not choose" the Faber & Faber 1967 and Putnam's 1968 change of title to *Welcome to Mars!* See "Correcting the Record on Blish," *Foundation*, no. 29 (November 1983): 55. In fact the *Anywhen* introduction does not support his assertion; it simply notes the two titles. The magazine title, "The Hour Before Earthrise," *If* 16 (July, Aug., Sept., 1966), is certainly more poetic; but the present book title (with or without the exclamation mark which the 1978 Sphere reprint and the current Avon edition drop) is punchier, more informative, and derives directly (without the exclamation mark) from the novel's final words (p. 153). The screenplay which Blish wrote, based on this work, is also entitled *Welcome to Mars*.

11. Paul Shackley writes (letter to Ketterer, 9 August 1984) that the proposed film version "would have begun by mentioning the Apollo moon landing but then said that government-sponsored manned spaceflight was discontinued."

12. According to Shackley (letter to Ketterer, 9 August 1984), in the film version, "The heroine would have become pregnant and given birth on Mars. Jim described some scenes which were written, then cut for length reasons—masses being sung on Earth while the children's air was believed to be running out on Mars; one country (I think China) testing an antigravity device that backfires and goes downwards while agents of another country (I think Japan) photograph it."

13. *A Case of Conscience* (London: Arrow Books), p. 199; the phrase provides the title of the first section of *The Day After Judgment*.

14. The discussion that Blish had with Suvin regarding the popularity of "Surface Tension" is recalled in Blish's "Aristotelean Spheres," *Seldon's Plan* 40 (September 1976): 48–50, which is Cy Chauvin's combination of two Blish letters, the first from *Speculation* (Spring 1973) and the second from *Cypher* (May 1974); and again in "The Pantropy Series: Introduction by James and Judith Blish," in *The Great Science Fiction Series*, ed., Frederik Pohl, Martin Harry Greenberg, and Joseph Olander (New York: Harper & Row, 1980), pp. 112–13.

15. Cp. *Cities in Flight*, p. 129.

16. "Nor Iron Bars," in Blish, *Galactic Cluster* (New York: The New American Library, Inc., 1959), p. 90.

17. *A Case of Conscience*, p. 100.

NOTES TO CHAPTER 9

18. Ibid., p. 93; "A Case of Conscience," *If* 2 (September 1953): 117.
19. "This Earth of Hours," in *Galactic Cluster*, p. 173.
20. *The Star Dwellers* (New York: Avon Books, 1982), p. 34.
21. "A Dusk of Idols," in Blish, *Anywhen* (New York: Avon Books, 1983), pp. 87, 91.
22. *Mission to the Heart Stars* (New York: Avon Books, 1982), pp. 43, 44, 103.
23. Headnote to "No Jokes on Mars," in *Anywhen,* p. 119.
24. *The Quincunx of Time* (New York: Avon Books, 1983), p. 61.
25. Ibid., pp. 97, 57.
26. PS, 23 June 1970; *The Quincunx of Time,* p. 85; "Beep," in *Galactic Cluster,* p. 150.
27. *Midsummer Century* (New York: Doubleday & Co., 1972), p. 90.
28. *The Quincunx of Time,* p. 95.
29. *Cities in Flight,* p. 89.
30. *The Vanished Jet* (New York: Weybright & Talley, 1968), p. 1. Subsequent page references are to this text, the only edition. The jacket design—a blank cut out of the plane superimposed on a portion of the Earth as viewed from the stratosphere—is by Judith Lawrence. The manuscript had been rejected by Faber & Faber in 1967 on the basis of its being thin and unoriginal, and Blish's foisting his political views (an anti-Arab position?) on juveniles (CM 51). There would seem to be no basis for Raymond J. Wilson III's speculation that *The Vanished Jet* was an unpublished manuscript from early in Blish's career. See "James Blish (1921–1975)," in *Part 1: A–L, Twentieth-Century American Science-Fiction Writers,* ed. David Cowart and Thomas L. Wymer (Detroit: Gale Research Company, 1981), p. 52. Judith Blish writes (letter to Ketterer, 11 September 1984), "*The Vanished Jet* was written on commission for an editor who was looking for juveniles and was a personal acquaintance; it wasn't based on any old story that I know of." In a letter to Karin Laflin Adams Blish mentions that "for a six-month period in 1968 I was loaned by my pr. agency from my regular account to the Saudi Arabian account" and that much of what he learned as a result got into "a juvenile (non-sf) I was writing at the same time" (KLA, 24 February 1973).
31. P. 62. Cp. this line from Blish's poem "Oryx in Phoenix:" "The new tombs of some Mada'in Salih awaiting an earthquake." While working on the Saudi Arabian account, Blish learned "that King Faisel had given the States a dozen oryx and that they were going to the Phoenix zoo" (KLA, 24 February 1973). In an earlier note to Karin Laflin Adams (who had turned the poem into a serenade), Blish points out that "Oryx in Phoenix" (Adams's home town), first published in the British literary quarterly *Priapus,* no. 19 (Spring 1970), was written about 1966. Blish comments: "Downright eerie to see it turned into a serenade, with so many apposite turns inside, to you, and still retain the quite different feelings it sprang from." During the Blish Memorial Evening (19 February 1976) John Brunner led off his reading of what Judith Blish claimed were Blish's favorites among his own poems with "Oryx in Phoenix" (the others were "Song of the I," which includes some of the famous anagrams in which Galileo concealed his discoveries concerning the planets, "Theory of Right Action," and "Taby Dead"). Brunner concluded his reading with a poem that Blish loved—William Dunbar's "Lament for the Makaris" (c. 1508).
32. *More Issues at Hand,* pp. 59–66. In "The Enemy Within" by Richard Matheson (the sixth episode from *Star Trek*'s first season) a transporter malfunction creates a duplicate Captain Kirk. The story figures in Blish, *Star Trek 8* (New York: Bantam Books, 1972). At the same time Blish claimed, "I stole the whole question [of whether the transporter can transport the soul] from Larry Niven" (PS, 23 June 1970).

NOTES TO CHAPTER 9

33. A related metaphysical question, "What is the shape of the soul?" appears in "A New Totemism," in "Four Fugitive Pieces by James Blish," ed. David Ketterer, *Vector*, no. 120 (June 1984): 11–13; reprinted in *The Tale That Wags the God*, ed. Cy Chauvin (Chicago: Advent, 1987), pp. 67–71. Here Blish asks which artists might best help us to appreciate the human soul, or its equivalent, in alien forms.

34. *Spock Must Die!* (New York: Bantam Books, 1970), pp. 2–3. Subsequent parenthetical page references are to this edition. The third of Blish's "Writing Accounts" ledgers indicates that he received an advance of $3,000 for this book—$1,000 more than the sum he was paid for each of the *Star Trek* collections (Dep. Blish 440/3). The further *Star Trek* novel based on "the two Mudd scripts," that Blish mentions in two letters to Shackley (PS, 22 May 1974, 17 June 1974) was partially completed at the time of Blish's death. It finally appeared as *Mudd's Angels* (New York: Bantam Book, 1978), adapted by J. A. Lawrence and "Dedicated to the Memory of James Blish." It comprises adaptations of the Stephen Kandel scripts "Mudd's Women" (17 October 1966) and "I, Mudd" (3 November 1967) and an original third section by J. A. Lawrence.

35. PS, 23 June 1970. In a letter to Karin Laflin Adams Blish refers to his surprise at the fact his two explanations for the "female passion for Spock" "have not drawn much comment . . . I thought a lot of people would be livid over the racial one" (KLA 12 December 1974).

36. Cp. Blish's "The Box," discussed p. 41 herein.

37. Pp. 91, 111. *The Vanished Jet*, p. 103.

38. Judith Blish mentions this number in a note on a draft of chapter 1 herein.

39. Blish, "Song," *The Hopkins Review* 5 (Autumn 1951): 32.

40. Blish, "In Memoriam: Fletcher Pratt," *The Magazine of Fantasy & Science Fiction* 12 (January 1957): 94.

41. Blish, "Venice Observed, 1969," *Open Places*, no. 11 (January 1972): 12.

42. Robert A. W. Lowndes, "An Index to James Blish's Contributions to the Mailings of the Vanguard Amateur Press Association" (unpublished), pp. 3, 15.

43. Blish specifies the number of sonnets in a 1969 letter to Charles Monteith. Monteith mentions the title of the collection and its rejection in a letter to Blish's English agent, Gerald Pollinger (14 November 1969). Christopher Hudson had harshly characterized the poems in his 12 November 1969 report as "wordy, romantic and ultimately rather colourless" (CM 84). In a letter to Virginia Kidd Blish refers to a poetry collection now entitled "The Building of the City" (Dep. Blish 423/3, 28 April 1957).

44. Blish, "A Prayer for James Joyce," *James Joyce Quarterly* 7 (Summer 1970): 379.

45. Blish, "A Science Fiction Coming of Age," in *The Tale that Wags the God*, p. 155.

46. Ibid., pp. 118–19.

47. Ibid., pp. 119–20.

48. These poems appeared in the mimeographed *Stony Point Workshop*. Virginia Kidd writes (letter to Ketterer, 11 September 1984): "(A group of us, all published poets, met at Sony [Sonya] Dorman's in Stony Point, New York.) Each of us brought a group of poems and we very seriously workshopped them. We had a great time. The nature of the work was such that it was eminently publishable. I was an amateur press publisher from way back and I published a Proceedings. That was the first issue of *Kinesis*." Dorman is a poet and SF writer.

49. Blish, "Serenade for Telephone," *Prairie Schooner* 44 (Summer 1970): 167.

50. Blish, "All Hallows Leave," *Ball State University Forum* 16 (Autumn 1975): 45.

51. The same autumnal image occurs at the end of "A Reprise," *Open Places*, no. 11

(January 1972): 14, where the poet, in response to an "un-augered letter" from his beloved (the "distant breath" of summer competing with winter at the "mail-slit"), proclaims "Let's praise the treacheries by which we are foredone./ Write me down again, leafling, in mirth and applefall."

52. For data on the fifteen "Captain Video" scripts, see note 31 to chapter 1, p. 323 herein. For the twenty-nine-page script of one of the radio plays, "The Gold Frame," see Dep. Blish 393/6. The two Okie film scripts, the property of John Flory of Spacefilms (who had bought the screen rights to the Okie saga, and also has the rights to *Welcome to Mars*), are entitled *A Life for the Stars* and *The Space Witch*. "*A Life for the Stars* would have been the first Okie film, by-passing *They Shall Have Stars*." It "would have contained a romantic interest since 'you can't make a film without one.' This was not Jim's idea but he accepted it" (Shackley to Ketterer, 9 August 1984). "*The Space Witch* was a completely original Okie story. . . . In it, New York docks in a Tortuga-like Okie spaceport run by a woman, the Space Witch. Amalfi loses his city while gambling with the Space Witch and then has the problem of getting the city back" (Shackley to Ketterer, 2 August 1984). Judith Blish writes (letter to Ketterer, 18 August 1983): "The two scripts [Jim] did were not quite the novels—the events of the books were recast, so that the scripts are combinations. They were written between 1962 and 1966, with Mr. Flory in frequent consultation. The intent was that Mr. Flory would produce the films he had bought from various authors upon his retirement, aiming at what was then the SF film market—drive-ins." The opera libretto, "Eros and Psyche," was written around 1966. Until he was advised otherwise, in 1969 Blish entertained the hope that Benjamin Britten might set this libretto to music. According to a brief account of Blish's life prepared by Judith Blish for Charles Monteith, once Blish heard that Benjamin Britten was up for a knighthood, there was no halting his plan to move to England (CM 84). Judith Blish writes of the TV series, "The Man Without a Planet." "This was an outline for a TV series submitted to Krantz Films in 1965 for what they tentatively called 'The Survivors.' There is neither contract nor rejection in the file" (memo to Ketterer, 1 October 1984).

53. Since the papers relating to "The True Faust" (Dep. Blish 426/5—correspondence, notes, and a few pages of drafts) are restricted, my information about this play derives from a telephone conversation with William Morris.

54. Blish, "A True Bill," in *Ten Tomorrows*, ed. Roger Elwood (Greenwich, Conn.: Fawcett Publications, 1973), p. 157. Subsequent parenthetical page references are to this text.

55. William Atheling, Jr., *The Issue at Hand*, ed., with an introduction by James Blish (Chicago: Advent, 1964), pp. 8–9. Subsequent parenthetical page references are to this text. For the correction, see *More Issues at Hand*, p. 8.

56. *More Issues at Hand*, p. 21.

57. In his foreword to "Private Eye" by Lewis Padgett (joint pseudonym of Henry Kuttner and his wife, C. L. Moore), Blish's selection for *The Mirror of Infinity* anthology, he claims that, during their correspondence covering the last ten years of Kuttner's life, he learned more about writing from Kuttner than from any other person. See Robert Silverberg, ed., *The Mirror of Infinity: A Critic's Anthology of Science Fiction* (New York: Harper & Row, 1970), p. 98. It was Kuttner who pointed out the need for more "sensual detail" in Blish's work (KLA, 27 February 1973). As for when and how Blish first made contact with Kuttner: "I was taken for a pen name of Kuttner's, by a fan named Entrekin, in September 1948—a very fortunate mistake, from which emerged my decade of correspondence with Kuttner." See Blish, "Moskowitz on Kuttner," *Riverside Quar-*

terly 5 (February 1972): 143, n3, and the fifteen or so very long letters from Kuttner (Dep. Blish 424/3, 29 September 1948–6 April 1952). *Thirteen O'Clock (and Other Zero Hours)* (1970) is Blish's collection of Kornbluth's "Cecil Corwin" stories.

58. Blish, "Poul Anderson: The Enduring Explosion" (part of a Special Poul Anderson Section), *The Magazine of Fantasy & Science Fiction* 40 (April 1970): 53, 54. Another Anderson story, "Security Risk," is dismissed as a mechanical, clichéd exercise in *More Issues at Hand*, pp. 90–91.

59. *The Magazine of Fantasy & Science Fiction* 5 (November 1953): 101.

60. *More Issues at Hand*, p. 8. Subsequent parenthetical page references are to this text.

61. Pp. 25–28 and 36–39. A regressive tracing of the positive review of Kingsley Amis's *New Maps of Hell* (1960), which also appears in this chapter, reveals that it first appeared in *Xero* and was previously reprinted as part of "SF: The Critical Literature," *SF Horizons*, no. 2 (Winter 1965): 38–48. A complete listing of Blish's attacks on Moskowitz would include the following: "The Future in Books," *Amazing Stories* 42 (June 1968): 135; "The Great Historian," *Australian SF Review*, no. 14 (June 1968): 8; and "Moskowitz on Kuttner," pp. 140–43.

62. *The Issue at Hand*, p. 79.

63. Robert Edward Colbert, "A Case of Conscience: The Literary Criticism of James Blish, *Essays in Arts and Sciences* 9 (August 1980): 255.

64. P. 1. Unless otherwise identified in this discussion of "The Agent as Patient," parenthetical page references are to the manuscript of "Kritike Antikritikos." I am grateful to Cy Chauvin for providing me with a copy of this manuscript, which he had obtained from Judith Blish. While Blish's main title smacks of T. S. Eliot, his subtitle, "Seven Subjects with an Object," is taken from the title of a book projected "some thirty years ago" by "my dedicatee" (p. 7). Since the dedication page is missing, I have not been able to identify the dedicatee.

65. "The Long Night of a Virginia Author," *Journal of Modern Literature* 2 (February 1972): 395, 393. Subsequent parenthetical page references in this and the following paragraph are to this text. One of the correspondence files in the Bodleian Library reveals that Blish had earlier submitted this article to *The Southern Journal*. The editor, Louis Rubin, explains in his rejection letter (21 January 1970) that paralleling one work with another is of less academic interest than a case for direct influence.

66. A listing of Blish's substantive *Kalki* contributions may be found in the "Criticism, Reviews, and Literary Concerns" section of my Primary Bibliography.

67. "Rituals on Ezra Pound," *Sewanee Review* 58 (Spring 1950): 188. Subsequent parenthetical page references in this paragraph are to this text.

68. In a letter published in Bruce Gillespie's Australian fanzine *The Metaphysical Review Seven* (1972?): 10, Blish refers to his presentation copy of the first edition of *The Recognitions* as "one of the most valuable items in my estate when I kick off." Gaddis was a friend of Virginia and James Blish. Thus, in a letter to Charles Monteith (25 May 1959), in which he tries to interest Faber & Faber in publishing *The Recognitions*, Blish is able to report Gaddis's claim never to have read Joyce (CM 51).

69. For Blish's claim that Anthony Burgess's *A Shorter "Finnegans Wake"* augments the feeling that *Finnegans Wake* is a "naturalistic novel," see Blish's positive review, *A Wake Newslitter* 3 (August 1966): 87–89.

70. This and subsequent parenthetical page references in this paragraph are to "Formal Music at the Wake": parts 1, 2, and 3, *A Wake Newslitter* 7, nos. 2, 3, 4 (April, June,

August 1970): 19–27, 35–43, 51–58. Blish first read *Finnegans Wake* as a teenager in 1939, according to *More Issues at Hand*, p. 145.

71. "Kram Revisited," *A Wake Newslitter* 4 (August 1967): 77.

72. *A Wake Newslitter* 8 (December 1971): 91–93.

73. "The Climate of Insult," *Sewanee Review* 80 (Spring 1972): 340.

74. Ibid., p. 346. The Hyman quote became something of a tic. It also crops up in *The Issue at Hand*, p. 28; and in a letter (22 March 1974) reacting to my criticism of Blish's implicitly (albeit unwittingly) rating Budrys's *Rogue Moon* up with Joyce's *Ulysses*. See Ketterer, "*Rite de Passage:* A Reading of *Rogue Moon,*" *Foundation*, no. 5 (January 1974): 56, n3; and Blish letter, *Foundation*, nos. 7 and 8 (March 1975): 155. This may be a symptom of fatigue. Likewise, the reference to the "tension curve" in "Usher" ("The Climate of Insult," p. 342) also occurs in *The Issue at Hand*, p. 14.

75. Lowndes, "Introduction: Science Fiction the Hard Way," *The Best of James Blish*, ed. Lowndes (New York: Ballantine Books, 1979), pp. xiii–xiv. The original or near original title was "The Semantics of Music."

76. Professor Wolfgang Bottenberg of the Department of Music, Concordia University, Montreal, writes, "The basic idea of Blish is absolutely superb, and merits full attention by anyone who wants to have deeper insight into music as a language of communication. . . . The book is almost a revelation to those who seek an answer which can be tested . . . The knowledge of Mr. Blish in music is perfectly sound" (memo to Ketterer, 4 November 1984). Cy Chauvin tells me (letter to Ketterer, 2 September 1986) that he "was able to interest" Serconia Press.

77. Pp. 110, 117; these and ensuing parenthetical page references are to the manuscript, "The Sense of Music."

78. *The Tale That Wags the God*, p. 134.

79. "The label 'gas giant' for a Jupiter-type planet . . . was my own creation," Blish asserts in "Future Recall," in *The Disappearing Future*, ed. George Hay (London: Panther Books, 1970), p. 102. Blish's interest in astronomy, space exploration, and science in general led to his becoming at one time or another a member of the American Rocket Society, the Association of Lunar and Planetary Observers, the British Interplanetary Society, and the History of Science Society (*Contemporary Authors* entry, 1963).

80. "Tiger Ride," *Astounding Science Fiction* 42 (October 1984): 143.

81. "1984 and Beyond," *Playboy* 10 (July 1963): 34.

82. "In Tomorrow's Little Black Bag," in *7th Annual of the Year's Best SF*, ed. Judith Merril (New York: Simon & Schuster, 1962), pp. 304, 307.

83. Judith Blish to Ketterer, 10 February 1983, 18 August 1984.

84. Telephone conversation, 21 February 1983.

Chapter 10

1. Blish to Nicholls, 10 and 12 August 1974. I am grateful to Gregory Feeley for sending me a copy of his copy of this letter and of the lengthy 26 June 1972 Nicholls letter to which Blish was replying, both obtained from Peter Nicholls. In his accompanying letter (14 September 1983) Feeley writes, "Virginia Kidd says that Blish worked on the novel, by then bearing its present title, through the 1950s. It was, she reports, a much fuller text than the one she now has, and she feels the paring that constituted so much of Blish's later artistic method was in this case detrimental."

2. Pollinger relayed this information to Gregory Feeley, who in turn relayed it to me in a letter dated 14 September 1983.

3. An extract from one of Henry Sostman's poems is quoted in *Cities in Flight* (see p. 187 herein).

4. I am grateful to Gregory Feeley for sending me a copy of his copy of 26 pages (including pp. 1–21) of this draft of "Cage" in the possession of Josephine Saxton.

5. Satanic references appear on pp. 7, 90, and 96 of the final manuscript version of "A Cage of Birds." Subsequent parenthetical page references are to this text. I am grateful to Virginia Kidd for allowing me to make a copy of this manuscript.

6. Brunner to Ketterer, 6 October 1984. Brunner, who had first met Blish at an American SF conference in the 1960s, was an admirer of Blish ("one of my personal Top Ten" after "I found 'Let the Finder Beware' ") since reading "Sunken Universe" and "Bindlestiff" in his teens.

7. Saxton to Ketterer, 6 May 1984. Note that the theme of death as a result of misused medication also occurs in "A Cage of Birds."

8. Judith Blish to Ketterer, 10 February 1983.

9. It should be noted that one of the epigraphs to the Faber edition of *Doctor Mirabilis* is taken from *The Worm Ouroboros*. Aside from completing a thematic trilogy, Brian Aldiss observes that *Black . . . Judgment* provides the culminating instance of works by Blish remarkable for the visitations of either devils or angels. Such visitations would include the creatures released in *The Night Shapes* and the angels dancing inside the Greater Coal Sack in *Mission to the Heart Stars,* and embrace the possibility of a demonic Lithia in *A Case of Conscience*. See "Blish and the Mathematics of Knowledge," in *The Stellar Gauge: Essays on Science Fiction Writers,* ed. Michael J. Tolley and Kirpal Singh (Victoria, Australia: Norstrilia Press, 1980), pp. 142–44.

10. "A Science Fiction Coming of Age," in *The Tale That Wags the God,* ed. Cy Chauvin (Chicago: Advent, 1987), p. 165.

11. *"Black Easter" (or "Faust Aleph-Null") including "The Day After Judgement"* (London: Arrow Books Limited, 1981), pp. 12, 27, 14, 16. Subsequent parenthetical page references are to this edition. Gregg Press published a hardcover combined edition in 1980 with an Introduction by David G. Hartwell. *Black Easter* was first published by Doubleday (in the U.S.A.) and Faber & Faber (in the U.K.) in 1968. A shorter version (i.e., without the later written opening section for the book publication entitled "Preparation of the Operator") entitled "Faust Aleph-Null" had been serialized in *If* 17, nos. 8, 9, 10 (August, September, October 1967): 6–24, 106–42, 134–60. ("Aleph-Null," which also occurs in chapter 3 of *A Case of Conscience,* is the first transfinite number. This mystical mathematics associated with Georg Cantor is central to Blish's 1953 story "FYI"; see pp. 220–21 herein.) Blish explained to Charles Monteith that by this, his preferred title, he meant to suggest "Faust One and Faust Two [Theron Ware] and after this Faust no other" (CM 51, 3 October 1967). But Faber & Faber did not like Blish's title and opted instead for the title selected by Doubleday—*Black Easter*. *The Day After Judgment* was first published by Doubleday in 1970 and by Faber & Faber in 1972. A shorter version (i.e., minus the Jack Ginsberg half of the opening section entitled in the book publication "The Wrath-Bearing Tree") had appeared in *Galaxy* 30 (August–September, 1970): 4–68. Blish added titles and epigraphs to what are called "Stations" (i.e., chapters or sections) in the respective book publications of these two works. My combined Arrow edition, however, drops the term "Stations." (A reference to Roger Bacon, incidentally, also occurs in *The Day After Judgment,* p. 154).

12. "A Science Fiction Coming of Age," p. 165. In an "Author's Afterword" Blish

refers to Baines's voicing of this "ancient philosophical question" (p. 210) in *The Day After Judgment:* "A large part of the mystic tradition says that the possession and use of secular knowledge—or even the desire for it—is in itself evil . . ." (p. 171).

13. "A Science Fiction Coming of Age," pp. 168–69; Introduction to *Black Easter/The Day After Judgment* (Boston: Gregg Press, 1981), pp. v–vii.

14. A letter from Phyllis Eisenstein in *If* 18 (January 1968): 161, accused Blish of plagiarizing much of "Faust Aleph-Null" from Waite's *Ceremonial Magic,* a revision of Waite's *The Book of Black Magic and of Pacts* (London: G. Redway, 1898). Blish's unpublished notebook reply reads: "I used the same sources White [sic] did so some duplications are inevitable" (Dep. Blish 437).

15. Pp. 55–56, Arthur Edward Waite, *The Book of Ceremonial Magic* (1898; New York: University Books, 1961), p. 220 (the Triangle), p. 223 (the Circle). Blish informed Charles Monteith that all the figures in the *Black Easter* manuscript were done by Judith Blish (CM 51, 3 October 1967).

16. See Waite, part 2, chapter 4, section 1 (for his names and descriptions of demons), and part 1, chapter 4, section 2 (for his views on black and white magic.).

17. Doubleday had commissioned this work according to Damon Knight, *The Futurians* (New York: John Day, 1977), p. 241.

18. Of the other names in *Black . . . Judgment,* only the baneful Baines has occasioned comment. But in a reply to Ted White's review in *Amazing Stories* 43 (January 1970): 122–25, Blish scotches White's suggestion that Baines was named after the war-mongering President Lyndon (Baines) Johnson. See *Amazing Stories* 43 (July 1970): 137–38. Father Domenico Bruno Garelli was named after Domenico Garelli of Milan, a matter Garelli refers to in a letter to Blish written shortly before Blish's death. This letter, now part of the Blish Papers, may be found in the Letters of Condolence file. The name of a minor character of French ancestry, Dr. Šatvje, is, it is pointed out in *Black . . . Judgment,* "a Serbo-Croat transliteration from the Cyrillic of 'Chatvieux' " (p. 135). Perhaps the Dr. Chatvieux in *The Seedling Stars* (1957) is a descendent of the same family. Blish was concerned with weaving his various fictions into a complex tapestry by means of such subtle links.

19. This sentence is part of the "Preparation of the Operator" section missing from the serial publication of "Faust Aleph-Null" (see n. 11 above). However, the Gray Morrow cover illustration for the issue of *If* which began this serial corresponds exactly to the details of this sentence. Either Morrow had read the absent section, or Blish wrote the sentence to account for Morrow's inspired emblematically microcosmic illustration or, most likely, Blish had given Morrow particular instructions regarding the illustration. As noted earlier (p. 38), the opposition between science and the occult was first explored by Blish in a manner anticipative of *Black . . . Judgment* in "Mistake Inside" (1948).

20. *The Magazine of Fantasy & Science Fiction* 35 (December 1968): 17. Subsequently Russ wrote Blish a letter expanding somewhat on her review (Dep. Blish 431/4, 4 March 1975).

21. Cp. the painting, "The Burning of Los Angeles," with which Nathanael West's *The Day of the Locust* concludes.

22. Cp. William Gaddis, *The Recognitions,* a complex symbolic novel (see pp. 145, 283 herein) which also uses alchemy as a governing structural metaphor.

23. White objected that *Black Easter* was a bloated work, that its characters were stereotyped, and that its resolution was pulled out of a hat. See *Amazing Stories* 43 (July 1970): 122–25. Subsequently White found *The Day After Judgment* to be "a superior book" to *Black Easter* and suggested that the two books should be published as one. See

his reviews in *The WSFA Journal*, no. 77 (June–July 1971): 36–37, and *Amazing Stories* 45 (September 1971): 109–10.

24. *Amazing Stories* 43 (July 1970): 137–38.

25. This paragraph begins a section that only exists in the book publication of *The Day After Judgment* (pp. 122–25; see n. 11 above). Either the section was one of those inspired second thoughts that Blish tried to train himself out of, or he cut it for magazine publication.

26. *A Case of Conscience* (London: Arrow Books, 1972), p. 54; *Doctor Mirabilis* (New York: Dodd, Mead & Company, 1971), pp. 5, 309–10; *Welcome to Mars* (New York: Avon Books, 1983), pp. 32, 67.

27. "After Such Knowledge: James Blish's Tetralogy," in *A Multitude of Visions*, ed. Cy Chauvin (Baltimore: T-K Graphics, 1975), p. 27.

28. Bob Rickard notes (ibid., p. 28) that Blish often sends teams to planets so that arguments can take place and points to the "elaborate four-way-argument" in *A Case of Conscience* as similar to that in *The Day After Judgment*. The quotation is taken from William Atheling, Jr.'s description of *A Case of Conscience* in *The Issue at Hand* (Chicago: Advent, 1964), p. 51. On the subject of fours it will be recalled that *The Seedling Stars* consists of four stories and that *Cities in Flight* comprises four books.

29. *Foundation*, no. 13 (May 1978): 6–12. An article of the same title appeared three decades earlier in the Vanguard Amateur Press Association publication *(. . .)* [*Three Dots*]. Robert A. W. Lowndes writes (letter to Ketterer, 5 May 1984):

> Jim's "Probapossible Prolegomena to Ideareal History," in the first issue of *Three Dots* [September 1948] is a whimsical, mock-scholarly analysis of the arguments pro and con he had with himself and others in Vanguard about the feasibility of putting his mailing reviews (which were frequently quite extensive) into a separate publication, instead of in *Tumbrils,* where they would take up too much space that he could use to better advantage. I cannot be positive, but I do consider it very likely that by the time he wrote the article of the same title for *Foundation* he had completely forgotten having used that title before.

30. "Science in Science Fiction," *Science Fiction Quarterly* 1, nos. 1, 2, 3, 5 (May, August, November 1951; May 1952): 89–91, 83–86, 111–13, 49–53; "The Science in Science Fiction," *Quicksilver,* no. 2 (April 1971): 19–26. See also, Thomas Kuhn, *The Structure of Scientific Revolutions* (Chicago: Univ. of Chicago Press, 1962).

31. "Probapossible Prolegomena," p. 6.

32. Ibid., pp. 9–10. For a case in point see Blish's review of Colin Wilson's *The Occult:* "Eclectic Occultism," *The Spectator* 227 (6 November 1971): 654; and his review-essay concerning four books on demonology and the occult: "James Blish on the Decline of the Supernatural," *The Spectator* 229 (19 August 1972): 286–87. In the latter piece he refers to John W. Campbell's editorship between 1939 and 1943 of the supernatural magazines *Unknown* and *Unknown Worlds* as a "ghost [which] has been hovering over science fiction ever since" (p. 286).

33. "Probapossible Prolegomena," p. 10. See also Blish's "Science Fiction—An Uneasy Marriage," *Book Fair* (Massillon, Ohio: n.p., 1962), and "Think Me To Your Leader," *The Sunday Times Magazine* (22 November 1970), pp. 30–33. In the *Sunday Times* piece on ESP and science fiction Blish claims that science fiction grew out of the supernatural mystery story.

34. *The Issue at Hand*, pp. 54, 56.

NOTES TO CHAPTER 10

35. *A Clash of Symbols: The Triumph of James Blish* (San Bernardino, Cal.: The Borgo Press, 1979), p. 60.

36. David Ketterer, *New Worlds for Old: The Apocalyptic Imagination, Science Fiction, and American Literature* (New York: Doubleday Anchor Press, and Bloomington: Indiana Univ. Press, 1974).

37. David Ketterer, "Death and the Denial of History: The Textual Shadow of the SF Author," *Science-Fiction Studies* 9 (July 1982): 228–30.

38. *A Clash of Symbols,* p. 57. Such "Tuckerisms" are so called because of their prevalence in the work of SF writer Wilson Tucker, Cp. "We All Die Naked," pp. 150–51 herein.

39. In a letter to the Australian critic John Baxter, Blish identifies Selahny as Zelazny (Dep. Blish 411/10).

40. *Against Interpretation* (New York: Farrar, Straus & Giroux, 1966), p. 213.

41. For information about *Tesseract,* see Sam Moskowitz, *The Immortal Storm: A History of Science Fiction Fandom* (1954; rpt., Westport, Conn.: Hyperion Press, Inc., 1974), pp. 63–68, 75, 95, 124, 180–81.

42. In "Trilogy as Trinity," *Warhoon* 23 (May 1968): 13–17, Blish argues for the following shared features in the "After Such Knowledge" novels: (1) an "uncompromising Catholicism" (p. 14), (2) diabolism with Egtverchi as "a grotesque Anti Christ," (3) the immanence of Armageddon, and (4) the character of "theological novels" (p.15). He points to the example provided by Cabell's mixed "Heirs and Assigns" trilogy before concluding that "After Such Knowledge" "as a whole" and "each individual volume, deals simultaneously and successively with the Father of Lies, the Sons of Knowledge, and the Ghost of Unknowing" (p. 17). Blish had more in mind than what he admits is a way of selling three books instead of one. It might further be noted that the work which inspired Blish to write *Doctor Mirabilis* and *Black Easter, The Worm Ouroboros,* is also part of a mixed genre series. Eddison's Zimiamvian trilogy (*The Mezentian Gate* [1958], *A Fish Dinner in Memison* [1941], and *Mistress of Mistresses* [1935]), whose internal chronology reverses that of publication, is set in the heaven of *The Worm Ouroboros.*

43. Cy Chauvin, Preface, *The Tale that Wags the God,* pp. 4–5.

PRIMARY BIBLIOGRAPHY

This chronological bibliography is based on Judith Blish's alphabetical one, now available as "The Works of James Blish" in *The Tale that Wags the God,* ed. Cy Chauvin (Chicago: Advent, 1987), pp. 195–247. It previously circulated in mimeographed form under the title *James Blish: A Bibliography, 1940–1976* (1976). Among additional items, some listed in Robert A. W. Lowndes's unpublished "An Index to James Blish's Contributions to the Mailings of the Vanguard Amateur Press Association" (1979) are incorporated in sections II, V, and VI herein. Only in the interests of accessibility or in cases involving title or other substantive changes have I listed reprintings. For a virtually complete list of reprintings the reader is referred to "The Works of James Blish."

I. Fiction

Each of the items below is identified as belonging to one of twelve categories which are abbreviated as follows: SF (science-fiction stories and novellas), F (fantasy or marginal SF stories), D (detective stories), W (westerns), S (sports stories), P (parodies or satires), J (jungle stories), L (love story), R (realism), N (novels), C (collections) ST (*Star Trek* collections). Twelve corresponding numbering systems are used concurrently because, within each category, items are numbered consecutively.

SF1. "Neptunian Refuge" (by Jim Blish). *The Planeteer* 1 (Nov. 1935): 2–6, 8–9.
SF2. "Jungle of the Microcosm" (by Jim Blish). *Tesseract Magazine* 1 (April 1936): 7–9.
SF3. "Death's Crystal Towers" (by Jim Blish). *Tesseract Combined with The Planeteer* 2 (Sept. 1936): 7–10 (issue distributed in uncompleted form).
SF4. "Emergency Refueling." *Super Science Stories* 1 (March 1940): 101–4. Reprinted in *Yesterday's Tomorrows,* ed. Frederik Pohl. New York: Berkley, 1982 (pp. 32–36).
SF5. "Bequest of the Angel." *Super Science Stories* 1 (May 1940): 46–61.
SF6. "Citadel of Thought" (in C5). *Stirring Science Stories* 1 (Feb. 1941): 38–50.
SF7. "When Anteros Came." *Science Fiction Quarterly,* no. 5 (Winter 1941): 143, 146.
SF8. "Callistan Cabal." *Stirring Science Stories"* 1 (April 1941): 42–52.
SF9. "Phoenix Planet." *Cosmic Stories* 1 (May 1941): 6–26.
SF10. "Weapon out of Time." *Science Fiction Quarterly* 3 (Spring 1941): 135–40.

SF11. "The Real Thrill." *Cosmic Stories* 1 (July 1941): 67–73.
SF12. "The Topaz Gate." *Future Fiction* 1 (Aug. 1941): 51–63.
SF13. "Solar Plexus." *Astonishing Stories* 3 (Sept. 1941): 84–89. Revised version, in *Beyond Human Ken*, ed. Judith Merril. New York: Random House, 1952.
SF14. "Sunken Universe" (by "Arthur Merlyn" like F1, V:30, and VI:3; see N7). *Super Science Stories* 3 (May 1942): 49–62. Reprinted in *Worlds to Come: Nine Science Fiction Adventures,* ed. Damon Knight. New York: Harper & Row, 1967 (pp. 305–35).
SF15. "The Solar Comedy." *Future Fiction* 2 (June 1942): 53–66.
SF16. "The Airwhale." *Future Fiction* 2 (Aug. 1942): 93–97.
SF17. "The Bounding Crown." *Super Science & Fantasy* 1 (Dec. 1944): 60–75, 129.
D1. "Death off the Record" (by "Marcus Lyons"). *Crack Detective Stories* 6 (Nov. 1945): 49–52.
D2. "Murder Wears a Mourning Cloak" (by "Marcus Lyons"). *Crack Detective Stories* 8 (Jan. 1946): 40–45.
D3. "Hot Horn—Cold Heart" (by "Marcus Lyons"). *Crack Detective Stories* 7 (May 1946): 65–68, 93–94.
D4. "Red Chip for Blackmail" (by "Marcus Lyons"). *Crack Detective Stories* 7 (July 1946): 43–46, 86.
SF18. "Chaos, Co-ordinated" (with R. W. Lowndes; by "John MacDougal"). *Astounding Science Fiction* 38 (Oct. 1946): 36–57.
D5. "The Spirit is Killing" (by "Marcus Lyons"). *Crack Detective Stories* 7 (Nov. 1946): 53–57.
D6a. "Total Recall" (by "Marcus Lyons"). *Tumbrils,* no. 10 (Nov. 1946): 2–3.
W1. "Back-shot Legacy" (by "Luke Torley"). *Western Action* 2 (April 1947): 91–102.
D7. "Killer of Fire" (by "Marcus Lyons"). *Crack Detective Stories* 8 (April 1947): 18–27.
W2. "Barb-Wire Law" (by "Luke Torley"). *Blue Ribbon Western* 7 (May 1947): 78–86.
W3. "Sabers Are for Saps" (by "Luke Torley"). *Sports Fiction* 5 (June 1947): 47–51.
S1. "Backfield Business." *All Football Stories* 1 (Dec. 1947): 53–61.
S2. "Bats for Brains." *Sports Fiction* 5 (Dec. 1947): 31–39, 95.
S3. "Phanton Blades." *Complete Sports* 5 (Dec. 1947): 57–64.
S4. "Dribble Trouble." *All Basketball Stories* 1 (Winter 1947–48): 66–73.
S5. "Back Seat Hoopster." *Ace Sports* 16 (Jan. 1948): 85–96.
D8. "Death's Photo Finish" (by "Marcus Lyons"). *Crack Detective Stories* 6 (Feb. 1948): 28–33, 95–96.
F1. "Mistake Inside" (by "Arthur Merlyn," like SF 14, V:30, and VI:3). *Startling Stories* 17 (March 1948): 90–100. Reprinted (as by Blish) in *The Dark Side,* ed. Damon Knight. New York: Doubleday, 1965 (pp. 36–63).

W4.	"Bonanza in Lead." *Famous Westerns* 9 (April 1948): 24–35.
S6.	"Fullback Frankenstein." *Sports Leaders* 1 (April 1948): 60–69.
S7.	"Touchdown Destiny." *Real Sports* 1 (April 1948): 50–58.
S8.	"Puck Poison." *Best Sports* 2 (May 1948): 37–45.
S9.	"Ten Yards to Glory." *Big Sports* 1 (May 1948): 33–41.
P1.	"Bloody Pulp Stories." *Tumbrils,* no. 16 (June 1948): 9. Revised as "What's Happened to the Pulp Magazines" (satire of S, J, W, L, and pirate pulps), *Mad* 1 (Dec. 1956): 34–37.
S10.	"Scrapple at the Crease." *Sports Fiction* 5 (July 1948): 82, 84, 86–93.
S11.	"Slide, Sucker, Slide." *Big Baseball Stories* 1 (Aug. 1948): 64–77.
W5.	"Freedom Lode." *Six Gun Western* 2 (Sept. 1948): 40–56.
W6.	"Double-Clutch Danger." *Sports Fiction* 6 (Oct. 1948): 38–53.
W7.	"The Hustler." *Super Sports* 7 (Oct. 1948): 83–97.
SF19.	"No Winter, No Summer" (with Damon Knight; by "Donald Laverty"). *Thrilling Wonder Stories* 33 (Oct. 1948): 140–47.
SF20.	"Tiger Ride" (with Damon Knight). *Astounding Science Fiction* 42 (Oct. 1948): 142–53.
W8.	"Chinook Bill and the Shooting Woman." *Complete Cowboy* 8 (Nov. 1948): 79–81.
SF21.	"Against the Stone Beasts." *Planet Stories* 3 (Fall 1948): 74–89.
J1.	"Serpent's Fetish" (see N15). *Jungle Stories* 4 (Winter 1948–49): 60–69.
S12.	"Gridiron Workhorse." *Sports Fiction* 6 (Jan. 1949): 48–63.
D6b.	"I Remember Murder" (revision of D6a). *Crack Detective Stories* 9 (Jan. 1949): 77–79, 88–89.
S13.	"Touchdown Tenderfoot." *Super Sports* 7 (Jan. 1949): 40–51.
SF22.	"The Weakness of RVOG" (with Damon Knight; expanded as N10). *Thrilling Wonder Stories* 33 (Feb. 1949): 76–89.
S14.	"Cinder Saint." *Sports Fiction* 6 (March 1949): 49–54, 90, 94.
SF23.	"The Box" (in C2 and C5; see III:4). *Thrilling Wonder Stories* 34 (April 1949): 130–40.
SF24.	"The Homesteader." *Thrilling Wonder Stories* 34 (June 1949): 135–40.
D9.	"Ferry to a Funeral." *Crack Detective Stories* 10 (July 1949): 88–92.
L1.	"The Torrid Type." *The Link* 7 (July 1949).
W9.	"The Hound of Hades." *Blue Ribbon Western* 13 (Aug. 1949).
J2.	"The Snake-Headed Sceptre" (by "V. K. Emden"; see N15). *Jungle Stories* 4 (Summer 1949): 60–81.
SF25.	"Let the Finder Beware!" (expanded as N2a and b). *Thrilling Wonder Stories* 35 (Dec. 1949): 11–58.
SF26.	"Okie" (see N4). *Astounding Science Fiction* 45 (April 1950): 69–103.
SF27a.	"There Shall Be No Darkness" (in C3a and C5; see F2). *Thrilling Wonder Stories* 36 (April 1950): 72–94.
SF28.	"Battle of the Unborn" (as "Struggle in the Womb" in C2). *Future Fiction* 1 (May/June 1950): 65–69, 93.

D10.	"Killer Come Back to Me!" *Famous Detective Stories* 11 (June 1950): 52–70.
SF29.	"The Bore." *Fantastic Story Quarterly* 1 (Summer 1950): 124–29.
S15.	"Casey and the Second String." *Super Sports* 8 (Sept. 1950): 27–34.
SF30.	"The Secret People" (with Damon Knight). *Future Fiction* 1 (Nov. 1950): 46–61.
SF31.	"Bindlestiff" (see N4). *Astounding Science Fiction* 46 (Dec. 1950): 6–41.
SF32.	"Peace Declared!" *Man's World* 1 (Jan. 1951).
SF33.	"The Void Is My Coffin." *Imagination* 2 (June 1951): 140–50.
SF34.	"Blackout in Cygni." *Planet Stories* 5 (July 1951): 73–83.
N1a.	"Sword of Xota." *Two Complete Science Adventure Books* 1 (Summer 1951): 2–66.
SF35.	"Elixir." *Future Fiction* (combined with *Science Fiction Stories*) 2 (Sept. 1951): 38–46.
SF36.	"Bridge" (part of N5a and b). *Astounding Science Fiction* 48 (Feb. 1952): 57–82.
SF37.	"Surface Tension" (see N7, in C3a and b and C5). *Galaxy* 4 (Aug. 1952): 4–40.
SF38a.	"Beanstalk" (in C1b; expanded as N13). In *Future Tense,* ed. K. F. Crossen (New York: Greenberg Pub., 1952); 237–341.
N2a.	*Jack of Eagles* (expansion of SF25). New York: A Corwin Book, 1952.
F2/ SF27b.	"There Shall Be No Darkness" (expansion of SF27a; in C6). In *Witches Three* (New York: Twayne, 1952).
F3.	"Testament of Andros" (in C2, C3a and b, and C5). *Future Fiction* 3 (Jan. 1953): 70–84.
SF39.	"Turn of a Century." *Dynamic Science Fiction* 1 (March 1953): 82–84.
SF40.	"Sargasso of Lost Cities" (part of N4). *Two Complete Science Adventure Novels* 1 (Spring 1953): 2–57.
SF41.	"First Strike" (in C2). *The Magazine of Fantasy & Science Fiction* 4 (June 1953): 84–97.
D11.	"Claw of the Kidnapped Idol" (by "Marcus Lyons"). *Crack Detective Stories* 8 (Aug. 1953): 43–48.
SF42.	"Common Time" (in C1a, b, and c, C3a and b, and C5). *Science Fiction Quarterly* 2 (Aug. 1953): 34–49.
N3.	*The Duplicated Man* (with Robert Lowndes). *Dynamic Science Fiction* 1 (Aug. 1953): 10–104.
SF43.	"A Case of Conscience" (see N8). *If* 2 (Sept. 1953): 5–51, 116–17.
SF44.	"Earthman Come Home" (see N4). *Astounding Science Fiction* 52 (Nov. 1953): 86–122.
SF45.	"FYI" (in C2). In *Star Science Fiction, No. 2* (New York: Ballantine Books, 1953): 111–20.
N1b.	*The Warriors of Day.* New York: Galaxy Science Fiction Novel, no. 16, 1953.

SF46.	"Beep" (in C1a, b, and c, and C5; expanded as N26). *Galaxy* 7 (Feb. 1954): 6–44.
SF47.	"At Death's End" (part of N5a and b). *Astounding Science Fiction* 53 (May 1954): 6–43.
SF48.	"The Thing in the Attic" (part of N7). *If* 3 (July 1954): 4–30.
F4.	"The Book of Your Life." *The Magazine of Fantasy & Science Fiction* 8 (March 1955): 84–94.
SF49.	"Translation." *Fantastic Universe* 3 (March 1955): 123–28.
SF50.	"Watershed" (part of N7). *If* 5 (May 1955): 36–43, 103.
SF51/ P2.	"With Malice to Come: I. A Feast of Reason; II. The Billion-Year Binge; III. A Matter of Energy" (three vignettes). *The Magazine of Fantasy & Science Fiction* 8 (May 1955): 36–40.
SF52.	"One-Shot" (in C2). *Astounding Science Fiction* 55 (Aug. 1955): 127–37.
SF53.	"King of the Hill" (in C1a). *Infinity Science Fiction* 1 (Nov. 1955): 56–67, 130.
N4.	*Earthman, Come Home* (novelization of SF26, SF31, SF40, plus SF44). New York: G. P. Putnam's Sons, 1955.
SF38b.	"Giants in the Earth." *Science Fiction Stories* 6 (Jan. 1956): 6–91.
SF54.	"A Time to Survive" (see N7). *The Magazine of Fantasy of Science Fiction* 10 (Feb. 1956): 15–60.
SF55.	"To Pay the Piper" (in C1a, b, and c.). *If* 6 (Feb. 1956): 39–51.
SF56.	"Masks (essentially by Virginia Kidd; in C2). *Teke Life: Magazine for the Men of Tau Kapa Epsilon* (March 1956): 39–40. Reprinted as "The Masks," *The Magazine of Fantasy & Science Fiction* 17 (Nov. 1959): 111–14.
SF57.	"Sponge Dive" (in C2). *Infinity Science Fiction* 1 (June 1956): 83–99.
SF58.	"Tomb Tapper" (in C1a, C3a and b). *Astounding Science Fiction* 57 (July 1956): 88–102.
SF59.	"A Work of Art" (in C1a, b, and c; C3a and b, and C5; and IV: 2). *Science Fiction Stories* (as "Art Work") 7 (July 1956): 46–63.
SF60.	"Writing of the Rat" (in C4a and b). *Galaxy* 12 (July 1956): 54–66.
SF61.	"The Genius Heap" (in IV:2 as "The Dark Night of the Soul"). *Galaxy* 12 (Aug. 1956): 92–107.
SF62.	"Detour to the Stars" (see SF67). *Infinity Science Fiction* 1 (Dec. 1956): 20–38.
N5a.	*They Shall Have Stars* (novelization of SF36 plus SF47). London: Faber & Faber, 1956.
SF63.	"Get Out of My Sky" (in C6). Serialized in *Astounding Science Fiction* 58, nos. 5 and 6 (Jan., Feb. 1957): 6–38, 92–128. Reprinted in *Get Out of My Sky,* three short novels selected by Leo Margulies. New York: Crest, 1960 (pp. 7–85).
SF64.	"Two Worlds in Peril" (with Phil Barnhart). *Science Fiction Adventures* 1 (Feb. 1957): 6–38.

SF65.	"Nor Iron Bars" (see SF67). *Infinity Science Fiction* 3 (Nov. 1957): 34–45.
N6a.	*Fallen Star.* London: Faber & Faber, 1957.
N6b.	*The Frozen Year.* New York: Ballantine Books, 1957.
N7.	*The Seedling Stars* (contents: SF54, SF48, SF14, SF37, SF50). New York: Gnome Press, 1957.
N5b.	*Year 2018!.* New York: Avon, 1957.
N8.	*A Case of Conscience* (expansion of SF43). New York: Ballantine Books, 1958.
N2b.	*Esper.* New York: Avon, 1958.
N9a.	*The Triumph of Time.* New York: Avon, 1958.
N10.	*VOR* (expansion of SF22). New York: Avon, Inc., 1958.
SF66.	"This Earth of Hours" (in C1a and C5). *The Magazine of Fantasy & Science Fiction,* 16 (June 1959): 5–23.
N9b.	*A Clash of Cymbals.* London: Faber & Faber, 1959.
C1a.	*Galactic Cluster* (contents: SF58, SF53, SF42, SF59, SF55, SF67, SF46, SF66). New York: Signet, 1959.
SF67.	"Nor Iron Bars" (SF62 plus SF65). In C1a and C1c.
N11a.	. . . *And All the Stars a Stage.* Serialized in *Amazing Science Fiction Stories* 34, nos. 6, 7 (June, July 1960): 6–67, 8–131.
SF68.	"The Oath" (in C2, C3a and b, and C5). *The Magazine of Fantasy & Science Fiction,* 19 (Oct. 1960): 5–22.
SF69.	"And Some Were Savages" (in C4a and b). *Amazing Stories,* 34 (Nov. 1960): 113–33.
N11b.	. . . *And All the Stars a Stage* (revised). New York: Doubleday, 1960.
C1b.	*Galactic Cluster* (contents: SF42, SF59, SF55, SF65, SF46, SF38a). London: Faber & Faber, 1960.
SF70.	"A Dusk of Idols" (in C4a and b). *Amazing Stories* 35 (March 1961): 6–29.
N12a.	*The Star Dwellers.* Serialized in *Boys' Life* 1, nos. 6 and 7 (June, July 1961): 9–10, 245; 20–21, 40–42.
SF71.	"The Abattoir Effect." In C2, pp. 73–90.
C2.	*So Close to Home* (contents: SF28, SF57, SF52, SF23, SF41, SF71, SF68, SF45, SF56, F3). New York: Ballantine Books, 1961.
N12b.	*The Star Dwellers.* New York: G. P. Putnam's Sons, 1961.
N13.	*Titans' Daughter* (expansion of SF38a and b). New York: Berkley, 1961.
F5.	"Who's in Charge Here?" (as "None So Blind" in C4a). *The Magazine of Fantasy & Science Fiction* 22 (May 1962): 12–16.
F6a.	"On the Wall of the Lodge" (with Virginia Blish; cut version of F6b). *Galaxy* 20 (June 1962): 52–75.
N14a.	*A Life for the Stars* (see III:7). Serialized in *Analog* 70, nos. 1, 2 (Sept., Oct. 1962): 6–51, 111–61.
N14b.	*A Life for the Stars* (see III:7). New York: G. P. Putnam's Sons, 1962.

N15.	*The Night Shapes* (revision of J2 plus J1; see III:6). New York: Ballantine Books, 1962.
Clc.	*Galactic Cluster* (contents: SF42, SF59, SF55, SF67, SF46). London: Four Square/New English Library, 1963.
N16a.	*Doctor Mirabilis.* London: Faber & Faber, 1964.
SF72.	"The Shipwrecked Hotel" (with Norman L. Knight) (part of N20). *Galaxy* 23 (Aug. 1965): 151–85.
SF73.	"No Jokes on Mars" (in C4a). *The Magazine of Fantasy & Science Fiction* 29 (Oct. 1965): 71–77.
C3a.	*Best Science Fiction Stories of James Blish* (contents: "A Preface to Tomorrow" [revision in V:B2], SF27a, SF37, F3, SF42, SF59, SF58, SF68). London: Faber & Faber, 1965.
N17.	*Mission to the Heart Stars.* New York: G. P. Putnam's Sons, 1965.
SF74.	"A Hero's Life" (expanded as SF83). *Impulse* 1 (March 1966): 61–86.
N18a.	"The Hour Before Earthrise." Serialized in *If* 16, nos. 7, 8, 9 (July, Aug., Sept. 1966): 6–42, 76–113, 137–60.
SF75.	"The Piper of Dis" (with Norman L. Knight; part of N20). *Galaxy* 24 (Aug. 1966): 56–87.
N16b.	*Doctor Mirabilis* (mimeographed edition). New York: James Blish, 1966.
SF76.	"How Beautiful with Banners" (in C3b, C4a and b, and C5). In *Orbit No. 1,* ed. Damon Knight. New York: G. P. Putnam's Sons, 1966 (pp. 51–62).
SF77.	"To Love Another" (with Norman Knight; part of N20). *Analog* 79 (April 1967): 8–56.
N19a.	"Faust Aleph-Null." Serialized in *If* 17, nos. 8, 9, 10 (Aug., Sept., Oct. 1967): 6–24, 106–42, 134–60.
ST1.	*Star Trek* (contents: "Charlie's Law," "Dagger of the Mind," "The Unreal McCoy," "Balance of Terror," "The Naked Time," "Miri," "The Conscience of the King"). New York: Bantam Books, 1967.
N20.	*A Torrent of Faces* (with Norman L. Knight; novelization of SF72, SF75, SF77). New York: Doubleday, 1967.
SF78.	"Skysign" (in C4b). *Analog* 81 (May 1968): 137–61.
SF79.	"Now That Man is Gone." *If* 18 (Nov. 1968): 108–12.
N19b.	*Black Easter (or Faust Aleph-Null)* (expansion of N19a). New York: Doubleday, 1968.
ST2.	*Star Trek 2* (contents: "Arena," "A Taste of Armageddon," "Tomorrow is Yesterday," "Errand of Mercy," "Court Martial," "Operation-Annihilate!" "The City on the Edge of Forever," "Space Seed"). New York: Bantam Books, 1968.
N21.	*The Vanished Jet.* New York: Weybright & Talley, 1968.
N18b.	*Welcome to Mars* (see III:11). New York: G. P. Putnam's Sons, 1968.
SF80.	"Our Binary Brothers" (part of "King Log"; see SF81 and SF84). *Galaxy* 28 (Feb. 1969): 122–30.

SF81.	"The City That Was the World" (part of "King Log"; see SF80 and SF84). *Galaxy* 28 (July 1969): 69–97.
F6b.	"On the Wall of the Lodge" (with Virginia Blish; uncut version of F6a). In *Dark Stars,* ed. Robert Silverberg. New York: Ballantine Books, 1969 (pp. 242–74).
ST3.	*Star Trek 3* (contents: "Preface," "The Trouble with Tribbles," "The Last Gunfight," "The Doomsday Machine," "Assignment: Earth," "Mirror, Mirror," "Friday's Child," "Amok Time"). New York: Bantam Books, 1969.
SF82.	"We All Die Naked" (in C3b). In *Three for Tomorrow,* ed. Robert Silverberg. New York: Meredith Press, 1969 (pp. 153–204).
SF83.	"A Style in Treason" (expansion of SF74; in C4a and b). *Galaxy* 30 (May 1970): 4, 45.
N22a.	*The Day After Judgment. Galaxy* 30 (Aug.–Sept. 1970): 4–68.
SF84.	"Darkside Crossing" (part of "King Log"; see SF80 and SF81). *Galaxy* 31 (Dec. 1970): 5–25.
C4a.	*Anywhen* (contents: "Preface," SF83 (minus the prologue), SF60, SF69, SF70, F5, SF73, SF76). New York: Doubleday, 1970.
N23.	*Cities in Flight* (contents: N5a, N14b, N4, N9a). New York: Avon Books, 1970. New York: Nelson Doubleday, Inc., 1970.
N22b.	*The Day After Judgment* (expanded version). New York: Doubleday, 1970.
F7.	"More Light." In *Alchemy and Academe,* ed. Anne McCaffrey. Doubleday, 1970 (pp. 88–120).
N24.	*Spock Must Die!* New York: Bantam Books, 1970.
SF85.	"Statistician's Day." In *Science Against Man,* ed. Anthony Cheetham. New York: Avon, 1970 (pp. 131–40).
C4b.	*Anywhen* (contents: as C4a, plus SF78). London: Faber & Faber, 1971.
N16c.	*Doctor Mirabilis* (revised edition). New York: Dodd, Mead, 1971.
ST4.	*Star Trek 4* (contents: "Preface," "All Our Yesterdays," "The Devil in the Dark," "Journey to Babel," "The Menagerie," "The Enterprise Incident," "A Piece of the Action"). New York: Bantam Books, 1971.
N25a.	"Midsummer Century." *The Magazine of Fantasy & Science Fiction* 42 (April 1972): 5–65.
F8/ P3.	"Getting Along." In *Again, Dangerous Visions,* ed. Harlan Ellison New York: Doubleday, 1972 (pp. 554–79).
N25b.	*Midsummer Century* (expansion of N25a). New York: Doubleday, 1972.
ST5.	*Star Trek 5* (contents: "Preface," "Whom Gods Destroy," "The Tholian Web," "Let That Be Your Last Battlefield," "This Side of Paradise," "Turnabout Intruder," "Requiem for Methuselah," "The Way to Eden"). New York: Bantam Books, 1972.
ST6.	*Star Trek 6* (essentially by Judith Lawrence Blish and Muriel Lawrence) (contents: "Preface," "The Savage Curtain," "The Lights of

	Zetar," "The Apple," "By Any Other Name," "The Cloud Minders," "The Mark of Gideon"). New York: Bantam Books, 1972.
ST7.	*Star Trek 7* (essentially by Judith Lawrence Blish and Muriel Lawrence) (contents: "Who Mourns for Adonais?" "The Changeling," "The Paradise Syndrome," "Metamorphosis," "The Deadly Years," "Elaan of Troyius"). New York: Bantam Books, 1972.
ST8.	*Star Trek 8* (essentially by Judith Lawrence Blish and Muriel Lawrence) (contents: "Spock's Brain," "The Enemy Within," "Catspaw," "Where No Man Has Gone Before," "Wolf in the Fold," "For the World is Hollow and I Have Touched the Sky"). New York: Bantam Books, 1972.
R1.	"A Light to Fight By." *Penthouse* 3 (June 1973): 49–50, 52, 102.
C3b.	*Best Science Fiction Stories of James Blish* (contents: "A Preface to Tomorrow" [revision in V:B2], SF37, F3, SF42, SF59, SF58, SF68, SF76, SF82). London: Faber & Faber, 1973. Reprinted as *The Testament of Andros* (London: Arrow Books, 1977).
N26.	*The Quincunx of Time* (expansion of SF46). New York: Dell Books, 1973.
ST9.	*Star Trek 9* (essentially by Judith Lawrence Blish and Muriel Lawrence) (contents: "Preface," "Return to Tomorrow," "The Ultimate Computer," "That Which Survives," "Obsession," "The Return of the Archons," "The Immunity Syndrome"). New York: Bantam Books, 1973.
SF86.	"The Glitch" (with L. Jerome Stanton). *Galaxy* 35 (June 1974): 100–109.
ST10.	*Star Trek 10* (essentially by Judith Lawrence Blish and Muriel Lawrence) (contents: "Preface," "The Alternative Factor," "The Empath," "The Galileo Seven," "Is There in Truth No Beauty?" "A Private Little War," "The Omega Glory"). New York: Bantam Books, 1974.
ST11.	*Star Trek 11* (essentially by Judith Lawrence Blish and Muriel Lawrence) (contents: "Preface," "What Are Little Girls Made Of?" "The Squire of Gothos," "Wink of an Eye," "Bread and Circuses," "Day of the Dove," "Plato's Stepchildren"). New York: Bantam Books, 1975.
C5.	*The Best of James Blish* (contents: SF6, SF23, SF27a, SF37, F3, SF42, SF46, SF59, SF66, SF68, SF76, V:112). Edited by Robert A. W. Lowndes. New York: Ballantine Books, 1979.
C6.	*"Get Out of My Sky"* and *"There Shall Be No Darkness"* (reprints SF63 and F2/SF27b). London: Panther Books, 1980.
P4.	"The Art of the Sneeze" (reprinted in V: B3). *The Magazine of Fantasy & Science Fiction* (Nov. 1982): 63–64.

II. Poetry

1. "South Wind." *St. Nicholas: Scribner's Illustrated Magazine for Girls and Boys* 60 (July 1933): 438 (St. Nicholas League Role of Honor mention only).

2. "My God, the Greeks" (by "Marcus Lyons"). *Tumbrils*, no. 1 (March 1945): 6.
3. "Prayer for Joyce" (by "Marcus Lyons"). *Tumbrils*, no. 1 (March 1945): 6; *Renascence* 2 (April 1946): 40; as "A Prayer for James Joyce," *Stony Point Workshop* 1 (Jan. 1969): 3; *James Joyce Quarterly* 7 (Summer 1970): 379.
4. "Grandmother Always Wore Stilts, 5 Poems by C. Dale Hart" (by "Marcus Lyons"). *Tumbrils*, no. 3 (July 1945): 4–7; first poem, "Poem for the Man Who did not Recognize Death in a Slouch Hat," reprinted in *Renascence* 1 (Dec. 1945): 64.
5. "Thersites" (by "Marcus Lyons"). *Tumbrils*, no. 4 (Sept. 1945): 3.
6. "At the New School" (by "Marcus Lyons"). *Tumbrils*, no. 5 (Nov. 1945): 2.
7. "Votary" (by "Marcus Lyons"). *Tumbrils*, no. 6 (Jan. 1946): 9.
8. "White Night" (by "Marcus Lyons"). *Renascence* 2 (June 1946): 71.
9. "Breach" (by "Marcus Lyons"). *Tumbrils*, no. 10 (Nov. 1946):3.
10. "Exeunt" (by "Marcus Lyons"). *Tumbrils*, no. 10 (Nov. 1946): 5; as "Exeunt Omnes," *The Sewanee Review* 63 (Summer 1955): 465.
11. "Tabby, Dead." *Tumbrils*, no. 12 (Feb. 1947): 5; *Stony Point Workshop* 1 (Jan. 1969): 1.
12. "Goodnight" (by "Marcus Lyons"). *Discrete* 2 (May 1947): 4.
13. "Ringel, Ringel Rosenkrantz." *Tumbrils*, no. 15 (Nov. 1947): 21.
14. "Auto-da-Fe." *Quarterly*, no. 1 (April 1948): 2.
15. "Red April." *Tumbrils*, no. 16 (June 1948): 8; *The Beloit Poetry Journal* 2 (Winter 1951): 15.
16. "Ritornello." *Quarterly*, no. 3 (June 1948): 11.
17. "Die Einwichlung" (poem in German). *Quarterly*, no. 3 (Sept. 1948): 16.
18. "A Beautitude." *Occasional*, no. 1 (Sept. 1949): 3.
19. "Poem in Form of a Triangle." *Occasional*, no. 1 (Sept. 1949): 3.
20. "Song as Song." *Quarterly* 2 (Sept. 1949): 23.
21. "A Song for Music" ("For Ezra Pound"). *Quarterly* 2 (Sept. 1949): 22; *Poetry* 75 (April 1951): 14.
22. "Atalantidon." *Tumbrils*, no. 24 (Jan. 1950): 4; *Priapus*, no. 21 (Spring 1971): 29.
23. "Cinderella, or The Eye's Habit: The Poet as Voyeur." *Tumbrils*, no. 24 (Jan. 1950): 2.
24. "Come Away Death." *Quarterly* 3 (Jan. 1950): 2; *The Hopkins Review* 5 (Fall 1951): 31–32.
25. "Dispatch from Gaza." *Tumbrils*, no. 24 (Jan. 1950): 3.
26. "An Expectation." *Quarterly* 3 (Jan. 1950): 5; revised version, *Quarterly* 3 (March 1950).
27. "Song Called To Account of Darkness." *Tumbrils*, no. 24 (Jan. 1950): 3.
28. "Theory of Tragedy." *Tumbrils*, no. 24 (Jan. 1950): 4; *The Hopkins Review* 5 (Fall 1951): 31.
29. "Testament of Theseus." *Western Review* 14 (Spring 1950): 213.

30. "Caesura" (reprinted in V1:34). *Accent* 10 (Fall 1950): 224–25.
31. "Dies Irae." *Accent* 10 (Fall 1950): 225; *Saving Worlds* (New York: Doubleday 1973).
32. "Song." *The Hopkins Review* 5 (Fall 1951): 32–33.
33. "The Poet Waiting for Charon." *The Beloit Poetry Journal* 2 (Summer 1952): 16.
34. "Letter From a Selenite." *The Beloit Poetry Journal* 5 (Spring 1955): 21.
35. "In Memoriam: Fletcher Pratt." *The Magazine of Fantasy & Science Fiction* 12 (Jan. 1957): 94.
36. "The Coming Forth." *The Beloit Poetry Journal* 7 (Spring 1957): 9–10.
37. "Nocturne" ("to RB [Richard Bergeron, *Warhoon* editor] from JB"). *Warhoon* no. 17 (Oct. 1962): 82.
38. "A Mirror Without Cloud" ("on 'putting away' a cat"). *Stony Point Workshop* 1 (Jan. 1968): 1.
39. "Caprice After Ronsard." *Stony Point Workshop* 1 (Jan. 1969): 3.
40. "Homage to Wm. Carlos Williams." *Stony Point Workshop* 1 (Jan. 1969): 4.
41. "Sleepy Song." *Stony Point Workshop* 1 (Jan. 1969): 3; *Kinesis* 2 (March 1969); *Prairie Schooner* 44 (Summer 1970): 168.
42. "Theory of Right Action." *Stony Point Workshop* 1 (Jan. 1969): 2.
43. "Two Brands for the Burning." *Stony Point Workshop* 1 (Jan. 1969): 2; *Prairie Schooner* 44 (Summer 1970): 167.
44. "Oryx in Phoenix." *Priapus* 19 (Spring 1970): 14.
45. "Serenade for Telephone." *Prairie Schooner* 44 (Summer 1970): 167.
46. "Aubade for Radio." *Ball State University Forum* 11 (Fall 1970): 64.
47. "Misprisions." *Ball State University Forum* 11 (Fall 1970): 80.
48. "Antiphony." *Kinesis* 3 (Dec. 1970): 17.
49. "A Djinn of the Green Djinni." *Kinesis* 3 (Dec. 1970).
50. "Dove Sta Memoria." *Kinesis* 3 (Dec. 1970).
51. "A Long Convalescence" ("to the del Reys"). *Kinesis* 3 (Dec. 1970): 17.
52. "Retreat and Flourish." *Kinesis* 3 (Dec. 1970): 17.
53. "Sennet Before Carbonek." *Kinesis* 3 (Dec. 1970): 18.
54. "An Alembic." *Ball State University Forum* 12 (Fall 1971): 50.
55. "Husbandry in Heaven" ("Three Sonnets from XXXIII Valentines from Holofernes"). *Open Places*, no. 11 (Jan. 1972): 15.
56. "A Morning Song" ("Three Sonnets from XXXIII Valentines from Holofernes"). *Open Places*, no. 11 (Jan. 1972): 1.
57. "A Reprise" ("Three Sonnets from XXXIII Valentines from Holofernes"). *Open Places*, no. 11 (Jan. 1972): 14.
58. "Venice Observed 1969." *Open Places*, no. 11 (Jan. 1972): 12.
59. "Grand Pause." *Prairie Schooner* 46 (Summer 1972): 149; *Best Poems of 1972: Borestone Mountain Poetry Awards 1973* [25th annual volume] (Palo Alto, Cal.: Pacific Books, 1973): 15.

60. "Huysmans Discovers the Reciprocating Engine." *Counter Measures*, no. 2 (1973): 63.
61. "All Hallows Leave." *Ball State University Forum* 16 (Fall 1975): 45.
62. "Scenario: The Edifice." *Best Poems of 1975: Borestone Mountain Poetry Awards 1976* [28th annual volume] (Palo Alto, Cal.: Pacific Books, 1976).

III. Dramatic Work

1. "Carbonite Johnny" (half-hour detective radio play). CBS "Action Magazine on the Air," 1952.
2. "The Gold Frame" (half-hour detective radio play). CBS "Action Magazine on the Air," 1952.
3. *Captain Video and the Sub-Space Corsair* (fifteen half-hour scripts). Du Mont TV (31 Aug.–18 Sept. 1953).
4. "The Box" (teleplay of I:SF23). 1953.
5. *C.I.D.: Universe* script. 1953.
6. *The Night Shapes* (movie script based on I:N15). 1962.
7. *A Life for the Stars* (*Cities in Flight* movie script with John Flory; based on I:N14a and b). Space Films, written between 1962 and 1966.
8. *The Space Witch* (original *Cities in Flight* movie script with John Flory). Space Films, written between 1962 and 1966.
9. *The Man Without a Planet* (outline for a TV series, "The Survivors"). Krantz Films, 1965.
10. "Eros and Psyche" (unpublished three act libretto). 1966.
11. *Welcome to Mars* (movie script with John Flory; based on I:N18b). Space Films, 1967.
12. "A True Bill" (chancel drama). In *Ten Tomorrows*, ed. Roger Elwood. Greenwich, Conn.: Fawcett Pubs., 1973 (pp. 155–84).

IV. Works Edited

1. *Vanguard Science Fiction*. No. 1 (June 1958). Editorial: "In the Beginning," p. 2.
2. *New Dreams This Morning* (includes SF61 and SF59). New York: Ballantine Books, 1966. Preface, pp. xi–xii (revision in V:B2).
3. *Introducing James Branch Cabell* (with William Leigh Godshalk; 16pp. pamphlet of biographical and bibliographical articles reprinted from *Kalki*). The James Branch Cabell Society, 1970. Preface, pp. 2–3.
4. *Nebula Award Stories 5*. New York: Doubleday, 1970. Preface, pp. 6–10.
5. *Thirteen O'Clock (and Other Zero Hours)* (stories by C. M. Kornbluth writing as Cecil Corwin). New York: Dell, 1970. Preface, pp. 7–10.

V. Criticism, Reviews, and Literary Concerns

Blish's critical books (B) and introductions to books written or compiled by other people (IN) are numbered separately.

1. "Notes on Writing Science Fiction" (by "Niles [sic] H. Frome, Canadian Author. Adapted by Jim Blish"; in two parts). *Tesseract Magazine* 1, nos. 3, 4 (May, June 1936): 5–7, 13–17.
2. "Ode pour l'Election de Son Sepulchre" (essay on the Ezra Pound case). *Tumbrils*, no. 1 (March 1945): 1–6.
3. "Eblis in Bakelite" (on Clark Ashton Smith's poetry and prose). *Tumbrils*, no. 2 (June 1945): 12–13.
4. "Fapa and the Pamphleteers." *Tumbrils*, no. 2 (June 1945): 3–4.
5. "The Coming Struggle for Pound." *Tumbrils*, no. 3 (July 1945): 2–3.
6. "Comments from the Waiting List" (on conventions and devices in music). *Afterthoughts*, no. 2 (Sept. 1945): 3–4.
7. "Review: *The Air Conditioned Nightmare*, Henry Miller" (by "Marcus Lyons"). *Renascence* 2 (April 1946): 47–48.
8. "Field Reports" (review of premiere of Hindemith's "When Lilacs Last in the Doorway Bloom'd," by "Marcus Lyons"). *Renascence* 2 (June 1946): 77–78.
9. "The Wilderness of Mirrors" (on standards for musical evaluation). *Tumbrils*, no. 6 (Jan. 1946): 4–5.
10. "Debussy contra Berg" (by "Marcus Lyons"). *Renascence* 2 (Sept. 1946): 89–91.
11. "Dialectical Letter to Chandler Davis" (criticism of Ayn Rand's *The Fountainhead*). *Tumbrils*, no. 11 (Feb. 1947): 2–4.
12. "Discourse on Prosody" (in four parts). *Tumbrils*, nos. 15, 16, 20, 22 (Nov. 1947; June 1948; Feb. and Sept. 1949): 2–5, 5–7, 7–8.
13. "Peter Grimes: A Review." *Tumbrils*, no. 15 (Nov. 1947): 14–18.
14. "Let Them Say It!" *Writer's Digest*, no. 28 (Jan. 1948): 32–33.
15. "Wallpaper Listening" (excerpt from unpublished book, "Music the Hard Way"). *Discrete*, no. 3 (April 1948): 5.
16. "*Elektra:* A Record Review" (but mainly a long essay on Richard Strauss). *Tumbrils*, no. 20 (June 1949): 2–32.
17. "Appendices to *Electra* Record Review." *Tumbrils*, no. 22 (Sept. 1949): 12–17.
18. "The Pisan Cantos." *Tumbrils*, no. 22 (Sept. 1949): 1–6.
19. "Rituals on Ezra Pound." *The Sewanee Review* 58 (Spring 1950): 185–226.
20. "Dianetics: A Door to the Future." *Planet Stories* 4 (Nov. 1950): 102.
21. "Book Reviews." *Astounding Science Fiction* 47 (April 1951): 135–40.
22. "The Little Mag." *Kirgo's*, no. 1 (April 1951).
23. "Science in Science Fiction." *Science Fiction Quarterly* 1, nos. 1, 2, 3, 5 (May, Aug., Nov. 1951; May 1952): 89–91, 83–86, 111–13, 49–53.
24. "Readin' and Writhin'." *Future Science Fiction* 3 (Sept. 1952): 66, 74.
25. "Science Fiction Bookshelf." *Startling Stories* 27 (Sept. 1952): 140–41.
26. Book Reviews. Classic Features [no other information available] (22 March 1953, 17 May 1953).

27. "The Pound Scandal" (casebook review). *The Sewanee Review* 67 (Fall 1959): 703–6.
28. Articles on: Science Fiction, Bradbury, Clarke, Heinlein, Fantasy. In *The Grolier Encyclopedia*. New York: Grolier Press, 1959.
29. "Wine and Water" (review of Harry Roskolanko's *Poet on a Schooner*). *Prairie Schooner* 34 (Summer 1960): 172–73.
30. "The Secret Files of Captain Video" (by "Arthur Merlyn" like I:SF14, I:F1, and VI:3). *Xero Comics* 1 (January 1961): 17–20.
31. "Books" (nineteen book reviews). *The Magazine of Fantasy & Science Fiction,* 20 (June 1961): 105–9 (reprinted in B2); 38, nos. 2, 4 (Feb., April 1970): 44–49, 48–53; 39, nos. 2, 3, 6; 40, nos. 1, 3, 5; 41, nos. 2, 3, 6; 42, nos. 1, 2, 4, 6; 43, nos. 1, 5; 44, no. 1 (Aug. 1970 - Jan. 1973): 58–62, 16–20, 20–24, 22–26, 14–19, 38–43, 11–15, 41–45, 22–26, 27–31, 36–41, 101–5, 92–97, 59–64, 117, 17–21, 45–51.
32. "Theodore Sturgeon's Macrocosm" (reprinted in B2). *The Magazine of Fantasy & Science Fiction,* 23 (Sept. 1962): 42–45.
33. "Science Fiction—An Uneasy Marriage." *Book Fair* (Massillon, Ohio: n.p., 1962).
34. "Inchieste, Fantascienza e Cineme—Le Riposte." *Cinema Domani* 2 (Jan. & Feb. 1963): 20–21.
35. "Is This Thinking?" (reprinted in B2). *SF Horizons,* no. 1 (Spring 1964): 54–57.
36. "Music of the Absurd" (reprinted in B3). *Playboy* 11 (Oct. 1964): 140, 196–200.
B1. *The Issue At Hand* (by "William Atheling, Jr."). Chicago: Advent, 1964. Includes reprints from "The Issue at Hand" column in *Skyhook,* nos. 15–23 (Fall 1952–Winter 1954/55), and in *Axe,* no. 34 (1963), and from *Warhoon* and *Xero*.
37. "Review: Mary Ellen Bute: *Passages from* Finnegans Wake." *A Wake Newslitter* 2 (Dec. 1965): 29–30.
38. "SF: The Critical Literature" (reprinted in B2). *SF Horizons,* no. 2 (Winter 1965): 38–48.
39. Review of *A Shorter "Finnegans Wake,"* ed. Anthony Burgess. *A Wake Newslitter* 3 (Aug. 1966): 87–89.
40. "Kram Revisited." *A Wake Newslitter* 4 (Aug. 1967): 76–77.
41. "Eine Kleine Okie-Musik." *Australian SF Review,* no. 12 (Oct. 1967): 10–12.
42. "The Anagram Game: More About Mother and Elsewhere." *Kalki* 2 (1967): 17.
43. "The Anagram Game: Three More." *Kalki* 2 (1967): 39.
44. "At the Altar of Sesphra: An Approach to the Allegory." *Kalki* 2 (1967): 6–7, 17.
45. "The Economist" (reviews of Joe Lee Davis, *James Branch Cabell,* and Louis Rubin, Jr., *No Place on Earth*). *Kalki* 2 (1967): 32–33.
46. "Ettarre an Anagram?" *Kalki* 2 (1967): 49.

47. "The Jurgen Suite." *Kalki* 2 (1967): 61.
48. "Paranoia and Science Fiction" (a round-robin letter symposium, involving Alexei Panshin, James Blish, and Joanna Russ, stemming from the 1966 Milford Science Fiction Writers' Conference). Published by the Science Fiction Writers of America, 1967.
49. "Source Notes: A Horrible Quiet Noise." *Kalki* 2 (1967): 26.
50. "Source Notes: Birdsong." *Kalki* 2 (1967): 5.
51. "Source Notes: Cabell Gets One Wrong." *Kalki* 2 (1967): 31.
52. "Source Notes: Ninzian Gets One Right." *Kalki* 2 (1967): 2.
53. "Trinity as Trilogy." *Warhoon*, no. 23 (May 1968): 13–17.
54. "The Great Historian." *Australian SF Review,* no. 14 (June 1968): 8.
55. "The Future in Books" (seven book reviews). *Amazing Stories* 42, nos. 1, 3–6; 43, nos. 2, 3 (June 1968–Sept. 1969): 135, 138–39, 143, 73–74, 141–42, 142–43, 119–28.
56. "On Science Fiction Criticism." *Riverside Quarterly,* no. 3 (Aug. 1968): 214–17. Reprinted in *SF: The Other Side of Realism,* ed. Thomas D. Clareson. Bowling Green, Ohio: Bowling Green University Popular Press, 1971 (pp. 166–70).
57. "2001: A Note on the Music." *Warhoon,* no. 24 (Aug. 1968): 25–26.
58. "Comments on *Torrent.*" *Speculation* 2 (Sept. 1968): 6.
59. "On a Clear Day All You Can See Is Placards." *Warhoon,* no. 25 (Nov. 1968): 14–18.
IN1. "Credo: James Blish." *The Year's Best Science Fiction No. 1.* London: Sphere Books, 1968 (pp. vi–vii).
IN2. Introduction to Alexei Panshin, *Heinlein in Dimension.* Chicago: Advent, 1968 (pp. vii–ix).
60. "The Problem of Scoteia." *Kalki* 2 (1968): 48–49.
61. "Some Cabellian Tropes." *Kalki* 2 (1968): 66–67.
62. "Source Notes: More Spells." *Kalki* 2 (1968): 62–63.
63. "Source Notes: The Mirror and Pigeons Resolved." *Kalki* 2 (1968): 97.
64. "To Rhadamanthus, Snarling: Cabell Against His Critics." *Kalki* 2 (1968): 43–47.
65. "The Tolkien of the Twenties Returns" (Cabell revival). *Chicago Tribune Book World* (6 July 1969): 8.
66. "American Fantasy Boom." *Books and Bookmen* 15 (Oct. 1969): 20–21.
67. "Review of *The Silver Stallion.*" *Science Fiction Review* 33 (Oct. 1969): 32–33.
68. "Cabell as Historical Actor" (with James N. Hall). *Kalki* 3 (1969): 43–45.
69. "Cabell as Kabbalist." *Kalki* 3 (1969): 11–12.
70. "Cabell as Voluntarist." *Kalki* 3 (1969): 120–22.
71. "Did Cabell Use the Tarot Deck?" *Kalki* 3 (1969): 145–46.

72. "The Economist" (discussion of Cabell, *The Witch-Woman*). *Kalki* 3 (1969): 35.
73. "The Economist" (review of Arvin Wells, *Jesting Moses: A Study in Cabellian Comedy*). *Kalki* 3 (1969): 73–74.
74. "A Wildean Echo?" (with Paul Spencer). *Kalki* 3 (1969): 108.
75. Review of Brian Aldiss, *Barefoot in the Head* (reprinted in B2). *Speculation* 3 (Jan.–Feb. 1970): 24–26.
76. "Why Do Poets Bother?" *Books and Bookmen* 15 (Feb. 1970): 54–55.
77. "Some Fictional Descendants of Carroll." *Jabberwocky*, no. 3 (March 1970): 6–8.
78. "Formal Music at the Wake" (in three parts; reprinted in B3). *A Wake Newslitter* 7, nos. 2, 3, 4 (April, June, Aug. 1970): 19–27, 35–43, 51–58.
79. "High Fantasy—And Lots of It." *Vector*, no. 56 (Summer 1970): 6–7.
80. "The Good, the Bad, the Indifferent" (Speculation Conference, panel comments; revision in B2). *Speculation* 3 (Sept.–Oct. 1970): 21–24.
81. "Think Me to Your Leader" (on ESP and SF). *The Sunday Times Magazine* (22 Nov. 1970): 30–33.
82. "Manuel's Second Coming." *Cypher*, no. 3 (Dec. 1970): 5–8.
83. "The Tale That Wags the God: The Function of Science Fiction" (also as IN3; reprinted in B3). *American Libraries* 1 (Dec. 1970): 1029–33.
84. "Foreword" to Lewis Padgett, "P. Note Eye." In *The Mirror of Infinity: A Critic's Anthology of Science Fiction*, ed. Robert Silverberg. New York: Harper & Row, 1970 (pp. 95–98).
85. "The Geography of Dream." *Kalki* 4 (1970): 90–95.
B2. *More Issues At Hand* (by "William Atheling, Jr."). Chicago: Advent, 1970. Includes combination of prefaces to I:C3a and IV:2, material from *Axe, Xero, Warhoon, Science Fiction Times*, and *Science Fiction Forum*, plus 38, 35, 31, 32, 75, and 80, this section.
86. "The Stallion's Other Members." *Kalki* 4 (1970): 67–69.
87. "Die Wiederentdeckung James Branch Cabell." *Quarber Merkur*, no. 2 (Feb. 1971): 30–32.
88. "Poul Anderson: The Enduring Explosion" (reprinted in B3). *The Magazine of Fantasy & Science Fiction* 40 (April 1971): 52–55.
89. "The Science in Science Fiction" (reprinted in B3). *Quicksilver*, no. 2 (April 1971): 19–26.
90. "Another Book at the Wake" (ref. to Havelock Ellis). *A Wake Newslitter* 8 (Oct. 1971): 78.
91. "Eclectic Occultism" (review of Colin Wilson, *The Occult*). *The Spectator* 227 (6 Nov. 1971): 654.
92. "Announcement—A Wake Appendix." *A Wake Newslitter* 8 (Dec. 1971): 91–93.
93. "Special Announcement—A Wake Appendix." *James Joyce Quarterly* 9 (Winter 1971): 176.
94. "Cabell as Playwright." *Kalki* 5 (1971): 35–37.

95.	"Primitive Cabell—and Cabellians." *Kalki* 5 (1971): 10.
96.	"Source Notes: Witches, Demons and Spells." *Kalki* 5 (1971): 23.
IN3.	"The Function of Science Fiction" (see 83 and B3, this section). In *The Light Fantastic*, ed. Harry Harrison. New York: Charles Scribner's Sons, 1971 (pp. 1–13).
IN4.	Introduction to J. B. Cabell, *Figures of Earth: A Comedy of Appearances*. London: Tandem Books, 1971 (pp. 5–6).
IN5.	Introduction to J. B. Cabell, *Jurgen: A Comedy of Justice*. London: Tandem Books, 1971 (pp. 5–6).
IN6.	Introduction to J. B. Cabell, *The Silver Stallion; A Comedy of Redemption*. London Tandem Books, 1971 (pp. 5–6).
97.	"The Long Night of a Virginia Author" (reprinted in B3). *The Journal of Modern Literature* 2 (Feb. 1972): 393–405.
98.	"Moskowitz on Kuttner." *Riverside Quarterly* 5 (Feb. 1972): 140–43.
99.	"New Myth for Ulysses" (review of Richard Ellman, *Ulysses on the Liffey*). *The Spectator* 228 (26 Feb. 1972): 317–18.
100.	*"Figures of Earth/The Silver Stallion/Jurgen"* (review). *Shadow Fantasy Literature Review* 2 (March 1972): 18–19.
101.	"The Climate of Insult." *The Sewanee Review* 80 (Spring 1972): 340–46.
102.	"James Blish on the Decline of the Supernatural" (review of four books). *The Spectator* 229 (19 Aug. 1972): 286–87.
103.	"The Arts in Science Fiction" (reprinted in B3). *Vector*, no. 61 (Sept.–Oct. 1972). Reprinted in *A Multitude of Visions*, ed. Cy Chauvin. Baltimore: T-K Graphics, 1975 (pp. 58–67).
104.	"A Bough to Cabell" (unsigned). *Kalki* 5 (1972): 67–75.
105.	"The View from Mispec Moor." *Kalki* 5 (1972): 124–25.
106.	"A Transatlantic View" (a Brian W. Aldiss bibliography). *Vector*, no. 63 (Jan.–Feb. 1973): 25–28.
107.	"The Literary Dreamers" (reprinted in B3). *The Alien Critic* 2 (May 1973): 44–50.
IN7.	"Foreword" to *The Best of John W. Campbell*. London: Sidgwick & Jackson, 1973 (pp. 7–12).
108.	"The View from Mispec Moor: Footnotes to 'The Long Night' " (see 97, this section). *Kalki* 6 (1973): 29–31.
109.	"A Surfeit of Lem, Please?" (review of *The Invincible*). *Foundation*, no. 6 (May 1974): 95–96.
110.	"Book review" of the 1972 Swedish translation of Cabell, *Figures of Earth. Kalki* 6 (1974): 69–71.
IN8.	Introduction to Lester del Rey, *Psico Scacco (Pstalemate)*. Milan: Editrice Nord, 1974 (pp. 1–2).
IN9.	Introduction to Ursula K. Le Guin, *La Falce Dei Cieli (The Lathe of Heaven)*. Milan: Editrice Nord, 1974 (pp. 1–3).
111.	"Look Dear, He Found My Lost Necklace (or, Roto-Rooting in the

	Unconscious)." *Science Fiction Writers of America Bulletin* (Winter 1974–75).
IN10.	"John Brunner: A Colleague's View." Preface to *The Happening Worlds of John Brunner*, ed. Joe DeBolt. Port Washington, New York: Kennikat Press, 1975 (pp. 3–7).
112.	"Aristotelean Spheres" (Cy Chauvin's combination of Blish letters re: "Surface Tension" in *Speculation*, no. 32 [Spring 1973]: 48–50, and in *Cypher*, no. 11 [May 1974]: 31; reprinted in B3). *Seldon's Plan*, no. 40 (Sept. 1976): 6–8.
113.	"Probapossible Prolegomena to Ideareal History" (not the same as VI:9; reprinted in I:C5 and B3). *Foundation*, no. 13 (May 1978): 6–12.
114.	"A Bad Idea Trampled to Death by Ducks" (revised version of letter in *Disclave*, no. 80 [May 1972], re: genesis of . . . *And All the Stars a Stage*). In "Four Fugitive Pieces by James Blish," ed. David Ketterer. *Vector*, no. 120 (June 1984): 8–9.
115.	"A New Totemism?" (reprinted in B3). In "Four Fugitive Pieces by James Blish," ed. David Ketterer. *Vector*, no. 120 (June 1984): 11–13.
B3.	*The Tale That Wags The God* (contents: "Preface" by Cy Chauvin, John Foyster article [see Secondary Bibliography below]; 83, IN3, 89, 103, 115, 113, 88, 107, 97, 36, 112 above, plus I:P4 and VI:34 and 31; Blish bibliography [by Judith Lawrence Blish]). Edited by Cy Chauvin. Chicago: Advent, 1987.

VI. Science and Other Subjects

1. "Classroom Beachhead" (on education). *Agenbite of Inwit* 2 (Sept. 1945).
2. "Some Functions of Historical Rationalism" (about philosophies of history). *Tumbrils*, no. 5 (Nov. 1945): 3–6.
3. "Zombie . . . ?" (on viruses: by "Arthur Lloyd Merlyn" like I: SR14 and F1, and V:30). *Science Fiction* 1 (Jan. 1946): 7.
4. "WRL" (essay on the War Resisters League). *Tumbrils*, no. 8 (July 1946): 1–4.
5. "Invisbile Armada." *Air World* 5 (Sept. 1946): 13, 66.
6. "Scientific Method and Political Action." *Politics* 3 (Nov. 1946): 358–59; reprinted in (. . .) [*Three Dots*], no. 14 (Nov. 1947): 1–3.
7. "The Road to Death" (on the first draft-card burning demonstration). *Tumbrils*, no. 12 (Feb. 1947): 3–4.
8. "Language—Writer's Ivory Tower" (on and in regularized English). *Tumbrils*, no. 14 (Nov. 1947): 3–4.
9. "Probapossible Prolegomena to Ideareal History" (not the same as V:113). (. . .) [*Three Dots*], no. 1 (Sept. 1948): 1–2.
10. "What Is Evidence?" *Future Fiction* 1 (March 1951): 78–80.
11. "Our Inhabited Universe" (series of ten articles). *Thrilling Wonder Stories*, 38, no. 2 through 41, no. 2 (June 1951–Dec. 1952): 104–7, 42–44, 54–57, 64–69, 63–66, 112–16, 103–7, 48–51, 56–59, 44–47.

12. "Methuselah's Grandparents." *If* 3 (May 1954): 63–69.
13. "Tips to Trippers." *Scoot* 1 (Oct. 1957): 5.
14. "Sputnik and the Pharmaceutical Industry." *Drug & Cosmetic Industries* 31 (Dec. 1957): 741, 804, 824.
15. "Planet Earth." In the *I.G.Y. Teachers' Manual*. Reprinted in *Science Fiction: The Year's Best*, ed. Ralph Shikes (1958).
16. "The Shadowy Figure of Roger Bacon" (expanded as 25, this section). *Science World* 5 (April 1959): 11–12.
17. "Medical News Stories." *Factor* 1 (1960).
18. "New Drugs for Old Ills." *Catholic Digest* 25 (May 1962): 96–99.
19. "Five Answers." *New Comment* [BBC Third Programme] (17 October 1962).
20. "In Tomorrow's Little Black Bag." *7th Annual of the Year's Best S-F*, ed. Judith Merril. New York: Simon & Schuster, 1962 (pp. 304–9).
21. "The Playboy Panel: 1984 and Beyond" (discussion by Blish and others). *Playboy* 10, nos. 7, 8 (July, Aug. 1963): 25–37; 31–35, 108, 112–18.
22. "A Message from Loki." *Worlds of Tomorrow* 1 (Feb. 1964): 121–24.
23. "Let Joy Be Unconfined." *Playboy* 13 (Oct. 1966): 103–4, 134, 206–9. As "Toward a Technology of Pleasure," in *The Pursuit of Pleasure Anthology* (Chicago: Playboy Press, 1972), pp. 6–25; and in *The Sensuous Society* (Chicago: Playboy Press, 1973), pp. 51–56.
24. "The Strange Career of Doctor Mirabilis." *Australian SF Review*, no. 6 (Jan. 1967): 22–24.
25. "The Invention of Science" (expansion of 16, this section). In *Adventures in Discovery*, ed. Tom Purdom. New York: Doubleday, 1969 (pp. 47–60).
26. "James Blish." In *The Double: Bill Symposium*, ed. and pub. by Bill Mallard and Bill Bowers (1969).
27. "Future Recall." In *The Disappearing Future*, ed. George Hay. London: Panther Books, 1970 (pp. 97–105).
28. "All in a Knight's Work." *Speculation*, no. 29 (Oct. 1971): 5–12.
29. "James Blish Interviewed" (by Paul Walker). *Moebius Trip*, no. 13 (May 1972): 4–10.
30. "The Development of a Science Fiction Writer" (cut version of 34, this section). *Foundation*, no. 2 (June 1972): 17–23.
31. "In Conversation: James Blish Talks to Brian Aldiss" (reprinted in V:B3). *Cypher*, no. 10 (Oct. 1973): 6–17.
32. "If You Don't Like It Here, Why Don't You Go Back Where You Came From?" *Punch* (11–17 Dec. 1974): 1044–45.
33. "Interview with James Blish" (by Marty Klug). *Whizzard* 2 (June 1975): 6–11, 20, 41.
34. "A Science-Fiction Coming of Age" (uncut version of 30). In *The Tale That Wags the God* (V:B3), pp. 139–69.

SECONDARY BIBLIOGRAPHY

Reviews are included on a very selective basis.

Aldiss, Brian W. *Billion Year Spree: The True History of Science Fiction.* New York: Doubleday & Company, Inc., 1973 (pp. 237, 251–52, 310).
———. "In Memoriam: James Blish." *Extrapolation* 17 (December 1975): 5–7.
———. "James Blish: The Mathematics of Behaviour." *Foundation,* no. 13 (May 1978): 43–50. Reprinted (heavily revised) as "Blish and the Mathematics of Knowledge." In *The Stellar Gauge: Essays on Science Fiction Writers.* Edited by Michael J. Tolley and Kirpal Singh. Victoria, Australia: Norstrilia Press, 1980 (pp. 137–49); and (with "James" before "Blish") in Aldiss, *This World and Nearer Ones: Essays Exploring the Familiar.* London: Weidenfeld & Nicolson, 1979 (pp. 37–50).
———. "PEEP: An Introduction to *The Quincunx of Time.*" James Blish, *The Quincunx of Time.* New York: Avon Books, 1983 (pp. 6–10).
Aldiss, Brian, with David Wingrove. *Trillion Year Spree: The History of Science Fiction.* London: Victor Gollancz Ltd., 1986 (pp. 196, 226, 240–42, 243, 289, 465 nn. 9–11, 472 n. 17).
Ash, Brian. *Faces of the Future: The Lessons of Science Fiction.* London: Elek/Pemberton, 1975 (pp. 185–87).
Berger, Harold L. *Science Fiction and the New Dark Age.* Bowling Green, Ohio: Bowling Green University Popular Press, 1976 (pp. 130–32, 156–58).
Blish, Elisabeth. "Introduction." James Blish, *Mission to the Heart Stars.* New York: Avon Books, 1982 (pp. 7–10).
Blish, Judith. "Introduction by James and Judith Blish" to "The Cities in Flight Series" (includes extracts from Primary Bibliography, VI: 31). In *The Great Science Fiction Series.* Edited by Frederik Pohl, Martin Harry Greenberg, and Joseph Olander. New York: Harper & Row, 1980 (pp. 86–87).
———. "Introduction by James and Judith Blish" to "The Pantropy Series" (includes extracts from Primary Bibliography, V: 111). In *The Great Science Fiction Series.* Edited by Frederik Pohl, Martin Harry Greenberg, and Joseph Olander. New York: Harper & Row, 1980 (pp. 112–13).
Bradham, Jo Allen. "The Case in James Blish's *A Case of Conscience.*" *Extrapolation* 16 (December 1974): 67–80.
Budrys, Algis. "Bookshelf" (review of *Black Easter*). *Galaxy* 27 (January 1969): 186–89.
Burgess, Andrew J. "The Concept of Eden." In *The Transcendent Adventure: Studies of Religion in Science Fiction/Fantasy.* Edited by Robert Reilly. Westport, Conn.: Greenwood Press, 1985 (pp. 73–81).

Carter, Paul. *The Creation of Tomorrow.* New York: Columbia University Press, 1977 (pp. 19, 86–87, 158–59, 222).
Chauvin, Cy. "Preface." *The Tale That Wags the God.* Edited by Cy Chauvin. Chicago: Advent, 1987 (pp. 1–5).
Clute, John. "James Blish." In *Science Fiction Writers: Critical Studies of the Major Authors from the Early Nineteenth Century to the Present Day.* Edited by E. F. Bleiler. New York: Charles Scribner's Sons, 1982 (pp. 291–96).
———. "Scholia, Seasoned with Crabs, Blish Is." *New Worlds 6.* London: Sphere Books Ltd., 1973 (pp. 118–29).
Colbert, Robert Edward. "A Case of Conscience: The Literary Criticism of James Blish." *Essays in Arts and Sciences* 9 (August 1980): 247–56.
D'Ammassa, Don. Review of *A Case of Conscience. Delap's F & SF Review* (September 1975): 21–22.
Del Rey, Lester. "The Hand at Issue." *The Magazine of Fantasy & Science Fiction* 42 (April 1972): 72–77.
Eckley, Grace. "Black Easter." In *Survey of Science Fiction Literature.* 5 vols. Edited by Frank N. Magill. Englewood Cliffs, N.J.: Salem Press, 1979 (1: 233–36).
———. "A Case of Conscience." In *Survey of Science Fiction Literature,* 1: 303–7.
———. "The Day After Judgment." In *Survey of Science Fiction Literature,* 1: 497–501.
———. "Doctor Mirabilis." In *Survey of Science Fiction Literature,* 1: 569–73.
———. "*Finnegans Wake* in the Work of James Blish." *Extrapolation* 20 (Winter 1979): 330–42.
Feeley, Gregory. "Cages of Conscience from Seedling Stories: The Development of Blish's Novels." *Foundation,* no. 24 (February 1982): 59–68.
———. "The Unglimpsed Reign of King Log." *Vector,* no. 120 (June 1984): 14–21, 38.
Foyster, John. "Introduction: William Atheling, Jr.: A Critic of Science Fiction." In *The Tale That Wags the God.* Edited by Cy Chauvin. Chicago: Advent, 1987 (pp. 7–18).
Hartwell, David G. "Introduction." James Blish, *Black Easter/The Day After Judgment.* Boston, Gregg Press, 1980 (pp. v–x).
Hassler, Donald M. "Blish James (Benjamin)." In *Twentieth Century Science-Fiction Writers.* Edited by Curtis C. Smith. New York: St. Martin's Press, 1981 (pp. 55–57).
Ketterer, David. "Change, Truth, and Sex in *The Seedling Stars* by James Blish." *Métaphores,* nos. 9–10 (April 1984): 145–59.
———. "*Cities in Flight:* A Wagnerian, Spenglerian Space Opera by James Blish." *Foundation,* no. 31 (July 1984): 45–67.
———. "Covering *A Case of Conscience.*" *Science-Fiction Studies* 9 (July 1982): 195–214.

———. "From RVOG to VOR: A Coded Message from James Blish." *Science-Fiction Studies* 11 (July 1984): 220–23.

———. "*The Frozen Year:* 'A Piece of Spoiled Goods' by James Blish?" *Extrapolation* 26 (Spring 1985): 36–42.

———. "'Imprisoned in a Tesseract': *Black . . . Judgment* by James Blish." *The Missouri Review* (SF and Fantasy issue) 7 (March 1984): 243–63.

———. Introductions. "Four Fugitive Pieces by James Blish" (Primary Bibliography, V:112, 114, 115; VI:24). *Vector,* no. 120 (June 1984): 5–6, 7, 9, 11.

———. "James Blish, *Welcome to Mars,* and the Haertel Complex." *Science-Fiction Studies* 11 (November 1984): 284–90.

———. "The Last Inspirational Gasp of James Blish: *The Breath of Brahma.*" *Science-Fiction Studies* 11 (March 1984): 45–49.

———. "Pantropy, Polyploidy, and Tectogenesis in the Fiction of James Blish and Norman L. Knight." *Science-Fiction Studies* 10 (July 1983): 199–218.

Knight, Damon. *The Futurians: The Story of the Science Fiction "Family" of the 30's that Produced Today's Top SF Writers and Editors.* New York: John Day, 1977 (pp. 151–58, 178–79, 209–13, passim).

———. *In Search of Wonder: Essays on Modern Science Fiction.* 1956; Revised and Enlarged Second Edition, Chicago: Advent, 1967 (pp. 26, 150–57 [ch. 16: "The Jagged Blade: James Blish"], 265–73 [ch. 26: "Symbolism"]).

———. "Knight Piece." In *Hell's Cartographers: Some Personal Histories of Science Fiction Writers.* Edited by Brian W. Aldiss. London: Weidenfeld & Nicolson, 1975 (pp. 113–14, 117, 122–23, 134, 137).

Lowndes, Robert A. W. "Introduction: Science Fiction the Hard Way." *The Best of James Blish.* Edited by Robert A. W. Lowndes. New York: Ballantine Books, 1979 (pp. ix–xxi).

———. "Introduction." James Blish, *Jack of Eagles.* New York: Avon Books, 1982 (pp. 7–13).

———. "James Blish: A Profile." *The Magazine of Fantasy & Science Fiction* 42 (April 1972); 66–71. Reprinted (slightly revised) in *The Best from Fantasy & Science Fiction: A Special 25th Anniversary Anthology.* Edited by Edward L. Ferman. New York: Doubleday & Co., 1974 (pp. 317–22).

McClintock, Michael W. "Working for Pharaoh: On the Writing Career of James Blish" (unpublished ms. to form basis of Starmont Reader's Guide monograph).

Masson, David I. "Up the Jungle Down the Aeons" (review of *Midsummer Century*). *Foundation,* nos. 7 and 8 (March 1975): 182–85.

Meyers, Walter E. *Aliens and Linguists: Language Study and Science Fiction.* Athens: The University of Georgia Press, 1980 (pp. 19, 22, 30, 30, 41, 43, 71, 77, 116).

Moskowitz, Sam. *The Immortal Storm: A History of Science Fiction Fandom.* 1954; reprinted, Westport: Hyperion Press, Inc., 1974 (pp. 47, 55, 64–67, 70, 73, 79, 87, 104, 113, 141, 184).

———. "Nils Frome in *The Golden Atom.*" *Science-Fiction Studies* 13 (March 1986): 98–107.
———. "On Nils Frome and Blish, Lovecraft, *et al.*" *Science-Fiction Studies* 12 (July 1985): 229–36.
———. *Seekers of Tomorrow: Masters of Modern Science Fiction.* New York: World, 1966 (pp. 412–13).
———. *Strange Horizons: The Spectrum of Science Fiction.* New York: Charles Scribner's Sons, 1972 (pp. 14–15, 17–18).
———. "The Versatile Jim Blish." *Helios* 1 (June 1937): 7–8.
Mullen, Richard D. "Blish, van Vogt, and the Uses of Spengler." *Riverside Quarterly* 3 (August 1968): 172–86. Reprinted in revised and shortened form as the afterword to Blish, *Cities in Flight.* New York: Avon Books, 1970 (pp. 567–607).
Nicholls, Peter. "The Death of James Blish." *Foundation,* no. 9 (November 1975): 54–56.
———. "James Blish." In *The Encyclopedia of Science Fiction.* Edited by Peter Nicholls. London: Granada Publishing, 1979 (pp. 77–78).
Panshin, Alexei and Cory. *SF in Dimension: A Book of Explorations.* 1967; Revised and Enlarged Second Edition, Chicago: Advent, 1980 (pp. 27, 73–74, 320).
Parker, Helen N. *Biological Themes in Modern Science Fiction.* Ann Arbor, Mich.: UMI Research Press, 1984.
Parkin-Speer, Diane. "Alien Ethics and Religion versus Fallen Mankind." In *The Transcendent Adventure: Studies of Religion in Science Fiction/Fantasy.* Edited by Robert Reilly. Westport, Conn.: Greenwood Press, 1985 (pp. 93–104).
Reginald, R. *Science Fiction and Fantasy Literature, Vol. 2: Contemporary Science Fiction Authors II.* Detroit: Gale Research Company, 1979 (p. 820).
Reilly, Robert. "The Discerning Conscience." *Extrapolation* 18 (May 1977): 176–80.
Rickard, Bob. "After Such Knowledge: James Blish's Tetralogy." In *A Multitude of Visions.* Edited by Cy Chauvin. Baltimore: T-K Graphics, 1975 (pp. 24–34).
Rogers, Alva. *A Requiem for Astounding.* Chicago: Advent, 1964 (pp. 188–89, 195, 198, 200, 202–4, 206, 207).
Russ, Joanna. Review of *Black Easter. The Magazine of Fantasy & Science Fiction* 35 (December 1968): 116–18.
Shackley, Paul. "Some Early Blish" (unpublished ms.).
Silverberg, Robert. "Common Time." "Three Worlds of Wonder." *Foundation,* no. 38 (Winter 1986/87): 5–12.
———. "Opinion." *Amazing Stories* 60 (May 1985): 4–6.
———. Review of *Doctor Mirabilis. Amazing Stories* 39 (March 1965): 123–24.
Stableford, Brian M. "'Beep' $\times$ 2 = *Quincunx*" (review of *The Quincunx of Time*). *Foundation,* no. 9 (November 1975): 104–6.

———. *"Cities in Flight."* In *Survey of Science Fiction Literature.* 5 vols. Edited by Frank N. Magill. Englewood Cliffs, N.J.: Salem Press, 1979 (1: 358–62).

———. *A Clash of Symbols: The Triumph of James Blish* (expanded and revised version of "The Science Fiction of James Blish"; see below). San Bernardino, Cal.: The Borgo Press, 1979.

———. "The Science Fiction of James Blish." *Foundation,* no. 13 (May 1978): 12–43.

Suvin, Darko. "Books Against Common Sense: Levels of SF Criticism" (on *More Issues at Hand*). *The Magazine of Fantasy & Science Fiction* 42 (May 1972): 126–29.

———. "James Blish, 1921–1975." *Science-Fiction Studies* 2 (November 1975): 294–95.

Warner, Harry J. *All Our Yesterdays: An Informal History of Science Fiction Fandom in the Forties.* Chicago: Advent, 1969 (pp. 11, 26, 39, 46, 192, 201–6, 218, 228, 266).

Wilson III, Raymond J. "James Blish (1921–1975)." In *Part 1: A–L, Twentieth-Century American Science-Fiction Writers.* Edited by David Cowart and Thomas L. Wymer. Detroit: Gale Research Company, 1981 (pp. 40–53).

Wolfe, Gary K. *The Known and the Unknown: The Iconography of Science Fiction.* Kent, Ohio: The Kent State University Press, 1979 (pp. 59, 84, 109, 121–24, 208–14, 216).

———. *"The Seedling Stars."* In *Survey of Science Fiction Literature.* 5 vols. Edited by Frank N. Magill. Englewood Cliffs, N.J.: Salem Press, 1979 (4: 1888–91).

INDEX

"Abattoir Effect, The" (Blish), 342 n. 48
ACREFF-MONALES *(The Triumph of Time)*, 183, 190–91
"Action Magazine of the Air," 29
Adams, Karin Laflin, 25, 90, 152, 248, 286, 287, 294, 327 n. 72, 352 n. 16, 357 nn. 30, 31, 358 n. 35
Adapted Men *(The Seedling Stars)*, 57–62, 66, 171, 332 n. 8
Adlard, Mark, 327 n. 72
Adventures in Discovery (Purdom), 194
Aesop, 236
"After Such Knowledge," 19, 21, 29, 198, 265, 296, 318, 321 n. 8, 365 n. 42. See also *Black Easter/The Day After Judgment; Case of Conscience, A; Doctor Mirabilis*
Again, Dangerous Visions, 156
"Against the Stone Beasts" (Blish), 40
"Agent as Patient: Seven Subjects with an Object" (Blish), 29, 281–84, 360 n. 64
Agronski, Martin *(A Case of Conscience)*, 80–81, 87, 88, 91, 94, 100, 101, 335 nn. 4, 6
"Airwhale, The" (Blish), 329 n. 8
Air World, 36
Albertus Magnus, 193, 204–5, 208, 212
Alchemy and Academe: A Collection of Original Stories Concerning Themselves with Transmutations, Mental and Elemental, Alchemical and Academic, 154
Aldiss, Brian, 20, 24, 25, 27, 28, 151, 164, 171, 183, 196, 219, 230, 245, 279, 280, 293, 320 n. 3, 332 n. 9, 333 n. 15, 337 n. 5, 342 n. 43, 344 n. 2, 349 n. 1, 350 n. 2, 353 n. 19, 362 n. 9
Aldiss, Margaret, 24, 25
Aleph-Null, 103, 220–21, 362 n. 11
Alexander IV, Pope, 209
Alexander the Great, 205
Alice (Carroll), 220, 239
"All Hallows Leave" (Blish), 273

Altshuler, Harry, 56, 324 n. 46
Amalfi, John *(Cities in Flight)*, 162–63, 174–91, 219, 229, 233, 322 n. 30, 339 n. 17, 345 n. 13, 347 n. 31, 354 n. 30, 359 n. 52
Amazing Science Fiction Stories, 130
Amazing Stories, 1
Amazing Stories Quarterly, 37
American Libraries, 280
American Rocket Society, 361 n. 79
Amis, Kingsley, 17, 340 n. 20, 360 n. 61
Analog (mag.), 75, 165, 166
Anatomy of Criticism (Frye), 92
. . . And All the Stars a Stage (Blish), 17, 108, 109, 129–34, 340 nn. 19, 20, 341 n. 35
"And Death Shall Have No Dominion" (Thomas), 166–67
Anderson, Poul, 148, 151, 276, 360 n. 58
Andros, T. V. ("Testament of Andros"), 109–11
"And Some Were Savages" (Blish), 17, 138
Antigravity principle, 255–57, 356 n. 12
Antimatter, 185, 186–87. See also Dirac, Paul
Anywhen (Blish), 108, 114, 130, 138, 140, 145, 148, 151, 356 n. 10
Appleton, Victor, 156
Aquinas, Thomas, 212
Archimedes, 226
Aristotle, 204, 205
Armata: A Fragment (Erskine), 352 n. 16
Arnold, Edwin Lester, 256
Arpe Effect, 259, 260
Arrow Books, 111, 118, 299
"Arrowhead," 14, 16, 21, 323 n. 32
Arthur, King, 54
Arthur Ransom trilogy (Lewis), 276, 335 n. 2
"Arts in Science Fiction, The" (Blish), 280
"Art Work," 343 n. 75. See also "Work of Art, A"
Ashby, Ross, 141

INDEX

Ashmead, Lawrence, 130
Asimov, Isaac, 1, 8, 55, 65, 75, 157, 158, 163, 164, 182, 222
Association of Lunar and Planetary Observers, 361 n. 79
Asteroid Belt. *See* "Rings of Sol, The"
Astonishing Stories, 8
Astounding Science Fiction, 6, 13, 36, 116–17, 157, 160, 161–63, 275, 279, 288
Astounding Stories, 4–5, 10, 72
"At Death's End" (Blish), 163, 166, 168–70. See also *They Shall Have Stars*
Atheling, William. *See* Pound, Ezra
Atheling, William, Jr. (pseud. Blish), 6, 19, 154–55, 274–78, 280, 313, 315, 324 n. 47, 330 nn. 18, 20, 335–36 n. 11, 338 n. 8, 339 n. 18, 343 n. 70, 364 n. 28
Augustine, Saint, 183, 304
Australian SF Review, 194–95
Avalon Books, 45
Avon Books, 23, 118, 163, 183, 184, 190, 253
Axe, 275

Bach, Johann Sebastian, 188, 285
Bacon, Roger, 15, 71, 192–215, 219, 225, 266, 295, 319, 349 n. 1, 354 n. 30, 362 n. 11. See also *Doctor Mirabilis*
"Bad Idea Trampled to Death by Ducks, A" (Blish), 341 n. 34
Baines, Mr. *(Black Easter/The Day After Judgment),* 52, 297, 304–11, 313, 362 n. 13, 363 n. 18
Balboa, General, 321 n. 9
Ballantine, Betty, 15
Ballantine, Ian, 84, 85, 87, 88, 90, 95, 96
Ballantine Books, 15, 84, 118, 288
Ballard, J. G., 119, 151
Ball State University Forum, 269
Bangsund, John, 194
Bantam Books, 21, 249
Barefoot in the Head (Aldiss), 279
Barnhart, Phil, 55, 334 n. 32, 355 n. 2
Battle Aces, 4
"Battle of the Unborn" (Blish), 41–42
Baxter, John, 17, 109–10, 142, 157, 183, 250, 283, 334 n. 25, 336 n. 16, 365 n. 39

"Beanstalk" (Blish), 55, 69–70, 332 n. 11, 334 n. 25. See also *Titans' Daughter*
Beast Must Die, The, 44. *See also* "There Shall Be No Darkness"
Beatles, the, 157
"Beep" (Blish), 13, 23, 37, 52, 153, 227–32, 237, 245, 257–64, 352 nn. 13, 15, 16, 17, 353 n. 21. See also *Quincunx of Time, The;* Haertel Network
Beer, Blish and, 10, 16, 17
Believers' World (Lowndes), 276, 345 n. 12
Bell, Eric Temple, 219
Bell, Jonathan ("Mistake Inside"), 38–39
Beloit Poetry Journal, The, 269
Benford, Gregory, 55, 234
Benson, Hugh, 276
"Bequest of the Angel" (Blish), 328 n. 8
Bergonzi, Bernard, 92
Bernard of Chartres, 197
Bester, Alfred, 112
Best of James Blish, The, 34, 63
Best Science Fiction (Faber & Faber), 13
Best Science Fiction Stories of James Blish, 42, 111, 137, 146, 148, 150, 157, 277
Beyond Apollo (Maltzberg), 119
Beyond Genre (Hernadi), 92
Beyond Human Ken (Merril), 34
Beyond This Horizon Festival, 24
Bierce, Ambrose, 328 n. 8
Biggle, Lloyd, Jr., 21
"Big Sendoff, The" (Blish), 119
"Bindlestiff" (Blish), 161, 176, 179–80, 362 n. 6. See also *Earthman, Come Home*
"Biographical Notes on James Blish" (Saxton), 27, 320 n. 7, 321 n. 8, 323 n. 36, 323 n. 41, 324 nn. 44, 57, 324–25 n. 58, 325 n. 60, 326 nn. 65, 70
"Biological Story, The" (Blish), 55, 333 n. 20
"Birds, The" (Du Maurier), 239
Birn, Jorn (*. . . And All the Stars a Stage*), 131, 133–34
Bixby, Jerome, 330 n. 17
"Black Destroyer" (van Vogt), 164
Black Easter (Blish), 19–23, 30, 38, 52, 110, 120, 137, 150, 205, 265, 278, 281, 289, 295–319, 325 n. 59, 349 n. 7, 354

n. 30, 363 nn. 15, 23, 365 n. 42. See also *Day After Judgment, The*
Black Easter/The Day After Judgment, 299–319, 362 nn. 9, 11, 363 n. 18
Blackett-Dirac equations, 170, 171
Blackmur, R. P., 275
Blackout (cat), 10, 12
"Blackout in Cygni" (Blish), 254, 330 n. 17
Blake, William, 304
Blish, Abraham (ancestor), 2
Blish, Asa Benjamin (child), 12; death of, 322 n. 25
Blish, Asa Rhodes (father), 1–3, 340 n. 23
Blish, Charles Benjamin (son), 15, 24, 326 n. 65, 355 n. 4
Blish, Dorothea Schneewind (mother), 1–3, 124, 320 n. 7, 320–21 nn. 7, 8
Blish, Elisabeth (daughter), 14, 27, 253, 326 nn. 64, 65, 70, 327 n. 77, 348 n. 37, 350–51 n. 4, 355 n. 4
Blish, James (Benjamin): Army career, 9, 321 n. 16, 325 n. 61; "Arrowhead" flooded, 14; and *Astounding Stories*, 4; and cancer, 18–19, 24–27, 145, 248, 268–69; and cats, 10, 22, 324–25 n. 58; in Chicago, 2–6; childhood, 1–8; collaborations, 6, 10, 18, 25, 29, 33, 36–37, 40–41, 44–48, 52, 55, 72–78, 112, 124, 140–45, 156–57, 243–48, 330 n. 17, 355 n. 2; as conscientious objector, 9; criticism, 274–87; death, 27; divorce, 18; and Dorothea Blish, 320 n. 7, 320–21 n. 8; dramatic works, 273–74; drinking habits, 10, 16–18, 27; in East Orange, N.J., 6–9; in England, 19, 20–30; factual articles by, 287–89; failing health, 24–27; on *Finnegans Wake*, 283–84; first stories, 2; visits Florence, 26; as full-time freelance writer, 21–22; and the Futurians, 8–11; in high school, 7; wins Hugo, 15, 19, 92; and juvenile market, 145, 165, 173–76, 250–69; and Le Guin compared, 116; interest in limnology, 8, 21; marriages, 12, 19; and mathematics, 219ff; on medical science, 288–89; in Milford, Pa. ("Arrowhead"), 14; love of music, 4; writings on music, 285–87; musical compositions, 286; as musician, 361 n. 76; in New York City, 12, 14–15; on the occult, 289; as pilot, 14, 115; and *The Planeteer*, 6–7; poetry, 269–73; as public relations counsel, 16, 20–21; and pulp magazines, 4, 8–10, 33–54; and religion, 4, 22, 321 n. 8; at Rutgers, 8–9; first sale, 8; on science fiction, 17; first science fiction novel, 10; sexual symbolism in, 61–69, 223–24; and Spenglerian philosophy, 163–64, 168; on Strauss, 286–87; *Tesseract*, 6, 318; on time travel, 325–26 n. 63; as trade-journal editor, 12–13; work for TV, 13–14, 56, 254; unfinished work, 29; and Vietnam War, 21; in Virginia, 21; influence of Wagner, 161–62, 164, 168, 183; on writing habits, 25
Blish, James Knox (great-grandfather), 320 n. 1
Blish, Judith Ann Lawrence (wife), 18–27, 154, 156, 193, 232, 236, 238, 244, 249, 289, 293, 323 n. 41, 325 n. 61, 326 n. 70, 326 n. 72, 344 n. 77, 354 n. 30, 355 n. 2, 356 n. 14, 357 nn. 30, 31, 358 nn. 34, 38, 359 n. 52, 360 n. 64, 363 n. 15
Blish, Katherine Hosking (stepmother), 2
Blish, Matthew Rhodes (grandfather), 2, 320 n. 1
Blish, Virginia Kidd (Emden) (wife), 8, 10, 11–12, 15–16, 18, 21, 24, 28, 71, 140–145, 183–84, 187, 198, 293, 320 nn. 4, 7, 321 n. 16, 322 n. 25, 323 n. 40, 324 n. 49, 325 n. 61, 326 n. 64, 326 n. 70, 331 n. 36, 332 n. 5, 334 nn. 25, 26, 337 n. 5, 341 n. 34, 342 nn. 44, 54, 343 nn. 56, 57, 346 n. 28, 347 n. 31, 355 nn. 2, 4, 358 nn. 43, 48, 360 n. 68, 361 n. 1, 362 n. 5; divorce from Blish, 18; marriage to Blish, 12
Bloch, Dr. Hamilton C. *(Fallen Star)*, 27
Bloch, Robert, 123
Bloomer, C. Hamilton, 6–7
"Blowndsh," 10
Blue Ribbon Western, 38
Blythe, Matt ("Chaos, Co-ordinated"), 37
Boggs, Redd, 274
Bond, Tipton *(The Warriors of Day)*, 52–54
Bonfiglioli, Kyril, 151, 317
Book of Ceremonial Magic, The (Waite), 297–300, 363 n. 14
"Book of Your Life, The" (Blish), 112, 155, 353 n. 26

"Bore, The" (Blish), 329 n. 17
Boris Goudonov (Moussorgsky), 346 n. 28
Bottenberg, Wolfgang, 361 n. 76
Boucher, Anthony, 276, 317
"Bounding Crown, The" (Blish), 36, 329 n. 9
Bowen, Rowland, 240
Bowers, Bill, 21
Bowra, Maurice, 28
"Box, The" (Blish), 41, 330 n. 18
"Box, The" teleplay (Blish), 29, 274
Bradbury, Ray, 1, 79, 111, 158, 254, 255, 275, 276, 337 n. 5
Bradham, Jo Allen, 94–97
Brahe, Tycho, 192
Bramwell-Farnsworth, Commodore *(The Frozen Year)*, 120–22
"Brass Head, The." See *Doctor Mirabilis*
Brave New World (Huxley), 78
Brazen Head, The (Powys), 193
Break with Conscription Committee, 9
"Breath of Brahma, The" (Blish/Saxton), 23, 29, 243–48, 296
Brest, John ("On the Wall of the Lodge"), 142–44, 342 n. 55
"Bridge" (Blish), 163, 168, 170–73, 346 n. 20, 354 n. 30. See also *They Shall Have Stars*
"Brightside Crossing" (Nourse), 235
British Interplanetary Society, 361 n. 79
Britten, Benjamin, 359 n. 52
Browne, Sir Thomas, 230
Brunner, John, 24, 294, 327 n. 72, 357 n. 31, 362 n. 6
Brunner, Marjorie, 294
Buck Rogers in the 25th Century (Nowlan/Calkins), 344 n. 1
Budrys, Algis, 15, 16, 22, 158, 204, 254, 266, 278–79, 325 n. 60, 361 n. 74; critique of Blish, 158–59
"Building of the City, The" (Blish), 358 n. 43
Burgd, Joachim *(The Duplicated Man)*, 45–47
Burgess, Andrew J., 335 n. 3
Burns, Robert, 46
Burroughs, Edgar Rice, 134, 254–56
Burroughs, William, 144
Burton, Robert, 92

Cabell, James Branch, 19, 281, 329 n. 14, 350 n. 3, 352 n. 16, 354 n. 30, 365 n. 42
Cabell Society, 324 n. 51
"Caduceus" (Blish), 286
"Caesura" (Blish), 270–71, 273
Cage, John, 286
"Cage of Birds, A" (Blish), 12, 29, 287, 290–95, 362 n. 7
Caiden, Danny *(Jack of Eagles;* "Let the Finder Beware"), 48–53, 188, 354 n. 30
Caligari, Dr., 311
Calkins, Dick, 165, 344 n. 1
"Callistan Cabal" (Blish), 8, 328 n. 8
Cambridge University SF Society, 280
Campbell, John W., Jr., 4, 6, 36–37, 42, 44, 75, 107, 113, 117, 119, 161, 162, 165, 176, 182, 196, 276–79, 337 n. 5, 345 n. 7, 364 n. 32
Canaveral Press, 75
Cancer, references to, 47, 50, 59, 131, 132, 133, 171, 180, 188, 239, 246, 267–68, 332 n. 11. *See also* Blish, James, and cancer
Canopy of Time, The (Aldiss), 183
Canticle for Leibowitz, A (Miller), 276
Cantor, Georg, 220, 221, 229, 336 n. 26, 362 n. 11
Cantos (Pound), 282
Capgrave, John, 335 n. 1
"Caprice in February" (Klee), 102
"Captain Video," 13–14, 56, 254, 274, 321 n. 11, 323 n. 31
"Carbonite Johnny" (Blish), 29
Carroll, Lewis, 37, 117, 220, 350 n. 3
Carse, Hawk, 7
Carter, Paul A., 322 n. 30
Carter, Sir Lewis *(Jack of Eagles)*, 49–50
"Case of Conscience, A" (Blish), 13, 14, 15, 83, 133, 154, 229, 259, 260
Case of Conscience, A (Blish), 1, 14, 15, 19, 25, 29–30, 56, 61, 69–70, 79–104, 138, 220, 257–58, 259–62, 265, 269, 276, 295, 296, 311, 318–19, 321 n. 8, 332 n. 13, 335 nn. 1, 3, 336 nn. 16, 18, 349 n. 7, 350 n. 17, 354 n. 30, 362 nn. 9, 11, 364 n. 28; Christian aspects of, 93–97; containment imagery in, 97–103. *See also* Haertel Network
"Cask of Amontillado, The" (Poe), 284
Castle, The (Kafka), 140, 142, 282

393

"Cathedrals in Space" (Blish), 164, 276, 315
Catholic Church. *See* Roman Catholic Church
Cats, references to, 38–39, 52, 146, 150, 252, 256, 292, 331 n. 36, 354 n. 30. *See also* Blish, James, and cats
Caves of Steel (Asimov), 75
Cavorite, 255
Chambers, Robert W., 154, 343 n. 70
Chandala (A Dusk of Idols), 139
"Chaos, Co-ordinated" (Blish/Lowndes), 36–37, 44, 45, 170, 257, 350 n. 3
Chas. Pfizer & Co., 16, 120, 165–66, 169, 288, 323 n. 39
Chauvin, Cy, 280, 286, 319, 320 n. 3, 356 n. 14, 360 n. 64, 361 n. 76
Chexta *(A Case of Conscience)*, 81, 82, 86, 90, 91, 93–94, 96, 98, 100, 335 n. 4
Childhood's End (Clarke), 221
"Child's Christmas in Wales, A" (Thomas), 115
Child's Guide to the Galaxy, A (Blish), 151
Christ, 94–95, 274
Christian Science, Blish on, 4
Chronica majora (Paris), 202
Chronicles of the House of Borgia (Rolfe), 350 n. 17
Ciardi, John, 43
C.I.D.: Universe, 112, 157, 274, 352 n. 13, 355 n. 2
"Circles" (Blish), 243, 245
"Citadel of Thought" (Blish), 8, 34–36, 329 n. 8
Cities in Flight (Blish), 14–15, 19, 23, 30, 33, 47, 54, 110, 153, 160–91, 198–99, 219, 250, 253, 259, 263, 265, 314, 318, 333 n. 21, 344 n. 3, 345 n. 13, 347 n. 33, 348 n. 34, 349 n. 7, 362 n. 3, 364 n. 28. *See also Earthman, Come Home; Life for the Stars, A; They Shall Have Stars; Triumph of Time, The*
Cities in Flight (orig. title of *Earthman, Come Home*), 176
Cities in the Air (Hamilton), 160
"City That Was the World, The" (Blish), 151, 233–36, 353 n. 25, 354 n. 27. *See also* "King Log"
Clark, John D[rury], 83, 335 n. 10
Clark, John H., 240, 354 n. 33
Clarke, Arthur C., 1, 36, 55, 221, 242, 275
Clash of Cymbals, A. See Triumph of Time, The
"Claw of the Kidnapped Idol" (Blish), 33
Cleaver, Paul *(A Case of Conscience)*, 80–82, 90–96, 98, 100–103, 335 n. 4, 336 n. 11
Cleland, John, 156
Clement IV, Pope, 194, 211–13
"Climate of Insult, The" (Blish), 284, 361 n. 74
Cloning, 78
Close Encounters of the Third Kind, 160
Clute, John, 92, 132, 177, 342 n. 45
Cohen, Chester, 11
Colbert, Robert, 279
Cole, Julian *(The Frozen Year)*, 120–24, 340 nn. 24, 25
Cole, Lois Dwight, 206–7, 214
Collier, John, 156
Columbia University, 9
"Coming Forth, The" (Blish), 137, 266
"Common Time" (Blish), 13, 25, 34, 44, 61, 84, 147, 153, 222–27, 235, 253, 257–58, 259–62, 268, 351 n. 7. *See also* Haertel Network
Communia mathematica (Bacon), 210, 212
Communia naturalium (Bacon), 207, 211, 212
Compendium studii theologiae (Bacon), 213
Conceptual breakthrough 35–36, 41, 61, 63, 65, 66, 107–8, 211, 257, 307, 312, 318–19. *See also* Containment; Flight and birds, references to
"Conquest of Life: New Pathways in Medicine" (Blish), 16, 29, 288
Conrad, Joseph, 138
Consolidated Warfare Services, 42, 52, 297
Containment, 3, 35–36, 41, 50, 53, 58–59, 60, 67, 69, 97–103, 148, 149, 177, 179, 213, 221, 232, 269, 270, 282, 311–12. *See also* Conceptual breakthrough; Flight and birds, references to
Corlett, Ann, 20, 196–97, 206, 291–92
Cornelius, Mary Lucia S., 322 n. 19
"Corpse Planet, The" (Blish), 287
Cosmic Stories, 9
Cowper, Richard, 327 n. 72

Crack Detective Stories, 10, 33, 36, 38
Creative afterthoughts, 25, 71, 85–86, 90, 124, 191, 262, 295–96, 336 n. 23, 352 n. 17, 356 n. 6, 364 n. 25.
Crest, 116
"Crisis in Utopia" (N. L. Knight), 55, 72, 78, 334 n. 27
Crispin, Edmund, 13
"Critical Mass." See *Torrent of Faces, A*
"Crucifixus Etiam" (Miller), 276
Crusoe, Robinson, 256
"Cry in the Night" (Kornbluth), 10, 286
C. S. Lewis Society, 19, 22
Cummings, Ray, 4
Curfew (cat), 10
Curtis, Richard, 236
Cyrus the Great, 230

Daedalus; or Science and the Future (Haldane), 78
Dalton, Jack, 284
D'Ammassa, Don, 93, 96
Damnation of Theron Ware, The (Frederic), 299
Dane, John Hilary ("King Log"), 233–37, 292, 339 n. 17
Dane stories (Blish), 232–37
Danewort, Frederick, 29, 292
Dangerous Visions, 141
Dante Alighieri, 95, 153, 304–5, 313
Danton, Paul *(The Duplicated Man),* 46–47
"Darker Than You Think" (Williamson), 330 n. 20
"Dark Night of the Soul, The" (Blish), 280, 337 n. 5. See also "Genius Heap"
"Darkside Crossing" (Blish), 151, 233, 235, 353 n. 23. See also "King Log"
Dark Stars, 142
Darwinism, 82
D'Averoigne, Count *(A Case of Conscience),* 88, 90, 91, 92, 101–3
Davis, Chandler, 11
Day After Judgment, The (Blish), 19, 23, 30, 38, 52, 110, 120, 150, 257, 265, 278, 295–97, 325 n. 59, 349 n. 7, 354 n. 30, 356 n. 13, 362–63 n. 12, 363–64 n. 23, 364 nn. 25, 28. See also *Black Easter*
Day of the Locust, The (West), 363 n. 21
"Dead Issues at Hand" (Blish), 29

"Death's Crystal Towers" (Blish), 7
De Bono, Edward, 107
De Camp, L[yon] Sprague, 21, 337 n. 5
De Chardin, Teilhard, 303, 335 n. 3
De Civitate Dei (Saint Augustine), 304
Decline and Fall of the Roman Empire (Gibbon), 163
Decline of the West, The (Spengler), 26, 201, 285, 314, 316
Dedalus, Stephen (cat), 22
DeFord, Chris *(Life for the Stars),* 173–77, 185–86, 345 n. 13, 346 n. 22
DeFord, Miriam Allen, 346 n. 22
De Kuyl, Simon ("A Style in Treason"), 152–54
Delany, Samuel R., 279, 317
Dell Publishing Co., 296
Del Rey, Lester, 21, 84, 151, 191, 205, 250, 252, 339 n. 18, 351 n. 7
Demonology, 289, 298
De multiplicatione specierum (Bacon), 194, 210
Der Rosenkavalier (R. Strauss), 29, 287, 290–92
"Descent into the Maelström, A" (Poe), 226
De signis et causis ignorantiae modernum (Bacon), 211
Determinism, 229
"Detour to the Stars," 333 n. 18, 351 n. 11. See also "Nor Iron Bars"
Dianetics, 13, 49, 315
Dianetics: The Modern Science of Mental Health (Hubbard), 13
Dick, Philip K., 144, 316, 349 n. 2
Dickens, Charles, 7
Dilemma of Determinism, The (W. James), 229
Dillon-Wagoner gravitation polarity generator. See Spindizzies
Dimension, fourth, 220
Dionne quintuplets, 70
Dirac, Paul, 37, 52, 170, 185, 222. See also Haertel, Adolph
Dirac transmitter, 37, 52, 174, 178–79, 181, 227–30, 257, 259, 262–65
Disclave, 14, 129, 131
"Discord in Scarlet" (van Vogt), 164
Discrete, 12, 270

INDEX

Dispossessed, The (Le Guin), 116
Divine Comedy, The (Dante), 335 n. 4
Doctor Mirabilis (Blish), 15, 19, 20, 30, 73, 128, 145, 192–215, 236, 265, 287, 291, 294–96, 311, 318, 325 n. 61, 349 nn. 1, 7, 10, 350 n. 17, 354 n. 30, 362 n. 9, 365 n. 42. *See also* Bacon, Roger
Dodd, Mead & Company, 197–98, 287
Domenico, Father *(Black Easter)*, 300–305, 308–10, 313, 319
Don Giovanni (Mozart), 295
Don Tarquinio (Rolfe), 350 n. 17
Dorman, Sonya, 358 n. 48
Dorry, Stan ("Emergency Refueling"), 36
Double: Bill Symposium, 21
Doubleday & Co., 29, 75, 130, 141, 148, 289
"Dove Sta Memoria" (Blish), 231
Doyle, Sir Arthur Conan, 156
Drug Topics, 12
Drug Trade News, 12
Duchess of Malfi, The (Webster), 163
Duggan, Alfred, 198
Du Maurier, Daphne, 239
Dunbar, William, 28, 357 n. 31
Dunne, J. W., 49, 50
Dunsany, Lord, 156, 351 n. 5
Duplicated Man, The (Blish/Lowndes), 10, 44–48, 52, 266
Durant, William James, 175
Du Sautoy, Peter, 284
"Dusk of Idols, A" (Blish), 17, 138–39, 258, 260–61. *See also* Haertel Network
Dusk of Idols, A (Nietzsche), 138
Dynamic Science Fiction, 10, 45

Earth. *See* "Planet in Doubt, A"
"Earthman Come Home" (Blish), 161, 176, 182, 228. See also *Earthman, Come Home*
Earthman, Come Home (Blish), 13, 14, 132, 161–64, 170, 175–82, 184–86, 189–90, 341 n. 34, 345 n. 13, 348 n. 34. See also *Cities in Flight*
Earthmanist culture. *See* Okie stories
"Earths of Other Suns" (Blish), 287
Eastercon. *See* 21st British Science Fiction Convention
Easton, Stewart C., 194

East Orange, N. J., 1, 6–9
Eckley, Grace, 335 n. 9, 336 n. 18
Eddington, Sir Arthur, 285
Eddison, E. R., 197, 295, 342 n. 42, 365 n. 42
Edwards, Malcolm, 280
Egtverchi *(A Case of Conscience)*, 87–95, 98, 101, 336 n. 18, 365 n. 42
Egyptian Helen, The (Strauss), 287
"Eine Kleine Okie-Musik" (Blish), 346 n. 28
Einstein, Albert, 220, 231, 261
Eisenhower, Dwight D., 170
Eisenstein, Phyllis, 363 n. 14
Elektra (Strauss), 148
Eliot, T. S., 19, 57, 73, 191, 296, 360 n. 64
"Elixir" (Blish), 44, 248
Ellington, Duke (Edward Kennedy Ellington), 157
Ellison, Harlan, 156, 274
Elvers, Dr. *(The Frozen Year)*, 120–23
Elwood, Roger, 274
Emden, Jack, 10, 12
Emden, Karen Anne, 12, 332 n. 5, 346 n. 28
Emden, Virginia Kidd. *See* Blish, Virginia Kidd (Emden)
Emden, V. K. (pseud. Blish), 6, 134, 342 n. 44
"Emergency Refueling" (Blish), 8, 36, 248
Emerson, Ralph Waldo, 222
"Enemy Within, The" (Matheson), 266, 357 n. 32
England, Blish in, 19–30
English Milford Conference, 23–24, 26
Enterprise (Spock Must Die!), 267–69
"Eros and Psyche" (Blish), 29, 359 n. 52
Erskine, Thomas, 352 n. 16
Ertak, Helminth (*. . . And All the Stars a Stage*), 131–33
ESP, 240–41, 364 n. 33. See also *Jack of Eagles*
ESPer. See *Jack of Eagles*
Esquire, 2
E.T., 255
Euphues (Lyly), 135
Eurish, 269
Evans, G., 346 n. 28
Evans, Matthew, 287
Excalibur, 54

"Exile of Time, The" (Cummings), 4
Exorcism, 86, 89
Experiment with Time, An (Dunne), 49
"Explosive doctrine," Bacon's, 211
Exposition Press, Inc., 15
Extrapolation, 220
Extrasensory perception (ESP), 279. See *Jack of Eagles;* Telepathy

Faber, Ann. *See* Corlett, Ann
Faber & Faber, 13, 18, 19, 24, 92, 108, 118, 130, 148, 161, 175, 183–84, 190–92, 196–98, 270, 284–85, 287, 289–90, 317
Fallen Star (Blish), 27, 118, 340 n. 20. See also *Frozen Year, The*
Famous Detective Stories, 10
Fantastic Voyage (Asimov), 65
Fantasy Amateur Press Association, 10
Fantasy and science fiction, relationship between, 107, 315–19
Fantasy Legion, 7
Farnsworth, Duncan (pseud.). *See* O'Brien, David Wright
Faust, 214
"Faust Aleph-Null" (Blish), 362 n. 11, 363 nn. 14, 19. See *Black Easter*
Feather, John, 348 n. 43
Feeley, Gregory, 68, 131, 191, 236, 332 n. 12, 333 n. 18, 338 n. 7, 339 n. 17, 340 nn. 24, 25, 341 nn. 34, 35, 341–42 n. 42, 343 n. 74, 348 nn. 34, 37, 349 n. 2, 349–50 n. 12, 350 nn. 13, 17, 352 nn. 14, 18, 353–54 n. 26, 356 n. 10, 361 n. 1, 362 nn. 2, 4
Ffoni, Dr. ("Mistake Inside"), 38–39
Figures of Earth (Cabell), 281
Finnegans Wake (Joyce), 33, 96–98, 219, 269–70, 279, 281, 283–84, 335 n. 4, 350 n. 3, 336 n. 22, 360 n. 69, 361 n. 70
Firbank, Ronald, 293
"Fire Balloons, The" (Bradbury), 79
First Men in the Moon, The (Wells), 78, 255
First on Mars (Gordon), 256
"First Strike" (Blish), 111, 157
Flammarion, Camille, 67
Flight and birds, references to, 3, 14, 51–52, 240–242, 282, 284, 293, 307, 321 n. 9. *See also* Conceptual breakthrough; Containment

Flood, hurricane Diane, 14
Florence, It., 22; 26
Flory, John, 359 n. 52
Flying Aces, 4
"Folded and the Quiet, The" (Sostman), 348 n. 37
Food Field Reporter, 12
Food of the Gods (Wells), 70
Food Topics, 13
"Fool's Errand" (Payne), 276
Foote, Paul ("There Shall Be No Darkness"), 42–43
"Forever and the Earth" (Bradbury), 158
"Formal Music in the Wake" (Blish), 283
Formed Stool Conway (cat), 10
Fort, Charles, 49
Fortean Society, 8, 49, 331 n. 34, 349 n. 2
Foundation, 23, 26, 348 n. 43
Foundation series (Asimov), 163, 182
Four Quartets (Eliot), 73
Fourth dimension, 220, 311
"Four Variations on a Well-Known Theme" (Blish), 12
Frederic, Harold, 299
Fremd, Ellen *(The Frozen Year),* 120, 123, 340 n. 25
Freya, 173
Friar Bacon and Friar Bungay (Greene), 193, 295
Frome, Nils H., 6, 343 n. 70
Frome, Nilsson (pseud. Blish), 6
"Frontier of the Unknown" (N. L. Knight), 72
Frosted Food Field, 13
Frozen Year, The (Blish), 3, 14, 16, 108–10, 118–24, 126, 137, 153, 263, 278, 290, 294, 323 n. 35, 328 n. 8, 329 n. 17, 332 n. 12, 356 n. 8
Fry, Christopher, 158
Frye, Northrop, 92–93
Fuller, Edward, 2
Fuller, Matthew, 2
Fuller, Samuel, 2
"Function of Science Fiction, The" (Blish), 280, 284
Future Fiction, 9, 10
"Future Recall" (Blish), 33, 325 n. 61, 327 n. 1
Future Science Fiction, 109

INDEX

Futurian, The (mag.), 317
Futurians, The, 8–12, 22, 33
Futurians, The (Knight), 12
Futurian Science Literary Society of New York. *See* Futurians, The "FYI" (Blish), 220–21, 226, 231, 362 n. 11

Gabbard, G. N., 197
Gaddis, William, 140, 145, 283, 343 n. 56, 363 n. 22
Galactic Cluster (Blish), 109, 114, 117, 226, 341 n. 34
Galaxy Science Fiction (mag.), 26, 29, 56, 67, 68, 75, 114, 141, 142, 151, 233, 275
Galileo Galilei, 209
Galle, Johann Gottfried, 260
Gamow, George, 332 n. 10
Ganymede, 57–60, 69
Garden of Cyrus; or, The Quincuncial Lozenge (Browne), 230
Garelli Domenico, 363 n. 18
Garrard ("Common Time"), 223–26, 235, 237, 253, 259–61
Garrett, Randall, 276
Gas giant, 288, 327 n. 1
Geis, Richard E., 197
Genetic engineering. *See* Cloning; Pantropy; Polyploidy; Tectogenesis
"Genius Heap" (Blish), 337 n. 5, 344 n. 75
George, Henry, 72
Gerard of San Borgo, 209
Gernsback, Hugo, 1, 4, 7
"Gerontion" (Eliot), 296
"Get Out of My Sky" (Blish), 116–17
"Getting Along" (Ja. Blish/Ju. Blish), 156–57, 355 n. 3
"Giants in the Earth." *See* "Beanstalk"
Gibbon, Edward, 163, 175
Gilbert, Stuart, 297, 348 n. 33
Gilmore, Doris ("There Shall Be No Darkness"), 43
"Glass Night" (Blish), 29, 349 n. 2
"Glitch, The" (Blish/Stanton), 157, 343 n. 74, 354 n. 27
Godshalk, William Leigh, 19, 324 n. 51
Gold, Horace L. 75, 332 n. 5
"Gold Frame, The" (Blish), 29, 359 n. 52
Gordon, Rex, 256
Grahame, Kenneth, 28

"Great Dark, The" (Mark Twain), 331 n. 4
Great Earth Port Authority, 57
Greene, Robert, 193, 295
Green Exarchy, 23
Gregory X, Pope, 206, 212
Grolier Encyclopedia, 275
Grosseteste, Robert, 199–202, 205–6, 209
Grotesque, 7
"Guide to Pornographic Men's Clubs in London" (Blish), 354 n. 26
Gulliver of Mars (Arnold), 256

Hadrian IV, 335 n. 9
Hadrian the Seventh (Rolfe), 89, 335 n. 4, 350 n. 17
Hadrian VIII, Pope *(A Case of Conscience)*, 89, 93
Haeckel, Ernst, 192
Haertel, Adolph *(Welcome to Mars)*, 222–23, 231, 254–57, 260–64. *See also* Dirac, Paul
Haertel Complex, 261–64. *See also* Haertel Network
Haertel drive, 253–54, 257–60, 262
Haertel Network, 231, 257–65
Haertel transformation, 226
Haesermann, W. H., 282
Haggard, H. Rider, 37, 134
Haldane, J. B. S., 50, 78
Hamilton, Edmond, 4, 6, 160, 344 n. 3
Hamlet (Shakespeare), 102, 233
Harrison, Harry, 24, 151, 243, 245–46, 280
Hartwell, David G., 296, 362 n. 11
Hawthorne, Nathaniel, 38, 97
Hay, George, 23, 296, 325 n. 61
Heard, Gerald, 79, 100, 325 n. 1
"Heart of Darkness" (Conrad), 138
Heinlein, Robert, 1, 21, 33, 163–65, 246, 250–51, 275–76, 278, 280, 317
Heinlein in Dimension (Panshin), 352 n. 15
Heisenberg, Werner Karl, 50
Hennessy, Sean *(Jack of Eagles)*, 50–51
"Henry George Slipped Here" (N. L. Knight), 72
Henry III, King of England, 195, 200, 202–3, 210–11
Heraclitus, 201
Hernadi, Paul, 92

398

"Hero's Life, A" (Blish), 47. *See also* "Style in Treason, A"
Highet, Gilbert, 84
Hilary, Edmund, 233
Hill & Knowlton, Inc., 16, 20–21
Hillstrom, Dr. Ulla ("How Beautiful with Banners"), 146–48, 354 n. 30
Hiss, Alger, 173
History of Science Society, 361 n. 79
"History of Witchcraft, Demonology, and Magic" (Blish), 29, 289
"Histrion" (Pound), 344 n. 77
Hitchcock, Alfred, 239
Holding Your Eight Hands, 353 n. 18
Holm, Christian (*VOR;* "Weakness of RVOG, The"), 125–28, 341 n. 32
Holmes, Mycroft, 198
"Homesteader, The" (Blish), 329 n. 17
Homosexuality, 127–28, 292
Hopkins Review, The, 269
Hosking, Katherine. *See* Blish, Katherine Hosking
Hoskins, Robert, 142
Houdini, Harry, 49
"Hour Before Earthrise, The." *See Welcome to Mars*
"How Beautiful with Banners" (Blish), 146–48, 150, 354 n. 30
Hubbard, L[afayette] Ron[ald], 13, 49
Hubert's Arthur (Rolfe), 350 n. 17
Hudson, Christopher, 358 n. 43
Hugh Selwyn Mauberly (Pound), 148
Hugo (award), 1, 15, 17, 19, 92, 150, 323 n. 34, 354 n. 30
Hunt, William Holman, 280
"Hunting of the Snark, The" (Carroll), 37, 350 n. 3
Hurricane Diane, 14
Huxley, Aldous, 78, 93
Hyman, Stanley Edgar, 284, 361 n. 74

Icarus (cat), 22
Ice (Kavan), 119
ICSC (International Cosmos Science Club), 6
If Worlds of Science Fiction (mag.), 56, 83, 142, 289, 302, 363 n. 19
"Imagination of Disaster, The" (Sontag), 318

"Immortal Bard, The" (Asimov), 158
"Immortal Game, The" (Anderson), 276
Impulse, 151, 317
"Index to James Blish's Contributions to the Mailings of the Vanguard Amateur Press Association, An," 322 n. 21, 366
Inferno (Dante), 153, 304
Infinity, 113
"In Memoriam: Fletcher Pratt" (Blish), 270
Innocent IV, Pope, 206, 209
In Search of Wonder (D. Knight), 275, 279
International Cosmos Science Club (ICSC), 6
International Geophysical Year, 120–21, 123, 340 n. 23
"In This Sign" (Bradbury), 79
"In Tomorrow's Little Black Bag" (Blish), 288
"Into the Labyrinth of the Mind" (Clark, John H.), 354 n. 33
"Introduction: The Function of Science Fiction." *See* "Tale That Wags the God, The"
Introduction to the Eternal Gospel (Gerard of San Borgo), 209
"Invention of Science, The" (Blish), 194
Inverted World, The (Priest), 67
"Invisible Armada" (Blish), 36
"Iron Dwarf, The" (Blish), 287
"Issue at Hand, The" (Blish), 274–75
Issue at Hand, The (Blish), 19, 118, 124, 276, 277, 278–79, 321 n. 8, 361 n. 74, 364 n. 28
"Is That a Death?" (Blish), 29, 292–95
"I've Got a Little List" (Garrett), 276

"Jabberwocky" (Carroll), 117
Jack of Eagles (Blish), 44–45, 48–52, 170, 188, 220, 241, 264, 315, 326 n. 64, 331 n. 36, 339 n. 18, 354 n. 30. *See also* "Let the Finder Beware"
James, Henry, 124
James, William, 229, 299
James Branch Cabell Society, 19, 197, 281
James Joyce Symposium, 23
Jarmoskowski, Jan ("There Shall Be No Darkness"), 42–43

Javalin (. . . And All the Stars a Stage), 131–33
Jesus. *See* Christ
Jesus Christ, Superstar, 274
Joachim of Flora, 209
John, King, 200
John the Baptist, 95
Jong, Erica, 126
Journal of Modern Literature, 281
"Journey's Rupture: Poems 1949–70" (Blish), 270
"Journey to the Seedling Stars" (Blish), 356 n. 6. See also *Mission to the Heart Stars*
Joyce, James, 13, 19, 96–97, 140, 219, 249, 283, 286, 293, 360 n. 68, 361 n. 74. *See also* James Joyce Symposium
"Jungle of the Microcosm," (Blish), 332 n. 4
Jungle Stories, 38, 134
Jupiter. *See* "Poison Giants, The"
Jurgen (Cabell), 329 n. 14

K *(The Castle),* 283
Kafka, Franz, 140, 222, 282–83
"Kafka Scandal, The" (Blish), 140
Kalki (Cabell), 19, 281, 324 n. 51, 360 n. 66
Kavan, Anna, 119
Keikobad (cat), 22
Keller, David H., 37
Kemp, Earl, 17
Kennedy, Kit *(The Night Shapes),* 134–37, 354 n. 30
Kidd, Virginia. *See* Blish, Virginia Kidd (Emden)
Kinesis (mag.) 358 n. 48
"Kind of King, A." *See* "No Royal Road"
"King in Yellow, The" (Chambers), 154, 343 n. 70
"King Log" (Blish), 23, 24, 29, 151, 232–37, 287, 292, 348 n. 34, 353 n. 23
"King of the Hill" (Blish), 113
Kirk, Capt. James T. *(Star Trek; Spock Must Die!),* 267–69, 357 n. 32
Kirk, Capt. Pierre D., 250
Klee, Paul, 102
Knight, Damon, 2, 6, 8–12, 14–16, 21, 34, 40–41, 44, 61, 124–27, 129, 146–48, 223, 235, 275, 279, 323 n. 32, 324 n. 45, 329 n. 16, 341 nn. 27, 32, 34, 344 n. 5, 351 nn. 7, 8, 355 n. 2
Knight, Norman L., 18, 44, 55, 72–78, 150, 355 n. 2
Knight's Mare, 72
Kor beam, 37
Kornbluth, Cyril, 8, 10, 15, 276, 286, 288, 323 n. 35, 360 n. 57
"Kritike Antikritikos" (Blish), 281–83, 360 n. 61
Kuhn, Thomas, 103, 107, 231, 280, 364 n. 30
Kuttner, Henry, 21, 237, 276, 359–60 n. 57
Kyle, David A., 7

Lafferty, Donald. *See* Blish, James (Benjamin); Knight, Damon
Laflin, Karin L. *See* Adams, Karin Laflin
La Guardia, Fiorello, 174
"Lake of Light, The" (Williamson), 4
Lamentations, 285
Lament for the Makaris (Dunbar), 28, 357 n. 31
Lane, Erwin, 4
Last and First Men (Stapledon), 78
Latham, Philip. *See* Richardson, Robert Shirley
Lathrop, John, 2
Laverty, Donald (pseud. Blish and Knight, Damon), 6, 40
Lavon (The Seedling Stars), 65–68
Lawrence, J. A., 25
Lawrence, Judith Ann. *See* Blish, Judith Ann Lawrence
Lawrence, Muriel, 25
"Leaven of Power." See *Doctor Mirabilis*
Left Hand of Darkness, The (Le Guin), 335 n. 10
Le Guin, Ursula K., 116, 163, 333 n. 15, 335 n. 10
Leiber, Fritz, 119, 140
Lessing, Doris, 119
"Let Joy Be Unconfined" (Blish), 288, 332 n. 12
"Let the Finder Beware" (Blish), 48–52, 362 n. 6. See also *Jack of Eagles*
Levin, Ira, 296
Lewis, C. S., 19, 22, 79, 276, 317, 335 n. 2
Lewis Carroll Society, 220

Ley, Willy, 83, 122, 335 n. 10
Lieut. Gullivar Jones: His Vacation (Arnold), 256
Life for the Stars, A (Blish), 14, 164–66, 168, 173–77, 185, 186, 191, 250, 340 n. 20, 345 n. 13. See also *Cities in Flight*
Life for the Stars, A, screenplay (Blish), 359 n. 52
"Light to Fight By, A" (Blish), 156–157, 290
Limnology, Blish's interest in, 8, 21, 333 n. 20
Lipscomb, Thomas H., 287
Lithia *(A Case of Conscience),* 61, 80–103, 265, 362 n. 9
"Lithia" (Blish), 83
Lithium, 89, 103
"Little Black Bag, The" (Kornbluth), 288
Loftus, Jack *(Mission to the Heart Stars; The Star Dwellers),* 250–54
"Long Arc, The," 355 n. 5. See also *The Star Dwellers*
"Long Night of a Virginia Author, The" (Blish), 280–81
"Long Way Home, The," 351 n. 11. *See also* "Detour to the Stars"
"Look Dear, He Found My Lost Necklace . . ." (Blish), 325 n. 62
Lord of the Sea (Shiel), 276
Lord of the World (Benson), 276
"Loss of Breath" (Poe), 222
Lothar, Dan ("Citadel of Thought"), 34–35
Louis VIII, 200
Louis IX, 211
Lovecraft, H. P., 154–56, 343 n. 70
Lovelace, Richard, 227
Lowndes, Robert A. W., 6, 8–12, 23, 33–34, 36–37, 44–48, 63, 109, 123, 158, 169, 270, 276, 285, 321–22 n. 18, 322 nn. 21, 24, 25, 324 n. 46, 329 n. 10, 330 nn. 20, 21, 331 nn. 32, 33, 34, 338 n. 9, 343 n. 74, 344 n. 3, 345 n. 12, 348 n. 37, 349 n. 2, 352 n. 17, 355 n. 2, 364 n. 29
Lundgren, Christian ("There Shall Be No Darkness"), 42–43
Luros, Milton, 109
Lutz, E., 194, 349 n. 3
Lycanthropy, 42–44
Lyell, Charles, 134

Lyly, John, 135
Lyons, Marcus *(Finnegans Wake;* pseud. Blish), 6, 33, 45, 48

Macbeth, George, 352 n. 18
Macbeth (Shakespeare), 352 n. 18
McCaffrey, Anne, 24, 34, 154
McCarthy, Sen. Joseph, 170
Macdonald, Dwight, 9
MacDougal, John (pseud. Blish and Lowndes, Robert A. W.), 6, 36, 45
McFadden, Bernarr, 2
MacGregor, James Murdoch, 129
Machiavelli, Niccolò, 175
MacHinery, Francis Xavier *(They Shall Have Stars),* 167, 170, 172
McIntosh, J. T. (pseud.). *See* MacGregor, James Murdoch
Mack, David, 7–8
McKenzie, Anne, 274
Maeterlinck, Maurice, 197
Magazine of Fantasy & Science Fiction, The, 23, 56, 119, 237–38, 275
Magic, 289; white, 305–6
"Magic Hammer, The" (Blish), 29, 355 n. 4
"Magician, The." See *Doctor Mirabilis*
Magician Among Spirits, A (Houdini), 49
Mahrt *(The Warriors of Day),* 53–54
Mall, Henry *(Jack of Eagles),* 51
Mallard, Bill, 21
Maltzberg, Barry, 119
"Man, The" (Bradbury), 276
"Mankind Breaking through the Vault of Heaven . . ." (Flammarion), 67
Manning, Lawrence, 6
Man Plus (Pohl), 78
"Man Who Loved His Food, The" (Saxton), 27, 248
"Man Without a Planet, The" (Blish), 359 n. 52
Mardi (Melville), 222, 226
Mariner IV, 254
Marla *(Jack of Eagles),* 49, 51
Mars. *See* "Iron Dwarf, The"
Marsh, Adam, 199, 201–4, 207, 210
Martels, John *(Midsummer Century),* 238–43, 263–64, 354 n. 35, 355 n. 36
Martin, Oliver ("Mistake Inside"), 38–39
Marx, Karl, 175

"Masks" (V. Blish/J. Blish), 337–38 n. 5
"Masque of the Red Death, The" (Poe), 155
Masson, David I., 242, 351 n. 8, 355 n. 36
"Mathematical Story, The" (Blish), 220
Mathematics, 219–20, 241–42
Matheson, Richard, 357 n. 32
Maurey *(Titans' Daughter)*, 70–71
Mayflower, 2
Meid, Liu *(A Case of Conscience)*, 87, 89–91
Meister ("The Box"), 41
Melnik, Berthe, 11
Melville, Herman, 92, 222, 226
Memoirs of a Survivor (Lessing), 119
Memorial Evening for James Blish, 326–27 n. 72, 357 n. 31
Men and Machines (Silverberg), 34
"Mercy Death" (D. Knight), 124, 127
Mercury. *See* "Moon of the Sun, The"
Merlyn, Arthur (pseud. Blish), 6, 38, 56, 151, 323 n. 31
Merril, Judith, 8, 11–12, 14, 15, 21, 34, 83, 141
Merritt, A., 156
Merwin, Sam, 124–25
"Message from Loci, A" (Blish), 346 n. 19
Metamorphosis, The (Kafka), 222
Metaphysica (Bacon), 209
"Methuselah's Grandparents" (Blish), 289
Meyers, Walter E., 353 n. 22
Michel, John B., 10, 11, 324 n. 46
Michelis, D. *(A Case of Conscience)*, 80–81, 87, 89–92, 102, 335 n. 4
"Midsummer Century" (Blish), 23, 141
Midsummer Century (Blish), 47, 51, 231, 237–43, 257–58, 262–65, 293, 339 n. 18, 342 n. 42, 346 n. 17, 352 n. 16, 354 n. 31, 355 n. 3. *See also* Haertel Network
Milford, Pa., 14–16, 21
Milford Science Fiction Writers' Conference, 15, 16, 21, 285. *See also* English Milford Conference
Milky Way: Five Cultural Portraits (ACREFF-MONALES), 183, 190–91
Miller, Walter M., Jr., 276
Miller, William H., Jr., 6, 7
Millington's, 296
Milne, Edward Arthur, 261

Milton, John, 348 n. 39
Mission to the Heart Stars (Blish), 250, 252–55, 258, 260–61, 264–66, 340 n. 20, 341–42 n. 42, 356 nn. 5, 6, 362 n. 9, 363 n. 19. *See also* Haertel Network
"Mistake Inside" (Blish), 38–40, 143, 151, 289
Möbius strip, 220
Mokele-mbemba (The Night Shapes), 135, 137
Mona Lisa (Thayer), 349 n. 2
"Monsters of Mars" (Hamilton), 4
Monteith, Charles, 13, 17–20, 24, 27, 28, 41, 125, 316, 317, 327 n. 72, 349 nn. 1, 2, 356 n. 6, 358 n. 43, 359 n. 52, 362 n. 11, 363 n. 15
Moon, the. *See* "Sister of Terra"
"Moon of the Sun, The" (Blish), 287
Moorcock, Michael, 144–45
More, Thomas, 80
More Issues at Hand (Blish), 23, 148, 277, 279, 325 n. 58, 329 n. 16, 330 nn. 18, 20, 334 n. 26, 344 n. 3, 352 n. 15, 359 n. 55, 360 n. 58
"More Light" (Blish), 154–56, 324 n. 47
More Than Human (Sturgeon), 15
Morris, William, 274, 359 n. 53
Morrow, Gray, 302, 363 n. 19
Moskowitz, Sam[uel], 6, 154, 278–79, 343 n. 70, 344 n. 3, 360 n. 61, 365 n. 41
Moussorgsky, Modest Petrovich, 346 n. 28
Mudd's Angels (Ju. Blish), 358 n. 34
Mozart, Wolfgang Amadeus, 286, 295
Mufti (cat), 22
Muir, Willa and Edwin, 283
Mullen, Richard D., 164, 181, 183–84, 345 n. 13, 346 n. 23, 347 n. 29
Multitude of Visions, A (Chauvin), 280
Munch, Edvard, 115
"Music of the Absurd, The" (Blish), 280, 286
"Music the Hard Way." *See* "Sense of Music, The"
"My God, the Greeks" (Blish), 270
"My Kinsman, Major Molineaux" (Hawthorne), 38

Naysmith, Dr. *(A Dusk of Idols)*, 138–39
Nekronomikon (Lovecraft), 154

Nelson, Thurlow G., 332 n. 5
Neptune. *See* "Poison Giants, The"
"Neptunian Refuge" (Blish), 6
Nernst-effect, 259, 327 n. 1
Network, 88, 335 n. 8
New Age, The, 275
Newcliffe, Caroline ("There Shall Be No Darkness"), 42–43
Newcliffe, Tom ("There Shall Be No Darkness"), 42–43
New Dreams This Morning, 277–78, 280, 337 n. 5, 344 n. 75
New Jerusalem, 160, 174
"New Map of the Mind, A" (Clark, John H.), 354 n. 33
New Maps of Hell (Amis), 17, 360 n. 61
"New Totemism, A" (Blish), 358 n. 33
Newton, Jake ("The Box"), 41
New Worlds, 144
Nicholas IV, Pope, 213
Nicholls, Peter, 26, 290–91, 326–27 nn. 72, 73, 361 n. 1
Nichols, Philip, 346 n. 24
Nietzsche, Friedrich, 138–39
"Nightfall" (Asimov), 222
"Night Journey" (Blish), 29, 287
Nightmare Has Triplets, The (Cabell), 281, 350 n. 3
"Nightride and Sunrise" (Bixby), 330 n. 17
Night Shapes, The (Blish), 108, 109, 134–37, 342 n. 44, 354 n. 30, 362 n. 9
Night Shapes, The, screenplay (Blish), 274
"99.8%" (Blish?), 130–31
Niven, Larry, 357 n. 32
Nixon, Richard M., 173
"No Jokes on Mars" (Blish), 145–46, 258, 261–62, 354 n. 30, 356 n. 10. *See also* Haertel Network
No Man Friday (Gordon), 256
"None So Blind." *See* "Who's in Charge Here?"
Non-Stop (Aldiss), 333 n. 15
"Nor Iron Bars" (Blish), 226, 258–62, 327 n. 1, 333 n. 18, 339 n. 18, 351 n. 11. *See also* Haertel Network
"No Royal Road—for JB" (V. Blish), 28, 327 n. 76
"Notes on Writing Science Fiction" (Blish), 6

Nourse, Alan E., 235
Nova Express (Burroughs), 144
"No Winter, No Summer" (Blish/D. Knight), 40–41, 353 n. 25
Nowlan, Philip Francis, 344 n. 1
"Now That Man is Gone" (Blish), 149, 343 n. 62
Nullity of Magic, The/"On the Nullity of Magic" (Bacon), 209, 296

"Oath, The" (Blish), 137, 157, 266
O'Brien, David Wright, 340 n. 23
Occult, The (Wilson), 364 n. 32
"Occurrence at Owl Creek Bridge, An" (Bierce), 328 n. 8
"Okie" (Blish), 13, 161, 165, 176, 177–78. *See also Earthman, Come Home*
"Okie Children, The" (Karen Anne Emden), 346 n. 28
Okie stories, 13, 160–91, 228–29, 359 n. 52. *See also Cities in Flight*
One in Three Hundred (MacGregor), 129, 130, 341 n. 34
"One-Shot" (Blish), 113
One Two Three . . . Infinity (Gamow), 332 n. 10
"On the Wall of the Lodge" (J. Blish/V. Blish), 140–42
"Operas of Richard Strauss, The" (Blish), 29, 287, 290
Ophiuchi Hotline, The (Varley), 78
Orbit, 146
"Oryx in Phoenix" (Blish), 357 n. 31
Otway, Thomas, 158
"Our Binary Brothers" (Blish), 151, 233, 235–36, 341 n. 42. *See also* "King Log"
"Our Inhabited Universe" (Blish), 287, 355 n. 39
Ouspenskii, Petr Demianovich, 49
Out of the Silent Planet (Lewis), 79. *See also* Arthur Ransom trilogy

Pageant Press, 15
Palinurus *(Aeneid),* 356 n. 7
Palmer, John, 322 n. 19
Panshin, Alexie, 352 n. 15
Pantropy, 55–57, 59–61, 65, 69, 77, 171. *See also Seedling Stars, The*

"Pantropy vs. Terra forming" (Blish), 332 n. 7
Paracelsus, 192, 350 n. 16
Paradigms, new, 107–9, 280
"Parallax," 11–12
Pareto, Vilfredo, 175
Paris, Matthew, 202, 206, 210
Patchen, Kenneth, 11
Payne, Paul L., 276
"Peace Declared" (Blish), 329 n. 17
Peacock, Thomas Love, 92
Peake, Mervyn, 268
Peirce, Charles S., 334 n. 26
Penthouse, 156
"Penton and Blake" (Campbell), 6
Peregrine. *See* Peter the Peregrine
Perelandra (Lewis), 80. *See also* Arthur Ransom trilogy
"Persistence of Meaning, The" (Ju. Blish), 26
Petard, H. O. *See* D'Averoigne, Count
Peter the Peregrine *(Doctor Mirabilis),* 204–5, 211, 212, 214
Petrified Planet, The, 83
Petrucelli, Marty *(VOR),* 124–28, 328 n. 8, 341 nn. 28, 32, 353 n. 20
Phallic symbolism, 61–65, 127–28
Phantagraph, The, 7
Phantascience League Digest, 7
Philmus, Robert M., 332 n. 10, 336 n. 22
Philoctetes (Sophocles), 332 n. 12
"Phoenix Planet" (Blish), 110, 119, 328 n. 8
Piercy, Marge, 119
Pilgrim's Guide to Rome, A, 86
Piper, H. Beam, 83
"Piper of Dis, The" (Blish/N. L. Knight), 75. See also *Torrent of Faces, A*
PK (psychokinesis). See *Jack of Eagles*
Planck, Max Karl Ernst Ludwig, 50, 347 n. 31
"Planet Earth" (Blish), 340 n. 23
Planeteer, The, 4–7, 254, 330 n. 17
"Planet in Doubt, A" (Blish), 287
Plato, 167, 246
Playboy, 286, 288, 311
Player Piano (Vonnegut), 277
"Players of A, The" (van Vogt), 160
Plutarch, 175
"Pluto and Beyond" (Blish), 287

Poe, Edgar Allan, 7, 19, 155, 222, 226, 284, 285, 332 n. 4
Pohl, Frederik, 8, 15, 36, 37, 75, 78, 84–88, 91, 141, 142, 237, 323 n. 31, 324 n. 46, 325 n. 62, 333 n. 18, 341 n. 34, 345 n. 10
"Poison Giants, The" (Blish), 287
Polanski, Roman, 310
Pollinger, Gerald, 290, 358 n. 43, 362 n. 2
Polyploidy, 55, 70–71, 169. See also *Titans' Daughter*
Poor Original Curfew, 10
Pornography, 112, 235, 353–54 n. 26
Portrait of the Artist as a Young Man, A (Joyce), 336 n. 18
Pound, Ezra, 9, 11, 19, 140, 148, 249, 275, 282, 283, 293, 344 n. 77
"Pound Scandal, The" (Blish), 282
Powys, John Cowper, 193
Pragmatism, 300
Prairie Schooner, 269, 283
Pratt, Fletcher, 83
"Prayer for Joyce" (Blish), 270
Priest, Christopher, 67, 245
Prince of Taranto, The (Thayer), 349 n. 2
Principles of Geology (Lyell), 136
Pringle, David, 348 n. 43
"Probapossible Prolegomena to Ideareal History," 1948 (Blish), 364 n. 29
"Probapossible Prolegomena to Ideareal History," 1978 (Blish), 295, 314–15, 317, 364 n. 29
Progress and Poverty (George), 72
"Prophecy of Love, A" (Blish), 29, 293–95
Prospero *(The Tempest),* 312
Psyche and Eros, 118. *See* "Eros and Psyche"
Psycho (Bloch), 123
Psychokinesis (PK). See *Jack of Eagles*
"Psychological Story, The" (Blish), 13
Ptolemy, 211
Pulp magazines, Blish's work in, 4, 8–10, 33–54
Purgatorio (Dante), 304
Putnam's, 92, 161, 195, 206

Quantum mechanics, 220
Queenan, Bernard, 339 n. 14
Queens Science Fiction League, 123

"Quest for Saint Aquin, The" (Boucher), 276
"Question of Content, A" (Blish), 277
Quincunx, 230, 241–42, 257
Quincunx of Time, The (Blish), 19, 23, 37, 52, 113, 153, 229–32, 237, 245, 257–59, 261–64, 352 nn. 13, 15, 16, 17, 353 nn. 19, 21. See also "Beep"; Haertel Network
Qvant, the *(Midsummer Century)*, 239–41, 354 n. 35, 355 n. 36

Rabelais, François, 92
Rachelwiltz, Princess Mary de, 282
Ragnorak, 186
Rahner, Karl, 335 n. 3
Ransom, Arthur. *See* Arthur Ransom trilogy
Reagan, Ronald, 313
"Real Thrill, The" (Blish), 231, 258, 262, 264, 328 n. 8, 330 n. 17. *See also* Haertel Network
Rearguard Productions, Inc., 43
Recognitions, The (Gaddis), 145, 283, 360 n. 68, 363 n. 22
Reginald, Robert, 344 n. 2
Reilly, Robert, 335 n. 4
Renascence (mag.), 11, 270
Report on Probability A (Aldiss), 280
Reprobationes (Bacon), 209, 210
"Reprise, A" (Blish), 358–59 n. 51
Revelation, Book of, 165
Rhine, Dr. Louisa Ella, 49
Richardson, Robert Shirley, 165, 288, 346 n. 16
Rickard, Bob, 312, 364 n. 28
Rime of the Ancient Mariner, The (Coleridge), 293
Ring of the Nibelung, The (Wagner), 161–62, 165, 172–73, 186
"Rings of Sol, The" (Blish), 287
Ringworld, 23
"Rituals on Ezra Pound" (Blish), 9, 282
Robe, The, 338, n. 14
Roberts, Jane, 15
Robinson Crusoe on Mars, 256
Roger Bacon and His Search for a Universal Science (Easton), 194
"Roger Bacon's Contribution to Knowledge" (Lutz), 194

Rogers, Alva, 13, 163
Rogue Moon (Budrys), 254, 266, 268, 278, 361 n. 74
Rogues Gallery (Little Theatre group), 274
Rolfe, Frederick, 89, 350 n. 17
Roman Catholic Church, 85, 96
Rose, Mark, 334 n. 34
Rosemary's Baby (Levin), 296, 310
Rosenberg, Max, 43
Rosenblum, J. Michael, 317
Ross, A. Leslie, 224
Rothman, Julius, 324 n. 51
Rousseau, Jean-Jacques, 335 n. 1
Rubin, Louis, 360 n. 65
Ruiz-Sanchez, Father Ramon *(A Case of Conscience)*, 80–103, 335 nn. 4, 6, 336 n. 11, 354 n. 30
Russ, Joanna, 237, 303
Rutgers University, 8–9, 55
RVOG ("The Weakness of RVOG"), 124–26, 128–29. See also *VOR*

Sandburg, Carl, 7, 114, 271, 338 n. 13
"Sargasso of Lost Cities" (Blish), 161, 176, 180–82. See also *Earthman, Come Home*
Sarton, George Alfred Léon, 175
Satan, 81–82, 95, 297, 305, 316
Satellites, planetary. *See* "Systems Within a System"
Saturn. *See* "Poison Giants, The"
Satyricon, The (Petronius), 95
Saxton, Josephine, 24–29, 243, 246–48, 294, 320 n. 7, 321 n. 8, 323 nn. 36, 41, 324 nn. 44, 57, 324–25 n. 58, 326 nn. 64, 65, 70, 327 nn. 72, 77, 354 n. 26, 355 nn. 37, 2, 362 n. 4
Schneewind, Benjamin von, 2
Science Fantasy, 151, 317
Science Fiction Advancement Association. *See* SFAA
"Science Fiction Coming of Age, A" (Blish), 271, 295, 296, 331 n. 1, 353 n. 22
"Science Fiction Foundation, 23
Science Fiction League, 7
Science Fiction Quarterly, 10, 224
Science Fiction Writers of America. *See* SFWA

"Science in Science Fiction" (Blish), 13, 55, 107, 110, 133, 220, 314
"Science in Science Fiction, The" (Blish), 107, 108, 280
Science World, 194
Scott Meredith Literary Agency, 12, 331 n. 33
Screwtape Letters, The (Lewis), 22, 317
Seabury Press, 287
Second Part of Armata, The (Erskine), 352 n. 16
"Secret Files of Captain Video, The" (Blish), 151, 323 n. 31
Secret of Secrets, The (Aristotle), 205, 207–8
"Secret People, The" (Blish/D. Knight), 41, 226
"Secret Songs, The" (Leiber), 119
"Seeding Program" (Blish), 56–61, 64, 69, 171, 332 n. 12. See also *Seedling Stars, The;* "Time to Survive, A"
Seedling Stars, The (Blish), 8, 14, 34, 55–69, 77, 78, 130, 171, 198, 265, 332 nn. 5, 9, 13, 333 nn. 18, 21, 334 n. 32, 340 n. 20, 341 n. 34, 363 n. 18, 364 n. 28. *See also* "Seeding Program"; "Sunken Universe"; "Surface Tension"; "Thing in the Attic, The"; "Watershed"
"Semantics of Music, The," 361 n. 75. *See also* "Sense of Music, The"
Sena *(Titans' Daughter),* 70–71
"Sense of Music, The" (Blish), 12, 29, 285, 320 n. 4, 321 n. 8, 344 n. 76, 348 n. 39, 353 n. 23
Serconia Press, 285, 361 n. 76
"Serenade for Telephone" (Blish), 272
"Serpent's Fetish" (Blish), 134, 136, 342 n. 44. See also *Night Shapes, The*
Sewanee Review, The, 9, 269, 275, 282
SFAA (Science Fiction Advancement Association), 6–7, 318
Sf Impulse, 317
SFWA (Science Fiction Writers of America), 21
Shackley, Paul, 23, 83, 90, 112, 134, 140–41, 143–44, 151, 153, 163, 228–29, 231–32, 236–37, 251, 261, 263–64, 268, 280, 282, 288, 303, 321 n. 8, 329 n. 14, 343 n. 67, 346 nn. 20, 21, 348 nn. 34, 35, 36, 40, 41, 349–50, n. 12, 352 n. 15, 356 nn. 11, 12, 359 n. 52.
"Shadowy Figure of Roger Bacon, The" (Blish), 194, 204–5
Shakespeare, William, 7, 283
Shannon, Claude, 285
Shar *(The Seedling Stars),* 65–68
Shaw, Bob, 327 n. 72
Shaw, Larry, 11, 229, 275
Shaw, Noreen, 275
Shaw, William Harlan, 84
She: A History of Adventure (Haggard), 37
Shelley, Mary, 156
Sherman, Michael (pseud. Lowndes), 45
Shiel, M. P., 276
Ship Who Sang, The (McCaffrey), 34
"Shipwrecked Hotel, The" (Blish/ N. L. Knight), 75. See also *Torrent of Faces, A*
Siegfried *(The Ring of the Nibelung),* 172
Signet Books, 129
"Silence, The" (Poe), 155
Silverberg, Robert, 34, 142, 149, 209, 338 n. 7, 342 n. 54, 350 nn. 16, 20
Silver Stallion, The/Kalki (Cabell), 281, 354 n. 30
Sirens of Titan, The (Vonnegut), 48
"Sister of Terra" (Blish), 287
Skyhook, 92, 274, 315
"Skysign" (Blish), 130, 148–49
Smire (Cabell), 281
Smirt (Cabell), 281
Smith (Cabell), 281
Smith, Clark Ashton, 335 n. 7
"Snake-Headed Sceptre, The" (Blish), 134, 136, 342 n. 44. See also *Night Shapes, The*
So Close to Home (Blish, 41–42, 111, 113, 137, 338 n. 5, 339 n. 15, 342 n. 48, 351 n. 5
Socrates, 211
Solace of Pilgrims, The (Capgrave), 335 n. 1
"Solar Comedy, The" (Blish), 328–29 n. 8, 353 n. 25
"Solar Plexus" (Blish), 8, 34, 147
"Solenevich," 166
"Song" (Blish), 270
"Song of the I" (Blish), 357 n. 31
"Song of Worlds Unseen" (Davis), 11
"Sonnet: To Science" (Poe), 285

Sontag, Susan, 318
Sophocles, 332 n. 12
Sostman, Dirk, 348 n. 37
Sostman, Henry, 341 n. 34, 348 n. 37, 362 n. 3
"Sour William" (Blish), 275
Space Witch, The, screenplay (Blish), 164, 359 n. 52
Special Blish Issue, *Magazine of Fantasy & Science Fiction, The,* 23, 238
Spectator, 42
Speculation, 23, 279
Spengler, Oswald, 26, 30, 47, 54, 163–65, 168–69, 173, 175–77, 183, 186, 201, 219, 253, 285, 314–16, 319; philosophy of, 163–64, 169, 173, 176, 177, 178, 181–82, 188, 190, 253, 314–15, 318, 345 n. 12, 346 n. 23 347 n. 29. See also *Cities in Flight*
"Sphinx, The" (Poe) 332 n. 4
Spindizzies, 172, 174, 177, 179–82, 187, 259
Spock *(Star Trek; Spock Must Die!),* 267–69, 358 n. 35
Spock Must Die! (Blish), 266–69, 355 n. 3
"Sponge Dive" (Blish), 113
Stableford, Brian M., 63, 75, 77, 83, 110, 126, 130, 164, 241, 250, 289, 316, 317, 351 n. 8, 353 n. 21, 355 n. 3
Stanton, L. Jerome, 157, 343 n. 74, 354 n. 27, 355 n. 2
Stapledon, Olaf, 78, 332 n. 9
Star Dwellers, The (Blish), 250–55, 258, 260–62, 340 n. 20, 343 n. 67, 351 n. 4, 355–56 n. 5. See also Haertel Network
Starship Troopers (Heinlein), 251
Startling Stories, 44, 237
"Star Trek," 21, 25, 44, 249
Star Trek books (Blish), 24, 25, 249–50, 266, 340 n. 20, 355 n. 2, 357 n. 32, 358 n. 34
"Statistician's Day" (Blish), 151, 236–37
"Stenographers' Hands" (Keller), 37
Stephen Dedalus (cat), 22
Stephenson, Andrew, 244, 248, 327 n. 72
Stevens Institute of Technology, 7
Stirring Science Fiction, 8
Stirring Science Stories, 34
Stoker, Bram, 156
"Stone Guest, The" (Blish), 295

Stony Point Workshop (mag.), 358 n. 48
Storm *(A Torrent of Faces),* 73, 76–78
"Strange Career of Doctor Mirabilis, The" (Blish), 194, 197
Stranger in a Strange Land (Heinlein), 276
Strauss, Richard, 13, 29, 157–58, 286–87, 290
Stravinsky, Igor, 282
Structure of Scientific Revolution, The (Kuhn), 103, 107, 364 n. 30
Sturgeon, Theodore, 15, 324 n. 46
"Style in Treason, A" (Blish), 47, 151–54, 178, 231, 258, 262–63, 265, 342 n. 42. See also "Hero's Life, A"; Haertel Network
Summa salvatione per scientam (Bacon), 213
"Sunken Universe" (Blish), 8, 34, 55, 56, 63, 151, 331 n. 4, 333 n. 20, 339 n. 18, 362 n. 6. See also *Seedling Stars, The;* "Surface Tension"
Super Science Stories, 8, 56
Super Sports, 10, 38
"Surface Tension" (Blish), 8, 13, 21, 34, 56, 58, 61, 63–64, 66–69, 169, 257, 331 n. 4, 333 nn. 17, 18, 21, 339 n. 18, 354 n. 30. See also *Seedling Stars, The;* "Sunken Universe"
"Survivors, The." See "Man Without a Planet, The"
Suvin, Darko, 257, 280, 337 n. 4, 356 n. 14
"Suvin Looks East" (Blish), 280
Sweeney, Donald Leverault ("Seeding Program"; *The Seedling Stars*), 57–61, 69, 171, 265
Swift, Jonathan, 80, 92, 160, 165, 183, 336 n. 22
Swift, Tom, 156
Swinburne, Algernon, 183, 346 n. 29
"Sword of Xota." See *Warriors of Day, The*
"Systems Within a System" (Blish), 287

"Taby Dead" (Blish), 357 n. 31
Taine, John. See Bell, Eric Temple
Tale of a Tub, A (Swift), 336 n. 22
"Tale That Wags the God, The" (Blish), 280
Tale That Wags the God, The (Blish), 281, 286

INDEX

Talley, Truman M., 129–30, 265
T'ang Yaou-Shun (. . . And All the Stars a Stage), 133–34
Tannhaüser, 257
Tarrant, Katy, 75
Tate, Peter, 24
Tate Gallery, 304, 308
Taurasi, James V., 7, 123
Tectogenesis, 55, 72–73, 75
Teilhard de Chardin, Pierre, 303
"Telecast" (Blish), 29, 119, 140–41,. 143, 144, 283, 290. See also "On the Wall of the Lodge"
Telemachus, The, 254, 321 n. 11, 330 n. 17
Telepathy, 277, 339 n. 18; mathematics of, 220
Television, Blish's work for, 13–14, 56, 254
Tempest, The (Shakespeare), 312
Ten Tomorrows, 274
Teratology, 55
Terraforming, 57, 332 n. 7
Tertium Organum (Ouspenskii), 49
Tesseract, 311, 313, 318
Tesseract (fanzine), 6, 316, 332 n. 4, 365 n. 41
Tesseract Combined with The Planeteer, 7
"Testament of Andros" (Blish), 109–11, 119, 278, 328 n. 8, 338 n. 7
Testament of Andros, The (Blish), 111
Thackeray, William M., 7
That Hideous Strength (Lewis), 321 n. 59. See also Arthur Ransom trilogy
Thayer, Tiffany, 349 n. 2
"Theory of Right Action" (Blish), 357 n. 31
"There Shall Be No Darkness" (Blish), 42–43, 150, 330 n. 20, 354 n. 30. See also *Beast Must Die, The*
They Shall Have Stars (Blish), 120, 161, 163–64, 166–68, 170–73, 175-77, 180, 186, 190, 257, 288, 340 n. 20, 345 n. 10, 346 n. 24, 356 n. 8, 359 n. 52. See also *Cities in Flight*
"Thing in the Attic, The" (Blish), 56, 61–65, 69, 332 n. 5, 333 n. 21. See also *Seedling Stars, The*
Thirteen O'Clock (and Other Zero Hours), 323 n. 35, 360 n. 57
"This Earth of Hours" (Blish), 117–18, 131, 258, 260, 339 n. 18. *See also* Haertel Network
Thomas, Dylan, 115, 166
Thomas, Geoffrey *(The Duplicated Man),* 45, 47–48
(. . .) [*Three Dots*], 364 n. 29
Three for Tomorrow, 149
Thrilling Wonder Stories, 6, 124, 287
Thucydides, 175
"Tiger Ride" (Blish/D. Knight), 40, 288, 329 n. 15
Time Machine, The (Wells), 165
Timescape (Benford), 234
"Time to Survive, A" (Blish), 56, 332 n. 8, 338 n. 11. See also "Seeding Program"; *Seedling Stars, The*
Time travel, 325 n. 63, 328 n. 8, 353 n. 25
Time Traveller (Wells), 255
Titans' Daughter (Blish), 55, 69–72, 169, 332 n. 11, 334 n. 25. *See also* "Beanstalk"
Tobacco Institute, 20
Todd, Dr. *(Jack of Eagles),* 49–51
Tolkien, J. R. R., 22
"To Love Another" (Blish/N. L. Knight), 75. See also *Torrent of Faces, A*
"Tomb Tapper" (Blish), 115–16, 126, 137, 153, 157, 341 n. 33, 346 n. 20
"To Pay the Piper" (Blish), 86, 113–14
"Topaz Gate, The" (Blish), 328 n. 8
Torley, Luke (pseud. Blish), 6
Torrent of Faces, A (Blish/N. L. Knight), 18, 52, 55, 72–78, 128, 130, 150, 192, 245, 350 n. 2, 354 n. 30. *See also* "Piper of Dis, The"; "Shipwrecked Hotel, The"; "To Love Another"
"Torrid Type, The" (Blish), 33
"Towards a Technology of Pleasure." *See* "Let Joy Be Unconfined"
Toynbee, Arnold, 175
Tracy, Evelyn ("Mistake Inside"), 38–40
Tracy, Hugh ("Mistake Inside"), 38–40
Transfinite numbers, 103, 220–21, 243, 362 n. 11
"Translation" (Blish), 337 n. 5
Transmitter, Dirac. *See* Dirac transmitter
"Treetops," 22, 27, 284, 326 n. 70
Trial, The (Kafka), 140, 283

Tritons *(A Torrent of Faces)*, 72–78, 354 n. 30
"Trinity as Trilogy" (Blish), 365 n. 42
"Triumph of Time, The" (Swinburne), 183
Triumph of Time, The (Blish), 164–65, 182–91, 346–47 n. 29, 347 n. 31, 347–48 n. 33, 348 nn. 33, 36. See also *Cities in Flight*
"Trompe L'Oeil" (Blish), 270
Trouble (dog), 71
True Bill: A Chancel Drama in One Act (Blish), 273–74
"True Faust, The" (Blish), 359 n. 53
True Story, 2
Tucker, Wilson ("Tuckerisms"), 365 n. 38
Tumbrils, 10–11, 270, 348 n. 37, 364 n. 29
"Turn of a Century" (Blish), 337 n. 5
Turn of the Screw, The (James), 124
"Twayne Triplet," 83
21st British Science Fiction Convention (Eastercon), 23, 24
Two Nuggets to Boot Hill (Blish), 15
2001: A Space Odyssey (Clarke), 221
Twain, Mark, 331 n. 4
"Two Worlds in Peril" (Barnhart/Blish), 55, 78, 334 n. 32

Uhlan, Edward, 15
ULTIMAC, 112–13, 157
Ulysses (Joyce), 246, 279, 283, 361 n. 74
Unknown, 42, 364 n. 32
Unknown Worlds, 42, 364 n. 32
Uranus. See "Poison Giants, The"
Ussher, Bishop, 184, 348 n. 34
Utopia, 73, 116, 229, 246, 297, 310

Vance, Jack, 152, 317
Vanguard Amateur Press Association. See VAPA
Vanguard Record Company, 11
Vanguard Science Fiction, 14
Vanished Jet, The (Blish), 265–66, 269, 290, 341 n. 34, 357 n. 30
Vanity press, Blish and, 15
van Vogt, A. E., 21, 44–45, 160, 164–65, 275
VAPA (Vanguard Amateur Press Association), 10–11, 72, 269–70, 364 n. 29
Varley, John, 78

"Venice Observed, 1969" (Blish), 270
Venice Preserved (Otway), 158
Venus. See "Corpse Planet, The"
Venus Observed (Frye), 158
Vietnam, 274, 313; Blish opposition to, 21
Viking 1, 254
Vogue, 145
"Void is My Coffin, The" (Blish), 330 n. 17
Voltaire, 92
Von Braun, Werner, 344 n. 1
Vonnegut, Kurt, Jr., 21, 48, 277, 334 n. 31; Blish's possible influence on, 48
VOR (Blish), 41, 108, 109, 124–29, 328 n. 8, 353 n. 20. See also "Weakness of RVOG, The"
Voyage of the Space Beagle, The (van Vogt), 164

Wagner, Richard, 161, 165, 173, 186, 286
Wagoner, Bliss *(They Shall Have Stars)*, 167–70, 172–73, 346 n. 21
Waite, Arthur Edward, 297, 300, 363 n. 14
Walker, Paul, 21, 321 n. 8, 354 n. 31
Walter, Grey, 141
War Birds, 4
Ware, Theron *(Black Easter)*, 297, 299–300, 304–6, 308–10, 313, 316, 354 n. 30. See also *Damnation of Theron Ware, The*
Warhoon, 275
"War Is Over, The" (Budrys), 279
War of the Worlds, The (Wells), 255
War Resisters League, 9
Warriors of Day, The (Blish), 44, 45, 52–54, 135, 331 n. 36, 346 n. 17
"Watershed" (Blish), 56, 60, 70. See also *Seedling Stars, The*
Watson, Ian, 242
Wayne, Jane, *(The Frozen Year)*, 120–22, 340 nn. 25, 26
"Wayriver" (Blish), 14
"W. B. Yeats's Criticism of Ezra Pound" (Haesermann), 282
"Weakness of RVOG, The" (Blish/D. Knight), 41, 124–25, 129, 186. See also *VOR*
"We All Die Naked" (Blish), 149–51, 354 n. 30

INDEX

"Weapon Out of Time, The" (Blish), 40, 328 n. 8, 353 n. 25
Weaver, Warren, 285
Webster, John, 163
Welcome to Mars (Blish), 145–46, 254–58, 261–62, 264, 274, 311, 327 n. 1, 348 n. 37, 356 n. 10, 394 n. 30. *See also* Haertel Network
Welcome to Mars, screenplay (Blish), 274, 356 nn. 10, 11, 12
Wells, H. G., 22, 70, 78, 156, 165, 255
Wentz, Dr. *(The Frozen Year),* 121
Werewolves, 42–44
Wesso. *See* Wessoloski, Waldemar
Wessoloski, Waldemar, 4, 5
West, Nathanael, 363 n. 21
Western Action, 10
Western Review, 269
Westerns, Blish as writer of, 10, 15
Weybright & Talley, 265
"What is Evidence?" (Blish), 13
"When Anteros Came" (Blish), 328 n. 8, 341 n. 28
Whipple, Jonah ("Emergency Refueling"), 36
White, Kenneth S., 324 n. 46, 355 n. 5
White, Ted, 363 n. 18, 363–64 n. 23
White magic, 305–6
Who Killed Science Fiction? (Kemp), 17
"Who's in Charge Here?" (Blish), 139–40
Wiener, Norbert, 285
Wilde, Oscar, 155
Wild Talents (Fort), 49
Wilhelm, Kate, 21
Willey, Robert. *See* Ley, Willy
William Douglas McAdams, Inc., 288
Williams, Charles, 22
Williamson, Jack, 4, 330 n. 20, 332 n. 7
Wilson, Colin, 364 n. 32
Wilson, Raymond J. III, 357 n. 30
Wilson, William (cat), 325 n. 58
Wind in the Willows, The (Grahame), 28
Winks, Donald L., 288
Witchcraft, 289, 298

Witches Three, 43
"With Malice to Come" (Blish), 337 n. 5
Wodehouse, P. G., 351 n. 5
Wolfe, Gary K., 333 n. 21
Wollheim, Donald, 4, 7–12, 34, 36, 123, 340 n. 24; alienated from Blish, 12
Wollheim, Eleanor, 123, 340 n. 24
Woman on the Edge of Time (Piercy), 119
Wonder Stories, 7, 10
"Word for World is Forest, The" (Le Guin), 333 n. 15
Wordsworth, William, 251
"Work of Art, A" (Blish), 13, 157–59, 280, 287
World of Ā (van Vogt), 275
World Science Fiction Convention, 15, 20, 275, 277
World's Fair, Chicago (1933), 3
World's Fair, NYC (1938), 6
"Worlds in Collusion," 24
Worm Ouroboros, The (Eddison), 197, 295, 362 n. 9, 365 n. 42
Wright, Farnsworth, 340 n. 23
Wright, Jeremy ("Mistake Inside"), 38–40
"Writing Accounts," Blish's, 323 n. 31, 324 nn. 46, 55, 351 n. 11, 353 n. 23, 358 n. 34
"Writing of the Rat, The" (Blish), 114–15, 138, 340 n. 19
Wylie, Dirk, 324 n. 46

Xero, 275
"XI Effect, The" (Latham), 165
Xota *(The Warriors of Day),* 52–54

"Year Two Million, The," 243
Year 2018! See *They Shall Have Stars*
Yero ("Mistake Inside"), 38–39
"Yes" (rock group), 27
Ymouse (cat), 22, 324 n. 58

Zelazny, Roger, 149, 279, 317, 365 n. 39
Zissman, Judith. *See* Merrill, Judith
"Zombie . . . ?" (Blish), 151